THE MUSIC LIBEL
AGAINST THE JEWS

THE MUSIC LIBEL
AGAINST THE JEWS

Ruth HaCohen

Yale

UNIVERSITY PRESS

New Haven & London

This book was published with the support of the Israel Science Foundation and with assistance from the Louis Stern Memorial Fund.

Yale University Press books may be purchased in quantity for educational, business, or promotional use. For information, please e-mail sales.press@yale.edu (U.S. office) or sales@yaleup.co.uk (U.K. office).

Set in Electra type by Newgen North America.
Printed in the United States of America.

Library of Congress Cataloging-in-Publication Data
HaCohen, Ruth.
The music libel against the Jews / Ruth HaCohen.
  p.   cm.
Includes bibliographical references and index.
ISBN 978-0-300-16778-8 (cloth : alk. paper)   1. Jews in music   2. Music by Jewish composers—History and criticism.   3. Judaism—Relations—Christianity—History.   I. Title.
ML3921.6.J83H33 2011
780.89′924—dc22

2011015192

A catalogue record for this book is available from the British Library.

This paper meets the requirements of ANSI/NISO Z39.48–1992 (Permanence of Paper).

10 9 8 7 6 5 4 3 2 1

To my mother, Esther Pinczower,
And the blessed memory of my father, Eliezer Pinczower

Contents

PREFACE

It could start with a story I read as a little girl. A young and arrogant king fell in love with a princess from a faraway country by looking at her portrait. Sounds familiar—reminiscent of Tamino and a few other oriental princes? And the rest bears some likeness. This prince set out for that remote country to find out that in *Silentland* one is allowed to speak but ten words a day. A chatterbox, he could not abide by this law and was expelled from the country without ever seeing his beloved. He returned with a big army to conquer the state and the princess' heart, but discovered to his dismay that this taciturn girl refrained from indulging in ordinary amorous exchanges. For when he started his prattling, she disappeared; dumbfounded as he turned, she reappeared. This "silent treatment" conditioned him properly: her periods of stopover lengthened, until once, sitting silently together for a while, the young king heard a "soft melody that seemed to come from far away, and that was more beautiful than all the melodies he had ever heard." What is it, he asked the princess, and she delightedly replied: "This is the melody which the stars play, when they move in their heavenly orbits. Nobody can hear it, only those who can be still and silent. . . . This is the reason for Silentland's stillness—not to disturb those who want to listen to the melody of the stars."

I was highly intrigued by this beautiful story. What could it mean, that music of the stars? I pondered. I was not familiar, at the time, with the verse from God's answer to Job out of the whirlwind: "When the morning stars sang together, and all the sons of God shouted for joy." Access to Shakespeare or Mozart was even farther away. I cannot tell why I did not ask the people around me as to the meaning of this enigma. I kept it in my heart as a private secret, though my brothers should have come across it as well. We all liked the fantastic book that opened with this story, Ludwig Strauss' *Die Zauberdrachenschnur; Märchen für*

Kinder ("The Magic Kite-Tail" and Other Legends for Children), which we read in the exquisite Hebrew translation by the poet Dan Pagis.

I did not notice then that the book had first appeared in Germany. It looked so much like "our book," especially since its Hebrew title, different from the German one, was borrowed from its last story, "Ha-kad Ha-ʿatiq" (The Ancient Jar), whose plot takes place in Old Jerusalem, the walled-off city of my childhood. Though taking place in what seems like the late Ottoman period, the story carries its protagonists—father and son—through unknown subterranean burrows into ancient Jerusalem. There, assisted by Elijah, they find out precious secrets revealed by benevolent spirits.

Much less was I aware that it was published in Berlin, 1936, in the days when Jewish culture in Germany knew its last, coerced flourishing, the days of the Jewish Culture League (*Der Jüdische Kulturbund*), when children like my mother (the only Jewish girl in a Nazified gymnasium in Munich) could find a bit of solace in that fairy-tale substitute, richer and more meaningful than the Grimm Brothers' *Märchen* it meant to replace. Only years later, as a university student, did I encounter Arie L. Strauss' (as he was called in Hebrew) literary essays, among them his classical Psalms treatise, and read his Hebrew poetry. That in 1936 this bilingual literary persona (1882–1953) was already in Palestine/Eretz Israel, a kibbutz member paving roads of *zifzif* (coarse sand) with his wife, Martin Buber's daughter, Eva, and that he was also attracted to Yiddish literature, was information I came across much later.

How all these many details are related to the book they preface I cannot tell the reader in advance; I myself discovered some of these connections only once I finished writing it. I can only hint that Mozart and Shakespeare, Elijah and the Jewish Culture League, German Jewry, the Grimm Brothers, Buber's enterprises, Psalms, *zifzif*, burrows, and, above all—the music of the stars, or spheres, play their significant parts.

As a student, the discovery of the origins of the Music of the Spheres myth came to me as a *Menon*-like recollection—or wisdom learned from an angel (as the parallel Jewish tradition relates). I realized, of course, the Greek roots of the myth; but as I listened to what Western culture had to offer, all seemed "ours" and "mine," whether of Greek or Hebrew, English, Italian or German, Christian or Jewish origins. This continued the legacy passed on at home. Jewish and humanist traditions coalesced and enriched one another: the Bible and Shakespeare, the Midrash and Thomas Mann, and that which pertains in particular to this book—Jewish liturgical music and the music of the great classical tradition. All were thought to express human spirit at its best. In these worlds, the new Hebrew-Zionist culture found a special place and was connected to other legacies in ways that seemed obvious to us, since all was ever delivered in Hebrew (the only language spoken at my parents' home, both German émigrés of the 1930s).

That there could be tensions and conflicts between the musics I had learned to cherish, that the sublime vocal moments of the Days of Awe, at my parents' East European synagogue (they opted for that custom which seemed more authentic to them) not only dawned from a different horizon than that of the divine music of Bach or Beethoven, but were intrinsically "dissonant" to each other was only dimly grasped. As a performer and avid listener, with my father or alone, classical Western music became a major expression and exploration of self and spirit. Israeli folk music also found a place in this private pantheon, in part discovered in the small songbook *Shirej Eretz Israel* (Land-of-Israel Songs), edited by Jakob Schönberg, which was also published in Berlin in the mid-1930s, and which I eagerly seized from my parents' library as a treasure.

So the second beginning could emerge when this wholesome worldview began to crumble. Among several significant moments in that process of loss of "innocence," the most important was my increasing exposure to Wagner's galvanizing music—never heard and barely mentioned at my parents' home—and to his vexing ideas. They played against each other in various ways, and, since the 1990s, developed into thoughts and queries I began to share with my mother. This was part of a process whereby she opened herself more and more to memories, experiences, and insights related to her grim past in Nazi Germany and her ceaseless preoccupation with how German society fell under that terrible spell, and the fate that consequently befell those Jews who remained there. My mother's deep thinking, her willingness ever to unprejudicially analyze and understand, our mutual insights, and her trust energized my tortuous research, even before it really began.

The third and maybe more "practical" start followed a few years later, in 1997: an enchanting Oxfordian rainy summer evening spent with dear friends. They were interested in my research at the time on musical sympathy, on the figure of Echo, and related matters. At a certain moment during that lovely talk, Terence Cave, a literary scholar, turned to me and asked whether I had ever read George Eliot's *Daniel Deronda*; the answer was yes, as a young teen, though in a Hebrew translation. —Weren't you then too young for such stuff? Would you be interested in reading it again? It can contribute to your research.

The next morning I opened my pigeonhole at St. John's College, where I found a thick envelope containing the novel, edited by Terence Cave; I started to read it right away and discovered that, indeed, I never really had read it. The "English plot" of Gwendolyn and Grandcourt was entirely new to me, since the Hebrew translation, an abridged Zionist version, had skipped it altogether (abridged English versions, expectedly, did quite the opposite). Yet the eureka moment was different: it occurred while I was reading chapter 32, the "synagogue" chapter that, focalized through a "Gentile" outsider, tells of a staggering experience of a Friday night service in a Frankfurt Synagogue, containing details that only an insider could possibly fathom.

I immediately sensed it to be an "antidote" to Wagner and, deferring my other scholarly engagements, plunged into a study of both text and context, and their relevant Wagnerian counterparts. (This yielded an article published by the Hebrew *Teoria u'Vikoret* in 2001, translated and reworked for chapter 6, below.) Signs were strewn along the way that led to the insight that this contrast is revealing of even greater cultural meanings than those embedded in the contemporary horizons these authors partially shared. Only gradually did I perceive that there is a real story, or cultural history, lurking below, calling for narration: the story, or history (the German *Geschichte* has them both) of the "noisy Jews," as they were "heard" by non-Jews, and the way both Jews and non-Jews imagined the musical or nonmusical other as an outcome of this "hearing."

This then became a scholarly passion that engaged me in ways I could barely have envisioned beforehand: medieval history and Schoenbergian studies, ethnography real and fictive, psychoanalytic literature and history of German Jewry. It necessitated "world enough and time": the time, a fruitful one, was granted in Berlin, in my blissful *Wissenschaftskolleg* fellowship year (2004–5) in a city grimly burdened by its pasts, which paradoxically enabled profuse encounters with people, books, places, ideas, musical and stage experiences, as well as renewed Jewish life, that enriched this project immensely. The *Kolleg* with its warm and most devoted staff provided an optimal setting for creative work and enabled meeting of minds and the creation of lasting friendships. (The first fruit of this year was the programmatic article "Between Noise and Harmony: The Oratorical Moment in the Musical Entanglement of Jews and Christians," published in *Critical Inquiry* 32/2 [2006].)

I am pleased to further express my gratitude to various people and institutions. As will be evident below, the scope of my acknowledgments reflects the fact that the research and methodologies underlying this book engage diverse fields including history and musicology, literary studies, ethics and aesthetics, semiotics and cultural theories, and within musicology—an investigation into Western as well as Ashkenazi Jewish traditions.

If there is one person to whom I owe the inspiration for crossing disciplinary and conceptual boundaries, it is my sometime mentor, and eventual colleague and friend, Ruth Katz, with whom I have benefitted from a lifetime of significant intellectual discourse, and shared a few substantial projects.

Generous assistance of scholars in the abovementioned areas included David Nirenberg and Galit Hasan-Rokem in medieval and Jewish studies and history, who opened my eyes to important matters, and with whom, back in the Berlin year, I engaged, on the banks of Grunewald's beautiful lakes, in deep, thought-provoking conversations. Further in this field I have benefitted from a continuous dialogue with Israel J. Yuval. For the Christian musical aspects of the Middle Ages, the input of my colleague Yossi Maurey was vital. I would like to especially thank my colleague and friend Boaz Tarsi, whose profound understanding of Ashkenazi Jewish music turned out to be highly valuable for this study. David Nirenberg later on read the entire manuscript, as did Geoffrey Hartman, Doron Mendels, Gabriel Motzkin, and Michael P. Steinberg; their wise and trenchant comments improved the text in many important ways.

Other friends and colleagues who read significant parts of the manuscript and gave many knowledgeable and illuminating comments throughout various stages of this work and sometimes saved me from blunders are James Chandler, Richard Y. Cohen, Arnold Davidson, Carolin Emcke, Don Handelman, Ilana Pardes, Thomas Pfau, Edwin Seroussi, and Sarit Shalev-Eyni. I would like also to thank Steven Aschheim, Leon Botstein, Almut Sh. Bruckstein, John Butt, Ute Frevert, Michael Fried, Moira Gatens, Brian Gilliam, Alois Hahn, Roger Hurwitz, Yulia Kreinin, Lydia Liu, Reinhart Meyer-Kalkus, W. J. T. Mitchell, Noam Mizrahi, Felix Moeller, Doron Narkiss, Elchanan Reiner, Eliyahu Schleifer, Yael Sela, Assaf Shelleg, David Shulman, Michael K. Silber, Suzanne Stewart-Steinberg, Kenneth Stow, Naphatali Wagner, and Eli Zaretsky for fruitful conversations, suggestions, and comments.

Special thanks are due to my friend and refined literary scholar, Nita Schechet, for her thorough reading of a large part of the manuscript's first draft and for the improvement she brought to its form and rhetoric. Her devotion, combined with a profound sense of proper textual unfolding, yielded a gift of friendship of a rare kind. Many thanks are also due to Talia Trainin, a scholar and artist in her own right, for her highly sensitive and prudent editorial work on the entire book and for her numerous suggestions, poetic and otherwise, that enriched the book considerably. I am deeply grateful to my dear friend Barbara A. Schmutzler for her meticulous, highly professional, and devoted proofreading of the entire manuscript, and for her special contribution to the quality of the German translations. My thanks go also to Alexa Selph for her highly skilled compilation of the index.

Before and throughout the years of writing the book it was the Hebrew University of Jerusalem—my haven—where I always received great support and trust in enterprises that could have seemed idiosyncratic by established scholarship and research conventions. The Hebrew University provided also financial support for the publication of this book. My thanks go also to my colleagues in the department of musicology and in other fields for their friendship and for a congenial academic environment. I am most grateful to my research assistant Oded Erez, whose help in the final stages of preparing the manuscript for publication proved invaluable due to his technical and logistical help as well as his general wisdom and knowledge in music and critical theory. Adi Burtman complemented him later on, with no less devotion, accuracy, and sensibility. Mordechai Neeman set musical scores in electronic formats, faithfully and intelligently. Beyond them, my thanks go to many other students at the Hebrew University who studied with me in the last decade in various courses and seminars, and whose rich thoughts and responses reverberate in the following pages.

Many thanks are also due to other institutions and the people who hosted me there. They include the music faculty in Oxford, England and the Bach Network UK, both chaired at the time by Reinhard Strohm, who for years has been an invaluable source of professional insights and friendship; The Sara N. and J. Evans Israel Cultural Residency Program at Duke University, headed by the scholar and musician Eric Meyers; Jerusalem Institute of Advanced Studies in connection with the groups "Literature and Ethnography," and "Transmission and Appropriation of the Secular Sciences and Philosophy in Medieval Judaism"; The Cogut Center of the Humanities at Brown University, directed by Michael P. Steinberg; and the Center for the History of Emotions at the Max Planck Institute for Human Development, Berlin, chaired by Ute Frevert. I feel blessed, in the past two years, to have been a member of the Scholion Center for Interdisciplinary Jewish Studies at the Hebrew University, whose remarkable staff, headed by Israel J. Yuval, have created an engaging scholarly environment for creative work. My thanks also go to my colleagues in "The Hermeneutical Imagination" group for their illuminating discussions and their friendship. For the rare wisdom of tending to body and spirit I owe special thanks to Ephrat Michelson and her Yoga Iyengar group.

I am pleased as well to express my gratitude to the wonderful staff at Yale University Press, first and foremost to Senior Editor Jennifer Banks, for her kind and exquisite professional treatment of the manuscript, right from the start, for her responsiveness to the special needs of this book, and for the faithful investment of many other staff members, especially Christina Tucker, Piyali Bhattacharya, and Ann-Marie Imbornoni. Thanks also go to copyeditor Deborah Bruce-Hostler, for her superb judgment and thoughtful work.

My family members also contributed their part. My sister Zivia Seligman ever widened my psychoanalytic horizons, and her husband Michael Zakim engaged with relevant historiographic scope all the more significant because of our shared musical pursuits. I would like to acknowledge also the generous influence of my brothers Rami Pinchover and Yehuda Pinchover, in their love of Jewish music and their knowledge of Jewish classical hermeneutics. My niece Lotem Pinchover assisted me skillfully in bibliographic and other matters. Almost last but not least, my son Yotam HaCohen's spiritual and intellectual quest had a profound impact on the writing of this book. My innermost gratitude goes to one man, the man of my life, Yaron Ezrahi, whose emotional, intellectual, and logistical support all through this journey and beyond has surpassed all dreams and expectations. Our decision to merge our lives coincided with the genesis of this book project, and he was the first to read all the sections of this manuscript from the very first to the last, and more than once. He intuited the potential of this research even before I had fully conceived it, and was always there with his sharp and critical mind, his intellectual enthusiasm, vast knowledge, and deep musical and cultural sensibilities. Our endless conversations about shared and interrelated enterprises, and on other matters—worldly and otherwise—enriched this book in ways beyond description.

This book is dedicated to my mother, Esther Pinczower (née Fraenkel), and the blessed memory of my father Eliezer Pinczower, whose crucial role in this work the reader could already guess. My intellectual growth was inspired and nourished by their treasures of knowledge and insight, in both Jewish and general humanistic lore, their commitment to learning, and by the blessed combination of my father's rare musical understanding—classical and Jewish—and my mother's unique literary and historical sensibilities. I was blessed enough to receive their love and support throughout the work on this book and to share with them my discoveries and ideas.

Jerusalem, April 2010
Passover 5770

NOTE TO THE READER

Aiming to address a broad readership, I glossed necessary terminology—musicological, aesthetic, Jewish, historical, and so forth—en route, a glossary that might seem superfluous to the knowledgeable; I beg their patience. The resort to musical nomenclature should not hinder the nonexpert from getting the gist of the description, not to speak of the general argument.

Longer music examples feature in the book's appendix, marked app. 1, app. 2, and so forth.

On Hebrew transliteration: sources using Ashkenazi pronunciation were kept intact, otherwise Sephardic pronunciation was adopted, following either common spelling of terms and words, or rules in line with "general purpose style" of modern Hebrew.

Translations from Hebrew, German, French, and Latin are the author's, unless indicated otherwise. The biblical excerpts are mostly drawn from either the JPS (Jewish Publication Society) 1917 translation (sometimes with slight changes) or from the King James Version, according to context.

Introduction: Vocal Fictions
of Noise and Harmony

The Music Libel Against the Jews is a study of the historical categorization of the Jew as a producer of noise in a Christian universe conceived of as dominated by harmonious sounds. The accusation of the Jews as noisemakers originated in early Christianity, but it is apparently only in the second millennium, and mainly in western Europe, that it permeated cultural contexts that intensely engaged both accusers and accused. The book thus traces the path of the manifestations and roots of the noise accusations from the medieval period and examines their repercussions in modern times. I pay special attention to the opening up of the artistic sonic sphere towards the Jews in the wake of historical developments in the eighteenth century, a gesture which thereafter turned rather ambivalent. Pivotal to the Jews' struggle for aural inclusion are certain artworks—musical, literary, and, to a lesser extent, pictorial—created by both "invaders" into that common aural space and by those considered its privileged "inhabitants." My main objective is to reveal the symbolic configurations of noises and voices in the imaginary worlds constituted by these works, as they rehash old archetypal noise stories or work them through. Leading to the artistic enterprise of emancipating dissonance, or noise, as an integral part of musical expression, this path was ironically consummated (by Arnold Schoenberg among others) at a time in which "Jewish noise"—in Nazi Germany—had become politically more essentialized than ever.

HARMONY AND NOISE

That noise—prima facie an acoustic, sensorial concept—is, in terms of its perceptual content, a changing cultural construct is a long-accepted tenet.

While this study does not go against this grain, it presupposes a rather stable *cultural* notion of harmony—at least until the second half of the eighteenth century—whose *musical* content has changed in the course of the second millennium. As a classical heritage adopted and adapted by the church fathers from Greek and Latin sources, harmony invited the immediate association of a select sensory order with theological and political entities. It highlighted certain euphonious sonorities as the graceful emblem of the Lord's celestial true and charitable dominion and its embodiment on earth by the unified, ruling church. Hailing these sonorities through chants, hymns, chiming bells, processions, and carefully wrought polyphonic settings, the musical practices of the church were conceived to enhance this order in the souls of individual believers and in the community as a whole. Harmony, in other words, served the church—Catholic as well as Protestant—as a major mode of being and becoming throughout its history, defining, ideationally if not practically, its inclusive boundaries and exclusive norms.

The historical noise charge against the Jew was, then, necessarily complex, though often nonexplicit. In the course of the Christian-Jewish entangled histories, it became increasingly implicated with the ethico-theological dimensions of traditional anti-Jewish epistemology. The Jew, as Shakespeare's Lorenzo insinuated, "hath no music in himself": he is deaf, if not hostile, to the harmonious unfolding of sounds; he is pitiless, if not cruel, to those seeking sympathy and compassion; he is noisy, if not discordant, compelled to cry out to his God Jehovah, who had forsaken him and who could now barely hear him. Theology, indeed, was the basis of this "scheme," which sought empirical validation of the triumphant *ecclesia* over the abject *synagoga* through the various manifestations of the mark of Cain, believed to be borne by Jews' dejected appearance. Sonic marks of Cain could actually be heard in "real" synagogues throughout medieval Europe—those in proximity to churches, monasteries, and chapter houses. Seldom practiced according to a Christian perception of preconceived modes and modalities, notorious for their "yells" and "lamentations" and for their terrifying shofar (ram's horn) blasts, synagogues' vocalities would have been experienced by Christian auditors as issuing from an extraterritorial underworld. In a sonic universe that increasingly attempted to coordinate diversity according to prefigured concordant orders, the nonsynchronized soundscape of the *perfida synagoga* (a sonic texture termed, in professional musicology, as "heterophony") could not but become a symbol of offensive noise for ages to come: *Lärm wie in einer Judenschule* (noise/shouts/ado as in a synagogue). This exemplum was still powerfully reverberating in cities such as London and Vienna during the first half of the twentieth century.

Noise was thus more than merely a relative term against which the majority culture defined its identity and mission. There seemed to be something fixed, or, more accurately, something that had become persistent, in the practices of the accused. This, however, was, to a certain extent, a reactive state, mainly affecting Jewish communities located between Ashkenaz (as the countries in the Germanic speaking orbit were called by Jews) and England.[1] (This region is termed the "core" countries in the following pages). North Italy had its share in this history, especially at the turn of the seventeenth century. The case of (mainly medieval) Spanish Jews has its own characteristics, to which I will allude in chapter 1. I chose to concentrate on the northern countries because their history is culturally more cohesive, especially since early modernity.

In any event, while the 1492 expulsion from Spain and the subsequent Inquisition had been brutal and cruel, the most traumatic recorded events in European Jewish liturgical heritages which seem to have become vocally iconized as such were those that befell the Jewish communities in the core countries in the wake of the Crusades. It is not coincidental, as I will try to show, that crucial developments in church music took place at about that time and were symbolically canonized as hailing the church in its variety of holy missions.

Not much is known about the sonic-musical relations of Jews and Christians during long stretches between these early days and modern times, but, as far as the core countries were concerned, there seems to have been a rather strict aural separation between these neighboring religious communities, manifest in a professed refusal to borrow and lend their respective sounds.[2] This schism, including the Jews' nonacceptance of Christian musical notation, not to speak of church melodies, polyphony, and other musical procedures, has been taken for granted in modern research of Jewish music, and barely investigated in scholarly terms.

INCLUSIVE SPACES AND AESTHETIC CATEGORIES

A reflection of changing historical circumstances and ideologies, as well as of variegated musical practices and norms, the basic noise categorization underwent significant transformations in the course of subsequent centuries. Thus, for example, in the course of the sixteenth and seventeenth centuries, with the spread of reformist musical practices and the parallel "invasion" of Sephardic musical traditions from the Iberian Peninsula into northern European Jewish communities, new sonic norms and forms were introduced alongside new conceptions of vocal iconicity and separatism.[3] A similar infiltration in Italy, interacting with prevailing humanist trends, played a role in a variety of collaborations in the musical sphere between Jews and Christians at about that time.[4] These developments seemed to have affected the basic noise accusation by relativizing its grip, first and foremost through its dramatic staging. In addition, there were the sensuous encounters of the Europeans with the Ottomans from the sixteenth century onward—the first great modern encounter with "menacing" Islam—later followed by pivotal exchanges with Indian and American indigenous (sonic) cultures. These encounters partly took the edge off the clash with the Jewish soundscape, and in part shaped its unique character.[5]

During the second half of the eighteenth century, with Enlightenment projects well under way, a more crucial change took place in the mutual perception of the noise-harmony categorization. This period witnessed three major processes—intellectual, artistic, and political—that were highly conducive to the framing of a shared sonic sphere of Jews and Christians. They include the rise of modern aesthetics; the making of what was believed to be an abstract and universal musical language, and the introduction, in the core countries, of legal procedures that were designed to lead to an improvement in the legal status of the Jews in their various host countries.

All three processes were expressions of remarkable inclusive tendencies, at least as apprehended by those Jews and Christians who opted to be part of them. The development of normative aesthetics in the eighteenth century aimed to formulate universal concepts and categories for evaluating and classifying styles, genres, and individual works of art. These concepts and classifications include ontologically oriented categories (mimesis and illusion), formal ones (harmony and organicity), criteria related to social norms (moderation and taste), categories of feeling (pleasure and pain), and categories of overall aesthetic effect (the beautiful and the sublime).[6] These bifurcated pairs generally represent inherent dialectical relations, however veiled. They mark an attempt to tame self-propelling and unruly artistic entities within well-balanced and educative aesthetic environments that aimed to naturalize the prejudicial and rationalize the peculiar. Of crucial importance to the story being told here is the Aristotelian pair of pity (*eleos, Mitleid,* compassion) and fear (*phobos, Furcht*) that had already engendered a controversy in which the Jews in general, and the Jew as an aesthetic category in particular, had participated as absent-present entities. This is paradigmatically revealed in Moses Mendelssohn's contribution to the debate and in his presumed fictional embodiment in his friend's (Lessing) *Nathan der Weise.* (The "pity-fear" pair was eventually replaced by the modern "sympathy and abjection," as will emerge in my discussion of the case of Wagner and Eliot.) The fact that Jews, who at the time played only a marginal role in public social and cultural life, could participate in an intellectual exchange that became central to their further categorization in aesthetic terms is part of the irony of this history.

The making of an "abstract" musical language—known also as the classical instrumental style—should be viewed against this ideological background, to whose enhancement it largely contributed. This musical language elaborated through an interaction with dramatic and vocal music, crafted instrumental configurations that could stand unto themselves, unaided by textual labels and contextual frames.[7] These configurations not only "made sense" autonomously, but also conveyed meanings, even if their exact import was far from universal. Nonlexical by the very nature of the medium, these new musical meanings, seldom burdened by specific contents and ideas, seemed to defy specificity in favor of more transcendental significance.

Nonetheless, this musical language was never divorced from an emotional import, which, even if restrained, became highly nuanced. Nor did it subdue the dramatic disposition of its building blocks, as epitomized in the generic sonata form. Molding "narrative-less narrative" out of conflictual musical entities, the sonata-form mechanism, which had become so prevalent, guaranteed the satisfactory dénouement of these musical entities within a coherent whole. Moreover, the underlying logic that binds its progressions aimed (successfully) to be accessible to those who were duly exposed to it—growing bourgeois audiences of diverse ethnic affiliations and religious denominations.[8]

Within these expanding bourgeois audiences, in mid- and western Europe, members of Jewish origin began to find their place. What had been socially unthinkable prior to the eighteenth century, could now be entertained even before legal procedures of naturalization and emancipation were, however partially, finalized. Moderate financial capabilities and minimum citizenship privileges sufficed for such participation, which seemed not to encroach on the idiosyncratic modes of life that some Jews opted to adhere to, and others gradually abandoned. These groups (later further classified as "Orthodox," "Liberal," and "assimilated") could entertain the new and sublime art without being forced to adjust themselves to a foreign dogmatic content, when such a content existed (as in the case of Bach's Passions). They could ignore or transcend it by force of the overall musical-spiritual experience it engendered.

Moreover, well-to-do Jews—and Berlin, Paris, Budapest, Vienna, and London at the turn of the nineteenth century were home to more than a few—could privately rear a new generation of Jewish children on this musical heritage, which they absorbed as their own. This process of acculturation was not unique to music; it characterized other cultural avenues, especially trends in linguistic assimilation, not rejected by traditional Jewry. Yet music, with its unique spiritual potential, held a special attraction for them for generations to come.

POST-ENLIGHTENMENT REPERCUSSIONS

A shared sonic public space became, indeed, a fact. Precocious Jewish children (Meyerbeer, Mendelssohn, and Halévy are prime examples of this species) entered this space in the ardent belief that they could take part not only as consumers but also as artists and cultural leaders. The "Jewishness" of a composer such as Felix Mendelssohn (baptized at the age of seven) might, indeed, be debatable (and has recently provoked controversy in musicological circles). I allow myself to label him thus—as well as other authors and laypersons of scant Jewish affiliation—because they were all challenged by their Jewish ancestral roots, even when eschewing affiliation with a self-proclaimed Jewish community.

"The Jew" in this project also concerns an abstract Jew—the Jew as an aesthetic category—in his or her role as an overt or covert stereotype-prototype in literature, music, and the visual arts.[9] These two uses of the concept of Jewishness, as actual and abstract, are interrelated throughout this book, for the historical Jews that populate it were all challenged not only by their politico-ethnic classification but also by the "aesthetic" one that often directly targeted them, which they strove, not necessarily consciously, to rebut. It is, by and large, in vocal fictions they conceived that this rebuttal transpired, as the means whereby they sought to undermine personal and more general insinuations.

These struggles, however, took place in a dramatically modified environment, which no longer embraced the postulates of the Enlightenment that had launched the shared sonic spaces initially taken for granted by these authors. Indeed, in the course of the first half of the nineteenth century, major transformations in the three aforementioned dimensions—the aesthetic, the musical, and the political—seemed to erase or radically alter many of the projects of the seemingly optimistic and inclusive rationalism of the era that had preceded it. These include the rise to prominence of aesthetic categories that disrupted the well-balanced, ethically compatible, aesthetic universe of the Enlightenment; the destabilization and particularization of "abstract" musical art; and the various political reactions to the products of the ideologies of liberalism and egalitarianism, which included, first and foremost, nationalism and anti-Semitism. Let us examine these three major transformations in more detail:

(1) Among the "disruptive" aesthetic categories one finds the "bizarre," with its picturesque, grotesque, and gothic (partially overlapping) categories; the "indigenous," with its authentic, original, and local-folklore categories, and the "light" (or "Philistine") group with its popular, kitsch, and entertaining categories. And there were more. All seemed incongruent with the established Enlightenment

categories in varieties of ways, confusing notions of judgment and value. Later, the road was open to embrace entities such as the Dionysian, the uncanny (*Das Unheimlich*), and the transfigurative, which marked an attempt to transcend or annul aesthetic categorization by introducing new modes of theorizing art.

To a large extent, good bourgeois artists and audiences buttressed against these reconceived categories, perceived now as destabilizing by rejecting, rearranging, or subsuming them under the older, non-"Philistine" categories, sometimes renovating the latter by means of organic notions of origin, growth, and creativity. The irruption of the figure of the Jew and the Jew as author into the realm of art seemed to disturb this partially conscious effort, not by introducing radically new terms into this spectrum of old and new categories and criteria, but rather by changing their hierarchy and orientation. To introduce an alternative sublime, to problematize taste, and call into question the "benevolence" of art and its assumed origin, the presence of the Jew—both as an author and as an aesthetic category—destabilized the inclusiveness of the old aesthetico-social harmony.[10] Furthermore, Jewish manifestation in art challenged the notion of "sympathy." In the Jew's presence, specific fellow-feelings and the social behavior they promoted, such as compassion and friendship, became "contaminated" with their antipode, including abjection and alienation, as the "case of Wagner" demonstrates. There were, of course, other factors that contributed to transformations of the classical aesthetic ordering. Nevertheless, the very presence of the Jew as an historical and figurative entity marked predicaments in key ideas and ideologies of art, especially those concerning voice and sound.

(2) Like the more theoretical aesthetic realm, the musical (and literary) spheres—practical and ideational—that interacted with it had, in the course of the nineteenth century, radically reshuffled some of its accumulated assets, conferring on them new orientations and values.[11] Classical musical language was still carving its finest architectural edifices when its inherent cosmopolitical bent underwent a sort of Hegelian *Aufhebung*, granting its semiabstract contents an absolute metaphysical stance. Concurrently, the accessible structures of classical music could be adapted into, or adjusted to accommodate *Volksgeist* expressions of various kinds—such as domesticated folk-song genres and folk-choral repertoires (sung in glee clubs and choral societies in England, the *goguettes* in France, and in *Liederkranz* in Germany).

These idioms were rendered, in turn, within fictional (dramatic) music—German and Italian romantic opera, French grand opera and the like. Concomitantly, general emotional contents became more individualized, featuring the wanderer and the self-ironic lover (in the framework of a lied), or the desperate, inwardly torn heroine, who were either set apart from a historical society (mainly in the lied), partially historicized, or grafted into a mytho-religious environment (in opera and oratorio). The narrative bent of the musical language that had hitherto avoided programmatic scripts now tended to host stories of the fantastic and the phantasmagoric. Still, while local colors became increasingly desirable, they had to be painted so that common musical outlines would not be erased. This also affected the new banner of originality that challenged composers to forge their own, individualized style from the furnace of what gradually became defined as the people's spirit.

The ubiquitous bourgeoisie, the target audience of all this, did not always care for such nuances. They wished to have their good time, and had the means—both financial and cognitive—to do so in their salons as well as outside them. Cultured (*gebildet*) and sentimental, increasingly including Jews of various religious orientations, audiences rarely seemed to have been disturbed by their favorite artists' racial identity as long as good taste, entertainment, and status were maintained.[12]

(3) The new liberal spirit that seemed to nourish this class proved, however, much weaker in terms of its more general and concrete political agendas. The quick deterioration of liberalism, following the ascending manifestations of nationalism and rekindled anti-Semitism stemmed, among other factors, from the dialectic nature of the Enlightenment. The Napoleonic era and its consequences, the series of revolutions that ensued, contributed in different ways to these processes. The three societies that hosted our authors and their works—the German-speaking, the British, and the French—varied, of course, with regard to these processes. Consequently, they often generated different responses or approaches to similar states of affairs, as the case of George Eliot contra Wagner shows (chapter 5). In all these societies, however, waves of modern anti-Semitism turned the ancient hatred of Jews into modern xenophobic sentiments against those who, shedding their various marks of Cain, now dared to "look like you and me." For a Heine or a Meyerbeer, old *rishes*,[13] as the Jewish jargon termed the traditional hatred of Jews, had never left the stage; it only changed its colors and masks.

From the point of view of those who opted to be so identified, Jewish selfhood could not be assumed as it had in earlier times. No matter how "observant" or "progressive" one conceived oneself, one wished to be both inside this identity and outside it (or sometimes to strictly dichotomize it, as reflected in the Eastern-Jewish poet and *maskil* Jehuda Leib Gordon's famous expression: "Be a man outside your dwelling and a Jew inside"). Whether negotiated from within or from without, one's Jewishness became an almost daily challenge, more intense than ever before. Individuals and communities thus contested had to refashion themselves accordingly by delving into Jewish cultural, religious, and liturgical matters, choosing and mixing elements according to their ideological and practical needs. Music and vocal performativity played a special role in this trial both as a symptom of traditional Jewish existence (whether rejected or accepted) and as a tool to renew it. Whatever the attitude toward it—from within Jewish territory (synagogues and the like) or outside it, in relation to communal practices or individual expression—the ancient noise accusation could not be avoided. Like a genie released out of a bottle that had seemed sealed forever, it was set free in a myriad of ways by both friends and foes.

The most explicit and notorious upsurge of this specter surfaces in Wagner's *Das Judentum in der Musik* (*Judaism in Music*, 1850) lampoon. What is often regarded as his phantasmagoric invention is an expression of a far deeper substrate in the relationships between Jews and Christians, as I wish to demonstrate in this book. Of all anti-Semitic composers (and there were several) it was Wagner who ingeniously grasped an undercurrent of ambivalence regarding the sonic inclusion in the works of the Jewish authors he attacked (a group whose members included Felix Mendelssohn, Heine, Halévy, and Börne). Wagner combined this ambivalence not only with a sense of his own precarious position as musician and composer, and not only with surging anti-Semitic trends, but also with tarnished synagogal reports that now bore ethnographic corroboration (see chapter 3). Yet Wagner is an exception in this history, for while he elucidated the accusation, he also modernized and outwardly rationalized it. Earlier and later, most of its manifestations are either cursory or, as stated above, assume the form of a figurative plot that could generate a fictional world of its own or embed itself in an existing one.

VOCAL FICTION: ACCOMMODATIONS AND OPERATIONS

Why should noise accusations mostly inhabit a fiction, deploying its vocal resources? My answer is rather simple: to begin with, the noise accusation appears as a widespread story, a sort of narrated blood libel featuring a plot by Jews to murder an innocent Christian victim in order to silence the boy's harmonious musicality. The most pervasive motivation imputed to the Jews in this "plot" was that, allegedly, they could not endure a virgin boy's pure singing of Marian antiphones and, therefore, killed him. This archetypal schema was iterated in various versions and guises, and found, still in the Middle Ages, reverse echoes in at least one famous Jewish martyrdom story. The basic plot is itself a reverberation of the Passion story in contemporary (twelfth to sixteenth centuries) musical terms (see chapter 1). Hence, the *com*-passion motives and motifs are inherent in it and are subsequently emphasized.

From a generic point of view, in the literary medium, the plot (or anti-plot) could appear as a short story (rhymed or simple), a play (a Passion play, a religious drama, or their amalgamation with other genres and forms), a poem, or, later on, as a novella or as part of a novel. When musicalized, it could emerge or be counteracted in an oratorio—the genre par excellence for featuring inclusive and exclusive gestures, through a contemporary dialogue with a biblical story along an intricate temporal dynamics. From the time of Bach and Handel, the oratorio was handled so as to powerfully pile up diverse communal sediments and work through or enhance their import (by means of well-formed "oratorical moments"). Opera could subsume such procedures while further dramatizing and concretizing inherent vocal conflicts. Halévy, Meyerbeer, Wagner, and Schoenberg opted to so effect them. Echoes of the sonic plight could also find a significant expression in the more modest lieder and songs (as in the case of Nathan-Byron's *Hebrew Melodies*) and in certain programmatic music. In all these, the clash between the libelous (fictive) element and the fictional one is destined to bring about ironic effects and dramatic uncertainties.

Whatever medium or genre, the plot's unfolding and the inner communications it embodies are approached here in terms of a "fictional world"—a concept that addresses the nature of both "fictionality" and "world" as well as their conjunction.[14] In the following discussion, "fictionality" stands for the illusionary allure whereby certain artistic devices wrap the occurrences related, described, or depicted by the works that enact them, separating them from "lived reality" while granting them vivacity. "Worldness," on the other hand, relates to the degree of wholeness, regulation, and coherence a fictional work bestows on the succession of occurrences to which it refers, affecting their boundaries with other worlds, whether "real" or "fictive."

Despite attempts to keep fictional worlds apart both from one another and from real ones, they tend to blur, overlap, intersect, interpenetrate, and coincide with each other through various cognitive and semiotic bonds.[15] Fictional worlds often serve as models and inspiring modes of imagining "real" ones, and "real" worlds provide much of the fabric of fictional ones. This is theoretically significant for the analysis of the "mental universes" engendered by works of art and other artifacts, affecting larger cultural and intellectual itineraries. The role of sympathy, solidarity, alienation, and abjection—the communal modes, as I term them henceforth—is crucial in this connection. Central to the noise plots, the present study considers these modes in their double role as both ethical and aesthetic mediators, linking insiders and outsiders within and outside fictive worlds. Within each world, they function as emotional and moral attitudes toward "friends" and "interlopers," either separating or grouping them together. Between worlds, they act as regulatory forces, drawing their audience into their respective spheres or eliciting negative responses to them.

Thus the blurring of traditional borders between the real and the fictive, the aesthetic and the ethical, abjection and sympathy (as prime communal modes), as I argue elsewhere,[16] substitutes the mirror metaphor, so central to mimetic art, with a "spiral" one—a flexible, formative principle, overcoming ontological barriers. The spiral, I maintain, implies a concentric configuration in which internal protagonists and external audience are located along the same, continuous line. Such a line measures distance, but at the same time enables a smooth passage from one circle of the spiral into the next. Sympathetic projections from each and every point along the route of the spiral may be imagined as individual trajectories toward the object of compassion, located at the center of the spiral and mobilizing it. At the same time, expansions of spirals in space emanate various sympathetic dynamics (or the opposite, a dynamics of alienation) and *foci* of repulsion and attraction.

Each such spiral has its own ethical, aesthetic, and political advantages or hindrances. It may encourage judgment and thus a "proper" aesthetic distance. It may sensitize to varieties of human predicaments, thereby enriching one's moral sensibility. By virtue of all this, an aesthetic-experiential spiral is able to evoke awareness of political misuses and abuses. Through the magnetic fields it activates, however, such a spiral is capable of forcefully drawing the audience into the fictional, blurring its sense of reality. Immersing the audience in fantasy and mythology, it often does so while replicating the familiar and reproducing a seemingly homogeneous human texture.

The political implications of such configurations can be problematic, if not dangerous, as Friedrich Nietzsche and Bertolt Brecht long maintained. While I do not share all their convictions, their teachings nourish my analysis. In any event, "alienation," as it functions in this context, is a term both larger and narrower than Brecht's famous *Verfremdung*, firstly because it can be located in the fictional world itself, and secondly, because of its proximity to abjection and repulsion. On the whole, the possibilities of converging and diverging sympathy, compassion, solidarity, alienation, and abhorrence are not confined to single plots or ideologies, as we shall see, nor necessarily to redemptive or catastrophic stories, which often deploy these relational modes in more predictable ways.

PERFORMED VOCALITIES

Understanding the internal workings of a fictional world—its semiosis—calls for an engagement with its underlying symbolic logic. What could be an endless enterprise is limited in the present study to tracing vocalities as themes, structures, and carriers of performative gestures. The thematic components of vocal elements inhere in the archetypal plots of noise and harmony, becoming, in most of them, pivotal and well differentiated. Structured in the work's (world's) fabric—poetically, musically, or both—vocalities defy fictionality and often, if not always, become real: a voice singing *that* song (rather than a symbolic rendition of speech); harmonious sounds reaching our ears as well as those of the dwellers of their fictional world; Daughters of Voice speaking to us directly—all these and their like, reaching beyond ontological barriers, as pieces of the "real." Such a convergence of the real and the symbolic causes documentary and fictional ethnographic stories to exchange places (chapter 3) and assist sympathy in pulling us into the unreal. Bearing symbolic expression—in recitative, aria, or the like—vocality renders performative speech acts such as swearing, praying, anathematizing, and sanctifying audible; or even becomes the vehicle for performing identity: a Jesus, a woman, a Jew, or sometimes, as in the case of Halévy's Rachel—*La Juive*—a conflation of the last.[17]

Semiosis, in the present enterprise, is further constrained by reception history; by the way the works have been grasped and interpreted by performers (adding another layer to the performativity of voices) and their audiences. I believe that such interpretations should give vent to implied meanings in relation to new intertextual and contextual frames. Without strictly dividing the vocal-political unconscious from the more conscious and deliberate,[18] I have attempted to trace the broader contours of this history beyond intentions and reflections of its protagonists.

By and large, the order of presentation is responsive to the chronological, thematic, and generic coordinates discussed in this introduction. Chapter 1 addresses historico-theological roots and vocal manifestations of the noise accusation in the High Middle Ages up to the premodern era, alternating between medieval and modern viewpoints. From narratives, as well as liturgical and musical pieces dating from the first Crusades to the sixteenth century, I extrapolate the possible repositories of that time in subsequent collective sonic images shared by each community. These include iconic expressions of the Passion (*Pascha*)–Passover conflictual concurrence and versions of blood libels against those regarded as unmusical Jews. The chapter moves then to Shylock and some contemporary brethren who were accused of or represented as lacking musicality. On the whole, these narratives and rituals unveil the affinity of the nonharmonious with the dark and gloomy, calling attention to certain "benighted" elements they harbor.

The shadows of night will follow us throughout this journey, almost comprising an aesthetics of their own, that partially capsizes that of light and harmonious order. Phenomenologically speaking, night and noise share an otherness, a murkiness associated with the abject; the one whose voice does not cohere with those around him seeking refuge in obscurity. When coupled, night and noise can become ominous; through noise, a subjugated community terrifies its religious oppressors, who flee for their life. Then its members can freely engage with their traditional worship, with their forbidden *alter Brauch* (old custom; that is the Druids' successful strategy, in Goethe-Mendelssohn's *First Walpurgis Night* of 1831). Night associations reverberate throughout the book, calling for further exploration.

Chapter 2 first elaborates on the new intellectual climate that emerged with the Enlightenment, which nurtured ideas of sympathy and egalitarianism and new ideas in music aesthetics, encouraging Jews to join in and participate in what they believed would yield, for the first time, an inclusive sonorous world. It then discusses exemplary works effecting new historical sensibilities and interreligious tolerance—Bach's Passions, Lessing's "Jewish" plays, and Handel's oratorios—in relation to the communal modes they enact and the "oratorical moments" they could potentially evoke in their first and subsequent performances. Chapter 3 analyzes the resurfacing of vocal charges against Jews, and their rejoinders, in ethnographic and pseudoethnographic reports of synagogal "disharmonious" services by "enlightened" and Romantic writers as different as Christian Edelmann, Charles Burney, Heymann Steinthal, and Lion Feuchtwanger. It also discusses the internal, partly defensive harmonization of the synagogal service as well as the paradoxical search for its "authentic" element. Heine's *Hebrew Melodies* (in addition to other vocal poems) and their alleged model in the musical-poetical *Hebrew Melodies* of Isaac Nathan and Lord Byron are part of this real and fictional scene.

In chapter 4 I grapple with subversive responses to "vocal charges" in operas, oratorios, and novellas (Halévy's *The Jewess*, Meyerbeer's *The Huguenots*, Heine's *Rabbi of Bacharach*, and others). I analyze contemporary aesthetic-semiotic ideas concerning the expressivity of music and the modes of signification underlying the creation of worlds projected by these works as well as the covert and overt ideologies which uphold them. Against this background I also probe the sonic embodiment of imaginary prophets who voice their "negative theology" before a multitude hostile to their message (Mendelssohn's *Elijah* and Meyerbeer's *The Prophet*). In chapter 5, I examine the aesthetic categorization of the Jew as epigone, unmusical and uncompassionate, as propounded by Schopenhauer and Richard Wagner and deconstructed by George Eliot. The sonic ambience of the Order of the Grail and the Jewish synagogue that fosters the emergence of their respective "saviors"—Parsifal and Daniel Deronda—is assessed in terms of effecting mechanisms of sympathy and compassion in the two related oeuvres.

By way of concluding this turbulent history, chapter 6 concentrates on Schoenberg's creative career vis-à-vis the transformations of his (latent) aesthetic theology. Coping with the complex legacy of the noise allegation and its aesthetic-theological ramifications, the import of Schoenberg's oratorical works (including *Jakobsleiter*, *Moses und Aron*, and *Kol Nidre*) is assessed against the background of contemporary Jewish authors' works burdened by that legacy in different ways, including those of Freud, Kafka, David Vogel, and Theodor Reik. The chapter points to a possible transcendence of the old noise charge in Schoenberg's works, probably echoing Spinoza's political theology that intrigued Schoenberg's contemporaries. (Mahler is only marginally treated in this volume, for reasons of periodization and limitation of scope.) Chapter 7 shifts direction in discussing the ultimate essentialization of the noise accusation in Nazi propaganda films and concludes with a lesson learned from Thomas Mann's *Doctor Faustus*. The Epilogue ponders on voices and vocalities—some uttered throughout this volume, others unheard yet latent. It elaborates on their irrepressible nature in connection with their particular expressive load: as carriers of traumatic experience. The somewhat fuzzy demarcation line between the first seven centuries of the present history (chapter 1) and what follows, is reconsidered along these paths. I then briefly discuss the fate of noise charges in our present extremely boisterous world that has lost its aspiration for inclusive harmonies and overarching sympathies.

Before embarking on this journey, let me equip the reader with a synoptic view of the vast territory throughout which we are about to travel: at the outset, noise and harmony are rather diametrically opposed; aesthetics, theology, and politics converge in what appears, to a large extent, a Platonic universe, upholding the harmony-noise dichotomy in various spheres of life. External and internal soundscapes, celestial and terrestrial, seem to abide by its precepts, which loosen themselves up perhaps only in the orbit of the profane. In this "province," Jews, the pariahs, bear the acrimonious politico-theological burden of the noneuphonious Other almost alone. Eschewing the noise-harmony dichotomy, Jews appear to consider their own music rather favorably.[19]

On our way to modernity, these seemingly clear-cut divisions begin to blur. Also the cultural norms and practices associated with them are less easily categorized. Sectarianism increases, and with it plural harmonious forms. A noncongruent sonoric "federation" seems to emerge. However heterogeneous this process is, Western society turns gradually cacophonous. Towards the end of the second millennium, it even abandons dreams of uniform global sonority. In the external public sphere, with the growth of urbanization and industrialization, nondesirable sound — mechanical and human — proliferates; noise thus becomes a target of both legal and environmental consideration. In the artistic realm, reputable harmonious configurations turn conventional, losing their auratic status and cultural-theological primacy. New aesthetic categories enter the game, generating combinations incompatible with the sharp dichotomies of the past.

In its modernist attire, the old noise accusation may appear to the traveler to engage each of these realms separately or jointly. Thus the "noise-as-in-the-synagogue" defamation sometimes loses its sting in relation to the propagation of other particularistic communal sonorities. With the growth of ethnographic interest, synagogal soundscape evokes, at times, exotic curiosity, especially after going halfway to satisfy conventional harmonic sensibilities. Concomitantly, the comparative "as" (in "Noise *as* in the synagogue") applies itself to new vociferous elements abundant in modern cities and societies, exacerbating the old noise accusation. In certain orbits, one can discern that even conventional harmony is framed as "noise": those abiding by its rules are regarded as lacking authentic musicality, succumbing to mimicry or dead forms (Wagner on Mendelssohn).

In the Jewish department, we encounter individuals and groups, especially those that aspire to be integrated into the general Western culture, who are attracted to aesthetic forms that allow for multivocality and multitemporality: the oratorio and related genres. Without forgoing particularistic identity, they aesthetically join imagined communities from which they were formerly segregated. Oratorios play, however, dialectic games; we may observe oratorical works that transform into nationalist, or even racist configurations, performing mythological unities. In their own communal sphere, some Jews opt for the conventional harmonious, catering to both outsiders and insiders, while still seeking indigenous musical elements. Within the aesthetic, or even the purely musical, individuals appear to shatter the hierarchical order implied in the harmonious arts, questing for alternative aesthetic categories or new artistic values. Schoenberg's "emancipation of dissonance" is among them; his search, as he argues, stems from exploring untrodden modes of expressivity. Sometimes, his multivocal soundscapes turn unruly despite attempts to regiment them. Noise, in the urbane sense, is basically alien to his artistic visions; it does engage, however, creators around him, Jews and others. The Nazis attack wherever they can;

they are most blatant when abusing traditional Jewish sonorities. But there they become enmeshed in unavoidable ideological and artistic paradoxes.

These entanglements terminate abruptly when a millennium of Jewish settlement in Europe is cruelly ripped apart. Yet some of their reverberations continue, giving rise in other places to new artistic forms and sonic imaginaries. Moreover, notwithstanding the particularities of the musical conjunctions here portrayed and the conceptual and critical undertones they forbear, they may cast light on other politico-theological sonic environments and the contesting and converging soundscapes of the minorities and individuals that populate them.

Assessed from such a broader perspective, this book constitutes perhaps the first attempt to trace latent and manifest currents in the encounters of Ashkenazi Jewish and Christian Western music as aspects of the ingress of Jewish composers and musicians into classical music spaces. Examining both denied and desired reciprocal musical borrowings between these two sonic worlds, this volume purports to offer new perspectives on the problematics of continuity, discontinuity, and the exotic in the relation of modern music to past musical cultures.

———··◄∞►··———

RECIPROCATED RITUALS AND NOISY ENCOUNTERS: MUSIC LIBELS AND THEIR ANTIDOTES

Part I—LAMENTO. Decidedly of Jewish inspiration—[a] mixture of bitterness, violence and of pain. Don't fear an "excess" of expression. This old bruised race whose sufferings throughout the centuries cannot be measured! Recall the Bible, the ardour of the Psalms, of Oriental blood. Recall those poor old fellows which you have certainly met in the streets, on the roads . . . with their long beards, sad, desperate, dirty . . . and who still have some hope—(what hope?) as they *mumble their prayers in Hebrew.*

—*Ernest Bloch, program notes for the* Quatuor à cordes, *1916*[1]

Our story begins fragmentarily, in dim pictures and weak reverberations of medieval Jewish and Christian communities in midwestern Europe. It sketches sonic encounters between these communities, or avoidances thereof. It proposes a possible genealogy of the noise accusation from within the complex constellations in which the adversarial communities were entangled. This genealogy extends between the High Middle Ages and the premodern era, the turbulences in the wake of the Reformation and Counter-Reformation included. It dwells on some particular configurations, for their own sake, and sketches others, to expand the vista. Lenses are polished largely by modern scholarship: European and Jewish histories, musicology, literary criticism, art history, philology, theology, and liturgical studies. Sometimes perspective emerges from imaginaries[2]—rather than scholastic arguments—of Jews and non-Jews from the nineteenth century onward, such as the one above. The search, in this case, is conducted through modes of experience that have survived—however transfigured—in essentially different historical phases.

A distinction between the two perspectives is not always easy to keep, since the historiography we are engaging in has its roots in general imaginings that Jews have fashioned of their past. This holds true for the historians who mapped modern Jewish history within the paradigm of the *Wissenschaft des Judentums* ("Science of Judaism"), from Heinrich Graetz to Simon Dubnov. Fascinated by the discovery of the Hebrew chronicles from the First Crusade in the Rhineland towns (dating 1096, "the Tatnu Sorrows" in the insiders' jargon), they adopted these insiders' stories as history. Moreover, these historians applauded the narrated acts of immolation (*Kiddush HaShem*) as tokens of Jewish steadfastness, while concomitantly advocating the rootedness of the German Jews in the country, from whence they hoped to negotiate anew Jewish existence, with both church and state.[3] In a search for an indigenous musical lore, musicological research of Jewish music in the first decades of the twentieth century—in particular that of A. Z. Idelsohn—was deeply committed to a grand national vision. While the foundational historiographical paradigm has undergone significant transformations in subsequent generations, its counterpart in the sphere of music still holds for present-day researchers, despite obvious drawbacks. In both scholarly cultures, present-day ideological and methodological contentions, some harsh and uncompromising, do not render easy the grasping of a path in these Gothic mazes either.

This crux has led me to plunge into this intricate universe through one of its least explored yet highly intriguing knots: the rise, in the Catholic circles, of a new type of anti-Jewishness (or Judeophobia)[4] concomitantly with the development of new musical genres, in both church and synagogue. This concurrence, which could effect an unprecedented coalescence of identity and expression at crucial moments in the interactions between Jews and Christians, became musically iconized, to resurface as such in successive sonic encounters in future centuries. *Grosso modo*, these interactions seem to fall into three realms of becoming: (1) musical practices that played a role in the making of separate and mutual sonic identities; (2) specific aural components of established rituals in the respective communities—mainly those of Passover and Easter—that were formative in the perceptions of the collective Self and the collective Other for generations to come; and (3) widespread libelous narratives about Jews' "murderous unmusicality," and their subdued Jewish responses, assessed against the backdrop of the ritual murder accusations (blood libels) and host desecration allegations. The main part of the present chapter is structured around those three major concerns.

If the historical point of departure in this chapter is mainly the eleventh and twelfth centuries, it broadly drifts toward the High Middle Ages, with key imaginaries clustering in the course of the fourteenth century. The chapter's second part moves forward to the next two and a half centuries, elaborating on the premodern vocal fictions that featured "staged" noise accusations, attesting to the latter's persistence and reconfiguration in new cultural and theological contexts. Curiously, their fictional loci converge in northern Italy, where the first Jewish ghettos were erected. That northern Italy may stand here as the borderline of the core countries (meaning, in the present study, the German-speaking countries, France, and Britain, as discussed in the introduction) is a premise supported by extant historical evidence.

DISTINCT COMMUNITIES AND "CROSS"-COMMUNICATION BETWEEN NOISE AND HARMONY

Present historiography of the Jews of northwestern Europe since the First Crusade still debates the question of to what extent these minority groups entertained meaningful interactions with neighboring ruling Christian majorities, beyond (or between) the aggressive attacks launched by groups of the latter. All agree that long stretches of regulated coexistence interlaced with the martyrological and other gory events, yet the question regarding the extent of social, economic and cultural (including religious-theological) exchange between the two communities has remained significantly unsettled. Generally speaking, the Jewish twelfth-century revival in northwestern Europe is understood in terms of the contemporary renaissance in Christian society, but this in itself does not necessarily imply direct interrelations.[5] While commercial and other material transactions never stopped, cultural connections between the groups seem less widespread.[6]

In all symbolic transactions, save the financial one, Jews, always in inferior positions, were destined to be cast more as borrowers than as lenders, influenced than influential. Even here the picture varied, for Jews were filtering channels of influence. In what concerns artistic craftsmanship, in the pictorial realm—in light of the general restriction against figural representation of the sacred (following the second commandment) one would expect to find an avoidance of conspicuous contact. Less problematic should rank the exchanges of poetic forms and literary motifs within such schemes, whereas musical ones—the most abstract, less dogmatically "tainted" of all these media—could be expected to present no significant obstacle.

Here lies our first historical paradox: the scope of such deliberate exchanges seemed to go precisely in the opposite direction: scant musical transactions, marginal poetic exchanges and religiously acceptable pictorial ones. Concerning the latter, we find in the High Middle Ages rich Jews hiring Christian artists to ornament their sacred manuscripts—the Bible, prayer books, Passover Hag-

Fig. 1.1. *Yotser* of Shabbat Ha-gadol (heralding Passover), Maḥzor, Germany, 1300–30, Cod. Levy 37, fol. 169v. Courtesy of the Staats- und Universitätsbibliothek, Hamburg. Proselytizing widespread and heavily loaded Christian icons in their own holy books, Jews in the late Middle Ages subtly retorted Christian allegations. The illustration for a *piyyut* sung on the Eve of Passover shows a blinded synagoga becoming the beloved woman of the Song of Songs, dressed as queen, led by her beloved, wearing the *Judenhut* (by then decreed by Christian authorities), to the chosen lands of Lebanon and Amana.

gadahs, and more, with an eye ever open to proper transfigurations of the borrowed iconographical forms (see figure 1.1).[7] Liturgical literary borrowing was quite rare for Ashkenazi Jews; they had their own rich Hebrew poetic forms, which continued to flow from other diasporas, especially Spain, inspiring their own.[8] In music the scene was more extreme, with both communities becoming sonically estranged at least ever since the second millennium, declaratively but to a large extent also practically.[9] This paradox is intensified when approached through phenomenological lenses: in the small medieval towns, in which Jews used to settle within Christian populations, one could not avoid hearing sounds and voices coming from adjacent streets and houses of prayer. Furthermore, within the pretechnological aural environment that characterized medieval towns, "the effect of a single cry" must have been clearly felt, as Johan Huizinga has famously maintained, not to speak of that of the ever-dominating sounds of bells that "rose ceaselessly above the noises of busy life and lifted all things unto a sphere of order and serenity":[10]

> The bells were in daily life like good spirits, which by their familiar voices, now called upon the citizens to mourn and now to rejoice, now warned them of danger, now exhorted them to piety. They were known by their names: big Jacqueline, or the bell Roland. Every one knew the difference in meaning of the various ways of ringing. However continuous the ringing of the bells, people would seem not to have become blunted to the effect of their sound.[11]

Yet not for all did the bells toll similarly. The exclusion of the Jews from Huizinga's picturesque rendition replicates that of the reality drawn; typical, as such, to historians of Europe until quite recently. Cognizant of the denotations of these auditory signs, Jews in their narrow *Judengassen* would have interpreted them in their own way. They would have experienced differently the less direct messages emitted by sounds of street processions and other outdoor ceremonies, where the vocalities of plainchant reverberated; differently than their Christian neighbors would they have felt towards secular sound forms, though less alienated than in relation to the solemn and often inauspicious religious genres.[12]

And what about Christians? The phrase *ein Lärm wie in einer Judenschule* (noise as in the synagogue, or as loud and disorderly as in the synagogue), or in its late medieval form: *das geschray der Judischeit in irer synagog* (the cries of the Jews in their synagogues), an expression that continued to reverberate for many centuries,[13] apparently means that Christians did not wish to pay close aural attention to that which transpired there; this itself had a history since the first millennium. Noise, like dirt (following Mary Douglas' famous claim),[14] especially when attributed to the despicable Others, repels the perceivers who cease to discern in it variety and richness. It seems, however, that even such perceptual obstruction could not fend non-Jews off from noticing the shofar's (ram horn) strident blasts, blown during the period of the Jewish High Holidays. Indeed, this animalistic roaring must have aroused anxiety—a different sort of anxiety than the one purported to be religiously instigated within the community of their emitters. Leo Spitzer claimed that *fare un ghetto* meant to make uproar, attesting thus for similar defamation, proposing that the premodern segregation of Jews within a ghetto's confines seems to have been associated with the old defamation.[15] In any event, as late as 1871, Pope Pius IX accused the Jews, following the fall of the ghetto and the subsequent dismemberment of the Vatican state, of noisily polluting the sacred city.[16]

Though not explicitly referring to the shofar, a recent study by Kenneth Stow brings ample evidence to the entrenched presence of this noise aversion connected to the synagogue, issuing with Chrysostom, through Gregory the Great, increasingly and more overtly elaborated in the second millennium.[17] As Stow shows, this aversion was deeply connected to the image of the impure "Jewish dogs," whose origin refers to Matthew 15:26—those to whom Jesus' bread was not being thrown, who later took their revenge in devouring the host. It is worth quoting here a whole passage from Stow's description:

> So canine was the Jews' image that even synagogal chanting was likened to "barking." More than one papal text invokes the term for barking, *ululare*, to refer to the *clamore* attached to the synagogue service. A letter by King Henry III of England in 1253 employs *ululare*, as well as the companion term, *strepitum*, a racket. The term appears again in a text of Philip V of France in 1320, which speaks in nearly the same breath of "their braying" (*suos latratos*) and also "their barking" (*suos ululates*). Philip directed that the offending synagogue from whose walls these sounds were emanating be removed; its "noise competed" (*concurrenter emittere*) with the prayer of the nearby church. Jewish prayer, if not all Jewish practice, seems universally to have been sensed as the yelping of dogs "pra/eying" to devour the host.[18]

Without disrupting Stow's doggish environment, I propose a different interpretation to *ululare*, predominating in the papal texts. Taken among its etymological descendents in Spanish (*ulular*), Italian (*ululare*), English (*ululate*), and maybe also German (*heulen*), this onomatopoeic verb denotes a rather mournful, howling sound describing the hooting of owls and other nocturnal birds and animals, as well as the sound made by strong wind.[19] Curiously, the verb is used sometimes to define the sound emitted by the shofar's *t^erua'ah* as "a long ululating 'wailing' sound." "There are two main variants of the True-ah [*sic*]," explains an insider text. "One tradition uses nine separate short calls, in rapid sequence. The other is a single long call with nine wavering ululations."[20] This meaning can still be linked to dogs' howling via the coyote, whose Latin name is *Canis latrans*, a figure that will be resumed in chapter 6 via Kafka's story, "Investigations of a Dog."

Throwing light on Christian imaginaries, this invaluable evidence does not account for the Jews' reluctance to borrow non-Jewish sonorities, all the more so, since their brethren from eastern and southern countries—mainly, but not solely Muslim, were basically embracing them.[21] Also, it leaves unanswered the question of why the Jews abhorred lending their own auditory capitals to Christians when the latter craved them (as will be subsequently elaborated). Nor does it explain why these Jews eschewed learning the emerging technology of the notational system, so painstakingly developed in monasteries at least since the ninth century. Aimed to faithfully render crucial musical information, it could have been adopted by Jews for their own musical needs, the way they did with other foreign forms of inscription and encoding.[22] These quandaries should be further grappled with against the ascending new liturgical and paraliturgical genres and musical procedures in the neighboring institutions of the church. This series of queries was seldom—if ever—tackled in the research literature, and seldom diagnosed as such. The scarcity of written documents referring to relevant circumstances might play a role here; it definitely renders any attempt to cope with this complexity partially speculative (see fig. 1.2 and plate 1 for an exceptional illustration).

And yet there seems to be an important key to the harmony-noise encounters of Christians and Jews, whose relations qua adversarial religious communities—the subaltern of which adhered to its self-isolation as "pariah nation," to use Max Weber's well-known formulation in *Ancient Judaism*—underwent major transformations at that period. Though still debated, it is increasingly agreed among scholars that Jews in the Rhineland and related areas were not holdovers from Roman and early medieval settlements, but were mostly "newcomers" from Mediterranean homelands.[23] As part of these newly arranged communities' urge to shape their liturgical life—whether in the face of the horrific 1096 pogroms and subsequent events, or in relation to their innovative theological ideas and their reinforced religious commitments, they gradually and rather spontaneously formed what is known as the Ashkenazi *Minhag* (or religious custom, held as distinct from abiding *Halakha*).[24] In what concerns collective worship, these developments called for performative practices of a radically different nature from those of the neighboring churches. How did this yield the kind of soundscape characterized, if not categorized, as dominated by noise (*Geschray*, or *Lärm*, and their like)?

Fig. 1.2. (and plate 1). Parma Psalter, Emilia-Romagna (northern Italy), late thirteenth century. Parma, Biblioteca Palatina, Ms. Parm. 1870, fol. 213v. Courtesy of the Biblioteca Palatina. The words "Hallelujah, Sing to the Lord a new song," are exemplified in this Jewish psalter by a choir chanting under direction of a man who reads a manuscript with square notation of Hebrew words. The text in the manuscript reads: *ein kamokha ba-'elohim*, from Shabbat's morning prayer, sung upon opening the ark (this connects to, or connotes the occasion of, reading psalms on Shabbat, as designated by the heading of the psalter's page). It may well have been inspired by the Christian tradition of manuscript illumination whereby the phrase *Cantate Domino canticum novum* often received a pictorial complement in the form of an image of a singing choir. In any event, a Jewish-Italian psalter, it does not seem to reflect practices of Ashkenazi Jews. Whether it conveys real or "nonsense" music is hard to say.

One speculation can lead us to think about this space as characterized, from early times on, by "heterophonic chant-mumbling," an effect aptly deconstructed by Boaz Tarsi as occurring "when the members of the congregation quietly (almost to themselves) simultaneously mumble chantlike patterns, approximating the same musical gesture on the same text (although not clearly enunciating it) but not the same absolute pitch, speed, rhythm, or exact musical pattern."[25] While this sort of mumbling is evident in later descriptions of synagogal sonorities[26] the question is whether this goes all the way back to late medieval times. Litanies, loud lamentations, and other poetical genres composed in the wake of Jewish martyrology of 1096 and subsequently, might have been conducive to its instigation. As we shall see, the etymology of *Lärm* leads in this direction. Even more important have been the unique relations between the congregation and its emissaries (*shliḥei tsibur*)—the "carriers of prayer," (*ba'alei t^efilah*; *Vorbeter*), since late antiquity, if not earlier, that were distinct from any official order of priests or cantors. More spontaneous and egalitarian, more importuning and elegiac than their Christian counterparts' services, the aural gestalt of the responsorial modes of performance that emerged in the synagogue could have gradually become these communities' hallmark, which they guarded proudly and tenaciously.[27]

As for the musical content itself, the complex melodic system that characterizes the mature Ashkenazi liturgical music evolved in a totally different track than that of Catholic liturgy. Scant surviving documents notwithstanding, one can still argue that even in its early stages, this music's "mode of conduct,"[28] must have reflected highly nuanced calendrical forms of recitation especially for Shabbat and the various festival services. The renowned poet and cantor Jacob ben Moses Moelin (c. 1360–1427) gives musical instructions in his highly influential *Minhagei Mahril* (first printed 1556), attesting to a rather entrenched musical system, in his times, that had not developed overnight.[29]

Early in the history of this musical tradition, the most elevated and internally structured prayers—such as certain Kaddishim, *Tal* (Dew), and *Geshem* (Rain) prayers, and other central prayers of the Days of Awe—gave rise to individually shaped melodic configurations.[30] This group of tunes, labeled as *scarboves*, is known also as *Missinai Niggunim*—"Tunes given at Sinai," given to Moses on the Holy Mount of Revelation, together with other parts of the oral tradition. This label follows the thirteenth-century *Sefer Hasidim*'s instruction not to use the tune of Torah (Pentateuch) in other parts of the Bible, rather, that each tune will be sung "as established, all according to the law of Moses from Sinai, as written, and He [God] 'will answer [Moses] with a voice'" (Exodus 19:19).[31]

The attribution reflects the high esteem in which those musical entities were held in these communities, bestowing on them a special aura of sacredness and primordiality. Moreover, it may point to the role of the trope recitation of the Pentateuch, Prophets, and Scrolls, following the Tiberian *Masorah* signs and instructions of the ninth century, in the development of increasing text sensitivity in this vocal tradition.

The unwritten norms and forms reflected by such sonic procedures seemed to have rendered a semiotically rich tonal conduct, evoking specific religious emotions and inspiring identifiable communal moods associated with the various festivals and other occasions and celebrations, related both to annual and life cycles. These musical networks were shared, with local variations, by central European and—following expulsions and wanderings—also by the eventual Eastern European Jewish communities.[32]

In the adjacent churches, monasteries, and convents, sound was ordered in a very different manner. The new religious phenomena or developments of central importance in this context include the ascendance of the Eucharist as a key ritual and doctrine alongside the newly conceived Corpus Christi rituals, the emerging Marian cult, and new modes of devotion and narration to which it gave birth. The combative religio-political consciousness that gave rise to the Crusades seemed to have been partially inspired by these theological and performative elements.

The new modes of worship associated with these developments enriched and further enhanced the musically established world of the Roman Mass and Office, with its Ordinary (texts repeated daily) and its Proper (those specifically related to calendrical holidays and events). As indicated above, unlike the vocal world of the neighboring Jewish community, this one was managed through music manuscripts, which established and canonized the rendition of large parts of the musical entities involved in this centralized and hierarchically controlled ritual.[33] This was meant to encourage musical unity in and across communities, and a well-controlled ceremony whose character and dynamics were planned in relation to the "propriety" of the occasion.[34] While there was a certain flexibility in the choice of the chants of the Ordinary, high discipline aspired to preserve the well-established order of the entire event, in the spirit of what may be described as an Augustinian temporal unfolding within an Ambrosian synaesthetic space.[35]

Within the Mass (the liturgical occurrence of the Eucharist), parts of the Eucharist's calendrical Proper—the Introit, Gradual, Alleluia, Tract, Offertory, and Communion—are the oldest in the Mass cycle. As such, they bear traces—

both textual and musical—of ancient liturgies, of which the Jewish one could play a significant role, at least in the collective memory. Due to their function as accompaniment of ritualistic actions, they are considered the most consecrated, to be performed by a select few. These ancient and nonmetrical melodic forms stand in contrast to their counterparts in the Ordinary, whose melodies are usually dated later, many of them in the twelfth century, and which engage more communal forms of singing, allowing for a nonexpert choir or congregation to take part.[36] The Communion itself, despite its earlier origin, is musically rather simple,[37] accompanying the action of the congregation, which approaches the altar to receive the host. The combination of simple musical form and free procession of the congregation could itself embody a symbolic-ritualistic realization of the inclusive attitude of the church and a manifestation of its grace and openhandedness. Curiously, Christian self-perception of this part of the Mass as most attractive, especially for young souls, is attested by a Marian tale of a conversion of a Jewish boy. As a fourteenth-century source relates: "To the minster he came with others / the children surrounded him / the walls were curtained off / the images were nicely gilt / the glass was lovely / the altar beautiful / all this much delighted the Little Jew."[38] Ethnographically this story is not farfetched: such an event could have been imagined and performed.

The other side of this openhandedness was, obviously, the "cross"-communication implied by the Communion ritual, whose roots lie in the primordial "Jewish Crime": the Crucifixion. For Christians, the crime could always be repeated, either through the infamous ritual murders associated with Passover (see below), or by desecrating the host. As Sarah Beckwith argues, celebration of this sacrament in the late Middle Ages became increasingly related to the repudiation of skeptics who cast doubt on the miracle of Christ's real presence in the Eucharistic host; as such it became highly instrumental in reconfirming communal identity in Catholic Europe.[39]

The well-made Christian vocal world would conceal such tensions. Issuing in the ninth century, becoming more pronounced in the twelfth, this world gave rise to a crucial development in Western music: the birth of polyphony. Both the monophonic unfolding of the Mass and the Office and the polyphonic textures that gradually evolved were a genuine embodiment of the ideas of world harmony that the Christians took over from the Greeks and Romans. This harmony was musically conceived in terms of perfect intervallic proportions, structurally balanced forms, and well-tempered fusions. Beyond "proper" music, ideas of harmony permeated all avenues of theological, scientific, artistic, and linguistic medieval forms.[40] The harmoniousness bestowed upon the church by these ideas and the musical products that were considered as their incarnation spread beyond its liturgy to include an entire environment, both real and imaginary, in which birds, ecclesiastic bells, and choirs of angels fill the air, the atmosphere—*die Stimmung*—with their concordant sounds.[41]

Compared to such a self-assertive, harmonious sonic world, the music of the adjacent synagogue sounded duller, more dissonant, and noisy than any other alien musical world. The sounds emitted by the synagogue were cacophonous and unintelligible to Christians, who considered them as ongoing testimony of the *perfida synagoga*. No trained choirs, bells, or instruments adorned its services; no embellished musical manuscripts guided their unfolding. Moreover, as Bruce Holsinger demonstrated, from Guido of Arezzo onward, a singing that relied on rote memorization, rather than on notated solmization, was considered "blind," its practitioners demoted as "non-*musici*," their lack of musical proficiency a sign of sinful nature![42] The dichotomy of Christian/Jew could thus be superimposed on a seemingly natural and neutral divide of "discrete" and "indiscrete" sounds that became prevalent, distinguishing between pitched or musical sounds produced on stringed instruments, bells, organs, and the human voice on the one hand and nonpitched, noisy sounds including human laughter, *groaning, barking, and roaring*, on the other.[43]

Noise itself, in this connection, connotes all "symptoms of disharmony, lack of grace and unregeneratedness," as we learn from Spitzer's study of its etymology in Old French. It also connoted lamentation (*loud* lament), another precursor of "noise," itself originating from *nausea* (illness), grief, and quarrel.[44] It was also the characteristic soundscape of Hell, in sermons, preaching manuals, and other descriptions, both a cause and effect of the continuous chastising of the sinners, as Esther Cohen explains.[45] A counter-reading of a psalm verse nourished such modes of thought: "Why do the heathen rage, and the people imagine a vain thing?" Originally coined in opposition to non-Jews,[46] it was taken over by Christians "who considered themselves as the elect people, and who had then to look upon the Jews as miscreants." Though, as Spitzer claims, ancient and medieval cultures, but especially oriental ones, connected inner emotion with outer appearance, mourning with wailing, one may argue that in the late Middle Ages, the dominant Christian culture might have started to distance itself from such "brutal" behavior (compare the origins of the French *bruit*), and, in any event, viewed Jews' wailing as emblematic of their forsakenness by God.

In due time, certain Hebrew words in several European languages became fraught with infamous connotations related to noise, especially in the Italianate regions, as will be discussed below. In the context of a gruesome accusation of host desecration, Jews, upon witnessing the revelation of "a lovely little boy" in the heart they extracted from a Christian priest, "shouted so amazingly that nearby citizens came forth and saw the miracle." It is the Christian harmoniousness, this plot implies, which thus triggered its absolute antithesis in the Jews—horrible noise, a motif that will recur in relation to other hostile communities.[47] That the northern Christians, or their Gallic and Germanic predecessors, not so long before, suffered from similar noise allegations by their Roman conquerors raises the question to what extent such noise projections are effected through repeated collective "acting out."[48]

The historiographic literature dates ritual murder accusations (blood libels) as issuing in the year 1144 in Norwich, England, followed by Würzburg, Germany, in 1147. Such libels tended to associate the "murder" of a Christian child with Jewish rituals, mainly those of Passover, believing that Jews needed the child's blood for the special rituals of their festival of redemption. The association of the special ritual of the lamb's sacrifice as described in the Bible, in conjunction with God's redemption of his chosen people in Passover combined here with the entrenched belief in the primordial Jewish sin of Jesus' crucifixion. There were numerous versions of these stories and of their actual use against Jews; most of them, however, share the interpretation of existing Jewish rituals in light of distorted Christian conceptions of Judaism and Jewish law.[49]

One of the major controversial issues in recent decades concerning the background of these libels was launched by Israel Yuval, who argued that ritual murder accusations were a Christian reaction to Jewish self-sacrifice in the 1096 pogroms, in their refusal to Christianize. According to Yuval, the Christians held a distorted mirror up to Jewish parents, whose faith urged them to commit filicide and worship their brutal God by further murdering Christian children.[50] What seems pertinent to the thesis developed in this book is that Christians did associate Jewish fathers and mothers with mercilessness towards their children which, in turn, found a strong theological echo for generations to come, especially in relation to Eucharistic elements symbolizing the Passion along the lines of the sacrifice of the chosen. At the same time, the new cult of Marian devotion counterpoised this mercilessness with a maternal form of Christian compassion. The conflation and juxtaposition of compassion and violence, in relation to Christian and Jew, were, in turn, conceived in oppositions of harmony-disharmony, angelic and satanic affiliations, which then lent themselves to concrete musical associations.[51] On the Jewish part, the poetry of vindication, litany, and lament, mainly associated with the theme of Abraham's sacrifice of Isaac, seemed to fixate the traumatic events for ages, bestowing on its heroes and their deeds a glowing aura. As David Nirenberg maintained, it even established its own modes of memory that survived until modern times and beyond.[52]

PASSOVER'S STRAINS

My choice to compare more particularly the sonic worlds of Passover (Seder) and Easter reflects the proximity of the two memory-enacting holidays among their overt and covert, real and imagined sonic reciprocations and ruptures since the High Middle Ages in both religions.[53] They will keep resounding in the following chapters in various ways through Heine's *Rabbi of Bacharach* and Halévy's *La Juive* (*The Jewess*), Bach's Passions, and Wagner's *Parsifal*, respectively, and through other major works. Yet this comparison should be preceded by an earlier one: that of the Seder[54] with the Eucharist—both basically (or originally) night rituals, centered on sacrifices and their ersatz;[55] both are "media through which members communicate to themselves in concert about the characters of their collectivities."[56] Moreover, the Eucharist seems to have evolved from the Seder, at least partially, and continued to unfold in an evolving reciprocity. In each, distinct forms and practices of annunciation and renunciation were elaborated, accumulating specific modes of commemoration and celebration, potentially transcending the texts and occasions of their origins. The Jewish Seder—the first-night ritual of Passover, commemorates the story of the Exodus for the Jews. Matzah—"bread of the poor"—and wine are obligatory food in the ritual meal, yet the major part of it is vocal: the telling and chanting of the story of Exodus, its miracles, and God's grace. This comprises texts from various times and sources: biblical portions including psalms; prayers and eulogies; Midrash (homilies), and poetry.

The Eucharist is the sacrament of a single historical Seder of Jesus and his disciples, which turned out to be his last.[57] Bread (the wafer/host) and wine are essential in the Eucharist as well, taken in by the congregation after clergy sing and recite long and varied texts. Whereas the Eucharist ingestion of host and wine consummates in the miraculous transubstantiation, the consumption of matzah and wine in the Seder was kept free of mystical associations for long periods by major Jewish trends, as Gershom Scholem maintained, conjuring up only memory "and the identification of the pious with the founding generation which received the revelation."[58] The Seder is celebrated once a year by the family circle and its guests, whereas the Catholic Eucharist, though initially practiced in a similar way, became a daily ceremony rehearsed by a community, only metaphorically considered kin, and conducted by a chosen group of priests. Still, once a year, at Easter time (which usually converges with Passover), particularly on Good Friday, the entire Passion of Jesus is commemorated with the recitation of relevant chapters from the Old Testament and the Gospels. Christians are thus annually reminded of the intimate connection of the two festivals: Jewish Passover and the Christian *Paschae*—the *Pascha cruci-fixionis* (Good Friday) and *Pascha resurrectionis* (Easter).[59] Above all, they are reminded that Jesus was captured, judged, and crucified on the day of the Feast of Passover, and that the Jews could have saved him, but they chose not to. Jews are more subtly reminded of tragic outcomes of this association, through trau-matic resonances in their own ritual.[60]

Passover is an exclusivist festival par excellence, or a festival of exclusion; this basic trait was part of Jews' self-awareness in the generations here discussed. "*Passover* on account of what?—Because He *passed over* our ancestors' houses in Egypt when He plagued the Egyptians, and our houses He saved," they read in the Haggadah, the authoritative text for this ritual since ancient times. "As it is said: 'Ye shall declare, This is the Paschal offering unto the Lord who passed over the houses of the children of Israel when He struck Egypt and spared our houses. The people bowed in worship.'" The slaying of the firstborn was the epitome of God's plagues on Egypt and the obstinate Pharaoh would not let Moses' people go until he—himself a firstborn—was personally threatened. Gradual and systematic were Pharaoh's methods for excluding, subjugating, and torturing the Mosaic tribe, as the Pentateuch narrates, and the Mosaic tribe swore never to forget that ignominy.

Commemorations of the event are made daily, as for those of Jesus' cruci-fixion, in prayers and rituals of various kinds. But the Seder is different. From the very first night of the Exodus and onwards, the commandment is not only to remember, but to tell the story to the next generation in order to generate the collective memory—"and thou shall tell thy son in that day, saying, [i]t is because of that which the Lord did for me when I came forth out of Egypt" (Exodus 8:8). Over generations, the parents' narrative and the interrogation of the children grew in importance, diminishing the role of the sacrifice in the ritual: the more the atavistic offering receded, the larger the room for interpre-tative memory. The first historical sacrifice, that which the family members ate in Jerusalem, every year, in the days of the Temple, led to the memorial one: after the destruction of the Second Temple (70 CE), the lamb was super-seded by a small, relatively insignificant memorial relic on the Seder plate, and a celebrated annunciation[61]—the first in a triple annunciation, quoted above, formulated by Rabban Gamliel (the two others relate to the matzah and the *maror*).[62]

These sayings of Rabban Gamliel belong to one of the most ancient sec-tions of the Haggadah, themselves containing older layers—quotes from the Bible. This is typical of the Haggadah, which is structured as layers of texts

Fig. 1.3. (and plate 2). "Va-yikod Ha-'am," an illustration from the fourteenth-century Barcelona Haggadah. London, British Library, Ms. Add. 14761, fol. 61r. Courtesy of the British Library Board. The page illustrates the words "The people bowed in worship," quoted by Rabban Gamliel, and the initial words of his saying: "matza zo" (this matzah). Between the words a seated figure of an old man holding two matzahs, on the four corners four angels, blowing horns, the upper left one simultaneously plays the lyre. The horns thus constitute the diagonals of an edifice in the center of which a sphere that could symbolize the Seder bowl. Five musicians stand or dance below the structure, each located within an arched opening, and play five contemporary musical instruments. The whole picture thus stands for an imagined harmonious thanksgiving that Spanish Jews believed themselves to be part of; this was not a utopian vision, for Jewish instrumentalists were welcome at weddings. This illustration issued from Spain, where Jewish "noise" and sound were differently construed by insiders and outsiders.

nesting within older layers—or older texts enfolding into texts composed later.[63] (See fig. 1.3 and plate 2 for a late-medieval musical illustration of this quotation from the famous Barcelona Haggadah). Many voices are summoned on the imaginary stage set by the Haggadah: voices of historical rabbis and sages, of anonymous agents, of fictive protagonists, and albeit rarely, of God himself. An unseen authority, a biblical decreeing voice, occasionally addresses the reader in the second person singular and urges him to perform certain—mainly illocutionary—acts: Come and *learn* what Laban the Syrian sought to do to Jacob our Father; thou must similarly *expound* to him; thou shalt thyself *begin* for him.[64]

Above, beyond, and between all these voices one hears the voice of the collective, of the many—in the first-person plural—directly or through citations. This collective voice appears in the language of the Midrash (which structures the main part of the Haggadah), the psalms, and in that of the prayers and eulogies, to which every generation adds its deictic presence in an ongoing process of identification and collective memory-making, in "a fusion of present and past."[65] It is this fusion that can render a description of the Seder such as the one adumbrated above to appear ahistorical; an ongoing oratorical performance that could ever repeat itself among its rather fixed textual-ritual forms, without congealing into a static rite.

All these voices conduct and carry out speech acts of various kinds, including enunciating, announcing, praising, praying, telling, narrating, inferring, singing, blessing, teaching, asking, quoting, pointing, commanding, sanctifying, promising, prophesying, excommunicating, and, at a certain point, also cursing.[66] These illocutions cross, overlap, and reinforce each other, integrating ritual practices into the main action, the telling of the story. They invite further unwritten speech acts, encouraged by the canonical text: "The more a person tells of the coming forth from Egypt the more he is to be praised." These, of course, add further complexity to the interlayered ritual celebration. Yet even the official written text does not unfold as a continuous straightforward story; the telling goes in circles, back and forth, downwards and upwards, reaching its high points of the past (the crossing of the Red Sea, the arrival in Canaan, the building of the Temple) and the future (the salvation, the return to Jerusalem) several times, without arriving at a definite conclusion.[67] The hope and dream for salvation is felt throughout, like a contrapuntal voice that occasionally proceeds to the foreground—as a prayer, an announcement, or inference—becoming the main melody.

As for the real music element of the Seder—it is less uniform than the synagogal one, as it was developed and carried in the more intimate and varied circles of families. Still, one can identify older recitative-like layers, to which the more recent, more rhythmically organized ones were adjusted. Mostly they fall within the realm of "Adonai Malach" *steiger* (a musical mode of sorts, functioning as such within the modal system of Ashkenazi cantorial music), recognized by subdued exultation and solemn festivity (characteristic of Friday night).[68] The variety of melodic configurations and forms associated with the Seder attests to the attempt to mold the variety of the Haggadah's speech acts in a suitable tonal-oratorical expression. Another tacit musical association the basic mode of recitation suggests — at least for later generations — is the great moment of consecration of "The Beloved Friends" under the wedding canopy (*Huppa*), which, in the Seder night, allegorizes into the embodied union of the People with God.[69] This goes hand in hand with the custom of reciting, at the end of the Seder, the scroll of the Song of Songs, proclaiming the rejuvenation of this union.[70] All these musical elements are freely alternate and overlap with non-tonal speech, and other less-organized vocalities of this special, familial night.

Rabban Gamliel's homily is one of the high points of the Seder. It comprehends memory, thanksgiving, teaching, and, while acknowledging the unhappy present predicament, implicitly arouses hope for better days. It typically avoids announcing the toll exacted by God's choice of Israel as the elected people; God has promised salvation, and He is there, as a main savior, Himself — not through a messenger or mediator.[71] As such, it involves difference and otherness as a people's acknowledged self-identity, as a pledge of allegiance, for which salvation is more ideal than real, at least in light of the long history of persecution and libels that became associated with the festival and its related ceremonies.

This goes again in circles — a centripetal one, as in the "Ve-hi She'amda" declaration: Jews will be ever persecuted, God will save them, historical transformations notwithstanding; and a centrifugal one that pulls, through "wicked sons" outside of family, community, and story, to other places, folks, and legends. These contrary magnetic motions — largely related to "memory" on the internal path and "interrogation" on the external one — will mix with other movements that for generations of post-Enlightenment Jews will blur former defined boundaries of inside and outside being.

EASTER IN-VOCATIONS: FROM DRAMATIC RITUAL TO RELIGIOUS DRAMA

The more specific vocal worlds of the two Paschae — the *Pascha crucifixionis* and the *Pascha resurrectionis* — the oldest festivals in the Christian calendar, are products of medieval times, yet their presence as musically lived experiential forms perdures well into modern times, searing impressions on individual and collective consciousness for generations. True, the eventual schism of the church during the Reformation and Counter-Reformation gave rise to new, sometimes contrasting, forms and genres of festivity and commemoration, some of which will be discussed below. Yet the changes introduced into both traditions—the Catholic and the Lutheran—over centuries, did not intrude on the basic liturgical codes of these festivals.

Thus what distinguishes Good Friday ceremonies from other Catholic holidays has been the custom not to celebrate in it the Mass proper. Its omission, the *Catholic Encyclopedia* tells us,

> marks in the mind of the Church the deep sorrow with which she keeps the anniversary of the Sacrifice of Calvary. Good Friday is a feast of grief. A black fast, black vestments, a denuded altar, the slow and solemn chanting of the sufferings of Christ, prayers for all those for whom He died, the unveiling and reverencing of the Crucifix, these take the place of the usual festal liturgy; while the lights in the chapel of repose and the Mass of the Presanctified is followed by the recital of vespers, and the removal of the linen cloth from the altar.

The order of lessons, chants, and prayers for Good Friday dates from about 800 CE, and represents, as such, the order of the earliest Christian prayer meetings; that is, with no celebration of Mass. Paradoxically, this kind of meeting for worship was derived, according to the official Catholic tradition, from the Jewish synagogue service,[72] which, even at its most ceremonial, seemed to abstain—at least until modern times—from the kind of official ritual characteristic of the Catholic Mass.

This affinity with ancient synagogal rites, dating from the time before the church established its most structured liturgical order on the very day that commemorates, among other things, the Jews' betrayal of Jesus, could expose both communities in their most sensitive and vulnerable spots. Moreover, to conflate within the liturgy of the day chapters from Lamentations and Jonah (texts central to two other piously and emotionally charged Jewish holidays—Tish'a' b^e'Av [Ninth of Av, the fast commemorating the destruction of the Temples] and Yom Kippur [Day of Atonement]) rendered this approximation to major Jewish sensibilities rather sharp. One can surmise that this knowledge was kept alive within the Christian community through Jewish converts who could not refrain from noticing this proximity.[73] The Catholic Church coped with this vulnerability, this exposure to its preestablished forms and, above all, Jesus' wounds and sorrow, by resorting to a variety of solemn rituals and performative actions consisting of processions, prostrations, singing, and prayers culminating in the ceremonial unveiling of the cross.[74]

In the midst of this the choir sang the *Improperia,* a series of reproaches — built on verses borrowed mainly from the Hebrew Bible — that were supposed to have been addressed by Christ to the Jews.[75] Consisting of verses and refrain ("Popule meus quid feci tibi? aut in quo contristavi te? responde mihi!" [O my people, what have I done to you? How have I offended you? Answer me!] from Micah 6:3), the *Improperia* involved the whole congregation, musically and emotionally.[76] These striking sentences were rendered in a plainsong melody of a rather simple, iterative, lamentative melodic character (see music example ex. 1.1a). Werner, relying on Egon Wellesz, believes that the series of reproaches directly reflects an old rabbinic text, though with a "sharp anti-Jewish twist." The Jewish text considered here — central in the Haggadah — enumerates God's acts of grace towards his people, which the Roman Church views, in turn, as reason for reproach. For example: the Jewish text reads: "For had He divided the sea for us, and had not caused us to pass over on dry land — it would have sufficed." The contrasting Catholic text rebuts: "Ego ante te aperui mare, et tu aperuisti lancea latus meum" (I have opened the sea before you, and you have

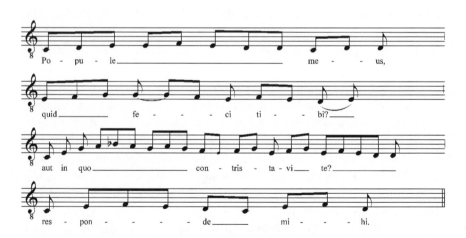

Ex. 1.1a. Good Friday liturgy: Adoration of the Cross, *Improperia* ("Popule meus"), plainchant.

Ex. 1.1b. Good Friday liturgy: Adoration of the Cross, *Improperia*
("Ego ante te aperui mare"), plainchant.

opened my body with a lance) (ex. 1.1b).[77] Werner, as part of his agenda, even
goes so far as to claim that the old tune of the Jewish poem "It would have sufficed" (*Dayyenu*) likewise wandered from the Jewish Seder table to the Good
Friday anti-Jewish vocal utterances. An affinity with certain "Adonai Malach"
tunes is discernable, without determining which music is the "original" and
whether the *Dayyenu* melody can claim such antiquity (ex. 1.1b first part, is a
good illustration).

Later, in 1560—the high point of harmonious, balanced, Renaissance style,
still within the time of the Council of Trent—Giovanni Palestrina gave these
sentences "such an appropriate and beautiful musical setting" that Pius IV ordered it to be performed in the Sistine Chapel. Palestrina's setting, extols the
Catholic Encyclopedia, is "unsurpassed in simple beauty, dramatic feeling, and
depth of impressiveness."[78] The music of the setting, in comparison to Palestrina's rendition of other parts of the Good Friday liturgy, is quite simple and
monotonous, demonstrating Counter-Reformation ideals: for the sake of clear
declamation it forgoes polyphonic complexity, highlighting certain chordal
progression (faux-bourdon), while preserving the character of the original chant
with a few short melismatic embellishments (ex. 1.2a and b, textually parallel-
ing the above plainchant examples). Such an experience of harmoniousness
sought to become, through its overt association with Jewish *impropriety*, an exclusivist expression, befitting the prevalent anti-Jewish atmosphere in the Papal
state. And yet, already at the time—the period of Reformation and Counter-
Reformation—the musical texture it celebrates became increasingly associated with musical heterogeneity (that of the Protestant chorale), which could
no more keep a strict division between noise and harmony. Ironically, subsequent Sistine Chapel music, composed in the style and spirit of Palestrina's
Improperia, would eventually become a commanding model of ecumenical

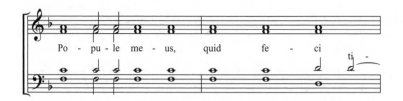

Ex. 1.2a. Giovanni Pierluigi da Palestrina, Good Friday liturgy: Adoration of the Cross, *Improperia* ("Popule meus"). *Giovanni Pierluigi da Palestrina: Werke*, ed. F. X. Harbel and others (Leipzig, 1862–1907/R), vol. xxxi.

Ex. 1.2b. Giovanni Pierluigi da Palestrina, Good Friday liturgy: *Improperia* ("Ego ante te aperui mare").

spirituality in nineteenth-century Britain, facilitating a more Jewish-friendly musical approach.[79]

Was this a cause, an effect, or a parallel development of the Jewish verses of the imprecations, recited after the Seder meal, on "the Gentiles who did not call your name"? The custom of reciting these imprecations, consisting of several verses from Psalms (89:6 and 69:25) and Lamentations (3:66),[80] probably originated in Ashkenaz around the twelfth century. While variations could occur in the choice and order of verses, it became ritualistically connected with the opening of the door for Elijah at the introduction to the fourth goblet.[81] The pictorial iconography it gave rise to in the Middle Ages and its distorted mirrored images in Christian illuminated texts show the extent to which this part of the ceremony became loaded for both Jews and Christians.[82] As for the vocal expression of these verses in the Ashkenazi communities, they seemed to be recited to the tune of the Haggadah; subdued, yet solemn and free, not giving vent to special emotion or religious feeling.

The vocalities of Easter seemed to unleash the somberness and further elaborate on the festive atmosphere associated with the ceremonies of the preceding week (Palm Sunday). Above all, they concerned a development that also took place in the course of the twelfth-century Renaissance: the birth of religious drama. As is well known, religious drama emerged from the tropes that began to flourish in the eleventh century, such as the highly celebrated Easter sequence — *Victimae paschali laudes* (attributed to Wipo of Burgundy, an imperial chaplain). Though sometimes regarded as lacking in musical individuality and dramatic consciousness,[83] the melodic sequence of this piece is one of the earliest examples of a rare combination of expressivity and well-balanced form. As such, it should have struck early listeners; its contour, reflecting a deliberate use of the modal scheme of the first mode (which is basically symmetrical), could probably be perceived, compared to more standard singing, as bold, directional, as well as harmonious. Through an unexpected, though compatible turn on the lower range of the mode, it breaks, after three introductory verses, into a dramatic dialogue between two clearly represented interlocutors. The first starts with:

> Dic nobis Maria, quid vidisti in via?
>
> [Tell us Maria, what did you see on the road?]

And is responded by

> Sepulchrum Christi viventis et gloriam vidi resurgentis.
>
> [I saw the tomb of the living Christ and the glory of the Risen.]

in a complementary melodic unfolding (ex. 1.3). This melodramatic complementarity would not escape a listener attuned to the vocal dimension of the ceremony, especially after hearing the more subdued, repetitive, and unsteady melodic contours of the previous chants. Within this new, emotive framework, the words in the seventh verse, which revert again to the higher part of the mode, would be most noticeable:

> Credendum est magis soli Marie veraci, quam Judeorum turbe fallaci.
>
> [It is better to trust only in Mary, the truthful one, than in the deceitful multitude of Jews.][84]

The temporal proximity of the composition of this sequence—words and music—to the First Crusade and the Jews' martyrology is noteworthy. Like the parallel Jewish *piyyutim* of vindication and redemption that became so strongly associated with contemporary Jewish martyrology, it too entered and remained at the core of the liturgy for centuries, engraving its strains in the generations to come, even beyond the Reformation.

Ex. 1.3. Easter Sequence, *Victimae paschali laudes* (attributed to Wipo of Burgundy, ca. 995–1050).

***

As a measure of how deeply this dramatic hymn became associated with Paschae, and as such with the Jews' destiny through to modern times, I quote here a few lines from Blaise Cendrars' *Pâques à New York*, that in a previous section sensitively interweaves a tapestry of humble East European Jews on a New York Easter, while loosening "aesthetic categories" associated with them: the shabbiness of their abodes and appearance, their noisy/nauseating aura, and the romanticizing, pictorial version thereof (Rembrandt).[85] He then pleads to the Lord—in a gesture that serves as a kind of refrain in various sections of the poem—to have compassion on them. Later in the poem, he quotes the question from the *Victimae paschali laudes* addressed to Maria, giving new answers, avoiding the malignant medieval line. The question is thrice repeated as a refrain in Latin, to which the following answers are given:

> *Dic nobis, Maria, quid vidisti in via?* / —La lumière frissonner, humble
> dans le matin.

> *Dic nobis, Maria, quid vidisti in via?* / —Des blancheurs éperdues
> palpiter comme des mains.

> *Dic nobis, Maria, quid vidisti in via?* / —L'augure du printemps
> tressaillir dans mon sein.[86]

The signs Cendrars' Maria gives are all natural, all humble, similar to all the wretched groups—Jews included—that populate the poem: thieves, whores, Muslims, and Chinese. In the new, hard, and alien world of New York in 1912, fraught with signs of Calvary and crucifixion, the Lord himself eventually ceases to be a point of reference, leaving human beings in general, and the poet in particular, alone to their urban miseries. By the same token, Jews are no longer considered signs of evil; they merge in the general picture of suffering. An unredeemed world, it is also music-less; all elements of harmonious sounds that once adorned the traditional, Christian holiday—bells, anthems, canticles, and so forth—are gone.[87] Arthur Honegger's 1920 setting of these lines gives rise to a sonoric environment at once fragile and compassionate, acoustically unfamiliar and yet redolent of other times and dreamlike territories.[88]

***

Thinking back to medieval times, the *Victimae paschali* is usually recognized as a harbinger of a long series of religious dramas, composed for the high holidays of the ecclesiastic year, above all, for Easter time. Easter, as a festival of resurrection and redemption, invoked the imaginative faculty of believers whose spirit was heightened by the previous related holidays, which were characterized by processions, prostrations, and most "treasured" ritual actions.[89] In terms of music, the story of the Passion itself which, according to existing manuscripts, was divided into three singing parts—the high pitch for the Synagoga, medium for the narrator-Evangelist, and low for Christ—vocally juxtaposes the same conflictual entities, bestowing a perceptual difference among them.[90] Even more acrimonious were later Passion and Easter plays caricaturizing Jews. In these the most elaborate and well known is the Lucerne Easter Play (mid-fifteenth to the end of the sixteenth century), containing about twenty-five *"Juden Gesänge."* Characterized by distorted Hebraic words and other deriding gestures, the major part of them resort to children's rhyme melodies, not uncharacteristic of other religious dramas. Few seem to adjust to elements of real "Jewish songs" (even Missinai tunes) as Werner contended.[91] They seem, however, to tell stories of mutual listening which might go a few centuries back.

COUNTERNARRATIVES, OR "NOTE AGAINST NOTE"

Within vocal-ritualistic environments of the kind illustrated above, the most explicit expression of the noise accusation against the Jews was first leveled in a subgenre of the ritual murder libel, in a narrative featuring music and miracles attributed to the Virgin Mary. It attests to the Christian vocal world of the late Middle Ages (from the late twelfth to the sixteenth century) that, along with new hymns, antiphons, sequences, and motets, gave birth to its young Orpheuses, whose devotional song would conquer death. These Orpheuses were mainly children whose voices were suitable for the performance of the new music, especially in its ascension to a high register (in contradistinction to the allocation of voices in the Passion practices, in this subgenre, a high register marked the innocent and the angelic). The unmusical Jews, so the plot would usually go, were not able to stand the pure, holy tune, the singing of a hallowed Marian antiphon—a "Gaude Maria," "Salve Regina," or an "Alma Redemptoris Mater" by a virgin clergeon or clerk, and would slit his throat, or kill him in a less symbolic fashion.[92]

These hymns, which were composed during the eleventh century and acquired popularity exactly at a time in which the ritual murder libels began to disseminate, could indeed embody, in words and music, the beauty and celestial purity associated with the Christian musical ideal. Displaying a similarly wide melodic range, tonal organization, and clear modal character, their melodies are even more elaborate than that of the *Victimae*.[93]

Inexorable exclusion is the inevitable sanction against the deed which the Jews are accused of: "[Y]vele shal have that yvele wol deserve," as the Prioress puts it in her tale, addressed below. Only if they choose (as some versions suggest) to enter the Christian harmonious universe they will be saved and included. And yet there is something obstinate in their aural nature, as one rather insidious later version of the story tells: "Sed licet *christ*iani sicud [*sic*] dic*tum* est vocem cantantis euidenter sunt experti, iudei *tam*en vocem et cantu*m* sunt penitus inexperti." (Though assuming that Christians, as is said, are obviously experts in singing, all the same Jews are totally ignorant of voice and song.) And further: "Miro quidem [*sic*] modo omnes *christ*iani melodiam et cantu*m* audierunt, sed sola iudeo*rum* obcecata perfidia non audiuit." (I wonder how it is that all Christians [had] heard melody and song, and only the blind perfidy of the Jews does not hear.)[94]

Historically, Jews molded their communal sonic self within their own cherished tales. Narratives of battles, or rebuttals, were transmitted through the High and late Middle Ages in various forms and themes. In *Gentile Tales*, Miri Rubin shows how the pervasive fear of the danger presented by the Jews to the crux of Christian worship—the Eucharist—was enacted and transformed into narratives that became constitutive of Christian communal identity and its ostensible harmoniousness.[95] Stow collected Jews' rebuttal stories, claiming that counternarratives, in this connection, were instrumental for the fashioning of self-reassurance.[96] Interestingly, in the case of the narrative of the postmortem singing boy, the source of the proto-plot could be Jewish: the *Aḥima'az Scroll* of 1054, prior to all the Christian versions, contains a narrative of a highly similar thematic structure, one however with no adversarial target, only of a singing beyond death, in search of redemption.[97]

Moreover, the well-known testimony featuring the tune of "Olenu [Aleinu] Leshabeah"[98] seems to be part of the more specific sonic counternarratives of immolations. It unfolded during the persecution of the Jews of Blois (France) in 1171 (long kept in the collective memory of Ashkenazi Jews), and was told by an eyewitness who wrote his testimony for Rabbi Jacob of Orléans:[99]

[A]nd as the fire ascended, they raised their voice in song, in one voice, and at the beginning the tune was low, becoming in the end high [*gadol*, literally, big] voice, and they came to us and said: what is it, your song, for we have never heard such a sweet melody. And we thus were able to identify it as Aleinu Leshabeah.[100]

From a musical perspective, there was probably something new and tantalizing about the tune—eventually entitled a Missinai tune—whose essential motifs

Ex. 1.4. "Olenu Leshabbeach" A. Beer, ca. 1765, in Idelsohn's rendition. The numbers refer to his divisions of the phrases according to major motifs.

and structure could make their way into written variants. Ex. 1.4 is the earliest written instance of "Aleinu," (transcribed by Aharon Beer, c. 1765). As Idelsohn argues, since these traditional songs are not essentially different from their present form, we may assume that they were already solidified in the seventeenth century, if not far earlier.[101] The major mode of the tune (with a slight Mixolydian bent) should have been dissimilar to the "lamentative," "noisy" tone associated with the synagogue, conveying instead a celebrated grandeur through the opening, descending arpeggio, the octave leap, the triumphant cadences, the unusual range (octave + sixth) and the overall "conquering" element, as reflected in the description of the "ear witness" reflected in the (Jewish) narrator's testimony. Though its exact shape cannot be known, the tune, a sonic figuration of the theological ideas conveyed by the text—the glorification of God, the celebration of his believers, the condemnation of idolatrousness (these parts were censured in certain periods), and the prayer for universal recognition and worship of the monotheistic God—must have constituted a source of pride and identification for the Jewish communities of the time, and was (at least according to the narrator's testimony) clearly distinguished as unique by Christians and Jews alike.[102]

Curiously, the lament of the satirized Jew in the *St. Nicholas and the Jew* religious drama (*Iconia-Spiel*), which scholars ascribe to the Blois (Fleury) area (composed c. 1170–95), could bear reminiscences of the "Aleinu" hymn sung by the Blois Jews, as Hélène Wagenaar-Nolthenium claimed (especially the two quoted phrases in ex. 1.5), thus corroborating the insider's report and the oral nature of this "borrowing."[103] Even more importantly, it could point to a differentiating characteristic of Jewish music which, in contradistinction to contemporary Christian genres, comprises a disarray of motifs and phrases, thus parodying Jews' laments.

All these events and records bring us to the first elaborate fictional world in the present study: "The Prioress' Tale" from Chaucer's *Canterbury Tales*, the most famous and artistic specimen of the music libel topos, relating the story of a seven-year-old clergeon, a musical saint, singing his sacred song to the Virgin unto death and beyond.[104] The literary rendition grants the tale a sophistication lacking in its models: interlacing mimesis and diegesis, history and myth, ethnography and ideology, it has perplexed many a reader, resulting in contradictory interpretations, spanning between a total dismissal of the anti-Jewish element as poetically irrelevant, and a harsh indictment of the author and his social circle as anti-Semites in a "no-Jews' land."[105] Yet it is the undecidability of the text that renders this work a gold mine for an understanding of the mutual reflectivity—or resonance—of the societies it implicates, and of possible reactions it could have engendered in individuals, from Chaucer's time onward.

Ex. 1.5. "Planctus Judei" (excerpt from Hélène Wagenaar-Nolthenium's transcription).

As Lee Patterson insightfully maintains, the tale, qua tale, involves various mimetic levels, first and foremost, the one embodied in the diegesis itself—by the Prioress, who through her rhetoric aspires to eradicate the gap between teller and protagonists, liturgy and history, ideology and ethnography. Innocent of any self-reflection, fully identifying with clergeon and mother, she also transmits the most blatant anti-Judaic prejudices of her times. Irony becomes the author's own tool to subtly expose her as such (starting from the *Tales'* Prologue); to show the futility of the world she fabricates, especially what Patterson views as a "nostalgic *desire* for innocence . . . frustrated in the moment of its conception."[106] Frustration, in this case, owes much to the tale's complicated fabric, raising crucial questions—put forward by Patterson—that are of special pertinence for the discussion of the Jewish-Christian sonic entanglements:

> To what extent is the "new" religion of Christianity an imitation of its rejected "old" form, Judaism? Has Christianity in fact superseded, even annulled its predecessor, or has it become simply another version of a Judaically defined monotheism? And has Judaism retained its original identity, or has it not undergone a process of "inward acculturation" to Christianity through the absorption of elements derived from its now dominant offspring?[107]

An interpretative strategy addressing such ruminations may urge us to enter into this work's world from within the sonic experiential dimension it both records and propels. Registered in different ways by the adversary communities, the sonic dimension conveyed by this world doubles. Twofold is also the projected world itself: one—that of the Prioress and her captive audience, the other—of the very story she narrates. Equipped with the ironic lenses the author provides, we may come closer to these worlds or distance ourselves from them: either listen "soberly," with the entire gang, to the holy woman's tale; be privy to the events her story unfolds, or reflect on the Prioress' manipulations, her creator's craft, and some of his inadvertent intimations.

In this two-tiered world, sound—mostly musical sound—is heard almost throughout. On its basic fictional level, it sets out in the children's "schole," where we hear them learning to "synge," then continues with the "Ave Maria" the little clergeon first intones, at home and outside. We then go on to listen in with him as the older children sing the complicated "Alma Redemptoris Mater" (ex. 1.6), which he devotionally covets, and then "prively" learns from his "elder fellow."[108]

> Fro day to day, til he koude it by rote,
> And thanne he song it wel and boldely,
> Fro word to word, acordynge with the note.

Twies a day it passed thurgh his throte,
To scoleward and homward whan he wente;
On Cristes mooder set was his entente.
As I have seyd, thurghout the Juerie
This litel child, as he cam to and fro,
Ful murily than wolde he synge and crie
O Alma redemptoris everemo. [544–54][109]

The music does not stop even when Satan incites the Jews against the singing lad; only when they "kitte his throte"—the very singing throat (imitating
their own self-immolation in the 1096 events, as Patterson suggests)—it ceases,
for a very short while. Cries of the poor, widowed mother are then heard, to be
replaced, miraculously, when she finds him, "with throte ykorven lay upright,"

Ex. 1.6. Marian antiphon: "Alma Redemptoris Mater."
"Loving mother of the Redeemer, that passage to heaven, gate of the morning, and
star of the sea, assist the fallen people which is trying to rise again: you who bore to
the wonderment of nature, your holy Creator, Virgin before and after, who from the
mouth of Gabriel received that joyful greeting, have mercy on us sinners."

with more "Alma redemptoris" that he begins "to synge / so loude that al the place gan to rynge" (611–13). Taken later from the Jewish privy by folk and provost, "pitous lamentatcioun" mixes with that of the child's, who continues with "his song . . . with honour of greet processioun," throughout the Jewish street and further down into the abbey, to be finally laid upon the bier.

Music breaks off again very shortly, giving way to another violent act:[110] Jews are punished for their deed, at the provost's command, drawn first by wild horses, then hung "by the lawe." But the song resumes "anon," and continuously; even when the dead saint tells his tale, it should reverberate somewhere, maybe through the voice of the Virgin, whom he quotes. When the miraculous grain that the "blissful Mayden" put on his mouth after his killing is finally taken by the holy abbot (together with his singing tongue), so that She will be able to "feeche" him to herself, the singing comes to an end. Weeping and more music praising "Cristes mooder" is heard, until the burial is completed.

As listeners, we would experience this musicality even beyond this burial and prior to the narrated events, in the Prioress' *musical* voice, from the first famous psalm she rehearses, through her apostrophe to the "blisful Queene" in which she complains of her expressive limitations ("as a child of twelf monthe oold, or lesse") and pray the queen to guide "my song that I shal of yow seye." Vocal presence would be strong throughout, in her heightened voice and exclamations. This must strengthen our sonic-harmonic persuasions, reassure our joint *Stimmung*. Vocality, we may reflect from a more distant plane, is filtered here through the characters' subjectivity. The little clergeon, Mother, provost, and Prioress herself are all granted inwardness. Jews, whose evil is ontologized through Satan's presence, are almost completely deprived of it. Even their will to kill the disturbing child is taken from them, not to speak of their painful screams.

Vocalized almost throughout, this well-made world reveals not only a process of self-differentiation but also, I believe, a Christian anxiety regarding the possibility of establishing reciprocal relations—actual and imaginary—between the two communities. The author's ironic distance, staging the Prioress' piousness and affectation, renders this anxiety more palpable than parallel folktale versions. I would like to offer two complementary conjectures regarding the nature of such anxiety: the first relates to the penetration of Jewish "noise" into the church, the second—to the infiltration of "harmony" into the synagogue. According to the first one, the kind of tunes that were developing at the time in the neighboring Ashkenazi synagogue, the abovementioned Missinai tunes, which harbor a new lamentative element, could eventually become identified—by foreign ears—with the synagogal soundscape. Other parts of the Jewish prayer were probably also cast in minor modes (maybe already exacerbated through an

Ex. 1.7. "Gaude Maria" (plainchant).

"Ahavah Raba" flavor), rather than the solemn Dorian mode, characteristic of "Salve Regina," or the Ionic (major) of "Alma Redemptoris Mater" that became increasingly widespread in the Christian religious music of those regions. (In the synagogal recitations, a "major" unfolding, as in "Adonai Malach" often leads to a "minor" development.) This might account for the zeal that characterized the Christians' endeavor to safeguard their new music against that which they experienced as noise and lament. (Though, listening to the "Gaude Maria," one can hear plaintive motifs, some of which prevail in later Jewish Ashkenazi tunes [ex. 1.7].)[111]

If one applies Louise Fradenburg's critical reading of the basic anxiety that the story's rhetoric bears on the musical element, one may argue that what the Christians apprehended as Jewish noise/lament led them to (unconsciously) project their own cruel actions against these Jews through centuries of persecutions and libels. Moreover, the mourning mother—imitating the Virgin herself (and competing also with famous Jewish mothers)—and, for that matter, the story as a whole, is "most profoundly mourning for the losses inflicted by Christian culture on itself, its self-repressions and self-silencings."[112] The noise-nausea reaction becomes thus a classical abjection case (in the sense elaborated by Kristeva), a way to repress Christian society's own cruelty, under the false presumption of an all-inclusive harmoniousness and purity of its believers—the basic trait of the Virgin Mary and her related musical (and extramusical) cult.

And yet, to include all Christians within this category may do another wrong, though smaller; at least some among them could have marveled, even unwittingly, at some of the achievements of their humble neighbors, as divulged by the Blois testimony. Prior to the above identification of the tune in *Planctus Iudei*, by Wagenaar-Nolthenium, Idelsohn identifies a Christian melody such as "Sanctus" IX as a borrowing from the "Aleinu" tune (ex. 1.8, especially the third "Sanctus").[113] Of course, the order of things could have been the reverse.

Sanc - - - - tus. sanc - tus, sanc - - - - tus: - - -

Ex. 1.8. "Sanctus" IX.

Bearing the second conjecture in mind, I would like to call attention to a basic element in the "Prioress' Tale"—that the child goes through the Jewish street which is "free and open to either end" and sings the song aloud and repetitiously ("everemo"). This motif iterates in many versions of the story, emphasizing the ethnographic inevitability of "passing through" the Jews' street (mainly in the versions of the A and C groups, in Brown's study) or the forbidden "overhearing" by the Jews in the neighborhood of the church (group B in Brown's study). In the majority of the versions, the boy goes through the street or sings in a procession innocently and inadvertently; only in one version does he deliberately seek to insult the Jews.[114] Obviously, tunes are endowed with the disposition to trespass determined borders, especially those in close proximity.[115] If melodies are not inherently promiscuous (much as Jewish women, "attracting" Christian men, were considered at the time by both Christian and Jewish authorities),[116] they are at least vagrant and collaborative—with the neighbor, the foreign, the Other, easily prone to becoming deterritorialized and reterritorialized, to borrow Deleuze's and Guattari's fertile terms.[117] This view is congruent with the medieval conception of sound, as expressed by Thomas Aquinas: unlike other "sensibles" whose "potentiality" and "actuality" reside in the object as such, sound is divided between the object (which carries the potentiality) and the medium which actually transmits it from object to hearer.[118]

Viewed from this perspective, the fictional dispatching of the seven-year-old clergeon into the marked territory of the Jew is paramount in anthropomorphizing the melody, granting it agency, weightless and innocuous as the pure melody appears to be. In the chain of agencies the story concatenates[119] this is, in fact, degree zero. Is the emission of the virgin-child to the Jewish neighborhood indeed so innocent? The collaboration of the "tune," in our story, with the other agent in action—Satan—could prima facie mean exonerating the singer from any responsibility for the transference of consecrated melodies into abject territories.[120] And yet Satan's intrusion into the story at this particular point discloses perhaps a deep suspicion set in the Christian culture itself in relation to the connection between musicality, emotionalism (the child's devotion to Mary) and the transgression of communal, dogmatic borders. This intrusion recalls other transactions of Satan and similar inciters endowed with musical powers.[121] Moreover, the clergeon's idiosyncratic performance, which defies, as some writers noticed, so many church regulations, inadvertently renders him a Jew: since he studies the song by rote and further intones it, without notes, he naturally belongs in that illiterate musical community. Be that as it may, music here acts as a willful power, a missionary agent defiantly deployed beyond the harmonious order within which it was supposed to be kept and controlled through scores and pedagogical or ritual strictures. What could happen, the story seems to ask, if indeed the Jews covet the melody, or any other tune or hymn, co-opting it for their own sacrilegious purposes?[122] What will remain of the providential origin assumed by the holy Roman music, by grace of the incarnated Dove who whispered it all in Saint Gregory's holy ear? Melodies, as part of reterritorialization, are easily governed by new texts and annexed to foreign rituals, collaborating with both friend and foe. Once governed by the sacrilegious, additional sacred values and cherished qualities could break away from their "proper" place and become contaminated. This, indeed, is bound to happen a short while later, as we shall soon see. Beyond that, it points to the inability of church authorities—hypostatized in the story by the figure of the narrating Prioress herself—to safeguard what Fradenburg discerns as "the desire of the *Tale* . . . for a language that erases the difference between word and thing, for a language that, in effect, escapes the difference in symbolicity."[123] It is music, I would add here, that aesthetically epitomizes this condition, while concomitantly undermining it, which renders it suspicious.

The two anxieties—related to noise penetration and melo-harmonic diffusion, respectively—seem to have worked simultaneously. While the transgression of the harmonious takes place, the noisy-nauseating melody of the adjacent synagogue could likewise creep into the church's consecrated service, letting *diaboli in musica* inside.[124] This was especially pertinent in the High Middle Ages, when the church had relaxed its strictures regarding music newly composed. In any event, the fact that in Chaucer's version the lad sings an "Alma Redemptoris Mater" rather than a "Gaude Maria"[125] supports my interpretation, for it is only the latter that contains an anti-Jewish text, which is highlighted in the versions that feature it. By omitting the controversial text, as well as by emphasizing the child's attraction to the song even before understanding the text (a detail found only in Chaucer's version), the distinctly musical clash between the two cultures looms larger.

That Jews, in the wake of new ascetic movements (mainly *ḥasidei Ashkenaz*) from the late twelfth century, also harbored "musical" fears, expressed in their own terms, should not surprise us: in their case, they seemed to dread their symbolic treasures' incorporation within the powerful, dominant church body, and likewise were concerned about contaminating their own musical vessels and souls. *Sefer Hasidim* contains several restrictions related to interborrowing of music between Jews and non-Jews; sec. 429 (3), for instance, prohibits the "lending" of synagogal tunes to non-Jews, and recounts, almost verbatim, the Blois story: "A foreigner who says to a Jew: sing for a me a pleasant tune (*niggun na'im!*); sec. 768 (7) warns not to sing foreign tunes "for it is a transgression"; sec. 238 forbids singing Christian lullabies to Jewish babies, and 238 warns against the very use of "idolatry tunes" (meaning Christian) before the Almighty.[126] Both restrictions indicate an ongoing practice of some mutual borrowing, but there is not much musical evidence to this effect, especially not of contemporary sacred Christian music. With all due differences, in both neighboring cultures, it was the melodic, ineffable element that carried the purity, pity, piety, and devotion associated in the Christian context with Mary and through her with the Trinity and church, as well as with the wholeness of worship in Jewish religious practice, and its memory culture, respectively.[127]

So we have here double reflections, or resonance: this doubleness raises the musicological question whether the music of the two separated communities was, at the time, indeed so distinct. Looking at the songs in the "Prioress' Tale" and the Blois testimony respectively, we find parallel developments mainly in terms of melodic range and expressive boldness. Thus the rivaling stories both "highlight" the use of high pitches for heightened expression of the religious text.[128] Beyond incidental borrowings and competitive musical strokes, however, our counternarratives serve to reinforce the rule that the Christian hymns under consideration are the product of a generic development, which seemed to detach itself from previous synagogal elements—psalmodic or responsorial elements—that formerly may have provided a source of influence. Though it could not ignore the next-door neighbor's music, synagogal music similarly aimed to cherish indigenous musical expression.

Focusing on the noise rather than on the harmonious element, the musical clash between the communities can be regarded from yet another angle, as that which enabled them to restrain real murderous impulses, sublimating these into symbolic, mutual inclusive or exclusive forms, which make room for restricted modes of violence. From Nirenberg we learn that Good Friday riots against the Jews in fourteenth-century Spain were mainly carried out in attacks accompanied by great noise. Yelling, screaming, clamoring, clanging of noisy bells—in addition to stoning the walls of the Jewish quarter—were the main weapons employed in riots defined by various medievalists as "ritualized aggression." For years they were annually launched, mainly by children and youth, and were strictly kept within temporal, spatial limits with a certain amount of physical aggression. The Jews, in turn, though for all intents and purposes more confined in their manifestation of aggressive noise, found their reciprocal outlet, especially in Purim.[129]

We should reexamine at this point the notion of noise, as it relates to the worlds being surveyed here. There is the ritualized noise of the Other (the synagogal noise in the case of the Christians) and there is, at the same time, a ritualized noise produced so as to *overwhelm* the noise of the Other. Psychoanalyst Theodor Reik—a student and colleague of Freud—deduces (quoting Robertson Smith) an affinity in Hebrew, Arabic, and other Semitic languages between the root *yalel* (wail, weep, howl) and *halel* (praise, thanksgiving: the root of "Alleluia"). The two, he argues, are deeply interconnected through mechanisms of aggression and repression; they can be shown to be phonosemantically, if not etymologically related to the Latin "ululare" attributed to Jews.[130] Noise, adds Jacques Attali, is by and large a governing principle for the production and circulation of music; it is a universal form of violence, and, as such, is a weapon, "and music, primordially, is the formation, domestication, and ritualization of that weapon as a simulacrum of ritual murder." Thus music "symbolically signifies the channeling of violence and the imaginary, the ritualization of a murder substituted for the general violence, the affirmation that a society is possible if the imaginary of individuals is sublimated."[131] If this statement is too sweeping in its relegation of music to a single genealogical principle, it seems applicable to cases in which, by defining the Other's music as noise, one confines it (if one has the power to do so), or overcomes it by "our noise," even though only temporarily and symbolically. The last option, as in the case of Goethe-Mendelssohn's *Die erste Walpurgisnacht*, is particularly open to the persecuted minority sometimes even more than to the hegemonic majority. It could be argued, then, that the sound worlds of both Jews and Christians, in the course of long centuries of segregation, reciprocation, and subjugation constituted forms of expressing, allegorizing, and preserving difference within restricted ritual modes. Exclusive as these sound worlds were in relation to each other, as noise they allowed to give vent to certain emotional impulses which, as music, they could subdue.

Continuing with the vein of longue durée reflections and anticipations, it may be added, at this point, that Christian anxieties of the kind the "Prioress' Tale" seems to harbor, would be summoned to nurture, say, a cloistered fictional medieval Order of the Grail, that would celebrate Good Friday ceremonies

on an operatic Montsalvat, is not self-explanatory. And yet, unwittingly, the innocent, virgin child of the "Prioress' Tale," now christened Parsifal—the *reine
Tor* (innocent fool)—will be transfigured there, in his association with angels'
music and his agonizing, *Herzeleide* mother (herself exhibiting certain "Jewish
mother" traits). Through an unheard "space-time" music, he will appear in the
Castle of the Grail—the order that predestined him aurally as their savior. We
will return to this unique vocal world in chapter 5, where it will be heard against
the background of a "nearby," likewise imaginative, synagogal music, similarly
evoked by a roaming Gentile—Daniel Deronda. The vocal resonance of old
beliefs and audible memories, and their emotional residue—including, respectively, medieval Parsifal, and ancient Missinai tunes—will interlace in these
newly conceived imaginative worlds. The changed status and role of noise and
ordered sound, as cultural constructs of the foreign and the familiar, should
partake in the comparison.

Altogether, the antipodal images of the two communities here portrayed
deeply imprinted themselves and their "associated commonplaces" in the consciousness and the subconscious of both communities, and were summoned at
certain historical moments.[132] Thus the motif of the sacrificing or murderous—
depending on point of view—parents would come to the fore in vocal fictive
worlds, in which the sacrificing parent is usually portrayed ambiguously, if not
sympathetically. After all, the terrible deed of infanticide entails a "redemption
in advance" in the parents' eyes—redemption from lapsing into a false and foreign faith. Despite the crucial difference between murderous parents and those
who cannot save their children from death once they refuse conversion, the psychological and theological link between them is strong. In the Jewish culture,
both could take inspiration from the first willing-to-sacrifice father, Abraham, as
well as from some wittingly and unwittingly sacrificing mothers, such as Hannah
and Rachel.[133] Modern fictional parents who will engage us later, as different as
Nathan the Wise (father of six children murdered by the crusaders in Palestine,
and adoptive father of Recha, an orphan Christian child),[134] Éléazar (father of
Rachel in *La Juive*), and the Catholic Comte de Saint-Bris (father of Valen-
tine in *Les Huguenots*), belong to this group, to whom some neglectful Jewish
parents—Mirah's father and Daniel's mother in *Daniel Deronda*—should be
added. Titurel, the sacrificing father of Amfortas in *Parsifal*, also belongs in this
category. How deeply this tortured legacy was engraved in the hearts of Jews
and non-Jews can be attested by the words George Eliot gives her character
Mirah Lapidoth, the Jewess—in the counternarrative to *Parsifal*—telling her
own "passion" story that almost culminated in suicide. Justifying the desire for
self-destruction, Mirah later recounts:

Then I thought of my People, how they had been driven from land to land and been afflicted, and multitudes had died of misery in their wandering — was I the first? And in the wars and troubles when Christians were cruelest, our fathers had sometimes slain their children and afterwards themselves; it was to save them from being false apostates.[135]

Dyads of sacrificing/killing/abandoning parent and sacrificed/murdered/forsaken child, prominent throughout the nineteenth century, lead back to the paradigmatic story of Abraham, Hagar, and Ishmael, enlisted in the "compassion controversy," contending for opposing views. The ubiquity of such dyads, mostly father-daughter, in the vocal fictions of "Jewish noise," is not coincidental, as it enabled the subversion of predetermined immolation stories through the enactment of emotively oriented feminine vocalities. The paradigm of many of the modern father-daughter dyads is that of Shylock and Jessica, whose musical reciprocations will engage us in the following pages. A fictional representation of the vocal behavior of other north Italian Jews, as heard by the neighboring "goyim," is briefly discussed in the chapter's coda, which also brings the lament of the cruelest of all: that of a Hebrew mother, devouring her own child.

Before plunging into these premodern aural worlds, a historical assessment of the gap in between, which seems to harbor some crucial implications on modern sonic universes in general, and the Jewish-Christian one in particular, is due. In the edgy mid-fifteenth century, one would still find a well-made sonic world projected from Flanders onto Spain, in which deities, angels, venerable Christians and undignified Jews are clearly ordered and bounded. The mid-fifteenth-century Flemish altarpiece *Fountain of Grace and the Triumph of the Church over the Synagogue* (based on Revelation 22:1), variously attributed to the school of Jan van Eyck, is the case in point (see plate 3). On the face of it, the painting is a three-tiered image, as the Prado Museum website informs its visitors:

> At the top, Christ [is seated] on the throne between the Virgin and Saint John the Evangelist with the Lamb at his feet, from which a spring flows. In the middle plane is a heavenly choir with its musicians. On the left side of the bottom plane are kings, noblemen, popes and theologians, while the right side shows various confused, fleeing Jews, one of whom is blindfolded.[136]

Christ, in fact, is present everywhere; among the various symbolic forms, the golden hosts floating on the octagonal font, which divides the lower plane (outside paradise) between Jews and Christians, loom large.

The typical angelic instrumentalists (as seen in Hans Memling's *Christ Surrounded by Musician Angels*) fill the air with their harmonious music, avoiding the use of harsh wind instruments. Rather than embodied—as in the "Prioress' Tale"—the miracle is, in this case, sonically corroborated. Its effect is reflected on the contented Christian entourage, immersed in the host-fountain vision, eschewing (Jewish) discombobulating letters.[137] In the corresponding Jewish group, old decorum might still be discerned (in colors, robes, scheme; above all, in the high priest's biblical *Ḥoshen* adornment), a decorum that connotes, however, excessive literality, as maintained by David Nirenberg.[138] The Jews, disarrayed by the miraculous sight, seem also to forfend harmonious sound: one Jew covers his ears; a (conventional) band shields the ears of the blindfolded high priest; other Jews gesticulate with disgust, or are preoccupied with the doubly-fallen letters.

Structure seems to further accentuate difference and potential shareability. The conflation of symbolic hierarchy with incipient perspectival technique seems to yield, in this case, an Escher-like effect, in which the musicians' plane is basically horizontal (though a bit lower to that of Christ, the Virgin, and St. John's), while the flanking turrets' cells are meant to be read vertically. This illogical spatial construct renders the musical aspect of the scene both close and remote, depending on the elected point of view, partially solving the theologically unbearable space-sharing of Jews and Christians, and yet facilitating a possible transition from one group to the other (theologically, it should be unidirectional, but the symbolic space opened by the painting does not guarantee that). All in all, the imagined universe shared by Prioress and listeners still prevails for the later altarpiece onlookers: the "Alma Redemptoris Mater" clergeon could take part in the angelic orchestra, to the Jews' pervasive aural dismay.

Could listeners or onlookers of this kind still uphold such a universe, about a half-century later, when Martin Luther would make his appearance on the European scene? Something crucial must have changed at that historical moment. Threatening to bury any part of those synagogues that were not burned down "with dirt so that no one ever again [saw] a stone or cinder of it in eternity"[139] (though elsewhere he referred to Jews in different terms), Luther, despite himself, dug inroads into the eventual inclusion of Jewish music, and music of Jews into the general European music, more than any other Christian leader before him, and probably after.

A short explanation for a longer thesis (not included among Luther's famous ninety-five): what seems to distinguish the case of Lutheran music is the acknowledgment that the sacralization of music involves a process, whereby its sonic configurations—be they melodic or even polyphonic—can draw their fabrics from any source and setting, provided they undergo a procedure through which they are adapted to the proper text and context, and invested in their sanctioned values. Once they have been so regulated, the improper or degraded origin of such contrafacta is purged or forgotten. The new sphere in which they sediment endows them with new functions, sentiments, sublimity, not easily dislodged. This regulation, or habituation, is communally brought about, though seeking sanction from an authoritative seal. Once the process is consummated, the converted sound objects become the treasure-house of an entire congregation; its spiritual coinage. This process, in turn, calls for the reappropriation of novel musical materials, whether borrowed or invented, to make room for spiritual rejuvenation.[140]

Rendering communal, vernacular music a constitutive religious principle, Luther irrevocably undermined the Catholic assumption of musical homogeneity. That presumptive homogeneity—as indicated above—was part and parcel of the church's hegemonizing and uniformizing aspirations, ascribed to Pope Gregory the Great. If earlier papal rule allowed the adoption of limited particularizing tendencies of its sonic liturgy, as well as a certain amount of (basically unacknowledged) contrafacta, now the dam was broken and music could freely flow from one territory to another, divorcing itself from words to which it was faithfully wed, permeating new texts and contexts. Catholic leaders felt this crisis; that is why they devoted time and concern to musical counter-reformation. But while dealing with the nitty-gritty of text-underlay and other formal matters, the verdict had already been irreversibly passed. Reverting to its inherent "promiscuous" nature, music could wander around unconfined; Catholics and Protestants mingled their styles and creations, and *contrafacta* contracted new musical facts.

Also, Jews began to enjoy, maybe for the first time in their long sonic exile, the new musical free-for-all bargain conditions. The exclusiveness of Christian music had loosened its grip. Revolutionary scientific and epistemological ideas contributed as well to the decline of old metaphysical notions that buttressed world harmony ideals. All this may account for the fact that towards the end of the sixteenth century, Jews began to borrow auditory capital from Christian neighbors, including relevant procedures of its manufacturing: musical notation, compositional strategies, polyphonic structures. While this was limited to northern Italy, and only peripherally touched the core countries, the leash had slackened—now also from the Jewish gatekeepers' side. Also here there was a theological shift, mainly among Kabbalists, not unrelated to what transpired in parallel occult Christian circles, encouraging an even more open sacralization of music qua music.[141] With each community adhering to its own sonic treasures, while further developing them, noise accusations turned more relativistic and self-conscious, even in Catholic kingdoms, a precept further buttressed by European (colonial) explorations. This process is already felt in the vocal fictions analyzed below.

THE JEW THAT "HATH NO MUSIC IN HIMSELF": SHYLOCK AMONG PREMODERN BRETHREN

> How sweet the moonlight sleeps upon this bank!
> Here will we sit, and let the sounds of music
> Creep in our ears; soft stillness and the night
> Become the touches of sweet harmony.
> Sit Jessica. Look how the floor of heaven
> Is thick inlaid with patines of bright gold;
> There's not the smallest orb which thou behold'st
> But in his motion like an angel sings.
> Still quiring to the young-ey'd cherubims:
> Such harmony is in immortal souls;
> But, whilst this muddy vesture of decay
> Doth grossly close it in, we cannot hear it.
> (William Shakespeare, *The Merchant of Venice*, V.i)

The touches of sweet-harmonious Belmont's night have become a title, a motto, an inspiration, and a source for scholarly books and artworks alike. Whether appraised as a sublime expression of an eternal, universal idea, or described as a vestige of a lore increasingly replaced by new ideas regarding constellations, tuning, animation—its sincerity, benevolence, and splendor have seldom been surpassed.[142] Love and light, sight, sound and touch, form and motion characterize the night, and sweetness invests them all. Not a mere simple harmony of notes is conjured up in Belmont, but rather a total synaesthesia, a *Gesamtkunstwerk*. One sense-formation turns into another. All combined conjure up the basic imagery—that of the floor of heaven. The fabric of the scenery is darkness, thick darkness, acting as ground for the main figures—the "patines of bright gold." Stillness is its equivalent in the realm of sound: the backdrop on which *musica instrumentalis* is better heard. Yet unlike the eye, the ear is granted only a replica of the sonorous *harmonia mundi*. Unlike the eye, it does not overcome "its muddy vesture of decay"—its material nature—its opacity. But while this is a universal condition of humanity, of its essential "flesh and blood," the night of the spirit, the "dark night of the soul," the obscurity of affections, is not so. It marks the exceptional, the aberrant: the man "that hath no music in himself," who "is not moved by concord of sweet sounds," whose heart is "fit for treason, stratagems, and spoils," as Lorenzo tells Jessica. "Let no such man be trusted," he admonishes her. "Mark the music," he finally instructs her.

External darkness and surrounding stillness function thus as factors of in-clusion — cloaking all in a *musica universalis*. Only obscure affections, rather than complexions, exclude; the Prince of Morocco had his chance. Night, or blindness of the spirit, is concomitant with dearth or deafness to the delight of music. *Musica humana*, in this Boethian scheme, is in full concordance with *musica instrumentalis*.

Many have lent such an innocent, Boethian ear to this musical text, for which evil is abstract and dark people remote. When "played" out of context, the Shakespearean text metamorphoses into a sweet, euphonious *Serenade to Music*, as in Sir Ralph Vaughan Williams' work of 1938–40. Lorenzo and Jessica, and those who share with them the first four acts of the play, know, however, that evil is clear-cut, and that expulsion from their paradise — Belmont — is personal. Lorenzo's "man who has no music in himself" reverberates with the Duke's "inhuman wretch, who is incapable of pity," an allusion to Jessica's father, Shylock (IV.i.5).

The fictive world of *The Merchant of Venice* thus entertains an aesthetic that highlights a bright, luminous, harmonious visual and musical Platonic order that conquers the inner night, against which the obscure, dissonant, immoral, and antimusical order of the Jew looms large. The ostensibly inclusive thus turns out to be rather exclusive; not all take part in this enlightened harmoni-ous aesthetic, at least according to some of this world's dwellers.[143] (Angels and cardinals from within the world of the *Fountain of Grace* would concur.)

For indeed, in this threshold work/world all seems to depend upon the ques-tion of whether the Jew's conduct is the offspring of his original, primordial sin, or of the contingent conditions in sixteenth-century Venice, which have brought him to such wretchedness.[144] The play hinges on this question, and Portia apparently decides in favor of the circumstantial: approaching her house upon returning from Venice, she hears the music Lorenzo has her musicians play for her — "her music," as Nerissa notes. And so Portia remarks: "Nothing is good, I see, without respect; / Methinks it sounds much sweeter than by day." Nerissa elaborates on her mistress' phrase, replying: "Silence bestows that virtue on it, madam." But Portia goes further, claiming:

> The crow doth sing as sweetly as the lark,
> When neither is attended; and I think
> The nightingale, if she should sing by day,

> When every goose is cackling, would be thought
> No better a musician than the wren.
> How many things by season season'd are
> To their right praise and true perfection. (V.i.102–8)

Raised by her father on an ethic of "leaden caskets" rather than gilded ones, Portia professes beauty to be in the ear of the listener. The Lady of Belmont clearly substitutes the relative and the contextual for the absolute and the ideal. This, however, does not stand the test of Portia's own choices, as her essentialist remarks on the Prince of Morocco testify. Are liberal aesthetics and the more ideologically entrenched political one at odds with one another? Will the first ever overcome the second, banishing racial prejudices? Shakespeare's text leaves these questions open.

Young Lorenzo, on his part, "lives on manna," both heavenly and absolute (V.i.294). Thief and orator, perhaps even an exorciser of evil spirits, he subscribes to an uncompromising truth, which he introduces to ignorant and melancholic Jessica, who, untrained in the lore of how to perceive such music, tells him innocently that she is "never merry to hear sweet music." Lorenzo, her instructor, responds: "because your spirits are attentive."

This reply is unclear: why attentive, and to what? Or if "attentive" in the sense of "polite," or even of "assiduously attending to the wishes of others"[145] — does music arouse in her this sympathetic orientation, or is she a sympathizer by nature? Why does this resolve in her being not merry? Is she different, in this sense, from "native" Christian girls? Jessica never asks and we remain uninformed.

Sensitive to this point in the text, stage director Jonathan Miller ended his 1970 production in an unexpected way. He draws our attention to Jessica's silence after Lorenzo's "harmonious" speech, and how it speaks volumes when other couples arrive in Belmont celebrating their reunion in quarrels and love. When Shylock's will, which was composed and imposed on him, arrives and is read aloud, Jessica hears it, deducing her father's imminent death. Upon which we hear an Ashkenazi Kaddish—a synagogal hymn in its most exemplary form, sung for the dead, here, by an unseen cantor. In the context of 1970s England, such an ending of the play was politically *in*correct.[146]

Interestingly, another director followed in Miller's footsteps, filling the vocal/emotional void of displaced Jessica with a Jewish voice that encroaches upon a present, which until that point had seemed self-contained. In his 2000 production of the play, Trevor Nunn opts for ellipsis and addition: Jessica is so agitated by Lorenzo's "harmonious" speech, even before he mentions "[t]he

Fig. 1.4. Gabrielle Jordan as Jessica singing in *The Merchant of Venice*, a Royal National Theatre production directed by Sir Trevor Nunn, produced for television by The Performance Company (Richard Price and Chris Hunt Ltd) © 2002.

man that hath no music in himself," that Lorenzo "spares" her this part.[147] This, of course, only works if one knows the original text; otherwise it is a rather questionable politically correct gap. Then, upon reading the will, an unexpected, unwritten—musical—gesture is superposed: Jessica falls to her knees in front of everybody (fig. 1.4), defiantly singing what can be heard to English ears as a variation on the "Greensleeves" refrain (compare ex. 1.9a with ex. 1.9b). Once she continues with the second phrase, however, a foreign element comes forth, redolent with eastern European Jewish melodic associations (ex. 1.9c). The text itself quotes (with a mistake) verses from Proverbs 31, a hymn to the "excellent wife" ("Eshes ḥayyil"), sung in its entirety in Jewish houses every Friday night in praise of the "mistress of the house."

The meaning of this quotation in Jessica's utterance is, needless to say, desperately ironic;[148] so is the way she performs it: as a bitter, affective Jewish lamentation. Unlike the bystanders in this scene, the spectator may recall that this is not the first time the song is heard in the play, being privy to its first rendition in act II, when Shylock summons Jessica to take care of the house, before he goes out for the supper transaction. Shylock utters (and Nunn reorders the text): "I am bid forth to supper, Jessica: / There is some ill a-brewing towards my rest." Then, after Jessica helps him with his coat: "There are my keys. But wherefore should I go? / I am not bid for love; they flatter me: / But yet I'll go in hate, to

Bo - tah bo lev — bo - a - lo____ ve-sho - lol lo____ ye - ḥe - sor____

Ex. 1.9a. "Eshes ḥayyil" eastern European *niggun*, second verse.
The heart of her husband doth safely trust in her, and he hath no lack of gain
(Prov. 31:11).

Ex. 1.9b. "Greensleeves."

Gmo - la - s'hu tov ve - lo ro kol - ye-mei__ ho ye - ho__ ye - ho

Ex. 1.9c. "Eshes ḥayyil" third verse.
She doeth him good and not evil all the days of her life (Prov. 31:12).

E - shes ha - yil mi____ yim-tzo ve-ro-hok mi - pni - nim mikh - ro

Ex. 1.9d. "Eshes ḥayyil" first verse.
A woman of valour who can find? for her price is far above rubies (Prov. 31:10).

feed upon the prodigal Christian" (II.v.12–15). There is a pause, then he continues in a most tender tone—"Jessica, my girl," and subsequently quotes the first verse of "Eshes ḥayyil" that she will later skip, in a tune immediately recognizable as "Jewish" (ex. 1.9d).

In the midst she joins him in a most devoted, loving tone, and so they continue with the next two verses in a responsorial form of cantillation, as if commemorating not only her dead mother (whose photograph is part of Nunn's setting,

Fig. 1.5. Gabrielle Jordan and Henry Goodman as Jessica and Shylock singing "Eshes Ḥayyil" in *The Merchant of Venice*, a Royal National Theatre production directed by Sir Trevor Nunn, produced for television by The Performance Company (Richard Price and Chris Hunt Ltd) © 2002.

emphasized by the camera's gaze in the film version), but all the good that father and daughter have shared (fig. 1.5). Even this first musical interpolation falls under what I term an "oratorical moment"—the enrichment of the present with a cluster of voices and beings from other times. Only then does he utter, "Look to my house. I am right loath to go" and, with his next lines, painfully destroys that precious moment they have just experienced—this production thus triggers the question of whether she would otherwise have decided to stay.

Thus the voice of Kaddish that in Miller's version alights from another world, time, and community, in Nunn's production bursts out from Jessica's body, instantiating her other, Jewish, familial self in the presence of the Christian community. Moreover, for the spectator, this is a voice carried from that scene between father and daughter, thus more concretely "past-tensing" the present. External or internal, these alien musical, vocal moments in both Miller's and Nunn's respective versions enrich the fictional present, revealing its probable antecedents and possible consequences.

These sounds mingle with the underlying affect that permeates the entire play, like a persistent, almost unheard—more precisely unattended—musical drone. This emotional drone starts even before the play begins and pervades beyond its ending, long after the touch of sweet nuptial nights of three happy pairs has evanesced. During the play, this tone never leaves its bearer—the melancholy outsider, Antonio.[149] He strikes it with " [i]n sooth I know not why I am so sad," and then comments in a typical Shakespearean mode:

> I hold the world but as the world, Gratiano:
> A stage where every man must play a part,
> And mine a sad one. (I.i.77–79)

Antonio is coupled thus to Jessica; closest to the sad events in Venice, both are "never merry" despite the fact that one of them is getting married. Could the melancholy of the "agency of evil" coincide with that of its indirect victim? What does this reveal about the playwright's apprehension of Christianity and Judaism in terms of aesthetics, sensibility, essentialism, and vocality?

Heine, who eventually struck his own famous lines, "Ich weiß nicht, was soll es bedeuten / Daß ich so traurig bin" (I do not know why I should be so sad)— the opening lines of his famous poem *Die Lorelei* (1822), likewise addressing betrayal and the power of music—heard it, this drone. In his ethnographic-poetic ears, when visiting Venice's ghetto, at the synagogue, unable to see Shylock, his ears perceived

> a tearful voice, of the kind eyes can never pour out. . . . It was a sob that could move a stone to compassion. . . . Sounds of pain that could come only from a breast that sealed inside all the martyrdom which a tortured people has borne for eighteen hundred years. . . . It was the moan of a soul tired to death, collapsing in front of heaven's gates. . . . And this voice was familiar to me, as if I had heard it just as it desperately yelled: "Jessica, my daughter!"[150]

The entrenched association of Jews, as a people, with their noisy prayers, finds its peculiar fictional construct in the Italian peninsula. There it became associated, first and foremost, with *barucaba* —a distortion of the Hebrew *Baruch haba*, (*benedictus qui venit*, welcome, literally: blessed be the comer) that stood in northern Italy as a mock term for the Hebraic prayer expression (associated also with the beginning of the ubiquitous Jewish blessings: *Baruch atta*). Drawn from a psalm central to both Jews and Christians (118:26): "Blessed be he that cometh in the name of the *Lord*," it seems to have pulled together other distorted and fictitious Hebraic words and names (badonai, tadonai [for Adonai, the Lord]), many of which have a phonosemantic matching with Italian words. As Don Harrán has recently argued, the connection with the circumcision rite, in which *Baruch haba* functions as a major expression, is crucial here, engendering further sexual insinuations.[151] This doubling of sensual (obscene) distortion of the Jew bred its repercussions in later periods, as we shall see. What is of interest in the present connection is how the fictive-dramatic rendition of a Jewish prayer, through such Hebraic hullabaloo, both relativizes and aestheticizes the basic noise defamation, while, paradoxically, domesticating it. Modeled after a commedia dell'arte plot, the works featuring *barucaba* scenes (generically termed *ebraiche*) should point to a rather widespread oral practice that has largely remained undocumented. Of the extant three pieces, the earliest features in Ghirardo da Panico's *villotta* (crude song), published in 1569 in a collection of *villotte* edited by Filippo Azzaiolo; the second dominates the twelfth scene in Orazio Vecchi's (1550–1605) madrigal comedy *L'Amfiparnaso* (printed in 1597, first presented in Modena in 1594); the third appears in Adriano Banchieri's (1568–1634) *Barca di Venezia per Padova* of 1605.

I chose to focus on the second, which could have been a model for the third, and creates a more distinctive fictional frame than the first does. The scene featuring the Jews (III, iii) is described in the argument in the following words: "Francatrippa (Pantalone's servant) goes to the Hebrews to make a pawn. He batters loudly on the door, and one hears a jumble of voices and dreadful speech."[152] The scene is musically rendered as an extensive madrigal.

All Jews are typically Shylockean, the argument implies; in this farce, however, none is considered malicious. The emphasis lies not on their avarice, but rather on their stubbornness: the Jews will refuse to transact with the *Goi* because of Shabbat's law. The dramatic intention is clear; the scene is meant to be noisy, from the knocking on the door (vocally rendered) to the last word of the Jews' vehement refusal to take the pawn; yet, taken as a whole, the scene should be more farcical than spiteful. The underlying style—imitative polyphony in five parts—fits the dramatic action even more than other scenes (as was advocated, a few years before, by the Florentine Camerata's members), many of which consist of a dialogue between two lovers, or even of a single lover's monologue. The linguistic components of the Jews' responses containing distorted "noisy" words are rooted in a similar phonologic distortion: distorted names (Bethel for Bethuel, Merdochai for Mordecai); words (Baruchai, Adanai for Adonai, Lord); and nonsensical curses that could sound "Hebrew" to poet, composer, and audience—"Oth zorochot / Aslach muflach / Iochut zorochot / calamala Balachot."[153]

Interestingly, the music is not, strictly speaking, dissonant; rather, it is set in C major (or Ionian mode)—the key of the whole work—and deviates only slightly from it. (Compare this with the mid-sixteenth-century *Juden Tanz*, "the Jews' Dance," by the German composer Hans Neusiedler, which most exceptionally conflicts two tonal realms, D-sharp and E-natural, effecting harsh dissonances, while melodically repeating monotonous ululations.)[154] It is rather the

disturbed polyphony of changing rhythms on syllabic melodies, and varieties
of *stretti* entrances that produce a semblance of vociferous prattle (reminiscent
of Bach's *turba* choirs). To a lesser degree, similar procedures characterize the
dialogue of other farcical scenes in the comedy. Curiously, the loving couples,
who naturally gain our sympathy above all other figures, speak in the language
of tortured love—what Monteverdi will soon term *seconda pratica*—a compositional strategy exploiting unprepared dissonances and nonuniform modal space
for effective expressivity. Within this semiotic universe, Jews are thus associated
with the ridiculous and the ignoble; but they are not exceptional as such in a
commedia dell'arte. What is different in their case, compared to other farcical
figures, is their representation qua group, rather than as individual personae
(they, too, lack subjectivity). Furthermore, the argument's instruction regarding
a "jumble of voice and dreadful speech" should behest performers to enhance
vociferousness, even if the tone combinations remain within a harmonious
scheme.[155] Some performers follow suit; the result is noisy anyway. Had there
not been contemporary parallel attempts to brutally convert distinguished Jewish musicians (as in the case of Abramino Levi, court musician in Mantua,[156]
though later, Salomone Rossi entertained a rather respectable office there),
such scenes could have remained a sign for a "contained" otherness of the Jews
within Christian communities.

Relativism becomes even more pronounced in Banchieri's boat, which celebrates a carnival of dialects and genres.[157] With a similar text to that of Vecchi,
its synagogal scene avoids the latter's plot, contented with the typical *barucaba*
wordings. Nonsense syllables prevail in many songs, and also the Jews have
their fa la la, but theirs is different: *La (con) trainana . . .* sounds Jewish to your
ear? But those who sing it are the *cinque* (five) singers, who move from one
musical region to the other, adjusting themselves to its peculiarities, yet abiding by their euphonic triads. After all, it should sound enjoyable, throughout.
Theology recedes before aesthetics and pleasure.

* * *

When she mounts the stage, the tone becomes, however, different. Alone,
she will bemoan. Nothing is exceptional here: mid-seventeenth-century singers
thrived on *lamenti*. Once they are a queen's, another time a madwoman's; a
Dido or an Olivia can likewise intone them. Tonight she will turn into a *Madre
Ebrea*, a Hebrew mother: the renowned Antonio Cesti (1623–69), a sometime
Franciscan friar, is the composer of her cantata, poet unknown. This mother
plunges into a long soliloquy. Not immediately: first she gets a fair introduction by a narrator, in much the same way as her fictional mate, an anonymous
nymph, received (by three tenors) courtesy of Claudio Monteverdi.[158] The nar-

rator contextualizes her story: ancient Jerusalem, the time of Titus' siege. It is inspired by an unmentioned, yet well-known verse to those familiar with Lamentations (2:20): "Shall the women eat their fruit, the children that are dandled in the hands?" The narrator tells the listeners, in unruffled G major, that the desperate hunger of this mother brought her to kill her son. From this moment, the mother starts to recite her plight in real time, as she waits for the horrendous dish to be ready. It is all in style, "well done": a voice against a continuo accompaniment, properly structured, exhibiting the beauty of the singer's voice. Characteristically, she begins with a change from the declamatory (recitative) style of the narrator, to a rather jolly, G major bel canto 3/2 meter, urging the flames to burn her son: *su su carboni ardete*.[159] This will become the refrain, interspersed within proselike (recitative) and other poetic sections, with varying meters and tonalities. In style and spirit, this structure reminds one of contemporary Venetian works, like Monteverdi's Poppea's monologue,[160] in which the heroine fantasizes her future as the empress of Rome. Not an exemplary woman either, but one whose lust still drives her in the normal direction: sex, control, power.

Madre Ebrea is not unreflective. Revealing her subjectivity, she touchingly confesses: a wicked mother, she is indeed a tigress, who wants her son to flame and burn. "Ah non son io che così voglio e desio! Fame ria, fame esecranda\ così vuol, così comanda" (Ah I am not myself to so wish and desire! Foul hunger, curse hunger, [it] so wishes, so commands), she further exclaims, gradually descending from high G. She desires it *so*: the word *così*, becomes the hinge carrying this terrible craving. It is not the lament, the loud lament, of a Jewish mother that evokes the nausea, the noise, in this historical moment. Laments are all over, the pleasure of the day. It is *this* lament, on *that* sacrifice. It becomes especially nauseating when she describes that her tears quench the fire she wishes to rekindle. A familiar musical icon quenches the imaginative fire, a descending chromatic fourth, thrice repeated (twice on A minor, once on D major), telling us a crucial lesson: we can both enjoy and abhor. It is all a matter of compliance of signifier and signified. Signifiers in this case are not to blame. In this baroque universe, severed from their entrenched metaphysical connection to world harmony, they become free-floating. Thus they could shift even to designate an abominable object. This *impropriety* becomes even more horrifying than former ones, as Brecht will eventually recognize, begetting a new source of noise: mental noise. Only on the very last phrase of hers, when all inhibitions are gone, expression becomes more directly emblematic: "ruoto il dente, apro il labro e ti divoro" (I move my teeth, open my lips and devour you; see ex. 1.10, second page [ms. p. 32], second system); C major, speeding up motion, abrupt ending. Listeners are left dumbfounded.

O mio caro figlio tu che gia fosti il sol degli occhi miei hor'in si gran periglio del mio ingordo appe

tito sarai trofeo gradit'o e se gia ti diss'io mio ben mia vita hor di mia fame ar=

dita vitte ma diverai e tu mia vita un si gran core havrà = = i

e voi labra mi baci cangiar potrebain fieri morsi j ba=ci Bengo con labro in=

degno à ragion ti chiamai unico mio sostegno se sostenermi in vita hor tu potrai

ma' fame tiranna ti gia mi condanna con barbaro esempio à far di te mio figlio

Ex. 1.10. Antonio Cesti, Lamento della Madre Ebrea ("Del famoso oriente"), concluding part. Christ Church Mus. 83:32. Courtesy of the Governing Body of Christ Church, Oxford.

It is at this moment that the narrator takes over. To further describe the cruelty, while calming down, rationalizing, and reassuring that such a great excess perpetrated by a wicked Hebrew woman should not surprise anybody, since—and here the narrator reverts to a melodious 3/2 phrase (ex. 1.10, last phrase): "chi uccise un Dio può divorar un figlio" (one who killed [a] God can devour a son). In the beautiful parlors of Innsbruck, Vienna, or Venice, where this could have been performed, the ladies should not be worried. These are the ancient Jews and Jewesses, who forty years before the Jerusalem siege killed our God. These are the Jews from old Ashkenazi times, who murdered their own children, and some time later, around Passover, also ours (so maybe nonetheless a cause of concern?). A people deprived of compassion, then as probably now, should not be trusted, even if their music is incorporated into "ours," or we adapt ourselves to "theirs."[161]

—————··❮∞❯··—————

Rethinking and Enacting Sympathetic Worlds: The Eighteenth-Century Oratorical Legacies of Bach, Lessing, and Handel

It was the result of a very serious reflection about the disgraceful oppression under which a people must suspire that a Christian, I should think, cannot view without a kind of reverence.

—*Gotthold Ephraim Lessing on his play* The Jews

The transition from medieval to premodern time marks the growing predilection for the embodiment of the noise accusation through dramatic genres, in line with what Jacques Rancière calls "the representational regime of the arts."[1] It also bore witness to the release of musical hegemonic culture in Western Christianity, which took place with the introduction, by the leading reformists, of diverse communal liturgies that differentiated musical collectives from one another, and favored "bottom-up" expression over "top-down" harmonization. Both changes, which had some repercussions in the neighboring Jewish community, affected the destiny of the noise accusation in various ways. The representational mode, as indicated by Aristotle, is experienced through a distance, calling for measured immersion in the fictional reality, encouraging reflection. Its "embodied playfulness," moreover, separates actor from protagonist, concomitantly marking their affinity: some of the protagonist's properties are bequeathed on the performer, whether he or she wishes to be endowed with them or not. This works, to a certain extent, against the essentialist grain, especially in the comic genres.[2] The new liturgical forms, however, accentuated the "choral" regime of art (in Rancière's terminology) or "oratorical," as I call it. While sanctifying the communal, its blurred demarcations between performers and audiences, original and adjacent members, enable, under certain circumstances, more inclusive trajectories.

And yet, these tendencies, though moving towards the democratization of the sonic sphere, would not work, in the present case history, without a social-political change in the relations of the European countries to their Jews, within the framework known as the processes of emancipation.[3] Moreover, as will become clear in the following, such democratization also involved an ideological transformation, related to deistic tendencies and the emergence of the modern concept of sympathy, and its role in bringing new and renewed forms of art.

This takes us into the mid-eighteenth century, a transitional period in Berlin and other urban centers, in which some Jews and non-Jews had jointly hoped that the murky sides of their mutual religious and cultural pasts would be tempered in the present. Fostering new forms of dialogue and reciprocity, the main actors of this drama wished to set aside old barriers, political and practical, creating, instead, common spaces, both public and private. The public spaces included bank, library, streets, theater, and concert hall; the private consisted of office, study, atelier, salon, and private garden. All soon became arenas for encounters and fertile exchanges of artistic, intellectual, and ethical sensibilities. These changes and exchanges, however, of which Moses Mendelssohn and his generation were both witnesses and major catalyzers, already proved rather shaky and questionable in the time of their inception, as testified by the famous Lavater affair and its subsequent repercussions.[4] And yet, for Mendelssohn and his close circle it seemed, or it was at least possible to hope, that this affair was an exception to a new rule rather than a deeper violation; for some, the enterprise of emancipation gained thereby even more impetus and thrust.

FROM DISCRIMINATING COMPASSION
TO UNIVERSALIST SYMPATHY

It is thus no coincidence that one of the major manifestations of the new horizons that seemed to open up for this generation was related to the belief that the discriminating forms of compassion based on religious identity were increasingly being replaced by naturalistically encompassing codes of sympathy. The main part of this chapter will discuss vocal embodiments of sympathetic worlds produced by Christian authors—all of them German (Bach, Lessing, and Handel) that became iconic for Jews who sought sonic inclusion. All these works benefited—directly or indirectly—from new modes of thinking of sympathy and compassion. Mendelssohn and Lessing were both central to this development, which included major philosophical figures of the time, starting with Descartes and Spinoza, achieving trenchant and encompassing elaborations by Rousseau and Adam Smith. In the first part of this chapter, we will attend to their elaborations on these concepts, heeding especially the ways these thinkers connect sympathy/compassion with musical and vocal notions, or implications thereof.

The concept of compassion, which since Plato and Aristotle linked theater, rhetoric, and ethics within a shared mental frame, had highlighted the role of the imagination in the formation of a merciful, benevolent attitude towards the other. Only when one imagines the other's emotional and existential position can one become compassionate, argue the ancient philosophers: through the imagination one puts oneself in the other person's place and, concomitantly keeping a proper distance, distinguishes oneself from the other. It is this simultaneous double position of involvement and detachment that breeds moral behavior towards another person, at least according to Aristotle.[5]

This rather complicated mental configuration called attention to its aporias, which seemed to increase in complexity with the introduction of God into the picture. Ancient "theologians" of the Jewish God—from Abraham, through Moses and Job—wrestled with the inner struggle within the Divine Being, between God's unstinting grace and absolute justice; between omnipotence and omniscience; between God's choice and love of the few, and commitment and commiseration for all. Moreover, for the nonrepresentable God, who can be approached only through negative attributions, the mechanism of human compassion could be considered of a rather precarious theological status. The division of divinity in Christianity into separate agents appeared to resolve these aporias; the hypostasis of Christ and the subsequent Passion called for a reciprocity of compassion, eliciting grace (from the Lord) and devotion (on behalf of the believer).

Despite the discrepancy between Judaism and Christianity in this regard,[6] God's mercy and grace are seen to aim to resolve human suffering and soften the harsh judgment in both religions. Central ancient prayers were conceived in this spirit in musically distinguished tunes that vocally aimed to traverse the unbearable distance between God and humankind. Among them are the "Kyrie eleison, Christe eleison" (God have mercy, Christ have mercy—the Greek addresses to the divine being in the opening Ordinary part of the Mass); the even more ancient sections in the services for the Jewish Days of Awe ("pity your creations, and you will rejoice in your creations"), or God's Thirteen Attributes (Exodus 32) repeatedly recited during Yom Kippur and the days of S^eliḥot. Furthermore, in both Judaism and Christianity there is ambivalence regarding those entitled to God's pity: whether it applies only to the select—those who chose to be part of the church, or God's people, who keep his laws and adhere to his dicta, or whether his mercy extends to all.

The vocal elements related to pity and compassion within the religious polemics of Jews and Christians were already discerned in the medieval tales discussed in chapter 1. They will surface again in the course of the nineteenth century with its rehashing of traditional claims and the reintroduction of ancient
themes and figures within a new polemical environment.

For Enlightenment thinkers, however, such theological considerations became secondary. Whether empiricists or rationalists,[7] they investigated human
nature, leaving aside, to a considerable extent, God and his qualities.[8] Their
analysis articulated the insight that compassion is a composite emotion, which
includes "being with" (on the part of the compassionate person) and the "emotion of" the object of compassion: sadness, mourning, pain. Since the "being
with" clearly concerned a make-believe gesture, linking compassion with theatrical representation seemed unavoidable, as is clear already in Descartes'
Passions of the Soul (1649).[9] Once deconstructed, the suffering component of
compassion—the "tragic" emotional condition of the object of compassion—
could be substituted. Thus Spinoza, in his 1677 *Ethics*, observed that the "pleasure arisen from another's good" is complementary to the pain "arisen from the
hurt of another"; the second is *commiseratio* (compassion) but for the first, he
complains, he does not find a name.[10] Moses Mendelssohn, in his *Rhapsodie
oder Zusätze zu den Briefen über die Empfindungen* (1761), was perhaps the first
in the history of modern aesthetics to fully recognize the compound nature
of "fellow-feeling" in general, and in particular its emotional implications in
terms of different possible combinations of its elementary components.[11] Lessing seemed "sympathetic" to Mendelssohn's ideas, as expressed in their correspondence in the 1750s.

Thus the role "enlightened" Jews played in the discourse of sympathy is not
negligible, nor is it incidental.[12] It is against this background—the fine embroidery of the intellectual, spiritual friendship of the two great men, Mendelssohn
and Lessing—that one should read the famous and recently much quoted sentences written by Lessing to his friend Friedrich Nicolai in those early years:
"Der mitleidigste Mensch ist der beste Mensch, zu allen gesellschaftlichen
Tugenden, zu allen Arthen der Großmuth der aufgelegteste" (The most compassionate man is the best man, the best disposed towards all social virtues, for
all sorts of magnanimity). This comes as a conclusion of previous ruminations
about tragedy's main goal, as an artistic genre:

> Sie soll unsre Fähigkeit, Mitleid zu fühlen, erweitern. Sie soll uns nicht blos
> lehren, gegen diesen oder jenen Unglücklichen Mitleid zu fühlen, sondern
> sie soll uns so weit fühlbar machen, daß uns der Unglückliche zu allen Zeiten,
> und unter allen Gestalten, rühren und für sich einnehmen muß.

[It is supposed to increase our ability to feel compassion. It must teach us not only to feel compassion towards this or that unfortunate person, but rather, (it must) make us sensitive to such an extent that the unfortunate will touch and win favor with us at all times, among all characters.][13]

Expanding the boundaries of sympathy to include other times and places, a suffering to which one is not immediately related and for which one is not accountable, introduced a new perspective into the European scene. In Lessing's case, as we shall further see, it must have been the basic moral premise on which he founded his benevolent attitude towards the Jews in his dramas. In a way, though not explicitly, Lessing seemed to take a certain responsibility for generations of discrimination and persecution of Jews and others.

Later, however, enhanced as a reaction to Rousseau's ideas and to other intellectual developments of the time, the gap between Lessing's and Mendelssohn's respective positions regarding *Mitleid* became apparent. We therefore turn to Rousseau and Smith, the great secularizers of compassion/sympathy, before reviewing how the German-Jewish discussion profited from them, and how they differed. Mutual to Jean-Jacques Rousseau's and Adam Smith's analysis of compassion/sympathy is the relatively neutral and natural context of their discussion, interested as they were in the social and the political (rather than in the historical and the cultural). Seeking to establish human morality on the benevolent principle of compassion/sympathy, both thinkers proved highly influential for generations of philosophers and artists, and therefore both play a vital role in the facilitating of cultural-aesthetic developments, discussed below. Their arguments, emerging on the European stage of the eighteenth century,[14] later reverberate in the writings and works of Schopenhauer, Wagner, George Eliot, Nietzsche, Max Scheller, and even in those of Schoenberg. Rousseau's and Smith's respective thinking delineates new avenues for emotional existence, and, as such, may help analyze philosophically less elaborate expressions of similar emotional complexities.

Out of the two, however, it was Rousseau who sought to render compassion an inclusive and universal principle in human ethics and behavior, granting it a central role in the education of the individual. The natural foundation of sympathy, he claims, is its activation by the human agent through "a gentle voice," which "must be the mother's as well as nature's," as Derrida puts it. While this precondition is innate and prior to any concept or image, it is through the imagination, Derrida indicates, that pity becomes a social factor: "Without imagination . . . pity is not accessible to passion, language, and representation, [it] does not produce identification with the other as with another me."[15] Moreover, it is only through entering into human discourse that compassion might become "the last refuge of nature in our state of greatest estrangement from it," as Clifford Orwin argues.[16]

As regards the special role music may have in the imaginative formation of sympathetic worlds, we may gain insight from Paul de Man's interpretations of Rousseau's ideas in his *Essay on the Origin of Languages*. Rousseau, de Man maintains, posited music as a model for language and art precisely because music entails an autonomous play of relations, free of predetermined signification or reference.[17] It is not that Rousseau overlooked the mimetic element in music signification (as Derrida emphasizes). Following the late-sixteenth-century Florentine Camerata's members and others who furthered their ideas, Rousseau observes that "by imitating the inflections of the voice, melody expresses pity, cries of sorrow and joy, threats and groans. All the vocal signs of passion are within its domain." But he also said (as de Man indicates) that "not only does [music] imitate, it bespeaks. And its language is lively, ardent, passionate; and it has a hundred times the vigor of speech itself."[18] De Man construes this mode of signification in terms of the sequential unfolding of music, and its interrelated power of metaphorical substitution.

Until the eighteenth century, the unconsummated, asymbolic nature of music was concealed behind texts, contexts, and given patterns, as if out of fear to expose a basic emptiness and self-negating principle that seemed to underlie it. It was the undertaking of many a composer, theorist, and a receptive audience, since the late seventeenth century and onward, to focus on music's mode of "successive impressions"[19]—which prevents it from collapsing into a simultaneous, self-identical object (the kind of self-identity underscored by the rhetoric of the "Prioress' Tale," in Fradenburg's reading)—a nonsimultaneity that leaves it "hollow in its core,"[20] unless abducted by topics, programs, or technical forms. Aspiring to such an "empty" condition did not render music meaningless; on the contrary, the fixation of its symbolic creations in narratives and other verbalized renditions was gradually apprehended as an aesthetic drawback, a limitation on music's emancipatory expressive aptitude. Music's ability to continually enact, or articulate anew, the emotional substratum to which it refers turned into its great advantage. If the paradox of compassion lies in the inherent gap between the successive projection of the sufferer's mental state upon a temporal axis and another person's reaction to it in "real time," according to de Man, then music is phenomenologically capable of reflecting such reciprocity.[21] It does so by projecting emotional change, which is concomitantly polyphonically surrounded with a related sympathetic environment. (This argument, though conceptualized somewhat differently, will later be taken by J. J. Engel; see chapter 4). This principle of "emotional adjustability" will be elaborated to an extreme by Emanuel Levinas' ethical approach regarding the infinite call to face the Other, to ever encounter it face to face without fixating or thematizing it, or, conversely, merging with it.

The fluid, nonfixable nature of the musical unfolding, its basic freedom from predetermined semantic identities, rendered it central also in the modern vocal fictions which are the foci of the following chapters. These vocal fictions, embodied in oratorio, opera, lieder, novels, poems, and their like, could grapple with the aesthetic categories the Jew and noise allegations were connected to by using the very medium these categories struggled to fixate: sound, now embodying a transcending-identity phenomenology. This basic condition of the new music was also conducive to unleashing less stereotyped reactions to the Jews within fictive worlds (by the personae populating their imagined arenas) and outside them (by readers, listeners, and service goers). It depended, however, upon the extent to which this propensity of music was realized and geared— that is, upon the modes of highlighting its nonessentialist nature along with the relentless thwarting of its inevitable tendency towards reification.

An addendum to Rousseau's ideas, of interest for the present history, is his refutation of the Christian concept of musical harmony, in the way it was technically developed in the course of the Middle Ages.[22] Elevating music's capacity to render, through melody, the undulations of the heart, and exalting languages whose flexible phonological constitution enhances this condition, Rousseau contends against the northern Europeans' "barbaric" languages for being hard, harsh, graceless, and rigid. Their way to conceal these noisy qualities, he explains, brought their speakers to elongate their vocals—thereby acoustically rendered as (musical) pitches. To these emotionally meaningless sounds, he speculates (while historically in line with the bare facts), they fortuitously added even more euphonious vocals—embarking on polyphonic texture. This sort of polyphony, he concludes, was all about resolution of dissonances (*concordia discors*). Western harmony is thus founded on "barbaric noise," whose antiemotionalism, and lack of moral basis thereof, still accompanies its later products. Rousseau thus undermines the superiority of Western harmony; moreover, he argues that melody-oriented musical cultures (which the Ashkenazi liturgical one may exemplify) are aesthetically, no less than morally, more commendable.

In contradistinction to Rousseau, the empiricist Adam Smith subjects sympathy to "commonsensical" scrutiny, without, however, losing its foundational role in the formation of his moral theory.[23] Smith embraces the inclusiveness of Spinoza's definition of fellow-feeling, placing "positive sympathy" above "negative compassion" on a scale of natural propensities. "Nature," argues Smith, "when she loaded us with our own sorrows, thought that they were enough, and therefore did not command us to take any further share in those of others, than what was necessary to prompt us to relieve them."[24] Far from idealizing human nature, but also from disparaging it, Smith is undisturbed by "theatrical" compassion, which Rousseau deemed a waste of ethical energies, a draining of the resources necessary for real moral action. The Scottish Smith is more preoccupied with ethical "proprieties" and acknowledges what was already recognized by Aristotle, though in different terms: that sympathy can be evoked only when one "is in perfect concord with the sympathetic emotions of the spectator." He further states that "the person who feels none [no emotion] that bears any proportion to mine, cannot avoid disapproving my sentiments, on account of their dissonances with his own."[25] Note the musical metaphors: concord, dissonances, and proportions, bearing witness to the intimate affiliation of compassion with the notion—scientific and poetic—of "sympathetic vibration."[26] Smith, however, invests the metaphor with new content: What blocks sympathy and breeds indifference, he argues, are different sets of values regarding what should "merit" our sadness or joy. It also concerns the cognizance of the circumstances that brought about affliction or fortune; for such awareness sometimes abates our sympathy, sometimes elicits it.

But "propriety" concerns not only the sympathizer's attitude; it also involves its target, the "emoting persona," who is called upon to "turn away his eyes from whatever is either naturally terrible or disagreeable in his situation" so as to keep his expression "within the bounds of moderation." Only with such a predisposition would he be able to win the "complete sympathy and approbation of the spectators," argues Smith, interestingly deploying a theatrical term. Smith even goes as far as to reproach "the intrepid Duke of Biron," brave in war and battle, who "wept upon the scaffold" in disgrace.[27] What would Smith have to say about Jesus on the cross, weeping (according to St. Matthew), in Hebrew: "Eli, Eli Lama Azab[v]tani" (My God, my God, why have you forsaken me)? Avoiding the religious, Smith is interested solely in the socially proper. He performed this transition so well that we almost overlook the fact that "proper" and "propriety" were, not long before, still largely associated with the liturgical, religious realm. In terms of our story, the Proper (of the Mass) and *Improperia* (of the Jews) became thoroughly secularized and only culturally and psychologically bound in Smith.

Indeed, considerations of propriety contextualize sympathy as a cultural virtue without denying its central role in society's well-being. They imply shared values and emotional norms, and render social relations dependent on dynamic changes of position and the traversing of nonuniform personal distances in varieties of emotional combinations. As such, propriety considerations also include cultural and aesthetic norms: "He who admires the same poem or the same picture, and admires them exactly as I do, must surely allow the justness of my admiration." Unintentionally, Smith here paves the road for the antithesis of this stance—for "cultural aversion," or even *volkstümliche Abneigung* (popular aversion)—of the kind advocated by Wagner against Jewish presence, though Wagner's essentialist orientation and nationalistic aspirations were virtually foreign to Smith.[28]

Though not exactly an "invisible-hand" explanation, Smith's understanding of sympathy is guided by a tacit principle of economical distribution of emotional loads and resources, executed for the benefit of all.[29] According to Smith, both sympathizer and sympathized-with should relegate their emotional expression according to their counterpart's avowed state; continuous attentive adjustment should result in alleviating pain and eliciting joyfulness, as Smith promises. Aesthetically speaking, such flexibility indeed fits the "condition of music" as Rousseau, in de Man's version, advocated. Likewise, it aspires to the fluid worlds of narrative—ever mediated by a narrator's voice—rather than to the straightforward and more rigid ones realized on stage.

Noteworthy is Smith's projection of "sympathetic interest" beyond that of a rather "domestic" fellow feeling; the nearby poor, the suffering neighbor, or the fortunate or unfortunate compatriot. His well-known deliberation concerning the genuineness of the "man of humanity's" sympathy with the suffering of the distant ones—the (speculative) earthquake-stricken Chinese—anticipates modernist and postmodernist preoccupation with limits and predicaments of humanitarian interventions. His ruminations already gear towards queries such as: how does cultural otherness (religious, national, or the like) affect fellow-feeling? What happens when Aristotle's basic condition of compassion—similarity of background, age, and status—is not fulfilled? And, above all, how should one face the calamities and suffering of Others of all kinds, close and distant, privileged and unprivileged denizens of this globe?[30] This, inevitably, would subsequently lead as well to considerations regarding the power of sympathy to read the others within the "Western standard": women, Jews, slaves.

Lessing and Mendelssohn, each in his own way, though still located in the "presentimental" if not "naïve" world of the Enlightenment (according to Schiller's famous distinction), did not shun this problematic. Lessing, who basically accepted Rousseau's natural principle of compassion, delved into the mysteries of Greek catharsis, coming up with the notion that in theater in general, and tragedy in particular, fear and pity—*phobos* and *eleos*—should mitigate each other so as to create a viable middle way. In a way, his own dramatic works attest to this conception, containing within them certain seeds of cultural sobriety, if not enlightened resignation.[31] Mendelssohn, who wrote the abovementioned letters at a time when he was troubled by religious prejudices of some of his Jewish brethren,[32] became suspicious of natural compassion as a social regulating force. "In uns liegt keine ausdrückliche Bestimmung, an den Schwachheiten anderere Geschöpfe Mißvergnügen zu haben. Nein!" (We lack an explicit disposition to commiserate with the infirmities of other creatures. No!) says the Jewish scholar to his readers, mostly Christians. But then he adds the following crucial statement: "Mitleiden gründet sich auf Liebe, Liebe gründet sich auf die Lust und Harmonie und Ordnung" (Compassion is based on love, love bases itself on desire and harmony and order)[33] and these two—both love and the yearning for harmony and order—are the presence of the Divine in human beings, a transcendental rather than an immanent principle, which is, however, what should bind human society and sociability along communal differences. Wittingly or unwittingly, Mendelssohn's concept of harmony aims to refute the old exclusivist Christian harmony that rejected that which is not in unison with its abiding strictures. In a certain way, the notions of these thinkers, however conservative they may appear—especially those of Mendelssohn—could be interpreted as trajectories hurtling beyond their immediate futures to alight in a post-Enlightenment and postsentimental world, suspicious of sympathetic whims and condescending compassionate gestures, in the search for social-political solutions founded on human solidarity and rights.

This, however, will not concern us now. At stake are the modes through which the aesthetics of sympathy found expression in the course of the eighteenth century in artistic products that projected sympathetic worlds. Auguring a new culture of religious tolerance and social inclusion, vocal art seemed to provide new frames of reference for Jews seeking "sonic" integration. Such vocal works and their universes bear, thus, a special significance for the developments discussed in this volume insofar as they have become normative models and objects of identification for later generations. Three groups of such works will engage us in the following pages: Bach's Passions—*St. Matthew* and *St. John Passion*; Lessing's "Jewish plays"—*The Jews* and *Nathan the Wise*; and three of Handel's biblical oratorios—*Samson*, *Israel in Egypt*, and *Judas Maccabeus*. A juxtaposition of these works may point to their common components while highlighting the unique elements of each. Together they exemplify and anticipate artistic articulations of "communal modes" of sympathy, solidarity, and redemption in the centuries to come. Concomitantly, they also harbor latent modes of alienation and discrimination.

The genre of the oratorio is the linchpin connecting these oeuvres. Paradigmatically exemplified in Bach's and Handel's works, it opens a new exploratory path into Lessing's dramas within an auditory-religious framework, revealing hidden dimensions of their affective power. The theatrical environment of his work, in turn, sheds light on pertinent thematic-dramatic elements implicit in the musical texts.

The role of successive performances and interpretations of these opuses is crucial for an understanding of their historico-cultural import and implications. The following discussion refers also to some paradigmatic performances that harbor indications of the worlds of meaning that their producers and intended audience could fathom. Felix Mendelssohn's interpretation of the *St. Matthew Passion* looms large here, but the analysis includes other, less famous "production events," which, in different times and places, point to changing conceptions regarding auditory inclusion or exclusion of others and attest to the various attempts to engage in a confrontation or dialogue with their spiritual-religious legacies (as is the case with the productions of *The Merchant of Venice* discussed in chapter 1). The world of Mendelssohn's *St. Matthew Passion* will be the first to be approached through an interpretation of this kind.

A CRISSCROSSED *MATTHÄUS-PASSION*

At the Center for the Performing Arts, the Opera Hall, Tel-Aviv, February 2002,[34] a special event: tonight, the *St. Matthew Passion* (BWV 244) is performed in an operatic production. Throughout the hall, an immense bridge comprised of curving rails leads from the stalls (approximately row twenty) down onto the stage above the orchestra, situated, as usual, in its pit. The conductor takes his place there and the famous E minor ritornello of the grand overture emerges. With the very first, well-grounded arpeggio cry of the chorus "Kommt, ihr Töchter" (Come, ye daughters), the curtain opens. The double choir is disclosed—men and women standing on two juxtaposed four-tier scaffolding-like constructions, in typical though variegated costumes of eastern European Jews from the first half of the twentieth century (see fig. 2.1). The stage itself is strewn with wooden crosses of various dimensions, tied with white bandages. The choir on the left is singing, while the second choir is mute, as if awaiting an invitation from its counterpart. Upon the first sounds, consciously interrupting the music, *they* arrive, one after the other, from the very end of the

Fig. 2.1. Jesus at the Cross, disciples and other "Jews" around and above, in Friedrich and Uecker's 1999 staging of the *St. Matthew Passion*. With permission by the photographer, Bernd Uhlig.

railed bridge—a group of thirteen German youths, some blond, some brunette, casually dressed.[35] One, however, more typically Aryan-looking, is distinguished by his special, white attire, while another is dressed like a Lutheran pastor. Astonished by what they see, they are driven along the bridge into the arena of martyrdom, ready to start playing their role. Germans, Jews, Israelis; perpetrators, onlookers, victims; performers, audience, congregation—all seem to blend tonight, crossing visible and invisible roads on the way to the Crucifixion.[36]

The groups are situated, by and large, along the huge beams of an imaginary cross. The "Germans" are mainly positioned along its vertical beam, the one leading to ancient Jerusalem: Gethsemane, Golgotha, and other sites. The "Jews" are located on the horizontal pole, seeking heaven from the terrestrial level upwards. Each group embodies both its quasi-contemporary self as well as its traditional other: the vertical "Germans" conflate with the Hebrew biblical personae—the Evangelist, Jesus, his disciples and followers. The roles of the horizontal "Jews" are even more complicated: in the turba choirs, they represent the biblical Jewish priests and crowd, allegorically metamorphosing (in the chorus' sections) into the "Daughters of Zion" and the "Faithful," and, metonymically (in the chorale parts), into Christian (Lutheran) believers. From within both groups new individual voices, unmentioned in the Scriptures, come forth. Some of them are new and abstract; some rewrite roles of scriptural personae; together they provide a variety of affective perspectives on the unfolding drama.[37]

The opening scene in this production becomes a colossal cry. One sits in the audience and weeps as it touches a most sensitive, vibrant nerve wrung by the music. Listening to the *cori spezzati*—the divided choruses' exchange in the overture[38]—it seems as though it had always been there, aimed at that moment in which Germans, dressed as Jews from concentration camps, would engage in a bizarre dialogue paraphrasing ancient verses of the Song of Songs, introduced by Picander (Christian Friedrich Henrici) and Bach, and by a subsequent tradition tenaciously adhering to its cultural treasures:[39]

> Kommt, ihr Töchter,
> helft mir klagen, seht,
> Wen?
> den Bräutigam, seht ihn
> Wie?
> als wie ein Lamm.[40]
>
> [Come, ye daughters, help me lament, behold,
> Whom?
> The bridegroom, behold him
> How?
> Like a lamb.]

The turbulent ups and downs of this gigantic E minor slinging 12/8 three-partite aria—a grand, plodding pilgrimage, as a Schweitzer would have it,[41] onto the agonizing mount of Zion—lead one repeatedly to the summit from which one can have a vantage point of Jewish-Christian martyrology. In one of its first pinnacles, when you expect the soaring chorale "O Lamm Gottes, unschuldig" to be carried by angel-like child-sopranos, as if directly gazing at the eternal place of crucifixion, you will be deceived.[42] The innocent (G major) voices turn in this performance into a women's choir with no distinguishable voices breaking through the mass, singing from the bottom, the first tier of the "concentration-camp" construction as if mediating between the two groups and the variety of worlds they inhabit—one ancient, one traditionally Lutheran, the world of the Shoah, and a contemporary postmodern world. It is from within this group that individual voices will later emerge.

Is this a legitimate interpretation, one wonders as it unfolds, feeling some professional musicological qualms. Is not an operatic staging of an oratorio, however dramatic, a contradiction in terms, even a blasphemy—both theological and musical?[43] One has always assumed that the vocal differentiations the work carries along with its generic characterizations avail for an imaginative visualization of the agonizing events. Does one really need to *see* Christ distribute the bread (matzah) and the wine, and later chained, tortured, bleeding, and crucified? In this performance, the audience seems to be divided between those expressing doubt and those enthusiastically endorsing it. The division is not necessarily along "professional" lines. Later one discovers that the director and stage designer of the production—Günther Uecker and Götz Friedrich—were aware of a possible transgression of the genre's boundaries, linking their interpretation of the original theological constraints concerning representation and idolatry.[44]

Friedrich and Uecker justify their interpretation by linking it with the work's epochal Mendelssohnian 1829 Berlin *Singakademie* revival and its subsequent reception. How does this association relate to their experiment, and how did it seek to grapple with the theological predicament of representation that it seems to transgress? At the moment, it will suffice to note that the producers used, indeed, Mendelssohn's version (or "urtext" as Christopher Hogwood called it[45]) of the work, following its cuts and orchestration;[46] and that they felt obliged, by the Berlin connection, to interpret it in terms of twentieth-century history. Apprehending the palimpsest-like nature of the enterprise, they collapsed at least six layers of interpretation of the Crucifixion within a single hearing: St. Matthew's, Luther's, Bach's, and Mendelssohn's; crucial events in twentieth-century history as reflected in poetry and prose, and present-day approaches. Mendelssohn's intermediate layer, they seem to suggest, is the key to all others.

In the course of rehearsals for the premiere, Mendelssohn addressed his friend and collaborator in the enterprise, actor and singer Eduard Devrient, in words recorded by the latter. Those words, though lately overquoted, remain enigmatic: "und . . . daß es ein Komödiant und ein Judenjunge sein müssen, die den Leuten die größte christliche Musik wiederbringen." (And [to think] that it has to be a comedian and a Jew-boy who return the greatest Christian music to the people.) (!)[47] The designers of the Berlin production seemed well aware of this Jewish connection without overtly declaring it. The Jewish element could not have escaped Felix, who would have certainly remembered who first gave him the work: his observant Jewish maternal grandmother, Bella Salomon (née Itzig),[48] on his fifteenth birthday. For five years, Mendelssohn would dream of this revival.[49] His grandmother, not informed that her daughter's family had converted to Lutheranism, purchased this precious manuscript from an acquaintance, George Pölschau.[50] Apparently, this seemed quite natural for a family that so adored the works of the great Lutheran cantor, especially the vocal ones.

Between the stages of Bach and Mendelssohn in the six layers of the work's cumulative hermeneutics, one thus finds a "Jewish" intermediate layer; more precisely, that of the Berlin Itzig family, whose daughters Bella (Babette) Salomon and Sarah Levy were among the first to cherish the Bach legacy.[51] Why were they so drawn to this heritage? The theological solution for the dilemma of idolatrous representation of the holy through voice, image, and gesture, as it developed within the German Lutheran church and its adopted oratorio, could have appealed to Jews. At the same time, the poignant Christian martyrology, along with its anti-Semitic tones and overtones, would certainly deter them. Thus the early affinity of Jews for Bach's *Passions* must have surmounted such theological predicaments and reached other cultural sensibilities and burgeoning aspirations that poured into young Mendelssohn's historic production.

* * *

While the ears of the Itzig girls had been initiated into the sounds of the Leipzig cantor and his sons, their eyes were trained in a similar direction, toward a visual version of the "oratorical mode." In their wealthy father's salon, the sisters could find valuable biblical paintings, and works by Rubens, Hals, and Canaletto. One painting was the *Presentation in the Temple* of 1671 (depicting Elkanah and Hannah bringing their son Samuel to Eli, the high priest in Shiloh, as related in 1 Samuel 1–2) by the Dutch painter Gerbrand van den Eeckhout (1621–1674); another: *Moses Drawing Water from the Rock* by the Antwerpian Jacob Beschey (1710–1786).[52]

In the great tradition of Rembrandt and his school, Eeckhout's painting highlights the psychological element of each of the depicted figures through gesture, position, and facial expression. The artist chose a potent moment in the story: Hannah, once a sterile mother, now brings her offspring, Shmu'el (Samuel), whom she vowed to pledge to God's service (see fig. 2.2, plate 4). Here she is kneeling in a typical posture of prayer and piety, her eyes downcast; she may already have uttered her beautiful "Ode to Joy" (1 Samuel 2–10). Attentive, half-facing her, Elkanah rests his loving, devout gaze on her, expressing meekness, but the main focus of the composition, slightly to the left of the geometric center of the painting, is the baby, lying in the arms of a venerable but still vigorous Eli, whose expression reveals utmost joy. The baby is too small in

Fig. 2.2. (and plate 4). Gerbrand van den Eeckhout, *Presentation in the Temple*, 1671. Oil on canvas. Courtesy of the Szépművészeti Múzeum, Budapest.

relation to its age, according to the biblical story; the painter must have known better, but wished to provide an allegorical reminder of another consecrated infant in Nativity paintings such as by Raphael, Correggio, or Murillo. The figure behind the others, an old woman (modeled perhaps after St. Anne), could be a witness who would later tell the story, so that the ode to joy composed by

Hannah would subsequently be echoed by various personae, including the Virgin Mary (Luke 1:46–51).

This allegorization was not necessarily part of the cluster of associations evoked in this observant Jewish house; its members could naturally connect it, instead, to the reading from the Prophets on the first day of Rosh Hashanah, the Jewish New Year. For the modern, though still observant Berlin Jews who attempted, even unconsciously, to defend themselves against the old accusation of Jewish synagogal noise, the quiet form of Hannah's prayer (in her imploration for a child, she "was speaking in her heart; only her lips moved, and her voice was not heard"—1 Samuel 1:13) could have held a special appeal (though, as we shall see in the following chapter, some outsiders saw even this form of prayer as particularly Jewish). A similar role could have been played by Beschey's *Moses Drawing Water from the Rock*: the faithful shepherd, who has already watered the people and their animals (their thirst is quenched and they look satisfied), is now nursing the young boy in his arms in a gesture of compassion and care (plate 5, and fig. 2.3, detail). The people are peaceful and contained. "Noisy" elements that otherwise characterize their behavior have disappeared.[53] Compassion and harmony prevail.

Fig. 2.3. (and plate 5). Jacob Beschey, *Moses Drawing Water from the Rock* (detail). Oil on canvas. Courtesy of the National Gallery–Alexandros Soutzos Museum, Athens.

ORATORIO AS A COMMUNAL GENRE

Such pictorial embodiments of biblical stories, a moment (containing other moments) of expressive dramatization in a narrative told by an omniscient narrator, would have touched the imagination of those culture-thirsty Jews, who were among the first in modern times to search for ways to connect classicist and Christian imaginaries with their own sacred traditions. The musical oratorio would take them into a universe in which expressive religious gestures would be further hypostatized through concrete utterance and voices.

Without delving too deeply into theories of genre, I would like to suggest that, as highly encoded forms of expression open to variation and change, genres invite both creators and audiences to decipher the new in terms of the familiar.[54] These encoded forms acquire their amazing resilience in the history of cultures by functioning as inexhaustible vehicles for dealing with pertinent predicaments as well as diverse and shared imaginaries. As such, genres always have a prehistory and a post-history; their embryonic forms and aftermath. Yet the modalities, that is, the artistic ways in which raw materials are welded before crystallizing into established forms (later dissolving into new artistic habitats), appear in variegated disguises and forms even during the genres' heydays.

The oratorio, an expressive form typical of the Counter-Reformation, christened in seventeenth-century Italy, aimed to dramatize religion while retaining ecclesiastic boundaries. At the same time, its creators endeavored to distinguish their works from the then flourishing, secular theatrical genres through intricate dialogues offered by the oratorio—between time and place, text and commentary, representation and expression, ritual and dramatic form. Time and temporalities are determined, first and foremost, by the position of narrator or Evangelist vis-à-vis the audience. While situating the story in the past, the narrator/Evangelist concomitantly brings its related occurrences into the present through vital narrative tensions. Once temporal cohesiveness is achieved, space becomes similarly superposed. In the oratorio, past and distant places are grafted onto the immediate present, creating a nonrealistic, transhistorical chronotopoi. The sacred text delivered by the narrator, however sealed and canonized, becomes, even through its sheer secco recitation, a commentary, an interpretation, and a message. Inviting impersonation through distinct vocal intonations (the roles of Jesus, Samson, Elijah), it also calls for textual mediations and meditations on the narrated and enacted subject matter, enhancing the active role of the actual, contemporary believer—the designated audience of the performed work. Time, in an explicit non-Aristotelian way, becomes further mixed,[55] while representation turns out to be rather loose. Actual voices are potentially divided among personae belonging to different temporal and spatial categories, as others ventriloquize preexisting voices (beyond their original utterances). The same performing voice could, in principle, represent both a *historia sacra* figure as well as a host of contemporary subjective feelings about it, cast in a mixture of expressive ecclesiastic and secular modes.

It was largely the avoidance of the directly mimetic, of a fictive reality "out there," and the interrelated emphasis on the hermeneutic process so central in the Lutheran tradition, that endeared the oratorio genre to German Lutheran pastors, composers, and their congregations (though it has also known its moments of decline).[56] Centered on the altar and the chorus' place, the performance of an oratorio revived the spirit of medieval religious dramas for a Lutheran Baroque congregation within a contemporary religious context that considerably underplayed the role of ritual, filling the figurative, emotional gap left open since the stormy iconoclastic attacks of the Lutheran reformers. Sometimes embodying the community, sometime inviting it to join forces, the chorus highlights the blurred boundaries of the real and the fictive, the individual and the communal, the sacred and the mundane.

The circular, only partially mimetic presentation bypassed the idolatry predicament, yet enabled emotional identification and mobilization. Speaking from a more strictly semiotic point of view, the oratorio and its related genres made explicit the following interrelated stages in the construing of the communal experience of the holy:[57]

(1) The oratorical text deploys a plethora of speech acts inherent in the biblical text, such as narration, exclamation, ordaining by decrees, interrogation, prayer, supplication, glorification, blaspheming, blessing and incantations, to which an array of meditative, expressive, and declarative speech acts of various kinds are annexed by means of new poetic supplements. The narrative frame renders salient this variety of speech acts, and generic musical-dramatic distinctions (such as recitative, arioso declamations, choral proclamations, and the like) further mold them.

(2) These generic distinctions, in turn, give rise to musical gestures that not only convey and animate the speech acts, providing their "sonoric seat," but often embed them—especially in the "through-composed" movements (arias, choral fantasies, and fugal choruses)—within an encompassing dynamic texture.

(3) Generic and gestural means further concretize "virtual agents" (dramatis personae performing speech acts) without, however, over-reifying them. (It is these special properties that drew Devrient to the *St. Matthew Passion*, maintaining, that the "impersonation of the several characters of the Gospel by different voices is the pith of the work.")[58]

(4) Situated in a variety of chronotopoi—biblical, contemporary, timeless— each such "persona" becomes affiliated with a certain fictional plane, or following Heidegger, *Daseinsebene*, or plane of existence,[59] thus conversing both with fictional-plane "peers" (such as Jesus addressing Pontius Pilate), as well as across them (two female voices, descending from the choir, embodying "believers" who accompany the bound Jesus after Judas' betrayal).

(5) The connection between such planes and personae is made through musical syntactical-rhetorical means, facilitating recursive nets (such as through tonal means, in which the higher section in the hierarchical order usually becomes the encompassing one), subjunctive proclamations (through generic superimpositions, conferring a "would-be" status on their utterances), cross-relations to previous sections (through motivic association), and the like.

When such a conflation of planes and personae occurs, it often gives rise to "oratorical moments." Such moments show forth a vocalized alchemy in which a voice (or voices) from a certain time, context, and configuration pierce through series of pasts, presents, or futures—or a mixture thereof, carrying embedded existential layers, and project them onto an ever-renewed present tense.[60] Their appearance can be experienced as a miracle, an aural epiphany spiritually radiating on those exposed to its vocal light and open to deciphering its aggregate meaning. They can, however, also function as both ominous harbingers and repositories, summoning voices from time immemorial, prefiguring sounds of unknowable futures.

THE *ST. MATTHEW PASSION*'S SYMPATHETIC SPIRALS

Only few oratorios and cantatas embody the entire plethora of these rhetorical-musical means, but they are all employed, in an unsurpassed way, in the *St. Matthew Passion*. The initial Leipzig years (1724–1727) during which Bach unfurled the potential of the genre in three cycles of annual cantatas were crucial in preparing him for this colossal enterprise. In this sense, the work is sui generis; it is the kind of oeuvre that, in Walter Benjamin's terms, comes closest to the embodiment of its overriding aesthetic idea, containing within itself "the index of a particular, objectively necessary artistic structure."[61]

This structure is intimately related to the import issuing from such a magnum opus, and to a certain encompassing religious experience and spiritual process it aspires to proffer. The ideational import and experiential input go beyond the traditional, dogmatic beliefs that initially nurture both composer and librettist.[62] It relates, first and foremost, to the idea and experience of compassion, or *Mitleid*, or, even more generally, to sympathy, *Mitgefühl*. Comprehending a dramatic-emotional strategy, it seems to transcend the feelings of repentance and suffering, of guilt and revenge that are expressed in the course of the drama. By means of emotional trajectories vocalized by various agents, virtual and historical, and within the subjectivities of one's own self (as Naomi Cumming proposed),[63] it momentarily hypostatizes the main subject and object of compassion — Jesus, animating the story and co-opting the congregation within the narrative.

If, indeed, such a theologico-aesthetic conception resonated powerfully with the renovators of the work and their audiences in the first part of the nineteenth century, it should have been reflected in some of the choices that guided the historic 1829 performance and subsequent productions.[64] I wish to argue that Mendelssohn's and Devrient's choice of movements reveals such a resonance. Earlier scholars concentrated on what Mendelssohn left out in his production. Thus Michael Marissen's claim that the "cutting" expresses an attempt to mitigate the anti-Semitic import of the work has been convincingly refuted by Jeffrey Sposato;[65] similarly persuasive is Sposato's general contention that, above all, the omissions reflect an attempt to reduce textual redundancy and avoid theological difficulties.

Yet neither Sposato nor Marissen grapple with the experiential process that the revived work could offer to a growing post-Napoleonic bourgeois German audience. I therefore propose to examine what Mendelssohn chose to include in this historical performance rather than focus on his omissions. Following Schleiermacher's theological teaching too closely, Sposato maintains that arias evoking present-day viewpoints were basically eliminated by Mendelssohn in favor of those parts that represent biblical voices or emphasize the unity of the Lutheran community, in the spirit of Schleiermacher. Schleiermacher himself, however, as Sposato rightly emphasizes, viewed the *individual* believer's relation to the congregation in terms of *Gemeindetheologie* — the unique contribution each individual believer brings to the ever-accumulating body of the church, on her way to resembling her redeemer.[66]

All the arias in the work could be perfectly consonant with this criterion. As it turns out, however, those in Mendelssohn's final version involve both individual and community by mobilizing and fusing distinct Dasein planes, sweeping individuals and congregation into ever more attractive spirals of mutual compassion and redemption, breeding powerful oratorical moments. Mendelssohn did not omit a single one of these multilayered parts. Take, for example, the closing numbers of the first part of the work (no. 27–29 NBA).[67] These crucial oratorical moments are loaded with much of what has hitherto transpired. Voices, forces which have appeared earlier, actions that have taken place, find a new outlet and reconciliation here. But only temporarily; new predicaments would arise that would activate the drama of the second part, in which the Passion reaches its apex and denouement. As we shall see below, this multiplicity of voices, planes, and forces had and continued to hold a powerful rhetorical impact on other works and the worlds they purported to summon.

Let's examine how this actually works. The two main numbers (27, 29) are closely related; they share the tonality of E in its double major-minor appearance. At the same time, they project an imaginative arch back onto the opening E minor chorus and comprise a (plegal) link to the second part, which starts in B minor.

Bach calls the first number "Aria" and the second "Chorale." The aria, in fact, is a duet interrupted by a contrasting choir, which takes over at a certain point and harnesses the other choir to the action. The solos never return, and with them all traces of da capo are eliminated. The traditional sense of balance is lost as well. The closing choral fantasia "O Mensch" forges ahead within huge swells of a perpetuum mobile ritornello. Its homophonic texture constantly breaks from within into quasi-heterophonic waves. Its AAB infrastructure seems lost among these surrounding forces.

These are only frames, yet their shapes reflect the content of the pictures they encompass. The first focuses on Jesus, who has just been arrested at the culmination of a disgraceful betrayal. Some imaginary voices, in line with a long pictorial tradition, plea in reaction: be with him in this horrible moment, accompany him and see how all that surrounds sympathizes with him. The others cry: avenge him, give expression to the rage aroused in you and call on nature to join forces. The first are the solo souls—soprano and alto; the second are the milling crowds, the choirs (ex. 2.1).

The two perspectives cannot be merged on their own subjective spheres, yet they share the same texture. This is a sign Bach gave us to mark their co-existence in the same temporal and spatial plane. Their respective affects are too divergent for their actions to coordinate.[68] The first two souls stumble in an appoggiatura syncopated texture, avoiding as much dissonant clashing as possible. There are four main thematic parts in this ritornello. The first gesture consists of a double fugato which builds up a typical rhythmical, tonal, and melodic tension. The underlying motif may be identified, following the tradition, as a gesture embodying a speech act of sighs. It is momentarily resolved in a balanced, monothematic gesture of solacing responses, which bursts forth into a semicadence, closing the first part of the ritornello. It is this moment of soft and balanced echoes of the underlying ritornello that Bach chose for the rival choir's intrusion (compare mm. 5–6 to mm. 21–22). This creates a

Ex. 2.1. J. S. Bach, *St. Matthew Passion*, I, 27a, Aria,
"So ist mein Jesus nun gefangen," mm.1–25.

second-order dissonance between diametrically-opposed speech-acts—solace and exhortation—which calls for its own resolution. The two appoggiatura souls walk further and further, merging in parallel sixths.[69] They never return along the same thematic route, and they never revert to their initial tonal starting point. Their lonely walk, unsupported by the basses, is self-sufficient by way of affording mutual, momentary consolation.[70]

The tonal energy leashed within the meddling crowd is released in section 27b ("Sind Blitze . . ."). The singers use the same figure (outcry) as before, but within a 3/8 metric system it gestures differently (ex. 2.2). This musical speech act comes close to a tribal dance which amasses circles of dancers as it proceeds, becoming fiercer and more fervent through the input of the juxtaposing choirs, as though the participating dancers move closer and closer to an invisible object on which all are concentrating. The break (in m. 104) that comes so abruptly (following the rhetorical *abruptio*) launches them into a final, terrifying, boisterous cry: "Eröffne den feurigen Abgrund" (Open the fiery abyss). In the kind of musical speech acts they use, they resemble the turba choirs. The virtual congregation thus achieves its utmost involvement in the drama: they overcome all recursive barriers and invade the basic fictional territory, attempting to rewrite a history that had long been sealed. The vocal expression of this break is *Lärm*—outcries, alarum—as much as could be achieved within the stylistic boundaries of the time; noisy Jews and devout Christians converge in the same gesture, in the same vociferous behavior.

Fascinating, in this connection, is John Butt's interpretation to the first turba chorus of the *St. Matthew Passion* (4b), where

> the word 'Aufruhr' (uproar) is literally evoked in a way all eight voices sing semiquaver patterns together (b. 13) . . . The fact that the high priests and elders are insisting that the killing of Jesus should not coincide with the Passover feast—since this would cause an uproar—makes the *actual* sound of an uproar all the more potent.

Ex. 2.2. *St. Matthew Passion*, 27a (coro I) and 27b (coro I, II), derivative speech acts.

The music, continues Butt, "does something above and beyond what the words alone would have done."[71] Indeed it does, for it is that coincidence that took place in the holiday, which created the uproar in all senses of the word, and made the Jews, theologically speaking, into a "community of uproar."

Musically, this movement traverses an immense virtual distance without moving at all. It descends the circle of fifths and then ascends again; never arriving at a destination, these progressions build momentum and create an image of gravitation towards a fathomless abyss. Though *Mond und Licht* have been sought in sympathy, and *Blitze, Donner und Wolken* have been summoned in revenge, they haven't altered Jesus' predicament. What should these virtual souls do, where should they go now?

In the last number of part 1, again all forces are enlisted to close in on that ring within which Jesus seems to be, initiating an act of atonement and redemption, however transcendental. The perspective is enlarged; larger parts of Jesus' story and the history of every man since Jesus—the Man whose sins are great—are now being enlisted: "O Mensch," they cry, "bewein' dein' Sünde groß." The forces geared for this purpose include organs, one real and another virtual, encompassing an entire universe of Baroque sound.[72] (It is in this case a sonic universe without trumpets; there is no place for them in this sympathetic atmosphere of death and loss.) The soprano in ripieno from the first chorus, who sang from the upper gallery (and a different Dasein plane) in the opening chorus ("O Lamm Gottes"), now joins forces with the other soprano group and the two choirs merge into one.

It is again in the ritornello that one should seek the dialogical momentum. Its fundamental motif echoes the preceding aria and more (see music example ex. app. 1, in appendix). By intersecting the melody at the very beginning by dramatically opposing forces (moving in contrary directions and in contrasting registers and timbres), built-in tension is created and furthered by hinting at the parallel minor in the second section of the theme. This engenders the leap in the third section, which enhances the tension that has been aroused. A sequential vicious circle is avoided by imposing in m. 5 a pedal point above which a turbulent, implacable passage hovers, falling again and again into the underlying pedal note (mm. 5–7). An effect of reverberation is thus introduced. The ritornello returns twice, in a typical way, in order to reestablish the tonic.

When the chorale enters, the lower voices, as mentioned above, produce a condensed, simultaneous (though subdued) echo. This coextends with the first part of the ritornello; and when the ripieno closes the phrase and the pedal part is heard, the lower voices burst forth in minor, unleashing their subdued echo, almost literally crying (to paraphase): "Bewein. Bewein für euch, bewein für ihn"—Cry for your lack of sympathy in the past, and as an expression of the sympathy which is aroused in you now (mm. 20–23). In the remainder of the chorale, the same locus subsequently appears five times. Two are heard without the chorus and three hold other pivotal sympathetic words: *Krankheit* ("Und legt' dabei all' Krankheit ab,"—and healed all illness), *geopfert* ("bis sich die Zeit herdrange, daß er für uns geopfert würd"—until the time press forward that he for us be sacrificed), and "wohl an dem Kreuze lange"—and on the cross (our sins He was to bear).[73] The degree of sympathizing with Jesus reaches an apex.[74]

As the *Passion* unfolds, it becomes gradually filled with emotional surges projected from various planes and positions, rendering a kind of negative image (in the photographic sense) of Jesus—who becomes, from the moment of betrayal, an absent subject. The subsequent combinatorial numbers enhance this tendency. By listening to their own voices and those of others vis-à-vis the elusive, suffering subject—the butt of their indifference, denial, or cruelty—the *Passion's* personae realize more than their own and others' emotions: they create an emotional bridge, otherwise barred, to the sufferer. In his own oratorios, though they never literally use the same effects, and while remaining in a more homogenized chronotope, Mendelssohn, nevertheless, employs complex continuities and interrelated polarities for construing his imaginary community of believers.

Bringing this understanding of the work to bear on the rise of sympathy as a new, emancipatory belief, one can begin to understand the great attraction the work could have had for Jews since the generation of Felix's grandparents, his parents, through to Felix and Fanny, A. B. Marx,[75] Giacomo Meyerbeer, and others.[76] This, however, was not confined to composers; professional musicians and other cultural celebrities were drawn to this "most perfect creation of German art," as Ludwig Rellstab defined it.[77] In their enthrallment with its rich spiritual and emotional import, subsequent generations of Jews, especially in Germany (Liberal, Orthodox, and ultra-Orthodox alike), were not deterred by the intensely Christian character of the work. For, it is this type of work that seems, once and for all, to dissolve the homogenized, exclusive harmonious universes that had barred their doors before the Jews unless they accepted its hegemonic patterns. The metadialogical, and only partially mimetic form of presentation of the opus seemed to bypass the idolatry predicament while fostering emotional identification, mobilization, and participation.

Self-exposure to the work's powers could thus resolve into a spiral dynamics. Along Jesus' Via Dolorosa, various protagonists stand, each devising his or her distance from the Lord and projecting his or her own compassionate expression of his agony. New participants can join the spiral and fathom their position vis-à-vis the protagonists; Jews likewise could accommodate themselves into its circuit, especially since the emotional parts—the arioso and arias—transcend the particular historical and theological narrative, achieving a more universal spiritual expression.

It is true that in order to produce the work in 1829, Mendelssohn had to become a Christian, inasmuch as Mahler, though in a different way, had to convert for his position as director of the Vienna Philharmonic sixty-eight years later. Yet Mendelssohn considered himself as thoroughly Christian (Lutheran) and might not have regarded his Jewish identity, which burst forth precisely at that "Christian" hour of rearing towards the performance, as contradictory to his new loyalty. There certainly was a dynamic aspect to his complex sense of identity that seems to amplify in the course of his brief life, especially following the death of his father, and which surfaced, among other ways, in his reissue of his grandfather's *Gesammelte Schriften* in the early 1840s.[78]

In the debate held in the late nineties in the pages of *Musical Quarterly*, launched by Sposato's criticism of Eric Werner's 1963 Mendelssohn biography, Sposato cast doubt on some of the "Jewish elements" attributed to the composer by the renowned researcher of Jewish music. Sposato's revisiting of Mendelssohn's letters and other documents led him to conclude that, though interested "in the ultimate political fate of the Jews, Mendelssohn tried to distance himself from this heritage as much as possible."[79] Despite some important qualifications and reappraisals of major events in the life of the composer (including a reconsideration of some of Mendelssohn's statements as well as of aspects of his works—especially the oratorical ones) made by Sposato, the issue of the composer's identity emerges as far more complex than Sposato would admit.[80] One cannot but agree with Leon Botstein who not only endorses Werner's contextualization of Mendelssohn's biography (vis-à-vis the still prevalent remainders of a long anti-Semitic history, including Nazi distortions of the composer's biography and the deprecation of his work), but wisely rebuts some of Sposato's claims. Above all, Botstein argues that Mendelssohn's personal construing of Protestant Christianity via his religious opuses (including Psalm 113, the *Lobgesang*, *Paulus*, and *Elias*) "was designated to fit a crucial criterion—that it be the modern moral equivalent and logical historical outcome of Judaism."[81]

One of the implications of this debate is, as formulated by Michael P. Steinberg, that Jews continued to hold on to their special cultural-religious sensibilities even beyond baptism.[82] Thus the inclusive, spiral oratorical presentation could especially appeal to the sensibilities of Jews, those with slight connections to their heritage, as well as those who opted to abide by it. The latter could find in the *Passion*'s concatenation of speech acts, welding a variety of textual and temporal layers, an echo to the familiar Seder, likewise suffused with a variety of "oratorical moments" which transcend particular historical specificities (see chapter 1).

Paradoxical as it may appear, the most cherished, exclusive, and anti-Jewish of Christian rites, could become in its "Bachian" attire a gravitational center of ecumenical, inclusive dialogue. Oscillating between premodernity and modernity, as John Butt argues, and between old susceptibilities and new possibilities, the work could encourage profound reconsideration of Christian-Jewish relations within an underdetermined yet historically laden vocal experience. The embodiment of Jesus as both martyr and savior, object and subject of compassion, engenders the Jew as a complex aesthetic category: ur-insider as well as radical outsider, a center of attraction, a self-staging agency whose martyrological destiny renders an ever-growing number of suffering compassionate believers into a congregation constantly redeemed through an emotional participation enacted both individually and communally.[83]

Jews, of course, were not alone in their attraction to the work, and the work itself was not the only oratorio to appeal to them. There were others who were drawn to it, and, as we shall see, at a certain moment it relinquished its inclusiveness, for Jews as well as for other Others. By and large, however, the general inclination toward the oratorio and the modalities it generated, as they became embodied in different musical and literary genres, opened up a continuous musical dialogue between Jews and Christians throughout the nineteenth century and beyond, as we shall see in the following chapters.

ST. JOHANNES PASSION IN THE SHADOW

Four years after the premiere of this production of *St. Matthew Passion*, in the wake of the increasing popularity of Bach's oeuvre, the Singakademie chose to perform its older sister work, the *St. John Passion* (BWV 245).[84] The conductor this time was the newly appointed C. E. Rungenhagen (1778–1851). Mendelssohn, whose intimate acquaintance with the work eventually yielded the "Es ist genug" aria of *Elias* (modeled after the central aria "Es ist vollbracht" from the *St. John Passion*),[85] had just severed his ties with the academy following his defeat at the elections.[86] For fifty years, Bach's interpretation of the Passion according to John had never been publicly performed in Berlin. In the following, I propose a short theological-phenomenological assessment of the *St. John Passion* in order to further illuminate the appeal of the *St. Matthew Passion* both for that time and later.[87]

The *St. John Passion* is usually considered the more anti-Semitic of the two works. The story here centers on Jesus' incarceration and judgment and on the Jews who, stubbornly and ferociously, do not accept Jesus as King and Lord, demanding his death by crucifixion. (In *St. Matthew* Christ is portrayed as a guiltless "suffering servant" and his death is brought about by collective guilt—Jews', Romans', and, to a certain extent, also his disciples', as attested by the concluding chorale of part I).[88] The more intensively dramatic occurrences in the *St. John Passion*—especially Pilate's addresses to the Jews throughout the trial—and the far fewer meditative chorales and individual sections, also contribute to its general harsher effect. The sense of alienation that the work might have triggered in Mendelssohn's milieu calls for a few more considerations.

In comparison with the dialogical, resonating structure of *St. Matthew*, *St. John* is basically a monolithic and, in many sections, thematically repetitive work. It attempts to say everything and at once, containing in almost each and every utterance an overt statement and its opposing hidden theological meaning. Though as a musical composition it is also temporally structured along its tonal and dramatic *Herzstück* (core), it is primarily the macrocosm that strives to enhance that which is already defined in the microcosmic elements. The final form is, thus, more static than dynamic. A big cross is erected throughout the various tonal sections of the work, creating a huge chiastic structure mainly felt through the turba choruses.[89] Chorus and orchestra are one, and seldom divide themselves into echoing *cori spezzati* structures. Rather, they alternate between powerful homophonic statements (as in the first "Herr, unser Herrscher" chorus) and polyphonic turba sections. Individual, abstract voices only seldom interact with others—whether the congregation's or individual's. No sallies from fictional, Dasein planes are enacted and there is almost no traversing of them.[90]

All seems to happen at one and the same time, one and the same place, or in all times and all places concomitantly—*Zu aller Zeit, in allen Ländern.* It is as if all has always been there, predetermined: the Lord's crucifixion, his kingship, our salvation—all collapsing into the tremor-provoking opening "Herr unser Herrscher, dessen Ruhm in allen Landen herrlich ist," a psalmist declaration of "old" Israel's God's kingship (O Lord, our Lord, how majestic is your name in all the earth! [Psalm 8:1]). Recited by Jews in their Days of Awe as a verse closing the Kᵉdushah (sanctification),[91] this verse is here reinterpreted through a new Christological eighteenth-century ending: "Zeig uns durch deine Passion daß du, der wahre Gottessohn, zu aller Zeit, auch in der größten Niedrigkeit, verherrlicht worden bist." (Show us through your Passion that you, the true Son of God, at all times, even in the greatest abasement, have been glorified).

This double verse attests to the congruence of the God of the Old Testament with that of the God of the Passion—"the Word incarnates in the man, Jesus of Nazareth, Son of God." The basic foundation of Lutheran Christology, it originates in St. John, the only Gospel that declares "He who has seen me has seen the Father" and for which the Son is the Father, the Martyr is the Redeemer. It is there that the revelation is ever present; in the humiliation of the Lord, in the abasement of his *Herrlichkeit*. The power of faith, according to Luther, lies in its ability to see the truth through such appearances; more particularly, through the negation of his affirmation: the Yes hidden (Gospel) behind the No of the Law, as Chafe put it.[92]

This basic oxymoronic structure finds several musical allegorizations in the course of the work. Thus behind the Jews' apparent rejection of Christ there lies a hidden recognition of his true nature; as Chafe showed, the relation between text and music in the series of turba choirs engaging identity—"Jesum, Jesum, Jesum von Nazareth" (2b [3]; 2d [5])—points clearly to such recognition. Such hidden recognition is also manifest in the use of *ich bin es* (I am that person) by Jesus and, in a negative way, by the denying Peter (as Marissen indicates) and surfaces also in other strategic moments in the work.[93]

St. Augustine taught the Christian world that Jews, in their obstinate, sacrificial presence, bear witness to their own punishment and desolation, while at the same time continuing to serve as custodians and librarians of the biblical books, like a "blind man in the mirror," whose face can be seen by others but not by himself.[94] This basic theological doxa, which since the early Middle Ages has found its expression in the famous opposition between the faithful *ecclesia* and the perfidious *synagoga*, here too renders the Jews in their paradoxical predicament as Jesus' deniers as well as the earthly testament of his *größte Niedrigkeit* (utmost abasement, lowliness).[95]

Though perhaps driven by theological reasoning alone, Bach construed along its lines a powerful musical embodiment—that of the *St. John Passion*, even if, as Marissen argues, he wished to mitigate the burden of Jewish responsibility,[96] in accordance with new theological trends in eighteenth-century Leipzig.[97] And yet, as a recipe for a successful integration and assimilation of Jews in a general, liberal society, such a structure would fail to offer a viable strategy. Moreover, the Lutheran teaching it implies, that "Christian belief is a gracious undeserved gift from God, and that there is no justification before God by human good works"[98] is a counterproductive premise for those who attempted to find favor—social, cultural, political—through what they deemed their "good work." Furthermore, in contradistinction to the *St. Matthew Passion*, redemption in the *St. John Passion* resides in the very act of crucifixion. The long way to resurrection, designated in the later *Passion* work, is annulled here, for victory is secured at the cross. For Franz Rosenzweig in his *Star of Redemption*, the first long-term (even eternal) road to future salvation would be identified as a Jewish conception, whereas the second—living already in a redeemed reality—as a Christian one.[99] I believe this controversial theological argument has deep phenomenological roots that theologically unsophisticated Jews could identify with, even if not consciously or overtly.

It should not surprise us, however, that later, once the cult of Bach became entrenched and its overall aesthetics permeated into a nondogmatic "religion of music," Jews could more easily bypass the *St. John Passion*'s blatant theology and endorse its more general, spiritual message. The arias, with their abstract, emotional appeal, could thus render the text into an allegory of a more general, universal, and thus inclusive message. They could even directly touch a Jewish nerve, as, for example, the heartbreaking "Zerfließe mein Herz" (Dissolve my heart) could evoke the verses from Jeremiah's book of Lamentations read on Tish'a' be'Av and its accompanying affect.[100]

This brings us again to present-day approaches to the Passion music: in an attempt to mitigate the questionable import of the *St. John Passion*, a "musical-theological" experiment was performed by Cantor Hans-Jörg Hahn in collaboration with HaAtelier group (directed by Almuth Sh. Bruckstein and myself). On Good Friday of 2005 in Stuttgart, in a gesture prompted by the desire to broaden and contemporize the oratorical appeal of the *St. John Passion*, the aria texts were successfully superseded by Jewish, Muslim, and nonreligious equivalents, communicating kindred spiritual-emotional messages.[101] The new texts were recited and then visually projected while the music was played instrumentally. The congregation at that *Karfreitag* (Good Friday) performance, though deprived of its familiar *St. John*, reacted enthusiastically to the new rendition. But this was not an exercise that liberal Jews and non-Jews could have conceived of in the first half of the nineteenth century.

JEWS ON STAGE (LESSING'S JEWISH PLAYS)

THE JEWS: PREJUDICES VOCALIZED

—Ich bin ein Jude.
—Ein Jude? Grausamer Zufall!
—Ein Jude?
—Ein Jude?

[—I am a Jew / —A Jew! Oh cruel mischance! /
—A Jew? / —A Jew?][102]
(Gotthold Ephraim Lessing, *Die Juden*, xxii.4–7)

No real music accompanies these utterances in the denouement of the short, ingenious *Lustspiel*, or comedy, *Die Juden*, written by the precocious, twenty-year-old playwright Gotthold Ephraim Lessing. As a brief echoic scene, however, the music of its speech almost transfigures into real music; the recognition moment in *The Marriage of Figaro*'s sextet comes to mind as a sonoric frame for its performance. Unlike the famous sextet, however, no relaxing cadential statement assures us of a satisfactory dramatic or familial resolution.[103] On the contrary; the young lady in love with "him," the Jew who has just revealed himself as such, understands only the music, not the meaning of this revelation, exclaiming thus in bewilderment, if not horror:[104]

> Ei, was tut das?
> [Oh, what is the meaning of that?]

Only towards the end of the scene, about forty lines later, is there an answer. The Jew's servant, the Christian Christopher, rhymes a delayed cadence to the vocalized "Jude" sequence, which ends, however, in a "false" cadence:

> Es gibt doch wohl auch Juden,
> die keine Juden sind.
>
> [There are Jews, after all, who are not Jews.]

A drama of identities, it brings all to bear on the title, *Die Juden*, which both alienates and invites, labels and hides, opening up the complex structure of meanings of the work. Who are the Jews? And who, or rather what, is Jewish? That is the main question this *Lustspiel* puts forward, suggesting that wrongly categorized *Vorurteil* (prejudice)[105] — whether moral or aesthetic — leads to mistaken identifications and misleading expectations. For, as it turns out, those who are expected to be Jews — the "band" of criminals — are revealed as Christians, whereas the enigmatic nobleman — *ein Reisender*, a traveler — turns out to be a Jew.

This chiastic bifurcation is crucial. In a way, it resonates with the very predicament that characterizes the *St. John Passion*, whose renewed, second performance was scheduled — still in Bach's lifetime — the same year *Die Juden* was written (1749)[106] and in the same city, Leipzig, where Jews were permitted entry only for its famous fair. Dressed in contemporary attire,[107] we encounter here a generous, sacrificial hero of Jewish origin, modeled both on Jesus and the Wandering Jew, and we also meet scandalous fake "Jews," who do not hesitate to crucify noble people. Not unlike Jesus, the real Jew, though revered, remains alien, outside the general social sphere of home and wedlock, whereas the "Jews," though exposed as delinquent Christians, are not expelled from it.

In the play, they also evoke associations with the two robbers who were crucified on Jesus' left and right (according to St. Matthew), themselves expecting—not crucifixion—but that which comes closest to it: the gallows.[108] As part of the work's chiastic structure, it is the Christian villain (the one initially dressed as a Jew), who expresses the most intolerant views against the Jews. Ironically, the harshest feelings that the *St. John Passion's* type of Jews could arouse in the heart of good Christians is voiced in the Jew's ear by this "Jew." Indeed, contemporary typical anti-Jewish preaching is clearly heard here:[109]

> Darum ist es auch ein Volk, das der liebe Gott verflucht hat. Ich dürfte nicht König sein: ich ließ' keinen, keinen Einzigen am Leben. Ach! Gott behüte alle rechtschaffne Christen vor diesen Leuten! Wenn sie der liebe Gott nicht selber hasste, weswegen wären denn nur vor kurzem, bei dem Unglücke in Breslau, ihrer bald noch einmal so viel als Christen geblieben? Unser Herr Pfarrer erinnerte das sehr weislich, in der letzten Predigt. Es ist, als wenn sie zugehört hätten, dass sie sich gleich deswegen an unserm guten Herrn haben rächen wollen. Ach! Mein lieber Herr, wenn Sie wollen Glück und Segen in der Welt haben, so hüten Sie sich vor den Juden, ärger, als vor der Pest.[110]

> [That's why they're a people cursed by God. Luckily I'm not king, or I wouldn't leave a single one, not one, alive. Ah! May God protect all righteous Christians from people of their sort! If God himself didn't hate them, how come only a short while ago, in the Breslau disaster, almost twice as many Jews as Christians perished? Our local pastor very wisely pointed that out in his last sermon. It is as if they had been listening and at once decided to take their revenge on our good master. Ah, my dear sir, if you seek grace and good fortune in this world, protect yourself against the Jews more than against the plague!]

A rich drama of identities enables the semiotic embodiment of this duality, reverberating long after the play ends. It happens again "on the cross" and at the crossroad. Two "Jewish" criminals attack a baron; they apparently wish to kill him and then rob him, with the assistance of his coachman. He is saved by a passing traveler: The Traveler. The trajectories of these three agents—Baron, robbers, Traveler—could stand for three axes in a triangle: one (the Baron) is unwittingly moving towards the other, awaiting him (the robbers); the third (Traveler) fortuitously arrives at the point of concurrence. The saved Baron goes home, wondering about the identity of the miraculous rescuer, whom he has invited to his abode. The Jew now stands in front of the "Jew," who, in the meantime has got rid of his "Jewish" appearance and launches his diatribe against the Jews (quoted above). This "Jew," the bailiff of the Baron's estate, a traitorous Judas allegorically named Martin Krumm (crooked), now substitutes a major sin with a small crime: striving to pickpocket the Traveler's watch, he ends up stealing his snuffbox.

More triangles are then created: the treacherous bailiff, Krumm, now lusts after Lisette, the maidservant, who will cunningly obtain from him the snuff-box—a Jewish property, the Jew's property, of which she is unaware. At the same time, the Baron, who seeks to unmask the Traveler's identity, entrusts Lisette with this sensitive inquiry. Lisette, who thus connects two, even three "passion triangles"—the erotic passion of Krumm and Christian (the Jew's ser-vant) and the inquisitive passion of the grateful Baron[111]—uses the object of exchange, the snuffbox, to spy. She chooses for this purpose an ersatz subject—Christoph—employing two seductive objects, herself and the box. As it turns out, Christoph is unaware of the box's original owner as well as oblivious of the latter's identity.

The Jew is thus the common vertex of two or three triangles of violence and desire. The various discoveries should all focus on him—the center of a cross. As the box returns to the owner's vicinity, semiotically loaded with the com-municative acts it gradually releases, it enables him to retrace identity and lust. In the course of his search, the Jew will inspect the "Jew," who will involun-tarily drop his fake "Jewish" beard. With the Baron's aid, the various triangles of communication and transaction will come to light. This anagnorisis, how-ever, forgoes any straightforward disclosure of the two main characters'—the Baron's and the Traveler's desires or riddles. Another, more "elevated" triangle hovers above them, consisting of the young lady, the Baron's daughter, who, encouraged by her father, orients her erotic passion toward the Traveler. Like the Shulamite in the Song of Songs, she invites him to her garden; like the biblical character, she painfully learns that the Wandering Jew was not meant for her. Senta of the *Fliegende Hollander* and Elsa of *Lohengrin* will be similarly conceived (and deceived).

The search for the lover's identity, the attempt to establish him as property, will lead to the Wanderer's vanishing. Before this happens, when the Baron is still attempting to yoke his savior with his property (if not with his daughter), the Jew typically replies:

> Auch dieses Anerbieten ist bei mir umsonst, da mir der Gott meiner Väter mehr gegeben hat, als ich brauche. Zu aller Vergeltung bitte ich nichts, als dass Sie künftig von meinem Volke etwas gelinder und weniger allgemein urteilen.
>
> [That offer, too, I fear, is pointless in my case. The God of my fathers has given me more than enough for my needs. In full recompense, if you will, I

ask only that, in the future, you should be milder and less sweeping in your judgment of my race.]

The Jew, an Abraham (in his remark that "The God of my fathers has given me more than enough for my needs" he echoes Genesis 24:1 "And the Lord had blessed Abraham in all things"), asks the Baron, an Abimelech (though he ironically paraphrases Abimelech's words to Abraham), not to deal falsely with him, his people, or descendants,[112] and he proceeds:

> Ich habe mich nicht vor Ihnen verborgen, weil ich mich meiner Religion schäme.
> Nein! Ich sah, aber dass Sie Neigung zu mir, und Abneigung gegen meine Nation hatten.

> [The reason I concealed my identity from you was not that I am ashamed of my religion. No! It was because I perceive that, while well-disposed towards me, you were averse to my nation.]

This is indeed the quandary, and the words themselves—*Neigung* and *Abneigung*—will continue to resonate in German culture; Richard Wagner will choose to falsify this tract a hundred and one years later, coining a general, sophisticated term for the hatred of Jews, already mentioned above: *volkstümliche Abneigung*. As far as he is concerned, this includes both the many and the select few, the people and their poets and prophets; the latter, in fact, were the main object of his disdain and hostility.[113]

This is the oratorical moment of the play: vocally transcending its immediate, contemporary present, it embraces an entire history, people, and beliefs. The voice of the Traveler resounds through all the successive presents in which Jews and Gentiles, Jews and Muslims, make a covenant, whether overt or covert. The strong allegorical bent of the play thus achieves its apex; with it, the figures—nameless, abstract titles—radiate beyond their Dasein moment. It is here, therefore, that realism is permeated by ideology, an ideology that is subversive in its historical context.[114] The treasure, a Jewish treasure, remains in Christian hands in this version of the Jewish Merchant play; so the Jew chooses to bequeath it, voluntarily and magnanimously. Unlike Shylock and later, Nathan, the issue here is, indeed, generosity and friendship rather than compassion and grace, prefiguring Moses Mendelssohn's ideas quoted above, and the eventual friendship between the two great Enlighteners:

> Und die Freundschaft eines Menchen, es sei wer es wolle, ist mir allezeit unschätzbar gewesen.

[For my part, I have always considered the friendship of a fellow human, whoever he may be, precious beyond measure.][115]

Before leaving, the two great men will rhyme again; chiastic echoes will once more find voice on stage and beyond, becoming the piece's most famous lines:

Der Baron: O wie achtungswürding wären die Juden, wenn sie alle Ihnen glichen!
Reisender: Und wie liebenswürdig die Christen, wenn sie all Ihre Eigenschaften besäßen!

[Baron: How worthy of respect Jews would be, if only they were all like you!
Traveler: And how lovable Christians would be if only they all possessed your qualities!][116]

THE AESTHETIC THEOLOGY OF *NATHAN THE WISE*

Nathan! Nathan!
Ihr seid ein Christ!—Bei Gott, Ihr seid ein Christ!
Ein besser Christ war nie!

[O Nathan!
You're a Christian! As God lives, a Christian!
There never was a better Christian!]
—(*Nathan the Wise* IV.vii.3066–3086)[117]

Articulated through the magic of blank verse, *Nathan der Weise* (1779) creates a self-resonating world through a system of self-allusions; in some crucial lines, it also echoes lines from Lessing's juvenile, more prosaic play, *Die Juden*.[118] Well-made blank verse calls attention, here, as elsewhere, to the sonoric, musical aspects of the text, which in more than one sense correlates with the Shakespearean tradition so revered by Lessing. Voices and vocalities are not only heard, rhyming and reverberating; they are also thematized throughout the play. Especially, though not exclusively, they touch on father-daughter relations. The story of Recha's (Nathan's daughter) rescue from fire, reported to Nathan in the play's first scene by Daja, Recha's devout Christian companion, contains the following poignant lines:

Diesen Morgen lag
Sie lange mit verschlossnem Aug' und war
Wie tot. Schnell fuhr sie auf und rief: "Horch! Horch!
Da kommen die Kamele meines Vaters!
Horch! Seine sanfte Stimme selbst."

> [Long she lay in bed
> This morning, eyes shut, motionless—as though
> She'd died. Then suddenly she starts and cries: "Hark!
> I hear my father's camels coming;
> Hark! the gentle music of his voice!"] (I.i.70–74)

And when Recha later appears on stage she addresses her father thus:

> So seid Ihr es doch ganz und gar, mein Vater?
> Ich glaubt, Ihr hättet Eure Stimme nur
> vorausgeschickt.
>
> [So, Father, you've returned. Are you safe and sound?
> I thought perhaps you'd only sent your voice
> Ahead of you.] (I.ii.169–171)

The voice that precedes the body, twice imagined soft and comforting, the second time hypostatized,[119] is the voice through which this redeeming figure probably first revealed himself to her, an adopted baby. A father, he is a great believer in vocalities, in the power of the ear over that of the eye, of hearing over sight, as his disciple and daughter Recha later tells Sittah (Saladin's sister and her eventually discovered aunt), explaining "why her wisdom is not from books derived":

> Mein Vater liebt
> Die kalte Buchgelehrsamkeit, die sich
> Mit toten Zeichen ins Gehirn nur drückt,
> Zu wenig.
>
> [Father sets
> Little store by cold book-learning which,
> He says, imprints itself upon the brain
> Through lifeless symbols.] (V.vi.3533–3536)

Hers is an oral, living wisdom, she later explains, hence the innocence and piety attributed to it. A Jewish quality? Not according to the medieval theologians we have encountered in the previous chapter, rather an ecumenical one: throughout the play, voices stand for the natural and the primordial, for human utterance previous to particularistic meanings, sectarian contents and ideas. This vocal quality and the way it connects Recha with natural compassion call to mind Rousseau's beliefs; Lessing was familiar with his French contemporary's writings on the subject, perhaps through Mendelssohn's translation. "But reason gradually gained the upper hand. She spoke with a gentle voice," reports

Nathan to the Lay Brother, recalling his reaction to the massacre of his family by the crusaders.[120] Indeed, Nathan's compassion is encompassing, natural and rational; typical of an enlightened person. It is so innate in him that it could vanquish emotions of vengeance as they arise. His Hebrew name bespeaks this inborn quality: he who has given; already, before it all starts. He who gave his life for the Christian girl, unconditionally, thereby overcoming his own horrible affliction brought about by the vicious, dogmatic Crusades.

The motif and motive of compassion connect *Nathan* to two Shakespearian father-daughter plays: *The Merchant of Venice* and *The Tempest*. Immensely affluent and remaining so even after lending his treasures, Nathan is, in contradistinction to Shylock, beyond usury and profits. His generosity surpasses material possessions extending to his own beloved daughter, whom he never chained to his own, sectarian religious beliefs. In this too he stands in diametric opposition to Shylock. This again goes into the question of essentials; Nathan lives by his faith, but he keeps it only to himself, refraining from discussing its contents.

Friendship, loyalty, and liberty, according to Hannah Arendt's interpretation of Nathan's choices, transcend claims of particular truths. Property, progeny, tradition, all seem *verzichtbar*, dispensable; universalistic moral values are above them. Are they indeed?[121] Where are particular sentiments and attachments, memories and commitments located and preserved, not to speak of more essential beliefs and truths? Regarding relations between daughter and father—Recha and Nathan—is there a possible *Eshes ḥayyil* they entertain or any other shared cultural-religious-familial form, of the kind we find represented in Trevor Nunn's production of *The Merchant of Venice?*[122] Shylock too remains with nothing, but under coercion; humiliated, he is excommunicated from all societies—both Christian and Jewish.[123] In this respect Nathan is closer to Prospero, also an elderly father who chose to renounce his material and spiritual possessions: his kingdom, his daughter (though only through marriage), his magic, and even his status as injured party. Like Nathan, Prospero too endorses isolation in the education of his daughter, and likewise trains her in compassion.[124] But Prospero is Christian whereas Nathan is not. Yet Prospero needs an Ariel—a magic spirit—to instruct him in compassion, whereas Nathan—a Job (like Job, Nathan sat in ashes for three days and nights), an Abraham (arguing with God), and victim of cruel Christian crusaders—has only to listen, as we have seen, to his inner *rational* voice, as he tells the Lay Brother the old story in which the latter plays an important role (giving Nathan the baby):

Als
Ihr kamt, hatt ich drei Tag' und Nächt' in Asch'

Und Staub vor Gott gelegen, und geweint.—
Geweint? Beiher mit Gott auch wohl gerechtet,
Gezürnt, getobt, mich und die Welt verwünscht;
Der Christenheit den unversöhnlichsten
Hass zugeschworen

[When you arrived, I'd lain three days and nights
Alone, in dust and ashes, weeping before God—
Arguing with God . . . I raged and ranted,
Cursing myself and the world,
Vowing irreconcilable hatred for Christendom.] (IV.vii.3045–3051)

And then:

Doch nun kam die Vernunft allmälig wieder.
Sie sprach mit sanfter Stimm': "Und doch ist Gott!
Doch war auch Gottes Ratschluss das! Wohlan!
Komm! übe, was du längst begriffen hast;

. . .

Steh auf!"—Ich stand! Und rief zu Gott: ich will!
Willst du nur, daß ich will!—

. . .

          Was Ihr
Mir damals sagtet; was ich Euch: hab ich
Vergessen. So viel weiß ich nur; ich nahm
Das Kind, trug's auf mein Lager, küsst es, warf
Mich auf die Knie' und schluchzte: Gott! auf Sieben
Doch nun schon Eines wieder!

[But reason gradually gained the upper hand.
Its gentle voice proclaimed 'Yet God exists!'
That, too, was his decree. So brace yourself!
Come, practice what you've long well understood—

. . .

'Stand up!' I stood and cried to God, 'I will
If it be Your will I should!'

. . .

          What you (the lay brother)
Then said to me and I to you, I have forgot.
I only know I put the child to bed
And kissed it. Then I knelt and sobbed, 'Oh, God,
For seven lost, here's one returned.'] (IV.vii.3052–3066)[125]

In his natural compassion and forgiving nature, Nathan, as the lay brother says in the epigraph above, is more Christian than the supposed compassionate Christians. But is he indeed? Or perhaps he inversely paraphrases the famous quarrel that the Jewish mother of seven sacrificed sons had with God, in which, according to the Midrash, she professed herself better than Abraham, whose sacrificial act was miraculously forestalled?[126] Or maybe he deems himself thus "beyond Jews and Christians"?

What is a Christian and who is a Jew? The play hinges on these questions and much ink has been spilt over it. The question of essentials brings us—how else?—to the ring parable. The parable seems to have been devised by Nathan for such an occasion, in which he will be involved in a religious debate concerning the superior monotheistic religion, not unlike the magic play Prospero had fashioned for a fortuitous occasion, in which his brother and ship's company would come close to his island.[127] Nathan again lives up to his name: Nathan the prophet of 2 Samuel, who speaks the voice of reason and morality, through parable, to King David. I will not engage here in the genealogy of the ring parable;[128] its well-known affinity with the caskets trial of Portia is here pursued only to the extent that it can be related to a content-free aesthetic theology. True, the trial of Portia's suitors emphasizes the deception of the ornamental and the gilded rather than the open-ended sacred history of religions stressed by the ring parable.[129] Still, the question of true essence emerges there as well. True essence? Portia herself is skeptical as far as art and particularly music are concerned. Before Bassanio makes his fateful choice, she voices her nonessentialist aesthetics (consonant with her words in act 5, quoted in chapter 1, and with the ideas professed by Descartes not many years later[130]):

> Let music sound while he doth make his choice;
> Then, if he lose, he makes a swan-like end,
> Fading in music: that the comparison
> May stand more proper, my eye shall be the stream
> And watery death-bed for him. He may win;
> And what is music then? Then music is
> Even as the flourish when true subjects bow
> To a new-crowned monarch: such it is
> As are those dulcet sounds in break of day
> That creep into the dreaming bridegroom's ear,
> And summon him to marriage. (III.ii.46–56)

Music is devoid of a fixed signified. Its immense associative powers, proposes Portia, reflecting a contemporary end-of-the-sixteenth-century aesthetics, render it pliable to the expression of both plight and pleasure, regardless of its inherent content. And yet once tinged by that with which it was affiliated, then, as Portia understands, it is difficult to detach this associated gist.[131] Are religions susceptible to a similar semantic shift, at least as far as their affective import is concerned? The ring parable points to a basic emptiness and parity at the core of the monotheistic religions which, however, are destined to become loaded over time with rich and apparently rather fixed contents.[132]

What does this comparison mean, however? Do stratified ineluctable differences between religions create an unfathomable rupture between their adherents like the accumulated differences of their respective music (if they insist on such differences)? Furthermore, does music, "being hollow in its core," as Paul de Man put it, lack indigenous emotive contents, in other words, are its affective powers merely conventional? Take first the religious element: Nathan also provides us here with a hint through a most powerful oratorical strategy, built up into his monologue (Lessing added this finale to the *Decameron* story), in which the Judge urges the three sons to regard the rings as a potential that radiates only through their internal, spiritual-moral aspirations and achievements:

> Komme dieser Kraft mit Sanftmut,
> Mit herzlicher Verträglichkeit, mit Wohltun,
> Mit innigster Ergebenheit in Gott,
> Zu Hülf! Und wenn sich dann der Steine Kräfte
> Bei euern Kindes-Kindeskindern äußern:
> So lad ich über tausend tausend Jahre,
> Sie wiederum vor diesen Stuhl. Da wird
> Ein weisrer Mann auf diesem Stuhle sitzen,
> Als ich; und sprechen.
>
> [(The power of the ring grows) with gentleness,
> With heartfelt agreeableness, with charity
> And deep submission to the will of God!
> Then, should the magic opal's power one day
> Imbue your children's children's children,
> I invite them—thousands of years from now—
> To stand before this judgement seat, whereon
> Will sit and speak a wiser man than I.] (III.vii.2044–2053)

The interplay of states of present tense is rather complex here, with voices going back and forth through them, launched towards a far future and then back into a distant past. Here stands Nathan, who in his fictional plane is located in the twelfth century. The temporal present of his parable's lessons backtracks at least

a few centuries (when Islam was already well on its way). The Judge he summons imagines a far distant present into which he projects the sons' remote descendents. These entangled temporalities impinge, in turn, on the spectator's
present (that of Lessing's contemporaries), but then diverge into subsequent
presents of generations of spectators.[133] Projected as a rich simultaneous cluster
of temporal sounds, it encroaches on the actuality of a "present" spectator and
beyond. It is a cluster of moments, of voices rather than a chord, for it cannot
simply harmonize within itself. Each present is different; moreover, in each the
degree of similarity and divergence between the three brothers, the three rings/
religions and their related music (both real and metaphorical) is different, and a
contrapuntal consciousness should retain, juxtapose, measure, and judge them
all.[134] Subsequent audiences and readers of the play should have been affected
by this predicament.

Yet the voice of the Judge, or God, pierces through this complexity, reverberating throughout. Ominous, sublime, it is an ecumenical Divine Voice, an
Enlightenment version of the Voice that, according to the Midrash, carried
"from one end of the world to the other" at the time when the children of Israel
received the Torah, sharply differentiating Gentiles from Israelites:

> When the Torah was given to Israel its sound [voice] traveled from one end of
> the world to the other, and all of the idolatrous kings were seized with trem-
> bling in their *hekhalot* [palaces] and recited a song, for it says *while in his hek-
> hal all say "Glory!"* (Psalms 29:9). They all gathered together by the wicked
> Bilam (Balaam) and said to him, "What is that sound of a multitude that we
> hear? Perhaps a deluge has come to the world? *The Lord sat enthroned at
> the Flood?* (Psalms 29:10) He told them: *The Lord sits enthroned, king forever*
> (29:10)—The Holy One Blessed Be He has already sworn not to bring a flood
> to the world. They said to him: He will not bring a flood of water, but He may
> bring a flood of fire, as it says: *For with fire the Lord will contend!* (Isaiah 6:16)
> He told them: He has already sworn not to destroy all living things. And what
> is that noise of a multitude which we heard? He told them: He has a precious
> thing in His treasure-house that he kept stored away for 974 generations be-
> fore the world was created, and now he wants to bequeath it to his sons, for it
> says, *May the Lord grant strength to His people* (Psalms 29:11). Immediately,
> they all began saying: *May the Lord bless His people with peace* (29:11).[135]

The Voice conjured by the Midrash was heard by both Jews and Gentiles, but
was addressed to Jews alone by force of their commitment to a severe system of
laws, which the Gentile, according to this anti-Christological Midrash, could
only contemplate with awe. Whereas Luther juxtaposes the Law to the Gospel,

Freud, in his oratorical essay *Moses and Monotheism* (in accordance with this Midrash), will hail it as *Triebverzicht*—renunciation of the drives; the epitome of what a people can aspire to share as a group. The Midrash ties this further with the noise of multitude, *hamon*, not necessarily harmonious, which this exalted, momentous event must have brought about. Half way, Moses Mendelssohn, who, as evidenced by his *Jerusalem*, was acquainted with this famous Midrash or its like, would certainly agree with the vocal distinction it intones. Religions are not free floating, nor are the musics they adopt to express their underlying sentiments, Portia's lesson notwithstanding. Moreover, difference becomes further entrenched through human choice and trauma, affecting subsequent changes and exchanges in and between religions. (And if their music is flexible, or "hollow" enough, it might be able to follow suit.)

Even Lessing, his ecumenical approach set aside, has his clear religious priority, which also transpires here, despite his harsh criticism of institutional, contemporary Christianity.[136] This seemingly contrasting understanding of the sublime vocality—Lessing's (biased) ecumenisms on the one hand and that of the particular Midrash on the other—will return in subsequent chapters of this history, sometimes dialectically, sometimes dialogically. At the present stage, the voice of difference, of a Jew (Nathan) resisting the shedding of difference despite the liberal, skeptical epistemological framework he entertains—is "backgrounded"; giving vent, as his drama consummates, to voices of familial reunion and festivity in which the dominant religions found a quasi-harmonious concord, leaving the Jew behind.[137]

HANDEL'S ARCHETYPES: A HARMONIOUS SUBLIME

Handel bequeathed his own oratorical worlds to the centuries to come. They were populated by a rich gallery of biblical figures and types whose Old Testament character appealed to their original, relatively homogeneous British audience no less than to subsequent, more heterogeneous European listeners who entertained diverse beliefs and convictions. Though *Messiah* was the most popular of these works during the nineteenth century, *Samson* (HWV 57), *Judas Maccabeus* (or *Maccabaeus*, HWV 63), and *Israel in Egypt* (HWV 54) were held in high esteem, especially by the audiences that engage us here, and were regarded by composers as structural and thematic models.[138] Their overall impact issued from their general oratorical qualities no less than from their dramatic appeal, as evinced by the responsiveness to certain aesthetic qualities and sentimental values with which they were continuously associated. Similarly crucial was their ideological gravitation which, though underdetermined in terms of specific political commitments, has borne a correspondent impact on different and, at times, diametrically opposed groups. In any event, tracing the cultural-intellectual infrastructure of the Handelian oratorio at its inception (and not only through its later modes of reception) should not be regarded, in the context of this book, as a mere prolegomenon for its later continental reception. Its originally inscribed qualities transcended its immediate context, radiating into later British milieus—that of Lord Byron, Thomas Rowlandson, George Eliot, and other Britons who will step into our story later.[139]

The Anglican anti-Papist tendencies of the early eighteenth century (as related to both Royalists and "dissenters") endeared Hebrew biblical songs of devotion and thanksgiving to British audiences, casting those songs as prescriptive models of religious music, both in the church and outside it.[140] As early as 1710, Robert Tate, apostrophizing church music, summons with it an entourage of Hebrew, biblical musical symbols: "return coelestial charmer, resume thy Royal psalmist's harp and to the songs of Sion, join the song of the Lamb . . . for thus may we maintain a commerce between earth and heaven, and commence our heaven upon earth."[141] The song of Sion (Zion) and that of the Lamb are evoked here, conjuring up the old covenant between Heaven and Earth (expressed through the similarly sounding "commerce" and "commence") whose renewal is urged by the preacher. Calling to mind the big *Passion's* overtures of Bach, it echoes Miltonian motifs and other seventeenth-century musical clichés prevalent in English poetry.[142]

It is within such a devotional atmosphere, which laid so much emphasis on sublime poetry, on the Old Testament, and ancient Hebraic culture, that one should assess the meteoric success of the Handelian oratorio and the esteem of Handel as "a true heir of the priestly King David's lyric psalms."[143] Through his British librettists, this Germanic-British King David summoned a protective, benevolent Old Testament God—"the just ruler of mankind"—in sharp contradistinction to the hitherto prevalent continental Christian violent image of the deity.[144] The Israelites, led by this God in the imagined worlds projected through such textual scaffolding, are, correspondingly, "not a debased rabble but a nation conscious of a natural right to freedom, and endowed with all the sensibilities of the eighteenth-century man of feeling as well as with the heroic courage and epic potential of a noble past," as Ruth Smith puts it.[145] Cast in the libretti as more resourceful, united, and militarily just than their original textual models, Handel's Israelites became an ideal image for his contemporary Protestant British audience seeking an appropriate nationalist paradigm (lacking in the New Testament) that would buttress their colonialist ambitions.[146]

In line with eighteenth-century biblical commentaries and theological decrees, this interpretative bent was not unrelated to the actual state of the Jews in the British Isles and the increasingly conciliatory attitudes towards them. It is evident that in the heyday of this trend, Jews began to profit from this political "naturalization," and that the decline of this hermeneutic trend was connected with a countertendency to block this process.[147] By that time, however, the Handelian oratorios had become autonomous entities, independently impinging their dramatic-emotional contents on their "occasional" listeners.[148]

In one of the most moving moments of this Hebraist phase, which had issued already in the mid-seventeenth century, one finds a poignant apology by D'Blossiers Tovey addressed to the Jews. Reminiscent of Lessing's compassionate decree, it is more specific. Tovey recalls the famous 1135 martyrdom of Jews in York where, as he describes it through the prism of the Masada model, Jews were coerced into communal suicide by cruel crusaders and reacted in a way he utterly justifies, complaining:

> Now can any one that reads this, believe himself in a *Christian* Country? or conceive why a Sett of People worshiping the same God with our selves, shou'd have been *bought and sold like cattle*, for no other Reason, but because in some Parts of His Law, they differ'd from the *Christian* Exposition of it?[149]

This goes beyond the Leipzig theologians who purged the Jews of the ritual murder defamation, for it assumes a direct responsibility for the history of Jewish persecution. We will see how this conciliatory approach eventually permeated vocal fictional worlds authorized by British creators.

As for the Handelian vocal fictions, what did subsequent British and non-British listeners (who had no concern with moral justification for colonial wars) read into them? Which aspect of their original messages transcends their time, and what was newly ascribed to the works in the course of their subsequent reception? The answers to these questions are partially documented, granting us hints for a deeper analysis of the aesthetic categories and communal modes these works offered both to those engaged in "harmonizing" Jewish existence as well as to those acting against it.

On the face of it, the benevolent image of ancient Israel and their choosing God, tonally embodied in these oratorios, never failed to speak to actual Jewish audiences or their supporters.[150] This image bespeaks a resistance to anti-Semitic distinctions between ancient and modern Jews, the original chosen people before and after Christ. It issues from the very revival in these oratorios of the Hebrew Bible stories otherwise rarely presented on European stages, and coincides with their growing centrality in the wake of the Jewish *Haskala* (enlightenment; literally, *Bildung*, education) and later Zionism.[151]

The stories themselves (of Joseph, Moses, and Joshua; Deborah, Jephtha, and Samson; of Saul and Solomon, Belshazzar, Esther, and Judas Maccabeus) convey, in various ways and despite tragic moments, an "Israel triumphant," glorifying its valiant, chosen leaders.[152] Redolent of the Land of Milk and Honey, incorporating biblical poetic lines alongside their real and metaphorical fauna and flora, these tales substitute heroic deeds for immolation stories, fostering utopian notions that envisage a visionary future as well as reflect a glorious past.[153] Part of these stories concern major Jewish holidays otherwise celebrated and commemorated only in Jewish circles. Passover (in *Israel in Egypt* and *Joshua* and, indirectly, also in *Solomon*), Hanukkah (in *Judas Maccabeus*), and Purim (in *Esther*), are all considered festivals of redemption, and two holidays (Passover and Purim), as we have seen (and will consider further), are especially associated with the noise/harmony dialogue of Jews and Christians. All musicalize central biblical poems—familiar from prayer and from the congregational reading of the Bible (the weekly Parashah and Haphtarah)—the Song of the Sea, the Song of Deborah and Barak, the Song of Songs, David's lament for Saul, Solomon's majestic prayer, and central Psalms—highlighting their sublime, artistic value.[154] Elevated through solemn sound, rather than debased as repugnant noise, unfold the major Jewish lamentations, so frequently cited in the oratorios (*Esther, Saul, Israel in Egypt, Samson, Judas Maccabeus, Susanna*).

The sublime value of the oratorio was culturally recognized not only by the original British milieu (including Handel himself)[155] and subsequent Gentile and Jewish ones, but was also canonized by German philosophers and aestheticians, of whom the first was probably Kant:

> Even the presentation of the sublime, so far as it belongs to fine art, may be brought into union with beauty in a *tragedy in verse* (*gereimten Trauerspiele*), a *didactic poem* (*Lehrgedichte*) or an *oratorio*, and in this combination fine art is even more artistic. Whether it is also more beautiful (having regard to the multiplicity of different kinds of delight which cross one another) may in some of these instances be doubted. Still in all fine art the essential element consists in the form which is final for observation and for estimating. Here the pleasure is at the same time culture, and disposes the soul to ideas, making it thus susceptible of such pleasure and entertainment in greater abundance.[156]

While this evaluation, as far as Kant is concerned, would apply to the genre of oratorio by and large, and would continue, as such, to reverberate in the course of its future history, it seems particularly relevant to the Handelian case, which even more than its "local" German counterparts aims to wed beauty—harmony—with the sublime, and pleasure and entertainment with didactic import.[157]

SAMSON SYMPATHIZED: SOLIDARITY IN THE MAKING

Harmoniousness is indeed central to the aesthetic categorization of a Handelian oratorio. Dissonances, as in the English tradition, are fused in favor of a sour-sweet flavor of otherwise euphonious unfoldings, and seldom impinge on overall attempts to mitigate them.[158] Conferring on the multivocal choruses of arms, men, and women the craved-for unity of its allegorized groups, musical harmonious strategies are conceived in Handel's oratorios by way of deepening the sense of communitarian cohesion that was so central in the British Commonwealth. Beyond old contrapuntal techniques, which Handel, the German, had mastered so well, he geared a variety of echoing procedures in order to enhance sympathetic effects between individual protagonists, between a protagonist and related groups, and among associated groups. The difference between Handel's *Samson* and *Samson Agonistes*—its Miltonian source—looms large when seen (or better, heard) through this auditorial prism. As literary critic Stanley Fish argues, the seventeenth-century poetical configuration of the biblical story by the blind Puritan poet evokes mainly wonder—wonder at the nature of the motivation of the main actions the poem narrates (mainly Samson's actions, but also Delilah's and Manoah's), conveyed by the chorus, thus directing the reader's reaction. In terms of the *St. Matthew Passion*, the sense of wonder elicited by the momentousness of Samson's fall amounts to the basic theological existential complaint that concludes its first part: "O Mensch, bewein' dein' Sünde groß," leaving its actual interpretation open even after Samson's equipoise is finally achieved.[159]

The eighteenth-century musical transformation of the text (by the "ecumenical" composer,[160] likewise in the process of becoming blind) replies in a non-theological way to the basic query about the cause of this fall. It enfolds the hero within an encompassing sympathetic environment which imbues the drama throughout. This sympathy is of a different kind than the one embodied in the *Passion*. Less engaged with redemption of the believer through compassion, it attempts to support the suffering individual by means of enveloping sympathy, which partially mirrors, partially relativizes his agony by rendering it, in the way Adam Smith will advocate, a communal matter. This Handelian Samson is never really alone, but for the very beginning. He is surrounded by his comrades, represented by the choir, to whom Newburgh Hamilton, the librettist of *Samson*, added Micah as a more individualized agent of compas-. sion, appearing immediately after Samson's first lament. Every utterance of the agonized hero is affectively responded to by those around him, who, through a variety of emotional, individualized reactions, communicate by means of the by-then entrenched semiotics of musical affections. Already in act I, Samson is able thereby to rise above his Job-like torments, for which Hamilton supplies him with suitable verses, paraphrasing Psalms and Job: "Why does the God of Israel sleep? Arise with *dreadful sound*." Rendering these verses as an aria adds another instance for the "war through noise" prevalent in the history narrated here, sharpened through the otherwise harmonious choruses of both Philistines and Israelites.[161]

Even when his musical utterances are sung without instrumental accompa-niment—as a musical iconography of loneliness and isolation—he can feel the surrounding emotional presence; for to begin with he is carried and embraced by the symbolic voices of the orchestra (ex. 2.3).[162] Though in a total eclipse, the Handelian Samson's night is never fully dark. Musically, indeed, it is not; nature, environment, *Stimmung*, is with him, pre-echoing his plea. When he utters his lonely complaint, the conventional, major close of a minor opening phrase will not deceive him, reinforced by the orchestra. We thus anticipatorily hear that he will be saved, redeemed—if not in this world or phase, then in the world to come, or for posterity.

Contained between encompassing reverberations and echoing wholes, the balanced relation between the individual and the community is never threat-ened. This again concerns the condition of the oratorio: speech acts, animated through tonal gestures and carried by a variety of virtual personae, are prevalent in Handel's opus no less than in Bach's.

One may wonder, however, whether these personae assume different Dasein planes, the way they did in Bach's second Passion, or whether they rather tend to populate the same imaginary world. Elucidating their role in Handel's ora-torios, Winton Dean argues that, as far as the choruses are concerned, their op-eration (following the classicist model of Racine) is at once "within and above the action," deriving power from "the fact that they are participants before they are commentators," a power that endows them with "sublime unity."[163] Again we find the aesthetic categorization of the sublime (perhaps overly used); in the terms suggested here it may be better interpreted by the profusion of oratori-cal moments that emerge through the double, sometimes triple Dasein planes (biblical Israelites, "transcendental" observers, and contemporary British, Ger-man, Jewish congregations) encroaching on real and imaginary futures and

Ex. 2.3. George Frideric Handel: *Samson* I, 12 "Total Eclipse," mm. 1–7.

pasts beyond their virtual present. Listeners could thus feel that the principal protagonists in this poem are not only their progenitors, but also their representatives, attesting to the pervading deictic modality of listening to the oratorios—the repeated instantiating of the listening first-person singular or plural (the audience) by the singing performing ones.

The moment after "Total Eclipse," when the quasi-transcendental ancient Hebrew—or perhaps contemporary Christian—choir intones "O first-created Beam, and thou great Word, 'Let there be light, and light was over all,'" is a case in point. In Milton's poems these were part of Samson's soliloquy (l. 83).

Hamilton not only "choralized" it but also added to it the paraphrase and prayer "one heav'nly blaze shone round this earthly ball: to thy dark servant, life, by light afford!" which, by its devotional, awe-inspiring opening harmonies, the chorale a cappella effect (on the words: 'Let there be light!'), and triumphant "and light was over all," immediately transports Samson beyond his miserable existence. At the same time, transcending human sins and plights, it reminds listeners of both creation and redemption while involving them in prayer, a powerful communal form of attending to and alleviating individual distress.[164]

Thus in dialogue with (or even articulating the primacy of) the "Israelite" people, this contemporary choir, unlike its counterpart in the *St. John Passion*, sonically embodies a new theological idea, prevalent in England at the time—the view that the two Testaments are in fact one, mutually signifying each other: "for the New is veiled in the Old, and the Old revealed in the New. The Old sings that the holy Lord has promised; the New sings that the holy Lord has performed. The Old praises the Father who gave the law; the New praises the Son who preached the gospel, and both say, '*Holy is the Holy Ghost that penned both Law and Gospel to make men holy.*'"[165]

When it all ends, after heroic Samson is solemnly brought to his grave and Manoah and Micah exhort the congregation not to weep but to rejoice, the Israelite women exultantly sing "Let the bright Seraphim in burning row, / Their loud, uplifted angel-trumpets blow / Let the Cherubic host, in tuneful choirs, / Touch their immortal harps with golden wires" and are responded to by the men: "Let their celestial concerts all unite / Ever to sound his praise in endless blaze of light." The union of heaven and earth, past and present, ancient Jews and modern Christians is triumphantly achieved.[166] No wonder the work had such an appeal for New Christians and New Jews in the century to come.

MUSICALIZED SUBJECTIVITIES: CONFUSING THE EVIL AND THE JUST

And yet this dialogical element of Testaments, people, and protagonists could capsize, when applied to individuals and groups in the fictional worlds beyond the circle of those associated through "correct" theological and moral ties. Sympathy is everywhere. In *Samson*, it applies to the Philistines as a group no less than to Delilah as an individual; only Harapha, the brutal Philistine giant, is outside this musical-emotional order.[167] The element of entertainment is mixed with that of the benevolent acceptance of friend and foe, a crucial part in the ascending culture of sympathy.[168] In *Israel in Egypt* it furnishes us with one of its most beautiful moments, again touching on darkness: even the sinful

Egyptians, we learn, should be compassionately appraised. The chorus' report, "He sent a thick darkness . . . even darkness which might be felt," invites an envisioning of the darkness from the benighted perspective of those afflicted by it, rather than from the vantage point of those who could relish it (ex. app. 2). With its casting-in-the-dark harmonic opening, followed by bold chromatic progressions, on a passacaglia-like looping, effected through the gentle, pleading, reverberating gestures of benighted voices, this chorus comes closer to "total eclipse," a moment of night's aesthetics which could, as such, touch a poignant chord among those sharing its sensibilities.

Against this background it may appear surprising that it was Felix Mendelssohn who was disturbed by this sympathetic Handelian approach, complaining to Sterndale Bennett in 1839 that the moving music of *Delilah* "[w]ith plaintive notes" and "[t]oo fleeting pleasure" "was not meant in earnest."[169] He had sound grounds for this complaint, however. Uniquely for his time, he sensed that musically expressive contents are themselves morally neutral, enlisted as they are to depict the subjectivities of those to whom they are ascribed. This he could have already learned from the *Magic Flute,* in which not only the magic musical instruments can be equally manipulated by both "night" and "light" personae, but where "villains" are no less, sometimes even more, musically-expressively attractive than their "virtuous" counterparts, evoking morally and politically confused and confusing sentiments.

This insight is crucial to an understanding of the fate that befell the Handelian oratorio in Germany, when darkness, real darkness — "even darkness that might be felt" — invaded those people whose progenitors were once the mythological inspiration of this genre. In *The Great Dictator* (1940) Charlie Chaplin clearly indicated how the celestial opening music of *Lohengrin* furnishes the subjectivities of both "Hynkel" (Hitler) and, in the happy finale, of the still agonizing, albeit redeemed, Jews. Chaplin deliberately points to the fact that in music, as sometimes in politics, perspective is a question of framing. The qualifying emotional gesture is basically nomadic, a floating coinage that can either ridicule its bearer (as in the case of Hynkel's hallucination of becoming the World's emperor) or ennoble it (when Hannah, the Jewish barber's girlfriend, looks at the sky, as if listening to his liberal/liberating speech, delivered in annexed Vienna).

Sometimes, as in the case of this highly optimistic, if rather naïve, Hollywood movie, all ends well; for unlike musical doubles, the realistic, human doppelgangers in this movie (Hynkel and the Jewish barber) are fortuitously decontextualized, prompting a blessed mistake.[170] Yet doppelgangers also evoke the "doubling, dividing, and interchanging of the self" that is at the heart of the *unheimlich* (uncanny) symptom or effect, as Freud famously maintained.[171] What seems related to the emotional history of the individual will turn out to apply no less to the cultural and political body. The same music can serve two opponent masters, two adversarial collectives, confusing the evil and the just.

Prefiguring some of the ethnographic materials that will be discussed in the next chapter, the story of Martin Stern poignantly illustrates this roving between the *Heimlich* (of home; secretive, mysterious) and the *Unheimlich* (eerie; shocking; terrifying) that German Jews must have felt in darkened times, combining musical (Handelian) doubling with the communal:

> When I was about ten, one of our maids, with Mother's permission, took me with her to Sunday services in a Lutheran church near our house. After a few minutes, my mind wandered agreeably once again, until suddenly I was brought up short—indeed, startled—by the choir and organ intoning a hymn that I had first heard in Temple [Reform synagogue]: the words were different, but the tune was exactly the same. How could they use a Jewish melody? Surely this indicated that these two religions, and perhaps others, had much in common, and that too much emphasis was placed on their differences. The melody was Händel's "Hail! The conquering hero comes" from his opera *Judas Maccabeus*. It seems that at that time Judaism was, in my mind, more identified with certain music than with particular rituals or teachings.[172]

Reflecting a century of avid Handel reception by the Jews in Germany in both concert hall and synagogue, as well as the centrality of his oratorios in the repertoire of the *Jüdische Kulturbund* (Jewish Culture League, established by the Nazis after 1933, and further controlled by them but administered by the Jews), Stern's reminiscence also unwittingly attests to the most bitter irony of its use by both Nazi Germans and subjugated Jews, seemingly serving contradictory purposes.[173] For the Jews, Handel's oratorios connote all the values of a happy union of Jewish and European cultures, serving as a source of pride, the object of nostalgia and the lodestone of a visionary future, all within a familiar entertaining frame. This continues well into the war years, as in the repertoire of the Theresienstadt ghetto.

For the Nazis, as Pamela Potter persuasively indicates, they stood for another specimen of Aryan culture and as powerful, affective symbols for an exclusive national, even military, union led by its *Führer*. Purging Handel's works of a Jewish presence and individualistic, democratic connotations, they recast *Israel in Egypt* and *Joshua* as *Der Opfersieg bei Walstatt* and *Die Ostlandfeier*, respectively, and *Judas Maccabeus* and *Samson* became, in their hands, *Wilhelmus von Nassauen* (or, in another version, "simply" *Der Feldherr*) and *Wieland*.[174] Between the British imperialists and Nazi Germany, the Weimar period of post-World-War-I Germany continued the tradition, initiated in the nineteenth century, of engaging Handel's oratorios in the active role of community building. Once conceived democratic and inclusive,[175] the communal model embodied in these oratorios became, in the dark period of the Third Reich, a kind of a double mirror, in which victim and perpetrator were self-portrayed in a glass darkly, each rarely noticing the expression of their Ultimate Other reflected in it.

Introducing Handel to the synagogue[176] was part of a more general trend, throughout the nineteenth century and the early twentieth century, of harmonizing Jewish prayer. The beginnings of this practice are not clear, but presumably it overlapped with its contrary move from synagogue to concert hall, with Jewish singers performing Handel oratorios in concert. John Braham was one such singer, whose 1821 performance of the aria "[a]nd the Children of Israel went on dry land through the sea" in *Israel in Egypt* evoked an "imperfect sympathy" in Charles Lamb, as he "boldly confessed," through a fictive figure, Elia.[177] For, as far as this alter ego confesses, he does not "relish the approximation of the Jew and Christian which [had] become so fashionable:"

> Jews christianizing—Christians judaising—puzzles me . . . B[raham] would have been more in keeping if he had abided by the faith of his forefathers. There is a fine scorn in his face, which nature meant to be of—Christians. The Hebrew spirit is strong in him, in spite of his proselytism. He cannot conquer the Shibboleth. How it breaks out, when he sings: "The Children of Israel passed through the Red Sea!" The auditors, for the moment, are as Egyptians to him, and he rides over our necks in triumph. There is no mistaking him.—B[raham] has a strong expression of sense in his countenance, and it is confirmed by his singing. The foundation of his vocal excellence is sense. He sings with understanding. . . . He would sing the Commandments, and give an appropriate character to each prohibition.[178]

Embracing difference, it is clear that Lamb's hero tries to keep the "Shibboleth" boundaries, clinging to "natural" inborn difference as a checkpoint guarding against the flooding of foreigners into his civil society.[179] The liberal, pluralistic social structure contradicts his inclinations, and he would do nothing to overcome them. His sympathies, as Elia "modestly" declares—referring to that given, natural, moral disposition, becoming, after Smith, a "household" of British people of letters, are imperfect; an imperfection which extends, in his case, also to Scots, Negroes, and Quakers. It is not that he cannot account for such imperfections. He does. His stance, indeed, bespeaks ambivalence: on the one hand, it exudes admiration for a primordial, "strong" element that Jews signify

Fig. 2.4. Thomas Rowlandson, "Family Quarrels or the Jew and the Gentile," published January 25, 1803. Etching, hand colored with watercolor and gouache. Courtesy of the Jewish Museum, London.

as a "piece of antiquity," dating "beyond the pyramids"; on the other—fear, xenophobia, prejudice. To the latter, the renowned adapter of Shakespeare's plays openly admits: "I have not the nerves to enter their synagogues. Old prejudices cling about me." And then comes the root of it all, which, as we have previously seen, a few Thuringian theologians, a century earlier, had dismissed as false:

> I cannot shake off the story of Hugh of Lincoln. Centuries of injury, contempt, and hate, on the one side,—of cloaked revenge, dissimulation, and hate, on the other, between our and their fathers, must, and ought to affect the blood of the children. I cannot believe it can run clear and kindly yet; or that a few fine words, such as candour, liberality, the light of a nineteenth century, can close up the breaches of so deadly a disunion.

And surely he was in good company (going all the way to Chaucer's Prioress), and could have even been directly prejudiced by the caricature by the renowned Thomas Rowlandson—his compatriot—which appeared in London about twenty years before, in "Family Quarrels or the Jew and the Gentile" (fig. 2.4, the title referring to Dibdin's opera *Family Quarrels* of 1802). It shows us rather clearly who sings genuine, healthy, proper, and folksy *moderato con espressione* music (C major, diatonic melodic steps, three-quarter meter though with slight incongruity of pitch and stress—the native English tenor Charles B. Incledon—and who has a sophisticated but distorted and degenerate kind of noise (nonmetrical, with an "unnatural" vocal range, impossible coloratura including unfeasible melodic jumps, misplaced arpeggio and a nonrelated cadence with a ludicrous "shake for seventeen minutes" instruction!). The Jew, hunched and exhausted by the physical effort, is a representation of our Mr. John Braham, who began his professional life as a choirboy at the Great Synagogue in London.[180] He is singing in "Allegro Squekando," and in order to intensify the noise, the Jews, his supporters, exclaim, or rather, *mauscheln*: "Mine Cod, How he shing!" (Whereas the "Gentiles" in the left corner exclaim: "encore, encore!" The cat holding the placard may be a symbol of ridiculed music (compare the artist's "musical cats"), thus degrading the entire scene.[181]

The caricaturist, indeed, has found new means to accentuate the old breach, while essentializing difference. Whether one should overcome these breaches, and if one should, how to do so—by clinging to differences or by blurring them; abiding by old liturgical customs or creatively mixing them with imported forms and new vocalities—is a question with which many have engaged in response to such claims. If a creatively evolving conservation is the way, where should it lead, both for individuals and congregations? In other words, what is the price of religious-auditory openness? For Lamb—and he, curiously enough, echoed some Orthodox Jewish opinions—the answer is clear: church and synagogue should not "kiss" or "congee" in "awkward postures of an affected civility." The old medieval isolation has not abated. And yet, even he was willing to listen to Jewish music and could not but marvel at a Jew "that hath music in himself." The oratorical culture operated here, as elsewhere, as a subliminal pedagogy of inclusion, preserving difference, bringing to the fore potent experiential moments, transporting individual and community beyond their immediate present. By the same token, however, in reviving pasts and mythologizing the present, they could rekindle entrenched prejudices and biased positions. In the next chapter we will witness how tortuous it was for Jews facing discriminatory opinions such as Lamb's (but also the relativist openness that such opinions inevitably disclose) to find their way between "harmonizing" their music into the ostensible new "candor" and "liberality" of the nineteenth century, and keeping a core they deemed, in various degrees and forms, their indigenous, "stubborn" elements that constituted an identity they were loath to renounce or obliterate.

NOISE IN THE HOUSE OF PRAYER: ETHNOGRAPHY TRANSFIGURED

By the rivers of Babylon, there we sat down, yea, we wept,
when we remembered Zion.
Upon the willows in the midst thereof
we hanged up our harps.
For there they that led us captive asked of us words of song,
and our tormentors asked of us mirth:
'Sing us one of the songs of Zion.'
How shall we sing the Lord's song
in a foreign land?
If I forget thee, O Jerusalem,
let my right hand forget her cunning.
Let my tongue cleave to the roof of my mouth,
if I remember thee not;
if I set not Jerusalem above my chiefest joy.

—*Psalm* 137

In his book *Das Ritual*, published in Vienna in 1919, in the section entitled "Das Shofar," Theodor Reik (1888–1969)—Freud's student and colleague—narrates the following: "Incidentally it may be remarked that the phrase 'there's an uproar here like in a synagogue' [*Es geht zu wie in einer Judenschule*], which originated in the Middle Ages . . . has obtained such peculiar popularity in our beloved city Vienna."[1]

We met this phrase earlier, in chapter 1, in connection with the roots of the old noise allegation. It is, however, its persistence in modern times that will engage us in this chapter. Within the new intellectual, political, and cultural environment, the old accusation resurged against the embedded tensions between the aestheticized and the authentic, the assimilated and the segregated, diaspora and exile, and contaminated versus consecrated ethnographic lore. Following my analysis of the reactions to the noise charge by Reik and a few Viennese contemporaries (similarly secularized modern Jews), I return to some of the early modern "ethnographic" manifestations of the synagogal soundscape, documented by both friends and foes, outsiders and insiders, which should have nourished the spectral enduring nature of the charge, or the attempts—musical or literary—to ameliorate it. Whether constituting "real" or fictional vocalities, the musical and literary attempts to address the "noise" charge, which this chapter analyzes, concern the synagogal soundscape or its recognized vocal products. Hence they are all "ethnographies" that elaborate upon a common network of themes, loci, rumors, texts, and subtexts, transfiguring old lore into contemporary cultural and artistic practices and coinage.

EIN LÄRM WIE IN EINER JUDENSCHULE

In the Vienna of the early twentieth century, Theodor Reik was not the only one to experience these words as disturbing noise. He never ceased to recall the sounds of the synagogues he had attended in early childhood,[2] and, in his maturity, would address the charges against the Jewish house of prayer, albeit indirectly, in his own professional work. So did another native Viennese Jew, Leo Spitzer (1887–1960), the eminent philologist and literary scholar, and, in yet a different way, the Hebrew poet and writer David Vogel (1891–1944), who lived in Vienna after the Great War, and whose masterpiece, *Ḥayei Nissu'im* (*Married Life*, 1929–30), is set in Vienna in the twenties.[3] And there were others. *Ein Lärm wie in einer Judenschule* (the phrase as quoted by Spitzer[4]) yields, when deconstructed along its linguistic components, two comparable phenomena—*Lärm* in a particular place (city, school, streets, church—the sentence is deictic, implicitly pointing to a certain "here"—a context, a place that changes according to the situation) and *Lärm in einer Judenschule*—a perpetual phenomenon, which enables the comparison, the *wie*. *Lärm* itself, a polysemic word, signifies (1) *sehr lautes Geräuch*—a very loud noise, not necessarily of human origin; (2) *Geschrei*—shouts, exclamations, loud sounds emitted by humans (pointing to *Lärm*'s etymology in the Italian *allarme*, from *all'arme* or *all'armi*, or French *alarme*, *à l'arme*); and (3) an aural state located somewhere between "alarum" (as in warning or alarm) and "ado" (as in bustle, fuss), as, for example, in the expression *viel Lärm um nichts*—"much ado about nothing."[5]

In whichever way one may interpret *Lärm*, the expression that conveys it clearly signifies noise in the synagogue as an essential, unavoidable fact, such as "barking dogs" or "the tumultuous sea." *Lärm*, this common wisdom imparts, originates in the synagogue and characterizes its basic soundscape—the sound-scape of a defeated people—as is often its denotation in Luther's translation of the Hebrew Bible, such as in the verse from 1 Samuel 4:14: "*Und als Eli das laute Schreien hörte, fragte er: Was ist das für ein großer Lärm?*"—When Eli heard the sound of the outcry (Hebrew: *Kol Hatse'akah*) he said: What is the noise of this multitude (*hamon*)?[6]

In the medieval world, as we have seen, the synagogue became not only the acoustic organ of the noise—the animal-like uproar of a resonating body. It also functioned as a circumscribed location, marking and guarding its emission from within and from without. Marked topographically, ethnographically, architec-turally, and jurisdictionally, the synagogue provided a warning to Christians against its aspiring, transgressive sounds. A site excommunicated from the outer world, serving as a noisy exile but also as a spot of confinement, its vociferous qualities were extended, however, to the entire Jewish community. The para-doxical coexistence of spatial circumscription and aural transgression became more salient precisely at a time in which the Jewish people had began—espe-cially in northern Italy—to be less clearly conspicuous, aspiring to economic integration, if not to a limited social one.

And yet, the phenomenal nature of noise in its most neutral sense, as was already stressed, is to diffuse beyond walls and confines—of both synagogue and ghetto—to resonate, penetrate, reverberate. Jewish noise has been no excep-tion; the very coining of the simile "noise as in the synagogue" implies that syna-gogal noise could circulate, or even originate, anywhere. (This is not unique to sound, or noise, as such: stories, proverbs, rumors, plagues share these basic fea-tures with noise, although noise is less semantically loaded than these similarly transmittable and often elusive public properties.) Despite restriction and con-finement, "Jewish noise," as was indicated, "defiled" Christian essences, while their "harmonious" sonorities could not hush at the gates of a Jewish ghetto.

It is the categorization implied in the simile, and its extended "ethnographic" manifestation, then, that helped maintain the essential sonic separation be-tween Jews and non-Jews, even when in reality it was no more (if ever) the case. For the phrase itself seemed to fixate its dichotomous elements: while the sound that emerged from the Christian house of prayer was ever conceived and perceived (by the Christians) as harmonious, created out of distinct, pitched components properly combined (and ostensibly in accordance with universal, mathematical-physical and metaphysical laws), traditional Jewish sound cannot avoid its categorization as a cacophonous, indefinably obscure mixture. Its clamor, which could still be heard in some synagogues in modern Vienna and other contemporary European cities, would be perceived to convey impoliteness, if not barbarism; its typical laments—pain, and the suggestion of an unredeemed, quarrelsome existence; its unregulated vocalities—a lack of solemnity and decorum. The praying Jews were quarreling with their God, and this was why they yelled, cried out—but to no avail; the Jewish God, according to a joke still in vogue through the twentieth century, and even told by self-mocking Jews, was too old to hear them.[7]

As was pointed out in chapter 1, if there is one particular sonic phenomenon that epitomizes Jewish noise, it is that of the "ululating" shofar.[8] Christians— medieval Christians in the small towns of Ashkenaz—could not help but hear it, though they could surely prohibit its use. Modern Jews did not avoid it, despite their attempts to otherwise modernize and harmonize their rituals. It is the sound of the shofar that Reik set out to explore in the aforementioned study; a sound that was reclaimed by Jewish composers at the turn of the twenty-first century, as a peal that symbolizes Jewish existence.

LÄRM AS MODERN NOISE: REIK, SPITZER, VOGEL

This brings us back to the starting point of this chapter, when Jews were no longer confined to one place, and noise—irksome, frightening, discordant— seems to have sprawled everywhere. Does the ubiquity of the noise-accusation phrase in "our beloved Vienna," to quote Reik again, bespeak that noise, modern noise, post–Great War noise, was tacitly associated with Jews? Could it be that Jewish noise disseminates everywhere and the city as a whole—strewn with Jews of various origins and types, associated as they were with the city's accelerated urbanization—unwittingly becomes a large, vociferous synagogue? David Vogel opens a window to the city's aural dimension:

> Not far off, the park band was playing, and the tune united with the rattling of the trams and the hooters of the cars outside to form a curious medley of noises and sounds. By concentrating intently on the music it was possible to weed out the foreign elements and return it, with a strenuous effort, to its pristine state. But Gurdweill actually preferred it the way it was, with the pulse of the life of the city beating outside it. Thus he imagined the music of a band playing on a ship at sea, and absorbing into itself the pounding of the mighty waves.[9]

Something radical happened in the realm of noise, or *Lärm*, around the mid-nineteenth century, with the emergence of industrialization, steam engines, and a generally intensified life pulse that was exacerbated at the turn of the twentieth century, irrevocably transforming the entire soundscape of human civilization.[10]

World War I played a crucial role in this metamorphosis and seems to have altered the basic auditory sensibilities of large sectors of the population.[11] Noise became an issue. Although, like plagues, noise could be attributed to a clandestine originator, the noise allegation against the Jews seems to have been systematically rekindled only by Pope Pius IX, in 1871, as noted in chapter 1, and by the Nazis, both along the traditional lines.

In an increasingly suffocating anti-Semitic environment, however, intellectuals and creators such as Theodor Reik, Leo Spitzer, David Vogel, Arnold Schoenberg, Gustav Mahler,[12] and Franz Kafka could not but be under the sway of this insidious accusation, which encompassed both ancestral Jewish habits of worship and modern Jewish existence. They responded to it "professionally," that is, through the legitimized and socially sanctioned way of living that each of them had adopted as a modern Jew, and yet they all disclose moments of what seem to be involuntary *confessions* of a repressed identity or past.[13]

Thus, Reik's main attempt in "The Shofar" is to psychoanalyze Jewish noise by focusing on the meaning of the shofar customs, a most sacred practice associated with the holy Days of Awe, whose poignant echo, dating from an Orthodox childhood, still reverberated in his mature years. Reik analyzes the shofar's related sources from the Bible throughout subsequent texts—homilies, prayers, laws, and customs, revealing his great expertise and insider understanding of this lore.

His starting premise lies in the subsidiary place allotted to Jubal, "the father of all those who play the lyre and pipe" (Genesis 4:22) vis-à-vis the central place and deified status of analogous "musical fathers" in other ancient cultures. Jubal, Reik observes (pronounced in Hebrew "Yuval") is a derivative of *Yovel*—both words standing for a ram's horn. The latter is inextricably connected with the shofar in the description of the Mount Sinai revelation.

Reik sensitizes his readers as to the textual contradictions inherent in this cryptic description, especially those pertaining to its sonic dimensions: "And then the voice of the shofar sounded louder and louder; Moses speaks, and God answers him by a voice" (Exodus 19:19). Who blew the shofar and who spoke there, he asks, and if the two were simultaneous—how could the speech have been intelligible? Reik solves the query by boldly suggesting that the shofar's blast was God's own voice. A refined version of a totemic god, Reik claims, biblical God was blowing His own horn.

Reik traces three stages in the historical development of the conception of the divine voice as noisy blast: the first is "the voice of the ram" [the totemic god]; the second, "the sounds which God made by blowing a ram's horn," and the last is "the incomparable voice which is removed from all that is human and animal, the voice of God purified of all earthly dross" (254). The shofar-blowing on Mt. Sinai, he adds, corresponds to the intermediate level, and is thus comparable to "the wild songs sung by savages, when they imitate the noise of the animal who is their totem god" (257).

Experienced by Jews as an extremely awesome and powerful sound, in Reik's view, the shofar's blast "unconsciously recalls to every hearer that old outrage, and awakens his hidden guilty conscience"—of the irredeemable and unforgettable crime of humanity—the murder of the father-god.[14] While closely drawing on Freud's *Totem and Taboo* (1912), Reik's argument prefigures some of Freud's own in *Moses and Monotheism* (1938). Reik's casual reference to "Jewish synagogal noise" opens up the possibility of interpreting his own attribution of noise to God in psychoanalytical terms. At the onset, it can be regarded as a transference of the charge against him (the author), and his parents' and grandparents' synagogue (and the Jews in general as the *patient* in this case), onto the *Autre* (to use the Lacanian term), *the lawgiver*, the One above all—the *Archtherapist* (however castrated).

Such an act of transcendental transference is fraught with meaning—first and foremost because it unwittingly reiterates the prime insinuation of the Christian claim: God does not answer; there is a fundamental "repressed" lack of communication with Him, which "returns" (with a vengeance) in the new clinical environment of scientific, professional research (comprised of Biblical criticism, modern psychology, ethnographic knowledge, and the like), and is transferable to the newly conceived authorial entity—the totemic god. He is the original noisemaker, rather than his people. It is noteworthy that, in contradistinction to the Christian imputation, Jewish noise is connected in Reik's view (as well as in Freud's) to the atavistic murder of the Father, rather than with the betrayal or murder of the Son (the source of Jewish noise according to the Christians).

A deeper insight into Reik's essay will, nevertheless, reveal a more complex aural genealogy, entailing an even more radical transposition of "noise." We will return to this point in chapter 6 and proceed now with the other aforementioned authors. Leo Spitzer also chose to "distance the testimony," as a medieval Hebrew expression would describe it, enlisting his tools as a philologist and etymologist to unearth the roots of this phenomenon.[15] Spitzer's analysis of the term *noise* (briefly surveyed in chapter 1) summons a whole range of related words: *noise, nausea, anger, boredom, seasickness, loud laments,* and *quarrel*— all relating to what he views as the inseparability, in ancient times (including, for him, the Middle Ages), of the experience of inner emotions of disturbance, awe, or the like, and their outward, vociferous manifestation.[16] Spitzer, the great upholder of harmony, in what Sander Gilman would term as a "double bind" self-hatred gesture,[17] also reminds us of the important notion that "noise in the Middle Ages was considered a symptom of disharmony, of lack of Grace, of unregenerateness."

This leads Spitzer to a discussion of the accusation against Jews, for which he finds further linguistic sources and parallels, but relegates it to a footnote, however extensive.[18] He thus transcribes noise, projecting it onto a different time and location, and onto other languages and communities, transmarginalizing its Jewish element (in the sense of rendering it subliminal, pushing it to a historical moment that remains on the fringe of consciousness) and vehemently refuses to connect it to contemporary anti-Semitic notions.

As for David Vogel, in a most revealing, atypical section in *Married Life*, his antihero, Rudolf Gurdweill, communicates—in fact confesses—the following in the ears of cruel Thea ("goddess"), his Christian wife, with whom he leads an increasingly horrifying sadomasochistic life:

> In a little village, unlike a city, religion still plays an important role in life. The boundaries are well-defined. Jews are Jews and Christians are Christians. You can't possibly confuse the two. Especially in the little settlements of Galicia and Poland. My parents weren't Orthodox but nevertheless they had nothing to do with Christians. In short: the Christians fascinated me in their strangeness. When I grew a little older, I would hang around the church on their holidays, moved and excited, waiting for something. The singing of the choir, threatening and obscure, would come pouring out into the fresh summer air like a slow stream of thick black tar. By then I already knew about the Inquisition, the Crusades, the persecution of the Jews, and I was constantly afraid that they would suddenly seize me and drag me inside and force me to do something terrible. . . . Once I dared to approach the door and look inside. I saw nothing but dense darkness, dotted with weak candle flames. I could see people kneeling, too. From that day on, whenever I thought about Christians I would see something dark with flickering candles.[19]

"The singing of the choir, threatening and obscure, would come pouring out into the fresh summer air like a slow stream of thick black tar." The image of black tar contrasts sharply with the Christians' own self-image of such music— harmonious, light, and transparent. Tarnished in his mind, Gurdweill/Vogel reflects, in terms of the collective memory of the Jewish persecution, the association this music bears to a Jewish boy in a Galician shtetl on the brink of the twentieth century is clear: a repository issuing from the roots of the antimusical accusations—the time of the Crusades, when Jews began to distinguish themselves musically through their singular lamentations/noise, while Christians, boasting of their new euphonious hymns and antiphons, safeguarded them from heretic Jewish ears. (Concomitantly, this experience also connotes a sense of ambivalence, of fascination and fear, marking that which eventually will attract Gurdweill to Thea's sadistic embrace.)

An allegation that could have been rebuffed by the counterargument that "all is in the ear of the listener," and that noise, like other cultural phenomena, is relative, reveals here a far deeper rupture. "Transplanting" noise—according to the medical etymology as "the supposed curing of a disease by causing it to pass to another person"[20]—entails, for Gurdweill/Vogel, the "remedy" for the Christian accusations he was exposed to. Interestingly, this is the only instance in which the protagonist refers to his own past, beyond the novel's temporal boundaries, which are primarily confined to the duration of its major narrated events.

The reader may notice, in the above discussion, the predominance of verbs carrying the prefix *trans-*: *transference, transcendence, transpose, transcribe*, and *transplant*—to which others could be added. The essence of sound, as noted, is to transit space. That is part and parcel of its phenomenal nature—a fact that has given birth to some of its derivative mythologies. Confine it, constrain it, contaminate it—and it will find a way to free itself, to be transported, transformed, transfigured.

Three prominent semantic fields related to the prefix *trans-* are pertinent to this discussion: the religious or theological field—including *transcend, transmute, transfigure, transgress*, and *translucence*; the musical and audial context, with words such as *transpose, transcribe, transmit, transform*, and *transfigure* (the last one especially relevant to contemporary Viennese music);[21] and the political-punitive that includes again *transgression*, but in which *transmigration, transfer, transplantation*, and *transportation* are also relevant. These three orbits of music's "going beyond" interchange and interpenetrate, disclosing aesthetic-theological-political structures that have been infused with new meanings in modern times.

In the unbearable lightness of its trans-figuration, music oscillates between two poles; it may soar to the transcendental sublime or descend into the abject, bestial, or criminal, sometimes as a vehicle of punishment, or as the last resort of the condemned prisoner.[22] The act of transcription or transposition of extant music from one location to another may in itself connote either elevation or disgrace, as, for instance, among certain Jewish and Christian circles, depending on whether they had supported religious reformation or fought it.[23]

"ENLIGHTENED" VISITS IN THE SYNAGOGUE: EDELMANN
AND BURNEY IN FRANKFURT AND AMSTERDAM

Only in early modern times, in the wake of the renewed accusations of "noisiness," did Noise in the House of Prayer become more available to cultural transaction. This is not only because Jews or their supporters felt more empowered, but also because the old complaints became more explicit and transparent, partially through ethnographical tools, whether authentic or fake. The extant ethnographies of synagogal soundscape—both admiring and dismissive—tend to concentrate mainly on two well-known synagogues, the synagogue at the Judengasse in Frankfurt (fig. 3.1–3.3) and its "branch," the Ashkenazi (*deutsche*) synagogue in Amsterdam. Historically and ethnographically, the venerable Frankfurt Synagogue was indeed the stronghold of old Ashkenazi custom, as attested already by the desire of one Johann Christian Edelmann, an eighteenth-century traveler, to be taken there to satisfy his "appetite" for such an experience.[24] In his ethnographic tour around the country, visiting a variety of religious communities and sects, he could have met Lessing's fictional Jewish *Reisender* (both "traveled" in "Germany" the same year), though Edelmann too would probably not have recognized him as a Jew.

Edelmann's description indeed presupposes the Jews' otherness to a great extent, reflecting, and maybe reinforcing, extant stereotypes. He concentrates on the bizarre choreographic element of the service—the strange body movements of the people and the cantor, the shabby and disordered synagogue—and, above all, the noisy elements, which he describes in animalistic terms of cat yowls and goat bleats, in addition to shouts, complaints, and other vocalizations. The animal element (resuscitating the medieval ululating dogs), we shall realize, is crucial to the modern allegation. Edelmann opens his report as follows:

> Die vielen Juden, die allda lebten und nicht weit vom Bornheimer Thore eine eigene große Gasse bewohnten, machten mir, da ich noch keine Synagoge gesehen hatte, einen Appetit, dieselbe zu besehen. Br. Düsterweg führte mich also in das Abendgebeth dieser armen verdüsterten Leute. Der Ort dieser Juden-Schule schien ihrer innerlichen Gemüthsbeschaffenheit ganz gleich zu seyn, denn er war überaus dunkel und sahe überall unter den Stühlen und Bäncken so unsauber und unordentlich aus, als wenn man hätte ausziehen wollen.

> [The many Jews who lived there and inhabited a long lane of their own not far from the Bornheimer Gate, gave me, since I had never seen a synagogue,

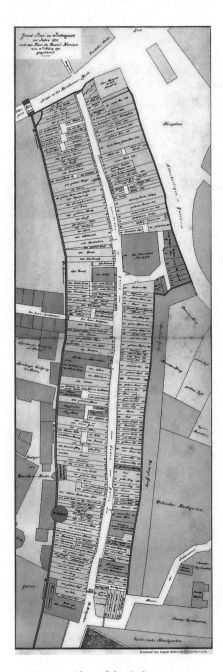

Fig. 3.1. Plan of the Judengasse in
Frankfurt, 1715, according to a drawing
by Merian. Courtesy of the Jüdisches
Museum, Frankfurt am Main. The location
of the synagogue is marked by the hexagon
on the upper right-hand side of the *Gasse*.
Bornheimer Gate is on the top left, marking
Edelmann's way into the long lane.

Fig. 3.2. The old synagogue (interior) in Frankfurt, Judengasse, 1855.
Aquarelle by Oscar Fischler. Courtesy of the Historisches Museum,
Frankfurt am Main. Photograph: Horst Ziegenfusz.

an appetite to see it. Hence, Br. (Brother?) Düsterweg led me to the evening prayer of these poor, benighted people. This Jewish *schul* (synagogue)[25] seemed to be identical with their inner disposition, as it was extremely dark, and looked so dirty and messy under the chairs and benches, as if they were about to move out.]

While Edelmann's report gives certain details—such as that it is evening prayer in the Frankfurt Synagogue—he is mainly concerned, as befits an enlightened man, to convey his own "compassionate" and condescending view to his equally enlightened readers: his ostensible ethnographic acuity casts this impoverished, marginalized group in advance as "poor benighted people." Their spiritual darkness is reflected in the décor—dark and dirty—and in the allegorical name of the guide, Düsterweg, "dark road." This grim description replaces ethnographical lacunae in his report, such as an accurate rendering of the service and the liturgical occasion. The occasion could have been Tish'a' be'Av—the (annual) mournful commemoration day of the destruction of the Temples in Jerusalem—in which darkness is part of the actual setting—and in which benches and chairs are turned upside down as a sign of mourning. But for Edelmann this single service captures the essence of Jewish religious and

Fig. 3.3. Frankfurt Judengasse, houses near the synagogue (at the far left in the photo), after the destruction of the houses on the western side, 1870. Courtesy of the Jüdisches Museum Frankfurt am Main.

aesthetic existence, leaving out the impact of the Jews' wretched economic, legal, and political conditions.

This biased rendering culminates in the revelation of the actual service:

> Ehe ihr *Geheule* angieng, stunden etliche neben uns, die heimlich beteten, wobei sie beständig mit dem ganzen Leibe vor und hinter sich wackelten, nicht anders, wie die trunckenen, die nicht mehr auf den Beinen zu stehen vermögen. Sie *plapperten*, so viel ich sehen konnte, sehr geschwind, schlugen sich einmal über das andere auf die Brust, daß es pufte und wackelten immerfort. Dieser elende Anblick hätte mich bald zu Thränen bewegt, wenn ihr Vorsänger nicht endlich vor den Tisch getreten und seine Comoedie angefangen hätte, denn da hätte es wenig gefehlet, daß ich nicht überlaut zu lachen angefangen.

> [Before their *wailing* started, several people stood next to us praying silently, constantly swaying back and forth with their entire bodies, not unlike drunkards who are no longer able to stand on their legs. As far as I could tell, they *babbled* very quickly, beating their breasts over and over so hard that it made a thumping noise, and kept on and on swaying. This miserable spectacle could have moved me to tears, had not their cantor finally stepped in front of the table[26] and started his comedy, for by that time little was missing and I would have burst out laughing loudly.]

The scenery consists of swaying bodies and babbling lips—*Lärm* in the sense of much ado, Luther's *hamon*. Even silent prayer becomes contaminated by the image of drunken behavior, calling to mind the story of Hannah in Eli's tabernacle (1 Samuel 1), celebrating silent communion with the Eternal, the happy ending of which hung as a sublime historical painting in Daniel Itzig's salon (chapter 2). Unlike their rendering in the book of Samuel, neither the content nor the context of prayers is given to us here; in its mixture of pathetic and bathetic elements, the sight can only evoke laughter, ridicule, or *Abneigung*, aversion—the word "scientifically" analyzed by Wagner in the first part of his anti-Jewish lampoon. Indeed, the vocabulary of noise deployed here foreshadows Wagner's description of the synagogal audial space. Words such as *plappern*, *Geheule*, and *Gurgel* were onomatopoeically concatenated by Wagner, to create one noisy sentence, imitating its object of vilification.

This lexical similarity raises the possibility that Wagner was familiar with Edelmann's account, or that this ethnographic genre was sufficiently prevalent to breed a specific vocabulary that circulated beyond its "scientific" boundaries. The choice of words—*Geheule*, *Kater-Geschrey*, and the image, in the paragraph that follows, of the scarecrow that frightens invading birds—bring to mind Goethe's and Mendelssohn's vision in the *Erste Walpurgis Nacht*, where noise itself—actual, musical noise—becomes the weapon of the subjugated Druids against their Christian oppressors, who succeeded, hitting at their prejudices, in frightening them away:

> Kommt mit Zacken und mit Gablen
> Wie der Teufel, den sie fablen,
> Und mit wilden Klapperstöcken
> Durch die leeren Felsenstrecken!
> Kauz und Eule
> *Heul* in unser Rund*geheule*!!
>
> [Come with prongs and pitchforks
> Like the Devil of whom they prate
> And with furiously rattling sticks
> Let us charge through empty mountains gorges.
> Let owl and hoopoe
> Screech amidst our roundelay!]

Do Edelmann's report and the genre it seems to represent betray an unconscious fear related to the ancient Jewish noise, connected to, for example, the festival of Purim, or even to a more primordial xenophobic dread of the Jews?[27] Consciously, at least, despite darkness and animal shouts, Edelmann is well protected by his prejudices and privileges:

> Dieser Kerl vermummelte erstlich den Kopf mit ein paar Tüchern in solcher Geschwindigkeit, als wenn ihn jemand jagte. Wie er nun in dieser Positur nicht viel besser aussahe als ein Popanz, den man auf die Kirsch-Bäume stellet, wenn man die Sperlinge verscheuchen will; also wurde er noch tausendmal lächerlicher, wie er in derselben mit wunderlichen Verbeugungen des Leibes ein ordentliches *Kater-Geschrey* anfieng und mit der rechten hand immer an die *Gurgel* schlug, das *Bocks-Triller* herauskommen musten.

> [First, this fellow covered his head with several kerchiefs so fast, as if somebody were chasing him. Looking in this condition not much better than a scarecrow one puts on cherry trees to scare away the sparrows, he became a thousand times more ridiculous when he started a veritable racket, accompanied by bizarre bends of his body, constantly hitting his *throat* with his right hand, which inevitably produced *goat trills*.]

Edelmann's gaze now focuses on the cantor and on the way he wears the prayer shawl, the *tallit*, or "kerchief." He resorts to a hyperbolic style in order to create his impression; the cantor could not have worn more than one tallit, though the way he dressed it quickly—or above his *kittel* (the gown worn by cantors and men during the Days of Awe service)—could so appear. Be that as it may, his report insinuates that the sight of Jews at prayer recalls a dance of an exotic tribe, a circus, a farce:

> Wer dergleichen seltsame Arten von Gottesdienstlichkeiten noch nie gesehen und sonst von Natur kein Saurtopf ist, der hat in der That Mühe, das Lachen zu verbeißen, zumal wenn er mit ansehen muß, was ich gleich weiter erzeh- len will. Denn wie dieses *Geheule* vor der Tische durch alle möglichen *Kazen-Töne* eine ziemliche Weile gewähret und der große Haufe oder die Gemeine bey gewissen Worten ein Paar Zeilen ganz zetermäßig mit darein *geschrien* hatten, lief dieser Psalmist auf einmal hinter den Tisch, sezte sich platt nieder auf den Boden, kehrte sich mit den Rücken nach der Wand, zog die Knie bis vor das Maul, faltete die Hände über die Knie und fieng in dieser Positur, ohne ein Wort zu sprechen, dergestalt an auf dem Hintern vor und hinter sich zu wackeln, daß mich Wunder nahm, daß ihm kein Seufzer entfuhr.

> [He who has never seen strange kinds of worship like this and otherwise is not lacking in humor by nature, will have to make an effort to restrain his laughter, especially when he has to witness what else I would like to tell. For when this *wailing* in front of the table in all kinds of *cat-like noises* had gone on for quite a while and the big crowd or congregation had screamed several lines along with him at certain words in a nagging sort of way, this Psalmist suddenly ran behind the table, sat down flat on the floor, turned his back to the wall, drew his knee up to his mouth, folded his hands above his knee and began in this position, without uttering a word, swaying to and fro on his be- hind in such a way that I was surprised no sigh escaped him.]

It is hard to imagine when such a scene or something slightly similar could have taken place. The only radical body movement this could be is the one on Yom Kippur day, in the Musaf prayer, when the hazzan—the cantor—(and congregation) kneel whenever the words "kneeling and prostrating" are uttered throughout the description of this holy day's ritual in the Temple.[28] And yet, its choreography is different. The following paragraph evokes, however, more as- sociations in this direction.

Edelmann now calls the cantor/hazzan a "psalmist" and describes the con- gregation in an act of semiresponsorial singing, however distorted it sounds to his ears. Unlike the increasingly prevalent descriptions of exotic tribes by Euro- pean travelers, this tribe shares something crucial with the Christian congrega- tion: psalm recitation. A key mutual heritage of Jews and Christians, the vocal rendition of Psalms might disclose an original ancient practice. But Edelmann's use of the word "psalmist" suggests an ironic, mocking comparison between this poor specimen and the sublime King David.[29] The comparison, however, seems to elicit a surprising skeptical undertone, with which Edelmann concludes his testimony:

> Dieses Gewackele daurete ungefehr eine Minute, während welcher Zeit die andern auch stille vor sich wegwackelten, bisweilen die Augen verdreheten, an Bärten zupften und der Brust einen Puff gaben. Das daurete so lange, bis der Erzwackeler wieder aufsprang, vor dem Tisch lief und seine lieblose Musik vollends zu Ende brachte.
>
> Mein Gott, sagte ich, zum Br. Düsterweg, ists möglich, daß Menschen, die noch ein wenig von gesunden Verstande übrig haben, glauben können, daß dem höchsten Wesen mit dergleichen Narrens-Possen gedienet sey? Wir hatten unsere Betrachtungen noch weiter: Sie giengen aber zur selben Zeit, zum wenigsten bey mir, weiter nicht, als daß ich dieses arme blinde Volk, meinen Vorurtheilen zu Folge, als ein von Gott verworfenes Volk betrachtete, ohne zu bedencken, daß sie uns, in so fern wir einen gekreuzigten Menschen vor Gott hielten, vor weit blinder anzusehen Ursache hatten.

> [This swaying lasted about a minute, during which time the others also silently wiggled about, occasionally rolling their eyes, plucking their beards and giving their breasts a thump. This lasted until the arch-wiggler jumped in front of the table once more and brought his unfeeling music to an end.
>
> My God, I said to Br. Düsterweg, is it possible that people who still have a little bit of common sense left should believe that the Supreme Being can be served with such fool's pranks? We continued our observations: however, at that time they went no further, at least as far as I am concerned, than my considering, following my prejudices, this poor, blind people as forsaken by God, without thinking that they had reason to view us, since we take a crucified man for God, as even more blind.]

Associating the acoustic phenomenon he describes with music and not merely with noise for the first time, however derogatively, Edelmann brings his report to a surprising relativistic ending. Unlike the preacher who the fictional Krumm heard in Breslau (in Lessing's *Die Juden*), Edelmann is radical enough, or deistic enough, to cast doubt on the most sacred theological principle of his own confessional frame, for which Jews were accused and persecuted: the deification of the (crucified) man Jesus.[30] He was not able, however, to further entertain the thought that their miserable situation—including what he experienced as a ridiculous vocal performance—could be the historical consequence of his brethren's belief. Thus Edelmann's otherwise deprecating report

nevertheless makes an opening, however small, towards cultural-religious tolerance and a more encompassing perception of nuanced aesthetic-theological
categories.

This kind of relativism is also present in the report of another cultural traveler, the Englishman Charles Burney (1726–1814), a renowned music critic and
historian of the time (and father of Fanny Burney, herself an observer of some
repute). Appearing in the second volume of his *Musical Tours in Europe* (devoted to central Europe and the Netherlands), his report is rendered in human
musical terms, in addition to noisy-animal ones. Though still uncomplimentary
to his described subjects, his report is ethnologically more faithful, conveying,
in a way, "the state of the art" of musical synagogal practices of the time.[31] Burney enters the Ashkenazi synagogue in Amsterdam:

> At my first entrance, one of the priests was chanting part of the service in a
> kind of ancient *canto firmo*, and responses were made by the congregation, in
> a manner that resembled the *hum of bees*.

Mr. Burney is a knowledgeable musician and professionally perceives the predominant recitative — traditionally termed *nussaḥ* — as a *cantus firmus* of sorts,
though his presupposition that priests are those who lead the service betrays
an unreflective transference of familiar Christian practices onto the unfamiliar
Jewish ones. As for the role of the congregation in this responsorial singing, the
image here is borrowed — twice in the course of the report — from zoology: the
hum of bees.[32] Whether it is more pleasant than Edelmann's cats yowling or
not, it certainly refers to a prevalent quality of the synagogal soundscape — the
simultaneous, heterophonic "chant-mumbling" which, as discussed above, can
sound to the untrained ear like senseless noise. Once the derogative tone infiltrates, the report develops into an elegant travesty:

> After this, three of the sweet singers of Israel, which, it seems, are famous
> here, and much attended by Christians as well as Jews, began singing a kind
> of jolly modern melody, sometimes in unison, and sometimes in parts, to a
> kind of *tol de rol*, instead of words, which seemed to me very farcical. One
> of the voices was a falset, more like the upper part of a bad *vox humana* stop
> in an organ than a natural voice. I remember seeing an advertisement in an
> English newspaper, of a barber, who undertook to dress hair in such a manner
> as exactly to resemble a peruke; and this singer might equally boast of having
> the art, not of singing like a human creature, but of making his voice like a
> very bad imitation of one. Of much the same kind is the merit of such singers,
> who, in execution, degrade the voice into a flute or fiddle, forgetting that they
> should not receive law from instruments, but give instruments law.

This description is rich in impressions. First, it notes an important sociological fact: at that time Jewish musicians were already well-known for their capabilities and were not only regarded by Christian society as ethnographic objects of curiosity but were also employed as singers.[33] This partly accounts for the fact that "jolly modern melodies" also find their way into the synagogue (though criticized by rabbis over the centuries, this practice become at that time even more widespread);[34] it also sensitizes the reader to the fact that harmony, in its technical meaning, has similarly become part of the synagogal soundscape. This could reverberate from part-music[35] performed in the nearby Portuguese synagogue on special occasions.[36] The *tol de rol* technique brings another element to the report: the singing of nonsense syllables that seems strange to Christian but not to Jewish ears, which later became even more prominent, with the increasing influence of Hasidic music. Burney then introduces the reader to another practice—a rather ubiquitous one, at the time, that of the *meshorerim* (singers)[37]—young apprentices (one singing falsetto, one bass) studying to be cantors and practicing in the services, enriching the auditory space through response and accompaniment. An evidence of these practices can be traced in Idelsohn's *Thesaurus*, vol. 6, which contains selections of tunes from cantors' manuscripts (see music example ex. 3.1).[38]

Burney rightly perceives this accompaniment in terms of imitations of musical instruments. Indeed, the popularity of the technique of vocal imitation of instruments seems to increase over the course of the following century due to the famous (east European) cantor (Hirsch Weintraub of Berlin, 1811–82), who cultivated the tradition.[39] The fact that it sounds farcical to Burney bespeaks a gap, in this regard, between ecclesiastic and synagogal decorum. (The origin of this cantorial technique may be ascribed to the prohibition, in Jewish rituals, to repeat or add words in sanctioned prayer, thus resolving melismas through nonsemantic utterances.) This difference is highlighted against the backdrop of his preceding visit to the New Church in Amsterdam where a "real" *vox humana* in the organ of that church, Burney tells his readers, "has been so much celebrated by travelers that I determined not to quit Amsterdam without hearing it."[40]

Indeed, as he says, prevailing aesthetics allow, even recommend, the imitation of vocal music instrumentally (as illustrated by the *cantabile* instruction) but not vice versa, certainly not the imitation of an instrument imitating a voice. (Obviously this is historically wrong, as Burney himself must have known, for coloratura arias of the eighteenth century imitated to a large extent instrumental idioms, especially of strings.) Referring to the New Church, Burney reports that not only is its chorus a "very noble one," but the *vox humana* of its organ "is one of the best stops, of that kind, which [he has] ever heard."

Ex. 3.1. A Kaddish, from Scholom Friede's manuscript, Idelsohn, *Thesaurus* vol. 6.

Beyond technicalities and decorum, two important aesthetic categories are introduced by Burney. The first relates to the epigonic nature of Jewish music permeating other forms of Jewish creativity—(a theme that will be repeated in the following century), the second addresses the proper aesthetic order, which should proceed from the natural (voice in this case) to the more artificial (instrument). This category, strongly advocated by music theorists at least since the Renaissance, is, according to this eminent historian of music, violated in the synagogue. While acknowledging the Jews' ingression into a shared musical space, Burney's text sensitizes its readers to their confusion of its prime categories and orders. Music, it insinuates, does not suit the Jews "naturally" and "harmoniously." This becomes even more explicit in the following paragraph (italics added):

> The second of these voices was a *very vulgar tenor*, and the third a *baritono*. The last imitated, in this accompaniment of the falset, a *bad bassoon*; sometimes continued on one note as a drone base, at others, divided it into triplets, and semiquavers, iterated on the same tone. But though the tone of the falset was *very disagreeable*, and he forced his voice very frequently in an *outrageous manner*, yet this man had certainly heard good music and good singing. He had a facility of running divisions,[41] and now and then mixed them with passages of taste, which were far superior to the rest. At the end of each strain, the whole congregation set up such a kind of cry, *as a pack of hounds when a fox breaks cover*. It was a *confused clamour*, and *riotous noise*, more than song or prayer.

It is this improper mixture of the ordered with the disordered that seems to draw this congregation back into their bad noisy habits—the images of which are again borrowed from zoological sources, bespeaking ferocity and foreshadowing alarming political undertones ("confused clamour," "riotous noise"). But precisely here, as if feeling the political incorrectness of the last sentences, enters Burney the polite, enlightened musician, speaking, like his German counterpart, in the tones of cultural relativism:

> However, this is a description, not a censure, of Hebrew music, in religious ceremonies. It is impossible for me to divine what ideas the Jews themselves annex to these *vociferations*. I shall, therefore, neither pronounce it to be good or bad in itself, I shall only say, that this is very unlike what we Christians are used to in divine service.

While I cannot vouch for Burney's sincerity, his retraction should be considered as a manifestation of an increasingly tolerant cultural-ethnographic atmosphere in which Christian European practices will still, and for a period to come, count as having the upper hand, but which will make more room for the music of the Other.[42]

The lithograph of the synagogue in Nancy (fig. 3.4a) seems to belong to the same ethnographic genre—in this case embodied visually. It is clear that the ethnographer is again an outsider. Though he aims to render a faithful

Fig. 3.4a. Interior of Nancy Synagogue, lithograph, 1810.
Courtesy of the Jewish Museum, London.

Fig. 3.4b. Interior of Nancy Synagogue
(detail). Cantor following "a score." The
young men surrounding him could be
his *meshorerim*. Courtesy of the
Jewish Museum, London.

Fig. 3.4c. Interior of
Nancy Synagogue
(detail). Faces in the act
of responsorial prayer.
The one in the right
corner bears a rather
sober "Rembrandtian"
countenance.
Courtesy of the Jewish
Museum, London.

depiction of the scene, this anonymous lithographer makes no effort to evoke sympathetic feeling toward the praying congregation. (If the synagogue is the new one of 1790, which was a rather spacious one, why are they so crammed?) Only men are standing in the rather crowded front. Some wear fashionable top hats, some oriental turbans, one, at least, is dressed as a soldier; the women are standing behind the barrier. The scene certainly depicts a holiday service, maybe Shavuot (parallel to Pentecost, the holiday honoring the giving of the Torah) as the synagogue seems to be adorned with special garlands. There are two hazzanim; their simultaneity is unwarranted, as is the coexistence of other illustrated occurrences—the opened Torah or a Megillah scroll, carelessly unfolding beyond the stand in front of one hazzan, falling in elegant flourishes almost to the floor, in a manner unthinkable under most circumstances. The second hazzan, apparently reciting from a book, is standing in front of a table on which a seven-branched candelabrum or menorah[43] is placed; a closer inspection of the book reveals that it may be a musical score (see fig. 3.4b), again highly improbable.[44] The two hazzanim are wearing *tallitot*, but no other man seems to be wearing one, which is also quite unusual (it could be a night service, but then no scroll is removed, except on Simchat Torah's night, or indeed on Purim). The congregation seems to be engaged in a responsorial gesture, with many of the facial expressions distorted due to the vocal act involved (see fig. 3.4c).[45] Concomitantly, the merger in this image of hats, head coverings, and their like, of "ancient Jews" from the classical period with modern Jews, heralds the new, ambivalent fascination for the exotic among foreign listeners and onlookers.

My emphasis on the outsider's alienated gaze disclosed by this picture may be exaggerated, for acculturated Jews will soon find themselves outsiders estranged from forms of worship of their own brethren, which they will find obsolete and unedifying.

VOICES FROM INSIDE: HEYMANN STEINTHAL AND LION FEUCHTWANGER

The division between Jews and non-Jews across the aesthetic categorization of Jews as noisy worshippers was never rigid or unchanging. In the course of the nineteenth century, some Gentiles became more sympathetic onlookers (or even participants) of Jewish traditional practices, while many acculturated Jews, ill at ease with their conspicuous cultural and religious heritage, sought to emphasize and even widen the gap between their modern forms of life and that of old-fashioned Jewish custom, increasingly associated with eastern European Jews (*Ostjuden*).

The picturesque and moving "autoethnography" (as Mary Louise Pratt terms this genre)[46] by the Jewish scholar Heymann Steinthal (1823–1899), referring to synagogal practices in Saxe-Anhalt in the early nineteenth century, accentuates what seems as a self-evident correlation between the observer's positioning (inside or outside) and the appraisal of the action depicted (benevolent or malevolent). Of his rich report I quote here the section portraying "Tishe Bow" (Tish'a' beʿAv) service—the evening on which Edelmann's visit may have taken place[47]—which Steinthal juxtaposes to Yom Kippur as a day in which all the glory associated with the latter "sinks into dust":

> Obwohl ein Hochsommerabend, war es doch in der Synagoge, wenn man eintrat, schon dunkel. Kein Kronenleuchter brannte, nur ein einziges Licht war angezündet auf dem Omed, dem Pulte des Vorbeters, wo doch sonst immer zwei Kerzen leuchteten. Ich sah den Chason ohne den gewohnten Gebet-Mantel (Tallis), ganz geräuschlos, in Filzschuhen, wie auch wir andern entweder in Filzschuhen oder in Strümpfen standen. . . . Ganz leise, stimmlos, begann er: borchu; und wie schaurig war es, wenn in dem hohen dunklen Raume, die Gemeinde dumpf murmelnd antwortete: boruch.[48]

> [Though a midsummer evening, it was already dark in the synagogue when one entered. No chandelier was lit, and only a single light had been kindled on the *Omed*, the prayer leader's lectern, where otherwise there always were two candles shining. I saw the hazzan, without the usual prayer shawl (tallit), utterly quiet, in felt shoes, just as we others were standing either in felt shoes or in our socks. Very softly, voicelessly, he began: *borchu*; and how eerie it was, when in the high, dark room the congregation replied in a muffled murmur: *boruch*][49]

He then describes the reading of Lamentations (*Eicha*), in small groups seated on the floor or on upside-down benches in front of a curtainless ark, that suffused the young boy with the poignant feeling of loss that the memory of the destruction of the Temple has evoked for millennia. Certainly, narrated from a distance (the text was written in old age), this text can be read as a highly romanticized, or at least nostalgic, description. And yet it not only adequately reflects prevalent liturgical customs, but clearly bespeaks the power of a deeply rooted tradition, of "long sanctioned forms quick with memories and sentiments that no argument could lay dead," as George Eliot put it,[50] pointing to the sublimity and meaning it carries for its bearers, and its far-reaching consequences for their existential choices.[51] Moreover, Steinthal's report intimates that detached from the "total" musical-religious experience and its embedding cultural system, the ritual beauty and sublimity would have been lost upon the hearer. Does this mean cultural hermeticity? We will come to this query later in this chapter to examine how this kind of experience, once reported, is bound to open itself up from within, acknowledging cultural reciprocity at its very basis.

This reporter, in any case, is highly sensitive to the vocal element and makes an effort throughout to define the experience of his audient youth, as if refuting the kind of accusations Edelmann amassed:

> Der Chason begann das "Eicho" leise in abwechselnd kurzen, schmerzhaft zitternden und langgezogen klagenden Tönen; ausserdem war alles still, was sonst in der Synagoge nicht vorkam.

> [The hazzan began the *Eicha* [Lamentations] softly, alternating between short, painfully trembling notes and long, drawn-out ones; other than that, there was utter silence, which did not usually happen in the synagogue.]

He also distinguishes the kind of bodily movement characteristic of this service, and, instead of ridiculing it, highlights its unique semiotic qualities:

> Der Chason bewegte sonst das ganze Jahr hindurch beim Gebet den Oberkörper langsam nach vorn und unten; heute aber gingen die Schwing-ungen seitwärts nach rechts und links.

> [Otherwise, throughout the entire year, the hazzan would slowly move his trunk forward and downward; today, however, the swaying went sideways, right and left.]

This, explains Steinthal, expresses an utmost concentration of distress. These accumulated impressions thus conjure in the young boy's imagination the scenes narrated by the Scroll of Lamentations. He could hear the daughter of Zion inexorably "crying in the night" and see "her tears on her cheek," observe her unconsoled, secluded, restless, and helpless—she had sinned! (Lamentations 1:2, 5) He proceeds to describe the increasing amplitude of the cantor's voice as he continues reading and closes with the observation of the particular vocal qualities of the Hebrew words *ach bi*, the guttural sound [ch] (in German phonetics) and then the sharp [i], how they penetrated the heart, concluding with the quote: "Look and see if there is any sorrow like my sorrow."[52]

Over a century later, for Lion Feuchtwanger (1884–1958), author of the historical novel *Jud Süß*, about the eighteenth-century Jewish banker Joseph Süß Oppenheimer (like many other in this history, the son of a renowned cantor), the sounds of lamentation and litanies are far more ambiguous.[53] This ambiguity, it seems, reflects his protagonist's own ambivalence. The Duke of

Würtenberg's treasurer was among the first modern Jews who inhabited both Jewish and non-Jewish worlds, ending his life at the gallows, choosing to die as a Jew rather than convert to Christianity. The audial attention is granted, in this case, to the synagogal "noise" of contemporary Jews attempting to cope with an impending calamity of destruction. Because it reverberates with so many themes discussed in the present and earlier chapters, I quote the description at length here, italicizing words and expressions similar or equivalent to those found in Edelmann's rendering and elsewhere:

> They gathered in their synagogues, *beat their breasts*, acknowledged their sins, fasted on Monday, on Thursday and again on Monday, from sunset to sunset; ate nothing, drank nothing, did not touch their wives. They stood *crammed tight*, in their *evil-smelling synagogues, wrapped in their prayer mantles*, or in their grave clothes, *frantically rocking or groveling*. They *cried* to God, they *cried* to Adonai Elohim with *shrill, despairing voices* which reminded one of the *shrill, discordant sound* of the ram's horn which they blew at the festival of the New Year. They reckoned up their sins, they cried; "Not for our sake, Oh Lord, be gracious to us, not for our sake! But for our forefathers' sake." They reckoned up the endless lists of their predecessors who had been tortured by the Syrians, stretched on the rack by the Romans, slaughtered, strangled, exiled by the Christians, the martyrs from the Polish communities to those of Trier, Speyer, Worms. They stood veiled in their white grave-shrouds, their heads strewn with ashes, all their *limbs jerking ecstatically* until they were exhausted; they *bargained with God, importuned* him with *outcries*, when the day dawned greyly; and when in the melancholy dusk it faded away, they still stood and *cried with their discordant, shrieking voices:* "Remember the covenant with Abraham and the offering of Isaac." But by a hundred ways all *their prayers returned always to the wild, shrill chorus of avowal:* "One and eternal is Adonai Elohim, one and eternal is the God of Israel, the everlasting, the infinite, Jehovah."[54]

An insider, Feuchtwanger knows the *alte Brauch* better than foreign onlookers, most of whom never studied them in detail, nor understood their background and meaning. Feuchtwanger is acquainted with the custom of the triple congregation fast (*ta'anit tsibur*) on consecutive Mondays, Thursdays, and Mondays (on occasions of distress), with the role litanies and lamentations play in the related services, and the central place of recalled martyrdoms used in "bargaining with God." Like Vogel and Heine (see below) he makes the inevitable association of traumatic events (above all, martyrdoms in the time of the Crusades) with the vocal quality of the phenomenon he depicts.[55] The lists he recounts are all typical, as is the description of the "beautiful wives" that "fluttered in

corners, and gazed at their husbands full of trust." This more competent ethnography, while still not precisely evoking sympathy, confers some dignity and
historical depth on a mise en scène that appeared utterly absurd to the (actual)
contemporary Christian traveler (Edelmann).

Interestingly, Feuchtwanger calls the place neither a synagogue nor a *schul*,
using instead the more ecumenical term, already used by the nineteenth-
century reformists, *Betsaal*—a hall of prayer,[56] thus putting it on a par with
parallel houses of prayer, and maybe even echoing a verse from Isaiah 56:7,
central in the High Holidays' prayer: "Even them will I bring to my holy moun-
tain, and make them joyful in my house of prayer; their burnt offerings and
their sacrifices will be accepted on my altar; for my house shall be called a
house of prayer for all peoples." Even then, these *Betsäle* are no better than the
one described by Edelmann and depicted in the lithograph from Nancy: tight-
crammed and even evil-smelling. But here, within the frame of the novel, this
is set within the context of the Jews' political and economic circumstances—as
in their being denied purchasing a better lodging. The choreographic elements
also fall into place. Feuchtwanger not only applies better words to describe what
was mere *Gewackele* (wiggling) for Edelmann—"den Leib fanatisch schaukelnt
und werfend" (frantically rocking and groveling) or "alle Glieder ekstatisch
geschüttelt bis zur Erschöpfung" (all their *limbs jerking ecstatically* until they
were exhausted)—he portrays the entire context, a desperate attempt to change
the wicked edict, for which the Jews can turn only to the divine Ruler, as the
earthly one is of no avail.

The noise is quite terrible. And in the original German it sounds worse than
in the English translation. It begins a page earlier with "Ai" shouts appearing
from within the narrated words themselves. As the description proceeds, they
seem to grow louder and louder, more desperate, importuning, and ecstatic.
Typical is the association of this noise with the discordant, terrifying sound of
the shofar, which recalls not only Rosh Hashanah, but also the revelation on
Mount Sinai, "which sounded louder and louder";[57] similarly, the final, vehement blast refers both to the end of Yom Kippur as well as to the event at Mount
Sinai, with Feuchtwanger's own free theological paraphrase. But Feuchtwanger
does not refrain from dramatizing the discordant vocalities, silenced by the "triumphant procession" of the dominant culture, to paraphrase the famous words
of Feuchtwanger's great contemporary, Walter Benjamin.[58] Handel, as we have
seen above, had already taught Westerners that the shouting of the tortured and
the dejected can be most compellingly set to music, as was probably known to
the musical Feuchtwanger, whose novel was published in the same year that
Alban Berg's *Wozzeck* was premiered.[59]

JEWISH "CONFESSION" PROFESSIONALLY
HARMONIZED: *SCHIR ZION* IN A FOREIGN LAND

We will return to a horrific, uncanny metamorphosis of this scene by the Jews' ultimate detractors—the Nazis—in their version of *Jud Süß*. The reason for introducing a twentieth-century quasi-ethnographic testimony to the discussion at this point is to emphasize the extent of the noise legacy's fluidity, and how deeply and widely the Jewish Reform movement ideology permeated Jewish circles, determining their modes of perception and association with their own vocal and aural heritage. Indeed, the most prominent way to cope with the noise charges that Jews, aspiring to integrate into general European culture, could not have helped but internalize, was to renew the synagogal soundscape and harmonize it in terms of prevalent Christian practices. Change began in Berlin and Hamburg, and Vienna soon followed, albeit differently. In the course of the long process of metamorphosis and transformation, even in its most radical forms, some older musico-liturgical layers were preserved and, even in the most conservative forms of worship, a more musically "harmonized" public ritual was adopted. Jews in growing numbers conceived such transformations as crucial to their self-image and to their image in the eyes of Christians, and as necessary for survival in the face of increasing assimilatory tendencies in their communities.

If I choose to concentrate on the Viennese synagogal scene it is because it enriches our perception of the modern Jewish Viennese authors who struggled with the noise accusation in artistic, scholarly, and psychoanalytic ways (discussed above and in chapter 6). It is also because Vienna became a model, in this sense, for many other Jewish communities in central Europe and beyond. The first call to reform services (*Gottesdienst*) in the newly formed Israelitische Kultusgemeinde Wien (Vienna Israelite Community) employed the following terminology:

Die täglich fühlbar werdende Nothwendigkeit unsere gottesdienstlichen Verrichtungen verständlicher, erbaulicher und mehr dem Zeitgeist gemäß einzurichten, hat bei den Unterzeichneten den Wunsch erregt, den zu Berlin und Hamburg mit so günstigem Erfolg enstandenen israelitischen neuen Kultus nachzuahmen, und auch hier in der k.k. Residenzstadt Wien einen ähnlichen Gottesdienst einzuführen, wo das höchste Wesen auf eine, den Geist und das Gemüth mehr ansprechende Weise angebetet wird.

[The daily-felt necessity to render our service functions more intelligible, edifying and fitting the spirit of our time, has evoked in the undersigned the wish to imitate the Israelite ritual[60] that was newly formed in Berlin and Hamburg with such auspicious success, and to introduce also here, in the city of the imperial-royal seat, Vienna, a similar service, through which a praying mode more suitable for the spirit and the emotions will be offered.][61]

The subsequent detailed proposal that discusses, among other matters, the introduction of sermons in the German language and the translation into German of some of the prayers, contains also the clear requirement to have the service musically shaped by professionals in order to improve the mode of performance as well as its musical contents. It is in the context of this scheme that the young cantor and musician from Hohenems (a small Austrian town on the Swiss border), Salomon Sulzer (1804–1890), was hired in 1826 to officiate in this old-new role in the evolving Viennese community.[62] Sulzer held this post throughout his long life, becoming a model for the renewal of synagogal service in central Europe and beyond (including America and Odessa) through his extraordinary singing, admirable compositions, professional choir training, pedagogical skills, and compelling personality.

Interestingly, Sulzer, arguing for the importance of preserving the community undivided, restrained his colleague, the "preacher" Isaac Noah Mannheimer (the state authorities did not allow the community to hire a rabbi), who wished to reform the service more radically. Thus women, for whom a beautiful gallery was built, continued to be separated from the men, and most of the prayers were in Hebrew. But the service was shortened by removing many of the older *piyyutim*, leaving only the most liturgically (and musically) important ones, such as the *Tal*, *Geshem* (recited respectively on Passover and on Shmini Atseret), and the *Ne'ilah* (the final Yom Kippur prayer). While the introduction of an organ was suggested and vetoed,[63] a high-level choir of men and boys was established and trained.

At the same time, members of the congregation were forbidden to interact with the cantor vocally (through intonation, anticipation, and the like), or to sway during prayer or shake their bodies. Also, the noisemaking in response to pronouncing Haman's name during the reading of the Esther Scroll on Purim was considerably limited. This compromise was regarded as a thoughtful and workable balance between maintaining traditions while removing many of the causes for the repeated complaints against the Jewish house of prayer. With the exquisite range of Sulzer's baritone voice, his cultured yet emotional singing, and his admirable choir, it is no wonder that the Viennese synagogue became an outstanding musical attraction of Vienna at the time.[64]

Here, as throughout Germany, the general endeavor to renew the Jewish service was endorsed by state authorities—whom the reformists in Vienna, among others, were eager to satisfy,[65] as indicated by the subsidized nineteenth- and twentieth-century Jewish seminaries for training—according to partially standardized public (ecumenical) criteria: *Kantor-Lehrer*.[66] This development was probably associated with contemporary ethnologic awareness and the desire to control indigenous customs within a general, more pluralistic devotional framework.[67] Questions regarding precise changes in the Jewish service in the move towards Reform, in what ways, how far, and how deeply it spread, whether it changed the Jews' self-image and their image in the eyes of others, and what consequent relations developed between Western and Eastern Ashkenazi Jews, are beyond the scope of this study. My concern here is with Jewish noise, both alleged and figurative, and with understanding the underlying aesthetic-theological values that were enlisted in response to its "resurgence." Two short musical examples can, perhaps, provide a taste of this musical transformation, and may throw some light on the enthusiastic reception of Sulzer's music by both Jews and non-Jews. The underlying source of the widespread belief, expressed by Friedrich Uhlin (1866), that Sulzer's songs, like the famous "words of Lessing's Nathan," were so conducive to creating "proselytes for the legacy of humanity" and a "tolerant brotherhood" among Jews and Christians in Vienna lies, in the final analysis, in the music itself.[68]

The two examples belong liturgically to the heart of the polemic between Jews and Christians concerning the compassion of the Hebrew Bible ("Old Testament") God and His intimate relations with the Jewish congregation, as it seeks forgiveness and acceptance. Both are borrowed from Sulzer's *Schir Zion* 1 (1840), his first collection of synagogal compositions.[69] While also comprising music commissioned from other composers, Jews and non-Jews, the collection attests to the young composer-performer's attempt to forge a musical idiom enriched by prevalent musical styles, in a striving to achieve "decorum"—the dignified, solemn style so desired by these "new" Jews. By the same token, it aspired to cater to the ascending Jewish bourgeoisie, now exposed to a variety of musical experiences in the city, while preserving the expressive, and, to a certain extent authentic, core of Jewish music.

The first musical example, "Adonai, Adonai" (ex. 3.2), is the Thirteen Divine Attributes of God, proclaimed at the opening of the Ark on festival days; the second is the introduction to the Yom Kippur "Confessions" (*viduyyim*) sung by the community, or its representatives, in the first-person plural.

The piece opens with the choir, followed by a recitative by the cantor.[70] Set in a madrigal-like texture, Sulzer—a friend of Franz Schubert[71]—has it delicately oscillate between the major (B-flat) and its relative minor (G) through light chromatic steps (mm. 3–6, with the augmented sixth, "Italian" chord on

Ex. 3.2. Sulzer, *Schir Zion* I, 214, "Adonai, Adonai."

E-flat, connoting a Phrygian "Jewish" element) reinforcing the major as the recitation of God's merciful qualities proceeds, ending in a choral declaration: "nose owôn wofescha w'chatto-oh w'nakke" (forgiving iniquity and transgression and sin). While the community progresses towards the brighter realm of the major (a synecdoche for the increasing presence of the major mode in the "new" synagogal music over the course of the century), its emissary, the individual cantor, remains in the grimmer precincts of the minor, giving voice, in the following recitative (after the double bar line), to an imploring, entreating vein, long associated with the agony of Ashkenazi synagogal music (sometimes referred to as the "lachrymose" element).

At the same time, the piece draws on prevalent classical musical coinage correlating with lament and sadness, such as the cantor's descending melodic line on "el rachum w'chanun" (God merciful and gracious)[72] and the bold arpeggio, tonicizing the fifth degree in minor,[73] on "nôzer chesed lo^{a}lofim," sensitive to the words' meaning—keeping steadfast grace for thousands—retreating immediately, again through the poignant E-flat (functioning both as the lowered second of D, in line with the "exotic" Phrygian mode, and as a melodic shift back into the tonic). The stepwise progress down to the finale, through typical embellishments, concludes this recitative with a "succumbing to the verdict" (*kabbalat ha-din*) or "remembering the Jewish tragedy"—the "horrific *Judenschmerz*" gesture associated with the enormous pain bequeathed by Jews from one generation to another, as Ludwig Börne (born Juda Löw Baruch, 1786–1837) put it.[74] This recitative, however, remains isolated—the chorale closes it again with its more optimistic, contemporary mood, which could have been experienced, at the time, by those entertaining the renewed service, as marking a new orientation in Jewish rites and life: an A B A form, in which the exilic element is framed by a better past and future Jewish existence.[75]

The musical craftsmanship of "Ono Towo"[76] (ex. 3.3), whose three-part texture brings to ear the hazzan–bass singer (the *meshorerim*) tradition, consists of a gentle interweaving of the accompanying voices with a melody that aspires to extricate itself from the gloomy A minor through majorization and a two-step "diesic" (*dur*, in the German musical jargon) progress up the cycle of fifths.[77] Four measures before the end it alights at a poignant shift on *nu* of *^{a}nachnu* (we)—on the sixth degree of the original minor key (identical to a deceptive cadence progress) that leads, with a twist, the soaring towards a brighter horizon, back into the tragic, albeit solemn, tonal center.

This harmonic progression thus symbolically implies that dissonance is created not by tonal aberration but rather by the "back to normal" progression to

Ex. 3.3. Sulzer, *Schir Zion* I, 421, "Ono Towo."

which Jews were accustomed, as for example, in the way they returned to their hard labor and lot at the end of the Shabbat.[78] The melody, based on a motif in the class called by Tarsi "cross-repertory motifs" of Jewish Ashkenazi music[79] is symmetrically configured, creating a [4 + 4] + [4 + 4 + 2 + 2] phrase structure intensified through rhythmic acceleration and an upward sequence progression. The second, longer phrase (starting at the end of m. 8) creates a musical equivalent of the counterfactual utterance carried by the repenting congregation (". . . that we are not audacious and obstinate to say to you, our Lord and the Lord of our Fathers, we are just, and have never sinned"), bringing, in the last three measures (after the crisis in 17–18), to the inevitable factual confession "but we have sinned," a condensed musical gesture the contour of which enfolds the archlike melodic shape of the three preceding phrases. Piety, devotion, beauty, solemnity—and, above all, decorum. Synagogal music after Sulzer, enriched by the significant contributions of Louis Lewandowski, Emanuel Kirchner, Edward Birenbaum, and many others, was believed to have been redeemed from its shameful noisy environment—and integrated into its auditory present, with the wish to "renew its days as in the (old, glorified) past," a past believed to have preceded the fall into "noisy" existence.[80]

HEINE'S WHIMPERING KETTLE

Heinrich Heine (1797–1856), Sulzer's contemporary, seems not to have approved of these changes in synagogue prayer. Expressing serious reservations about attempts to "Christianize" the ancient Jewish service, he was even more critical of what he deemed as Felix Mendelssohn's direct submission and capitulation to the Lutheran harmonic deity.[81] Although a Protestant convert since 1825, the already famous author of the *Buch der Lieder* was active for a while in the kernel group of a few young Jews who undertook to renew Jewish life and lore—the founders of the *Wissenschaft des Judentums*.[82] He was not insensitive to the noise charge against Jews and their synagogues. The position he opted for in this and similar matters was rather dialectical; viewed in terms of "Jew as pariah," as Hannah Arendt suggested (an existential position she juxtaposes to the "Jew as parvenu"), Heine serves as a prime example of those "who have had practical experience of just how ambiguous is the freedom which emancipation has ensured, and how treacherous the promise of equality which assimilation has held out." Moreover, he was part of a group of contemporary "bold spirits" of Jewish decadence that "[i]n their own position as social outcasts . . . reflect[ed] the political status of their entire people."[83]

Discussing his case, the literary examples Arendt chose for proving her points concern music, or, more precisely, the vocal and auditory aspects of Jewish diasporic-exilic existence. (She does not seem cognizant of this choice.) Inevitably, such vocal diasporic existence, whatever its fictional temporal setting, involves ethnographic elements that are transfigured into the appropriate poetic-literary domain. Among the examples that Arendt mentions and briefly discusses are the poem "The God Apollo" and sections from the *Hebrew Melodies* (part of the *Romancero*), which I analyze below in some detail. Instructively, Heine's misgivings concerning renewed synagogal music were later expressed by the devotees of "authentic" Jewish music, among them the founding father of Jewish music ethnography, Abraham Zvi Idelsohn.[84] Heine, however, sensed the treachery and danger of romantic adoration of the indigenous folk element. This is manifest in his complicated reaction to the Grimm Brothers' enterprise, as Elliott Schreiber has shown.[85]

The poem stages many of the "ethnographic" ingredients described above, most ironically, through a reversal of a core Germanic figure: the Lorelei (mentioned in chapter 1), whom the poet had acerbically eternalized twenty-seven years earlier in "Ich weiß nicht, was soll es bedeuten / Daß ich so traurig bin" (I do not know why I should be so sad), a poem in which he tells the story of the vindictive siren who sits on a cliff above the Rhine with her lyre, and musically tempts passing boatmen who, mesmerized by her music, are shipwrecked and killed on the rocks below. Now Lorelei is transfigured, becoming the object of others' actions. Again, sitting on a cliff above the Rhine, she is a pious nun who, *listening* to a passing boatman, is enchanted by him, though still clinging to her cross. He is a beautiful blond Apollo, himself engaged in singing, surrounded by *neun marmorschöne Weiber* (nine beautiful as marble women, like the nine muses in the famous fresco by Raphael), as the narrator of this modern fairy tale reveals to us:

Der Goldgelockte lieblich singt   [Sweetly he of the golden hair
Und spielt dazu die Leier;   Sings and sweeps the lyre;
Ins Herz der armen Nonne dringt   Into her heart the lilting air
Das Lied und brennt wie Feuer.   Pierces and burns like fire.
Sie schlägt ein Kreuz, und noch einmal   She crosses herself, and yet again
Schlägt sie ein Kreuz, die Nonne;   She crosses herself, poor sister;
Nicht scheucht das Kreuz die süße Qual,   Her heart's entwined in sweetest pain,
Nicht bannt es die bittre Wonne.   Torments of rapture entwist her.][86]

And then his voice is heard, first person (reminiscent of well-known operatic characters[87] and other musical and literary personae), performing as if within a fitting mythological surrounding:

Ich bin der Gott der Musika,	[I am the god of music, I,
Verehrt in allen Landen;	Beloved by lads and lasses,
Mein Tempel hat in Grächia,	My temple under the Grecian sky
Auf Mont-Parnaß gestanden.	Stood on Mount Parnassus.
Vokalisierend saßen da	My daughters round about would lie
Um mich herum die Töchter,	Singing songs and chaffing,
Da sang und klang la-la, la-la!	Sigh, and cry Heigh hi, heigh hi!
Geplauder und Gelächter.	All chattering and laughing.
Mitunter rief tra-ra, tra-ra!	Sometimes we heard Tu-ru, tu-ri!
Ein Waldhorn—-aus dem Holze;	And from the trees saw glisten
Dort jagte Artemisia,	A hunting-horn, and we would spy
Mein Schwesterlein, die Stolze.	Artemis, my proud sister.]

Thus seduced, the *arme Nonne* must leave her secluded cliff and, masked and muffled, seek this chanting and enchanting god on the Rhine. Nobody knows who he is or where he stays. Like the Shulamite in the Song of Songs, she is ridiculed by some passengers, pitied by others, until she arrives in Amsterdam where she meets an old, ragged man, "counting on his fingers as if reckoning" and singing a "nasal ditty." Have you seen him—she asks him again—"he wears a scarlet mantle [recalling Jesus]; sweet he sings, and plays the lyre, and he is my darling idol."

The old man replies, disclosing, through the German, his indigenous Jewish accent:

Ob ich ihn gesehen habe?	[Have I seen him? What a question!
Ja, ich habe ihn gesehen,	Sure I've seen him, seen him often.
Oft genug zu Amsterdam,	Why, it was at Amsterdam,
In der deutschen Synagoge.	In the German synagogue.
Denn-er-war Vorsänger dorten,	There he was my leading cantor,
Und da hieß er Rabbi Faibisch,	And was known as Rabbi Faibisch,
Was au Hochdeutsch heißt:	Which means Phoebus [Apollo]
Apollo—	in High German—
Doch mein Abgott ist er nicht.	But he's certainly not my idol.
. . .	
Seinen Vater Moses Jitscher	I'm a good friend of his father,
Kenn ich gut. Vorhautabschneider	Moses Yitscher—circumciser

Ist er bei den Portugiesen.
Er beschnitt auch Souveräne.

For the Portuguese, and also
Just as good at clipping sovereigns.

Seine Mutter ist Cousine
Meines Schwagers, und sie handel
Auf der Gracht mit sauern Gurken
Und mit abgelebten Hosen.

His old mother is a cousin
Of my brother-in-law; she deals in
Sour pickles at the market
And in second-hand old trousers.

Haben kein Pläsier am Sohne.
Dieser spielt sehr gut die Leier,
Aber leider noch viel besser
Spielt er oft Tarock und L'hombre.

But their son is no great comfort.
Sure, he plays the lyre with feeling,
But, alas, he's even better
With the omber card or tarots.

Auch ein Freigeist ist er, aß
Schweinefleisch, verlor sein Amt,
Und er zog herum im Lande
Mit geschminkten Komödianten.

And he's one of those freethinkers-
Gobbled pork, and lost his post,
And he knocked about the country,
With a bunch of painted players.

In den Buden, auf den Märkten,
Spielte er den Pickelhering,
Holofernes, König David,
Diesen mit dem besten Beifall.

In the stalls and at the markets
He played clowns and merry-andrews,
Holofernes, and King David—
It's the last got most applauded.

Denn des Königs eigne Lieder;
Sang er in des Königs eigner
Muttersprache, tremulierend
In des Nigens alter Weise.[88]

For he sang the psalms of David
In the king's own mother language
With the tremolando quavers
Of the *niggun's* old tradition.]

And the poem goes on to explain the dubious origin of his accompanying girls—the "marble muses"—in a manner reminiscent of various anti-Semitic publications, as in the "Going to Sin-agog" caricature (fig. 3.5).

Heine's cross-textual plot is performed on various ethno-literary levels: names are exchanged and blurred (Faibisch/Phoebus); roles are crossed over—man and woman, holy and profane, bathos (farcical musical noise) becomes pathos (song of a classical god) and reverts to a low bathetic rank (the music of the *Komödianten*, in which Jews were active, as fig. 3.6 demonstrates).[89] Musical techniques—what Burney called "a kind of *tol de rol*, instead of words," which seemed to Burney "very farcical," here signify idyllic, pastoral music. The admired object (the fake god) is literally demythologized only to be finally placed in a no less glorified mythological environment, his original one: that of King David, with his ancient Hebrew *niggun* (spelled here *nigen*).[90] It is this *Nigen alter Weise*, we finally learn, that is the secret of the lad's affective powers,

Fig. 3.5. "Going to Sin-agog! Or Solomon in his Glory!!" From J. L. Marks, *Marks' Caricatures*, no. 52, London, c. 1820. Engraving, hand colored with watercolor. Courtesy of The Library of The Jewish Theological Seminary, New York. The cartoon shows a stereotyped Jew ("Jewish" nose, thick lips, long beard, and a coarse, dark countenance, wearing a variation on the medieval triangular Jewish hat and a kaftan (coat), with two moneybags protruding from his pockets, going from synagogue (in the background) to "Sin-agog," to prostitution. The bubble above him represents him as saying (or rather *mauchel*ing) "Pless min heart vot a pargain"; beneath the rouged lady is a sign, "Lodgings to let," suggesting that even if the lady is no harlot, Solomon will treat her as such.

Fig. 3.6. Jewish *Komödianten* at the Canstatt folk festival. Lithograph,
1835 (Archive Dr. N. Gidal). This traditional (and still flourishing) festival
was one of many folk festivals that played a crucial role in creating
nationalist orientation in nineteenth-century Germany, according to
historian George L. Mosse. The bathetic appearance of Jews
in this image is noteworthy.

however dubiously he has disengaged it from its natural mooring. The dynamics of displacement, misplacement, and replacement is central to this ballad, stemming from Faibisch's promiscuous behavior which, like his music, is contagious. It blurs social boundaries, breaks entrenched identities, discombobulates emotions, and shakes established norms.[91] In addition to all this, the ragged old Jew hints to another important sociological fact: the parents' trades—a circumciser father and a *schmates* dealer mother—point to the eastern European origin of this enchanting Jewish performer, held in ambivalence by western European Jews.

Dressing up a Jewish *niggun* as a classical ballad calls attention to the role of ideology and social atmosphere in designating or possessing melody. Within an exotic, that is, ethnologically open framework, the formerly noisy Jewish elements sound attractive as the early nineteenth-century English caricature "A Visit to the Synagogue" shows (fig. 3.7).[92] The status that Sulzer and his synagogue gained in the course of the century owes to a similar approach. The harmonization of the service renders the music more tantalizing to Gentile ears, themselves perceiving the renewed synagogal soundscape as genuinely

Fig. 3.7. "A Visit to the Synagogue," possibly by Rowlandson (1809). Hand colored
engraving. Courtesy of the Jewish Museum, London. The Dukes of Cumberland,
Sussex, and Cambridge (with dummy heads marked "Cumberland lead, Cambridge
butter ("buttur"), and Suffolk cheese), make a clandestine visit to the synagogue,
dressed à la mode, hats in hand. They are greeted—"Welcome, thrice Welcome
Bretheren to the Synagogue"–by five Jewish figures, headed by the chief rabbi of the
Great Synagogue in London, Solomon Hirschel (1761–1842). They are stereotypically
depicted, with kaftans, beards, hooked noses, and bulging eyeballs, giving them a look
at once fierce and terrified, but without skullcaps, which is historically unwarranted
and incompatible with the rabbi's portrait at the National Portrait Gallery.

authentic, as is evident in this description by Franz Liszt, otherwise known for
his rather anti-Semitic views:

> Only once we witnessed what a really Judaic art could be, as the Israel-
> ites would have poured out their suppressed passions and sentiments, and
> revealed the glow of their fire in the noble art forms of the Asiatic Genius, in
> its full majesty and fantasy and dreams. . . . In Vienna we heard the famous
> Sulzer, who served in the capacity of leading-cantor . . . in the synagogue. . . .
> For moments we could penetrate into his real soul and recognize the secret
> doctrines of the fathers. . . . Seldom were we so deeply moved by emotion as
> on that evening, so shaken that our soul was entirely seized by meditation and
> given to participation in the service.[93]

Seeking the exotic and the authentic element, hailing the unique and the indigenous, breed, in turn, antagonistic exclusions. As in the case of the Brothers Grimm, and later in that of Wagner, such a search leads to rejecting otherness in the name of an undefiled pure substance.[94] Such a rejection, within a sonic universe which, for all intents and purposes, was permeated by the foreign and permeating into it, was inevitably a phantasmagoric vision, as the Nazi case would clearly demonstrate (see chapter 7). Old anxieties, mixed with contemporary ones concerning cultural singularity and belonging, both aggravated the old noise accusation and modernized it.

Heine seemed to foresee it all when in the *Rabbi of Bacharach* he poetically insists that all folk traditions are syncretic and no lore is kept solely for its appointed, or self-appointed, holders. An anthropological truism, this recognition prematurely dawned upon Heine, who concomitantly acknowledged the less obvious notion that cultural mixtures known as "traditions" do not become, perforce, arbitrary. The fact that he made this observation in the subliminal universe of sound renders his ideas even more valuable. In his various "essays" on Jewish sound, he sensitizes his readers to the existence of a persistent cultural hard core, on both perceptual and cultural levels, that yet defies pristine and lasting sameness.

Recognitions of this kind call, in turn, for a new set of queries, encompassing semantic, cognitive, historical, aesthetic, as well as psychoanalytic aspects that have been only partially examined as such in cultural configurations of this kind. One may ask, for example, by what process do traditions undergoing change and transformation preserve core elements, and how these are discerned. Why is the "authentic" element—genealogically a fusion—affective for insiders and, albeit differently, for outsiders? To what extent does the process of such inevitable change affect a tradition's meaning and significance? Such questions will engage us below; we should presently return to the Judengasse synagogue in Frankfurt, to an imaginary visit paid there towards the end of the fifteenth century. The fictional visitors are a special kind of outside-insiders: they are the beautiful Sara and her husband, Rabbi Abraham, from Heine's *The Rabbi of Bacharach* fragment, arriving in Frankfurt on Passover day as refugees from Bacharach, fleeing a blood libel unleashed against them in the midst of Seder (related in the story's first chapter (discussed in chapter 4).

As they enter the Jewish lane, the "ethnographer" intervenes in voice and overview: in those days, he tells the readers, the lane was still "new and nice, and lower than now, in which only later the Jews, when they multiplied in Frankfurt and, at the same time, were not allowed to extend the quarter, built there one floor above the other, and crowded like anchovies, crippled in both body and spirit" (for the Frankfurt Judengasse after the demolition of some of these overcrowded houses, see fig. 3.3 above). While echoing the notorious portrayal of Goethe's youthful visits to the Judengasse reported in *Dichtung und Wahrheit*, this rendering is, like Feuchtwanger's account, better histori-cally contextualized than Goethe's impressions,[95] supplying the reader with a narrative sympathetic to the Jews while adhering to a mostly faithful ethno-graphic report. This holds true even when relating Rabbi Abraham's perception of the synagogal voices from afar as "vielen, verworrenen und überaus lauten Stimmen" (the buzz of many loud voices) again—now from the "benevolent" pole—pre-echoing Wagner's description of the synagogal voice that appeared in press ten years later, while granting it a fairer contextualization.

It is against this background that one should read the following description of the synagogal service itself, reflecting turn-of-the-nineteenth-century practices (those familiar to Heine from childhood) or later ones, rather than practices of over three hundred years earlier. Focalized through beautiful Sara (sitting above, in the women's gallery), the narration succeeds in integrating an "objec-tive" description of customs and scenery together with a subjective accompani-ment of feelings and associations, thus rendering it both faithful and sympathy-provoking:

> The walls of the synagogue were uniformly white-washed, and no ornament was to be seen other than the gilded iron grating around the square stage, where extracts from the Law were read, and the holy ark, a costly embossed chest, apparently supported by marble columns with gorgeous capitals, whose flower-and-leaf work shot up in beautiful profusion, and covered with a cur-tain of purple velvet, on which a pious inscription was worked in gold span-gles, pearls, and many colored gems. Here hung the silver memorial-lamp, and there also rose a trellised dais, on whose crossed iron bars were all kinds of sacred utensils, among them the seven-branched candlestick. Before the latter, his countenance toward the ark, stood the leading-cantor, whose song was accompanied, as if instrumentally, by the voices of his two assistants, the bass and the treble. The Jews have banished all instrumental music from their church, maintaining that hymns in praise of God are more edifying when they rise from the warm breast of man, than from the cold pipes of an organ.
>
> Beautiful Sara felt a childish delight when the choir-leader, an admirable tenor, raised his voice and sounded forth the ancient, solemn melodies, which she knew so well, in a fresher loveliness than she had ever dreamed of, while the bass sang in harmony the deep, dark notes, and, in the pauses, the treble's voice trilled sweetly and daintily.
>
> Such singing Beautiful Sara had never heard in the synagogue of Bacha-rach, where the presiding elder, David Levi, was the leader; for when this

elderly, trembling man, with his broken, bleating voice, tried to trill like a young girl, and in his forced effort to do so, shook his limp and drooping arm feverishly, it inspired laughter rather than devotion.[96]

Many of the themes in this description are now familiar to us: unlike Burney, Heine portrays the *meshorerim* technique in more favorable colors, or tones. Unwittingly, he refutes Burney's mockery of the *vox humana* falsetto of the *meshorer* by supplying the reader with a theological-aesthetic reason for the prevalent practice: "The Jews have banished all instrumental music from their church, maintaining that hymns in praise of God are more edifying when they rise from the warm breast of man, than from the cold pipes of an organ." He even echoes, and yet mitigates—through the imaginative listening of sympathetic Sara—motifs from Edelmann's report when describing the ludicrous practice of the elderly cantor in Bacharach. Well-acquainted with the Jewish melodies, we hear, she had, however, never heard an uplifting performance thereof, until that very service in Frankfurt. It is again the combination of "long sanctioned forms quick with memories and sentiments that no argument could lay dead" that transfigures, *through the music,* the entire audiovisual scenery into a sublime spectacle, integrating romantic images of nature, which in the Western tradition have long been associated solely with harmonious church music:

> The choir-leader took the Book, and, as if it really were a child—a child for whom one has greatly suffered, and whom one loves all the more on that account—he rocked it in his arms, skipped about with it here and there, pressed it to his breast, and, thrilled by its holy touch, broke forth into such a devout hymn of praise and thanksgiving, that it seemed to Beautiful Sara as if the pillars under the holy ark began to bloom; and the strange and lovely flowers and leaves on the capitals shot ever higher, the tones of the treble were converted into the notes of the nightingale, the vaulted ceiling of the synagogue resounded with the tremendous tones of the bass singer, while the glory of God shone down from the blue heavens. Yes, it was a beautiful psalm. The congregation sang in chorus the concluding verse, and then the choir-leader walked slowly to the raised platform in the middle of the synagogue bearing the Holy Book, while men and boys crowded about him, eager to kiss its velvet covering, or even to touch it.

The scene portrays the removal of the Torah scroll from the Ark, which is conducted with much solemnity and splendor during Shabbat and festivals. (The "Adonai Adonai" piece of Sulzer, referred to above, is sung at the beginning of this part of the service). Through the Torah scroll, likened to a child lovingly carried by his parent, one is reminded of Sara's deep longing for a child of her own (reminiscent of the biblical Sarah), hinted in the first chapter; this trope intermingles with Sara's childhood imagery of forest and countryside, not different from that of a Christian girl of her fictive time, or perhaps Heine's time.[97] The scenery becomes cosmic, all-inclusive, transcending persecutions and particular sorrows, as well as the specificities of time and place. As Schreiber notes, "the transformation of the cantor's tones into nightingales is reminiscent of "das Übergehen in eine andere Gestalt" that the Grimm Brothers list as one of the principal characteristics of the pantheistic worldview of their *Märchen*.[98]

Transformation, if not transfiguration: while this reinforces the sense of hybridity predominating the experience, it also fits the spirit of Psalms, such as those sung on festivals (the series called *Hallel*, chapters 113–118). Well known to Sara, it is again a psalm that connects religions and beliefs, now, however, in a highly positive way. Unlike the parallel description by Edelmann, the responsorial singing of the congregation here seems to harmoniously complement the psalm. No less interesting are the final lines of the above description, in which Heine—knowingly or by mistake—confused the reading of Rosh Hashanah with that of Passover, including the change of tune, which characterizes the former, and not the latter:

> On the platform, the velvet cover, as well as the wrappings covered with illuminated letters, was removed, and the leading-cantor, in the peculiar intonation which in the Passover service is still more peculiarly modulated, read the edifying narrative of the temptation [trial] of Abraham from the opened parchment-scroll.

His mistake (like other, more famous ones in his Jewish texts) is instructive, for it reflects the conflation of the most emotionally charged moments of the Jewish year. The final trial of Abraham—the sacrifice of Isaac—is the prototype for later Jewish martyrology, especially in medieval times (as noted in chapter 1), exemplified in the case of Heine's Sara and *her* Abraham, associated here with Passover and Easter sacrifices as they were long engraved in the consciousness of Ashkenazi Jews.[99] Typically dreading pathos and self-glorification, the author brings this solemn moment back to the earthly—and ethnographically characteristic—occurrence: the trivial chatting of the women surrounding Sara.

The type of life-in-exile related by the story seems outwardly different from the kind of Jewish life celebrated in *Jehuda ben Halevy*, the second poem (fragment) of Heine's *Hebräische Melodie*. The dreary history of persecution surrounds and imbues *The Rabbi of Bacharach*, whereas *ben Halevy* apparently dwells on the flourishing world of twelfth-century Spanish Jewish-Muslim-Christian semiecumenical culture. A cradle of suffering, sacrifice, and lamentation, the Ashkenaz portrayed in *The Rabbi of Bacharach* finds a more natural affinity with the world depicted in the last poem of the *Hebrew Melodies* cycle—"Disputation." Leading this line of argument, Bluma Goldstein maintains that *Jehuda ben Halevy* dwells on the conceptual difference between exile and diaspora, and that by and large it suggests that "an integrative diasporic life may very well be able to ameliorate or even overcome the grief and paralysis of exilic existence."[100] The unequivocal distinction Goldstein makes between exile and diaspora, especially in this connection, seems to me ideologically biased, overlooking nuance and ambivalence.[101] Not only was Heine well aware of how precarious the situation of a Jew in "liberal" or, for that matter, "diasporic" Europe (or medieval Spain), his perception of the origins of his own poetic inspiration seems to draw here on far more ambiguous sources. Time and again Heine is attracted, especially in relation to the musical, ineffable basis of Jewish creativity and vocality, to precisely what Goldstein calls Jewish "exilic" moments as a source of inspiration and admiration, rather than to "diasporic" ones. *The Rabbi of Bacharach* is one example; another is the opening stanzas' paraphrase of Psalm 137 (quoted in the epigraph to this chapter) that opens the second part of *Jehuda ben Halevy*:

Bei den Wassern Babels saßen	[By the waters of Babylon sat
Wir und weinten, unsre Harfen	We and cried, our harps
Lehnten an den Trauerweiden—	Leaned against the weeping
	willows—
Kennst du noch das alte Lied?	Do you still know the old Song?
Kennst du noch die alte Weise,	Do you still know the old tune,
Die im Anfang so elegisch	Which at the start so elegiacally
Greint und sumset, wie ein Kessel,	Whimpers and hums, like a kettle
Welcher auf dem Herde kocht?	Which is boiling on the hearth?
Lange schon, jahrtausendlange	Long already, millennia long
Kochts in mir. Ein dunkles Wehe!	Has it boiled in me. A dark woe!
Und die Zeit leckt meine Wunde,	And time licks my wound,
Wie der Hund die Schwären Hiobs.	As the dog did Job's ulcers.
Dank dir, Hund, für deinen Speichel-	Thank you, dog, for your spittle—
Doch das kann nur kühlend lindern—	But that can only coolingly
	soothe—
Heilen kann mich nur der Tod,	Only death can heal me,
Aber, ach, ich bin unsterblich!	But, alas, I am immortal!]

By virtue of the powerful use of the deictic "we," the first three lines of this section are inherently equivocal: are we now hearing the original voices of the

"Hebrew Slaves" down in Babylon; is it a quotation of that song or perhaps a modern incarnation of the slaves? The rhetorical question at the end of the first stanza (following a dash suspended after the "weeping willow") indicates that a long time has elapsed since that primordial wailing, and it is not clear whether the old song, *das alte Lied*, is still practiced or even remembered. The rhetorical gesture is typical of a poet known for combining sublime expressions and quasi-colloquial utterances. Echoing the famous "Mignon's Song" by Goethe (and precursor of Wagner's *Tristan*, where the mortally wounded hero indulges in memories, awakened by the old melody of his childhood played by a shepherd), the second stanza begins where the "God Apollo" ended: "Kennst du noch die alte Weise?" And, instead of continuing in the same sublime vein, it turns to a domestic setting, one found later in the "exilic" poems of Chaim Nachman Bialik (1873–1934).[102] It is at this point that the *alte Weise* turns into noise: the elegy whimpers and hums like a kettle boiling on the hearth. The noise is cozy; it has no real melody, and yet it is meaningful to the insiders—the dwellers of the house. A stranger would probably not understand it, especially not its ancient, elegiac layers. Instructively, insiders of Jewish liturgical music in Germany substituted in their terminology *alte Weise* for the (old) Hebraic term, *nussaḥ* (the melodic formulas of the recitative for daily prayers, Shabbat, and the festivals). All three uses of the term—Wagner's, Heine's, and the Jewish cantorial one coalesce in identifying the old tune with existentially significant origins.

The third stanza turns the image upside down. The kettle becomes an insider, *kochts in mir*: it is located within the poet's body—its habitat. Devouring song, noise, and kettle, he also consumes time; *Jahrtausendlange*, embodying an extended oratorical moment issuing in Babylon and winding through a variety of moments he himself has recited or transfigured, including those of Jehuda ben Halevy, Rabbi Abraham from Bacharach, Goethe's traumatized feminine figure, and others. This *alte Weise*, or those *alte Weisen* (there are many of these melodies intoned and intimated in the course of the *Melodies*) are boiling relentlessly inside. It is as if Heine had deeply internalized the broken, nasal, lamenting voice of the old Rabbi Chaim, who he heard with Ludwig Börne in 1827, singing "By the Waters of Babylon" in the Frankfurt Judengasse.[103]

Time thus figured becomes a double-edged entity, at once the medium through which the song is prolonged and exists—the source of the pain and its lingering duration—and concomitantly the rather dubious consoler: the dog that licks the Job-poet's wounds but obviously cannot heal them. (This becoming-animal element is eventually taken up by another famous Jewish writer, as we shall see.) At this point, the millennia-old suffering poet, bearing with him "exilic" rather than "diasporic" stories as his ineluctable curse, transmutes into the *ewige Jude*, into Heine's Flying Dutchman: the accursed seed of Cain, who can never settle down and may only wish for his own death, his own *Untergang*.[104] Possessed by these boiling melodies, the poet still cannot dispose of them; melodies have indeed the cognitive power to obsess one's mind, and sometimes the minds of many. The presence of these melodies, an ever-renewed present tense, does not allow the poet to die, yet won't allow him to rest[105]—the kind of rest he could dream of when still flying, alone or with the "enormously talented" Mendelssohn, on their famous "Wings of Song."[106]

"THEY DEMANDED THE SONG": NATHAN AND BYRON'S "HEBREW MELODIES" COLLABORATION

The "wings of song" have, in the case of Heine's *Hebrew Melodies*, more than one sense. One of the famous inspirations of this cycle is Lord Byron's own *Hebrew Melodies* (1815–16), a work that engages some figures we have already met. Usually the affinity of the two cycles—Byron's and Heine's—is dismissed as external;[107] yet the "Hebrew *melodic*" element they share goes beyond title, general idea, and some common thematic and textual elements. Both are deeply interested in the issue of Jewish noise, self-referentially opening it up to a Christian, though not necessarily supportive audience. Exchanging real melodies and texts of Hebrew/Christian origins, they associate art and ethnography, present with past in a novel way, concurrently problematizing other entrenched dichotomies, above all that of dignity and disdain.[108]

Lord Byron's *Melodies* cycle draws on "sacred biblical models"; it embodies crucial moments in Jewish memory, and is also famous for its "proto-Zionist" orientation. Less known is that the cycle was literally inspired by "Hebrew melodies" of real ethnographic stature, although, to be sure, they were not as ancient as their collector Isaac Nathan (1790?–1864) pronounced them, that is, "upward of 1000 years old and some of them performed by the Ancient Hebrews before the destruction of the temple." A composer, singer, and music theoretician—and, like many of the nineteenth-century protagonists of the present history, the son of a cantor, Menachem Mona—Nathan gathered these melodies from Ashkenazi synagogues in London and Canterbury, supplying, though indirectly, interesting testimony of the musical practices of these synagogues at the time.[109]

Clearly, as Frederick Burwick and Paul Douglass maintain in their excellent introduction to the facsimile edition of the cycle, Nathan was aiming to profit from the stereotypical "wildness and pathos" attributed to the Jews and their music, well aware of the folkloristic trends in vogue in Britain at the time.[110] As an appraiser of Nathan's music put it, the music he presented to the public was sung by the Jews "ere our blessed Lord and Savior came into the world to be the cause of the persecution of these bearded men."[111] This pseudohistorical categorization was a clear attempt to make the music agreeable and accessible to Christian ears, to redeem it from its "perfidious" sound and the discordant noises long associated with Jewish existence. Nathan knew how to cater to his audience beyond antiquarianism; trained in Purcell, Handel, and the Viennese classics and relying on John Braham's bravura mode of performance,[112] he aspired to appeal to the taste of both amateurs and connoisseurs of poetry and music, enlisting for this the collaboration of Byron. The fact that the latter found genuine interest in both Nathan's music and in the ideas related to it should be seen not only against the background of the still prevalent Hebraic trends in England, discussed in the previous chapter, but equally in the context of new national and revolutionary causes associated with Byron's heroic life and death.

The mode of composition the two embarked upon was unique—a two-way process in which Nathan both set preexisting poems by Byron to music and furnished tunes to which Byron composed new poetry.[113] The two consulted each other in the course of working on their joint pieces, and the result of this transactional collaboration in ideas, languages, and media is evident throughout. One cannot overestimate this double gesture of reciprocity. The question of the authenticity of the melodies notwithstanding, what is important in the present context is that along with the contemporary Western musical models adapted by Nathan in these poems, the Jewish materials he used are of real ethnographic standing, and that the great poet was attentive to the undulations of the original text attached to the melodies that Nathan delivered, furnishing them with proper linguistic embodiments.

The melodic source of "Jephtha's Daughter," for example, could indeed be, as Burwick and Douglass claim, that of the Ashkenazi leining (chanting) of the Song of Songs according to the Masoretic *te'amim*, befitting the spirit of joy and courage with which this heroine faced her tragic fate. Other melodic borrowings are even more apparent, such as the late medieval "Maoz Tsur"—the well-known Hanukkah hymn mentioned in chapter 1—for "On Jordan Banks," certain High Holiday tunes (for example, in "The Harp the Monarch Minstrel Swept"), and more.[114] Constraining both composer and lyricist, these tunes color the cycle with an atmosphere and tones that were identified by its original listeners as both exotic and "passionate." Still, by means of its adjustments to the general and familiar European musical language (a process that obviously began long before Nathan's conscious adaptation and harmonization of the melodies), the *Melodies* also became engaging salon music.[115]

There was no antecedent for collaboration on such a scale, and few subsequently made a conscious attempt to reconcile these conflictive traditions.[116] (The authors' aspirations to personal profit is nothing exceptional in general, or in relation to arrangement of "ethnic" material in particular, Haydn and Beethoven included.)[117] This rich harvest of over twenty-four "melodies"— synergetic poetry cum music songs—defined anew the boundaries of Hebraism, or Jewishness, extricating it from previous stereotypical categorizations. Thematically, the songs include the realm of the "aesthetics of the night," sublimely portrayed. This is contrary to the *verdüsterte*, antienlightened imputation of Hebraism on behalf of censurers such as Edelmann.

The *Melodies* highlight the struggle, agony, and dignified bearing of the tragic fates of individuals and groups (Saul, Jephtha's daughter, Jews facing exile and subjugation).[118] They also glorify an ultimate aspiration—usually denied to Jews—to transcendental, immortal being. All of these are of interest to the present discussion; in what follows I will limit myself to a short analysis of two song-poems, "Oh! Weep for Those" and "We Sate Down and Wept," both directly concerned with the music/noise issue in its intersection with the exile-diaspora antinomy. I quote them in full:

Oh! Weep for Those

Oh! weep for those that wept by Babel's stream,
Whose shrines are desolate, whose land a dream;
Weep for the harp of Judah's broken shell;
Mourn—where their God that dwelt the godless dwell!

And where shall Israel lave her bleeding feet?
And when shall Zion's songs again seem sweet?
And Judah's melody once more rejoice
The hearts that leap'd before its heavenly voice?

Tribes of the wandering foot and weary breast,
How shall ye flee away and be at rest!
The wild-dove hath her nest, the fox his cave,
Mankind their country—Israel but the grave!

We Sate Down and Wept

We sate down and wept by the waters
Of Babel, and thought of the day
When our foe, in the hue of his slaughters,

Made Salem's high places his prey;
And ye, oh her desolate daughters!
Were scatter'd all weeping away.

While sadly we gazed on the river
Which roll'd on in freedom below,
They demanded the song: but, oh never
That triumph the stranger shall know!
May this right hand be wither'd for ever,
Ere it string our high harp for the foe!

On the willow that harp is suspended,
Oh, Salem! its sound should be free;
And the hour when thy glories were ended
But left me that token of thee:
And ne'er shall its soft tones be blended
With the voice of the spoiler by me!

Both lamenting the fate of Israel in exile and featuring music as their main theme, subject and object are located along various positions in these two poems. In the first they are distinct; the speaker/addresser is an outsider, speaking to one or more addressees, likewise outsiders, in a hortatory imperative: weep. Raising his voice, he seems to exhort the addressees to join him in mourning, to undertake lamentation that was long borne alone by the object of the lament. In the second poem, subjects and objects are one. The exiles are speaking for themselves, not through reported speech (as in Heine's *Melodie*); they seem to be the original spokespersons of the famous psalm: "We sate down and wept by the waters / Of Babel." Their mourning becomes a song of defiance, the promise and oath of a resisting collective voice drawing on vocal resources as their mainstay of rebellion.

Both poems have indefinite temporal settings. The first is clearly located in a prolonged present (the repeated tense of the first stanza) between past destruction and redemption in an undetermined future (to which the second stanza points), reflecting the agony the song relates. The gloomy ongoing, exilic existence of the agonized tribe to which the third stanza returns us is worse than that of animals and beasts—so the speaker says, and no hint of hope or consolation is granted. The second poem, on the other hand, abruptly modulates from past to future (in the poem's zenith; line 9, after the colon), from lament to song of resistance, implying again an extended, "suspended" present in which nothing takes place ("on the willow the harp is *suspended*") other than the self-referential song itself. The temporal scope in both poems/melodies is thus epic, historically unlimited, thereby inviting the emergence of oratorical moments. Do such moments occur? Should the instance of voicing these laments be so considered? What kind of message did it convey, say, for the British listener addressed by the creators of the poems?

The listener hears the poems musicalized, vocalized. Unwittingly, he or she is exposed to Nathan's unique brew of Jewish and Western musical elements and motifs, including their respective semantic import. Accessible as such to a select few, their general communicative appeal, with its embedded exoticism, could, nevertheless, reach the average contemporary listener. In "Oh weep" the listener could hear them "weep" even before he or she joins the weepers in action (ex. app. 3, piano prelude; see appendix): the first stanza, set to a subdued melody that wanders through repetition, gradually and slightly swells, but to sink again, after a short while, in the basic lamenting notes. It seems, indeed, as the *Jewish Encyclopedia* proposes (based on Francis Cohen's findings), a "clever empirical adaptation of the chant of the Blessing of the Priests"[119] (ex. 3.4). In even fuller form, one finds it in Scholom Friede's Kaddish, probably for the Days of Awe cited above (ex. 3.1). Retaining the solemnity of this melody and its related sublime liturgical moments, the adapted melody intensifies melancholy through its unredeemed expressive gesture, reminiscent, for non-Jews' ears, of a bleak funeral march. The second strophe (ex. app. 3, m. 24) echoes a Passover melody of the *piyyut* "Tsena Urena" (paraphrasing on Song of Songs,

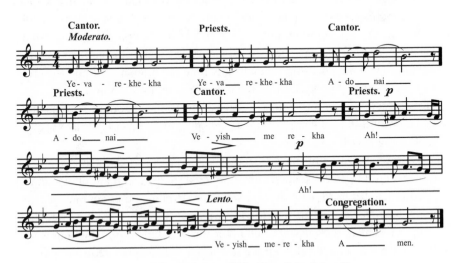

Ex. 3.4. Birkat Kohanim ("Blessing of the Priests"),
Jewish-Polish melody (seventeenth century?).

3:11).[120] Mitigated by major chords, it lilts like a lullaby with sequential repetitions that render it more comforting. Does the melody contradict the "Melody" that bemoans the absence of such pleasant tunes? Or perhaps it gives the taste of that longed-for joyful melody, similar to the original text it venerates, and which the text alludes to and signifies? The third strophe responds to this query in what seems a sinking-back into the previous agony, while utilizing the not over-used augmented-second at that early time (on the words: "foot and weary"; ex. app. 3). Effectively combining motifs from the first and the second strophes, the song ends with a clear lamenting signature, echoed by the piano.

"We sate down and wept" should sound like a heroic hymn throughout. Its melodic elements recall the "Magen Avot" *steiger*—a modal strategy dominating the last section of Friday night service (ex. app. 4). This modal strategy, located in the "minor" realm, includes, as Tarsi shows, distinct musical characteristics of which three conspicuous ones can be identified here: (1) ascending (motion) (fifth) from 1 to 5 (2), leading to a half (melodic) cadence on 5 (here on the word "by," beginning of third system, upper part) to turn (3), on a continuing phrase (here the second phrase) to the parallel major.[121] Together they comprise a tonal-melodic environment not foreign to Western ears, as they converge with a concerto-like gesture of a modulation from G minor to B-flat major. That gesture conveys that the cruel fate "[w]hen our foe, from the hue of his slaughters, / Made Salem's high places his prey" was heroically met.

Shifting back to the minor,[122] the heroic arpeggio now resolves into a musical painting on "were scattered all weeping," leading to a subdued cadence. Other Jewish motifs are hinted at later, adding up to a rather paradoxical statement: "They demanded the song: but, oh never / That triumph the stranger shall know! / May this right hand be wither'd for ever, / Ere it string our high harp for the foe!" Here the poet shifts dramatically from the original psalmodic expression, now connecting the oath to the defiant refusal to play music for the ears of their "captors and tormentors" (which in the biblical context appears only as a mournful state of being), while its melody intones precisely "that song" in such foreign ears!

The last stanza ("On the willow that harp is suspended, / Oh, Salem! its sound should be free") becomes an antiphonal singing, with a hint of another Jewish melody, the "Loeni Yigdal," well-known to the composer, one, according to him, that was adapted to English words for the service of the Protestant church.[123] The melody repeats itself in the next two lines ("And the hour when thy glories were ended / But left me that token of thee") before moving into a series of concluding gestures on "[a]nd ne'er shall its soft tones be blended / With the voice of the spoiler by me!" This oath deconstructs itself while being sung to music that is a hybrid of such tones and voices par excellence. Written for two voices and accompaniment, the melody makes use of the trio sonata texture. Deploying, in line with this genre, a series of echoing responses, it creates an internal sympathetic environment precisely on the harshest words of the poem.

Altogether, this paradoxical, partially unbearable, partially conciliatory state of musical-poetic affairs the song embodies becomes a daring testimony of a special historical moment, enabled by an implicit invitation to outsiders to take part in the internal, agonized experience and momentarily undergo it as their own.

The voices thus blend in varying degrees, depending on the time, the audience, the vocalizer. The story of emancipation and acculturation from and into the surrounding soundscape made this merge inevitable, sometimes profitable, at other times less so, and often highly creative. And while this took place, noise, as concept and reality, became a much wider phenomenon, transcending sectarian exclusions. As for the old "Jewish noise," not a single author, reporter, reformer, or reviewer along the path we have traveled in this chapter heard, reproduced, or transfigured it in the same way as any other. In the matrix proposed at the opening of this chapter, which includes the binaries insider/outsider, real/fictive, benevolent/malevolent, and traditional/transfigured ethnographies, most of the logical combinations it comprises have been virtually realized. If Steinthal's insider, real, traditional, and benevolent testimony is taken, however, as one pole in this matrix, the other pole, combining outsider, fictive, transfigurative, and malevolent "ethnography,"—the Chaucerian story-type that initiated the noise accusation in the Middle Ages—was left mostly vacant, at least for the time being. The happy moment in all of these transactions seems that of Nathan-Byron, for it blurred most of these dichotomies without annihilating affiliations. Like Sulzer and Heine, these authors themselves seem to undergo self-transformations in the course of their creative enterprise, functioning as a possible model for generations to come.

Listeners, for their part, became freer to engage their auditory vantage point in relation to the new (real or imagined) sonic phenomena, whether drawing on an oratorical-moment strategy or a less culturally complicated mode of listening. An ongoing dialogue among Jews and between them and their surrounding sonic cultures characterizes the cases analyzed above. The Jew as an aesthetic category thus gained new qualities, both negative and positive, while the borders between the two became blurred. This phenomenon in itself becomes the source for further anxieties. While Jews began to assess the price of their reforms, the loss of earned vocal traditions that could serve them as resources for configuring their problematized communal belonging, Christians—Germans and otherwise—began to be apprehensive of their vexed worlds, similarly, under the siege of growing secularity and assimilatory processes. Associated with the hegemonic culture, they increasingly recognized unwelcome others as trespassers into their patrimony.

Composers and writers of the stature of Mendelssohn, Meyerbeer, Halévy, and Heine were tacitly or explicitly recognized as such trespassers. Their fictional worlds grapple with their double fate as both inheritors of the noise allegation, and heralds of new sonic environments. The next chapter maneuvers between these poles, in the attempt to deconstruct the ideological and emotional motivations that produced these worlds and sustained them.

4

"JEWS (AND JEWESSES) LIKE YOU AND ME": VOCAL IMAGINARIES OF MENDELSSOHN, MEYERBEER, HEINE, AND HALÉVY

In Germany, France, the Jews are people like you and me; their religion, their customs have been so melted down in the processes of social progress they were part of, that all that renders them [Jewish] has disappeared, except for his commercial competence, his greediness; but his greediness wears yellow gloves, his competence becomes French: he is a poet like Heine, a musician like Meyer-Beer and Halévy, collector like a Fould, generous like Rothschild; whereas from Krakow and onward, the real Talmudists are revealed.

—*Honoré de Balzac*, Letter on Kiev, 1847[1]

THE "GROUP"

Between the generations of Moses and Felix Mendelssohn, Jews from Berlin and westward increasingly attempted to look "like you and me," as Honoré de Balzac (1799–1850) notes in the epigraph quoted above: like modern European citizens. Sensible to minute differences in the gallery of human characters, the arch-portraitist of the *comédie humaine* seems disoriented by the disappearance of external marks of Cain on his fellow Jews.[2] Indeed, that generation of emancipated or partially emancipated Jews[3]—those born, like the renowned Parisian novelist, in the postrevolution decade—had easily shed external signs of their old identity. These included general appearance, clothes, names, religious customs, linguistic forms, and social demeanor. These newly recognized, if not fully legitimized, *Bürger/citoyens* came to realize that they could "adjust to everything" and become "everybody," as Hannah Arendt put it.[4] They seemed now to fit into the noncategory of elusiveness and evasiveness, the very category that, curiously enough, gradually became the ultimate definition of music and all that "aspired to its condition."[5]

As rarely before in European history, Jews achieved the status of "public" musicians, composers, and poets, of authors in their own (modern) right of independent agency, recognized as such by a civil audience. They had been preceded in the previous century by a few Jewish scientists, philosophers, and all but forgotten court-musicians; at the moment referred to by Balzac, Jews had also become bankers, collectors, industrialists, politicians, and critics; some eminent Jews had also become revolutionaries. In these and other professions and vocations associated with the production, accumulation, and redistribution of capital, knowledge, and experience, they—or, at least, the most gifted and fortunate among them—aimed to succeed on a grand and public scale.

Perhaps that ambition was their new distinction; Balzac seems to imply it when he associates their new practices with an old cliché: their greed and avarice. Deep down, he insinuates, they remain the same old Shylockean Jews, though with their new exterior and etiquette it had become harder to discern their essential Jewish identity. No longer "real Talmudists" (aspiring as they did to enlightened *Bildung*) in essence, Balzac tells us, they are still connected to their zealous and bigoted eastern European siblings.[6]

These born-as-Jews "liberated" burghers thwarted such insinuations as far as they could. In their vigorous attempts to integrate into the allegedly egalitarian Gentile society, they staved off associations with a coerced fraternity—those of their people later branded *Ostjuden:* eastern European "ghettoized" Jews who began to flow into western European cities while retaining old "tribal" signs.[7] Suspicious of, if not alien to their blood-brothers and sisters, the Mendelssohns, Halévys, Meyerbeers, and Heines rarely cooperated with or supported each other in their aspiration to success and recognition; envy, rivalry, and even contempt often prevailed.

Relations between Heine and Mendelssohn,[8] Mendelssohn and Meyerbeer,[9] and, to add another example, between Börne and Heine, were all problematic; more generous and mutually appreciative were Meyerbeer and Halévy.[10] Whether it was their problematic relationships that kept them apart or the fact that most of them belonged to different artistic contexts, one seldom finds, even in subsequent scholarship, a discussion linking them beyond some obvious factual historical references.[11]

It is the aim of this chapter to bring them together, to regard them as part of a unique generation exposed to new ideas and modes of thinking that contributed to their further development, and also to show how, in their turn, they contributed to the advancement of innovative cultural and intellectual sets of mind. Obviously, the scope of this chapter is limited and it is to be hoped that more studies will pursue similar directions. The following discussion opens with a short profile of that generation of Jews who sought integration within the range and energies of the moods and modes of thinking that characterized European society. (Moods, in this connection, are understood as publicly related emotional reactions to new social configurations.)[12] Against this backdrop, I will consider a few instances of the imaginary worlds created by these artists in the 1830s and 40s, from the viewpoint of their attempts to undermine prevalent aesthetic categorizations of Jews in terms of dichotomies such as noise-harmony, inclusion-exclusion, compassion-revenge, and originality-mimicry. Additional reasons for choosing the works discussed will become clearer as the chapter unfolds. At this point suffice it to note that all works seem to have been in Wagner's immediate mind when he conceived his *Judentum in der Musik* lampoon, shedding light on some of his deeper presuppositions and motivations.

The four main authors discussed here all flourished already in the 1820s—a generation characterized by a certain sociopolitical profile.[13] The precocious and short-lived Mendelssohn, a decade younger, matched Meyerbeer, Heine, and Halévy in terms of span of creative productivity. The agenda of these artists was complex. They strove to succeed not only on a personal, vocational level—that is, to justify their professional choices to parents and other family members; they also aspired to immediate recognition as first-rate artists, as well as to canonical posterity. In different ways, they aimed to be meaningful and true to self and, concomitantly, to play leading roles in grand artistic as well as sociopolitical or spiritual arenas. All in all, it was far more than the pursuit of worldly success and material profit that steered them as a beacon in their artistic navigations. In their attempts to debunk old prejudices against their tribe and the stereotyped implications, they reflect in part a utopian thrust, in part a revolutionary fervor, while their personalities ranged from devout neoconservative to cynical cultural critic. From the perspective of a shared cultural map, the transformation to which they all contributed may cluster them in a profoundly creative grid, a grid consisting of certain aesthetic beliefs, semiotic premises, and practical notions of artists well prepared for their tasks in terms of ideas, craftsmanship, and institutional pragmatics.

Born after "the" event, they must all have taken into account (unlike their parents' generation) that revolutions can and do burst out, that social order is precarious, and that violence is one of the ways through which momentous changes are introduced. Meyerbeer, Halévy, and Heine took great interest in subsequent revolutionary events and rioting;[14] Mendelssohn might have been a victim of one such incident.[15] In their new world, the old social stratification had indeed collapsed, while social codes and cultural practices had undergone major changes. These young men could thus trust their potential to meet opportunities to excel (whether or not they needed to convert for this goal remained an open issue). The education and professional training they received was on a par with, or even surpassed, that of their peers. In the case of young Mendelssohn this included, in addition to a superb musical and humanistic education, an early exposure to the great minds of his time, including Hegel, the Schlegel brothers, and Goethe, who adored the prodigy. For Meyerbeer, who grew up earlier in almost the same milieu, the highly refined and sophisticated members of the salon of his revered mother—Amalia (Wulff) Beer—was a stimulus taken for granted later in his life.[16] Heine, the most self-made of the four, also stood in the most precarious social position; nevertheless, he interacted with illustrious European personalities throughout his life.

Their Jewishness mattered to them, even if they seemed outwardly to forgo it. I have already indicated how Mendelssohn's and Heine's respective Jewish background, however scant, reasserted itself at some crucial moments in the course of their creative lives—though these moments differed considerably. Meyerbeer, in whose parents' house Reform Jewish services took place on a rather grand scale during 1815–17, remained faithful to the Jewishness of his ancestors, however abstract his faith and unobservant he became.[17] Prayers and cantorial traditions were part of the spiritual environment in which Halévy grew up, and this, in his case, seemed to mesh well with the formal musical training he had been receiving at the Paris conservatoire since the age of nine. Jewish texts and contexts had thus some early imprint on all of them, and some of them continued to renew contact in the course of their adult lives.

In the new challenging environment in which they immersed themselves, the old *rishes* (Jews' traditional insider term for Christian hostility, a Yiddish form of the Hebrew word *Rish'ut*, meaning evil, maliciousness) never subsided. Young Mendelssohn seems to have experienced it directly, and Meyerbeer was very explicit about suffering from it throughout his life.[18] His admonition to his young brother in 1819—the "hep hep" riots year—is most telling of that generation, for which, in this sense, he may stand as spokesperson: "Never forget the iron word *rishes*," writes Meyerbeer to his beloved brother Michael, "[f]rom individual to individual the word can be forgotten for a while (although not for long), but by the collective public never, since it requires only one who remembers to bring it back into general consciousness again."[19]

The Halévy brothers, while enjoying the utopian comradeship of the Saint Simonian fellows for some time, were not immune to the effects of this *rishes* (according to the French press, the composer was not elected to the Institute in 1835, which the press ascribed to anti-Semitism).[20] Neither was Heine, as is famously documented. The more specific noise charge which interests us in this volume would explicitly torment Meyerbeer, Heine, and Halévy even before Wagner's lampoon—as in Theodor Uhlig's (1822–1853) review of Meyerbeer's *Prophète* published in *Neue Zeitschrift für Musik,* which inspired Wagner considerably.[21] This turmoil skipped Mendelssohn, who died three years before this affair began, but he too definitely experienced an alteration in the climate, during the forties, in the cosmopolitan universe that for a considerable time had seemed so receptive to his works and person.

The central works discussed in the following—Halévy's *The Jewess,* and, once again, Heine's *The Rabbi from Bacharach,* Meyerbeer's *The Prophet,* and Mendelssohn's *Elijah*—are all expressions of some hesitation, disillusionment, or sobering on behalf of their creators vis-à-vis the possibility of the integration of Jews into the Gentile world. Viewed from this perspective, these works attest to reactions wavering between the conscious and the unconscious, as well as to overt and covert aesthetic categorizations of Jews. Addressing several interrelated theological and historic themes, it is their dramatic-musical and poetic configurations that call for an assessment of the oeuvres in terms of the artist's possible confutation or negation of such categorizations. Despite the fact that—except for Heine's—all the works considered here involve intense collaboration with other creators, not necessarily Jewish, "our" authors are justifiably considered their main creators. At any event, the subjects and modes of expression through which these works came into being were by definition communal, attesting to interactive mental processes at work. The well-entrenched and highly expressive languages of art—above all, that of music—facilitated the configuration of complex cultural messages, perhaps inaccessible through other media.

RETHINKING AESTHETIC CATEGORIES

Jewish artists, thinkers, and critics projected themselves onto their surrounding cultural universe by way of three main avenues: (1) through what they deemed as universal terms and ideas; (2) in terms complementary to, or even conflictual with, competing Christian or nationalist notions; and (3) in subversive ways, undermining preestablished categorizations, both general and specific. Each author reflects his own predilections, yet often all three options worked simultaneously, albeit in different doses and relations. In the more analytical-aesthetic terms of the present context, these possibilities signify: (1) an aspiration to artistic integration and coherence, transcending local differentiations and distinctions; (2) a multiplication of aesthetic categories, practices, and forms of being culminating in the remapping of the entire aesthetic field; (3) a calling into doubt of the very idea of categorization, replacing it with new modes of recognition and creation.

Let us look more closely at these three possibilities:

(1) *Artistic integration and coherence:* Developments in aesthetics, especially in the first part of the eighteenth century, hailed coherence—understood in terms such as "unity within variety"—as the prime artistic principle.[22] Symmetry, harmony, embellishment, and balance were highlighted, within this frame of thought, alongside generic homogeneity and stylistic decorum. These principles also implied the rejection of lower expressive forms in the aspiration for sublime beauty and an ideal nature. Drawing on Renaissance and neoclassical legacies, they were buttressed by rational arguments and enlightened ideals, claiming a universal purview.

Felix Mendelssohn, an aesthetic elitist, embraced these leading ideas, which rendered him, in the eyes of contemporaries and later generations, "conventional" or sometimes even passé. Himself an elaborator of new aesthetic categories (primarily that of the "enchanted magical"),[23] his essays on various eighteenth-century musical genres and his insistence on formal perfection reflected his belief in the cosmopolitan appeal of such music.[24] In the Vormärz period in which Mendelssohn's creative life unfolded, such beliefs were newly redefined—especially by Goethe and Hegel, who were part of the immediate circle of young Mendelssohn—in terms of the organic conception of *Bildung.* According to Thomas Pfau, this pervasive idea was conceived as a self-generating, teleological principle of edification (and education) inherently entailing the idea of transformational sequence.[25] This influenced the old ideal of coherence, which was gradually imbued with national (German) aspirations and social (bourgeois) sensibilities, and with the Romantic-existential aura pertaining to both.

(2) *Multiplication of aesthetic categories:* Towards the turn of the century, with the growing acknowledgment of the entertaining effect and social function of the bathetic ingredients of art and their revolutionary potential, an alternative aesthetics seemed to emerge. The way had already been paved through the reintroduction (by Edmund Burke in 1757, and subsequent writers) of the sublime as a critique of the beautiful, and its orientation toward dreadful, horrifying, and painful objects. With the ascendance of the picturesque, the aesthetic qualities or categories of the trivial, exotic, popular, caricatural, and carnivalesque found their place within artistic production itself and in theoretical assessments thereof.[26] At first, the picturesque applied solely to objects of nature, but gradually it was extended to human beings, first those embedded

in pastoral scenes (shepherds, farmers, peddlers, and their kin) and later also to their urban counterparts. A new gallery of types and characters including gypsies, bandits, prostitutes, witches, ragged children, and beggars began to populate works of art, demanding new modes of perception and evaluation. As Luc Boltanski aptly argues, this new collection of qualities and figures is no longer "only an opportunity for the spectator to reveal his interiority, for a representation of his own feelings and his tenderheartedness in the face of suffering," for they become "the subject of a description which focuses upon their external appearance in order . . . to pick out the character, to make them seen as the painter sees them."[27] Boltanski further explicates:

> By the power of the gaze which is able to frame it as it were, the object being contemplated is extracted both from the situation in which it is found and from the series of worldly objects to which it is attached by connections of use, in order to be connected to a different series which is that of objects already painted.[28]

The ability to detach the picturesque object from its conventional surroundings and transport it to a new, unfamiliar environment—that of the aesthetically created object—was of crucial significance for the social meaning and function of the new art. The ensuing shift must have entailed a dialectics whereby hitherto sanctioned objects of imitation were degraded and demystified, *entzaubert*, while "mere real things" were elevated, *verzaubert*. The picturesque thus conceived seemed to play a major role in the "aesthetic education," or, perhaps, reeducation "of man." Such an education, however, was understood in terms different from those defined by Friedrich von Schiller in his famous *Letters* on the subject.[29] Whereas Schiller's utopian treatise still adhered to old notions of beauty and the happy union of content and form, in more socially revolutionary utopias the emphasis fell on aesthetic qualities that should, as such, ignite the imagination—both scientific as well as practical—which would in turn shape and maintain a more egalitarian and productive modern society. Unlike the concept of *Bildung*, exposure to the divergent aesthetic qualities of the "picturesque" family did not necessarily entail a process converging in a certain telos, *Bild*, or unified worldview.

(3) *The calling into doubt of the ideas of categorization and identity* and the social and epistemological hierarchies that they imply would be deferred to the modern and postmodern era. But under the domain of general, official aesthetics, there lurked alternatives that could find expression in rather unwitting ways, sometimes stemming from exploring artistic technicalities, suggesting modes of thought that undermined some well-entrenched aesthetic categories of the time. Music was central here because of its semantic freedom. By destabilizing

notions of subjectivity and objectivity, cause and effect, meaning and use, form and content, such ideas and practices shook essentialist conceptions of art and encouraged dynamic modes of creativity and perception.

In contemporary aesthetics of music, one could find all three trends, though in different degrees of emphasis and self-awareness. A paradigmatic treatise to this effect that caught the attention and imagination of Meyerbeer while he was working on *The Prophet* (and which might have been known to the other artists in the discussed "group") is that of the Berlin philosopher Johann Jacob Engel, *"Über die Musikalische Malerei"* (1780).[30] It will serve us as an ideational platform from which to examine the expressive values of musical forms and procedures employed by the works under discussion.

Through the concepts he introduces, Engel proposes to understand the modalities of consciousness embedded in the major components of contemporary vocal music, implicating semiotic strategies and aesthetic considerations. These pertain in particular to the mixed genres of the works discussed here, operas included, which deploy oratorical modes and well-prepared oratorical moments. Like Daniel Webb, whose treatise on the *Correspondence between Music and Poetry* (1769) seems to have inspired him,[31] Engel postulates that music is "the most adequate to paint the impressions of the soul." Engel accepts Webb's notion about the special ability of music "by a joint effort of all its means to define 'classes' or 'types' of feelings" in the most accurate and refined way;[32] but he emphasized, even more strongly than Webb, music's inability to define both the object producing the depicted affect and the circumstances related to its generation.[33] Engel further delves into this paradoxical condition—which may be termed music's "unspecified specificity"—emphasizing that musical imitation draws on what he calls "transcendental similarities" shared by music and its objects of imitation (formal and dynamic qualities that eventually constituted the idea of music's isomorphism).[34]

Such transcendentalism serves an aesthetics that highlights universal emotional values, rising above historical, political, and theological barriers.[35] The legacy of Viennese instrumental music was the paradigm of this conception, which became even more poignant when a composer like Mendelssohn chose to produce *Lieder ohne Worte*—stressing that within the new, more aesthetically confined *Biedermeier* world that had reattached itself to textual specificities, pure musical qualities should emerge as the underlying spiritual force. Inspired by ideas such as those of Webb and Engel, Mendelssohn famously hailed music's semantic distinctness over the linguistic one:

> So much is spoken about music and so little is said. For my part I do not
> believe that words suffice for such a task, and if they did I would no longer

make any music. People usually complain that music is too many-sided in its meanings; what they should think when they hear it is so ambiguous, whereas everyone understands words. For me, it is precisely the opposite, not only with entire speeches, but also with individual words. They too seem so ambiguous, so vague, so subject to misunderstanding when compared with true music, which fills the soul with a thousand better things than words. The thoughts that are expressed to me by the music I love are not too indefinite to put into words, but on the contrary, too definite.[36]

And yet Mendelssohn himself could not entirely rely on such pure "transcendentalism"; time and again he was driven to "textual" music, well aware of the intricate semiotic relations it engenders. By and large, Mendelssohn's creative process seems to convey that universalism is not a sufficient basis for creating the social and cultural inherence he so craved. When assisted by text, music's transcendental appeal is endowed with context and belonging; but, as Engel explained, this endowment does not work by a simple division of labor between music and verbal text, because the verbal text, becoming vocal, is tonally suffused, and its instrumental mate is lexically pinpointed. In the lyrico-dramatic genres, maintains Engel, the voice represents a first-person singular that owns the emotion and expresses it, whereas the musical accompaniment depicts the surroundings in which it acts. (As implied by the specific verbal components of each piece, this can be internal, external, or both.) This division of labor, he continues—anticipating salient points of E. T. Cone's ideas in *The Composer's Voice*[37]—is thus between "subjective expression" and "objective painting" (what Cone terms, respectively, vocal and instrumental personae). But even these categories are not stable:

> The idea of an emotion, be it somebody else's or our own, can become the cause for a new emotion—sometimes a different, even opposite emotion. Somebody else's joy may arouse my own anger . . . In such cases joy and pleasurable feelings are the objective, anger and sadness, the subjective.[38]

Lyrico-dramatic music thus supplies more than a descriptive ambience for the internal occurrences of its protagonists. Its interplay between subjective and objective stances entails a shifting and sometimes multivalent point of view. This pertains in particular to oratorio, from which Engel drew most of his examples (especially those of Graun and Hesse). The role of the choir (not discussed by Engel) is of special interest in this respect, as it embodies an intersubjective focal point (the voice of the many), projected from inside or outside, or hovering between the two.

The problem of sympathy and its ambivalent nature, as discussed in chapter 2 of this book, can now be assessed from this perspective. As stated above,

Mendelssohn's complaint that the moving music of *Samson's* Delilah "was not meant in earnest" misses the basic dynamic element of music's expressivity—the location of subjectivity in relation to other voices. Engel preempted such claims by indicating that sometimes the expression of the subjective cannot take place without the painting of the objective to the extent that the subjective and the objective even merge; "the entire soul," in this case, resembles "the object as much as possible." At other times, however, "the subjective and the objective clearly face one another." Whereas the "merging" state gives rise to "homogenous" emotions, the "opposing" one generates "heterogeneous" states. In the final analysis, the criteria for artistic coherence are psychological rather than purely musical or "aesthetic," according to Engel, and are themselves open to a variety of interpretations depending on elective points of view.

All in all, Engel's ideas sensitize his readers to the notion that subjectivity is never fixed and is ever roving; it can always subsume other objects and subjectivities or be subsumed by them. Thus even the painter's point of view, from which the picturesque as aesthetic category was meant to be assessed, has no priority in aesthetic contemplation. This, as argued by Michael Steinberg, is indeed a major insight of composers at the time.[39] In other words, the way to ironic manipulations—"Romantic," political, or otherwise, was technically paved, but it took imaginative, bold creators to significantly realize them.

Some of Mendelssohn's *Lieder mit Worten* illustrate the precariousness of subjectivity and the instability of its extension, production, and affiliation. Let us look at a "homogenous" moment in Mendelssohn's early oeuvre—homogenous also because of its apparent unperformativity (not presupposing a "staged" protagonist to deliver it)—the popular lied "Frühlingsbotschaft" ("Spring's Message," sometimes called: "Gruß") set to Heine's famous words[40] (op. 19 no. 5, pub. 1833). Closely following Zelter's approach to the genre, Mendelssohn's lieder are known for their strict adherence to the strophic frame of the poem, ever revealing the autonomy of music over the dictates of the text, as Hegel advised the young composer.[41] Eschewing word painting in voice and accompaniment, Mendelssohn opted musically for the expression of the poem's overall mood rather than the representation of its dramatic content.[42] The little "Frühlingsbotschaft" follows this aesthetic but concurrently becomes entirely iconic; for here the text unfolds a metamusical narrative (and not the representation of an external object) that becomes its dynamic emblem. Poet, musician, and singer merge in one persona, parallel to the amalgamation of text, melody, and accompaniment.

Self-referential, the lied is about a special song: a spring song that functions as a message of its bearer. Basing itself on a D-major tonal block in the

Ex. 4.1 Felix Mendelssohn: "Leise zieht durch mein Gemüt."
(second strophe)

Zieh hinaus bis an das Haus,	[Go forward till you reach the house,
Wo die Blumen sprießen,	where the flowers bloom;
Wenn du eine Rose schaust,	and if you see a rose,
Sag, ich laß sie grüßen.	give her my greetings.]

four-measure introduction, it opens vocally with "Leise zieht durch mein Ge-müt" (softly filling my soul) by lilting the spring melody between scale degrees 5 and 3, like a child who starts playing with a yo-yo (see music example ex. 4.1).

Gradually filling in the gaps, it climbs to 6, to reverse the move on a similar path in the second tinkling phrase "Liebliches Geläute" (sweet chimes), now starting from the upper tonic without touching the finale ground. With the third phrase ("Klinge, kleines Frühlingslied," Ring, little springtime song) a symmetrical, chimelike progress, down and up, embitters the song's sweetness with the minor-second environment. Winding up this phrase with a tailpiece on 3–4, it prompts an upward stepwise gesture that sends the melody ("Kling hinaus ins Weite," Ring out: far and wide) even beyond its "natural" horizon of an octave, to safely collect it there. The homogeneity of subject and object seems so full, at once self-projecting and self-containing (the local convex and concave small arches grant this and so does its tonal scope) that its underlying hiatus eludes its listener: the subject releases the melody from within himself, like a bird from a cage in which it was imprisoned. He, however, remains behind, in prison, or as prison, watching the melody making its way into the world. Their division becomes clearer in the second strophe, when he gives it specific orders.

Spring takes place out *there*, in the garden—the melody's destination, perhaps also its very origin. What could be considered an extension of or substitute for the poet-composer-singer's light and innocent self is detached from him and by him; for some reason, he does not follow. Will a sign of recognition be returned? The poem-song stops there, as if indeed the upper tonic could receive the pent-up longing, like a bird or a butterfly received by its botanic host. The self-alienated poet, who never really saw himself as part of the garden (as in the Weimar classical "garden," associated with Goethe), Heine thus projects himself, by the outwardly nonironic façade of this poem, on Mendelssohn, who seems to naturally belong there.[43] Or is it the other way around? Perhaps, after all, the chorale-like, naïve melody seems to achieve what the text can only aspire to.

Iconic—to draw on Charles S. Peirce's semiotic categories more fully—the song remains indexically open forever. Who is its referent or its bearer? The answer seems simple, if not banal: every "I" who engages with it. What is true for lyric genres by and large, however, pertains here to an implied subject who must share the belief that he or she can be so iconized, that he or she generates or owns such *liebliches Geläute* and is able to project it in this way. When many a poet, composer, or singer—professional or amateur—sees himself or herself reflected in this description, the indexical, self-referential piece becomes a symbol of that society (again, in the Peircian sense) becoming a folk song or cliché.[44] Once, however, the subject of the song realizes, to her dismay, that though she generates the song, she is left out of the garden, the most *heimlich* object (both secretive and homey) becomes, before her ears, *unheimlich* (eerie and uncanny) in Freud's terms. The sweet-embittered melody—an embodied libidinal quest—turns into an unfulfilled, open sign (similar to the roving sign in search of its object, in "Die Liebende schreibt" [Letter from a Girl in Love], op. 86/3, written 1831, in Laurence Kramer's interpretation).[45] The semiotic mechanism that has upheld this order to this point now dwindles, and she can either gravitate out of the system (through irony or a new language) or become melancholic.

I do not aim to argue that the eventual dispossession of popular poem-songs of this kind from their real authors by the Nazis is foreshadowed here (though this dispossession is a startling political realization of this semiotic mechanism), nor that a straight line can be drawn from such lieder to Schoenberg, whose garden-lieder are songs of the isolated individual, well aware of his expulsion.[46] What I wish to argue is that in the midst of the coziness of the *Biedermeir* drawing room or garden there lurks the recognition that, sweet as such melody is, it is not its subject's individual property (not in the socialist or nationalist sense of unbelonging but rather in the private, *unheimlich* sense). Such a recognition would be less likely to dawn on the German-born Romantic (narcissist) artist, who could have felt alienated from society, yet less estranged from his own art/self. (Again, the woman artist is a different story, and, in that sense, closer to the Jew, as argued below.) Heine and Mendelssohn, from whom musical-poetical euphoniousness sprang so easily (a fact acknowledged by Wagner, among others)[47] would have subliminally experienced themselves, according to this interpretation, as less in possession of that which they achieved.

Perhaps this interpretation makes too much ado about one little song; and yet it is symptomatic in the way Marx, and later Freud, taught us about symptoms, and of the slippery interchangeability of *heimlich* and *unheimlich* objects, expounded by Freud. It is symptomatic, in Thomas Pfau's words, of the underlying dialectics that dawned upon some authors at the time, especially Heine, between "affect and rhetoric, between a vision of pure and noncontradictory inwardness and the historical forces at once obstructing its material realization."[48] In the case considered in this volume, this dialectics seems to yield a special kind of affective rhetoric and new relations between inwardness and historicity. In this, Mendelssohn eventually joined some of the Jewish artists whom he earlier seemed to oppose, as we shall see.

NOISE, TABLEAU, AND SHOCK — GRAND OPERA AS PARADIGMATIC SPACE

Unfortunate Pharaoh! You are the cause of my misfortune. Had you not allowed the children of Israel to depart out of the land of Egypt, or had you only had them all drowned in the Nile, I should not have been crowded out of Berlin by Meyerbeer and Mendelssohn and should still be conducting the Grand Opéra and the court concerts there! Unhappy Pharaoh! Vacillating king of crocodiles, it was due

to your half measures that I am now an utterly ruined man- and that Moses and
Halévy and Mendelssohn and Meyerbeer have conquered!

—Heine's satire on Spontini[49]

As part of their emancipation from old Jewish traits, "the Jews like you and
me" of that generation struggled to acquire not only an impeccable lingua
franca, but also to dispose of those nonverbal sonorant peculiarities that gave
them away: "Jewish" accent and intonation. This struggle was fraught with a
symptomatic paradox that led to an inevitable failure. Attempting to sound like
"everybody," Jews sounded like "nobody": their "High" German turned out to
be devoid of locality and dialect, exposing the new Jews' linguistic extraneous-
ness (though Jewish idiom was satirized in other European languages including
sometimes German). Universalist standards thus capsized, designating the Jews
as a particular, separate group.[50]

Felix Mendelssohn's attempt to avoid the pitfalls of language—all verbal languages (as stated in the above quotation from his 1842 letter)—highlights this
predicament, though even this strategy did not spare him from a similar trap. To
abide by what was considered as classical and universal criteria was ultimately
perceived as an aping of the original models. Another aesthetic category was
thus launched against Jews—epigonism (already insinuated in Burney's synagogal report, described in the previous chapter)—which seemed to be part of
the baggage of anti-Jewish rhetoric for at least a few centuries.[51] Though, as in
the case of Heine, proof was demanded from the accusers; that is, to demonstrate how the models were formulaic from inception, and so, by extension,
should be their derivatives.[52] In the interplay between text and music, rhetoric
and affect, there lurked another semiotic possibility for negating such a defamation: to engage subjectivity in a more oblique way, less indexically open
than in songs like "Frühlingsbotschaft." One such possibility was to search for
moments of homogeneity in a transcendental religious dimension, rather than
in an immediate social or existential one, inviting an "imagined community"
to join in. A different possibility was to assume the separation of subject and
object, and that of subject and subject, as a starting point; to abide by heterogeneity and dwell on it.

By and large, most European Jewish-born composers did not follow the path of
classical, abstract universalism; they opted for textual or highly "characteristic"
music, grounded in localities and programmatic contents of various kinds.
Their followers in subsequent generations (including Offenbach, Paul Dukas,
Schoenberg and Mahler, continuing in the twentieth century with famous Jew-

ish musical and film composers) drew on words or other labels for dynamic des-
ignations of emotional states and their context in a variety of "heterogeneous"
ways, allegorical, ironic, and so forth. This was not limited, of course, to Jewish-
born composers; Romantic and especially post-Romantic composers opted for
local colors and heterogeneities of different species. To be sure, dramatic composers always had a predilection for motley elements.

In the threefold aesthetic scheme proposed above, however, more autochthonous composers and writers could safely remain within the second plane—
the domain of multiple aesthetic categories, depicted from an external viewpoint, and still subservient to an all-inclusive harmonious sublime effect. What
I suggest here is that, as inside-outsiders, the composers-writers intrigued by
their Jewish origins tended to problematize categorization, often earlier and
more powerfully than "insider" artists did.[53] In other words, heterogeneity of
the kind advocated by Engel was for them an actual way of being and acting in
the sociopolitical world; its projection onto their created worlds was bound to
bewilder their middle-class audiences, especially the *bürgerlich* German one.
Moreover, their engagement with history, as part of their creation of "local"
picturesque spectacles, seems more poignant and exploratory than that of their
peer insiders. Living in times of change and revolution "brings a sense of inse-
curity to individuals, groups and leaders alike," the historian Doron Mendels
argues, generally stimulating "a symbiosis with one's past"[54] and sometimes,
I would add, also with a projected future (as in the case of Wagner). Such
symbiosis with the past, so self-evident to writers, scholars, and composers as
different as Rellstab,[55] the Grimm brothers, Chopin, not to speak of Wagner,
was much less so for those never-entirely-belonging artists. The histories they
took upon themselves to cast in their works are thus often demythologized and
fragmentized between subjectivities and factions, internal and external points
of view.[56]

In France, the generation of July (1830) revolutionists, witnessing the transition from constitutional monarchy to popular sovereignty, was perhaps the
first to experiment with this new array of imaginaries. The Saint Simonians'
influence—in ideas and practice—was felt among them, especially in the new
role they granted to art and artists, high in the hierarchy of the custodians of
the utopian commonwealth, sometimes soaring above leading politicians and
industrialists, sometimes alongside them.[57] The imaginative power of art was
deemed crucial to secure emotional control of the new society and the moral
political education of its citizens. A communal vision, it sought to guide the
audience's attention towards the proper revolutionary values through folk songs

and choral music, in the spirit of singing associations then in vogue in France, Germany, and England.

Notably, all our artists found interest in these ideas, though to different degrees, and even partially contributed to their enhancement, but no one adopted them literally.[58] Too doctrinal for their artistic goals, they rather opted for fictional realities and protagonists endowed with heterogeneous subjectivities and voices, thereby avoiding a subsuming external political-moral viewpoint. This preference, clearly discerned in the cases of Halévy, Heine, and Meyerbeer, would bring to the fore the problem of sympathy: with whom is the audience called to identify? Should their sympathy be guided by the artist or left to their discretion?[59]

In strictly musical terms, heterogeneity of voices yields inevitable noise. But it is a different kind of noise than the one hitherto discussed. It is different from the "synagogal noise," as perceived by outsiders, due to the latter's nonsynchronized soundspace, foreign musical material, and the different modes and genres of its musical elaboration. It is also distinguished from nature's turbulence, as produced by falling water, hurling wind, or a stormy sea (marked in German by *Geräusch*, distinguished, to a certain extent, from *Lärm*), which for the *Frühromantiker* connoted the sublime.[60] This new noise partakes, to a degree, of the traditional clash—pinpointed by Attali—of "Carnival and Lent" (as portrayed by Pieter Brueghel). In the Christian mind, this clash was associated with cyclical seasonal change related to the jurisdictional division between sacred and profane, celestial and mundane orders.

In the far less hierarchically ordered world of postrevolutionary (1830) Europe, noise became more poignantly an urban, sociopolitical phenomenon, an auditory reflection of the coexistence of groups and individuals of different orientations, affiliations, and histories. It mixes voices and sonorities emitted by various ethnic and religious groups, military forces, tradesmen, and official authorities as they encounter each other in heightened moments of celebration or trepidation. A live emblem of clashing interests, habits, moods, and expressivities, in the dramatic arena such sonorities become the backdrop and target of select individual action.

Such extended moments of encounter always verge on, or even engage the carnivalesque (in the Bakhtinian sense); hence, and more poignantly than in the old world, they involve anarchy and death. This yields oratorical moments of a new kind, fashioned and consummated in a way different from the more "harmonious" ones considered in previous chapters. Discussing the main genre which so engaged the new milieu—grand opera—Carl Dahlhaus describes its major modalities in terms of tableau vivant and "shock." Dahlhaus' main aim (though he never mentions anti-Semitism explicitly in this connection) is to defend grand opera against its libelers, mainly Schumann and Wagner (the former accused it of eclecticism, the latter—of consisting in "effects-without-causes" drama devoid—among other things—of characters developing psychological depth through dialogue; both writers directly criticized Meyerbeer).[61] The principle of tableau vivant is embodied in the grand opera by the living mass scene that operates mainly through mimicry, creating "frozen configurations" in which "time stands still, whether from terror, expectancy or exaltation." Shock, on the other hand, is "the law of motion governing the progress of the plot," consisting of a "sudden switch from one mood to the other." It is here that the genre's modernity resides, and what makes it so akin to the belief that "major political decisions are made in the street."[62] Dahlhaus summarizes these principles accordingly:

> It is the éclat, the unforeseen event, breaking in like a thunderbolt, that drives the plot forward with a jolt and supplies the premises for the arrangement of the next tableau. And like the tableau, the shock is not a deficient dramaturgical species, but a legitimate principle in its own right.[63]

Only music, emphasizes Dahlhaus, is capable of such moments, granting them experiential reality and a lived presence.

Meyerbeer mastered these principles and further developed them. A moment of this kind takes place in the opening of *Les Huguenots* (1836), act III: in the midst of the great upheavals related to the Huguenots' uprising in sixteenth-century Paris, they come one after another—Catholic promenaders, soldiers, Huguenot zealots, nuns, Gypsy girls, students, a wedding procession, each with their own particular and identifiable mode of vocality. They are noisy, especially at moments when the accumulation of all kinds of sonoric expressions is polyphonically or sometimes cacophonously construed.[64] Having as background a disarray of sounds and groups, a turbulent plot is clandestinely conceived against Raul and the Huguenots, crystallizing in a short tableau that brings in a new scene (*le Couvre-feu*), as evening sets, to an apparent moment of reconciliation, when the constable exhorts the crowd:

Rentrez habitants de Paris,	[Go to your homes, citizens of Paris,
Tenez-vous clos en vos logis;	Shut yourselves fast in your houses;
Que tout bruit meure,	*Let all noise cease,*
Quittez cez lieu,	Leave this place,
Car voici l'heure	For this is the hour
Du couvre-feu.	Of curfew.] (italics added)

And they reply in exactly the same way through text and music. "Let all noise cease," they sing in unison, almost a cappella (ex. 4.2). Both mode of performance and its musical content comprise a clear paraphrase of the "finale" of

Ex. 4.2. Giacomo Meyerbeer, *Les Huguenots* III, 18, "Couvre-feu"
(The Curfew), mm. 1–20.

the Friday night Jewish religious service, with which Meyerbeer was well acquainted. This finale begins with the first verses of Genesis 2:

> And the heaven and the earth were finished, and all the host of them. And on the seventh day God finished His work which He had made; and He rested on the seventh day from all His work which He had made. And God blessed the seventh day, and hallowed it; because that in it He rested from all His work which God in creating had made.

Silence, rest, peace, and the Jewish synagogue on Friday night: the melody draws on its typical, "Magen Avot" *steiger,* and its mode of rhythmic and melodic unfolding as pertinently shown in Boaz Tarsi's analysis:[65] the typical opening fifth, becoming the tone of recitation, the slight slide down and return for a short cadence; the subsequent (second or third) phrase of the parallel major arpeggios (F) moving up to the seventh, and the final cadence (of the choral section) that moves from the sixth, through a pause on the fifth, to the lower tonic.

The mode of singing, almost a cappella, is typical of what Meyerbeer believed a Jewish service should be: "[T]he praying man should approach his God without any intermediary. The Jews have maintained that opinion since the destruction of the Temple and we should not introduce any innovation," as he wrote in a letter to the Viennese Kultusgemeinde, stressing that the "human voice is the most moving."[66]

Meyerbeer thus turns the old story upside down: Hurly-burly and upheaval are outside, in the streets, among Christian factions; serenity and harmony dwell inside—at home, as Jews had always had them. Though here this inside is coerced, a shelter from ensuing *rishes* against the solitary, defenseless, young Huguenot (with some pariah traits parallel to those of the persecuted Jew), it points beyond the actual plot, to the underlying threat from which Meyerbeer was never free.

MOVING OUTSIDE: EASTER'S CLATTER IN (FICTIONAL) LATE MEDIEVAL FRANKFURT AND CONSTANCE

As distinct "dramaturgical categories" or modalities, tableau and shock extend to other musical and "musicalized" media and genres—whether directly influenced by the opera or not—especially those heralding, or embodying, modernism. They may partake in the oratorio and the symphony; the novel and the novella likewise host them. So do other theatrical genres (such as classical-inspired tragedies and melodramas) and, later, film. The rest of this chapter is devoted to two pairs of such works, each sharing thematic and structural principles while engaging them in different ways. Embodying the aforementioned modalities, these oeuvres bring to the fore some repressed elements—in the history and culture that they engage—which they work through in the course of the pieces. The first pair includes a literary work, again Heine's *Rabbi of Bacharach,* and a grand opera, Halévy's *La Juive.* The second pair includes an oratorio, Mendelssohn's *Elijah,* and another grand opera, largely conceived in the spirit of the oratorio: Meyerbeer's *Le Prophète.*

The first scene that will engage us is taken from the *Rabbi of Bacharach*'s second chapter, depicting the events that precede the entrance of the rabbi and his wife to the Frankfurt synagogue (discussed in the previous chapter). The two now enter the city on Passover/Easter morning, on their way to the Judengasse. Their encounter with the big merchandising city, following a night of horror, takes place on the river's noisy shore, whose *Lärm* is richly characterized: "ein betäubender Lärm, das beständige Hallorufen der Barkenführer, das Geschrei der Kaufleute vom Ufer her und das Keifen der Zöllner" (deafening noise, the constant hallo cries of the steersmen, the screaming of the traders from the shore, and the bickering of the custom-house officials). The narrative mode is cinematographic and, concurrently, operatic. Apparently focalized through the newcomers, it is often presented from a broad panoramic shot that periodically zooms in on the two tiny figures swallowed in the throngs through which they carve their way. Serpentlike sentences confer the effect of simultaneity, the Lessingian *nebeneinander* (simultaneous, "one next to the other") linear principle, while the momentary perceptual vantage point of the walkers, hurrying to their destination, endows it with a *nacheinander* ("one after the other") effect.[67] Whereas on the real opera stage the voices acoustically blend, here the noises are heaped one on top of the other through an overtly dense description. The multifarious noise continues to stem from many agents, groups, and instruments: they consist of trumpets and horns (mainly of rulers), flutes and drums (of guild processions), of talking, laughing, and transacting voices, emitted by characters from all walks of life—doctors and comedians, heralds and harlots, the latter singing their promiscuous witch-songs in shrill tones. As a counterimage, an Easter procession of monks passes by, in the midst of which,

> under a beautiful canopy, marched priests in white robes adorned with costly lace, or in bright-colored silk stoles; one of them held in his hand a sun-like, golden vessel, which, on arriving at a shrine by the market-corner, he raised on high, while he half-sang, half-spoke in Latin—when all at once a little bell rang, and all the people around, becoming silent, fell to their knees and made the sign of the cross.[68]

This description, consisting almost of stage instructions for a Wagner *Parsifal*, is imbued with the spirit of grand opera and its tableau vivant principle, also in its sudden shifts, when the camera zooms in on our walkers, who continue to be at odds with these sights and sounds. Sara is attracted here and there to eye-catching articles (jewelry and cloth), but, like Shakespeare's Jessica, seems never to be "merry to hear [the crowd's] sweet [or festive] music." The reader is "shockingly" reminded of the abyss between the haunted pair and the surrounding rejoicing masses, and the thrice operatically repeated refrain, Rabbi Abraham's soft command to his wife: "Mach die Augen zu, schöne Sara!" alerts the reader to the fact that, while Sara can choose to avert her eyes away from her surroundings, she can hardly close her ears.[69]

The masses dwindle when they come close to the Gasse's gate. A more chamber-music-like encounter, though no less carnivalesque one, is staged there, in which a grotesque drummer appears:

So the fellow sat and drummed to the melody of a song which the Flagellants had sung at the Jewish massacre [*die Geißler bei der Judenschlacht*], while he gurgled, in a coarse, beery voice—

"Our dear Lady true
Walked in the morning dew,
Kyrie eleison!"[70]

Rather than examining the couple's reaction to this fantastic scene (vocally—and thus ironically—characterized by the verb—*gurgeln*, common, as we have seen, in both malevolent and benevolent synagogal ethnographies), another bathetic figure appears onstage—a Jewish fellow called "Nose Star" (Nasenstern), expressing the feelings that would arise among the alarmed Jewish travelers in response to those horrific sounds, the connotations of which they would have been familiar with:

"Hans, that is a terrible tune," cried a voice from behind the closed gate of the Jewish quarter. "Yes, Hans, and a bad song too—doesn't suit the drum; doesn't suit it at all—by my soul—not the day of the fair and on Easter morning—bad song—dangerous song—Jack, Jacky, little drum—Jacky boy—I'm a lone man—and if thou lovest me, the Star, the tall Star, the tall Nose Star—then stop it!"

These words were uttered by the unseen speaker, "now in hasty anxiety, now in a sighing drawl, in a tone which alternated between mild softness and harsh hoarseness, such as one hears in consumptive people." The drummer was not moved, and went on drumming and singing—

"There came a little youth,
His beard had run away, in truth,
Halleluja!"

To be urged again to stop by the desperate Nasenstern. In an almost operatic setting whose actual music—that of the melody itself—might have been known to the novella's readers, the scene possesses imagined musical qualities also through the abiding song of the drummer, the vocally qualified entreating recitatives of Nasenstern, and the intensifying rhetorical structure, wherein comic relief effect contrasts sharply with its actual content: Nasenstern's dislike of the melody betrays a deeply ingrained fear that transcends its fictive setting in the fifteenth century. To the accompaniment of such songs—Heine reminds his German and Jewish readers—the Jewish quarters were invaded during the dangerous time of Easter, sometimes only by carnivalesque jesters, sometimes by hooligans who wreaked dreadful attacks, as we saw in chapter 1. Only through drink will this bloke be appeased and stop his horrible song. Iterating an internal commonplace held by Jews about Gentiles (*goyim*), the scene draws into full cadence.

The synagogal scene, quoted in the previous chapter, ensues. The juxtaposition of these two scenes again indicates that noise is outside there, in a world alien to the gentle and traumatized Jewish couple. The rumbling city noise is indeed real noise, *Lärm*—in the modern sense of the word—and not that of the interconnected, however loosely, sound waves of the Judengasse synagogue, whose moaning tunes and festive hymns, as the tale insists, are profoundly meaningful to its faithful members, across communities and time.

A direct, interactive sound of clashes between Jews and Gentiles in Easter-Passover time opens the first dramatized scene in *La Juive*, set in a similar fictive historical time. Heine should have been acquainted with this work; it was premiered in Paris in 1835 and immediately became a hit. But the dates of both works and the time lapse between the writing and the publication of Heine's fragment imply that the authors were incognizant of their respective works while engaged in their composition. The similarities are noteworthy; they pertain, in the present context, both to the juxtaposition of Passover and Easter in their different musical strains and to the degree of mutual partaking of Christians and Jews in each other's musicality. Oratorical modes characterize *La Juive* throughout. It is built within dual historical dimensions: a fictive one of the Council of Constance of 1414[71] and an actual one, Paris of the July Monarchy. A third layer is superimposed here—the history of its staging, mainly the famous 1999 Wiener Staatsoper "epoch-making" production.[72] The historical scope opened through the commemorated events, mainly the Passover Seder and the auto-da-fé, adds further dimensions. These layers and dimensions open each moment to an intricate dialogue between past and present, memory and vision, reenactment of traditions and their ongoing critique. Actual oratorical moments are projected by an active chorus that mostly assumes the role of a performative Catholic community, as well as by individuals who fuel it through public declarations, prayers, and trials.

"Staged" music frames the first act of Halévy's opera. It opens and also brings it to a closure, while its clamor seems to reverberate in the hall throughout the act. "Te Deum," St. Ambrose's fourth-century hymn, is its content—a hymn of universal religious values expressed in an Old Testamental language:

> We praise Thee, O God: we acknowledge Thee to be the Lord.
> All the earth doth worship Thee and the Father everlasting.
> [To Thee all Angels: to Thee the heavens and all the Powers therein.
> To Thee the Cherubim and Seraphim cry with unceasing voice:
> Holy, Holy, Holy: Lord God of Hosts.[73]]
> The heavens and the earth are full of the majesty of Thy glory.

Like other Ambrosian hymns, it celebrates and constitutes an ever-present, timeless Christian community that embraces and encompasses all living creatures.[74] Even more blatantly than in similar paeans (such as Lorenzo's soliloquy), its harmonious inclusiveness is deceptive, for it excludes all who do not abide by the Trinity dogma it announces in its subsequent (unsung) lines. Compared with a contemporary work such as Berlioz's *Te Deum* (1848–49), the music here is a simplified version of its genre (sung a cappella, with stock harmonic and polyphonic progressions in the organ prelude) functioning as a quote or a cliché. A "religious" tableau vivant, in which music is actually played on stage (henceforth called "real" music, what Carolyn Abbate dubbed "phenomenal" music, known in film studies as "diegetic"), it provides the spur for the instigation of people in the crowd to attack the self-excluding Jews (Rachel and Éléazar). Now the music becomes "symbolic" (or noumenal, in Abbate's terminology, or nondiegetic)—heard as music in the nonfictive world, but perceived, in the fictive one, as mere talk. The apprehension of the oscillation between real and symbolic music is crucial for the appraisal of the meaning of voice, sound, and noise in this work.[75]

Father and daughter—again, two lonely Jews in the midst of a Gentile host—are modeled on Shylock and Jessica, Nathan and Recha, as well as Isaac and Rebecca (from Walter Scott's *Ivanhoe*),[76] and share some of their traits. Here, however, the daughter is mature and takes care of her aging father who, like Nathan, has survived a pogrom and the murder of close family members, though he is far less magnanimous toward the perpetrators than his "enlightened" counterpart. (As becomes clear, unlike Nathan, Éléazar does not "receive" his adopted Gentile daughter; he rescues her, but never seems to have considered giving her back before the atrocious events.) Even more poignantly than the other dyadic families mentioned above, Éléazar and Rachel inhabit a hostile Gentile public sphere which, while exploiting the father's resources, covets his daughter. Apparently, they do not belong in any community, at least not according to act I; their social phenomenology is thus "modernized," though the nature of their struggle ostensibly partakes of both modern and medieval. In a more arresting way than their fictional prototypes (Shylock and Jessica, Nathan and Recha), they speak the same social-emotional language that their oppressors do, embodied in musical (symbolic) expressive codes. Fathomed, thus, by their fellow Gentiles, they, in their turn, understand them.

In other words, Éléazar and Rachel integrate perfectly in terms of particular musical motifs, which they sometimes borrow, sometimes lend, and sometimes counteract. Their interiorities as individuals and Jews seem, for the first time in the history of art, to be as overt and transparent as those of any operatic figure, though their referent—to draw again on Engel's ideas—is not always clear. (This musical shareability of the Jewish father-daughter dyad within their Gentile environment turns, in a caricature ["The Piano Lesson," fig. 4.1], into a modern motive for an anti-Semitic diatribe.)

The religious tableau vivant recedes to the background when the lens zooms in on the secretive meetings between Albert and Prince Léopold, disguised as a Jew. Their dialogue reveals part of the historical context of the events portrayed—the Hussites' uprising and the arrival of the Emperor to impose the pope's order and announce the victory of the Catholic Church. The real and the symbolic continue to interchange; from the musically symbolic dialogue of the two, the masses will emerge again in a triumphant, updated hymn of praise and glory: "Hosana, plaisir, ivresse, Gloire à l'Éternel!" (Hosanna, joy, rapture, glory to the Lord). Upon hearing this, the Jews, now inside their shop, could tell each other (though we cannot hear them) "It is our song: we are the only ones here who understand the meaning of this Hebrew collocation *hosanna* (*hosha na*—save us). Indeed, it is we that should pray so; we will do that, tonight, at the Seder, tomorrow in our prayers." (Curiously, one of the psalms Halévy composed for the Paris synagogue is 118, in which the words "Ono adonoi hoschioh no" are central.)[77] "For you Christians, hosanna is an empty word; a flag to wave, a triumphant slogan for those who have won it all." Triumphalism and festivity will increase, after Ruggiero, the zealot Provost, still in the grand introduction, will read the day's order.[78]

In this symbolic world, the potential of such musical sharing is too overt to be reckoned with and is therefore denied, repressed. It is denied when it is most explicit—in the emotional communication of the counterreligious lovers. It is what deceives Rachel, who is so taken by its half-false, half-true, gestures: Léopold-Samuel, the deceiving lover, sings a serenade ("Loin de son amie," far from your sweetheart, no. 3)—"real" music with an oriental profile, a sonic

Fig. 4.1. "The Piano Lesson," 1850. From the weekly
journal *Fliegende Blätter* (Stauber), no. 276. Courtesy
of the Universitätsbibliothek, Heidelberg. Piano
teacher: "you are not paying attention, you have here
an eighth note and you make it a quarter. Father (in the
background): Entirely my nature, why should she
take it an eighth, when she can have a quarter?"
A mundane Shylock-Eléazar can "measure" music
only through his "ducats" or gold.

masquerade. Identifying his voice ("quelle voix chérie si douce à mon coeur me
rend à la vie"—this dear voice so sweet to my heart gives me life), she joins him,
as do all operatic lovers, in parallel sixths (music appears now symbolic again).[79]
It is this performative emotional togetherness that so confuses her, compelling
her to declare: I love you because "notre culte est le même, / Le même Dieu
nous bénit tous les deux" (we follow the same creed / the same God blesses us
both), adding to the grounds of her attraction his talent as a painter (another apparent rejection of the "artless" Jew, this time his visual-aesthetic deficiency).[80]
When in the middle of act II she becomes disillusioned by him (learning his
true identity), this will be uttered in her particular emotive idiom, which he will
try to accommodate, but then she will be swept again into "his" music, overcoming the acknowledged difference by adopting the dominant voice.

It is this vocal-musical dominance that renders so weird, so uncanny, and yet so smooth the appearance of Léopold—dressed up as Samuel, the fake Jew—as a man of power (revealed onstage, in the finale of act I) when his beloved is in danger. This takes place prior to her and her father's realization of his Christian identity. (This is the third time they are saved from a threatening mob; the second is due to Cardinal Brogni's appearance, discussed below.) The confusion shared by both Jews and Christians is profound and nourishes two substantial ensembles, each of which is issued and led by one of the Jewish figures; the first even partially sounding "Jewish."[81] In the great Rossinean tradition it slides, through a triumphal procession, from an aria-like melody to a sweeping cabaletta stretta, expressing the subjective astonishment of the Jews against a background of collective "objective" festivity. A vocal drama of identities, so common in the operatic world, becomes loaded here with political-theological-aesthetic questions, existentially experienced, relating to cardinal questions such as primogeniture, betrayal, and victimization that stand between the two religions. The composer's own vocal affiliation, in real life professed as operatic and to a lesser extent, Jewish, remains unfixed.

A well-established operatic convention enables this sliding back and forth from real to symbolic music, emphasizing, as the opera unfolds, the "unbearable lightness" of mobilizing religion and its effective props for bloodshed, or, more specifically, the use of organized sound in what appears to be spontaneous, communal murder (in the first part of the drama; henceforth, execution becomes "official"). It is instructive that the main provocation in this direction is the real, apparently nonsymbolic sound emitted by the Jew: the noise of his workshop, perceived as the profanation of the Christian holy day (see Introduction). What is this noise, *ce bruit*? It is the pulse of the goldsmith's anvil, manufacturing jewelry of the kind a princess (Eudoxie) would buy that night. It is certainly gentler than the noise of the Nibelungs' hammer (in Wagner's *Rheingold*); like the latter, it is partially integrated into the symbolic musical order (it determines the musical pulse but its G octave remains "out of tune" though reinforced by two *cors à piston* and harmonically acclimatized by the augmented sixth chord preceding it). To the provoked Christian's interrogation, demanding to find out the source of the din, the Jew will rejoin by advocating religious freedom, as if versed in Spinoza, Moses Mendelssohn, or Voltaire:[82]

> Et pourquoi pas? Et pourquoi pas?
> Ne suis-je pas fils d'Israël
> Et le Dieu des Chrétiens m'ordonne t'il à moi?

> [And why not? And why not?
> Am I not a son of Israel
> And shall the Christian God give me orders?]

Which he winds up with a dismal exclamation, forgoing enlightened niceties:

> Et pourquoi l'aimerais-je?
> Par vous sur le bûcher, et me tendant les bras,
> J'ai vu périr mes fils!
>
> [And what should I care for your law?
> At your behest, stretching out their hands to me
> from the stake,
> my sons died before my eyes!]

The chromatic line of the orchestra, accompanying Brogni's reply, marks the vehemence of the Christians' threat; the inclusive hymn of praise ("for our city what a happy day") becomes sarcastically exclusive.[83] The Jews will be saved this time by the sudden entrance of Brogni, the former foe, now as "Supreme President of the Council," who is willing to forgive the "prodigal son" despite the Jew's deep grudge against and hatred of him.

This willingness to forgive—typical of performative Christian compassion—is staged as a tableau vivant whose shocking impact is felt by all, through oratorical intensification. Having been ruthlessly denied forgiveness by the Jew, the cardinal starts his cavatina: "Si la rigueur" (no. 2). A public prayer in F major, enveloped, as it moves, by soft woodwind waves (with a poignant touch on "*le* pardon"), its periodic structure subsumes the ever-extending imploring gestures of its first half into a general convex contour, reinforced and mellowed (through abducting the accelerated triplets of the preceding cadence) in its second phrase (see music example ex. app. 5, in appendix):

> If harshness and revenge
> Make them hate Thy holy law,
> Let forgiveness and mercy
> Bring them back to Thee, O God, on this day!

Everybody is enmeshed within it and by it, above all—literally and figuratively—Rachel, whose voice hovers above the singing body-operatic:

> So much goodness and mercy
> Soften my heart in spite of myself
> And the Christians and their beliefs
> No longer terrify me so much!

Subjectivities seem to converge in a grand harmonious moment. Only Éléazar excludes himself, but even he does not appear discordant. Time stands still, and each is left to his or her own while still under the spell of the revelatory anagnorisis. And yet harmoniousness is fraught with tension and shock (also musically). What is it that Rachel senses? Is it, as she declares—and many critics, then as now, believe it to be the case—her simple realization that, after all, Christians can be good and receptive? Or, perhaps, the fact that this "sweet music" does not make her "sad" (unlike its influence on Jessica) is telling of her own, unknown Christian identity (as other critics claim)? Or maybe she is deceived again, failing to read the power relations that this ostensibly compassionate and encompassing gesture discloses—the dominating (and proselytizing) Christians dispense magnanimity towards their unforgiving victims and then betray them in the name of the God, whose forgiveness they now beseech on behalf of the "sinners"?

Be that as it may, the expression *is* genuine. The cardinal does believe he is compassionate. It is only through a critical "transcendental" perspective that the third option emerges. But this *verfremdet*, distanced perspective is built into the operatic text, and its auditor is in no need of a Brecht to reveal it. Those who are sufficiently sensitive to its presence (Rachel is later included) cannot allow themselves to be merely seduced by this communal music.

STEPPING INSIDE: PASSOVER STRAINS IN THREATENED ENVIRONMENTS

The "countermusic" of the Easter "Te Deum" in the fictional setting of Constance (in Halévy's opera) and the sonic expression of the holiday's carnival in the imaginary late-medieval Frankfurt streets (in Heine's novella) is the music of the homely Jewish Seder. The juxtaposition of these two aural worlds—the Christian and the Jewish—is salient and goes deep into the allocation and re-allocation of harmony and noise in Jewish and Christian spaces. It is part of a fabric of images long associated with these high holidays, images that include the blood libel, the noise libel, and hidden and overt religious practices (discussed in chapter 1). The abduction of objects and sounds from one sphere into the other is central here, as well as the *heimlich* and *unheimlich* effects of their displacement. Chronologically, the opera and the novella run counter to one another in this connection: in the novella the Jewish Seder is the point of departure, its exposition (set in chapter 1 of the story), whereas in the opera it follows the huge spectacles of act I. The different plot rationales, as well as the specific nature of their artistic medium, dictate this difference. In the *Rabbi*, an epic overture opens the stage in a grand historic and geographical panorama and brings in, as a "promissory note," the following reminder, concerning the two major medieval accusations against the Jews, that of the host desecration and that of the ritual murder:

> There was another accusation which in earlier times and all through the Middle Ages, even to the beginning of the last century, cost much blood and suffering. This was the ridiculous story, recurring with disgusting frequency in chronicle and legend, that the Jews stole the consecrated wafer, and pierced it with knives till blood ran from it; and to this it was added that at the feast of the Passover the Jews slew Christian children to use their blood in the night sacrifice.
>
> Consequently on the day of this festival the Jews, hated for their wealth, their religion, and the debts due to them, were entirely in the hands of their enemies, who could easily bring about their destruction by spreading the report of such a child-murder, and perhaps even secretly putting a bloody infant's corpse in the house of a Jew thus accused.

From here onwards the narrative modulates smoothly, shifting its setting to the brilliantly adorned abode of the rabbi and his wife, where they celebrate with "relatives, disciples, and many other guests" the "great feast of Passover." A sympathetic insider, Heine provides a description (skipped in the following excerpt) that is adequate in terms of the ritual's *alter Brauchen*, while concomitantly rich and sensitive in terms of the emotional world it evokes, and thus self-revelatory:

> Mournfully merry, seriously gay, and mysteriously secret as some old dark legend, is the character of this nocturnal festival, and the traditional singing intonation with which the *Agade* [sic] is read by the father, and now and then reechoed in chorus by the hearers, first thrills the inmost soul as with a shudder, then calms it as mother's lullaby, and again startles it so suddenly into waking that even those Jews who have long fallen away from the faith of their fathers and run after strange joys and honors, are moved to their very hearts, when by chance the old, well-known tones of the Passover songs ring in their ears.

Though the melody of this singing/leining is not written, it should not be very different from the basic Seder tune (as noted above in chapter 1). It is probably the old, Ashkenazi "Adonai Malach" tune, along its specific mode of unfolding, which indeed both lulls and awakens its hearer concurrently, connoting melodically both the Jewish wedding ritual (*sheva b*e*rakhot*) and the ushering in of Shabbat, the Sabbath queen and bride. These associations hover above Heine's enigmatic legend. The "bride" (Sara), a childless (a fact poignantly referred to in the course of the evening because of the central role of children in the Seder ritual) and ever-beautiful woman,[84] remains throughout the story the girl who was clandestinely wed, who then waited alone for seven years (the period of time initially set for the biblical Rachel's expectation for Jacob) for his return from Spain. At the Seder, we read,

> she sat on the high velvet cushion with her husband, as hostess, had on none of her jewelry—nothing but white linen enveloped her slender form and innocent face. This face was touchingly beautiful, even as all Jewish beauty is of a peculiarly moving kind; for the consciousness of the deep wretchedness, the bitter ignominy, and the evil dangers amid which their kindred and friends dwell, imparts to their lovely features an expression of soulful sadness and watchful, loving anxiety, which particularly charms our hearts.[85]

Wedding as well as death similes are interwoven in the splendid embroidery of the evening to create a carnivalesque effect:

> While Beautiful Sara sat devoutly listening to and looking at her husband, she saw his face suddenly assume an expression of agony or horror, his cheeks and lips become deathly pale, and his eyes harden like two balls of ice; but almost immediately he regained his previous composure and cheerfulness, his cheeks and lips grew ruddy, and he looked about him gaily—nay, it seemed as if a strange, wild humor, such as was foreign to his nature, had seized him. Beautiful Sara was frightened as she had never been before in all her life, and a cold shudder went through her—due less to the momentary manifestation of dumb horror which she had seen in her husband's face, than to the cheerfulness which followed it, and which was now gradually developing into jubilant hilarity [*jauchzende Ausgelassenheit*]. The Rabbi cocked his cap comically, first on one ear, then on the other, pulled and twisted his beard ludicrously, and sang the *Agade* texts as if they were tavern-songs [*Gassenhauers*]; and in the enumeration of the Egyptian plagues, where it is usual to dip the forefinger in the full wine-cup and flip off the drops that adhere, he sprinkled the young girls near him with the red wine, so that there was great wailing over spoiled collars, combined with loud laughter. Every moment Beautiful Sara was becoming more amazed by this convulsive merriment of her husband, and she was oppressed with nameless fears as she gazed on the buzzing swarm of gaily glittering guests who were comfortably enjoying themselves here and there, nibbling the thin Passover cakes, drinking wine, gossiping, or joyfully singing aloud.

In a narrative entirely focalized through Sara, with sight and sound intermingled as if in a wild nightmare, we are seized by her horror. The sudden disruption in the reading of the Haggadah is visually expressed by the horrified expression on the rabbi's face, but it must have been accompanied by a sonic rupture as well, however restrained. (Had it been operatically staged, a harsh chord could have signaled it.) And there comes a real musical "shock": the sudden shift of the rabbi's solemn tune into a ludicrous tavernlike singing. What does this mean? Sara is flabbergasted; only later that night, when the two are far away from their home, on a cliff over the Rhine (!), will she entreat him for an explanation, which turns out to be simple enough: his discovery of the Christian child's corpse under the table, slipped into the house by the two mysterious guests who had arrived in the middle of the evening.

Why does a musical change mark this moment, and what does it signify? Sara does not ask and we never receive an answer. We can only guess. Again our speculation will comprehend at least three different levels: that of the story's possible world, that of the author's perspective and voice, and that which has since evolved, both artistically and interpretatively. In the story's reality, the musical change can function as a time-saving strategy aimed at diverting the victimizers' attention through what is for them familiar and entertaining and, perhaps, also as an internal Jewish encoded signal: move, run away, there is danger here. Whereas the first conjecture seems quite plausible, the second is less so—no one takes it as a warning, as we infer from what is subsequently told. In any event, it indicates again the extent to which noise and harmony should have been considered as relative by the adversarial religious groups. It also discloses the fact that the counterculture's music was known even to most pious learned Jews like the rabbi, or perhaps especially to them, for they, as this story indicates, moved more than others between worlds.

This brings us to the author's perspective and his critical view of *volkskundlich* (folklorist) values, mentioned in chapter 3: what appear to their owners, or collectors of folk songs (like Achim von Arnim and Clemens Brentano) to be jovial, convivial folk songs, the author intimates, could be contaminated by the blood of victims whose wine (so central to the festivities of this night) and property were looted to the sounds of such melodies during just such horrible nights. This could be the melody sung the following day by Johann the drummer near the Judengasse gate; contaminated, plagued—music cannot jettison that import, as poor Nasenstern insists (and Portia agrees). In the time gap and the forgetfulness they represent, it is perhaps the songs, above all, that remain as a living testimony to what transpired on such nights. Between Jews and Germans there remain such melodies that have accrued horrific meanings, though their façade is sometimes totally innocent.[86]

Is there indeed a difference between "our" and "their" songs? — one may ask again, once the curtain opens and we are privy to the secret ritual taking place in Éléazar's house (act II, no. 8, *Entr'acte, Prière et Cavatine*).[87] The opening flute configurations connote femininity and orientalism, with the typical augmented second; again, not yet a cliché when Halévy wrote it. The cellos wrap us in their warmth, and the harp connotes airy scenes of queens and princesses in enchanted gardens as well as King David's psalms (see fig. 4.2 for a vicious representation of a Jewish harp, or Jewess' harp).[88] But we are in a darkened hall, where the assembled people are ready to eliminate every sign of their religious rites being practiced at the moment, if a stranger appears; the Marrano legacy of clandestine Seders in Christian Spain is summoned here. Unlike Heine's description of the traditional Seder, we find here only the typical wine and the distribution and eating of the matzah, and the solemnity of a festival, celebrated within a familial gathering. The text is an invented one, barely reminiscent of the Haggadah; so too its music. Yet the moment is oratorical. Again "real" music; Éléazar sings, blesses, prays, and curses (the typical speech acts of the Seder), all in "real" sounds. A connoisseur's ear can detect a Jewish strain, such as on the words "parmi nous descends" or in the way the tune approaches the much stressed sixth (upper G) and feels comfortable with the narrow range of the melody. The unfolding, however, is chorale-like, responsorially carried, with Éléazar intoning his solo part a cappella and the small congregation harmoniously responding. They follow him verbatim: word for word, sound for sound (as in the constable's edict in *Les Huguenots*). The harmonies are simple, but here and there a poignant chord is introduced. If it recalls any Jewish soundscape, it would be that of Sulzer's synagogue and the related "reformed" liturgical music of the nineteenth century, familiar to Halévy, to which he himself contributed a few chapters.[89] This harmoniousness of the music figuratively covers the blatant content of Éléazar's words:

> Ô Dieu, cache nos mystères à l'oeil des méchants!

> [O God, hide our mysteries from the eyes of the wicked!]

And yet the musical phenomenology in its entirety could fit well into Heine's description of the affect that traditional music evokes: it is both "mournfully merry, seriously gay," concomitantly lulling and awakening its listeners. Halévy, it seems, searched for solemn affect, with which he was well acquainted, and

Fig. 4.2. "Brass and String Instruments from Munich," 1851. *Fliegende Blätter* (Stauber), no. 302. Courtesy of the Universitätsbibliothek, Heidelberg. In this caricature, a harp is portrayed as stemming from the Jewish nose-beak and the over-elegant shoe (the medieval *crackowes?*) of its player, coalescing visual and musical stereotypes of Jews into an emblem of the innate false musicality of a "Jewess who looks like you and me." The player's plucking fingers and her pelican-like stool enhance her ridiculed birdlike appearance. The pelican, traditionally symbolizing both the self-sacrificing Jesus as well as a murderous parent insinuates hypocritical (if not uncompassionate) piety, as does the player's devout glance. What can such an open mouth intone other than discordant sounds? Alternatively, the coexistence of girl and poor bird in the caricature could serve as a travesty of Leonardo's *Leda and the Swan.* Maybe in a grotesque reversal of roles the Jewish girl herself becomes the rapist—of music. Curiously, Eduard Fuchs chose this caricature for the frontispiece of his *Juden in der Karikatur, Ein Beitrag zur Kulturgeschichte* (Munich: Albert Langen, 1921).

was less concerned with ethnographic accuracy. Again, real and symbolic music interchange. In the midst of the subsequent litany a free arioso, enveloping the subjective plea with a Bach-like agitated accompaniment on "Si trahison ou perfidie osait se glisser parmi nous" (if treachery or perfidiousness dared to steal amongst us), when all *faithfully* eat the matzah, a counterprofanation occurs: Leopold furtively throws away the unfamiliar, strange food, an act perceived by an astonished Rachel. Éléazar continues with the cavatina "Dieu, que ma voix tremblante / S'élève jusqu'aux cieux" (God, let my quavering voice rise to heaven); again "real" music embodied in the tremulous voice, carried in the entreating, cantabile mode (more befitting the content and atmosphere of the Jewish Days of Awe than those of Passover).[90]

At this moment the princess and Léopold's wife Eudoxie arrives, seeking to purchase a piece of jewelry for her triumphant husband. The scene is a typical operatic one. The husband is hiding from all, while his voice is still audible to us, in this unbearable moment, whereas Éléazar, whose inwardness is likewise hidden from other protagonists by operatic convention, is alternating between a buffo-like pronunciation of the coveted capital and his cursing the Christians (as he is supposed to do during the Seder, according to tradition).[91] What follows is less typical operatically: before all leave—the father already senses Samuel's nonbelonging—they pray together, recapitulating the opening hymn (again an invented ritual). The chorale-like structure leaves room for Samuel's foreign voice and strain to intervene—in his private talk to himself, contrapuntally balancing Rachel's own "asides." We hear: "Ah! Leurs prières troublent mes sens!" (their prayers confuse me)—an ineluctable parallel between food and music is thus created, emphasizing his perfidiousness. Then he apostrophizes the "God of his Fathers" to take pity on his torment. Unwillingly included within the small Jewish group, and musically coinciding with them, he feels himself excluded from both Christian and Jewish universes. Oratorical moments burst from within, opening up to previous moments in the opera and to various liturgical instances of the summoning of "Gods of the Fathers" by both Jews and Christians. The harmoniousness of this solemn celebration is only a façade, screening something quite discordant that will transpire soon.

THE LIMINALITY OF MUSICAL POWER
AS A JEWISH-FEMININE ZONE

What ensues is a chain of (mainly performative) speech acts that capsize the power relations of the two factions. Whereas in the first two acts it is the powerful, triumphant Christians who dominate and determine the public and private agenda, life and death, love and betrayal, in the remaining three acts the Jews, and, in particular the Jewess, lead the action and its momentum, determining life, death, love, martyrdom, and, even worse, torture. In the first part of the second act the Jews' speech acts are mainly ritualistic. The series of trios that unfold (of Éléazar, Rachel, and Léopold), in which the extent of Léopold-Samuel's fraud is shockingly revealed, are carried by his confessional illocutions, which cast him in an already weakening position. Henceforth, the initiative and the power are transferred to Rachel and Éléazar—the power of the informed subjugated, who can abide by their innermost convictions wherever they lead them. The crucial moment is when Rachel, in the finale of act III ([a] *chorus*), appears on the public stage, in the most blatant, though spontaneous, speech act, confessing what had previously been revealed within their secretive domestic circle: the calamity of the love affair that the celebrated Christian prince had carried on with a humble infidel Jewess—herself. Shock is introduced to the cumulative, previously ritualistic, tableaux. This moment of revelation is framed by chromatically descending parallel octaves that may have been an inspiration for a no less powerful illocutionary and self-sacrificing moment in the life of an operatic heroine: Brünnhilde, in her final soliloquy, at the end of *Götterdämmerung*.

The following section—sextet with chorus—is a tableau vivant *of* shock, expressed in the language most accessible to the participants and bystanders (council members, church prelates, soldiers, and so on), that of the religious *mysterium tremendum*,[92] a language both religions have co-opted for their most formative moments: the Christian "Dies Irae"—the famous twelfth-century sequence that was annexed to the requiem Mass, and the Jewish "Un^etane tokef"—the seventh-century *piyyut* that was adopted, at about the same time, by the Ashkenazi Jews in what eventually became one of the culminating points in the Rosh Hashanah and Yom Kippur services.[93] Like a Jewish cantor in the days of awe, Leopold starts the plea that opens the section, sotto voce, in a series of tensed, abrupt, ascending gestures, in the basic tonality of the opera—E-flat major, hued here and there by secondary, chromatic chords:

> Je frissonne et succombe et d'horreur et d'effroi
> et j'appelle la tombe qui va s'ouvrir pour moi!

> [I shudder, overwhelmed with both horror and fear
> And I call for the tomb to open for me!]

Anxiety in the face of death and God seizes them all, each in his or her own individual mode of expression and prayer, contrapuntally organized to be perceptually intelligible. (The same harmonic progression will reiterate throughout the number, reinforcing the effect of the stillness of time while withholding a waning of tension; Éléazar, however, is exceptional in modulating to a distant tonality, emphasizing his difference, while magnetizing all to "his" place.) The chorus that upholds this oratorical moment as sonic pillars opens it to the respective mysterium tremendum moments of both religions: "Ô jour d'horreur et d'effroi" and later "Ô jour de deuil, Ô jour d'effroi" almost literally translating "Dies irae, dies illa" (Day of wrath, that day) and similarly recalling "[a]nd we will make mention of the mighty holiness of this day, for it is tremendous and awful," the opening phrase of "Un^etane tokef."[94] Among the protagonists, there are those still hoping that heaven will save them (the Jewish and Christian women and the religious officials) and those who do not (Éléazar and Léopold). In the final moment, they all unite in the exclamatory speech act: *Grand Dieu.* Even Éléazar and Brogni, separated from the rest by an audible time lapse, rhyme ironically on these same words.

The irony of the "oneness" of the Jewish and Christian God that the operatic conventions coerce them to proclaim is exacerbated by the fact that this horrifying moment revolves around the severe boundaries of exclusiveness that each religion imposes on its believers. All are seized by the disastrous impending outcome: the anathema.[95] It was first heard in the opera by Éléazar, who in the previous act excommunicated under malediction the impersonating Samuel. Now, in the number following the "Dies Irae" chorus, the pretender is also excommunicated from the Christian congregation by Cardinal Brogni. Brogni performs this illocutionary act as the man in power; in fact, he is compelled to do it by Rachel's public confession, and, however ferocious he sounds, he fears the outcome of the deed for all. Boundaries were transgressed, and easily so; voices and sounds were conducive in the committing of the transgression and also will be in its unearthing. What was so shielded against in the fictions of the "real" Middle Ages (as Chaucer's "Prioress' Tale" attests) is revealed as highly fragile in the "reality" of its fictional representation.

Here the modern predicament lies, which the feminine, empathetic figure of Rachel embodies so poignantly: identity is optional—one opts for it led by sentiment and commitment to a group, individuals, and their shared forms of life, rather than by blood and dogma. The individual is the one to mark the boundaries and she is responsible for the outcome of her choices. Indeed, there is no categorical outward sign that separates her from her feminine Other, and the other soprano, princess Eudoxie (beyond their social-political inequality, as also reflected operatically); hence their sympathetic duets and mutual understanding, however bitter their outcomes. The Jewess marks the boundaries and chooses, again and again, where to position herself and her Others, attuned to her own inner voice. The others follow her: they accentuate their vocal performativity in their main illocutions and addresses. Thus, among other utterances, Eudoxie will exhort (act IV, no. 19): "Ah que ma voix plaintive fléchisse votre coeur!" (Ah! Let my plaintive voice melt your heart), whereas Brogni exclaims (act III, finale [b]): "C'est l'Éternel lui-même qui vous a par ma voix rejetés et proscrits!" (It is the Lord himself who has rejected and proscribed you by my voice). Above all, Rachel's choice will affect her father, caught in deep ambivalence—between his love for her and his desire to grant her a good life on earth, and his craving for heroic self-sacrifice and vengeance. This overwhelming predicament draws from him one of the most famous operatic numbers of the entire century: "Rachel, quand du Seigneur" (act IV, no. 22) whose melodicity and rhythmical configuration are of the type prevalent in Yiddish songs, bringing what could be perceived as "symbolic music" to the precincts of the real. It is this embedded vocality, with its melodic gestures of pleading and imploration (as in the leaps of sixth and the fermata, ritardando style), that brought Neil Schicoff, a celebrated tenor and the son of a well-known cantor (a Viennese émigré), to perform this aria in 2003 in a Vienna synagogue in a spirit akin to the "torn and boiled heart" quintessential to a Jewish Ba'al T'fila of the Days of Awe.[96] However sentimental this aria may appear, its popularity for generations of Jews and non-Jews bespeaks the extent to which the "unspecified" affective world of precarious existence, epitomized by Jewish experience, became more universally shared.

At the end of the day, Rachel embraces the old sentiments and commitments—to die with her father, thrown into a cauldron of boiling liquid. Librettist and dramaturge Eugene Scribe's initial idea was to end it with her conversion. This change is crucial. It is less important who introduced the changes, for it is clear, as Hallman writes, that the changes, in general, went in the direction of intensifying the Jewish-Christian opposition, thus enabling a more straightforward artistic engagement with the aesthetic categorization of the Jew.[97] Is this martyrdom or glorified suicide, in line with opera heroines such as Dido who preferred the funeral pyre to the life of a humiliated, rejected lover? Or is it more akin to the self-immolation of a Brünnhilde, whose genesis she may have inspired? It is clear that the concepts and affects of Rachel are not medieval, though she is undoubtedly connected to anonymous ancient Jewish heroines as well as to fictional succeeding ones: Jessica, Sara, and Mirah. In the finale of act V, to the sound of the oratorical accompaniment of her impending execution sung by the Christian spectators (responsorially, first by Brogni and then by the congregation)—

> Au pécheur Dieu soyez propice,
> Saints et Saintes intercédez,
> du ciel appaisez la justice,
> Seigneur tout puissant, pardonnez!

> [God be merciful to a sinner,
> saints, intercede,
> mitigate the justice of heaven,
> almighty Lord, forgive!]

—Rachel moans to her father:

> Ah! Mon père, J'ai peur! Leurs lugubre prières
> glacent mon coeur d'effroi!

> [Ah! My father, I am afraid! Their gloomy prayers
> strike icy terror into my heart!]

The lugubrious internal pararhyme creates an imperceptible yet terrifying slip-page between *her père* and *their prières*, both hinging on *peur*. The gap between full rhyme and pararhyme becomes a reflection of the gap, so narrow, yet so ab-solute, between "us" and "them." The middle phrases of the a cappella chorale to which she reacts "intercede" with mournful chordal progressions, overcloud-ing the brighter diatonic E-flat major tonality of its opening and closing verses (ex. 4.3). Yet, what renders this so ominous? After all, the musical language of this chorale is no different from that sung in the Seder, though deploying more emphatically its darker realms.

If there is no categorical difference, either religious or strictly musical, be-tween "their" and "our" music—what is it that, nevertheless, reinstates exis-tential barriers around the division's historical victims? A tentative answer may be vislumbrated in the final section of the unfinished *Rabbi*, a "non-finale" ending, eschewing sentimentalism. Gates, real and imaginary; sounds, sights, smells, and tastes—sexual and culinary—create the chain of imageries that build up towards it. Gates and music are interrelated in this fictional world, as we have seen, with the tavern songs that marked the couple's flight from martyr-dom on Jewish premises, and the Flagellants' ones that signal their reentrance into a Jewish milieu. The open-endedness of the story creates another such liminal zone of music and identity. It is "orchestrated" as a quintet, with few attending bystanders: a duo of a foreign "Spanish" knight and the beautiful Sara whom the husband joins to form a trio, the meeting of all with Schnapper Elle (a new quasi-grotesque acquaintance of Sara whom she met at the synagogue's

Ex. 4.3. Jacques Fromental Halévy, *La Juive* V, finale,
"Au pécheur Dieu soyez propice."

women's gallery), backgrounded by Nasenstern. It will come to a halt, uncompleted, with a short choir, from within her restaurant.

The knight opens this "ensemble" with a gesture worthy of Don Giovanni's approach to Zerlina accompanied by her faithful Masetto: hyperbolical praises of Sara's beauty, interwoven with a series of "Spanish" poetic clichés "in a tenderly gallant tone." She bitterly rejects them and him, modulating the gallant laudations into a *Sturm und Drang* rebuttal, claiming: "My noble lord, if you will be my knight you must fight entire nations, and in this battle there will be little thanks to be won and even less honor." Her husband now takes the lead, revealing the knight's hidden Jewish identity. Softening the exchange, he gradually leads the Spanish knight to a surprising recognition: Seven years earlier, Rabbi Abraham had rescued him—his friend Don Isaak Abarbanel—from the waters of the Tagus near Toledo. Sounds of the lute Abraham had played then, in his longing for his beloved, can be heard in the background, when the "music" resolves into a happy homophonic trio of the three, interrupted with a few remarks exchanged by the participants, bringing the rich exposition to an end. Eulogizing Jewish food that he—finding more affinity with the heathens than with either Jews or Christians—prefers to Jewish religion and prayer, the knight leads the hungry couple to Doña Schnapper Elle's kitchen. This comic interlude brings them to a "recapitulation"—to music similar to that of the opening quintet—while the Spanish knight now grotesquely compliments stout middle-aged Schnapper Elle's beauty yet she, though charmed by his words, remains unyielding. A new theme surfaces: that of the Amsterdam brothel into which she was mistakenly taken, apparently without ever giving away her chastity and virtue.

Poetry and music are associated with the Spanish Golden Age; sex and food function as their alternative id's life instincts (capsizing Orsino's famous opening to Shakespeare's *Twelfth Night*). "Und meine Seele schmolz," says Don Isaak—who may stand for the author's alter ego—raving about Jewish food, "wie die Töne einer verliebten Nachtigall" (and my soul melted like the sounds of an enamored nightingale).[98] Nobody, in the course of the events, tastes these corporeal dishes, and they remain unfulfilled objects of desire. The interchangeability of Jewish food and borrowed melodies will be later iconized in Heine's Schiller-Beethovenian "ode to the *Schalet*" parody, and the Amsterdam brothel's women will feature in the "Apollogot." These themes are repeated throughout his work. Both music and food are the cathected objects that follow the liminal Jewish figure who chooses to wander in foreign precincts. Liminality is music's basic trait, as noted above: it is easily borrowed, smuggled, and transferred. But it is also among the last to leave, last to lose the imprints of those who possess it. Spain embodies this contradictory predicament. In Spain, the pious rabbi used to play the lute and sing love songs to an abducted, distant wife; in the Iberian Peninsula many a Jewish poet flourished, among them those of the Abarbanel family (to whom Don Isaak is related). Yet the kind of music Abarbanel represents was later connected by Heine, in the *Hebrew Melodies*, to an authentic Jewish vocal lore, before it became an Ashkenazi "whimpering kettle." "Jehuda ben Halevy" studied it as a child (in the melodies of the antique biblical trope); this later ripened in his wonderful musicalized poetry that the cherubim adopted for their celestial songs.

The inn's guests summon Schnapper Elle inside; the tortured guests and their valiant friend will obviously follow her. Otherwise everything remains open: the barren couple—will they later be blessed with child? The destiny of their Bacharach relatives who remained behind—were they slaughtered or saved?—the story contradicts itself on this point. Will Abraham establish a new community, be the head of an old one, or will they remain survivors, bringing the old world to a new, seemingly more modernized (and assimilated) one? Perhaps they will move to Palestine, like Daniel and Mirah (in the next chapter, and, for that matter, Jehuda ben Halevy, from the previous one?) Isolated from their entire community, these liminal figures connect the history of the aesthetically categorized Jew with a new agent: that of the chosen leader and prophet, the group's utmost insider, who, at the same time, becomes its fated outcast.

Before moving there, let us try to collect the notions concerning sonic belonging that the preceding pages yielded. As objects of desire and their embodiment, the musics and vocalities portrayed in the works discussed above also *structure* desire, becoming its most palpable manifestation, marking as well its contradictory trajectories: those confined within the communal and those extending beyond it, those projected from the past and those produced at the moment, those coming from the outside as noise or harmony searching for a habitat, and those that threaten to destroy the house. (A "heimlich-unheimlich" rendition of some of these trajectories, and the themes that launched them, can be viewed in Moritz Daniel Oppenheim's lithograph, "Reinchen Returns from the Church Concert," fig. 4.3.[99]) All these sonic articulations have been coveted, or averted at a certain moment within these worlds. Together they map, perhaps more than any other form or medium, the existential meanderings of liminal Jewish existence these vocal fictions sought to figure out. And yet, with the disappearance of visible borders, and however shared the musical language became, still almost unheard sonic boundaries between those adversarial subjectivities seem to have been acutely felt. And through them, only scant sympathetic ripples seemed to reach those who dwelled on the less fortunate side of that sphere.

JUST AND UNJUST PROPHETS

Modernism gave rise to a secular conception of prophecy and to profane prophets. They came to the fore in works of authors associated with the

Fig. 4.3. Moritz Daniel Oppenheim, "Reinchen Returns from the Church Concert."
Oil on cardboard (grisaille), 1877 (illustration for Salomon Hermann Mosenthal's
story, "Raschelchen"). Courtesy of the Jüdisches Museum, Frankfurt am Main. The
competition between Jewish and non-Jewish sonorities in German Jewry at the time is
typically brought into this image in connection with the feminine zone and Passover's
strains: The girl, a talented player, accompanied by her Christian lover (here,
undisguised, unlike *La Juive*'s Léopold), has just returned home from performing
in church to find her mother (who avoids eye contact with her) sitting alone at
the traditionally set Seder table. She pleads for understanding, or forgiveness. The
domesticated piano, functioning as a pedestal for the matzahs, bespeaks the mother's
hope of a different kind of integration between these musical worlds.
The melancholic cat concurs.

breakthrough of revolutionary modes of art and thought around 1900, as well as in their authors' missionary awareness. There are several reasons for the revival of this antique profession within a frame of reference so at odds with its original content and context. Among them are the creation of new, iconoclastic modes of expression, discourse, and thought leading to the formation of new deities; the vehemence with which they were brought about and their defiant contents; and the precarious position of their authors within a society that was indifferent, inattentive, or even alien to the new message they wished to deliver or implement.

Within this general group, the figure of the Jewish author as a "prophet without honor," as Frederic Grunfeld branded him at the onset of a new wave of interest in fin-de-siècle culture, looms large.[100] The dishonor Grunfeld refers to in this connection goes beyond the characteristic opprobrium that befalls prophets "in their own town,"[101] for it amounted to burning the works of these "prophets" and annihilating their bodies. It has long become a truism that Jews earned such a precarious cultural position by viewing European society from a vantage point reserved for those who were never entirely accepted in it, yet were often defter in imbibing its cultural treasures than many an "inside-insider," and shrewder in molding revolutionary tools in their amplification.[102] The connection of this development to the vital interest that Jewish thinkers such as Hermann Cohen, Franz Rosenzweig, and Martin Buber found in the biblical idea of the prophet, and to the central place of the Hebrew prophets and their religion in Zionist thought, entails a rather complex dialectics. Yet such dialectics is not without precedents in two major "prophetic" works composed by the liminal Jews Meyerbeer and Mendelssohn around the turbulent events of 1848–49, and just before the first publication of Wagner's *Das Judentum in der Musik*.

The almost synchronized attraction that the diametrically opposed figures of Meyerbeer and Mendelssohn found in the idea and story of a prophet— whether a true or a false one—and their immersion in his adventures for a good number of years is far from self-evident.[103] It is, of course, expected that in their "division of labor" Mendelssohn opted for the just prophet and Meyerbeer for the false or unjust one; that Mendelssohn made it his mission to harmonize the harshness of a biblical story about a wild prophet who became a mythical figure in both Jewish and Christian traditions, almost without tempering that story with late New Testamental interpretations, whereas Meyerbeer made it his business to delve into the convoluted psyche of a fake diviner, and musically magnify it. Pitting the different protagonists against each other among the communal and psychological environments in which their authors located them may shed new light on the composers' struggle, only partially conscious, to render their own predicament as outside insiders into a meaningful and durable cultural message.

Where does the prophet come from? How does a new, nonconformist cognition dawn upon him? What prompts him to his great and often ungrateful task? Is a divine vision necessary for this, or is such a vision an outcome of and a climactic point within his odyssey? What distinguishes his style and rhetoric from less combative oratories? What is the place and form of affect in his deliveries? Does he come to warn or redeem, lead or designate a different existential possibility? As far as the Hebrew prophets are concerned, most of them were directly ordained by God, who was revealed to them in utter solitude. To Moses he revealed himself in the Burning Bush; he addressed Jeremiah vocally and intimately, and opened the sky for Ezekiel to view the Celestial Chariot. Many were sent, or arose, in order to fight corruption, speak truth to power, offer alternatives, and bring consolation. The alternatives they advocated, as inscribed in many biblical prophecies, link the spiritual and moral force of monotheism with political and social justice generated by its premises. When polity and society rejected their message—as was usually the case—they became aggressive, sometimes violent. From the biblical narrator's viewpoint, their violence—whether that of Moses, Samuel, or Elijah—is considered as a vicarious expression of God's own wrath. Even then, violence is mostly compensated by compassionate acts of mercy, consolation, and peace on the prophet's behalf or as a result of his prophecies.

Vocal fictions projected by oratorio and opera have an affinity with prophetic plots, embedded in the constitutive role played by illocutionary acts and their tonal enhancement. The centrality of illocutionary acts is most salient in *Elijah* (premiered 1846), which shuns even the regular oratorical narrative of evangelist or *testo*, while concomitantly still eschewing dramatic enactment. Contemporary critics objected that this narrative laconism renders it difficult to follow; more enthusiastic supporters—and there were hosts of them throughout the nineteenth century—thought otherwise.[104] They seemed to have been able to follow a sequence dictated by a unique vocal logic, transforming the original biblical story into a new, modern spiritual plot. Vocality is apparent also in *The Prophet* (premiered 1849), despite the grand opera sine qua non dazzling stagecraft that reached new heights in this opera.[105]

As in *St. Paul*, transitions from arioso to more aria-like parts within the same number are prevalent in *Elijah*. The interchangeability of the freer with the more melodically and rhythmically structured parts renders the protagonists into spontaneous personae of sorts, while bestowing on their interlocutions a special festive aura. Unique to *Elijah* is a similar approach to the communal parts—whether that of the group of soloists or of the larger chorus. Within the same number, they are transfigured from direct actors and reactors in the transpiring events into more contemplative participants, in the spirit of the Lutheran chorale, though never in its actual text and music.[106] In this way, the segregated fictional plans of a Bachian Passion mix into a dynamic scene that concomitantly becomes less realistic and historical. In terms of Engel's theory, *Elijah*'s protagonists transcend the subjective point of view of their emotions and desires, gravitating towards a more objective and encompassing position whose emotional span is mainly located in the realm of the sublime, which is still lyrical if not personal.[107] This stands in stark contradistinction to *The Prophet*'s protagonists, who remain insulated in their subjective bubble, though some of them pretend to speak as if from a transcendental height, or actually believe themselves to have been transmogrified. No less variegated in terms of transitions between genres and subgenres than *Elijah*, the historical scenery that *The Prophet*'s protagonists populate and revive becomes loaded with conflictual psychological and emotional trajectories that implode its fictional world.

ISOLATION, REVELATION, REDEMPTION:
ELIJAH'S ASPIRATION TO UTOPIA

Our prophets thus meander within their unique vocal fictional spaces into which they launch their prophecies, reveries, and more humanly generated expressions. Where does their power stem from? As far as Elijah is concerned, he does not have to be specially anointed or ordained by a divine entity. Like that of his biblical model, his prophetic consciousness seems to have been always with him, simple and compelling; God's verdict is reflected in his recursive delivery—"[a]nd Elijah the Tishbite, who was of the settlers of Gilead, said unto Ahab: 'As the Lord, the God of Israel, liveth, before whom I stand, there shall not be dew nor rain these years, but according to my word'" (1 Kings 17:1). His departure from the human domain will be the same as his arrival, always with God, born with his mission and dying while fulfilling it. In this, of course, he is the model prefiguring Christ, though Mendelssohn refused to grant him this role (that is, to conclude the work with a supplementary text from the New Testament about the revelation of Christ, as had been suggested to him by Julius Schubring, his main collaborator in writing the libretto).[108] But he may also be a paradigm for a precocious artist—as young Mendelssohn was globally recognized. Elijah's power, revealed in the cursing illocutionary phrase that begins the oratorio, is forceful enough to prompt the communal organ into a lengthy and complex series of vocal acts including lament, prayer, exhortation, and promise. This pattern returns in subsequent scenes—a short and concentrated illocution by Elijah or another messenger that engenders a plethora of vocal actions by both individuals and the multitudes.[109]

A complicated tonal structure qualifies the multifaceted illocutions, engendering continuities and discontinuities in and between sections. The dynamic is cumulative and with each new scene the overall sonic effect increases, traversing two extended vocal communal revelations (the fire and the rain miracles) that culminate in a solitary one—God's revelation to Elijah, which consummates them all. What follows is an imaginary communal revelation of Elijah's flight to heaven in a fiery chariot with fiery horses. (In the Bible, the only witness is Elisha, the prophet's disciple and heir.) The imaginary community remains there until the very end; while calling to mind the ending of Handel's *Samson*, which leads from Samson's burial to the reestablishment of Israel's unity in harmonious terms, here the chorus may be identified neither with the original biblical community nor with a particular contemporary Christian one. It is an ideal, utopian community, of the kind implied in Isaiah's prophecies, which supplies most of their verses. While bringing the audience from Elijah's flight back to earth, it does not provide them with a clear liturgical routine or national context in the way Bach's and Handel's oratorios do.

It is going to be harsh—the opening pair of diminished fifths linked through a rising semitone (the "curse motif") of Elijah's first appearance on the national stage tells us. The people echo the motif when they complain (no. 5): "Yet doth the Lord see it not; He mocketh at us; *His curse hath fallen down upon us.*" But these imaginary sufferers from the curse of God through Elijah (they do not appear complaining in the Bible; the verse alludes to Deuteronomy's series of curses) now turn to voice his own eternal utterances, as if accepting the verdict: "He is a jealous God" and He "visiteth all the father's sins on the children to the third and the fourth generation of them that hate Him"; their quote from the second commandment (against idolatry) is carried in a stern, "grave" choral declaration in C minor. They are quick, however, to disperse the gloomy clouds (note the lowered second, m. 87) into the bright light of a C major—singing the rest of this verse: "His mercies on thousands fall, on all them that love Him and keep His commandments" (Exodus 20:5). The contrapuntal waves, moving ever higher, mellow away the earlier rigidness.

Biblical Moses pronounces almost the same words when God reveals himself in the cleft of the rock in his third, solitary Sinai revelation; his verse—including the Thirteen Divine Attributes—became the Yom Kippur motto, also recited at the opening of the Ark on holidays (whose setting by Sulzer was discussed in chapter 3). The Israelites (and the contemporary audience trained to imagine themselves in their place), now metamorphosed into a Christian chorale-singing congregation, would usually not suspect a link to a Jewish layer of this kind (which traditional Jews would immediately recognize, and with other such associations, would urge an embrace of the work as "Jewish").[110] And yet the Christian German contemporary audience received the work with reservation, tempting some scholars to consider this as a sign of recognition, on this audience's behalf, of certain "Jewish elements."[111] The British audience, on the other hand—including Queen Victoria and Prince Albert—educated by Handel's models and long exposed to Hebraic tendencies, embraced it wholeheartedly.

Mendelssohn leads us again to experience the benevolence of God—and Elijah—in the prophet's interaction with the widow of Zarephat, whose child he compassionately brings back to life (no. 8). The violence against the prophets of Baal—as in the Bible, here too Elijah slays four hundred of them—is similarly counteracted by the benevolence of the water miracle. Such juxtapositions seep deep into the musical structure and content. The underlying accusation of ancient Israel's ferocious God and the uncompassionate Jew seems to underlie Mendelssohn's handling of these elements. The thematization of the vocal element throughout the work acts as a cohesive self-referential factor. It is a voice that mobilizes all, that instantiates the people as a communal entity, that becomes the vehicle through which the Baal-Jehova duel transpires, that serves both as mode and form for Jezebel's enticement and appears as the medium of God's ultimate revelation to his faithful prophet. The massive presence of the visual image of fire is rendered aurally, following God's own synaesthetic metaphor, as Elijah (through Jeremiah) tells us: "Is not His word like fire!" (no. 17).

More than *St. Paul, Elijah* is Mendelssohn's Passion, perhaps in a double sense.[112] That he identified himself with Elijah is a commonplace established when Prince Albert so anointed him.[113] Moreover, Mendelssohn deliberately draws on this tradition (that of Bach), with which he was so intimately connected, only to generate a radically new version of his own. This affinity is revealed in numbers such as "Es ist genug" (26; modeled after the *St. John Passion: Es ist vollbracht*, as Stoehlin has shown) or in no. 2—"Zion spreadeth her hands for aid" (which I perceive as structurally inspired by *St. Matthew Passion* 27a: "So ist mein Jesus nun gefangen"; see discussion in chapter 2). Concomitantly, and even in these specific numbers, it avoids not only a replication of that (Christian) theology but even a potential merging of the two adversarial traditions—the Jewish and the Christian Protestant.[114] Mendelssohn ends with almost the same verse that opens the *St. John Passion*—"Herr unser Herrscher wie herrlich ist dein Name in alle Landen" (O Lord, our Lord, how excellent is thy Name in all the earth, no. 42 m. 18).[115] He clearly avoids the rest of Bach's text, however: "Show us through your Passion, that you, the true Son of God, at all times, even in the greatest abasement, have been glorified." No abasement is presented here. No doubt, Elijah's enemies strive to kill him, but they do not succeed in doing so, and when he is called to leave this world, his ascent to heaven reflects God's miraculous summoning rather than a Via Dolorosa, a crucifixion, and an assumption of humankind's colossal guilt. The redemption this Elijah prophesies and signifies is encompassing enough to embrace a different version of the Day of the Lord, *Dies Irae*, a more benevolent and less apocalyptic one than that of the official Christian God's Day—a Day that may be fulfilled on earth. Elijah—and here the adversarial traditions do converge—is a messenger, as attested in the verse from Malachi 3:23, recited in no. 40 by the solo: "Behold, God hath sent Elijah the prophet, before the coming of the great and dreadful day of the Lord, and he shall turn the heart of the fathers to the children and the heart of the children unto their fathers, lest the Lord shall come and smite the earth with a curse." This text also features as the final, festive verse recited in the Haphtarah of the Shabbat before Passover—Shabbat Ha-gadol, which downplays the element of God's "curse" in this verse.[116] He will come again—Elijah, on Leil Ha-Seder, as an invisible guest, a harbinger of both private and national redemption.

If indeed, in the spirit of contemporary revolutionary moods and ideas, Mendelssohn envisioned here a more earthly mode of redemption—was it an image of a utopian state of affairs or of a gradually improved present; an ecumenical one or a more specifically denominational one? Again, a hint can be elicited from the medium itself—sound—which is the medium of God's "private" revelation to his prophet Elijah, "qol dᵉmama daqqa"—"ein stilles sanftes Sausen" (a still small voice) in no. 34, "Der Herr ging vorüber" (Behold God the Lord passed by). Following the threefold turmoil describing the aural signs that precede the appearance of God (tempest, earthquake, and fire)—powerfully embodied through vocal and instrumental means—a simple, if not naïve E major phrase, whose major part falls on a long pedal point on its triad, marks his coming, or better, his Voice (here translated as *Sausen*; see ex. 4.4). The too often taken-for-granted sonic interpretation of this verse raises the question whether Mendelssohn's God is symbolized, or even incarnated, through a Rameaunian *corps sonore*—the natural basis of all harmonious music, according to the renowned eighteenth-century French theorist. Perhaps this God is even nature itself—the way Wagner would soon embody it in his famous *Rheingold* prelude (a semitone lower).[117] Pointing beyond specific religion and denomination, it

Ex. 4.4. Felix Mendelssohn, *Elijah* II, 34 Chorus,
"Behold, God the Lord passed by," mm. 115–26.

unwittingly marks the desire to relegate God's presence to a primordial beginning, following both Handel and Haydn in the symbolization of Genesis' light
through a prolonged triadic exclamation. Everything seems to grow out of this
substantial sound—the entire possible musical world—that world that fits human consciousness so perfectly, through a Leibnizian preestablished harmonic
order.[118] Even the king, Ahab, and the queen, Jezebel, are part of it, despite
their avowed betrayal of him, and so are the prophets of Baal: they speak its
language and even call upon their gods through it.

How is this theologically possible? In what way do these transgressors partake
of the divine order? What is the difference, in terms of the language and medium

of revelation and prophecy—if there is any—between true and false, the just and unjust prophet (in the Pentateuch, the false prophet cannot be known by the form or medium of his delivery—his signs and wonders may come to pass— only by its content; in modern terms—he may be simultaneously "right" [in his particular propositions] and "false" [in his narrative]). Furthermore, the God of Mendelssohn's Elijah never speaks to his prophet after the revelation, and, un-like the biblical figure, this Elijah responds only with a prayer of thanksgiving, never traversing the infinite distance between himself and God by a more direct address. Though not exactly along the contemporary Kierkegaardian "Fear and Trembling" position,[119] the way this modern prophet chooses to communicate with his creator is through the mode of prayer (as with the famous "Herr, Gott Abrahams," Lord God of Abraham, no. 14), which he (paradoxically) believes will be fulfilled. With the destruction of the Temple, prayer became for the Jew the only possible way to communicate with God.

The power of prayer bridges the unbearable distance between God and hu-man being, between eternity and mortality, and provides salvation. The abstract fictionality of the work becomes at this point its theological raison d'être: Noth-ing actually takes place on the oratorical stage—no child is (fictionally) revived, no (spectacular) fire descends, fiery chariot and horses do not appear; but what should transport characters onstage and real-life audience beyond the fictional world (in which all are equal before God, all utter his harmonious being) is prayer—a prayer of entreaty, glory, and thanksgiving, as source of salvation. It is as if the prayer itself—"God's breath in man returning to his birth, / The soul in paraphrase, heart in pilgrimage"[120]—was its own reward, as modern theolo-gians, Franz Rosenzweig for one, maintain.[121] Hence the centrality of Psalms as the poetic accompaniment chosen by Mendelssohn for large parts of the oratorio, which he prefers to the devotional texts of the Christian chorale. Man and Woman are always alone; fear and agony are their only companions: only if they put their trust in God are they delivered from their torment. This is the main lesson, or motto, of most of the Psalms, especially those that were selected to accompany *Elijah*'s protagonists (and others that Mendelssohn composed). That is what renders the work so theologically modern, in a way reminiscent of Schoenberg's famous 1912 letter, expressing his wish to compose an oratorio that would center on modern man's wrestling with God, who finally succeeds in finding him—"learning to pray."[122] At the same time, the preestablished har-mony provides a safe-conduct to salvation.

In the final analysis, however, they remain alone: Elijah, Felix (and later Arnold), the epitome, or portrait, of modern man as a Jewish composer (or writer). Though celebrated by many, he is not redeemed by them, nor are they

Fig. 4.4. Advertisement by the Jüdischer Musikverein,
Breslau, for a performance of *Elias (Elijah)*, 18 April
1937; from my family's archives. My grandparents
Dr. Abraham-Adolf and Lotte Pinczower most likely
attended. (A relative, Herta Pinczower, sang the alto
part.) A month earlier, the work received a special
performance at the Oranienburger Straße Synagogue in
Berlin, an event documented by musicologist Alexander
L. Ringer, then age sixteen. His moving, unpublished
testimony reports a most powerful silent reaction to
the work, "interrupted only by some vainly suppressed
weeping." And he adds: "There was no doubt that in
1937 Jews believed they were hearing a Jewish work
written by a German Jew affirming the greatness of
Judaism." Indeed, the popularity of Mendelssohn in
the Jewish Culture Leagues in prewar Nazi time was
immense; such an experience was possible because
the work's semiotic infrastructure could lend itself to
"Jewish" readings.

saved by him. The community they convoke is ideal, utopian. It may, for a
while, reverberate in a Birmingham audience or even in a German chorale
society imagining a communal revival in the form of an integrative oratorio.
Later, in the nineteen-thirties, it would support German-Jewish strugglers when
they were gradually and systematically excluded from the European order and
sonic worlds they so longed to be part of (fig. 4.4). Within the framework of the
Jewish League (Jüdische Kulturbund) coercively organized by the Nazis, the
sounds and vocalities of the utopian ideal would redeem the listeners for a short

while, together with the excommunicated, anathematized Felix and Elijah, before they would awaken again into the inexorable reality of their worsening condition.[123]

IN THE VORTEXES OF VINDICTIVENESS AND COMPASSION: DYSTOPIA'S COLLAPSE IN MEYERBEER'S *PROPHET*

The role of the prophet falls on poor Jean of Leyden,[124] a dreamy inn owner, as a thunderbolt, while waiting for his betrothed Berthe and his mother Fidès to join him a day before his wedding. The wedding will never take place; instead, he becomes a cruel false prophet who will attempt, as a final act of self-redemption, to purify himself of crimes and agony by a "let-me-die-with-the-Philistines" act directed against his various enemies. In the seemingly clear-cut division between pastoral-carnival and Lent sonorities that opens the work (no. 1–2), in which villagers appear (including his future wife and mother) as musically representing the pastoral-carnival and the three inciting Anabaptists—Jonas, Mathisen, and Zacharie—as representing Lent, he seems to be attracted to both genres. But the vocal order of the Anabaptists closes in on him, as it does for many on and off stage. Their vocal manipulation is simple but compelling; they musically carry on the former flow (here symbolized by the immediate transition from E-flat major to C minor, no. 3), aggressively forcing their grim, unison plainchant, as a trope of their revolutionary agenda, on all sounds and echoes around (ex. 4.5). This is embodied in their tune's hypermetrical structure, which determines the nature of vocal utterances of all potential devotees, who are soon swallowed up in this compelling sonority.

Ex. 4.5. Giacomo Meyerbeer, *Le Prophète* I, 3, "Le prêche Anabaptiste."
Ad nos, ad nos, ad salutarem undam, iterum venite,
miseri! ad nos, ad nos venite populi!
(To us, to us, to the life giving stream, come,
miserable wretches, to us, to us, come people!)

Their cumulative sonic procession culminates in a massive singing of the tune, to which the vox populi adjoins its defiant vernacular text.[125] Now all are ready for mutiny: together they climb towards Count Oberthal's palace, equipped with pitchforks, scythes, and mattocks. Unlike the march of their Druid predecessors in *The First Walpurgis Night,* these rebels lack determination, faith, and clever tactics. Upon the sight of mighty Oberthal, they are paralyzed and later flee.[126] The three exhausted Anabaptists now feel the need for a more powerful, charismatic figure to lead the people in the execution of their grandiose, violent program. When they see Jean in his tavern later that evening, they are convinced they found the right person.

Jean—a devout Christian and a keen student of the Bible—has premonitions and visions of himself in which he features as a Messiah, Son of God, engulfed in blood, dragged by Satan and cursed by infernal voices, but then redeemed by a heavenly voice. The Anabaptists, struck by his visual resemblance to the portrait of King David worshipped in Münster, will decipher dreams for him, and eventually almost realize their insurgence. But at this stage their interpretation falls short of mobilizing him, the humble lover. It is only an atrocious moral blow that persuades him to join them: wishing to sexually devour Jean's betrothed, the lascivious Oberthal will cruelly exploit Jean's devotion to his mother, forcing him to choose between the two women. Desperate, he will sacrifice his beloved fiancé for his adored mother. In his frustration and surging desire for revenge, Jean will join the Anabaptist triumvirate in its war waged against oppressive dictators.

Sonoric drive, religious fantasies, and a mounting moral rage merge to build up a persona in the new capacity the three impostors (as they are correctly labeled by Oberthal)—bestow on him. We meet Jean again, this time deeply immersed in his new role and the dystopia he has brought about with his three comrades, persuaded now of his divine origin, which he continues to cultivate through the image of the musical King David. His vocal articulation remains heightened throughout. A tenor, he usually inhabits the higher notes of his vocal ambitus, speaking as if in delirium or verging on hysterical tones of a *Sprechstimme.* (This befits his speech acts that include expressions of reverie, worry, beseeching, denial, enforced resolution, prayer, confession, wonder, plea, apology, remorse, and other distressful emotions.)[127] A spiritual fantasist, he will only come to terms with his choices and actions upon reencountering his mother's voice. He was not really responsible for his actions as a bloody prophet, he confesses to her, in act V (no. 28): "Ah! It is my love alone that has made me guilty. At first, in my just rage, I wanted only to avenge the death and the honor of Berthe, and then the bloodshed makes you merciless, those demented masters, those proud tyrants, I wanted to punish them all."[128]

Once again, the work hinges on the role and power of voice and vocalities. Here are key examples: In act II (no. 11) the three promise him, "at your voice they will be annihilated by us" or "will turn to dust."[129] In act IV, *scène et duo*, no. 23, the recognition of the two women takes place primarily through voice, and the mother then raises her voice to the Virgin in lament and prayer ("Ma voix qu'à te conjurer," E-flat major). In the finale of that act, in the exorcism scene the chorus of the Anabaptists' followers is relieved, after Fidès' withdrawal from her initial claim to Jean's motherhood: "Sa voix, sa voix, rend la raison" (His voice, his voice restores reason). Finally, in the grand reconciliation between the two (act V, *scène et grand duo*, no. 28) her voice thematically (and physically) resounds again. Fidès sings: "À la voix de ta mère, le ciel peut se rouvrir" (At your mother's voice, heaven can reopen) to which Jean replies "C'est sa voix qui me l'atteste" (It is her voice that guarantees it [heaven's pardon] to me).

His mother's voice is indeed of a most compelling nature. Following his fatal choice in act II (no. 10), in a shy voice and weeping (Meyerbeer's stage directions are accurate and detailed in general and with regard to voice in particular), she starts, in an arioso-like manner, to praise her son, pray for him, and bless him. "Ah, my son, be blessed! Your poor mother was dearer to you than your Berthe, than your love! Ah! My son! You have just given for your mother, alas! More than your life, in giving your happiness! Toward heaven may my prayer rise, and may you be blessed in the Lord. . . ." A "fate" motif (in Wagnerian terms), harmonically ambiguous, opens her number, resolved through an augmented (French) sixth through the dominant, to F-sharp minor (mm. 6–7), bringing in a distinct two-part melodic motif (divided between the cello and the flute) that is reiterated verbatim three times in her recitation, and then more freely enters into the musical texture of both voice and orchestra. (ex. 4.6a)

The motif bears a "Jewish" profile. It is one of those "cross-repertory motifs"—in Boaz Tarsi's terminology, introduced in the previous chapter—that run through the entire liturgical repertoire of Ashkenazi Jewish music, independent of genre, mode, and occasion. (What distinguishes the motif is the 5–1–3–1 upward progression, preferably filled in with the 2 between 1 and 3, as in the present case, with the 3 falling on the downbeat.) In one of its known versions, one finds it as the second phrase of "Kol Nidre,"—a central, emotionally loaded Missinai Niggun. This motif looms large, for example, in Arnold Schoenberg's matrix of cantors' versions of "Kol Nidre," ex. 6.4 (see chapter 6), becoming salient in the composition itself.

Theodor Uhlig, in his diatribe against the work, condemns the composer's style and cunningly attributes his aesthetic failure to his Jewish origins (himself characterizing Meyerbeer as endowed with *"Schlangenklugheit,"* serpentlike

Ex. 4.6a. Giacomo Meyerbeer, *Le Prophète* II, 10, arioso.

cleverness), denying an intended affinity perceived by another critic of Fidès'
motif with the "Ad nos" melody. The melody of the "Ad nos" itself, he insinuates, is one of Meyerbeer's "thefts" of an original Lutheran chorale.[130] This affinity of motifs, not far-fetched, may point to an early interpenetration of Jewish and Christian musical elements (as indicated in chapter 1), consciously or
unconsciously so juxtaposed by the composer. While bespeaking again the
elusiveness of sentiments of belonging through music, it also sensitizes to the
difference between threatening mantra and entreating theme whose melodic
grain they might share (a wise Nathan's ring syndrome?). Be this as it may, this
recurring theme functions almost like a leitmotif, later heard a semitone lower
(F minor) when Jean comes to part from the mother while she sleeps; it symbolically stands for him as her murmured prayer which he joins with his own
voice (ex. 4.6b); it amounts to her "sweet [vocal] image" which he takes with
him, as promise, identity, as that which he can never actually betray. It is tempting to view this bond against the background of Jacob-Giacomo's promise to *his*
mother: "Take from me, in his [grandfather's] name, the solemn promise that I

Ex. 4.6b. Giacomo Meyerbeer, *Le Prophète* II, 11 (scène et quatuor).

intend to live always in the religion in which he died. I do not believe that we can honor his dear memory more through anything else . . ."[131] Such a mother-son dynamic will significantly surface in the next chapter; in the symbolic space of the present opera, it will eventually save the prophet from himself, even if too late to alter the course of catastrophic events.

When she reappears in his life on his great coronation day in Münster—Jean now considered as a Son of God, "not even of woman born"—itself an ultimate acting out of his guilt feelings—he will deny her. A grand scene of anagnorisis, recognition, follows, exposing this denial with regard to his own flesh and blood. For saving himself he will enlist his cunning ways of fake exorcism, playing on her emotions, in his version of Solomon's trial.

The Anabaptists will soon betray him while the fake world falls apart. In the beginning of act V, forsaken, destitute, and alien in the dungeon into which she is hurled (not before cursing the Anabaptists as "priests of Baal" (!), Fidès will anathematize him for his treason and blood-spilling. Even before he arrives, however, she will endeavor to regain him for herself through an inner process of compassion. It is a cavatina with cabaletta stretta (no. 27, "O toi qui m'abandonnes") that conveys the depth of a parent's existential plight: it betrays an immense effort to contain the prodigal son within her rather uncompromising ethical-emotional, still loving embrace. Her mood is changing throughout, yet through her grand vocal gestures, performed in part with great restraint, well supported and responded to by a rich orchestral body, her expression transcends conventional unfolding, giving vent to a psychological progress that aims to counterbalance the abuse she has just gone through (as reflected, among other things, by tonal means, basically by linking the confrontation numbers around A-flat major, the key of the denial scene). Full reconciliation will be achieved only reciprocally, however. Upon his arrival (no. 28), and after a tortuous dialogue, in which the mother confronts him and demands that he renounce his power, they plunge into a sympathetic echo-singing that signifies and reinforces their mutual vocal appeasement. What she entertains naturally with her future daughter-in-law in act I, the mother and her sinful son will have to work through painfully. Berthe, the betrothed, will not follow their example. When she discovers, to her dismay, the identity of her long-lost lover (the prophet whom she has attempted—unsuccessfully—to assassinate), the briefly entertained dream of a regained triangular trinity of mother, son, and wife collapses forever.

Compassion and reconciliation are revealed as a most problematic human strategy in the antiliberal environment that predominates. Compassion can no longer be neatly measured (as in the balanced Smithian society) or generously practiced (as in *Nathan der Weise*), nor can it wholly compensate for ferocious divine acts (as in *Elijah*, discussed above). When a man is coerced to be cruel to his own beloved, how then is he to behave towards the one who provoked this atrocity (as Jean, who considers what to do with the captive Oberthal in act III)? When one is confronted with an act of terrible betrayal, can one still be merciful and forgiving (Fidès to Jean, act V)? When a woman is cognizant of her lover's crimes against humankind, does she even have the right to sympathize with him in his distress? (This is Berthe's unbearable dilemma, caught up as she is between her love for the perpetrator and her moral disgust.) Berthe opts for suicide; the prophet, like Samson, finds a more triumphant mode of self-annihilation: he is deeply convinced that the immoral enemies who brought manifold disasters upon him (including his own immorality) ought to perish. No longer able to express compassion in the earlier enlightened frame, the opera marks the dire mid-nineteenth-century need to rethink the limits and nature of sympathy and compassion, in both communal and familial spaces.

It is for only a very short while (during act III and part of act IV) that the dystopian world fashioned by the prophet and his Anabaptist comrades works. From the very beginning, the Anabaptists' cum prophet's world is too heterogeneous to offer an all-inclusive sonic closure for those inhabiting it. Its dwellers employ incompatible musical-vocal idioms: militant marches and various devout chants, carnival songs, and dance music (they must be entertained, these Anabaptist followers, according to the Parisian public taste, for whom ballet in the third act was a sine qua non), while deep inside they are still the happy pastoral villagers of act I (represented by the peasant peddlers). Only briefly does Jean merge musically with his Anabaptist anointers—they do not usually cohere smoothly. At one important point—his public prayer (no. 19) against an ominous "Ad nos" prologue—he even touches upon a Jewish melodic vein, with a response by a choir of basses and tenors: "Miserere nobis!" The grand ensemble in the act IV finale performs a highly intense moment, feeding on oratorical constructions with which Meyerbeer was very familiar. It coalesces an arioso (sung by the publicly betrayed Fidès) with chorale-like singing (the people in the church) which, while cohering musically, dramatically creates a most antagonistic effect, confusing all neat generic divisions. No less painful than the *St. Matthew Passion*'s "O Schmerz," it runs in the opposite direction: protagonists sharing the same fictional plane find that they are galaxies apart, thwarting congregational unity. On the whole, tableau too often dissolves into shock or even creates it while unfolding. Such things enraged Richard Wagner, who reported, in retrospect, that he furiously left in the midst of the performance, never to watch the work again (though he expressed a very different opinion in his enthusiastic letter to Theodor Uhlig, just following the event).[132] Wagner would eventually strive to create an all-inclusive, predeterminately redeemed sonic world, overcoming generic variety and dramatic cracks.

With Meyerbeer the case was different, though he might not have been fully cognizant of the fact that with this internally shattered vocal fiction, the traditional aesthetic categories—of the beautiful and the sublime—seem to have utterly lost their former grip. It is only at the very beginning of the opera that the music sounds beautiful in the classical sense of the word, and, retrospectively, this appears as a naïve world that can later only be regarded sentimentally, as it is very briefly attempted in the above-mentioned fifth-act trio.[133] Religious, oratorical genres—traditionally hailed as sublime—are thereby tainted as hypocritical and become self-parody. Even innocent, chiming children's voices (also in the grand act IV finale ensemble) cannot recover it, the way they would later in a Mahler symphony. There is almost no resting point at which one can give oneself to the artistic show and be rewarded by a sanctioned aesthetic experience.

Perhaps only with Fidès can one find subjectivity worth identifying with, but even that is judged in terms of bitter, awe-inspiring human existence rather than of the heroic sublime. No longer taking for granted old aesthetic moorings, the link between aesthetics and ethics similarly slackens. This is not only because expression becomes contaminated by insincerity, but also because contradictory moral values cannot yield a transcending unitary point of view, one that could be aesthetically assessed. Expression, in this imaginary world, is always verging on the pathological, and Meyerbeer takes great pains to reflect this musically. The world that gave rise to it remains, however, inherently unredeemed, unlike in *Samson, Elijah*, or, later, *Parsifal*. Identity, compassion, religious devotion, and even revolutionary values of liberty and fraternity—household assets of older worlds—are all up for grabs. The ways in which they will be reintroduced later, together with contents pertaining to the Jew as an aesthetic category and related themes, will be discussed in the next two chapters.

Famous critics and artists—including Berlioz, the Escudier brothers, Gounod, Fétis, and Gautier could not fail to notice the moral-aesthetic challenge of this work, though not all of these illustrious figures could welcome it enthusiastically, apprehending its revolutionary potential.[134] Audiences in both Paris and Vienna, in that tumultuous political moment (about a year after the 1848 upheavals), seemed more progressive and less hesitant to embrace the work's powerful grip: with its overwhelming reception in both cities, and the numerous performances that followed (especially in the 1850s), Meyerbeer reached the pinnacle of his artistic career.

* * *

Like the roving, indexically open melodic fragments she carried within herself, the musical subject that turned to "look like you and me" searched for "a local habitation and a name"—an emotional destiny where old sympathies and new aspirations, traumatic nightmares and utopian dreams could meaningfully, if not harmoniously, converge. In her body, she marked the liminal zone between worlds—those she could not utterly relinquish and those to which she never fully wished to belong. Melody, her spiritual nourishment, no less than her embodied desires, sometimes remained the last vestige of what she deemed she had forgotten. Attending here to sounds and there to voices, she sometimes capsized them: that which sounded to *them* like noise and nausea appears to her euphonious, homey, aurally hospitable, while *their* harmony breaks down into multifarious, noncongruent alien sounds. In her universal reveries, into which she often fell, the trap of an all-encompassing harmonious state of being left her with a void inside; she figured out that genre and mode, through their particularizing powers, could serve her better than language, which drew her into a common, morally, and theologically neutral public sphere. Thus she prayed, and prayer itself became her protected, quasi-redeemed, private resonating shell.

While, in her mind's ears, she kept listening to voices that subliminally and sublimely cohered, when she came to her senses she could not shun the experience of the tragic dismembering of the assumed communal unity of these voices. Theology, like other human affairs, is interest bound, she intuited, and its aesthetic manifestations are thus forever contaminated. As she realized the omnipresence of power relations, even within the ephemerality of intersubjective being, she could no longer be seduced by compassionate gestures, however attractive, nor was she herself later able to make them simply or unconditionally, even to those close to her. If she still opted for conciliation rather than flagrant resistance, it would call for working through a tortuous emotional path among the moral choices involved. That often entailed a problematized relation with a parent of the opposite sex. Or she could resign, withdraw, and die. Her vocalities and sonic selves, revisited and played back in this chapter, delineate an aural universe in which the characters of the next will wander, searching for an echoing belonging.

The Judengasse Synagogue Versus the Temple of the Grail: Motives of Sympathy and Redemptive Modes in *Daniel Deronda* and *Parsifal*

All the great religions of the world, historically considered, are rightly the objects of deep reverence and sympathy—they are the record of spiritual struggles, which are the types of our own. This is to me pre-eminently true of Hebrewism and Christianity, on which my own youth was nourished.

—*George Eliot's letter to John Walter Cross, October 20, 1873*

[N]othing will bring us back to the path of justice so readily as the mental picture of the trouble, grief, and lamentation of the loser.

—*Arthur Schopenhauer*, The Basis of Morality

AN ABSENT EXCHANGE

May 1877 was a rather Wagnerian month for the Leweses—George Henry Lewes and Mary Ann Evans (George Eliot). Cosima Wagner—a "rare person" according to Mary Ann—came first with a message from her father, Franz Liszt. Later her husband—Richard Wagner—joined them, almost conquering London with his music. There were all kinds of events in honor of the Wagners: generous meals, trips and walks, balls, and a gala concert. It was a serious attempt, in which Mary Ann Evans took a considerable part, to entertain the honored guests from Bayreuth. In the Albert Hall concerts, Wagner conducted a huge musical body, which performed a selection of his works. For a small and select group he recited the text of his *Parsifal*, which he had recently completed, "with great spirit and like a fine actor," as the novelist Eliot testified. The intimate and the public, the artistic and the intellectual, the German and the

Anglo-Saxon, seemed to mingle that late spring in those Victorian parlors. They were expecting something. George Eliot may have thought that the encounter with the man in whose operas she found "an impressive embodiment of human psychology, a representation of the natural along with the supernatural, an expression of a law shared by all the arts" would amount to a revelation. Nobody spoke explicitly of disappointment, though the encounter was not an inspiring event. Later, Eliot remarked that Cosima was the genius and Wagner a mere *épicier*. Cosima, in turn, recompensed the writer's generous hospitality posthumously: looking at Eliot's portrait, she commented on her ugliness, pointing at her resemblance to Girolamo Savonarola, the preacher and reformer from Florence.[1]

To be sure, not much rapport existed between the two great artists of almost the same age, who were then reaping the fruits of long years of artistic and intellectual activity. There were some good reasons: in 1855, Eliot, at home in the German language and culture, wrote an article that would not have quite pleased Wagner. Despite her praise, she attempted to diagnose "the problem posited by Wagner's music." She argued that the highest degree of musical inspiration should "overmaster all other conceptions in the mind of the creative genius." In music, the "slightest hint of a passion or an action" should always merge with "all other modes of conception," for this is the only way to achieve in music that triumphant effect over "men's ears and souls," she incisively maintains. Wagner's music, she implies, is overly planned and contrived; it does not stem from the source out of which genuinely human art grows. Though she praises *The Flying Dutchman* ("a charming opera," she writes), and finds in *Tannhäuser* the "music of men and women as well as Wagnerites," she has less patience for *Lohengrin*, complaining that the music sounds "to ordinary mortals something like the whistling of the wind through the keyholes of a cathedral."[2]

It seems quite probable that Wagner, never free from paranoia, had heard about George Eliot's article and about the even less sympathetic reception of his works by Lewes and the couple's friends. For Wagner there could be no harsher criticism than a denial of the genuineness of his music's expression.[3] He had not read Eliot's novels, but he might have had some idea about them, especially her most recent—*Daniel Deronda*—whose final part was published half a year before their meeting. It seems indeed unlikely that Eliot was introduced to him without mention of the novel, as the 1876 serial publication was a central event in England's literary life. Moreover, it would not be a wild conjecture to assume that he thus could have come across the themes and plot of the book, the subject of much talk at the time. Readers, well versed in stories of "good girls" of marriageable age, were fascinated by the novel's first chapters, which followed this familiar plot-line. Subsequent serialization revealed how the novel would betray their expectations. A foreign element came to dominate the plot—a highly accomplished young man, who had grown up in the house of an English aristocrat, and who might otherwise have fallen in love with the gorgeous heroine (Gwendolyn), finds himself deeply touched by the afflictions and the personalities of some Jews he meets. As he becomes increasingly involved in their life-stories, visions, and traditions, he is not surprised to learn that he himself is a descendent of their tribe. Not only does he not deny his origins, he even undertakes a lifetime mission to pave the way for the national-spiritual redemption of his people, who had never found peaceful existence as an ethnic-religious group, despite the great promise of modern times.

That some of these themes could have reached Wagner's consciousness may be inferred from the conversation, quoted above, in Wagner's family: Cosima's remark on Eliot brings Wagner (during that lunch) to reflect, following Gobineau, on Savonarola's physiognomy, remarking how ethics, in his case, eclipsed aesthetics (whether or not she knew, for example, of the latter's overpowering influence on the mature Botticelli, Cosima clearly did not endorse this preference, reflecting fin-de-siècle aestheticism). The mention of Savonarola might not be incidental; it could attest to the couple's acquaintance with some of Eliot's literary themes: her *Romola* is set in Machiavelli's and Savonarola's Florence. At the same time, the indirect comment regarding the inappropriateness of preferring ethics over aesthetics raises the suspicion that Wagner was aware of a crucial element in Eliot's novels: the close and faithful tracing of the moral growth of her protagonists, which reaches its highest expression in *Daniel Deronda.*

The encounter in London took place during years of increasing anti-Semitism in Germany. Though Wagner partially regretted the new, fully signed second publication of his lampoon *Das Judentum in der Musik* (1869) for the harm it caused to his reputation among his Jewish admirers, he never actually doubted the righteousness of his arguments, and continued to view them as a real contribution to a "scientific" understanding of the subject.[4] It is not clear to what extent Eliot was acquainted with the upheaval provoked by the publication of this essay, but she could have heard about it, and might even have read Wagner's lampoon.[5] In any event, the gap between their views on the Jewish question was profound. Eliot, who by that point in her life had acquired much knowledge of historical and ritual Jewish matters, could forcefully invalidate the anti-Semitic folly, whereas Wagner obstinately clung to a "theory of antipathy," which he set as the foundation of any issue which touched on Jewishness.

The two, however, probably never exchanged a word on the subject. In this chapter I engage Eliot and Wagner on the Jew as a sonic-aesthetic category, an engagement that historically could have actually taken place. This imagined Eliot-Wagner interaction articulates many motifs elucidated in previous chapters on various discursive levels within the vocal fictions they hypostatized: the musico-literary, the aesthetic-philosophical, and the theologico-political. At the basis of this confrontation lies the fact that the two authors shared some basic psychological and metaphysical premises with regard to art and morality which, however, led them to opposing conclusions. These inferences are clearly demonstrated in their imaginary representatives' respective visits to the Jewish synagogue and the temple at Montsalvat, and in the way both artists assess the experience of Jewish ritual music in relation to ritual music of "their own."

Their shared premises concern the concept of sympathy (or its alternative— compassion, pity, and *Mitleid*), its ethical and aesthetic centrality, and the psychological mechanism linked with its activation in human behavior. The use of the same frame of reference for oppugning purposes makes it possible to observe how an abstract system of arguments translates into practical aesthetics of negation of the Other (the Jew), on the one hand, and his or her full affirmation, on the other. What makes this chapter different from previous ones is that the aesthetic categorization of the Jew has become concomitantly more external and explicit: now it is a confrontation between outsiders, engaging wider political contexts and ideologies. Eliot and Wagner differ in this respect because Eliot's artistic treatment of the Jew is more straightforward, though its meaning might be lost on many contemporary readers. In Wagner's case, it is not so much an allegorized embodiment of Jews in his music dramas that is of interest in this connection,[6] but rather modes of artistic experience and aesthetic values that his dramas foster as a reaction to the Jewish art and musicality he so resisted and condemned. From within their divergent ideologico-political moorings, Wagner's and Eliot's respective works will be examined in relation to the "actual" realities of their times as well as in the modes of experience involved in the process of their realization.

The following discussion concentrates on several theoretical texts—ideologico-political and theological, and two works of art, one operatic (*Parsifal*) and the other literary (*Daniel Deronda*). The two works parallel, intersect, and harbor shared allusions and repeated themes. As in previous chapters, the fact that the works belong to two different media is not a methodological hindrance; their common elements extend—far beyond a dramatic plot—to the conspicuous musical elements of Eliot's novel on the one hand, and to the narratological character of Wagner's music drama, on the other. As Beryl Gray writes, "[n]owhere in George Eliot's fiction is the pattern of musical allusion more delineated—more coherently Shakespearean in the unity it generates—than in her last novel."[7] Eliot, whose love of music and whose devotion to musical activity never ceased, viewed herself as the heir of Shakespeare and Milton in this regard. She ascribed to music and to the sensibilities entailed in its perception the key to the secrets of the spirit and the harmony of the soul. Thus she enlists real and imaginary musical works that function in the fictional world of her protagonists. At the same time, she incorporates musical modalities and procedures within the narrative texture. The musical elements thus interwoven create a rich and reverberating fabric of additional levels of experience and meaning. Exemplified in the following discussion, these experiential and semiotic levels are brought into relief by comparing similar such levels in *Parsifal*, some of which are construed according to narrative modalities related to both temporal unfolding and the author's voice.

These levels of meaning are intrinsic to the universes of consciousness in which these two artists moved. This comparative case thus brings the double tracing of the Jew as a sonic-aesthetic category in its British and German contexts, sought throughout this book, to another pinnacle. In other words, the levels of meaning in the two works partake in the molding of complex interrelations between part and whole, individual and community, the ceremonial and the expressive, uncontrolled impulse and deliberate resolution, thus pointing to larger tendencies within these authors' respective milieus. In the case of Eliot, these correlations relate to a liberal-conservative worldview, and in Wagner's case—to an odd welding of semi- (if not pseudo-) liberal and monarchic elements. The commitment of both to certain forms of conservatism should not mislead us. Without the pretense to absolute truth, Eliot constructs an infrastructure for a contingent world in which grace, though relative, can permanently embrace objects which are not "chosen," but whose subjects are constantly involved in moral choices. In the shadow of the absolute, Wagner engenders some selective, isolated moments of compassion, endowed with a mythological force that eclipses the need of their renovation and the moral environment involved in their realization.

THE BIRTH OF WAGNERIAN AESTHETICS FROM THE UN-SPIRIT OF JUDAISM

I begin with Wagner not only because he was the first of the two to attend to the Jewish question (and thus perhaps provides a point of reference in Eliot's eventual treatment of the subject), but also because his discussion is mainly

theoretical and seemingly detached from the artistic act, whereas Eliot's generally combined the two. This enables me to momentarily isolate the philosoph-
ical-ideological question from its artistic embodiment.

For this purpose, I will briefly summarize the well-known facts of the background and implication of processes of emancipation in both France and Germany, and what the parallel development had already achieved in England,
now from a slightly different viewpoint than that of the previous chapter. If
the French Revolution's *fraternité* could only materialize (and not successfully
enough) among a few communes of utopian dreamers, *égalité* and *liberté*, by
contrast, could be legally constituted. While *liberté* was primarily viewed as
respect for the *autonomy* of the individual to live according to his or her views
and beliefs (as long as they do not harm others), *égalité* was linked with the
heteronomous validity of the (relegating) law and the (granting) privilege, and
to the fact that these are homogeneously applicable to every citizen, regardless
of religion or race. These two liberal principles were interdependent in both
theory and practice, yielding new cultural norms and forms of life.

Capitalism merged with these liberal conceptions. It substituted assets acquired through labor for those inherited by natural birth rights, and a dynamic
system of competition and change for stability and social hierarchy. It thus
highlighted the importance of establishing criteria for success and excellence,
whether consciously obtained or tacitly acquired, and the need for systems
of judgment and control. The changes in the social infrastructure of music-
making reflect this constellation: The liberalization of the musical world entailed not only the substitution of the proclivity of the amateur listener (or the
musical administrator attentive to his consumer's wallet) for the sponsorship of
the artist by the noble patron, but also the emergence of a new authority—the
music critic. The latter sought to base his judgment on independent criteria,
and thereby to guide potential listeners. The proliferation of journals of "professionals," which aimed at consolidating such criteria or undermining them, was
a direct outcome of this development.[8]

At the time of writing "Judaism in Music," Wagner was half-liberal, half-
socialist, an exile paying for his participation in the revolutionary events in
Dresden of 1848–49 (with his Russian friend Bakunin). From his point of view,
the ideas cherished in this revolution contributed to the weakening of the capi-
talization of art he so condemned. In his *Judentum* essay he fused some of
these revolutionary ideas with others that he cultivated in relation to *Lohengrin*
(1848). Wagner now sought to attack the world that had treated him, as he
complained, with unjustified hostility, from a new angle that enabled him to
formulate the ideal process of art reception. Wagner was nourished by several

anti-Semitic treatises that linked the fallacies of economic liberalization with the products of legal emancipation.[9] His personal story—bitter and humiliating as he experienced it—of a composer knocking at the gates of various musical institutions, sheds an interesting light on the connection between liberalization and emancipation. While distancing himself from the principles of socialism in postrevolutionary days, he began to allot considerable weight to subjective experience—ever moving from the individual to the collective—and to generate from it new artistic norms as a liberal communitarian.

The Jewish musicians who Wagner had met along his tortuous trajectory—Mendelssohn and Meyerbeer above all—represented prevailing public norms on the source of authority of artistic excellence, within which they were able to rise to greatness and through which to gain power: Mendelssohn as chief director of Leipzig's Gewandhaus Orchestra, Meyerbeer as a chief composer in the Paris Grand Opera. Their success, as Wagner did not fail to understand, reflected the criteria and taste of their time, and the circularity of the feedback system in which they partook. Wagner thus believed that his verdict against these composers directly implied the rejection of the criteria of judgment that they represented and the system of reception that presupposed them, and vice versa; this is the root of his criticism of the German (and, by extension, the French) society that had succumbed to such conditions.

It is not a coincidence that Wagner published his essay in the *Neue Zeitschrift für Musik* (founded in 1834 by Robert Schumann, Mendelssohn's great admirer), inspired by Uhlig's review of Meyerbeer's *Prophet* (discussed in chapter 4), in which the term *Hebräischer Kunstgeschmack* (Hebrew artistic taste) was (derogatively) formulated.[10] In other words, K. Freigedank (as he famously signed his essay) was not misleading us when he declared that his point of departure was located in critical theory. The external framework in which his ideas are set was indeed its breeding ground—the place where innovative critical notions and radical aesthetic goals were elaborated. From this point of view, it is not coincidental that at the time in which Wagner concocted his invective against the Jews he also industriously formulated his aesthetic program, in which he sought to ignite a revolution in the constitutive elements of the work of art.[11] He was indeed convinced that in *Das Judentum in der Musik* he was weeding out from the public field of art noxious taste-determining growths in order to enable the desired musical species to flourish. Aiming to justify the very act of uprooting, he articulated the deepest elements of his aesthetic outlook.

Three main premises underlie Wagner's essay:

(1) Individuals, inasmuch as they are linked to an ethnically living group, incorporate a kind of "existential substance" as the main core of their existence.

Defined in terms borrowed from the psychic world (such as suffering, zeal, nobility), this substance is further qualified in terms of force.[12] Wagner speaks about a "genuine folk-spirit" (*wirklicher Volksgeist*) when he refers to the Germans, and of "total sterility" (*vollendete Unproduktivität*) and "decaying stagnation" (*verkommende Stabilität*) when referring to the Jews. An individual from the first group is delineated as "a wholesome, total, and warm person" [*ein vollkommener, ganzer, warmer Mensch*], whereas members of the second group are defined by an "impotent personality" (Wagner uses the term *Ohnmacht* in this connection), or as a "deceptive [or delusive] composer" (*täuschender Komponist*).[13] The implied juxtaposition is thus not between different kinds of emotions a composer should possess, but between emotion or passion possessed by or lacking in the composer, which corresponds, respectively, to the existence of substance and to its absence. In the absence of real emotion, Wagner tells us, the vacuum in the consciousness is filled by weak linkages activated by the "imagination" or, alternatively, by melancholy—the default option of a personality that has no sufficient vigor even to properly mourn its missing objects. (Back to classical elements of anti-Jewish epistemology, New Christian Mendelssohn is characterized by both.)

(2) This "existential substance" is known through certain ideas wrought into symbolic systems—language, music, poetry, physiognomy, gesture (and in later treatises, also myth). Language, and even more so music, reflect most explicitly the "natural" substance of a group or of single individuals who belong to it. [Song] "is no doubt the most vital and undisputably true expression of the personal emotional being."[14] The emergence of language and music as modes of psychic communication is dependent on the continuous historical affiliation of the individual and the ethnic group with their natural geographic location.

(3) As specific utterances, these symbolic messages arouse certain emotional responses in the perceiver, consisting mainly of either acceptance or rejection of the entity they represent. In other words, the listener reacts to substance with sympathy, if not compassion, and to "nonsubstance" with popular aversion (*volkstümliche Abneigung*). Commensurability in the structure of the argument is thus guaranteed, for the first and last stages in the process described are conceived in terms of correlated emotional states.

According to this interpretation, characteristics attributed to Jews such as ugliness, shrieking speech, or defective music are not abhorrent in themselves, but rather in light of their emptiness. The idea of parasitism follows here: entities lacking in substance are in search of souls full of substance in order to live at their expense. Jacob Katz's claim that, following the anti-Jewish precedents in the writings of Marx, Bauer, and others, one can see Wagner's essay as concentrating likewise on an "abstract Jew," while giving it additional meaning:[15] if the abstract Jew of Marx seeks to dominate the capitalist system, thereby capsizing the ideal socioeconomic structure, the abstract Jew of Wagner substitutes deceptive values for the true values of artistic communication, preferring imagination or mood to real emotion, entertainment to psychic depth—musical effects to symbolic content. In both cases the result is rot and corruption.

That Wagner's main sources for the above claims could be found in the writings of certain Enlightenment thinkers such as Rousseau and Herder, who argued for the connection between substantial existence and primal linguistic utterance, is not surprising. The two, especially Rousseau, linked primal linguistic capacity to powerful emotional communication. However, whereas Rousseau associated this primacy with a primordial stage of human development (childhood or a lost historical paradise) and Herder identified it with earlier phases in the crystallization of ethnic groups, neither considered their ideas an adequate description of any *chosen* group in a possible present. They therefore did not limit the link between existence and expression to a specific historical-political reality. Inasmuch as the model they created was designed to mold reality, it concerns, from Rousseau's point of view (1) the extrication of the individual from society in search of an authentic, transparent flow of the subjective self, otherwise covered in contrived social masks; (2) the reforging of society on the basis of natural emotional communication, which stems from such transparent flows. From Herder's point of view, it relates to a cultural program that consists of: (1) the exposure of rich universal contents as embodied in particularistic variants of ethnic groups in the distant past and in the veiled present, and (2) the construction of new modalities of psychic expression for the sake of enriching the cultural-spiritual life of existing groups. Altogether, it is a universal, quasi-utopian model of communication at the center of these thinkers' worldview, rather than one possessed by an exclusive group or individuals.

What enables Wagner to transform this idealistic-universalistic model that can only be embodied partially and contingently into a realistic-particularistic one, assumed to realize the transcendental in an absolute way? Apparently, Wagner engages the "empirical sensibilities" of his readers rather than metaphysical notions. Accessing the sociologically "given"—what he calls popular aversion, *volkstümliche Abneigung*—"empirically" he asks his readers how we can explain the measure of abhorrence that we, good Germans, feel toward everything Jewish. From Wagner's point of view, sympathy or its opposite (rejection, abhorrence) are the psychological aspects of the artistic message, inhering in the symbolic expression of the "substantial" utterance. Sympathy is revealed to the addressee who carries internally the same substantial elements possessed by the addresser. Only those who share the same substantial elements are able to empathically respond to a soul delivering such a message; for others the road is blocked. The symbolic expression itself—in both the way it is produced as well as in the mode by which it should be deciphered—is not open to the process of regular learning. It cannot be acquired externally, through the act of traditional baptism, for example. In the lack of "natural," almost inherent, substance, the only way to attain it—as artist or art consumer—involves a readiness to suffer, as Wagner tells us in connection with the case of Ludwig Börne.[16] According to Wagner, the suffering of such an individual stems from his awareness of the absence of substance and functions as a necessary stage in its procurement. It has the power to exact compassion for the sufferer and thus to attain an empathic response of the kind elicited by a true artistic message. By virtue of this psychological mechanism and the solidarity it creates, the merging of the foreigner in society, which carries the real flag of existential truth, becomes possible.

This circular if not tautological argument configures "sympathy" as reverberation of sameness. Its trope is that of a sympathetic string, made of an acoustic substance similar to that of a plucked cord, at the sound of which it resonates. A pre-baroque conception that was still highly in vogue during the seventeenth century, sympathy was sought to contract distances[17] between those sharing affinity, thus procuring new resources of individual emotivity. Nationalized and remystified, it sustained Wagner's aspiration to direct a listener to yield "unresistingly" to his work, so that he "involuntarily assimilates even what is most alien to his nature."[18] The partial autonomy Wagner granted his listeners was further limited, however, by his insistence on the role of the self-appointed artist (again a "prophet" of sorts—one however, whose sources of inspiration are never called into doubt) to guide his folk to what he views is best for them qua folk.[19]

TOP-DOWN COMPASSION VERSUS BOTTOM-UP SYMPATHY

In comparison to sympathy, a psychological and aesthetic disposition, *Mitleid*, or compassion, plays a fundamental moral role in Wagner's thought. As he had read into Schopenhauer's general epistemology, so too in his "compassion" Wagner found reinforcement for ideas he intuited as an artist. With Schopenhauer, compassion is developed into an overriding moral principle that frees man from his will or egoism. This all-affirming principle crystallized in Schopenhauer against the background of two main interrelated negations. The first negation is directed against Judaism, stemming from the motivation to purge Christianity from what he deemed as the Jewish, anticompassionate elements with which it was plagued. The second, directed against philosophy, aims at superseding the Kantian individual, who acts in accordance with a rational, categorical dictum, with an individual who is motivated by a voluntary emotional core.[20] Wagner appropriated these ideas, rather egotistically; in his famous 1858 letter to Mathilde Wesendonck, he writes about a shocking experience he had when he witnessed the decapitation of a poor hen, noting how our lives rest upon such a "bottomless pit of the cruelest misery." To this he adds:

> As soon as another's existence seems to me to be lacking in suffering and carefully calculated to keep all suffering at bay, I can follow it only with un-smotherable bitterness, so remote is it from what I regard as the real solution to man's task. And so, without feeling any envy, I have nevertheless felt an instinctive hatred of the rich. . . . With subtle intent they avoid anything that could possibly make them feel sympathetic towards the misery upon which all their longed-for contentment rests, and it is this alone that keeps me a world apart from them. I have observed the way in which I am drawn in the other direction with a force that inspires me with sympathy, and that every-thing touches me deeply only insofar as it arouses fellow feeling (*Mit-Gefühl*) in me, i.e., fellow suffering (*Mit-Leiden*). I see in this fellow suffering the most salient feature of my moral being, and presumably it is this that is the well-spring of my art.[21]

In what follows, Wagner writes that in contrast to the experience of love, compassion in its various expressions is not conditioned by the individual nature of the suffering object, but only by the perception of suffering itself. This is the reason why we are not really interested in the personality of the sufferer, which in other cases might have aroused antipathy in us. In the final analysis, Wagner claims, what is important in the case of compassion is not what the sufferer feels but what I feel towards her or him, that is, my own subjective position. For what we know about what exists is only what we can picture in our imagination, and the way we imagine something is the way we feel and understand it. In his words, "if I feel the other man's suffering to be deep, it is because I myself feel deeply when I imagine his suffering, and whoever imagines it to be insignificant reveals in doing so that he himself is insignificant." This is my essential property, declares Wagner, "and it means that I will always avoid hurting another." There is nothing that is more enjoyable, he writes, than "the harmony in fellow suffering" (*Übereinstimmung im Mitleiden*). Indeed, through compassion we feel the obliteration of all of personality barriers—our own as well as those of the sufferer. Moreover, the more morally developed one is, the greater the ability to overcome one's own suffering by resignation, rendering the individual less in need of compassion. This is not the case with respect to animals, whose suffering, Wagner says, is meaningless and terminable only by death. If the suffering of animals has any meaning, it is in instructing human beings to appreciate compassion (here Wagner refers the reader to the scene of Good Friday in Parsifal's epos).[22]

To this point it appears that the expression of compassion is directed to all sufferers, but particularly to those who, like the Jews, cannot transcend their plight. But Wagner is quick to indicate his abhorrence for people who eschew compassion—the true root of redemption. To the suffering of the uncompassionate, therefore, he is completely indifferent. He is even willing to reform such people by subjecting them to torture, thereby inducing suffering and enhancing their capacity to suffer. Though he speaks in general terms, he likely learned from Schopenhauer that it is the Jews who deride compassion; Abraham's treatment of Hagar, who was banished to the desert with her son Ishmael, illustrates the absence of compassion in the Jewish soul and its religious teachings. According to Schopenhauer, Jews do not deserve compassion because they lack not only the ability to be compassionate, but also its prerequisite—the ability to suffer.[23]

Wagnerian compassion is thus exclusive in its rejection of those who are incapable of experiencing it and symbiotic in its effect of collapsing the boundaries between those who act and those acted upon. It dwells on the lofty emotions of those who are moved by suffering, while marginalizing the sufferer. A fundamental tenet of universal ethics, rooted in natural human dispositions rather than in habitual duties, it is concomitantly applicable to lesser human beings who lack the capacity for resignation by "will."

All these features elevate the compassionate while diminishing those who deserve compassion, denying them alterity,[24] and thus, independent subjectivity. A universal principle, such a compassion licenses elitism, exclusiveness, and xenophobia. Marc Shell has noted the power of universalism as a strategy of radical exclusion[25]—the dark side of radical idealism whose origin is in the Enlightenment. It was Rousseau, as we have seen, who regarded natural, spontaneous compassion as the universal origin of all morality, grounded in a "pure movement of nature, prior to all reflection." For Rousseau the difficulties begin with reflection, which leads to comparisons and value judgments, and he was concerned that compassion, mediated by rational considerations of the relative worthiness of its objects, becomes selective. Moreover, he considered the replacement of genuine compassion with an illusory, theatrical one, which leads to an impoverishing of the moral resources of the citizen. While Wagner retained the natural, prerational component of enlightened compassion, the particularistic notions he drew from it rendered the theater as the pedagogical tool for its "correct" dissemination, influencing the desired behavior of the audience beyond its walls.[26] In a dramatic context, compassion can take a variety of routes, such as those of Elisabeth, Lohengrin, Elsa, or Brünnhilde, not all of which are "properly conducted"—as the drama itself unveils. With *Parsifal* it becomes the main dramatic trajectory, recording a process of growth in an individual in lieu of the formulated principles of these Wagnerian teachings: it commences with indifference to suffering, continues through the experience of personal pain and its observation in others, and ends by combining the two in an act that begets redemptive compassion. Whether, and to what extent, it is open to attend to others' subjectivities—using a musical language whose psychological nuances transcend those that an Engel could envision—outside that of the compassionate self, is still to be assessed.[27]

Wagnerian sympathy and compassion thus complement each other. Whereas compassion is a response to a particular condition of a suffering object, a moral reaction to real or fictional situations, sympathy mediates the transference of compassion from the theater onto the outer world. Sympathetic response thus moves in stages from attraction through reaction and enthusiasm to absorption in the artistic work—the affirmation of being as artistically represented. Its opposite is, therefore, a rejection or negation of being and the artistic experience to which it is related. Sympathy in this Wagnerian scheme is thus the effect of the encounter between the universe of the listeners-observers and the universe embodied in the artistic work. Affirmed, the listener internalizes the expressions of compassion in the interactions between fictional personae. Moments of internal compassion (between protagonists) usually, but not always, converge with those that should transpire externally (from listeners towards protagonists). The artistic rendition of such moments often climaxes in the unification of discrete artistic elements of the work, with the listener partaking in a revelatory experience of resolution. One can discern here traces of the Aristotelian identification–recognition (anagnorisis)–compassion (eleos)–catharsis process; aimed at an ecstatic experience, the entire process seeks to transform the emotive energies of the audience into a moral-political force.

In contradistinction to Wagner, in Eliot compassion is subsumed by sympathy as both a moral principle and an aesthetic strategy. The solid place of sympathy in the British tradition (as formulated by Adam Smith, discussed in chapter 2 above) enabled the mitigation of the ontological barrier between fiction and reality and the regulation of identification with the other—real or fictional—in terms of changing, flexible, and reciprocal criteria.[28] In the case of Wordsworth, sympathy searches for a new poetic language that would expand the boundaries of sensibility and compassion, while exposing its inherent paradoxes, as claimed by Geoffrey Hartman.[29] Well aware of the danger of compassion as a condescending attitude, Eliot, nonetheless never gave up on the attempt to create mental worlds on the basis of the wider realm of sympathy. *Daniel Deronda* is perhaps the most far-reaching of them all.

Rooted at the neural core of human existence, Eliot's view of sympathy encompasses both life and literature, branching out in all directions. "We have only insight in proportion to our sympathies," wrote G. H. Lewes; and, for his life-partner as well, sympathy is far more than an ethical principle that underlies the literary enterprise.[30] It is an epistemological principle of our encounter with "reality," the means by which reality sheds its masks and emerges as it "truly is." The very measure of reality is a function of the sympathetic affirmation of the personae populating this reality, alongside their traits or actions. As an ethical stance, it amounts not only to seeing the other from his or her own perspective, as the adherents of sympathy have always claimed; it is also to view sympathetically the relations between that other's ethical choices and fate in their fullest complexity. Whereas the strength of this viewpoint seems to be quite self-evident, its weakness resides in blunting the force of moral judgment and imposing on the human condition (rather than on particular individuals) a kind of uniformity, which could doom any choice of action or emotional investment to epistemological failure.[31]

It is instructive to discern the inner logic of this ethical stand as manifested in the complex world of Daniel Deronda as he faces his life choices:

> It happened that the very vividness of his impressions had often made him the more enigmatic to his friends, and had contributed to an apparent indefiniteness in his sentiments. *His early-wakened sensibility and reflectiveness had developed into a many-sided sympathy, which threatened to hinder any persistent course of action*; as soon as he took up any antagonism, though only in thought, he seemed to himself like the Sabine warriors in the memorable story—with nothing to meet his spear but flesh of his flesh and objects that he loved. His imagination had so wrought itself to the habit of seeing things as they probably appeared to others, that a strong partisanship, unless it were against an immediate oppression, had become an insincerity for him. *His plenteous, flexible sympathy had ended by falling into one current with that reflexive analysis which tends to neutralise sympathy*. Few men were able to keep themselves clearer of vices than he; yet he hated vices mildly, being used to think of them less in the abstract than as a part of mixed human natures having an individual history, which it was the bent of his mind to trace

with understanding and pity. With the same innate balance *he was fervidly democratic in his feeling of the multitude,* and yet, through his affections and imagination, intensely conservative; voracious of speculations on government and religion, *yet loath to part with long sanctioned forms which, for him, were quick with memories and sentiments that no argument could lay dead.* We fall on the leaning side; and Deronda suspected himself of loving too well the losing causes of the world. Martyrdom changes sides, and he was in danger of changing with it, having a strong repugnance to taking up that clue of success which the order of the world often forces upon us and makes it treason against the common weal to reject. And yet his fear of falling into an unreasoning narrow hatred made a check for him: he apologized for the heirs of privilege; he shrank with dislike from the loser's bitterness and the denunciatory tone of the unaccepted innovator. A too reflective and diffusive sympathy was in danger of paralysing in him that indignation against wrong and that selectness of fellowship which are the conditions of moral force; and in the last few years of confirmed manhood he had become so keenly aware of this that what he most longed for was either some external event or some inward light, that would urge him into a definite line of action, and compress his wandering energy.[32]

Sensibility is a prerequisite for sympathy, Eliot maintains, while reflectiveness accounts for its many-sidedness. But this multifaceted aspect can dim the choice of the object of sympathy and thereby undermine itself, not unlike the medieval Buridan's Donkey that dies from hunger because of its inability to choose between two piles of hay—bilaterally equidistant. Would one of the two piles suddenly glow with beautiful colors, leading the donkey out of the dilemma, or would his appetite finally be satisfied by the grace of arbitrary preference? Eliot hints at the possible solution to the predicament: Daniel is "loath to part with long sanctioned forms which, for him, were quick with memories and sentiments that no argument could lay dead." The weight of these elements upon the sympathizing person is expressed by the concept of sentiment:

He found some of the fault in his birth and the way he had been brought up, which had laid no special demands on him and given him no fixed relationship except one of a doubtful kind; but he did not attempt to hide from himself that he had fallen into a meditative numbness, and was gliding farther and farther from that life of practically energetic sentiment which he would have proclaimed (if he had been inclined to proclaim anything) to be the best of all life, and for himself the only life worth living. He wanted some way of keeping emotion and its progeny of sentiments—which make the savours of life—substantial and strong in the face of reflectiveness that threatened to nullify all differences. To pound the objects of sentiment into small dust, yet keep sentiment alive and active was something like the famous recipe for making cannon—to first take a round hole and then enclose it with iron: whatever you do keeping fast hold of your round hole. Yet how distinguish what our will may wisely save in its completeness, from the heaping of cat-mummies and the expensive cult of enshrined putrefactions? (chapter 32, 365)

In the inner world of a moral personality, sentiment is a vital and activating agent, both compass and driving force, a consequence of a long-term emotional bond; a connection loaded with memories[33] by virtue of whose vitality and scope a moral personality can be rescued from being locked in indifferent reflection on the contingent affairs of humankind. The fact that under the special circumstances of his development (above all, his basic, however glorified, orphanhood) Daniel Deronda lacks the stability that comes with natural attachment, may account for his search for a guiding sentiment. Daniel, at this stage of his life—the image of the cannon hole suggesting a void at the core of his orphan experience—believes in the power of sentiment, and searches for its possible anchorage. Despite Eliot's agnosticism, and not unlike in Wagner, the sentiment will be anchored in a realm redolent with religious feelings. One can expect to find here a story related to sacred heritage, memories engraved in the "substance" of some souls; the aesthetic impact on readers may act as a bridge between potential sympathy within an imaginative world and real sympathy within a living sociopolitical universe. But in contradistinction to the Wagnerian case, the narrative of sacred heritage in Eliot is not predestined, and the bridge between the imaginary and the real is laid first within the artwork, like a frame within a frame. Moreover, the religious bond comes through a moral attachment, reinforced by cultural shareability. It thus neutralizes the artistic illusion and places it before the sober judgment of both those within it and those pondering it from outside.[34]

Taken from a broader perspective, the full range of Eliot's sympathy fulfills the following functions: it animates the fictional characters of the novel, motivating their interactions and external actions; it weaves discrete narrative elements into a thick fabric of attractions and rejections, inducing a hierarchy in their relations; it energizes the pastoral, historic, and domestic living environment that the characters inhabit and dubs its setting—sometimes still and numbly narcissistic.[35] It also qualifies being and actions not only by juxtaposing the principle of sympathy against its polar opposite (as embodied in Deronda and Grandcourt, respectively), or by ordering its varied expressions, but also through the authenticity, transparency, and consciousness of its agents. It constitutes them as seeking the realization of their own goals within themselves and beacons to some of them to realize goals in the social sphere. Above all, sympathy establishes the external perspective of the author, who forgoes omni-science, leaving the projections of her characters' dispositions within the situa-tions in which they are placed beyond her authorial control. At junctures where a closed past meets an open future, freedom of choice is revealed as stemming from the protagonist's amalgam of moral judgments.[36]

In contradistinction to Wagner, in Eliot's work the same attitude is manifest both within the fictive world (by the protagonists) and in the author's narrative strategy. Both protagonists and author share the same reflective hesitancy, a vir-tue which, on the face of it, weakens the determination to act. Not surprisingly, Eliot was accused of sarcasm, the merciless criticism of her characters, and a welding of profound tenderness and bitterness that supposedly confused, disori-ented, and oppressed her readers.[37] Her powers of observation, intellectual in-tegrity, and sense of social responsibility took her far beyond conventional con-temporary wisdom concerning the position and attitude of the creative writer vis-à-vis the writer's creations—the kind of moral feelings fundamental in the literary configuration (and embodiment) of sympathy that was so significant to her contemporaries. In the final analysis, she adopted the stance that the writer has no epistemological advantage over her created characters or anticipated readers; both receive from the writer the appropriate tools and resources for judging and interacting with reality. This is the basis of the democratic disposi-tion Eliot ascribes to Daniel. Neither character, nor author, nor reader can rest unchallenged on past achievements. This complements Eliot's tone, which is soothing and irritating, calming and provocative, lofty and subversive, utopian and satirical, as her earliest critics observed.[38]

The apparent contradiction between the utopian and the satirical is a mani-festation of the relentless tension within Eliot's possible worlds—the strain be-tween the ideal and the real as revealed in human existence. This is the most fundamental tension in her worldview, the one she most cherished. The col-lapse of any one of the two poles upholding this tensile structure would have threatened the socio-moral vision of her enterprise. The foundations of Eliot's universe, a universe sustained by the intellectual force of Comtian positivism and its British followers (Herbert Spencer and John Stuart Mill) and the spiri-tual values of Christianity, are built on a gap between an objective natural world and human subjectivity. Any attempt to elide this by projecting human values onto the natural, contingent world, any effort to load physics with metaphysics, is, as far as Eliot is concerned, an epistemological fallacy. Following Feuerbach, she endorsed a "Religion of Humanity," adopting values sanctioned by religion without projecting them onto a transcendental source. She regarded this ap-proach as the only way to uphold moral and social purpose within an indiffer-ent nature. In her books, she aimed to embody this approach in living forms in which the compassion directed towards suffering mortals due to the inherent gap between human aspirations and their fulfillment is reflected in a central principle of her metanarrative.[39]

THE AESTHETICS OF ECHOING AND ACQUAINTANCE

If Eliot chose—especially in *Middlemarch* (published 1871–72)—a satiric mode, moderate detachment, and an indifferent position vis-à-vis the gap between the real and the ideal, she uses a different strategy in the world she construes in *Daniel Deronda*. Under the guise of a literary realism that draws on her readers' recent memory (the plot of the novel unfolds in "1866"), in this later novel she shifts to the register of romance, superseding ironic reasoning with a willingness to search for the transcendental, and the principle of verisimilitude with incursions into the occasional fantastic and mythical. She shifts from social intrigue to internal psychological struggle and crowns all those moves in glorious, prophetic, and allegorical allusions. The turn to romance reflects the disposition in *Daniel Deronda* to break away from the compatible parameters of canonical literature.

On the face of it, it appears as if Eliot endeavored to compensate here for the unfamiliar elements of the Jewish story and to justify this diversion by embedding it within a metaphysical framework of dreams fabricated and fulfilled. More fundamentally, it is the unique configuration of sympathy, typical of the genre of romance, that generates *Daniel Deronda*'s plot, inspired, as Terence Cave shows, by the late Shakespearean romance-dramas. Furthermore, as Cave indicates, the plot is partially constructed like the multilayered dramas that combine semimiraculous events and a magical atmosphere culminating in spectacular scenes of recognition.[40]

The legacy of Shakespearean romance manifest in *The Tempest* and *The Winter's Tale* is indeed fundamental to the understanding of compassion in *Daniel Deronda*. Friendship and family harmony are buried there because of fatal suspicion and subversive guile; the relentless undermining of trust shatters the illusion of reciprocally transparent minds[41] and exiles the protagonists from their natural habitat to a universe in which they lose their identity in confronting a precarious existence. The moments of recognition take place when the exiled character reveals himself or herself to his or her "friends"-detractors. Achieving thus a superior position in relation to them, he or she draws upon compassion— Prospero's toward the brother who deposed and expelled him, Hermione's for the husband whose blind jealousy drove him to kill their son and banish her. (A possible model for these romances is biblical Joseph, who forgave though did not forget, and made himself known to his brothers ungrudgingly).

Eliot anchors the innermost source of Deronda's compassion in a partly unconscious formative childhood experience of alienation and indifference on
behalf of his mother and an absent father, and in a deep uncertainty about his
identity and parentage. It is this experience—which he himself could work
through under the magnanimous surrogate fatherhood of Sir Hugo Malinger,
and the broad liberal education the latter found incumbent to provide him
with—she intimates, that had imprinted a compassionate disposition in him
and "had given a bias to his conscience, a sympathy with certain ills, and a
tension of resolve in certain direction which marked him off from other youths
much more than any talents he possessed" (chapter 16, 175). This predicament
becomes an axis in a novel fraught with issues of rejection, exploitation, and
parental abandonment. It links Deronda to the Ishmaelites through bonds of
fate.[42] It prepares his heart to experience moments of recognition in full awareness of the responsibility that these sublime and elating moments demand.
Still, although the two women in whose fate he becomes involved—women
he saves from literal or metaphorical drowning—are victims of paternal abuse,
Daniel's sentiment goes to Mirah, the small, exotic Jewess with the enchanting
voice, and not to Gwendolyn, the Englishwoman of a Van-Dyckian beauty, who
similarly evokes compassion (this happens before he learns of his own Jewish
identity). In other words, Jewish aesthetics, embedded within a full-fledged phenomenology, has greater appeal for Daniel than the European aesthetics with
which he is so familiar. How can one account for this elective affinity? What
is the psychological explanation for such a bent for the unfamiliar? What is
buried in Daniel's orphan soul that reverberates to strange symbols of a foreign
culture? Or, again, in Eliot's language, how could "long-sanctioned forms," remote from his own, become transformed in Daniel's soul into "sentiments"?
Compassion alone cannot account for this, since in both instances emotional
concern, directed to the Other's suffering, extends to the cultural universe in
which Mirah, the object of compassion, dwells.

Following Wagner, it is useful at this point to distinguish between human
compassion and sympathetic affirmation, and to examine their links and reciprocal empowerment. In contrast to Wagner, Eliot sought to purge the factor of
compassion from all mysterious elements and to found it upon mental elements
befitting those employed in current cognitive psychology. Yet she incorporated
an additional significant factor: if, according to recent research in cognitive
psychology, empathy stems from a circular action in the brain—an action that
begins with recognizing signs of emotions in the person to whom compassion is
directed—for Eliot signs of feeling in other persons cannot be recognized if "intelligence and mental vision" are not involved.[43] It is the imagination, enriched
by personal experience, that facilitates the capacity to recognize emotional

expression even when it lacks clarity and familiarity. In the point of convergence between sympathizer and the object of sympathy, where Wagner allows mystical resonance, and psychological theory would emphasize evolutionary themes, Eliot provides a model based on ethical orientation. Given the equal moral standing of the fictive and the real in her worldview, Eliot could expect that the reader would undergo, and therefore fully follow, the processes and struggles in Daniel's soul.

The expression of compassion towards the Jewish girl precedes the sympathetic affirmation of the aesthetic content that she represents. It occurs within an antinarcissistic setting, a setting that can be regarded as "echoistic." An integral part of Daniel's compassionate soul, echoism derives from a long legacy of "resonating" literary characters—the daughters of the Ovidian Echo. The dejected companion of Narcissus, Echo vocally replicates his failure—to become Western tradition's prototype of a compassionate and consoling persona searching for its lost voice in and through the act of identification. As such she has been alternately identified with compassionate saviors and abandoned lamenters.[44] When he is thirteen, Daniel sings a song to Echo before an honorable congregation, the song that the Lady sings in *Comus*; Milton's words, which do not appear in Eliot's text, are among the most expressive of this tradition:

> Sweet Echo, sweetest Nymph that liv'st unseen
> Within thy airy shell
> By slow Meander's margent green,
> And in the violet-embroider'd vale
> Where the love-lorn Nightingale
> Nightly to thee her sad Song mourneth well.

> Canst thou not tell me of a gentle Pair
> That likest thy Narcissus are?
> O if thou have
> Hid them in some flowr'y Cave,
> Tell me but where,
> Sweet Queen of Parley, Daughter of the Sphere,
> So mayst thou be translated to the skies,
> And give resounding grace to all Heav'n's Harmonies.

By contrast to the Ovidian counterpart, Milton's Echo, like other resonating figures of the Renaissance and the Baroque, not only listens (to the nightingale's lamentation and the anguish of the singing Lady) but also envisions and protects (the echo she carries to all places, which reaches all valleys and caves, will find the two lost brothers of the Lady and hide them). Above all, she is endowed with Platonic virtues of earthly harmony corresponding to its heavenly counter-part. As a Daughter of the Sphere, moreover, she is the sister of the Daughter of Voice, the Kabbalistic "Bat Kol," who, since the sixteenth century, "moves the mind and sets the reason to motion, and when it has been moved, the image or form is reflected and returns by the same path to intellectual unity, enlighten-ing, exciting and raising to God all the parts of the soul."[45] Like Daughters of Voice shaped in poetry, music, and painting, Deronda is endowed with a rich musicality, with the power to listen and envision, and unifying capacity. Like them, he is destined to be redeemed in the act of compassion. Seeking solitude, Daniel's experience is never narcissistic.[46] At the beginning of chapter 17, we meet him by the water, his eyes penetrating great distances, thus replacing Nar-cissus' mirroring surface with the movement of his boat that breaks momentary reflections. From within this experience Deronda rises with the musical experi-ence that anticipates the suffering soul he is destined to encounter:

> He was all the while unconsciously continuing the low-toned chant which had haunted his throat all the way up the river—the gondolier's song in the 'Otello,' where Rossini has worthily set to music the immortal words of Dante—
>
> > 'Nessun maggior dolore
> > Che ricordarsi del tempo felice
> > Nella miseria'[47]
>
> and, as he rested on his oar, the pianissimo fall of the melodic wail 'nella miseria' was distinctly audible on the brink of the water.

As he sings, he recognizes the woman who sinks in the depth of her agony, seeking to end her life. The marks of her plight are universal ("poorly dressed, melancholy women are common sights"), and her movements towards suicide easily discernible. But compassion, once aroused, goes well beyond mere res-cue, which is effected with great sensibility and delicacy. It gives rise to close-ness between these two souls, an intimacy built on a culturally bound, musical echoing. But such a sympathetic vibration soon unveils alterity in the unfamil-iar "Spanish" beauty of Mirah and in the exoticism of the culture which it rep-resents. Accordingly, the gondolier's song evokes both sympathy and difference; his singing having reached her ears, overcoming distance, she intones, "in a low sweet voice, with an accent so distinct, that it suggests foreignness and yet was not foreign":

> 'I saw you before'; . . . and then added dreamily, after a like pause, 'nella miseria.'

Deronda, who does not immediately grasp her intention and doubts her sanity, receives an explanation:

> 'It was you, singing?' she went on, hesitatingly—'Nessun maggior dolore' . . .
> The mere words themselves uttered in her sweet undertones seemed to give the melody to Deronda's ear.
>   'Ah, yes,' he said, understanding now, 'I am often singing them.' (chapter 17, 190)

The song is in G minor, the key of lamentations in Western tradition (see music example ex. 5.1). The circumstances of the song in *Otello* are significantly analogous to those in our chapter: water, boating, music heard by the suffering soul. Like Desdemona, Mirah also listens to the song and finds there resonance with her wounded soul. The song is diatonic, limited within the bounds of octave + fifth, stressing again Phrygian elements, especially in the wail described above: "felice nella miseria." The dotted, variegated rhythm and the adorning embellishments grant it a recitative quality associated with prayer. Combined with the Phrygian chromatics, the song subliminally meanders in the twilight zone between Italian European music and the Jewish music (both Sephardic and Ashkenazi) that evolved alongside it.

The encounter between Daniel and Mirah touches on all these traditions, to which, as we have seen in the last chapters, the cultured European could be rather attracted, as the song becomes the code of the conversation:

> 'I cannot see how I shall be glad to live. The *maggior dolore* and the *miseria* have lasted longer than the *tempo felice*.' She paused and then went on dreamily, '—*Dolore—miseria*—I think those words are alive.'

Ex. 5.1. Gioachino Rossini, *Otello* III, 10, Gondolier's song, "Nessun maggior dolore."

Suffering is real and conversation, despite its operatic garb, is transparent. I am not from the theater, Daniel allays Mirah's fear of the world of the stage, the world of masks and deceptions from which she came. I do not belong to the world of illusions, which lies and misleads, the world that has surrounded you all along. You and I, as imagined characters, skip over the barriers of the fictional to touch the real.[48] For you reality is the future, humanity's hope. For me it resides in the possibility of finding a significant path where my unique voice can be heard. "Great God," says Daniel uncontrollably while facing her wretchedness; "the words escaped Deronda in a tone so low and solemn that they seemed like a prayer become unconsciously vocal." He imagines the possibly kindred suffering of his unknown mother; his exclamation, the author notes, was of the kind "in which both east and west have for ages concentrated their awe in the presence of inexorable calamity." Though a bond of familiarity is created, Mirah remains an enigma to him. Who is that wretched figure? Will he transcend the compassionate act that is basically disinterested in the personality of the sufferer, as Wagner believed, and seek her subjectivity (overcoming thus also an orientalist bias)? And how is this connected to the community from which she came and its ritual music?

SYMPATHY AT THE SYNAGOGUE

From this chapter until the one suffused by the music of the synagogue, Eliot takes us through many adventures, most of them as alien to Mirah as she is foreign to them. We partake in them after we are privy to Mirah's sad story, which she tells her benefactor, Mrs. Meyrick. In the meantime, Gwendolyn has returned to a world that no longer adjusts itself to her caprice, searching for a new socioeconomic mode of living and discovering the musical stage. Klesmer, the genial Jewish musician—whom she greatly admires—shatters her illusions: the path from amateurism to professionalism is long and demanding and does not suit narcissistic girls. She then accepts Grandcourt's grand courting, well aware of the woman he has neglected and their four illegitimate children. In a Medea-like gesture, the latter woman sends her, on her wedding night, "poisoned" diamonds that Gwendolyn's groom had once given her as assumed love tokens.

The words that ended the previous chapter are still resounding in our ears— "[i]n some form or other the Furies had crossed his threshold"—still the heart is full of dread for the dire outcome of the relations between this accursed husband and wife; when Eliot, as usual, turns to other music—the interludes of her tranquil epigraphs, which preface every chapter in the book, characterized by a contemplative, majestic tone, cultured to the bounds of irony, rhetorical on the verge of enigmatic:

> In all ages it hath been a favourite text that a potent love hath the nature of an isolated fatality, whereto the mind's opinions and wonted resolves are altogether alien. . . . Yet all love is not such, even though potent; nay, this passion hath as large scope as any for allying itself with every operation of the soul; so that it shall acknowledge an effect from the imagined light of unproven firmaments, and have its scale to the grander orbits of what hath been and shall be. (360)

We too wonder whether she is speaking of a love that has already come to pass or that is impending. We are kindled when meeting Deronda again after so many chapters in which he was concealed from us. Through him we return to Grandcourt's house before it was so frenziedly stricken. The perspective is indeed that of love-seeking. As with Wagner's orphan heroes—Siegfried, Parsifal—Daniel's journey is similarly marked by the search for identity, for familial roots and belonging. Daniel, as it turns out, will deeply engage himself in deciphering the connection between love and identity; this is in fact the pivot around which the story revolves.

From here until we enter the synagogue with Daniel, we oscillate between the protagonist's consciousness and that of the author, as preparation for the mode of evocation of the reader's sympathy to the synagogal experience; one that moves—in analogy to certain musical genres described in the preceding chapter—between a personified subjectivity and a more objectified persona. A comparison to the way Wagner integrates the synagogue image in his "Judentum" essay is instructive here: after Wagner notes the Jewish capitalist conspiracy, he rants about the Jew's detestable appearance, corrupt language, distorted talk, ridiculous singing, and deficient plastic capabilities, expounding on the detachment of the *gebildet* (educated) Jew from any organic humane environment, on his sterile thought, and his lack of ethnic habitat. He then assumes his synagogal "ethnography" as the single source from which contemporary Jews could draw indigenous musical motifs and a *Volksgeist* intelligible to them. Still, Wagner, speaking through his unified, authorial voice, admonishes his reader:

> However noble and sublime we are inclined to imagine this musical Service of God to have been in its initial purity, with all the more certainty must we perceive that this purity has come upon us only in the most disgusting degradation: for thousands of years, nothing has developed here out of an inner fullness of life. Rather, just as with Judaism in general, it has remained firmly

stuck both in content and form. A form which is never quickened through renewal of its content disintegrates; an expression whose content has long ceased to be living sentiment becomes senseless and distorted. Who has not had occasion to see for himself the distortion of liturgical song in a genuine people's synagogue? Who has not been gripped by the most disagreeable feeling, made up of hideousness and ridiculousness, while listening to the sense- and mind-obfuscating *gargling, yodeling* and *prattling,* which no deliberate caricature could distort more disgustingly than it presents itself here in full, naïve earnest?[49]

The image of the synagogue is forged on top of an agglomeration of negations, piled on top of each other, all of which directly touch our perception. In our mind's eye we see a bunch of ugly people (lacking an organic connection, they cannot be considered a congregation) in unaesthetic surroundings, whose appearance, speech, and thought are loathsome, whose religious emotions lack substance, while the historical dimension of their existence evokes associations of ragged old age and death-in-life rather than a mysterious antiquity. Clearly, Wagner's description relies on "ethnographic" reports of the Edelmann type as well as internal Jewish discourse in the wake of the synagogal reforms debate. Lacking direct ethnographic evidence, Wagner's diatribe is a rhetorical construction utilizing an algorithm of distortion. Creating an all-inclusive synaesthetic sensation, it prepares its reader for dissonant tones even before they are actually described. When they appear on stage, they are degraded from a musical level (to which they were still ascribed even in Edelmann's text) to a prephonetic one, the lowest of human vocalization. Conveyed onomatopoetically, these vocalities create an image of sonic ado.

Eliot, on the other hand, takes into account her readers' prejudices against the Jews and plants them not only in the hearts of her more typical British protagonists but also in that of Daniel himself. But the sequence in which this is set is utterly different from that of Wagner's lampoon. In the first part of the chapter, Daniel's consciousness revolves around the distinction, which he deems fundamental, between flirtation and love (following the sarcastic comment of his adoptive father, Sir Hugo Malinger, about his relationship with Gwendolyn). This brings him to come to grips with the nature of his relations with Mirah, and from here the way is short to learning about the letter he received from Mrs. Meyrick describing Mirah's exceptional vocal skills, her charm, and the impact of her presence on their home. The omniscient author waits for us there, reporting on Mirah's visit at the synagogue, accompanied by the usually friendly Meyrick's daughters, unsurprisingly lacking in sympathy in this case.[50] Becoming momentary "ethnographers," they report their dislike of the women's seats behind the rail, and the men's head cover. To their mocking questions about Jewish rituals, Mirah, however, calmly replies in the spirit of Daniel's own reflections: "I like what I have always seen there, because it brings back to me the same feelings—the feelings I would not part with for anything in the world."

Like those for whom some of their best friends are Jews (such as Wagner), the Meyrick daughters nurse the hope that their love and care will cause Mirah to relinquish her Jewishness. Then, through a simple association (operating in a manner recalling a diatonic modulation in tonal music), we come back to Daniel's' own ambivalent feelings towards the Jews—what else can one expect of an English gentleman, however well educated?

Exactly at this point we are brought into the discussion of Daniel's moral growth and its predominant sympathetic attitude, analyzed above. Eliot then enables us to momentarily feel our own ambivalence towards Jews and their culture with Daniel, while infiltrating our consciousness with growing sympathetic feelings, reinforced because concurrently activated by Daniel and bestowed on him. In the transition to the synagogue—our already familiar Frankfurt Judengasse synagogue—in a modulatory progression that may recall the transfiguration of time into space in *Parsifal*, Eliot repeats a recurrent motif: Daniel, whose visionary powers are part of his sympathetic qualities, evokes in his mind's eye

> —the faint beginnings of faiths and institutions, and their obscure lingering decay; the dust and withered remnants with which they are apt to be covered, only enhancing for the awakened perception the impressiveness either of a sublimely penetrating life . . . or of pathetic inheritance in which all the grandeur and the glory have become a sorrowing memory.

We are exposed here to obscurity and decay rather than to the stagnation and distortion of Wagner's text, and to their partaking in an allegory of ruins, associated with the sublime. Daniel, accordingly, sets to search for the Orthodox synagogue, which he knows to be preserving the old traditions more faithfully.[51] This search must be active, conjuring the imagination to find in the present "what hath been and shall be," as the author advocates in the epigraph. Like Wagner in relation to Parsifal, Eliot lets Daniel play with the experience of time and enlarge it immensely into a resonating oratorical perspective. In her case it is qualified ethically: one should not sanction immediate sensations, but rather transcend them. The Jews whom Daniel meets along the Judengasse evoke in him repugnance and disgust (in response to their German dialect, among other, typical triggers)—not unlike the feelings experienced by Goethe, whose visit there about "seventy years" earlier the reader may recall; but Daniel deliberately avoids the impact of such contingent encounters on his genuine exploration into the "Hebrew destiny"—an entity recalling the Wagnerian "substance."

Eliot opts to introduce him to the synagogue on the solemn occasion of Friday night service (*Leil Shabbat*). His entrance to the *Rabbinische Schule* (as the Orthodox synagogue was called, see fig. 3.1–3.3) is marked by a significant, reciprocated glance with an impressive old Jew—of crucial importance to the evolving plot; however, Daniel attempts to concentrate on the service itself, a scene worth quoting in full:

> He immediately found an open prayer-book pushed towards him and had to bow his thanks. However, the congregation had mustered, the reader had mounted to the *almemor* or platform and the service began. Deronda, having looked enough at the German translation of the Hebrew in the book before him to know that he was chiefly hearing Psalms and Old Testament passages or phrases, gave himself up to that strongest effect of chanted liturgies which is independent of detailed verbal meaning—like the effect of an Allegri's *Miserere* or a Palestrina's *Magnificat*. The most powerful movement of feeling with a liturgy is the prayer which seeks for nothing special, but is a yearning to escape from the limitations of our own weakness and an invocation of all Good to enter and abide with us; or else a self-oblivious lifting up of gladness, a *Gloria in excelsis* that such Good exists; both the yearning and the exultation gathering their utmost force from the sense of communion in a form which has expressed them both, for long generations of struggling fellow men. The Hebrew liturgy, like others, has its transitions of litany, lyric, proclamation, dry statement and blessing; but this evening all were one for Deronda: the chant of the *Chazan's* or Reader's grand wide-ranging voice with its passage from monotony to sudden cries, the outburst of sweet boys' voices from the little quire, the devotional swaying of men's bodies backwards and forwards, the very commonness of the building and shabbiness of the scene where a national faith, which had penetrated the thinking of half the world, and moulded the splendid forms of the world's religion, was finding a remote, obscure echo—all were blent for him as one expression of a binding history, tragic and yet glorious. He wondered at the strength of his own feeling; it seemed beyond the occasion—what one might imagine to be a divine influx in the darkness, before there was any vision to interpret. The whole scene was a coherent strain, its burthen a passionate regret, which, if he had known the liturgy for the Day of Reconciliation, he might have clad in its antithetic burthen: 'Happy the eye which saw all these things; but verily to hear

only of them afflicts our soul. Happy the eye that saw our temple and the joy of our congregation; but verily to hear only of them afflicts our soul. Happy the eye that saw the singers when tuning every kind of song; but verily to hear only of them afflicts our soul.' (chapter 32, 367–68)

As in the experience of love described in the epigraph to chapter 32, the experience of worship also entails various "operations of the mind": the way we immerse ourselves in it as readers involves understanding and judgment no less than emotion and devotion. Our eyes, like those of Daniel, survey the space and examine the temporal unit ahead of us. Well aware of how vocal music operates, Daniel and his author make a "decision" to prefer music to text in the overall experience.[52] Once it has been performed, he (or his semi-omniscient creator) can evoke comparisons to the most contemporarily esteemed musical works of the Christian tradition—Gregorio Allegri's *Miserere* (1638) and a Giovanni Palestrina *Magnificat* (he composed several), rendering the experience more "audible."[53] The first work could be imagined along its alternation between verses sung to the monotonic asceticism of the Gregorian psalm recitation and its tonal harmonization (in a minor mode) for five or nine parts, carrying on their faux-bourdon texture a soaring, improvised melody.[54] Palestrina's *Magnificat*, perhaps less familiar, could be associated (through its balanced, restrained polyphony) with the great Shakespearean and Miltonic tradition of the music of the spheres.

Into these imaginative sonorities, Eliot pours her principles of humanistic religion whereby "God" is converted into "Good"—transcendental providence becomes human benevolence, while still seeking the spiritual heights of "Gloria in Excelsis." Further, the communion ritual transfigures into a "sense of communion," and God's suffering is replaced by "human suffering of long generations of struggling fellow men." In between she interlaces the idea of "sameness in difference" by emphasizing that Jewish liturgy contains all the ritual forms created by other peoples.[55] Concomitantly, she exhorts her readers to lend their ears to the internal musical nuances of the singing in the hazzan's peculiar vocal performance and the "outburst" of the sweet boys' chorus.[56]

The affinity between Palestrina's and Allegri's psalmody and that of the Ashkenazi Kabbalat Shabbat service is established despite the fact that polyphony and measured time are principally not shared. No longer apprehended in terms of noise, sonic similarity becomes more perceptible. This goes even deeper, embodying an historical irony foreshadowed in chapter 1: what was extraordinary about Allegri's oeuvre, a fact that could not escape Eliot, is that the notation (or musical transcription) of this highly cherished Catholic work was banned by the Holy See. While its abduction from the Sistine Chapel's premises into the secularized world, sometime during the eighteenth century, became a prime mythology of Western music, it bore proximity to, if not direct genealogy from another treasured Sistine oeuvre—Palestrina's *Improperia*—the anti-Semitic hymn that metamorphosed in the hands of the elect composer into a euphonious faux-bourdon delight. Like the *Improperia*, the *Miserere* was associated with Holy Week, serving as part of the *Tenebrae* services. But unlike its predecessors, and in line with baroque emotionalism, this psalm exerted new emphasis on the individual: *Miserere mei, Deus,* have mercy on me, O God, and on those entitled to Your mercy; and yet *miserere,* for I know my transgression, because I, the sinner, need God's wisdom and love;[57] a prayer of the person well aware of the worthlessness of his or her being. These new qualities were sonically iconized through the soaring, improvising voices, searching (ecumenically) for their individual expression and redemption, using free counterpoint—the *super librum* technique in which the chapel's castrati singers excelled.[58] Through a lineage issuing probably from Mozart, continuing through Burney and following via Anglican musicians and other Britons, the *Miserere* alighted at Eliot's personal pantheon, authorizing it as a prime example of affinity between the two adversarial religions, which the Catholic Church endeavored so hard to avoid. Moreover, as a basically oral work, this holy of holies aural vessel paradoxically exposed itself to the predicaments and mysteries of a live heritage's transmission, characteristic of the Jewish liturgical tradition. The shared psalmodic elements, which Eliot believed to have originated in the ancient Jewish Temple, were thus exposed.[59]

This psalmodic common denominator consists of expansions of the antique antiphonal recitation of psalms (as ex. app. 6 and ex. app. 7 demonstrate; see appendix). Serving as mere scheme or formula for a more elaborate performance practice, the affinity of the two traditions could extend to the soaring melodic element they gave vent to. In the first five synagogal psalms of the Kabbalat Shabbat (95–99), it could be demonstrated by extending the basic major based "Adonai Malach" *steiger* (ex. 5.2c and ex. app. 7, in appendix) even to two octaves (framed between two dominants). In its melodic heights, its melismatic elaborations touch the poignant "minor" (in the manner of Ukrainian Dorian mode), thus approximating the *Miserere*'s *Stimmung*.[60]

The rest of the service available to Daniel would comprise another three psalms bracketing the *Lekha Dodi* congregational singing. The melodic ambitus of the first psalms is echoed in them, giving vent to a rich heterophonic performance by the congregation. Their new tonal framework becomes, in turn, the basis for the evening prayer restrained within the lower range of the so-called *Arvit steiger* (which in the Frankfurt *Minhag*, according to Ogutsch, is even more solemn, verging on the High Holidays' tune).[61] The silent standing prayer is followed by the "Magen Avot" responsorial parts (mentioned in chapter 4 and 3 respectively in reference to Meyerbeer's *Huguenots* and Nathan-Byron's *Hebrew Melodies*) that festively wind up the service. All in all, the musical variety and its decorum could offer a sonic illustration of Daniel's declaration that "our religion is mainly a Hebrew religion" (chapter 32, 374). The encounter with the Judengasse Synagogue opens up for him a more flowing and spontaneous experience of worship than the one he was acquainted with in parallel Christian (supposedly Anglican) rituals, still deeply rooted in ancient traditions.

Through Daniel's ears, Eliot herself could overcome the harmony-heterophony barrier that separated Christian and Jewish liturgical music, becoming perhaps the first among known outsiders (and many insiders) to elevate the synagogal soundscape in aesthetic-theological terms. The orchestration of various voices, albeit sonically heterogeneous, merges in the author's portrayal into an overall unique synaesthetic-kinaesthetic tableau. Through an imaginary listening to the hazzan's voice and the choir's sounds, and the now positive experiencing of the body movements, modest hall, the host's warmth (taking care of the guest's prayer book), sounds heard in the mind's ear from different moments of the Jewish liturgical year, human life, and nation-history are summoned, forging a *gesamtkunst* experience of a participating community.

On the wings of this enriched oratorical moment, Daniel realizes the "splendid forms of the world's religion" that here find "a remote, obscure echo." He wonders at his own emotions as his fantasy carries him into primordial being in the night of divine darkness, antedating vision and light. (Night is here combined into an affirmative theology, skipping the redemptive creation of light in Handel and Haydn and through them, Mendelssohn.) "And this whole scene," intervenes the author in her omniscient voice, "was a coherent strain" for him, "and its burthen a passionate regret" (maybe here she resonates the *Lekha Dodi piyyut*, with its usually animatedly sung refrain), which, if he had known the liturgy for the Day of Reconciliation, he might have clad in its antithetic burthen: "Happy the eye which saw all these things; but verily to hear only of them afflicts our soul. Happy the eye that saw our temple and the joy of our congregation; but verily to hear only of them afflicts our soul. Happy the eye that saw the singers when tuning every kind of song; but verily to hear only of them afflicts our soul."

Here Eliot's readers might have lost the associative thread binding Daniel's subjective, sublime experience to the counterfactual one suggested by his au-

thor (through the subjunctive "if he had known"). It is doubtful that these readers could have identified the "Day of Reconciliation" as Yom Kippur (in common English terminology, the festival is called the "Day of Atonement" after
its Hebrew name, whereas the author translated the German *Versöhnungstag*,
also traditionally associated with the day), if they had ever heard of that holy
day. To be sure, they could not have been aware of the fact that she is quoting
an antique *piyyut* here, one that concludes the oratorical "Seder Ha'avoda"
(lit. "order of the work" or the "worship"), a high point in the holy day that
vocally, performatively, revives the high priest's ritual of atonement in the ancient Temple—with a sharp dissonance. The melismatic unfolding of this entire oratorical part follows a melodic sequence similar to that of the "Adonai
Malach" sections of the Kabbalat Shabbat described above, with the Ukrainian
Dorian (minor) part falling on the prostrating of cantor and congregation at
the words: "[A]nd the priests and the people, when they heard the great and
awesome Name come out from the High Priest's mouth, were kneeling and
prostrating."[62] Like the *messaggera* in Monteverdi's *Orfeo*, who strikes the pastoral conviviality of the celebrating Orfeo and his companions at once with the
message of Eurydice's death (through a minor chord sustained by an organ), so
too the sound of "Happy the eye . . . verily to hear" magically metamorphoses
the sublime spectacle into the "shabbiness" of the present scene (usually carried as a heterophonic low-key lamentation). Eliot goes even further, and, following Daniel's feeling, she hints at the possibility of reading this *piyyut* upside
down; that is, instead of "Happy the eye . . . verily to hear"—"happy the ear . . .
verily the eye." The ear hears, even from far away. It sees the voices, as in the
Sinai revelation, and they are "long sounding" like the ram's horn (shofar) that
dominated it or the voice that then "traveled from one end of the world to the
other," according to the Midrash.[63] Similarly to Rabelais' Pantagruel, Daniel
could thus hear sounds frozen in an imaginary past melting into his present.
The eye itself, Eliot intimates, lacks this reviving power; rather, it grants its visual force through listening to primordial voices.[64]

David Kaufmann, the Jewish scholar from Budapest and Breslau—two important centers of the by-then flourishing *Wissenschaft des Judentums*—from
whom Eliot draws much of her Jewish knowledge and inspiration, could have
been moved by these lines. So could other Jews for whom this auditory space
reverberates, the present author included.[65] And Eliot's English readers? And
Daniel? For those readers who wished to follow the author, the *piyyut's* in-
cantational dimension thematized in the last quoted strophe ("Happy the eye
that saw the singers when tuning every kind of song; but verily to hear only
of them afflicts our soul") reinforces the total imaginary sonic impression in

a powerful oratorical moment. Some of them could have been reminded of moments in the Nathan-Byron *Hebrew Melodies* and would have responded sympathetically.[66]

The fall from this high point is experienced by Daniel and the readers in the transition from this imaginary sonoric scene back to Frankfurt Jewry's mundane reality on a summer Friday night. Daniel discovers that he is perhaps the only one for whom this whole experience was more than "a dull routine." He is truly shaken. To the question of the bearded old man (Kalonymos) whom he had noticed upon entering the synagogue, "Excuse me, young man—allow me— what is your parentage"—he coldly retorts: "I am an Englishman." This reply reflects the embarrassment, and maybe defensive reaction of an individual who has not found his place or identity in his original habitat, rather than the alien and condescending reaction of an arrogant Christian. His discontent reverberates in his fears concerning the human quality of Mirah's close kin, whom he seeks. The complex relation between aesthetic affirmation of a community's ritual and sympathetic behavior towards some of its individuals burdens even a Daniel. No wonder he seeks Mirah herself to allay his turbulent spirits and share his overwhelming experience. So doing, he closes the cycle initiated at Meyrick's home in the first part of the chapter.

This meeting engenders another series of sonorities and echoes. The first in this series is Mirah's recollection of childhood voices: first the way her mother had called her brother Ezra, and his response—"Mother," which she enunci- ates with "loving intonation." (As we are told later, Ezra-Mordecai, Mirah's sick brother, embodies the figure of the noble prophet, "the mad man of spirit" and the enlightened scholar, who envisions the Jewish people's political-spiritual resurrection and thus plays a central role in molding Daniel's new identity and sense of mission.) Engrossed in her memories, she reflects how wonderful it is that she remembers "the voices better than anything else," adding that "they must go deeper into us than other things." She speculates, in agreement with Daniel, that "heaven might be made of voices." Vocal performance on a professional level occurs in the wake of this confessional moment—up to that point we had only heard about Mirah's superb singing. Now she "really" sings to Daniel, as if responding to "his" song—

> with a subdued but searching pathos which had that essential of perfect sing-
> ing, the making one oblivious of art or manner, and only possessing one with
> the song. It was the sort of voice that gives the impression of being meant like
> a bird's wooing for an audience near and beloved. (chapter 32, 372)

To her own piano accompaniment, she sings Beethoven, "per pietà non dirmi addio," then adds pieces by Luigi Gordigiani and Schubert.[67] At last she comes back, though initially reluctant, to what seems to be the beginning of her spiritual vocality: a Hebrew hymn her mother had sung to her "when she lay in her cot." Her singing of it mingles lisping nonsense syllables with a few Hebrew ones that she happens to remember, carried "in quaint melancholy intervals" by a voice "sweeter, [with] more cooing tenderness than was heard in her other songs." Again, the words are not important, according to the aesthetics advanced in this chapter—all emotion resides in voice and melody. In response, Daniel recalls his synagogal experience, which he then reports to Mirah. The chain of echoes resounding between them is rich. Some of its links are private, as when she echoes her childhood in her mother's home; some are shared, as in the "melancholic" intervals of the little hymn through which she brings the two of them, musically and emotionally, to the *felice nella miseria*'s Phrygian moments on the Thames. Yet others unite the two in a counterfactual existence in an imaginary synagogue. The separate past becomes thus more mutual. Inasmuch as Mirah is amazed at the way the synagogue ritual, which hitherto had seemed to her "all shut away like a river in a deep valley when only heaven saw" had touched Daniel's heart, Daniel is stunned by her singing. He listens to her with closed eyes as if striving to isolate the melody—that of Beethoven—from the bewildering sights and surroundings, and finds himself expanding his hitherto familiar musical world by the very fact that it flows now from the soul of the feminine Other. The roles represented in this particular aria are thus inverted: the plea of the rejected woman—"for pity's sake, do not bid me farewell"—is now sung by the saved girl, herself turning into a siren who attracts her savior with graceful, innocent magic so that he will never leave her.[68] Estranging the familiar and familiarizing the strange enriches the aesthetic space of both characters and weaves within ties that they could not have dreamt of. Thus "she becomes the single artificer of the world in which she sings"—to recall the enchanting lines of Wallace Stevens; with her voice she has created a world, not only a fictional one.

COMPASSION AT MONTSALVAT

Parsifal, too, is an uninvited guest who joins a ceremony. He, similarly, does not pass the test of first acquaintance with the community's old guardian, Gurnemanz, and is amazed at a ritual that draws its strength from ancient sources. His journey likewise involves a search for his identity, and though the rebellion against his mother initially goes in the opposite direction of Deronda's, it also leads him later to a grand act of pilgrimage headed eastwards.[69] As for Ezra-Mordecai, so for Parsifal, the mother's calling of his name continues to reverberate mentally, and more than any other Wagnerian hero, he too is activated by compassion. In his compassion, he brings redemption through a complicated series of echoes and Daughters of Voices' calls to a world that awaits his coming, intoning:

> Durch Mitleid wissend
> der reine Tor:
> harre sein
> den ich erkor!

> [Enlightened through compassion / the innocent fool / wait for the one that I have chosen]

Above all, in relation to Amfortas, the king of the Grail knights, he is like Daniel to Ezra-Mordecai: a hoped-for successor to a deathly ill person whose appearance at the right moment enables the originally chosen heir to die or quietly relinquish his office. Here, however, the fundamental resemblance between the two heroes stops. Parsifal is a *Tor*—fool and innocent (like the *Tam*—both fool and innocent—from the Passover Haggadah, who at the same time "is not able even to ask" a proper question).[70] Wagner fashions the element of compassion in his vacant personality around a series of experiences that take place almost entirely onstage; his three-act musical drama closely examines the way in which compassion, of the kind discussed in his letter to Mathilde Wesendonck, is sown, aroused, acknowledged, and acts upon the world. The relation between theory and practice in this matter is thus comparable to its counterpart in Eliot's novel.

Why does Wagner insist on Parsifal's ignorance? Is it an echo of Rousseau's notion regarding the origin of all morality in natural, primordial sympathy, "the way it resides in the natural movement of Nature, prior to all reflection"? What is the meaning of linking such compassion to the pedantic ritual of the Grail's knights? One can simply answer that, as for Rousseau, for Wagner a society that is entirely mediated through ceremonial acts cannot shed its skin (or masks) when asked for a genuine act of compassion. Yet the ceremony itself is part of Parsifal's spiritual revival—the airy shell that seeks the echoing figure, the Miltonian "Nymph that will live and enliven the dead shell."

In an attempt to understand Parsifal's initial detachment from the ritual he is witnessing (in comparison to Daniel's involvement from the very start), one should take the difference between their hosting media into account. Planting his protagonists in psychologically complex contexts, Wagner succeeds in indicating the undulations of their unconscious in relation to a gradually revealed encompassing being through an intricate leitmotivic system. Inasmuch as their

Plate 1. "Hallelujah, Sing to the Lord a New Song." Parma Psalter, Emilia-Romagna (northern Italy), late thirteenth century. Parma, Biblioteca Palatina, Ms. Parm. 1870, fol. 213v. Courtesy of the Biblioteca Palatina.

Plate 2. "Vayikod Ha-'am." Barcelona Haggadah. London, British Library, Ms. Add. 14761, fol. 61r. Courtesy of the British Library Board.

Plate 3. School of Jan Van Eyck, *Fountain of Grace and the Triumph of the Church over the Synagogue*. Oil on wood. Courtesy of the Museo Nacional del Prado, Madrid.

Plate 4. Gerbrand van den Eeckhout, *Presentation in the Temple*, 1671. Oil on canvas. Courtesy of the Szépművészeti Múzeum, Budapest.

Plate 5. Jacob Beschey, *Moses Drawing Water from the Rock.* Oil on canvas. Courtesy of the National Gallery–Alexandros Soutzos Museum, Athens.

Plates 6–9. Arnold Schoenberg's 1910 experiments in the transfiguration (back and forth) of the "realistic" self-portrait into a more abstract one, into a gaze, from which a roaming voice seems to emerge (as in the *Glückliche Hand*), transcending subjectivities, engaged Schoenberg from about 1908 to 1913; metamorphosed, these ideas found later expression in the author's musico-theological oeuvres. Courtesy of Belmont Music Publishers, Pacific Palisades, CA / VBK, Vienna.

Pl. 6. Arnold Schoenberg, *Self-Portrait*, oil on canvas, 1910.

Pl. 7. Arnold Schoenberg, *Green Self-Portrait*, oil on cardboard, 1910.

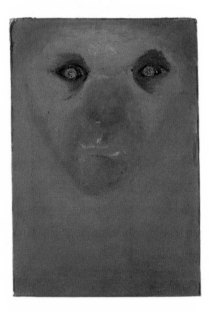

Pl. 8. Arnold Schoenberg, *Gaze*, oil on canvas, 1910.

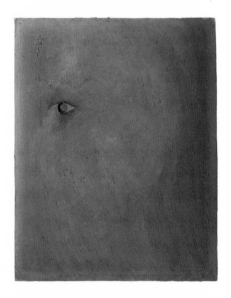

Pl. 9. Arnold Schoenberg, *Red Gaze*, oil on cardboard, 1910.

consciousness is profound, however, their introspective scope is cast in terms of music's semantic specificity (as explained by Engel), which has its limitations. Emotionally intensified to the furthest extreme, the protagonists' portrayal in musical drama cannot account for their moral development the way a novel can, and if the composer is not cautious enough to leave their moral deliberations to be read between the score's staves, or by other means, he will find his personae acting through overdetermined motives. On the other hand, these motives, both internal and external (related to environment, atmosphere, memories, feelings, drives, and insights), are reinforced and concretized through music in a way unattainable through other media. The seemingly clean background of Parsifal's consciousness increases the impression of the moments in which such motives act on him. These moments, embodied in a rich texture of echoing and compassion, will further our comparison between the two works and enable us to view the growth of personality in the characterization of the main protagonist.[71]

Three such superimposed moments in *Parsifal* comprise the essence of the drama: (1) the moment in which Parsifal's compassion is *not* aroused, despite the apparent existence of the necessary (external) conditions; (2) the moment in which "enlightened compassion" dawns upon him, alongside the knowledge of the action it requires; (3) the moment in which this action realizes itself. Each of these instances is built into a shell-like ceremonial and emotional construction that encompasses Parsifal from all directions.

But not only him; these constructions also embrace those listeners who open themselves to the process of sympathy and the affirmation of a world that demands its salvation. Wagner construes these designs in a special way. He lays their foundations in the overture—in the thematic array of the major leitmotifs along their density level, their position and interrelations. He establishes the sonic world of the Grail knights on an arpeggio texture that evokes associations with the universe of the Rhine's daughters and Valhalla's gods.[72] But it immediately turns out that the chordal basis in the present case is not deployed here in order to symbolize a primordial prehuman existence, but rather to create the resonating acoustic space of a well-made spiritual world. The first theme— the "communion" leitmotif—distinguishes itself by deviating in the fourth note from the chordal structure in line with the idiom of "innocent faith," as Deryck Cooke maintained (ex. 5.2a).[73] It structurally resembles the Introit of the third Nativity Mass (though the latter remains confined within the sixth), wrought to the famous words of Isaiah (9:5): "For to us a child is born, to us a son is given; and the government shall be upon his shoulder, and his name shall be called Wonderful Counselor, Mighty God, Everlasting Father, Prince of Peace"[74] (see

Ex. 5.2a. Richard Wagner, *Parsifal*, opening phrase ("Communion" motif).

Ex. 5.2b. Introit of the third Nativity Mass (plainchant).

Ex. 5.2c. Kabbalat Shabbat, "Adonai Malach"
(Psalm 93, Idelsohn, *Thesaurus* 7: no. 29).

ex. 5.2b). And yet it comes even closer to the *Adonai Malach* of Kabbalat Shabbat (ex. 5.2c) that welcomes with a fanfare (likewise confined to a sixth) the
revelation of God's kingdom in nature.

The communion theme *is* an Introit: an overture to an enormous Eucharist,
whose monophonic garments touch the monastic simplicity of the plainchant.
In its special convexity, extending beyond the chant here quoted, emphasizing
the three highest notes of the scale—from F to A-flat—it touches the parallel
minor, marking poignancy as an integral, natural part of the theme's diatonic
essence ("sameness in difference," George Eliot would say and carefully point
to the traditional Kabbalat Shabbat tune which similarly touches a minor element on the top of its ambitus).

The entire first part of the prelude is built on two double appearances of the
theme; the first double appearance is in the original key, the second—a third
above (C minor). Each immediate repetition is an orchestrated antiphonal response taken up by different instruments.

The double repetition of the theme and the intermediate undulating arpeggio sections create a symmetrical structure, well divided, ceremonial, and concomitantly insoluble. From the elongated pause that invites the last note to reverberate in our mind, a new diatonic-major leitmotif emerges at the beginning of the second part, in the tonic (the "Grail" motif). Its military orchestration (trumpets and trombones) is immediately balanced and softened through the echoing of its last tones in the woodwinds, and subsequently in the strings. With the sections of the "faith" motif,[75] heard between two such echoings, variegated through sequences and modulations, this whole part stands as a melodic, tonal, and dynamic solution to the previous one. The orchestration here fills the acoustic space with responses to previous instrumental sections until a full balance between them is achieved. A solution of this kind in the middle section is unusual; against this backdrop, the third part of the overture appears to be breaking the ceremonial barriers of the first two parts. It develops the first motif chromatically and deconstructs the textural homogeneity of the clear symmetrical division, while crafting a texture that recalls converging redemptive Wagnerian finales (like Isolde's *Liebestod* in *Tristan*) while lacking a conclusive ending. The ultimate quasi-monophonic appearance of the "communion" theme also deviates from its initial boundaries. As a totality, this prelude serves Wagner in constituting the musical-dramatic space in which not only will the impending events transpire, but also those related to more distant circles.[76]

Ritualistic and tense monophony; echoing that partially appears too late; premature resolution; chromatic fusion mixing all semantic elements together—what is the meaning of all these in a drama of compassion? Before considering this, two surprisingly missing elements within this shell-like construction should be marked: first, the lack of quasi-polyphonic configurations (of the kind deployed by Wagner's contemporaries in order to create an ecclesiastic atmosphere), and second, within this leitmotivic array, the "*Mitleid*" (sometimes called "fool" or "prophecy") motif is absent, despite its centrality in what follows.[77]

It is not coincidental that instead of Renaissance-Baroque polyphonic configurations (associated, then as now, with Palestrina), Wagner deploys the Venetian *cori spezzati* (referred to in previous chapters)—inherently associated with the acoustical phenomenon of echo, and as such, involving a different arrangement of space, balance and volume, acceleration and deceleration, segmentation and rhetorization. The *Mitleid* motif, which will gradually infiltrate the dramatic sequence like a distant echo, coming close and then appearing as a frontal vocal presence, accommodates into such an acoustic environment. The resonating saturation of the theme's first part—which hangs on a fine thread of two long same-tones (A) that function as momentary dominants, and builds a cumulative a cappella sonority mainly out of perfect fifths (ex. 5.3)—is rhetorically

Ex. 5.3. Richard Wagner, *Parsifal* (*Mitleid* motif).

mellowed in the ensuing phrase, which extends more leisurely in space. The gradual penetration of the motif into the acoustic shell plays a central part in assigning meaning to the circle of events that it is designed to support.

In Montsalvat, the knights, father Titurel, Gurnemanz and, above all, King Amfortas—the desperate, lone sufferer—are waiting for the savior. In Montsalvat there is no compassion. They demand insistently, even aggressively, the uncovering of the Grail, whose bared presence is necessary for the renewal of sanctified blessing, even if the deed would cause Amfortas unbearable suffering. Some salutary measures taken to alleviate his pain do not blur the impression made by these knight-priests of a community mobilized by the power of ceremonial routine, in which each knows his place, voice, and steps in a well-defined hierarchical order. They mock Kundry's strange, compassionate acts and her utter otherness. They are cruel to anyone who does not accept the local "laws of compassion"—against Parsifal who innocently hunts a swan. Their routine conduct does not allow them to fathom the relations between the circumstances of Amfortas' sin and between that sin and his tragic state. They are too inside or too outside. They are in need of holiness from a transcendental source because they cannot achieve it immanently. This transcendental holiness (unnourished by internal renewal) strikes Amfortas, who is exposed to its unavoidable tensions of intimacy and distance, desire and ascesis, emotion and devotion. The only one who understands the tragic situation is Gurnemanz, but even he is too eager to resolve it promptly; the shortcuts he takes in relation to Parsifal cannot condense intricate psychic processes.

And what of Parsifal? What does this tabula rasa perceive in all that takes place on Montsalvat? Parsifal arrives at the Grail ceremony, after he absorbs the shock of his first encounter with the mount's knights, experiences shame over his hunting transgression, and learns the news of his mother's death, which suffuses him with ineluctable guilt. Shame, guilt, and embarrassment—are they good stages in the initiation rite for the great deed that awaits him—redeeming bleeding Amfortas? In the grip of these affects, Parsifal is unable to act immediately as a free moral agent. The miraculous transfiguration of time into space, as it occurs in his transition from Montsalvat's natural environment into the ritualistic temple, cannot alleviate these feelings. Time is needed to process it all, and the spectacular ceremony will deepen his feelings of impotence and helplessness. His profound ignorance will not be of aid either; however entranced, he seems unable to fathom, at that moment, the meaning of Amfortas' painful cries, not to speak of act on his behalf.

Yet he will seize such a moment, if the scene continues to reverberate within him. The ritual has this potential. In its first part, Amfortas and Parsifal are present absentees. This is the most ceremonial stage, which creates the impression that Montsalvat's Grail rituals have always been thus performed (albeit once less gloomy). The metrically monophonic and predetermined structures divided among the groups and inside them—as in the first part of the overture—create this impression. It is so strong that we do not know whether the following, seemingly spontaneous dialogue between Titurel and Amfortas is not a routine plea of a retired *father* to an officiating *son* to uncover the Grail and a reiteration of a heartbreaking monologue of the responsive son. The *spirit*—that of compassion—is quick to rejoin. Amfortas' monologue, even if fixated formulaic, still bears the spontaneity characterizing the expressive arioso, increasingly granting meaning to the already familiar motifs quoted in its course. Its main, paradoxical import is: the suffering that I, Amfortas, bear brings me closer to Jesus' plight, while at the same time I am ashamed of and mortified by my sin— the cause of my suffering—before him and my community. Only he, Christ, can pity and redeem me—through death.[78]

Confession brings the compassion absent in the drama's overture and the ritual's first part, and introduces it into the sonic shell that increasingly envelops Parsifal. Without a moment's break, an invisible "Daughters of Voice" chorus responds to Amfortas in the motif that has become familiar—the *Mitleid* motif, whose words were first heard by Gurnemanz ("Durch Mitleid"). Yet the knights' present intonation, though of an echoing nature, is too demanding. Amfortas has no alternative, they say; he must uncover the Grail. In what follows, the boys (*Knaben*), singing from above to the communion motif, utter the crucial word *Mitleid* on the "minor" peak of the theme (ex. 5.2a). The Grail motif appears at the very end of the ceremony, right after a broad parading of the faith motif. It leaves Parsifal and Gurnemanz fixed in their places, while a leitmotivic plethora resounds in the musical space in front. (Do they hear it?)

Deeply disappointed, Gurnemanz pushes Parsifal outside the hall and furiously slams the door behind him. But where could Parsifal have broken in with the desired compassionate act, had he been able and willing to do so? When could he have asked the requisite question about the source of Amfortas' suffering? The ritual's participants did not leave an opening. The drama could have ended with the banishing of Parsifal from this arena, but an invisible Daughter of Voice appears high up, with half of the *Mitleid* motif, responded to by some of her fellows: "Selig im Glauben" (blessed in faith).

The moment missed by Parsifal has vanished before it actually took place. The moment during which the invisible Daughters of Voice sing the motif, following right after Amfortas' monologue, might signal that lapse, filling in the empty space in which this prospective redeemer was supposed to perform his act. Be that as it may, he and the entire congregation, inside and outside, internalize this oratorical moment. Like those outside, the insiders have also heard it as "real" (stage) music.[79]

Ceremonies unto themselves do not suffice to instigate Parsifal into action. All the flower girls in Klingsor's bewitched garden (act II), who stimulate their victims by means of a highly ritualized temptation, do not cause him to lose control. What could seduce him is a moment equal in emotional force to Amfortas' monologue, which could mobilize his sprouting compassion and combine it with the shame and guilt he bears, along with his search for identity and belonging. Why does Parsifal not succumb to Kundry (later in act II), when she makes the sophisticated link of eros with pathos and a woman's love with the missing mother's love? Why does Wagner, in the name of Parsifal, negate all the values that were central, for instance, in Siegfried's journey to Brünnhilde's cliff? What happens at that moment in which Kundry kisses him in the name of his missing mother, tapping on his guilt and orphaned feelings and connecting him to a most powerful eros—so that his compassion towards Amfortas is suddenly aroused?

At that moment Parsifal seems to fully and profoundly understand the situation in which Amfortas has lapsed. He is now situated in the same place where Amfortas had stood on the verge of sin. The meaning of all those longed-for gifts that were to fall into his lap—love, identity, and sexuality (identified with a primarily "missing object" from a psychoanalytic perspective)—is nullified in the face of this enlightening moment, the moment in which the internal decree and the role and mission it entails become plain as day, and from which the falsehood of this scene and Kundry's deceptive expression become clear to him. These instances, in which his feelings of desire, longing, anxiety, guilt, and shame illuminate those that had motivated Amfortas' sin, are not a time of aesthetic affirmation or anonymous compassion; they are rather moments of sympathy towards the individual he wishes to redeem.

Does Wagner contradict his own ideas when he posits compassion as emerging from introspection and the delving into the Other's inner motivation (rather than solely relating to the external manifestation of suffering)? This is apparently the case, but again the emphasis lies on abstracted suffering rather than on the suffering individual. On the face of it, it seems that Parsifal's treatment of Kundry goes in the direction of Daniel's treatment of Gwendolyn: Daniel is committed to her as a spiritual guide who clearly separates this role from that of a lover awakening vain hopes. The art of separation between various social and psychological roles is part of his moral growth. It emanates from the Weberian "ethics of responsibility," an ethics foreign to Parsifal, who lacks a distinct moral profile. Though moral growth is not beyond Parsifal's potential, his choices are of a magical nature, embodied in the closing acoustic shell reintroduced in act II and further magnified in the final act, in which Parsifal will eventually march forward and redeem the suffering king and his order through compassion.

This shell is the incarnated sentiment; it is both malleable and fixed, and concurrently flowing and enveloping, womblike, oceanic, thus defining space and fashioning belonging. The space that it opens wide lies within a community that lacks a redeeming element—similar to the space or gap felt in *Daniel Deronda* in the transition from the heights of Kabbalat Shabbat to the "passionate regret" of the real present. Once the redeemer steps forward into that space, the gap will be filled with his sounds. Against the background of the gloomy monophony that opens the Grail ceremony in the first act, the overture of the Good Friday ceremony in the third one sounds even gloomier, transforming into the funeral march accompanying Titurel, the old father, to his burial. The boys and the Daughters of Voice choir disappear. Concomitantly, the ceremony breaks through routine and becomes unique, like a mass that turns into a requiem. Amfortas' exclamations and protests are unprecedented, as are the knights' merciless demands to uncover the Grail. In its dense timbral and tonal configurations, it becomes, as Carolyn Abbate argues, a most noisy, vociferous dramatic scene—containing "every note ever imagined, all at once and almost louder than one can bear."[80] That such *Lärm* occurs in a Good Friday ritual, the most "Jewishly" sensitive time in the Christian year, is not a coincidence.

Shifting into an almost atonal sequence, the earlier thematic order is disturbed, as in the final part of the opera's overture. Parsifal penetrates this defective unfolding and, through his redeeming act, the middle part of the sonoric shell (as it appears in the drama's overture)—which had been the most reconciled of its components—is gradually reconstructed. But now the *Mitleid* motif merges with it, its reverberating fifths open ad infinitum, freeing the word *Mitleid* of the communion motif from its minor peak. The redemption of the redeemer ("Erlösung dem Erlöser") resolves the musical and dramatic noise and dissonances simultaneously and on various levels, entirely filling the shell's space. This does not mean that deep down the "disruptive voices are cured" thereby, as Arnold Whittall rightly insists,[81] and yet, as far as the authorial level is concerned, the basic Christian formula is maintained: noise is bad—a symptom of sin, decay, and of a God's forsaken people; harmony is good, providential, and inextricably associated with sacrifice, compassion, and exclusion.

Does a similar process take place in Daniel's case? Does the synagogal shell and its related cluster of echoes set Daniel's mission on a correspondent basis? The parallel plot leads to a concordant resolution: Daniel's attraction to the suffering soul is similarly enacted against the background of an impressive sonic ceremony through which the soul undertakes a mission of redemption. The group in his case, though more variegated and abstract, is no less in need of redemption. Will Eliot allow her sympathetic hero to fill the shell (more metaphoric in his case) that awaits his arrival?

FORM AND CONTENT: HIERARCHIC NARRATIVE VERSUS EGALITARIAN COUNTERPOINT

In *Daniel Deronda* the space is only partially filled with "redeeming" sounds. This spatial differential again sharpens distinctions within similarities between these two creators, their compassionate creatures, and the concept of compassion that they promote. The plenitude of Wagner versus the partiality of Eliot is first and foremost a consequence of divergent structural conceptions. Wagner builds his drama as a colossal ABA structure imbued with the principles of the sonata form. Wagner posits the two external acts in an extraordinary parallelism that includes the acting personae, the frame of the sequence of events, and their musical unfolding.[82] This parallelism stresses the gap between the opening and closing events and between the times in which they transpire, putting in relief changes undergone by the personae over the time lapsed. After the shattering experience in Klingsor's castle, and following a few wandering years searching his way back to Montsalvat, Parsifal is no longer the same innocent-ignorant character.[83] When he arrives on Montsalvat he learns that the Grail has long been covered. Suffering Amfortas never again allows its exposure. Gurnemanz has aged, Titurel died, and the knights are living an unblessed life. Everything that takes place acquires its meaning by comparison with the parallel episode in the first act. As in the sonata form, the thematic cycle changes through a recollection of its conflictive unfolding in the exposition (*Parsifal*, act I) and a dismembering on the verge of destruction (enacted mainly by other motifs) in the development section (act II). A providential power now determines—no more. With a supreme effort and exacerbation of its constitutive elements, it constructs (from the same or similar materials) a world on the verge of implosion, reconciling every intricacy and granting the sonoric whole a harmony that enables the consummation of the drama.

This structural conception has no place in Eliot's imaginative world. Her own formal predilection is for a powerful middle rather than glorified openings or apocalyptic endings. For Eliot, form resides in our discrimination of "the relation of multiple interdependent parts of a whole which is itself in the most varied and therefore the fullest relation to other wholes."[84] Things have no end and no beginning, every beginning is arbitrary, "no retrospect will take us to the true beginning; and whether our prologue be in heaven or on earth, it is but a fraction of that all-presupposing fact with which our story sets out" (*Daniel Deronda*, chapter 1, 7).

And so every ending is an unraveling, inherently connected to the concept of dénouement, as in *Daniel Deronda*'s ending: Mordecai has died; Gwendolyn is left alone with her wounded soul; Daniel, detaching himself from his natural mooring, sets off with his young wife on an enigmatic journey to an unknown land. Some of the earlier entanglements no longer exist, and the earlier intensity has abated. This is not an ecstatic experience. As we approach the novel's finale, the sounds reaching our ears do not increase, but rather are heard as if from a distance, echoing those encountered at its center as a primal, original experience. This is true for the general structure, and largely also for the individual chapters. Chapter 32, whose developments we have closely traced, is a case in point. It builds a wide-arched structure in which the synagogal experience stands as its capstone. All the events in its third part complement its first; parts of them remain an echo (allusions to the synagogue) and others—an "anticipatory echo" (we first learn here about Mirah's singing, and only later actually hear it). This ramified and complicated system unfolds gradually and contrapuntally. The peak is in the middle; the margins can give some resonance to a theme that has been heard or is about to be, but the effect of the ending is that of quiet resignation. The second and third time Mirah performs her songs (in subsequent chapters), some of which are the same songs and works, are less revelatory than the initial exposure in chapter 32. So is the appearance of Mordecai-Ezra, who later quotes his mother's call to him and his response to her, evidence supporting Mirah's story and voice rather than validating his own words.

In what way do these modes of construction reflect the question of compassion and affirmation of the ritual? I have already indicated that Eliot's ethical worldview is based on the understanding of a moral resolution, or an aggregate of such resolutions, as a psychic vector projecting possible future action. Daniel's essential resolutions have been made by the middle of the book. Congruously, for Daniel there is no deed—neither his nor others'—that is the single, ultimate, redeeming act. In contradistinction to Shakespearean romances, there is also no ultimate anagnorisis. Daniel's moments of recognition are multiple: with his discovery of his mother, himself as an abandoned, and still rejected child; with Ezra-Mordecai, himself as a certifiable Jew; with old Kalonymos, his status as grandson of a venerable Jew; through his reacquaintance with Mirah as bearer of all these lineages; refined again later, with Gwendolyn who, in addition to all the above-noted changes, is now faced with his matrimonial tie to Mirah. From the perspective of Daniel's "many-sided sympathy," all these moments compete with each other. In other words, the sequence of actions and events in the novel is not hierarchic; their sounds and voices are heard at varying volumes, and validate each other through the complicated system of echoing relations that interconnects them.

From the point of view of a theory of medium, Wagner and Eliot use opposing strategies: whereas Wagner deploys the sonata form's teleological narrative, Eliot opts for a polyphonic texture. According to Bakhtin, this texture fits the modality of the social-psychological novel, of which this book is a prime illustration. A hierarchic aesthetic conception, as embodied in Wagner's construction, is replaced in Eliot's work by a democratic, interactive foundation that flees indulgence of an extreme egalitarianism in favor of a gravitational principle of sentiment. Sentiment itself, as we have seen, is based on the convergence of powerful traditions with the vigorous vision of a moral, creative imagination that does not shun resolution. If, for John Morley, Eliot's writing is an illustration of how literature is able to embody the belief in the potential of a liberal set of actions, this literature itself grows out of the entrenchment of this belief in its cultural furnace. Eliot's worldview, imbued with the spirit of individualism of Montaigne, Shakespeare, and Spinoza, and also that of Wordsworth, Coleridge, and John Stuart Mill, lends her literary vision the dimension of a genuine search for the Other's proximity, all the while maintaining the unique features of her or his alterity.[85]

Though early in his life Wagner had assumed a liberal identity, he could never embrace a belief in a possible world constructed by individuals whose judgments are the product of a permanent combination of undiscriminating compassion and unbiased sentiment. In Wagner's Weltanschauung, sentiment is predetermined and compassion graded; the unique modes of spiritualization of a suffering other, as well as their impact on a soul mobilized towards the sufferer, could only take place within this frame.

AESTHETIC CATEGORIES AND UNIVERSES
OF CONSCIOUSNESS

The differences between Eliot's humanistic, liberal religion and Wagner's semireligious, communitarian one (concretized in their divergent conceptions of the Jew as an aesthetic category) should be assessed against the respective universes of consciousness that gave rise to them. In Eliot's case this universe owes much to British empiricism and its consequent aesthetics. Reducing epistemological dependence on innate or metaphysical factors, the British empiricists based the search into public and private realities and mentalities on foundations open to all. The individual's autonomy thereby granted, opened up before him or her horizons of experience with a potential for renovation of aesthetic and moral values. Regarding artistic experience, empiricist aesthetics aimed to sharpen the gap between art and reality in order to put artistic coherence on par with scientific rigor.[86] This answered a need to intellectually assess the creative effort of art-making, to tone down the festivity of artistic illusion, and to establish psychological distance as a fundamental principle of artistic experience. This is the source of the judicious authority Eliot grants her readers and the democratic platform on which she posits the virtual personae of her artistic world—from author to the least of characters. Still, the moral responsibility she demands of her characters is limited to the spectrum of their free choice within the constraints of their fates and their personal qualities, in response to the corresponding spectrum of their fellow creatures.[87] The continuity between real and fictional (as embodied in the romance-like frame) thus becomes the source of the objective dimension of Eliotian sympathy along its skeptical component.

On the face of it, the German philosophical legacy (especially the Kantian) similarly aimed both to enlarge the boundaries of the discretionary autonomy of the individual and support the principle of internal coherence of the artistic work. Concomitantly, it endorsed normative-categorical principles that reduced the boundaries of the individual's liberty in determining aesthetic value, depositing it in the hands of the creative genius. Schopenhauer, challenging Kant's categorical imperative—which Kant advanced at the cost of human warmth, loyalty, and friendship—set the principle of compassion at the center of ethical thought; he too, however, was hurled into a normative trap which further diminished the spectrum of humane values. His attempt aimed to charge the sober judgmental world of his predecessors with emotional force originating in Christian love (*agape*) and grace. Eliot needed this emotional component no less than Schopenhauer and Wagner; hence her adoption of the Feuerbachian philosophy that reinforced the principle of Christian love in its own way.[88] The centrality of the component of compassion in the divergent worlds of Wagner and Eliot partakes of this legacy. The difference in the inner structure of their respective worlds is what endows their respective "compassions" with such divergent characteristics.

With Wagner, this structure integrates a belief in the metaphysical status of aesthetic principles and the creator-genius' direct access to them with the conception of the potential for emotional spontaneity generating the listener-spectator's aesthetic affirmation. This integration is reflected in the transcendental pretension of Wagnerian compassion and its communitarian character, which paradoxically produces formulaic, abstract relations.

Turned upside down, these elements in Eliot's world are reflected in the multifaceted, immanent, and individual character of the author's sympathy and that of her protagonists. Hence their divergent views of the artist's role: for Wagner, his role is that of prophet and high priest who constitutes compassion and sympathy on a mythological level, whereas for Eliot her role is limited to opening individuals' eyes and ears to new options of personal-moral growth.[89] The mode in which each viewed the embodiment of content in form derives directly from this. Wagner's emotional world is a world of a dynamic hierarchy and its emotions are gravitational forces that demand correspondence for the sake of closure. For Eliot, emotions are needed for open-ended interactive animation of the worlds she creates, and act as independent vectors that affect each other. Hers is therefore a world lacking homogeneity, closure, or finitude, a world of powerful encounters whose kinetic charges gradually dissipate.

Still, Eliot is also engaged by questions of national redemption, the formation of a redeemer undergoing profound transfiguration, and the implications of ritual in establishing group identity and in eliciting individual sympathy and compassion; she too posits tradition as a constitutive element in society, and likewise wishes to create a link of amendment between the poetic inside and the prosaic outside. In short, she also has an interest in a human community as defined by its collection of individuals as well as the communal traditions that associate them. In a world lacking predetermined hierarchies, however, there is no advantage of one group over another. On the contrary, Eliot is aware that preference for one group over another may lead to the deprivation of that other.[90] Putting the Italian and the Jewish resurgence on a par, she implies the potential discrimination of the male members of these ethnic groups against their female members.[91] The Jew for Eliot is thus a paradigm of the Other in the same and the same in the Other, a *conditio humana* destined to ever evolve in varying historical circumstances. For Wagner, on the other hand, the Jew possesses a metaphysical nonsubstance which thus plays a role similar to that of the traditional Satan, against which the substantial plenitude of the German comes to the fore.[92] In less theological terms, Wagner's Jew is an abstract aesthetic category that must be overcome or marginalized, whereas for Eliot the Jew's aesthetic properties forever challenge a society that aspires to broaden its spiritual scope, bolstering and refining its moral vision.

The consummate "benevolent" and "malevolent" outsiders that Eliot and Wagner respectively embody in relation to Jewish ritual bring the history of the Jewish *Lärm* to one of its climaxes, yet pose a challenging query: their fictional benevolent outsiders—Daniel and Parsifal—ultimately partake in an action of redemption of the ritualistic community that had sought their sympathetic approval. As it turns out, they also discover their kinship to the community, Daniel as a descendent of a pedigreed dynasty, Parsifal as the founder of one. This bloodline transmutes their sympathetic reaction into a natural attraction, thereby weakening its sociopolitical and moral significance. Eliot seems aware of this, and it is precisely on this account that she deviates from the romance tradition: nothing magical or mystical is at work in Daniel's adventures, but rather a contingent sequence of events whose pattern emerges for Daniel at a certain point that he pursues. At any given moment he could resist and choose otherwise. That is why Eliot has to delve into his inner self, psychologizing and moralizing his pursuit. Wagner in *Parsifal* likewise does not emphasize tribal relations, but rather the role of a transformative process involving sense and consciousness in the making of a spiritual leader. Their respective orphanage is critical for their self-invention, for their acting outside familial bonds, Oedipal or otherwise, thus experimenting with the psyche's basic powers of social association and self-fashioning.[93] It is these elements that became so attractive to the subsequent generation of artists, who sought transfiguration as an evolutionary principle transgressing fixed identities and predetermined sympathies far beyond those revealed in the *Bühnenweihfestspiel* (stage-consecrating festival play) in Bayreuth. The cosmopolitan and, to some extent, Wagnerian Jewish composer Julius Klesmer in *Daniel Deronda* could sympathize with this. His archetypal character will penetrate deep into the concluding chapters of the present volume, which round the final portrait in this European history of Jewish sonorities and the Jew as an aesthetic category.

6

THE AESTHETIC THEOLOGY OF MULTIVOCALITY: ARNOLD SCHOENBERG AMONG ALTER EGOS

And the Ophanim and the holy Animals with rushing sound, rise up toward the Seraphim, over against them they offer laud and say . . .

—*From* Shaharit—*Morning Prayer*

[T]he terrible noise [*Lärm*] again had me in its power. . . . in the midst of all its majestic amplitude, which was terrifying, but still not unconquerable, a clear, piercing, continuous tone . . . came without variation literally from the remotest distance—perhaps the real melody in the midst of the noise [*Lärm*]. . . . Oh, the music these dogs made almost drove me out of my senses!

—*Franz Kafka, "Investigations of a Dog"*

VIENNESE SONORITIES—ONCE AGAIN

The soft interpretation made by some scholars of Wagner's Jewish annihilation behest (in *Das Judentum's* "finale"), using terms of cultural assimilation (rather than physical extermination), was actually implemented in the practice of many European Jews, especially in the generations following Wagner's republication of the treatise. While they could dispense with his explicit decree to move in this direction, they were more often than not taken by the narcotic love-death potion of his works and the emancipatory force of their stream-of-consciousness content. This was part of a general urge towards what may be termed as "mythological subjectivism": subjectivity empowered through mythological role models (Tristan, Tannhäuser, Zarathustra, and their like), their creators (Wagner, Schopenhauer, Nietzsche), or through metaphysical ideas or plots, expanding the self's existential space.[1]

Later developed into a more systematic thinking by Jung, such subjectivism could also imbibe the nationalistic tones and undertones of Wagner's works, transplanted them into other national arenas, or eschewed them in favor of a more cosmopolitan approach. The *Gesamtkunstwerk* ideal became one of his most inspiring influences on many fin-de-siècle artists who aspired to various kinds of synaesthetic-holistic ideals. The quest included also a search for a transcended sexuality, in androgynous or asexual modes of expression and existence (see below). Within this intoxicating post-Wagnerian atmosphere there was more than one reason for mid-European Jewish artists to believe in a redemptive artistic vision, transcending difference.

There were always those, like the renowned conductor of *Parsifal*, Hermann Levi—again a cantor's son—who, still in Wagner's time, would never part with his Jewish sentiments despite the pressure the Wagners exerted on him.[2] There were others, like Otto Weininger, Max Nordau, Karl Kraus, and Ludwig Wittgenstein, who, more Wagnerian than Wagner (at least in this respect), sometimes in a gesture of "Jewish self-hatred," sometimes in a more constructive approach, severely criticized their fellow Jews for their "degenerate" aesthetic predicament, its musical component included.[3]

Vienna—as briefly discussed in chapter 3—was a center of many variations on these and similar themes at the turn of the century. In a city known for its sharp contrasts and conflictual trends, one could find at the time tolerant policies towards Jews and other minorities (encouraging immigration from the Austro-Hungarian provinces) alongside burgeoning blatant anti-Semitism; it was a place where Zionism erupted and where the most radical assimilatory trends flourished; a center of particularistic Jewish culture and of outstanding Jewish-"Germanic" creativity. And, in what pertains to sonic works and surroundings, Vienna was a locus of a new, harmonized mode of Jewish service (established by Sulzer), as well as an arena in which sediments of older accusations regarding Jewish noise became explicit. It was also the empire's capital, where Jews were among the most avid amateurs of classical, conservative music, and, concurrently, the spearheads of the musical avant-garde.

Arnold Schoenberg—the Jewish composer considered as the emblem of the Viennese musical avant-garde, and likewise, as a young man, implicated in the Wagnerian craze—stands at the focal point of this chapter. I propose to view his creative journey as a highly profound, though only partially conscious, modernist endeavor to grapple with the complexity of the music libel against the Jews, through various vocal fictions—oratorical, lyrical, and dramatic. This goes beyond his famous "emancipation-of-the-dissonance" enterprise, as it is usually understood, that is, in terms of expanding the tonal universe and the evening-out of all tonal combinations. The term (coined by Schoenberg himself) can be seen, indeed, as translating Jewish "emancipation" from its original socio-legal and political environments into a sonic-artistic one, aesthetically empowering the nonharmonious element that Jewish existence stood for. Yet the new musical apparatuses involved in this sonic emancipation, and the works of art it yielded, should themselves be better assessed in light of other contemporary Jewish authors' wrestling with theological veins and liturgical strains that had long been associated with Jewish noise. This wrestling, never openly diagnosed as such, was inspired by newly conceived psychoanalytic notions, as well as by modernist theological and aesthetic ones. It was affected no less by the rapid sociopolitical changes of a period spanning from the last years of the nineteenth century to the Second World War.

Thus in addition to Schoenberg, other Austro-Hungarian and German Jews will populate this chapter, as Schoenberg's "alter egos"—a concept most pertinent to his artistic case, as we shall see. These authors include Sigmund Freud and his disciple, Theodor Reik, who bridge the psychological and the theological in some of their major treatises; the Jewish philosopher Hermann Cohen and (his disciple) Franz Rosenzweig; and via them, though also independently, Baruch Spinoza—resuscitated at the time within a theologico-political realm he himself launched—and Franz Kafka, a literary-existential "ego," who grappled with noise issues most poignantly in several short stories. Another abducted alter ego of the live composer—the fictional composer Adrian Leverkühn—will be shortly encountered at the end of this saga (chapter 7).

Unlike previous generations of Jewish composers and writers, Schoenberg and his "alter egos"—Mahler, Reik, and Vogel, to include others mentioned earlier in the present volume—came from a meager background of immigrants (or themselves were such immigrants), who could not afford the kind of education and cultural exposure the Mendelssohns, the Meyerbeers, and even the Heines entertained: less socially secure, they paradoxically ventured more boldly on new paths. Among other sociological and cultural causes, this change could be attributed to the more brazen end-of-the-century version of *Bildung* that many of them adopted. Partially detached from the social decorum associated with it by previous generations, and abiding more passionately by its existential aura, those still adhering to *Bildung*'s decrees often interpreted them as a self-within-world generative ethos, propelling its adherents to dreams of redemption or visions of annihilation, or, sometimes, to sober modes of mitigating both.[4]

Why should Judaism, or, for that matter, Jewish history and traditions, be of concern at all to these artists who projected themselves along such modernist trajectories? Converting at about the same time—Mahler to Catholicism (1897) and Schoenberg, more eccentrically in Catholic Vienna, to Protestantism (1898)—their Christianizing gestures were different, the former more touched by opportunist colors, the latter—by what he deemed an internal theological move.[5] Such a move followed in the progressive direction that Abraham Mendelssohn charted and Felix seemed to embody so well (only that they dwelled within a traditional Protestant milieu). The move to Lutheranism by many a "serious" Jew was popular at the time, Franz Rosenzweig included. Instructively, in Rosenzweig's and Schoenberg's eventual return to Judaism, Yom Kippur services played a significant role, however differently. But prior to that later stage, the Jewish element for Schoenberg would be culturally and theologically virtually repressed, though felt in the pervading anti-Semitic atmosphere of assaults against Jewish-born composers, artists, and authors fed by Wagnerian (and similar) anti-Semitic influences.[6]

In the case of Schoenberg, these assaults would become most salient in the infamous episode in Mattsee (1921), a resort town where the composer and his family were not allowed to stay on account of their Jewishness. Even more than the extremely humiliating episode itself, the most shocking element for Schoenberg at the time was what he perceived as the betrayal of his friend and spiritual mate, Wassily Kandinsky, with whom he shared modernist ideas and embarked on new enterprises.[7] The crisis within cosmopolitan modernism, a movement that aspired to uproot old allegations of Jews as nonartistic or a-musical, marked the unleashing of the aesthetic categorization of the Jew on a purely racist basis. The eventual classification of all modernists within the Nazis' *entartete Kunst*, including Kandinsky and company, as infected by the "Jewish plague," is another bitter irony of this turbulent history.[8]

Against this heightened background, which will be further portrayed, major themes and ideas discussed throughout this volume will emerge from within the vocal fictions discussed below. Aesthetic categories—or rather, attempts to transcend them—interpenetrate in these fictions with "noisy elements." Transfigured ethnographies would come once more to the fore as subgenres eliciting these noisy disruptions, leading, through acknowledgment of the sentiments they harbor, and the sympathetic/antipathetic feelings they evoke in humans and deities, to certain political insights. The three orbits of music's "going beyond," discussed in chapter 3, the religious/theological "transcendental" sphere, music's own transfigurative orbit, and the political-punitive realm of transgression and transmigration, will be polyphonically resumed in this penultimate chapter.

THE AESTHETICS OF TRANSFIGURATION

Did Schoenberg, Mahler, or, for that matter, the Jew-by-choice Alexander von Zemlinsky—that circle of leading, kin-related Jewish composers—ever believe in their normalization within Gentile society?[9] To a large extent they did, as various testimonies seem to account for; sometimes toying with cosmopolitan visions, sometimes with more local or pan-Germanic ones. From their point of view, they seemed to opt for the third option in the threefold scheme of aesthetic categories discussed in chapter 4: turning universal or multiplied aesthetic classifications into aesthetics of transfiguration, subverting fixed categorization. This aesthetics, whose major herald was the poet Richard Dehmel, hailed process over form, experience over object, and hard-won spiritual gratification over ready-made pleasure. And they adhered to it mainly because it transcended particularism and endorsed universalism of a new kind. Marking synaestheticism as the blurring of boundaries between artistic media, the new ideology was part of a more general modernist enterprise to emancipate art from sanctified models, coalescing contrary elements into novel experiential wholes.

What is unique to the case of Schoenberg is the continuous search for these values in the twilight zone of vision and sound, aesthetics and theology in genres and artistic modes, both traditional (string quartets, lieder, symphonic poems) and modern (monodramas, oratorical works, and chamber symphonies), opening the path for an experimental approach also through his paintings (Schoenberg was an avid painter in particular in the late 1900s, mainly of self-portraits, bringing the genre to the realm of abstract vision). What seemed to interest him most in that period is the gliding of the visual, through tears and crying, into the searching vocal persona, blurring boundaries of selves and genders (see plates 6–9).[10] The role of the eyes, the glance, and, if to expand the *Erwartung* (1909) experience, also the "doubling, dividing and interchanging of the self"—the heart of the *Unheimlich,* according to Freud, inhere in it.[11]

ALTER EGOS

The hegemony of consciousness over repressed and unconscious parts, which was so central to Freud's approach in general, and the *Unheimlich* concept in particular, was counteracted at the time by the precept that a person may entertain more than one consciousness, or a split consciousness. The latter theoretical position was held by Théodule Ribot, Alfred Binet, Pierre Janet, and later turn-of-the-century psychologists (Frederic W. H. Myers, Morton Prince, and

William James).[12] Holders of such multiconsciousness or multiple-personality theory, though driven by various theoretical and therapeutical interests, could maintain that certain psychological states, when rejected by the synthesis of the new personality (self) may remain outside the consciousness of the latter, but still arrive at an internal synthesis, and form a second consciousness, simultaneous with the first. This secondary consciousness may compete with the primary, be subservient to it or even dormant in it, but still claim an autonomous position.

Freud, who was following a path leading from Descartes, Leibniz, Kant, Herbart, Wundt, Husserl, and other believers that a transcendental self is coextensive with its phenomenal person, seems to be struggling against this subversive alternative, which had its own theoretical and therapeutic advantages. In short, here was a battle between a vertical or hierarchical (Freud and company) versus a horizontal or competitive/collaborative conception of consciousness.

We may assume that Schoenberg, his friends, and students were aware of the horizontal conception of consciousness. To his friend, the pianist and composer Ferruccio Busoni, Schoenberg wrote a few days before beginning to compose *Erwartung*:

> It is *impossible* for a person to have only one sensation at a time. One has *thousands* simultaneously. And these thousands can no more readily be added together than an apple and a pear. They go their own ways.   And this variegation, this multifariousness, this *illogicality* which our senses demonstrate, the illogicality presented by their interactions, set forth by some mounting rush of blood, by some reaction of the senses and the nerves, this I should like to have in my music.[13]

Schoenberg went even further, for he came to regard expressivity that does not aspire to the transcendental sublime as a wellspring of creativity. This was revolutionary even in terms of the most radical psychoanalytic theory of the time, as Simms rightly observes.[14] Added to that was the option of persons with one or several shared selves. Both options, and their effective combinations, imply a more flexible demarcation of consciousnesses and personae, and, concomitantly, more noisy elements, less harmoniously unified entities. Though Schoenberg tended to deny a redemptory potential to his experiments with "other minds," he certainly viewed them as containing emancipatory powers through a blurring of old demarcations and forms of thought.

In the realm of the vocally fictional, these beliefs could become a powerful moral force, intimating the belief in the ability to go beyond one's biographic and psychic heritages, beyond restored memory and long-term sentiments, creating ad-hoc communal conjunctions, associated through ever-evolving sensory and ideational networks. Whereas the self-visual (I/eye) leads again and again to the point of gouging out one's eyes, as Derrida has arrestingly shown,[15] the phenomenology of the vocal, on the other hand, leads from this point to the ability to go beyond one's own emotional territory into the depth of another's consciousness. The evolution of post-Freudian psychology, from Heinz Kohut up to contemporary relational and intersubjective clinical approaches, points to the potential to go in this direction inherent also in the basic psychoanalytic condition as formulated by Freud himself.

THE EMANCIPATION OF THE VOCAL THROUGH AN ORATORICAL TIME-SPACE

The introduction of the vocal by Schoenberg (and by Freud, despite himself, in his basic therapeutic technique) as a phenomenal entity revealing to a sensitive listener more than what simply meets the ear, led Schoenberg further to explore the "noisy" realms of vocality beyond well-defined musical sounds. In this he irretrievably transgressed the medieval dichotomy of "discrete" (pitched) versus "indiscrete" (nonpitched) sounds—the latter, according to medieval writers (later echoed by Wagner) including also human laughter, groaning, barking, and roaring.[16] Schoenberg's elaboration of the principle of *Sprechstimme* beyond its precursory uses (by Humperdinck) in *Pierrot Lunaire* (op. 21) and later vocal works—mainly oratorical ones—called for a reassessment of the tonal realm, which, even for Schoenberg himself, throughout his life, was still conceived numerically (although numbers functioned for him in a different way than in the old harmonic systems). Though the historiography of twentieth-century music has long normalized the new vocal expansion in terms of modern deterministic discourse, Sprechstimme and related techniques upset the exclusivity of the musical over the general sonic, opening it up for other kinds of "indiscrete" sound—mechanical, urban, and the like.

Bringing the expressivity of the modern individual to its furthest (hitherto artistically manifest) limits, Schoenberg seemed to be intrigued by what in this likewise highly synaesthetic work emerges again: the theological—revealed through religious modes (in various sections and structures of *Pierrot Lunaire* as well as in *Die glückliche Hand* (op. 18).[17] It is no coincidence, then, that the famous "oratorio" letter, addressed to Dehmel—Schoenberg's muse and collaborator in the previous stages—was written during the *Pierrot* (1912) year. This landmark declaration is worth quoting at length, in order to reinterpret it within the present context:

For a long time I have been wanting to write an oratorio on the following subject: modern man, having passed through materialism, socialism, and anarchy and, despite having been an atheist, still having in him some residue of ancient faith . . . wrestles with God . . . and finally succeeds in finding God and becoming religious. Learning to pray! . . . [A]bove all: the mode of speech, the mode of thought, the mode of expression, should be that of modern man; the problems treated should be those that harass us. For those who wrestle with God in the Bible also express themselves as men of their own time, speaking of their own affairs, remaining within their own social and intellectual limits. . . .

Originally I intended to write the words myself. But I no longer think myself equal to it. . . . I could never shake off the thought of "modern Man's Prayer," and I often thought: If only Dehmel . . . ![18]

The desired artistic collaboration is well-framed and apparently self-explanatory: the genre should be oratorio, since the mode of the prospective work is that of prayer and its plot concerns a spiritual search enfolding its own historicity, its own oratorical moments. The praying persona—the oratorical subject—is to arise there out of the ruins of modernist ideologies, in his or her backward movement to an antique, biblical state of being. "Having passed through"—stands as a necessary condition for this spiritual pilgrimage. What is not clear is whether one is requested, for this spiritual purpose, to mentally relinquish one's former selves, or rather to include them in the wrestling with God (or His angel). Furthermore, does the host of former selves become a choir, or, conversely, a community of welcoming believers, or is there another oratorical group, which the genre seems to demand, that accompanies this Pilgrim's Progress? The progress, in any event, is only dimly related to the great religions' agendas, as it aspires to a cosmopolitan, concomitantly futuristic and archaic vision.

Answers will eventually be provided, however not by Dehmel. Schoenberg himself provided them in the unfinished *Jakobsleiter* (Jacob's Ladder)—libretto written between 1915 and 1917, and work composed mainly during 1917—before he was conscripted again into the army.[19]

SLIDING METAPHYSICS: ORATORICAL UPS AND DOWNS

Apocalyptic revelation is the matter of the piece. Its creator was weaving it sonically, attempting to avoid older sublime forms and their ready-made sentimental trail, and yet rendering the unfolding affective. His inventions are epochal: the intensive use not only of Sprechstimme as such, but together with a singing voice; the introduction of a Sprechstimme choir, alone or with a singing choir against an instrumental background; basing much of the "purer" musical material on a complementary hexacordal kernel from which major parts of the vertical and linear configurations generate; and, finally, the deployment of various off- and onstage devices for special audial effects. The merged result consists of a vocally variegated heterophony reminiscent of synagogal chant-mumbling of unprecedented nature on a Western stage, sonorically unified through the governing hexacordal combinatorics.[20]

The oratorical events follow the content of the famous 1912 letter: the search for a praying mode, or voice. The dramatis personae—allegorical characters that populate the apocalyptic scene—include the one who is called, the one who is rebellious, the one who is struggling, the one who is chosen, the monk, the dying person, and lastly, the soul (which is eventually doubled). Comprising an ostensibly unconnected host of human destinies and choices, they animate, in religious-existential terms, the various phases of modern man that Schoenberg mentioned in that letter. These individualized personae are preceded and enveloped by the twelve-part mixed chorus, including the malcontents, the doubters, the rejoicers, the indifferents, and the quietly resigned. They appear on stage, waiting for verdict or for salvation. Thus they rehearse unaware, and in modernist attire, the vision, summoned in the central Jewish Days of Awe piyyut, "Un^{e}tane tokef" (alluded to in chapter 4 in connection with Halévy's "Ô jour d'horreur"): "those that come into the world shall pass before Thee as a flock of sheep," in God's Jewish Day of Judgment or its Christian *Dies Irae* counterpart (also reminiscent of the souls in Plato's myth of Er [cf. Dante]). The opening sustained polyphony of brass and flute punctuated by percussion, into which busy motions of string and woodwinds are interwoven, creates the sonic sphere portrayed by these texts, their presumed origin in John's Revelation and the eschatological tradition it represents.

Gabriel, as the traditional archangel of annunciations and visitations, is there to show souls the way. His conduct towards them, however, is in large part fierce, uncompassionate, foreshadowing the eventual role of the composer's Moses (only that Gabriel mingles singing and Sprechstimme recitation, whereas Moses slides into singing only once, and even this is ad libitum). In his opening command, he urges them to follow him: "Ob rechts, ob links, vorwärts oder rückwärts, bergauf oder bergab man hat weiter zu gehen ohne zu fragen was vor oder hinter einem liegt" (Whether to right or left, forward or back, uphill or down, one must go on, without asking what lies ahead or behind, without questioning).[21] Without questioning, they ask? This is untenable on their part, indeed untenable for those who went through the events of the First World

War—the Great War—and through other contemporary political upheavals, and for whom the world as it had been could never be restored.[22]

What are they looking for? What kind of answers will satisfy them? No one seems to be absolved in this trial—save for the pure soul, accompanied by a few anonymous Daughters of Voice, that could be brought here from their former, and more explicit metamorphoses in Bach's *St. Matthew Passion*, Wagner's *Parsifal*, and maybe even Zemlinsky's *Little Mermaid* (through Andersen) (1903).

Jennifer Shaw persuasively maintains that the work manifests Schoenberg's conscious struggle, as part of his Viennese milieu's quest for androgynous modes of expression, to find an expressive representation of the asexual in angels as well as in human beings. Shaw argues that Schoenberg by and large remained within older, or even reified, modes of sexual categorizations, especially the romantic Eternal Feminine.[23] Her analysis shows, however, that he was keen to transcend these categorizations. Shaw does not take into consideration that the failure of his imagined personae is the main point here—their obsoleteness, their inability to arise beyond their prejudices and old habits. Struggling with his own text, Schoenberg, upon returning from war the second time, never completed the piece, and let the concluding, feminine voices roam their way.[24]

These Daughters of Voice, and the doubled Soul with them, soar upwards, through an unseen thread of vocal escape. Shedding qualities, these voices, accompanied by soaring like instruments, lose clear tonal gravitation, beyond their immediate reciprocation. As they rise upward, their vocalizations, in this version of the work, leave mundane sonorities below; no words—spoken or sung—take part in their journey. And then, indeed, there is no way back to previous categories, structures, and reified ideals, no way back to the libretto. If the composer payed a price for it, by losing the possibility to evoke oratorical moments and the inclusive forces they release, it may be what he was, after all, unwittingly searching for, at least in that critical historical moment.

Even before the war broke out, and in the same legendary 1912, Freud published his groundbreaking *Totem and Taboo*, which relegated the religious quest of humans to phylogenic, preternatural drives, deriving from (or constituting) human beings' basic Oedipal condition. Even more than Schoenberg, Freud's exploration was *prima facie* universal: it traces the idea of religion in general, including that of the abstract, monotheistic, to the guilt feelings of primordial sons repenting for the assassination of their paternalistic, devouring father, worked through a chain of totemic ersatzes. Freud is less interested, at this stage, in spiritual struggles and gains. A quarter of a century later these will emerge as a follow-up of this theoretical endeavor in his *Moses and Monotheism*, when his personal life and lifelong enterprise would seem to be highly threatened by the mounting Nazi power. While such ideas seem to be inconceivable by the author in the last outwardly peaceful days of the Austro-Hungarian era, immediately by the end of the Great War, or as soon as it was over, his ideas led others to engage with more particularistic epistemology, as the case of his student Theodor Reik attests.

There was, however, another option: to insist on an oratorical inclusion of a Jewish strand within a Germanic one. During the war (1915) Hermann Cohen (1842–1918), the renowned founder of the Marburg school of neo-Kantian philosophy, chose this option. Immersed at the time in writing his monumental *Religion of Reason: Out of the Sources of Judaism* (1919, published posthumously), he was elsewhere suggesting a harmonious reconciliation of *Judentum* and *Deutschtum*—the subject of his article from which the following paragraph is borrowed:

> If we ask now how this achievement of German idealism is tied to other [cultural] tendencies, there can be no doubt about *the religious origin of our music.*
>
> . . . [In it] the *oratorio* is the prototype that incorporated all artistic means, absorbed all popular energies of song using dramatic forms as well. . . .
>
> The great *recitatives* that pervade our entire [Jewish] year are the *unique prototype of Jewish Music.* In them the peculiarity of musical idea and feeling, the characteristic solemnity, the Maestoso of the Jewish message. . . . take shape. . . . Through *Mendelssohn,* the non-Jew can get an idea of the great degree to which this musical uniqueness is in the Jew's blood. In the different melodies of "Lord God of Abraham," and "Israel, this day let it be *known that Thou art God,*" how he sings, especially the last words, and even more instructively in the *Lobgesang* than in *Elias,* should claim the connoisseur of Jewish music as an inherited property.[25]

Notice the overlapping indexical "our": once it is used as a referent of Jews-as-Germans, once—as that which is particularly Jewish. The transition from the first to the second is almost unnoticeable.[26] Almost a century after the musical reforms of Sulzer in Vienna began, transported and further elaborated by Cohen's father-in-law—the celebrated composer Louis Lewandowski in Berlin—the full integration, though not assimilation, of the two cultures was believed, by him, to be complete. Cohen—again the son of a cantor (Gershon Cohen from the small Saxony-Anhalt town Coswig, whose Tish'a' be'Av synagogal customs, discussed in chapter 3, were described by Steinthal)—believed that despite the musical adjustments the "Jewish recitative" underwent in the hands of the most prestigious musical personalities, represented by his father-in-law, its authentic core remained intact. What may seem astonishing—his appreciation of Mendelssohn's melodic idiom as an offspring from the same ancient spiritual well—ironically coincides with the eventual claim by the Nazis about the composer's Jewishness. That the soft gestures descending in arpeggio with their appoggiatura-like ending of Elijah's prayer—the universal "Oh Lord God of Abraham, Isaac, and Israel, this day let it be known that Thou art God"—sound to his ears like a synagogal tune is not surprising, because such melodic contours were rather ubiquitous in the liberal synagogue in Berlin and elsewhere in Western Europe. Such a recitative should convey, for Cohen, an inclusive sonic gift that the bearers of the ancient Jewish "Religion of Reason" (*Religion der Vernunft*) bequeathed to all those Germans who aspire to this enlightened religion's condition—be they affiliated with a synagogue or a church.[27] Since for Cohen, compassion plays a central, original role in this antique religion, he manages (though not explicitly) to thus completely capsize the noise accusation along its theological corollaries.

Whether knowingly or unknowingly, Cohen's outward ideological stance thus rather naively interpreted a typical nationalistic, if not essentialist, self-appraisal of the kind intoned by Carl Hermann Bitter (about forty years earlier) in his *Beiträge zur Geschichte des Oratoriums* (1872) as all-inclusive:

> That it was primarily German composers in whose works the art form of the oratorio has culminated in its completion and maturity will not lessen but increase the interest of the German readership in my work. . . .
>
> To our astonished generation it has been granted to view the fatherland in the moments of its highest brilliance. No one can believe that the triumph of German power, which we now celebrate with uplifted feelings, [is] a consequence of accidental circumstances. It rests on long and serious preparations through the work of the German spirit, which German power has toughened and directed.
>
> Also art has its part in this work and its effects. One of its most noble blossoms is oratorio. May the future fail [oratorio] as little as it will the other works of the secure German spirit.[28]

Cohen passed away in the same year in which the Second (German) Reich and the Austro-Hungarian Empire were defeated. I doubt if anyone—whether German Jews or German non-Jews—could have voiced an appraisal of this kind thereafter. Franz Rosenzweig, already a philosopher and scholar in his own right (who fought on the German side during the war and was wounded), upon writing his famous *Stern der Erlösung* (Star of Redemption) in the years following the war, discussed Judaism, the musical aspect included, in relation to Christianity rather than Germanness, and mainly as a parallel, separate spiritual route.

The Viennese context was different to begin with, because of its embedded multiculturalism (harsh anti-Semitism notwithstanding), resulting in a less celebratory notion of the Germanic essence. Still, Freud and Schoenberg saw themselves, each in his own domain, as belonging and contributing to the great German culture, even after the war. Unlike Cohen, however, they did not conceive, at that time, of any special Jewish idiom or ideas worth identifying with or elaborating upon in the context of an encompassing German culture. Nor were they apparently bothered by, or sought to reckon with, an aesthetic or anti-aesthetic categorizing of Jews. Yet the Cohen-Rosenzweig context is important not only for a further following of the northern German-Jewish authors' line, but also to pursue that of the Viennese authors, because later on the twain shall meet—on what seems a partially shared ideational ground.

The self-perception of Schoenberg as a German composer in the twenties is clearly expressed in his "odyssey" (Ethan Haimo's apt title),[29] towards twelve-tone music, regarding his invention as his quintessential contribution to German music, one that will assure its "dominance for the next century."[30] The invention, or method of composition, was sought to solve the problem of tonal organization (on both the horizontal and vertical levels) in what Schoenberg conceived as the demise of tonal harmony. It is significant that this method emerged from within an oratorical environment, integrating previous layers of the composer-painter's work and opening itself to new theological vistas.[31]

Seeking to go beyond dissonant and consonant, beyond dogmas, conventional sentiments, and categories in the search for the theological absolute, Schoenberg found himself, as we shall see, embroiled in the stubborn resurfacing of dogmas and sentiments, embodying deeply ingrained imaginaries of the collective. Such a resurfacing was manifested in opposing, and yet partially complementary ways, in two of his major oratorical works: *Moses und Aron* and *Kol Nidre*. As is well known, such resurfacing syndromes were theoretically and clinically recognized by Freud and his school, for some years. It is the conceptualization of syndromes of this kind that enabled an explicit consideration of the "noisy Jewish element," as Theodor Reik's "Jewish" studies, "Das Schofar" and "Kol Nidre" attest.

"HAIL TO THE PEOPLE WHO UNDERSTAND THE SOUND OF THE HORN": REIK COMES TO TERMS WITH ARCHAIC JEWISH NOISE

The hitherto rather compressed (if not partially repressed) mode of presenting Reik's ideas regarding the role of the shofar in the Jewish ritual (in chapter 3) should now resolve into a more elaborate consideration of his impressive thesis within the wider cultural context of its emergence—including Schoenberg's parallel treatment of ideas of noise, harmony, sin, Day of Judgment, the private and the collective soul—as well as of other contemporary endeavors to transfigure Jewish noise.

Modern Jewish reactions to the noise accusation of those mentioned in this chapter (Schoenberg himself, Freud, Reik, Kafka) and previously (Vogel) should be assessed against their basically eastern European backdrop. These authors' respective parents (and in the case of Vogel, he himself), had migrated from Galician and Moravian Jewish shtetls and towns to the empire's capitals (Vienna and Prague, in the case of Kafka's father) in quest of economic and social progress. Jewish life in these shtetls was generally more conservative, including liturgical music, which was mostly conducted in the traditional way.

Upon arriving in Vienna, or Prague, these *Ostjuden* often bore with them old habits, and centered around synagogues that followed the nonreformed musical tradition, including Ḥasidic ones. (Unsurprisingly, our authors' parents moved to more liberal-reformist environments.) In this sense, there was ever a living testimony in Vienna and Prague of the "aboriginal" Jewish soundscape, which became even more prevalent by the turn of the century, with the increasing flow of Jews from the empire's eastern parts. A Jewish-noise scene of the kind featuring in Richard Strauss' *Salome* (premiered in Dresden 1905; Vienna 1907) may have drawn its inspiration from the author's prejudiced perception of such synagogues' vocal manners.[32]

While ambivalence toward traditional Jewish sound was inevitable in these circles, the "modernized" ritual-Jewish sound also elicited a sense of alienation, as evinced by Vogel's Gurdweill and Kafka's letters. In Vogel's *Married Life*, the ḥazzan and choir heard in Gurdweill's wedding and at the funeral of Loti (Gurdweill's most beloved friend) also produce this effect. True, the emotions these dreadful events evoke for the protagonist are projected onto the music accompanying them, which does not make these events more favorable; for music and event become in these cases reciprocal metonymies (as Portia instructed).[33] Similarly, Kafka's "Letter to His Father" and some of his letters to Felicia reveal his deep reservation regarding the spiritually impoverished Jewish rituals of his childhood and youth, in both home and synagogue.[34] His posthumous *In unserer Synagoge* reveals, however, that even in such a dwindling, assimilatory Jewish life, the old, insisting *Lärm* never ceased, as witnessed by and figured through the imaginary terrifier-of-women "animal-in-residence," which cannot be expelled from that Jewish house of prayer. The "synagogue animal" turned out to be a "pet" shared by more authors, Theodor Reik among their most eloquent spokesmen.

Reik's position reveals a deep, though creative ambivalence with regard to "noisy" Jewish predicaments. This becomes evident upon a full consideration of the occasion that awakened his interest in the shofar as a cultural-religious practice. At a social gathering of people "greatly interested in music," Reik relates at the onset of his study, the question of the origin of music was raised. "Various theories [were] put forward," but were soon rejected; in the new spirit of the emerging ethnography and anthropology, one guest suggested to review ancient myths and legends, in search for new ideas. As customary to such soirées at the time, the friends consulted A. W. Ambros' authoritative *Geschichte der Musik*[35] in order to be replenished with "a bewildering abundance of myths describing the discovery of music among the Indians, Chinese, Egyptians and Greeks."

Common to all these myths, the friends found out, was the ascription of the invention of music to demigods: Orpheus, Arion, Hermes, Osiris, and their like. It was then noticed that no such myth was to be found in the Bible, except for the casual mention of Jubal/Yuval as the "father of all such as handle the lyre and pipe" (Genesis, 4:21). We have seen above how this reference motivated Reik's philological investigations, but on that occasion other matters were at stake:

> "And how does our scriptural authority explain this striking exception?" said our hostess, turning to me with friendly irony. The prohibition of images in the Old Testament immediately occurred to my mind, but was rejected—unjustly, as we shall see—and I had to admit with some shame that I could not give any explanation of this peculiar fact.[36]

"Friendly irony"; "some shame"; "had to admit"; "peculiar fact"—these words mark the charged atmosphere and emotional environment that hurled Reik—probably the only Jewish guest in that party—into the whirlwind of the shofar history (and prehistory), which inevitably evoked in him the ubiquitous Viennese *"Es geht wie in einer Judenschul"* categorization. Whirlwind indeed, since Reik, as he proceeds in the four-chapter study, meanders circuitously. Weaving insights into the basic circle of evidence, he attempts to solve not only the scholarly query but even more so, the shame/anxiety query that the host's seemingly innocent comment stirred up in him.

Shame harbors, in this case, an emotional complex, which involves guilt, but concomitantly also curiosity, longing, and eventually even pride. This emotional complexity is latent in Reik's professional discourse, which consists of both competence in Jewish sources, and expertise in the young psychoanalytic discipline. The two are interrelated: Reik's Jewish erudition—including liturgy, Halakha (Rabbinic Law), Midrash, and Kabbala—forms the substratum of the analysis itself, which even if at times exhibits a philological or historical nature, is aimed at the psychoanalytical level. And if transference may provide a starting point in his analysis, as suggested in chapter 3, it moves further into a full "working-through" of the rich evidence he has collected.

The starting point in this process is the author's personal experience, powerful, though partially repressed—Reik's own participation, as a youth, in the synagogue services and rituals, especially those of the Days of Awe, which had also motivated his Kol Nidre analysis (see the last part of this chapter). Reik's own intimate experience, in the case of the shofar, is never straightforwardly presented. It is projected onto the language of ethnographic report—clearly, however, an insider's language. Thus he portrays the ritual of the shofar blowing on Rosh Hashanah:

> It is difficult to overestimate the intensity of the effect of this ceremony on believers among the general mass of the people. The tones of this primitive, national and religious instrument are usually awaited with great tension, its reverberations are listened to with very deep and sincere emotion and contrition; yet these strong affects are quite out of proportion to the sounds which produce them. The importance of the rite in the mental life of the people is shown by their fasting right up to the conclusion of the shofar-blowing. It is necessary to have witnessed the praying multitude in order to estimate the effect as the people listen breathlessly to the Rabbi who pronounces the benediction before the blowing: 'Praised be the Lord our God, King of the Universe, who sanctified us with His precepts and commanded us to hear the sound of the shofar.'

Following his precise description of the order and procedure of the blowing, Reik adds: "The congregation, which as a rule does not spare its voice during the prayers [!], listens to these sounds in silence, breathes again when, without any interruption, the blowing of the shofar has been purely and clearly accomplished."[37]

The reason for the relief, Reik notes, is that the clear and unhesitant sound of the shofar is a sign for a blessed year. Unwittingly, Reik also betrays an indication that his childhood synagogal experience was not only Orthodox, but of the eastern European type, pertaining to the old "noisy," heterophonic chant-mumbling soundscape. And here comes the small, however meaningful, piece of confession:

> It is a long time since I heard the sounds of the shofar, and when recently, in the interest of this work, I heard the shofar blown on New Year's Day, I could not completely avoid the emotion which these four crude, fearsome, moaning, loud-sounding, and long-drawn-out sounds produced—I do not attempt to decide whether the reason for my emotion was the fact that I was accustomed to this sound from youth, or whether it was an effect which everyone might feel. The latter suggestion seems to be supported by the fact that Christians who have heard it for the first time, and to whom the rites of the feast as well as the significance of the ram's horn blowing are quite unintelligible, have testified to similar emotions.[38]

Reik transcribes his own emotional response as a scientific report of an impartial witness, rather than an autobiographic testimony of a participant, ascribing his communal-sentimental attachment to an *alte Brauch*. But even this cannot erase the empathy and astonishment with which the text is imbued, emerging, almost vocally, when major verses are recited and commented upon, as in the case of Psalm 89:16: "Hail to the people who understand the sound of the horn (*yod'ey t*^e*ru'a*), they shall walk in the light of your countenance."

Reik associates this verse with the beautiful Midrash of Rabbi Joshia (second century CE) that stresses the intimate connection between Jews and God. Unlike other peoples, who may excel in music, the people of Israel know how to "tempt" God with sound (!), says Rabbi Joshia, so that "He goes to the throne of mercy and compassion moves his heart." Vocal intimacy, mercy, compassion, and, no less, the original sonic knowledge, inaccessible to the noncovenanted,[39] capsizes the conventional Christian categorization of Jewish noise. If Reik had had further musicological license, he might have summoned here the traditional (Ashkenazi) melismatic vocal phrase attached to this verse (see music example ex. 6.1), mostly in the major mode, recited once the blasts (the first round of thirty) have been successfully completed, analyzing its festive (however modally undetermined) and maybe jubilant expressivity.[40]

The fact that Reik quotes Rabbi Joshia's Midrash three times in his study is telling, for it encapsulates, in a trenchant way, the entire argument: how to metamorphose, through the sonic medium, the rigor of God's severe judgment

Ex. 6.1. (Aschre Ho'om) אשרי העם

The melodic phrase of "Aschre Ho'om," recited by the cantor on Rosh Hashanah
following the first round of thirty shofar blasts, belongs to the older layers of Ashkenazi
liturgical music; variations abound. The above example is taken from Abraham Baer's
(1834–94) famous *Baal T'fillah oder Der praktische Vorbeter,* 2nd edition
(Frankfurt: J. Kauffmann, 1883), 255.

into the quality of mercy. Reik's study entails, in effect, a psychoanalytic deconstruction of this Midrash.

Reik's psychoanalytic tools include a primordial history and related interpretive strategies to decipher its traces and meaning in other contexts and
forms. The primordial history, as fashioned by Freud in *Totem and Taboo,*
originates, as indicated above, in the universal, phylogenic tribal parricide, the
origin of all religious impulses, caused by repressed Oedipal desires including
the fear of castration, the evolving competition of father and sons, and, once
the sons overpower their father and assassinate him, competition among the
remaining sons.

According to Freud, as a hereditary impulse in human societies, feelings of
guilt related to the primordial parricide are manifested as sin consciousness,
followed by repentance and a seeking for atonement and, as such, can be "displaced" or "generalized"; thus they are not easily discernable even to the scruti-
nizing eye. An important trace or clue for unveiling such processes, Reik clarifies,
comes from the psychoanalytic practice: as obsessional neurosis progresses and
is psychoanalytically treated, symptoms become even more exacerbated. Then,
explains Reik, "the highly complicated and very generalized symptoms of the
compulsive action approximate more and more to those relatively simple initial
actions of the compulsion, in which their mental origin may be recognized
by analytic methods." Then, in other words, the repressed material returns.[41]

This is the case of the shofar ritual as it has been practiced in later generations, argues Reik. In a condensed form, this ritual yokes together feelings of

sin, guilt, expiation, as well as unconscious tendencies of hostility and rebellion towards the father-god. How do all these atavistic feelings and impulses become entangled in a rather plain musical ritual? Here resides the ironic hinge of this rite, which could provide a latent rebuttal of the Viennese hostess' "friendly irony." It is a musical-totemic irony, of a new, young god (Ram), whose horn blow sonically imitates the death roar of a slaughtered old bull-god, whom he came to replace in the totemic ersatz.[42]

The old bull-god who was slaughtered, explains Reik, relying on new updated scientific findings, is the traditional Egyptian god; the new one—the ram—is that of the insurgent Israelite nation, heading towards Canaan. "In the usurpation of the divine horn, which is the most outstanding sign of the totem god, the murder is committed once more *in nuce*," Reik clarifies.[43] This functions not only as a collective reminder of the crime against the old god, but also enables a renewed rejection of forbidden impulses to kill paternal gods and fathers—eternally (and internally) recurring both phylogenetically and ontogenetically. Evoking it within controlled and containing frames, the shofar calls for the triple action of repentance, remorse, and conversion.

The working-through of the collective trauma by means of aural mimesis can thus be rendered as a fictional vocal performative act, in which the fictive element shelters the participators from the "real" thing while enabling its virtual collective experience to be publicly and palpably enacted. Whether or not Reik's argument is immune to internal contradictions and external (scientific) criticism is of less importance in the present context, for it clearly represents an intellectual endeavor to come to terms with the old noise accusation. Put another way, what Reik brands as Jewish life's "archaic structure" functions, in his analysis, as a communal mechanism for coping with a basic human predicament without repressing its symptoms. It should not come as a surprise that Reik downplays Christian sonic values—those associated with organs' and bells' harmoniousness, central in Spitzer's study of harmony, and extolled by Huizinga in his *Waning of the Middle Ages*. "It seems quite natural," argues Reik, "that this ancient instrument with its three crude sounds, the long-sustained tone, the interrupted notes and the tremolo, should make a greater impression on the listener than the sound of an organ or bells."[44]

Despite this fundamental dichotomy, Reik searches, nonetheless, for a modus vivendi between the shofar's sounds and the more harmonious Christian, classical music. Following the French archeologist Salomon Reinach, he brings Orpheus close to the Jubal/Yuval of Genesis: as a demigod and murderer of his father, Apollo. Orpheus was, in his turn, flayed alive and devoured by the Maenads, the father-god's agents. Reik connects this myth to the tradition according to which Orpheus led human beings to give up anthropophagy, and instead became associated with the appeasing of savage animals. Orpheus, Reik continues in this vein, embodies thus "the guilty conscience of the son who killed and devoured the father-god [and] instituted the law for the preservation of the totem, i.e., the prohibition against eating the fathers, which first assured the existence of community. Music is here the representative of morality." The Orphean myth, then, represents a wishful harmonious being in music that transcends its noisy source to celebrate reconciliation—a thesis not remote from that of Attali, discussed in chapter 1. Will this reconciliation be enacted historically as well—between Jubal/Yuval's adherents and Orpheus' followers? (Both traditions feature the usurpers with a string, rather than wind, instrument—Jubal/Yuval's *kinor* is an instrument not dissimilar from Apollo's and Orpheus' lyre.)[45]

Towards the conclusion of his study, Reik cursorily aligns the body movements of praying Jews—so derided by Christian viewers—with the most abstract, cosmopolitan, and artistic music of the time, in which the presence of the Viennese authors is conspicuous: the music of Bach, Beethoven, Bruckner, Mahler, and Mozart. Both, he implies, in the spirit of Cohen's reconciliatory mode, stem from the same deep religious impulses, hence the effect they exert over those who choose to be possessed by them.

KAFKA'S *LÄRM*

Appeasement and reconciliation are not Kafka's forte; his open-ended noise diagnoses will carry him beyond predestined environments, designating directions, rather than goals, while bringing ethnography back to the fore. First let us attend to a bull slaughter out in the open, one that takes place in an environment overrun by nomads, depicted in "Ein altes Blatt" ("An Old Manuscript," published in 1917). Elias Canetti defined it as "[t]he loudest passage in Kafka's work."[46] Focalized through the local shoemaker, the story tells us of wild, languageless nomads, who settled themselves ruthlessly in the central city square, in front of the emperor's palace, feeding themselves on the fresh meat of the nearby butcher's shop, which they and their horses brutally grab and swallow. The nauseating noise event takes place when

> the butcher thought he might at least spare himself the trouble of slaughtering, and so one morning he brought along a live ox. But he will never dare to do that again. I lay for a whole hour flat on the floor at the back of my workshop with my head muffled in all the clothes and rugs and pillows I had, simply to

keep from hearing the bellowing of that ox, which the nomads were leaping on from all sides, tearing morsels out of its living flesh with their teeth. It had been quiet for a long time before I risked coming out; they were lying overcome around the remains of the carcass like drunkards around a wine cask.

Interestingly, Canetti quotes this paragraph almost directly after he makes a reference to a genuine musical icon—traditionally situated on the other pole of the sonic universe we are discussing. In a note to be found in the fragment "Wedding Preparations in the Country" ("Hochzeitsvorbereitungen auf dem Lande," 1907–8), Kafka renders the brutal nature of power in a stupendous cosmic image in the following lines:

I was defenseless confronted with the figure, calmly it sat there at the table, gazing at the table top. I walked round it in circles, feeling myself throttled by it. And around me there walked a third, feeling throttled by him. And so it went on, right out to the circling of the constellations, and further still. Everything felt the grip at the throat.

Canetti explains the meaning of it all:

The threat, the throttling, spreads from the inmost center, where it originates, a gravitational force of strangulation, which sustains each concentric circle, "right out to the circling of the constellations, and further still." The Pythagorean harmony of the spheres has become a sphere system of violence, with human gravity predominating, each individual representing a separate sphere.[47]

Kafka seems indeed to allude to the structure of the spheres as envisioned by Er, in his temporary visit to the post- and prelife universe, as rendered in Plato's *Republic* (Book X). In that description, the concentric constellation of the planets' motion is accompanied by a unified chordal sound, the constituent tones of which are perpetually hymned by the heavenly sirens, each situated on the surface of a corresponding planet.

The breakdown of this system, which continued to accompany Western civilization as knowledge both physical and metaphysical until the seventeenth century, did not preclude it from concomitantly functioning as poetical myth in the centuries to come. Kafka, like Shakespeare, accepts its poetical existence, yet reads it gnostically, providing a complementary cosmic picture to Vogel's "black tar" church music. Rather than luminous, benevolent, and truthful, the Classical-Christian harmonious fashioning of the universe—and the music embodying it—appears to be dark and evil. The very words whereby Shakespeare's Lorenzo chose to describe "the man that hath no music in himself"—the one insinuated by him to be deaf to Christian, harmonious, music—are now rebounded at those controlling that system itself.[48] Could it be that the vociferous, carnivorous nomads of Kafka also descended from harmonious musical system (that was ethically capsized), or do they confirm the old metaphysical pattern?

The answer is not clear, at least not at first sight. In any event, what seems to stand as Jewish music in his writings is not at all elevated by the degradation of the "other" one. This becomes clear in several stories in which *Lärm* directly reads as Jewish, or allegorically, can refer to Jewish sound. I refer here to "In unserer Synagoge," to "Josefine, die Sängerin oder Das Volk der Mäuse" ("Josephine the Singer, or the Mouse Folk"), and to "Forschungen eines Hundes" ("The Investigations of a Dog"; all composed in his last years, between 1922 and 1924).

The intricacies and interrelations of these stories and the way they enact the thematic elements discussed above exceed the scope of this book. At any rate, they cannot be merely accounted for in terms of Jewish self-hatred, for their allegorical ambivalence resists formulaic deciphering. Rather, their sonic elements, as suggested by Deleuze and Guattari, drive them through "lines of escape" (*lignes de fuite*)[49] beyond recognizable forms of meaning. This is connected also to their "animal becoming" element; to the fact that these stories—part of a larger group of animal stories by Kafka that feature mice, dogs, apes, cockroaches, and so forth, are all distinguished only "by this or that threshold, this or that vibration, by the particular underground tunnel in the rhizome[50] or the burrow." Deleuze and Guattari add:

> In the becoming-mouse, it is a whistling that pulls the music and the meaning from the words. In the becoming-ape, it is a coughing that 'sound[s] dangerous but mean[s] nothing.' . . . In the becoming-insect, it is a mournful whining that carries along the voice and blurs the resonance of words.[51]

And in more general terms, "everywhere, organized music is traversed by a line of abolition—just as a language of sense is traversed by a line of escape—in order to liberate a living and expressive material that speaks for itself and has no need of being put into form."[52] Sound liberates—when the aesthetics of the beautiful is displaced by the aesthetics of the true, as Dahlhaus put it,[53] but exiled from its original habitat it also bespeaks otherness, if not transgression, as we have witnessed since the "Prioress' Tale" onward. Kafka's own linguistic utterances, as he records in his diaries, sound to him as belonging in that zone. "Kein Wort fast das ich schreibe paßt zum andern, ich höre wie sich die Konsonanten blechern an einander reiben und die Vokale singen dazu wie Ausstellungsneger"—the words he uses in his writing "jar up against each other"; he hears "the consonants rub leadenly against each other and the vowels sing an accompaniment like Negroes in a minstrel show."[54]

A key to Kafka's noise allegories (in Walter Benjamin's understanding of the term) may lie in that animal-in-residence "in our synagogue," the animal that becomes associated with the synagogal noise, in various strange ways. This animal ("in the size of a marten") grows accustomed to the house's permanent *Lärm*, tells the author, when it realizes that this noise does not threaten it, as he explains:

> And though divine service, with all its noise [Lärm], may be very frightening for the animal, because it recurs on a modest scale daily and on a grander scale during the festivals, always regularly and without even a break, even the most timid of animals could by now have got used to it, particularly when it sees that this is not the noise of pursuers, but rather a noise that has nothing to do with it.[55]

The animal gets used to the noise because of its regulative, cyclical repetitions; it thus learns the Jewish calendar, grows used to its undulations. It learns—as an outside insider—that it does not concern its own being. And yet it knows better about this *Lärm* and its meaning than those considered insiders, as an "objective correlative" of their repressed unconscious, of which the narrator, becoming momentarily omniscient, tells his readers: "And yet there is this terror [*Angst*]. Is it the memory of times long past or the premonition of times to come? Does this old animal perhaps know more than the three generations of those who are gathered together in the synagogue?"[56]

Kafka leaves this crucial and prophetic question open; he marks an oratorical moment—of *Lärm* carried by various generations coinciding in the animal's collectivizing memory—and then withdraws from it. He only tells us that the congregation's attempts to expel the synagogal animal had failed. In the final analysis, the animal is as much part of the synagogue's soundscape as its primordial noise is. And this is, as far as the author is concerned, the origin of it all, as well as its prospective tragic ending. Kafka thus echoes animalistic defamation of the synagogal soundscape, from the medieval *ululare* onward. Yet he embraces this noise, feels for its bearers, connecting it with its historical roots, as Heine did with his "whimpering kettle." Like Heine's, this reverberation occurs in German, but in the hands of Kafka it turns into what Deleuze and Guattari define as "a minor literature" (in which a minority makes use of a "major language"). It challenges this major language's hegemony, sublimity, and newly acquired flexibility, even in relation to those "minority" fellow-people who became its renowned spokesmen (like Heine, who was famously excused for loosening German from its "chaste" conduct).

Music, qua music, however, is transcendent in these stories. The musical dogs from the "Investigations of a Dog" seem to prove it. Their musical behavior is clearly upward oriented, in opposition to the regular downward conduct of the miserable dog folk: at the same time, a real suspicion is raised by the narrative, as to whether this spiritual endeavor is a valuable pursuit; whether there is not something essentially shameful in its performance, or in the incarnation of its ideal forms in sound (the way it was advocated "contemporaneously," by fictive Wendell Kretzschmar, in Mann's *Doktor Faustus*).[57] "Fie on them! They were uncovering their nakedness, blatantly making a show of their nakedness."[58] And yet, it is not clear whether there is music at all; this obfuscation becomes even more accentuated in the music of Josephine (in "Josefine, die Sängerin oder Das Volk der Mäuse"), the she-mouse whose music cannot be distinguished from more regular, mundane vocal behavior of the mouse folk.[59]

Transcendent music, music for music's sake, is dubious. Dogs, mice, and maybe also traditional Jews do not acknowledge it as a separate pastime and yet they admire it above all (though of course there is an aesthetic difference between their respective musics). Similar allegations were intoned by Rosenzweig, in a more straightforward way, directed towards the regular concertgoer, and against the *Religion der Musik*, as it had developed in mid-Europe through the nineteenth century. Spiritual noncommunal, or secular music "disintegrates real time with ideal times in its desire to be pure," admonishes Rosenzweig, and he further proceeds: "To be absolved of this crime [!] . . . it would have to integrate its ideal time into real time. This would however imply the transition of music from concert hall to church."[60] Music of the many—religious, choral music—creates, in Rosenzweig's imagined worlds, the right condition for a community-becoming. In the Kafkaesque world, on the other hand, the music made by the group qua group is not actually music; it is life itself—communal, strained, and persecuted.

The folk of dogs, the folk of mice; the fact that these animal herds are associated with the (noisy) Jewish folk did not escape the attention of some readers. They are not one and the same though: the Jews as "barking dogs" have been carried as an image, as we saw, since the Middle Ages. That of the mice, or *Mäuse*, is also connected to collective Jewish-vocal behavior, particularly to their speech, *mauscheln*. This will be further exacerbated when the Jews themselves will be metamorphosed into rats—in the Nazis' propaganda—producing an ultimate *Lärm*, ominously foreshadowed in Kafka's story of the synagogal animal. Of course, the relation animal folk–Jewish folk is not, and should not be regarded as a one-to-one identity. But certainly there is here an allegorical key, or starting point (not the only possible one) from which to move on, from which Kafka himself moved on, in addition to the internal logic of the narrated events, which transcends any figurative reduction.

This logic, in the three stories briefly discussed here, derives, among other things, from the position of the internal narrator in relation to the object of his story: the synagogue's animal, the singer Josephine, and the dogs' life in general and that of the musical ones in particular, as they all stand in relation to their uncanny music. In these stories the narrator is one out of many whom he by and large represents. In the first two stories he does not even have a separate, personal voice. He is the "congregation emissary" in the traditional Jewish way, speaking in a fundamentally empathic tone in relation to his narrated subjects. Even when he becomes individualized, as is the case in the "Investigations," his basic drive is to research the life of the many, and his secluded position stems from that drive.

No matter how cognizant the dog-author, the synagogue member, or the mouse-narrator is of his people's wretchedness, he is so much identified with their destiny that he cannot even imagine himself otherwise. And yet he searches for lines of escape, as Deleuze and Guattari tell us. Or perhaps it is not he who searches. He is only a witness, a chronicler, a researcher, and seems chained to his community, for better or for worse. That which escapes is the music, or perhaps, the sonic matter itself, in its ethereal, verging-on-nothingness nature. As with Reik, the sonic matter, however, always attests to a crime that was committed, a sinful existence, an unspoken angst; hence the need it evokes for expiation through fasting, the pool of blood, death. There is no other way out in this existential universe; the music, even when transporting, is not transforming, transfiguring. Oratorical moments are bound to be confined within themselves, and their meaning is opaque to most listeners (as it is to the synagogal animal).

While this last interpretation diverges from that of Deleuze and Guattari, it carries from their reading, in addition to the above-mentioned elements, their emphasis on these narratives' "sequence of intensive states, a ladder or a circuit for intensities that one can make race around in one sense or the other, from high to low, or from low to high."[61] While designating lines of escape, these ladders or circuits are not Jacob's ladder, not even Schoenberg's. Bypassing transcendence,[62] they pose the main question the discussion of modernist Jewish noise should address: the relation between transcendence and iconoclasm, which is, in another way, that between spiritual impoverishment and asceticism. If transcendentalism is forestalled in the iconoclastic gesture, does this inevitably order an ascetic existence, draining also emotional and spiritual life? Does it designate a dead end or maybe liberate new resources of creativity and sociability? These questions hover above the following discussion, which, however, far from exhausts the historical and theoretical aspects of this query.

SCHOENBERG'S AESTHETIC-POLITICAL THEOLOGY

The terrible groan of the slaughtered ox will not leave us so soon, despite Kafka's lines of escape. The attempt to redeem it will recur, and not only in psychoanalytical terms. The old Egyptian deity, which was superseded by the young and basically more enlightened ram god, was associated, in Reik's reading, with the Exodus, the revelation at Mount Sinai, and the forging of the tribes of Jacob into a nation. Elevation through sound—as signified by Psalm 47:6 ("God is gone up with a shout [t^{e}ru'a], the Lord amidst the sound of a Shofar")—was intricately associated, as we have seen in Reik's interpretation, with debasement, if not crime, and this is transmitted in the sound of the blast—the jubilee itself.

One cannot overcome this debasement because it is there forever. High and low sounds are one, and with them transcendence and transgression. The pagan god is contained within the True God; this inseparability may apply also to Kafka's animal sonorities. Schoenberg aimed to separate them, placing the two deities apart. This brings us to the first and fourth scenes of his *Moses und Aron* (composed 1930–32 and never completed). The idea of God presented in the first scene corresponds to the third stage in Reik's conception of the historical development of the idea of the divine voice, "the incomparable voice which is removed from all that is human and animal, the voice of God purified of all earthly dross." "Einziger, ewiger, allgegenwärtiger, unsichtbarer und unvorstellbarer Gott!" (only, infinite, omnipresent, unseen, and unfathomable God),[63] intones Moses; this God "embodies" Schoenberg's negative theology, and therefore cannot be vocally subsumed by harmonious sounds, so inextricably associated for the composer with an obsolete, if not coercive, conventional sublime.[64]

God's absolute being is vocally expressed by the noisy concurrence of musical voices and speech voices, similar to the soundscape of an eastern European synagogue.[65] This apparently unsynchronized, disjointed atonal soundscape uttered by many voices contrasts, in the opera, with the rhythmized, tonalized world of the golden calf rites. This seemingly vocally organized world commences with sounds of groaning, reminiscent of bulls at the slaughter, realized in densely repeating glissandi issuing from the strings (mainly cellos, later also violins) over

Ex. 6.2. Arnold Schoenberg, *Moses und Aron* II, mm. 334–38.

two octaves, and by trombones as in *Moses und Aron* II, mm. 334–36 (ex. 6.2), in the midst of a section starting at m. 320.

Schoenberg, however, gives the stage director the following instructions: "At many places in the foreground and background . . . herds of all manner of animals pass by. . . . Simultaneously, preparations for slaughter are to be seen at many places. The animals are decorated with wreathes. Butchers with large knives enter and with wild leaps dance around the animals"—signifying that the glissandi, a prima facie noisy sound, portray a multi-species animals' parade and/or the butchers' dance. Yet the use of low and bellowing instruments calls to mind the actual *voices* of heavy animals. Glissandi passages, it is noteworthy, subsequently mark the shrieking of the virgins, slaughtered by the priests (m. 823).

There is an absurdity in this scene. The bull is both slaughtered and idolized: the calf is the "son" in this genealogy of gods, and elevated to a deity status through its golden form. This absurdity may be heard in the words uttered by Aron just before the beginning of the orgy: "This gold image attests that in all things that are, a god lives. Unchangeable, e'en as a law, is the stuff, the gold that you have given. Seemingly changeable [e.g., from bulls to calf], as all else must be. Much less matters the shape that I have provided."[66] The preparation for the slaughter scene follows anon (as the glissandi are intoned). It is as if the noise of slaughtered beasts were mentally foreshadowed, even if they are not yet "actually" killed, as if massacre took place first and foremost in the imagination (of both animals and people), through these very sounds, while the image of the new god was already completed.

But what is the meaning of casting the new god in gold and yet leaving its actual shape open? In what ways does this lead to, or derive from the actual slaughtering of older, Egyptian gods—its fathers? Beyond this scene, do the transcended and the debased, both actualized through sonic devices, annihilate each other, in this opera? God—true God, the one, infinite, omnipresent, unseen—appears only once. Yet the "matter" of his revelation—mixed musical and speaking voices—iterates in various forms and by different agencies. Does this mean that "in all things that are, a god lives"—as Aron's "golden" pantheistic principle instructs? Or does it indicate that there is a basic fallacy in any ascription of sensuous, even sonic aspect, to the Almighty (as Moses realizes eventually with horror)?

These queries—and this oratorical work raises several more—are not unrelated to the work's unconsummated destiny, to the fact that it remained a torso. Though containing three full literary acts, the music to the third one was never written, despite Schoenberg's attempts to complete it, at various stages later in his life. The grappling with the question of how gold and voice, calf and ox, form and matter, song and speech, noise and harmony, oratorio and opera, biblical and modern sources conflate here in a heroic attempt to avoid aesthetic and theological categorization and yet envoice a message relevant to "modern man"—or maybe Jew—in a most crucial historical moment, will necessitate a more systematic look at the work.

In recent decades *Moses und Aron* has aroused great interest, generating appraisals of the work by musicologists, historians, theologians, and others. Yet not too often has it been examined beyond its avowed authorial intentions and its textual-musical manifestations, within the less immediate, though highly relevant, hermeneutic networks that it evokes. Fathoming the work's universe of meaning, the convergence of this moment in the composer's creative career and the historical timing of its becoming—the years just preceding the Nazis' rise to power—looms large. In terms formulated in the course of this study, this convergence means that the heightened consciousness of the author qua Jewish sonic creator "in dark time" brimmed with conflictive and contradictory elements, erupting from within the very dramatic métier he selected. This encompasses exodus, revelation, sacrifice, and compassion, as enacted by a biblical God through his emissaries, for the redemption of his chosen people.

Mobilizing the vocal to embody these themes—its functioning as aesthetic as well as theological medium—released a host of thematic components divulged in the course of the history of Christian-Jewish sonic entanglements along their aporias and predicaments.

The uncontrollability of the chosen subject matter is itself thematized in the work's world. The twelve-tone method, conceived in order to be in a position to control the evasive sonic material and direct its movement, camouflages this endemic unruliness.[67] Schoenberg, indeed, was dissociating the act of composing from that of manipulating the twelve-tone machine. The latter, he stressed, acts as a constraining apparatus, and cannot supply the creative vision and practice. But it does control the charismatic flow.[68] This becomes crucial in recording the doing and undoing of Moses and Aron in the oratorical opera they inhabit.

For on the other side of the twelve-tone machine stands the golden calf mechanism, in Aron's—Schoenberg's Aron—formulation of its essence, as indicated above. With its unchanging substance, its form, we were told, is secondary. Secondary indeed it is even in the biblical Aron's (or Aharon, as I call him below) perception of its nature:

> And Moshe said unto Aharon: "What did this people unto thee, that thou hast brought a great sin upon them?" And Aharon said: "Let not the anger of my lord wax hot; thou knowest the people, that they are set on evil. So they said unto me: Make us a god, which shall go before us; for as for this Moshe, the man that brought us up out of the land of Egypt, we know not what is become of him. And I said unto them: Whosoever hath any gold, let them break it off; so they gave it me; and I cast it into the fire, and there came out this calf." (Exodus 32:21–25)

Aharon teaches his brother Moshe a profound aesthetic rule. The convergence and interplay of artistic means and modes—poised, as they are, between what is physically, sensually, and culturally predetermined (gold, oil paints, musical sounds, stones, words) and what is fashioned by and as (cultural) techniques (forging fire, brushes, genres and styles, automatic writing)—could yield unexpected results for which the artist could be regarded as only partially responsible. At the very heart of artistic creation, then, lies an inherent unpredictability that often surprises creators and spectators alike.[69] In the Jewish tradition, this idea will be further developed in relation to the golem trope: that concrete creature, or automaton, is brought to life by words endowed with power; thus it can rebel or resist its own human creator, to the latter's horror and dismay.[70]

And yet Aharon's account leaves something missing, or incompletely explained: even if *this* particular kind of calf was not expected, some form of animal or creature of sorts had been there, to begin with, be it as a dim precept or as an object apprehended in retrospect. We note that the object is recognized both by Aharon as "this calf" and by the people who, according to Aharon's story (but not according to the preceding narrative) first demand: "Make us gods who shall go before us." And then, once the idol has been fashioned, they say: "These are your gods, O Israel, who brought you up out of the land of Egypt!" As W. J. T. Mitchell (following Abi Warburg) has argued, images are never without precedence or repercussion; their persistence over many generations stems from major religious, social, and cultural sources of creativity and control. At the same time, their actual form, combination, timing, and likeness are unlimited and unpredictable.[71]

Schoenberg must have been aware of Aharon's and Aron's basic misconception—the form is not secondary. Also the matter is not so permanent as Aron insisted. Certainly it is not divine, but rather comprises the mine out of which people create their images. In the creative act there are thus inherent tendencies of both matter and image that dictate their mode of evolution, and, as aesthetics taught long before, are not separable. Whether or not Schoenberg acknowledged the fact that even in the very theologico-political stuff he dared to (re)compose, there are those internal and thus contradictory tendencies that even in the most radically creative forging fire enforce their own evolutionary forms, his work, I argue, stands as a most impressive edifice for letting them go where they lead. His experience in this kind of creative laboratory, in his earlier synaesthetic, multiselves works, should have come to his aid.

Moses und Aron comprises, as such, a rich array of emotional-existential fluctuations that circumscribe the protagonists and issue an interpretive challenge to listeners/spectators. These fluctuations are not free-floating, however, but rather girded within prevailing coordinates, themselves marking irresolvable antinomies. Underdetermining the work's fundamental networks of meanings, they include textual antinomies pertaining to the work's fundamental textual, tonal, configurative, generic, and declamatory components:

(1) *Textual:* There is the biblical story, to which the Schoenbergian text stands as a commentary rather than as a text, living in its own right. It differs, in this sense, from the tradition of the opera in which, for example, the Shakespearean Othello does not threaten to compete with or intrude on the Verdian *Otello;* it also differs from the *Literaturoper* of Schoenberg's time,

which took scripts of plays as they were, only shortening them for the sake of their musical embodiment.[72]

(2) *Tonal:* The order, or orders, of the twelve-tone row and its derivative constructions, deliberately distance themselves from the gravitational forces of tonal or diatonic harmony, which nevertheless threaten their predominance.

(3) *Configurative:* At the same time, old musical habits, conventions, structures, genres, and the whole system of aesthetic (listening) expectations implicit in them (e.g., the baroque ritornello, folk dances, choirs, prayers, leitmotifs) continue to lurk behind a superficially "realistic" drama that purports to unfold an unstylized action.

(4) *Generic:* This antinomy concerns the oratorical versus the operatic drift of the dramatic presentation.

(5) *Declamatory:* Embodied by Sprechstimme or strict spoken parts, it obeys rhetorical and prosodic rules clearly at variance with those governing pitch-based musical structures.

A more careful examination of these five antinomian coordinates, as they articulate the phenomenological arena of the work, may yield the following observations: [73]

(1) *Biblical text vs. operatic libretto:* In her discussion and close reading of *Moses und Aron's* libretto, Bluma Goldstein addresses major issues such as the work's image-and-word dichotomy, the idea of a wasteland as a substitute for the land of milk and honey, and the skipping of major events told in Exodus. In her view, the last act of Schoenberg's work clearly shows a transformation in Moses' attitude, stemming from what had transpired in the first two acts. The lack of music in this act, she maintains, is consistent with this change, despite Schoenberg's claims to the contrary.[74] We will come back to this new Moses shortly. What should concern us here is that Schoenberg's deliberate changes in the original biblical plot, unlike the long, medium-oriented, operatic tradition of adapting literary text to libretto, were grounded primarily in politico-theological considerations and only secondarily conceived sonorously—that is, in what befits a *melo*dramatic medium. Schoenberg believed that an updating of this kind is an existential-spiritual necessity. Max Aruns, the main protagonist of his spoken drama *The Biblical Way* (completed 1927) argues in relation to the dictates of Jewish lore: "What is eternal in God's word is its spirit! The letter [*Wortlaut*] is merely phenomenal form, adapted to the moment, to the demands of wandering in the wilderness."[75] Aruns' claim for a spiritual, rather than a literal interpretation of God's words triggers criticism from another protagonist in the drama, who speaks for the relative distinction between the two.[76] This did not stop Schoenberg from being quite explicit in his insistence on the necessity for ever interpreting the old lore in terms of modern reality: "I believe

that the forms of the ancient Biblical language are no more convincing in our present use of language. One has to talk to the people of our time in our own style and of our own problems"[77] — Schoenberg thus paraphrases the idea he advocated in his 1912 "oratorical" letter.

The need for such textual updating means that the basic spiritual narrative embedded in the biblical narrative remains the same for both texts. The old theoretically lurks behind the new as a source to be constantly referred to, and to which the new should be compared. This diacritical structure, I argue, permeates *Moses und Aron* throughout. Thus, as Goldstein observed, Aron appears closer to the original Moshe than does the new Moses.[78] However unwittingly, Schoenberg adopted an interpretative approach akin to traditional Jewish biblical commentary, be it of the old rabbinic midrashic or the later medieval tradition, inspired, in his case, by new theological and philosophical trends.[79] Similar to these traditions, the Holy Scripture stood for Schoenberg as a source of meaning whose internal contradictions he endeavored to reconcile, in accordance with his own political theology.[80]

In this sense, Schoenberg's adaptation is categorically different from the kind of critical reading of the Bible advocated by Spinoza, often considered the initiator of biblical criticism. Spinoza, as Menachem Lorberbaum claims, interprets the story of Moses historically, aiming to derive from it an understanding of Moses as both theologian and statesman of his time.[81] At the same time, Schoenberg was not attempting to subsume older versions of myths within a new mythology in an aim to supersede them — as Wagner did. This has crucial implications, as it differentiates the protagonists' assumed consciousness from that of the listeners'/spectators' experience of it. It is by evaluating the new in terms of the old that spectators may apprehend the drama's vexed meaning.

(2) *The twelve-tone method*, as developed by Schoenberg, has long been considered the epitome of the modernist spirit in music. In the context of *Moses und Aron*, its aesthetic presuppositions and the procedures they imply gain a special significance. They imply a plethora of (endless) sound-combinations, symbolized in the more limited infinite space of possible chromatic twelve-tone orders, from which a certain row, *Reihe*, is selected. Within the boundaries of the chosen tonal world the composed work is a further selection (for an infinite number of compositions can be based on the same tone row), which exists, in relation to the sonoric universe, as a monad of sorts: closed within itself yet indirectly reflecting other such monads.[82] The forty-eight interrelated permutations the row yields are realized on the basis of strict rules and well-defined procedures. The further divisions of the row, including "hexachordal aggregates," allow for more freedom in relation to its predetermined order while still preserving its "selectivity." Adorno argues that these rules and operations betray the

spirit of cultic laws: more specifically, the law, *Gesetz*, of the Old Testament.[83] Indeed, the objectivity and strictness of the system goes beyond the traits characteristic of systems that developed organically, like the old tonal-harmonic system; in this sense they do aspire to the condition of a given law. Concomitantly, the free choice of the tonal material—both in terms of the chosen row as well as the specific configurations it yields—emphasizes its artificial and combinatorial nature and the author's sovereignty in regard to both.

The theological paradox underlying the work—that of prophesying the word of the omnipresent, yet elusive God—attains an emblematic embodiment through these tonal means: in each of its configurations the work realizes the unbearable tension between the idea of an eternal, unfathomable, and infinite God, and the limited, artificial, subjective human concretizations of His idea, which, at the same time, are theoretically endless. Once applied, the chosen tone row creates internal tensions akin to the perceptual gestalts it yields. In the case of *Moses und Aron*, these gestalts are drawn from the row's intervals, consisting of half and whole tones, two strategic tritones, and one minor third. The row's motivic derivations thus resemble melodic contours that are part of traditional operatic literature carrying their own expressive import and leitmotivic potential.[84] Moreover, Schoenberg's motivic elements facilitate perception through the affinity of their elaboration with long-established musical procedures, such as transposition and variation. Yet this last perception, as Michael Cherlin has pointed out, is, in terms of the work's epistemology, ultimately erroneous.[85] By the same token, when (through legitimate combinatorial procedures) a given row "fortuitously" emanates particular intervals, such as the fifth or the octave, or even a major chord, the result will be a sense of lost familiarity (on the level of old perceptual habits).

In other words, the abstract, atomistic compositional method yields, as Adorno maintained in relation to this work, despite itself, concrete and formulaic patterns that expose Schoenberg's musical design to the very tonal gravitational forces that the composer's serial method aims to avoid. Indeed, this dialectic is intrinsic to the basic compositional matrix of *Moses und Aron*; it seems no less intentional than the one involving source and libretto. What does it communicate? Are those who use it or are enveloped by it—the protagonists in their fictive world—aware, however slightly, of the nature of the medium in which they express themselves? Or is the medium a message solely addressed to those outside the protagonists' world, that is, to attentive listeners, called upon to scrutinize this world accordingly?[86]

(3) *Old musical habits or allusions*, as they evolve from within the new modern constituents, can be regarded as inherent rebellious "golems" but also as

part of a compositional strategy. In this latter sense, they amount to experiential procedures whose communicative and dramatic/emotional force derives from their cultural embeddedness and from their inherent, material qualities—such as motivic and leitmotivic elements that, in the listener's mind, suggest, anticipate, or recall traditional as well as pseudoarchaic musical elements and experiences. The first includes generic elements, such as a baroque ritornello, an arioso, and musical *topoi* conveying certain emotional connotations—enabling signification and communication. The second draws on "aboriginal" semblances, such as effected by a homogenized and perpetuating musical texture, exerting an incantatory effect of ecstatic rituals. These recognizable patterns come up against the erupting, perceptually uncontained musical prose, questioning its claim to verisimilitude and the negation of musical cliché.

(4) *The oratorical versus the operatic:* The work's genealogy features in this antinomy, for it was first conceived as oratorio and only in the course of making the libretto did Schoenberg realize he should cast it as a full, onstage drama. For Adorno, this determined the work's failure by its own internal criteria; for Lacoue-Labarthe, the oratorical elements persisted despite this change, propelling the work in the pursuit of a new sublime.[87] There is a grain of truth in both positions, but the result is not a hybrid. Schoenberg's deployment of what Adorno calls "bourgeois artistic means" (or "pagan" musical imagery, in his vocabulary), whose effect, invariably, is to anaesthetize sociopolitical awareness, exposes the composer, so Adorno states, to the charge of deploying musical elements for the sake of modern idolatry. Such a claim would be sustainable, if, indeed, the work aimed to glorify negative theology through a compatible aesthetic/stylistic conception (the way Bach's Passions are supposed to glorify the Crucifixion); but the very transformation of the opera from the oratorical shrine to the operatic stage divulges a different orientation. By featuring "floating" human figures and suspending the Aristotelian, spatiotemporal specificity of representation, the oratorio, qua genre, avoids reifying its protagonists and so proves a medium ideally suited for creating a spiritual community that perdures over time. While this configuration has its own advantages for certain artistic purposes, as this book proposes, it is only in the domain of opera that people directly and consistently confront each other; that their subjectivities, their experience of agonies, ecstasies, anxieties, and doubts, are materialized and made known.

I therefore venture to maintain that the transfiguration from the oratorical to the operatic in this case was meant to examine, in musico-dynamic terms, the meaning and effect of introducing, if not coercing, a theological principle into a certain kind of society, one that may be diagnosed as posttraumatic (a nation of slaves/children, as Aron calls them), that has been extricated from a nurturing idolatrous culture.[88] It is only in the illusionary condition of a full-fledged drama that such basic communal forces can fully respond to such coercion, expressing direct passions, instigating reaction. Thus occupying a dramatic terrain of the Parsifalian kind (to which Adorno critically refers), the operatic likewise intertwines with the oratorical, with vox populi, as it approaches the divine. But the result is a negative sublime, for the relation between emissaries and nations, between nations and deities, never consummates aural-communal harmonizing moments of the kind that have long become associated with the ecclesiastic genre and its related modes.[89]

(5) *The declamatory versus the melodic*: While the juxtaposition of the two — the pitched and the nonpitched elements — is not new (it is associated, in fact, with lighter genres, such as *Singspiel*, melodrama, and operetta), their simultaneous carrying of the same text, in even greater intensity and predominance than in *Jakobsleiter*, creates a special form of *turba*[90] (when dividing the people's group expression) or revelation (when used for embodying God's "voices"). As noted, the pitched and the nonpitched elements obey different rhythmical dictates, evolving inherent incongruity, which vexes listeners, ushering them, if not through direct realistic means, to consider the utterances as part of a nonunified universe. These divergent modalities signify a difference: speech is usually rougher and more direct, *melos* more pathetic and nobler. But not always; sometimes the latter will appear more appealing (and thus direct), and the former — transcendental and mysterious.

The order of these trajectories or coordinates remains unstable. Each claims priority from the point of view of the compositional process, and each carries its own inner tension, thereby highlighting or often exacerbating tensions inherent in the plot itself. Both the internal antinomies comprising each of these five coordinates and their relations to other coordinates vary throughout the work. They may be indifferently juxtaposed as if deaf to their mutual presence in the compositional matrix; they may replace or double each other, creating redundancy; and they can mutually illuminate each other, and work complementarily.

LEADERSHIP OF LOVE AND COMPASSION: AN IDOLATROUS LIAISON?

Let us examine how these antinomies impinge on the unfolding of the drama. Moses has just recovered from the opening Burning Bush scene, in which he seemed to reluctantly abide by God's assignment of him as his nation's spiritual leader. He is about to meet Aron in the wasteland. A grand opening sets the scene (see ex. 6.3, prelude to the encounter).

What does this music, played by flute accompanied by harp and violins, portray? It draws on something familiar: warm, transparent, and light. It supplies us with melody, with several "keynotes": musical, emotional, and ideational. The melodic element is not perceived as dodecaphonic. The first phrase (98–100) seems to reside in the happy precincts of B major. Enharmonically, it moves in the second phrase to F minor, a tritone below (this tritone is structurally at the center of the twelve-tone row), in which it continues, until it seems to switch again, in m. 105, to B. The tension and ambiguous tonal relations (between the minor and major areas) appear later in different, related temporary "keys." The melody organizes itself rhetorically: similar openings are found in mm. 100 and 101, in mm. 102 and 104, as well as in mm. 107 and 110. The rhythmic structure is also carefully woven, as is the registral dispersion. Throughout the polyphonic score, however, the twelve chromatic tones appear in each measure; yet they bear no direct relation to the melody above. Being so transparent, they render, however, a polytonal rather than an atonal feeling, particularly in relation to the flute line.

The music is picturesque and atmospheric, creating an aura of spaciousness. At the same time, it lulls us, in its 6/8 meter, despite hemiolic[91] disruptions. It creates an impression of restlessness, sacredness, and of the pastoral, while the tonal disruptions hamper an immediate sympathetic response. *Whose* music is it, we ask, seeing the brothers walking towards each other. [92] It may be Moses' music, Aron's music, or music that wraps them both; it can also stand for the composer's voice—his point of view. It may remind us of a grand ritornello in a Bach oratorio: a long opening section, which repeats itself, almost note for note, as an infrastructure, in the sections that follow (125–147). Schoenberg indeed conceived it as a distinct musical entity; the melody, we infer from his sketchbooks, preceded the other parts (see music example ex. app. 8, in appendix). The main iteration of the ritornello occurs when Moses and Aron start talking to each other. Aron, as many have noticed, sings on the notes of the dodecaphonic row, something he will not repeat to that extent. These very notes are carved from within the preceding music, as if they were part of it, dormant in it. The other tones of the ritornello change accordingly, to fit into the new "melody." But in the midst of each of Aron's phrases, the ritornello music stops and Moses enters, against a sparse orchestral backdrop, declaiming his reactions in Sprechstimme. The opening music seems thus to stand for Aron's music; Moses has almost no share in it. It may signify what the biblical God told Moshe in advance (Exodus, 4:14): "[Aharon] cometh forth to meet thee, and when he seeth thee, he will be glad in his heart." *He* (will be glad) and not you, interprets Schoenberg.

Had he been more enthusiastic, could it have turned the ensuing "dialogue" into a better conversation? Moses and Aron, it soon becomes clear, are not really listening to each other; Moses reacts to the first words of Aron, then he

Ex. 6.3. Arnold Schoenberg, *Moses und Aron* I, mm. 98–109.

bursts into his phrase, unheard by his *melo*dramatic brother. He appears out of "order": he neither belongs to the old tonal one, nor to the new dodecaphonic. What was still unclear in the first scene now becomes obvious—Moses is not part of the musical universe, but rather lives in its margins: "Now Moshe used to take the tent and pitch it without the camp, far off from the camp, and he called it the tent of meeting. And it came to pass, that every one that sought the

Lord went out unto the tent of meeting, which was without the camp," we read in Exodus 33:7. "Pitched without," or to be "out of pitch" (a pun possible in English alone and of no use to Schoenberg): the idea of being out of pitch, outside the public order, so as to reach that which is above being, has been time and again mentioned in the critical literature on this opera, with particular attention to the moment Moses "chooses" to enter into the row, disintegrating immediately into its *Sprechgesang* habits.[93] But unlike the biblical Moshe, this "heavy of tongue" leader, self-conscious of his "uncircumcised lips" whose "pitching without" served the people's religious needs, this Moses' going "out of pitch" conveys only little communal concern. Moses, it seems, has not learned much from the Burning Bush revelation. He reiterates, almost in the same form, his previous convictions, even more vehemently denying any concreteness that the divine voices allow. Does his autism stand in reaction to Aron's exaggerated emphasis on concrete, communicative elements in the religious mission—a refusal, on Moses' part, to live by the most fundamental antinomy—the one that inheres in God's message?

The final composed scene of the opera, following the confrontation over the golden calf, is a partial recapitulation of the second scene. After all that has transpired, the two brothers have no alternative but to listen more attentively to each other. Aron is full of judicious claims against Moses' stark purism, becoming an empiricist philosopher cognizant of the imagistic aspect of all human communication, including the purportedly divine one. Their musical environment becomes even more suggestive than in the former dialogue between them, highlighting the emotional flow and reinforcing its pictorial elements. This becomes clear in the opening exchange, which thematizes the idea-word-picture-miracle element in relation to both its visual and vocal embodiment, and its effect on the struggle over the people's spiritual guardian- and leadership:

> Moses: Aron, what have you done?
> Aron: Nothing new! Only, what my task has always been: when your idea brought forth no word, my word brought forth no image, I made marvels before their ears, before their eyes.
> Moses: Commanded by whom?
> Aron: As always: I heard the voice from within.
> Moses: But I have not spoken.
> Aron: But I still understood it so.
> Moses (*threateningly steps towards Aron*): Quiet!
> Aron (*steps back alarmed*): Your. . . . mouth. . . . You were long far from us . . .

Later, a variant on the wasteland ritornello even more clearly accompanies Aron's utterances alone, and he now directly reveals his emotions and motives—his feelings towards the people he was chosen to lead (act II, m. 1023): "You also would have loved this people, had you only seen how they lived if they [were] allowed to see, feel and hope."[94] And a few measures later (1043), in a freer paraphrase: "Let me present how I see the way the idea, your idea, should be communicated to the people," says Aron. "Indirectly, never specifically, guaranteeing stability while transfiguring necessity. Stern prohibitions that inspire fear yet may arouse hope, should anchor our thought. Unconsciously we have done thy will" (see ex. app. 9).[95] The idea, when communicated to the people, should be in accordance with the people's psychology, and never be straightforwardly commanded. It should glow emotionally. Fear, perseverance, hope, love—these would be, according to Aron, the emotional stages of the people on their way to attaining the divine idea as a guiding force in their life.[96]

EMOTION, SYMPATHY, AND IDEAL STATES

In the dialogue between the biblical Moshe and God, there is one exchange with tremendous theological implications, which Schoenberg chose not to include in his text. This occurs when Moses asks God (Exodus 3:13–14): "Behold, when I come unto the children of Israel, and shall say unto them: 'The God of your fathers hath sent me unto you'; and they shall say to me: 'What is His name?' what shall I say unto them?" Here, the 1917 JPS runs, following almost verbatim the King James version: "And God said unto Moses: 'I am that I am'; and He said: 'Thus shalt thou say unto the children of Israel: I am hath sent me unto you.'" New Jewish translations seem to be more faithful to the grammatical form: "God said to Moses, 'I will be what I will be.' And he said, 'Say this to the people of Israel, I will be has sent me to you.'" The aporetic nature of God's reply comprises a vast theological subject that nourished divergent commentaries of generations of theologians and scholars; in the present modernist context, it could be understood as a political-theological-aesthetic principle, itself open to a variety of interpretations. Luther seemed to understand the power of this utterance for his own Reformation project (deepening the gulf between God and his predestined creatures) when he translated it as: "Ich werde sein, der ich sein werde. Und sprach: So sollst du zu den Israeliten sagen: 'Ich werde sein,' der hat mich zu euch gesandt." Schoenberg could not be unaware of this version; the other Jewish translation he owned (Bernfeld) rendered it as a name of a God faithful to his people: "Ich werde sein, der bin ich." (Buber-Rosenzweig went beyond this translation, granting the verse an even more clear ethical-

existential sense: ich werde dasein, der als ich dasein werde.) Hypostatizing
God in name, image, content, or law is perhaps the root of all idolatry and of
social exclusiveness. The God of the Hebrew Bible is openness itself and, as
such, defies all patterns and fixity, or, at least, God can be thus conceived. This
could be easily adopted by modern trends of Judaism, including by Jews like
Schoenberg and even Freud.[97] A possible reason for Schoenberg's omission of
this biblical passage from *Moses und Aron* may be that he expressed it indirectly
elsewhere in the work, such as in act III in the idea of God's worship in the
wilderness. Wilderness, as Goldstein emphasized—a major trope of modern
Jewish authors—is an image mediating "between the phenomenal and noumenal realms, between the locus of the concrete activity and the attainment of
a spiritual goal."[98] Yet a careful reading of the third act's text does not yield the
impression that even this image is central to this Moses' thinking; the wilderness is an ambiguous place associated with both a community's failure and with
a locus for its education, rather than a mere trope for an indeterminate, open
existence. More generally, though the last word in the written text is Moses'
(who beforehand bemoaned his lack of the appropriate word), the missing music, and Schoenberg's prolonged wrestling with it suggests that something did
not work the way he thought it should. Though he did not intend it so, biblical
God's self-nomination is strongly suggested through the very aporetic, unconsummated nature of the work.

For what we have seen is that the conception of a God *ohne Eigenschaften*,
a universal God devoid of all traits, even negative ones, was in fact Moses' own
radical innovation, an idea of divinity incompatible with that of the God of the
Burning Bush who reveals His contradictory nature to Moses. In a paradoxical
way, Moses' vehement defense of *his* idea suggests an odd antagonism towards
the revelation of God who intends to historically appear on the political stage
and redeem the Volk, the people, from its oppression by Pharaoh. His failure
to hide his feelings points to Moses' underlying inability to recognize the two
essential faces of the monotheistic God—a conception of which Spinoza was
well aware. Spinoza developed an abstract notion of a monotheistic God, more
abstract than that of Maimonides, yet more immanent than the one advocated
by Schoenberg's Moses. At the same time, as Shlomo Pines indicated, Spinoza
understood that as a moral guarantor of the social contract of the modern, democratic state, the monotheistic God, if he were to be grasped by all people, wise
and ignorant, elevated and simple, had to make use of images. Only images
could generate the proper emotions, of love, fear, charity, and compassion, all
necessary for the balanced operation of the multicommunal, liberal state Spi-

noza espoused. Spinoza left unspecified which "subjective" God each member, or group, of his community would choose for itself.[99] But he knew well that emotions are necessary for the dynamic activation of a community obedient to God's moral decree.

As we noted, the life of the emotions is the main concern of Aron's religion and political style, a concern that prevents him from apprehending the overarching abstract spiritual idea that should govern it. Like Schoenberg's Moses, Spinoza believed that philosophers should dispense with the specific embodiment of God's ideas, and seek beyond the sentiments of a specific religious community. Like Schoenberg (though the latter was never explicit about it) and in a starkly anti-Platonic move, he maintained that "no men are esteemed less fit to direct public affairs than theorists or philosophers."[100] Schoenberg demonstrated that even the double rule of the philosopher and the statesman does not really work (though he himself personally aspired, however unsuccessfully, to be both).

Ironically, Moses cannot escape his own emotive element. Once we understand this, it becomes clear that the work was never aimed to cope with the question of a musical dramatic representation of God, but rather to grapple with the emotional and existential conflicts instigated by the idea of God once it irrupts into an earthly human world populated by individuals and multitudes seeking to enlist it to urge their redemption. (In this *Moses und Aron* comes close to *Moses and Monotheism*, only that Freud diagnosed traumatic break, and Schoenberg implements it.)[101] The perceptual nature of the conflictive musical operations explained above bespeaks a similar epistemological bifurcation; it thus grants a phenomenally distinctive expression to this philosophical idea. Such conflicts are compatible with the nature of the medium that expresses them—the opera. And yet, unlike traditional or even some modernist opera, *Moses und Aron* leaves its emotional conflict unresolved.

The modernist Jew, Schoenberg, has a certain advantage here over the modern Jew, Spinoza—the advantage of art over philosophy. Despite his philosophico-political stance, Spinoza, had he been able to, would have dispensed with all representation. He turned Moses into a Christ who directly communicates with God, soul to soul, rather than face to face or mouth to mouth.[102] Theology was for him a necessity, as long as human beings still cling to concrete phenomena, though he was well aware of the perceptual and psychological dimensions of human knowledge, and the nonrational elements it introduces into all human consciousness and action.

In the post-Kantian world, aesthetics, rather than theology, loomed large. All through the nineteenth century and well into the modernist era, philosophers and other thinkers endeavored to listen more carefully to the ever-engaging configurations of art, and adapted them for their purposes. They were, likewise, well aware that art and aesthetics are always in danger of being reified into personal or ideological forms. Adorno's abovementioned criticism of the *Gesamtkunstwerk* is drawn along such lines. But there was another line, parallel and compatible with this one, which tended to emphasize the role of images as embodying memories and sentiments "that no argument could lay dead," as George Eliot, through Daniel Deronda, maintained. Images granted the freedom to worship a communal God, thereby instantiating a freedom compatible with liberal convictions. Certain Jewish thinkers, as the German-Jewish, later American philosopher Leo Strauss maintained, attempted to reconnect these ideas back to the theological space opened up by Spinoza, granting them a more immediate sociopolitical dimension. Schoenberg was probably influenced by these trends when he construed his Janus-faced God as the ultimate emblem of these epistemological intricacies.[103]

Schoenberg's God, or better, his imagined Divine presence, indeed encompasses the entire gamut of possibilities to be expressed by voice and speech, dodecaphonic and free composition, operatic and oratorical techniques, the abstract and the concrete, new and old forms of expression. He thus appears much more a God with *unendliche Eigenschaften,* than the abstract, *unvorstellbarer* God of Schoenberg's Moses. And if one listens to the vox populi, in the *Zwischenspiel* between acts I and II, one hears how close God and the people are to each other. Placing this scene in the same strategic point in which the Burning Bush scene unfolds (before the real action of the following act), Schoenberg points to their complementarity. The people are impatiently waiting for an absentee Moses. "Wo ist Moses? Wo ist der Führer, lange schon hat ihn keiner gesehn!" (Where is Moses? Where is the leader? It has been a long time since he was seen.) Forty days are long enough for their feelings of frustration and anxiety to be awakened, feelings that will nurture, dynamize, the entire second act—the act of the golden calf. In a way, the people become themselves the revelation: God will not appear again. The bristling effect of their hissing voices, and the short *tremolos* in a chiaroscuro orchestration create a transparent, fragile texture, with the prevailing interval of the fifth, which foreshadows the orgiastic rites. Human beings are left to their own struggles, trials, and errors. But God, in the first and only epiphany he offers, expresses his compassion for the people, his tearing out of his perfect being—a gesture parallel to a Kabbalistic *Tsimtsum,* so fashioned as to redeem, through Moses and Aron, the needy, chosen, folk of slaves.

Schoenberg, like Aron, pays heed to the people, granting their experience of fear, suffering, hope, admiration, devotion, and ecstasy a central place in the world he creates. One may still argue that there is an element of ironic detachment, even mockery in the way he treats them. If this is the case, then all the protagonists should be so interpreted. Situated in their experiential world, all characters, Moses included, cannot extricate themselves from their fixated existential predicament, though some of them take steps in this direction.

In the debate between Cohen and Rosenzweig regarding Spinoza's interpretation of Judaism, as presented by Leo Strauss, the issue of these thinkers' sympathetic assessment of Spinoza looms large. Cohen accuses the excommunicated seventeenth-century philosopher of uncompassionate treatment of his own people and lore, of overlooking their agonized history and dire circumstances (which should be familiar to Cohen through the "Lacrimosa" element of contemporary Jewish historians),[104] a criticism that Rosenzweig subsequently rebounds on Cohen himself, claiming that Cohen had failed to take into account Spinoza's own situatedness in the historical context in which he acted and wrote.[105] Thus they transpose a problem that was central in the polemic between Jews and Christians in the nineteenth century (Jews' capacity for being compassionate) into an internal Jewish one. For George Eliot, as we have seen, the principle of sympathy centers on the requirement to balance our judgment of other people's minds and actions with our understanding of their "fate" or history. Schoenberg seemed to follow this precept to a certain extent; this may account for the fact that his dramas are left basically unresolved.

The compassion conundrum brings us back to his Moses, of whom we must now ask whether he really is so oblivious to the people's plight, and autistically locked in his own idealistic world. Yet God — or the divine voices — said that precisely this plight brought Moses to *his* idea of Him. Does he really go through a transformative process, the way Goldstein maintains, in which he returns to a more complex understanding of man and God? Maybe he does. Then there is a point to his speaking rather than singing, epitomizing thus the worship of God through *Wunschlosigkeit* or, as Freud was to define it in *Moses and Monotheism*, *Triebverzicht* ("renunciation of the instincts").

The experience of such a demanding ideal, both Schoenberg's Moses (and probably in this case also Schoenberg) and Freud maintain, epitomizes the essence of being chosen. Both Schoenberg and Freud, at this stage of their lives and common history (though one is a theist and the other an atheist), left the specific form of such renunciation open. In the case of Schoenberg's Moses this should be understood within the context of the opera's specific aesthetic properties. By speaking rather than singing, Moses, in fact, opts for a domain that is not yet part of the universe of musical sounds, though it partakes of its acoustic substance. Like the congregation's tabernacle, the spoken voices, from the point of view of music as art form, are, in principle, unsystematized, "out of camp." Like the broken tablets, they smash the sanctioned metaphysics of music, in particular that of Schopenhauer, who regarded music as the symbolic embodiment of the origin of all origins—the *Urwille*. Indeed Schoenberg, as Carl Dahlhaus has pointed out, moved away from such metaphysics; for him texts, programs, and their like "appear as interchangeable surface phenomena of the music."[106] The fact that the not-yet-aesthetic is included within that which is artistically well defined, is one of the many paradoxes and achievements that underrun this work. Put another way, noise inheres in harmony, threatening its hegemonic presumptions, pointing at its temporality and limitations.

KOL NIDRE: THE VOICE OF INVALIDATED VOWS

Six years elapsed between Schoenberg's preoccupation with his unfinished opera and the next moment in his creative career that will engage us here. In between, Hitler came to power, Schoenberg resigned from the Prussian Academy of Art, left Germany with his family, rejoined Judaism in Paris in a formal and public (though religiously unnecessary) act, immigrated to the United States, tried to settle on the East Coast, and because of health problems moved to Los Angeles, to be later naturalized as an American citizen. All the while he relentlessly initiated actions for saving Jews from the impending catastrophe that he so clearly foresaw, searching for cooperation with prominent Jews and institutions.[107] He barely composed during that period, ready to sacrifice his art to save his people. It was only in 1938, already well settled at Brentwood Park, that he plunged into a new compositional project: *Kol Nidre*. The work was commissioned by the liberal rabbi Dr. Jacob Sonderling (1878–1964)—himself a mid-European émigré—and scheduled to be performed on the forthcoming (1938) Yom Kippur.

The composer responded to the invitation enthusiastically. Following his wrestling, not only with the precariousness of Jewish existence, but also, in the wake of *Moses und Aron*, with a host of theological and aesthetic queries, this project gave Schoenberg the opportunity to further experiment in this direction. His growing appreciation of traditional forms of communal existence, of the people's need of palpable, collective modes of worship and solace, could find its consummation in a work—the only one in his entire oeuvre—that was explicitly intended for a liturgical function: the grand overture of Yom Kippur.

A loaded and problematic text, the saturated and highly emotive traditional tune, emplaced in probably the most awe-inspiring moment in the entire Jewish year—the elaboration of these three elements in this work marks a poignant convergence of the creative history of the individual artist with that of the turbulent life of the collective. Bringing the noise accusation history in the artistic domain to its apparently ultimate insider expression, it concomitantly points beyond itself, to a Jewish existence struggling to extricate itself from its encumbering European past. As such, it coalesces many of the themes and notions examined throughout this book, especially in the last chapter.

The vexed text was the target of many anti-Jewish and anti-Semitic assaults for generations. The reemergence of such assaults in modern times should not surprise us in the context of our discussion; though more openly and pointedly raised, it carries overtones and undertones similar to those raised by the resuscitated noise allegation. As such, it also provoked reactions from mid-European "New Jews" and rabbinic consultation of whether to change the text, explain its underlying roots, modernize it, or entirely remove it from the prayer book. The charge was rather simple: the text, a collective annulment of vows and promises that Jews, as individuals, have undertaken in the course of the preceding year,[108] proves the Jews' immoral nature, their epitomizing—in Shakespearian language (once again)—the (unmusical) people of treasons, stratagems, and spoil.

This is not the place here to delve into the internal history of the text and its legal and theological underpinning.[109] Unsurprisingly, like the noise allegation, this one also stirred Theodor Reik intellectually, in a way reminiscent of his grappling with the shofar ritual. Here, too, the provocation was external: the *Deutsche Volksblatt* used to quote it annually, Reik narrates, invariably availing itself of "the opportunity to deduce from this edict a moral depravity on the part of the Jewish race." As with his shofar reflections, the deeper motivation behind the Kol Nidre study lies in early impressions the rite engraved on him. This took place in his grandfather's little town, a place quite similar to Vogel's birthplace. The inhabitants of the Jewish street ("a relic of the old Ghetto"), we are told, in spite of recent emancipation, "held but little intercourse with the Christian population, and appeared absorbed in their families, the religious practices and the routines of business." And here comes the full autoethnography:

> During my visits to the little town I had often heard the ancient melody of the Kol Nidre, and there grew into my mind a picture of the primitive synagogue; of long-bearded men in white robes, moving their bodies rhythmically in prayer; and of my grandfather at my side. I remembered the mysterious

trembling that possessed the congregation when the cantor began the Kol Nidre. I remembered the visible signs of deep contrition exhibited by all these serious men, and their emotional participation in the text, and how I, child as I was, had been carried away by that specific wrongdoing that might have called for contrition, and moreover, was certainly incapable of understanding the full meaning of the words. Needless to say, my grandfather, a taciturn and fanatically pious man, had never explained to me the meaning of the Kol Nidre.[110]

The event as a *Gesamtkunstwerk* experience, with its vocal soundscape playing such a central role,[111] again intrigues the author with questions of incongruity: between "high" melody and "prosaic" text, between the text *cum* music and the congregation's intense reaction to it, between "the profound contrition . . . manifested in the tears of those who are praying"[112] and the apparent, irreproachable piousness of the people.

It is the melody that becomes the pivot of this reflection, for, as Reik asks (again), "[a]re the qualities of solemnity and impressiveness really to be attributed to the melody, or are they only perceptible for some obscure reasons to the adherents of the Jewish religion?" Reik believes in a certain universality that this music shares, and brings in a fascinating testimony of the Austrian romantic poet Nikolaus Lenau (1802–1850), a benevolent outsider, reporting a nonfictional experience—to draw on the terminology used in the exploration of "ethnography transfigured" in chapter 3 above—who describes the Kol Nidre service he attended in a most passionate language. Portraying the setting of candles and people—in sensitive terms that could compete with Steinthal, he recalls:

> Then the cantor began to chant that profoundly solemn and heartrending song of absolution, so fraught with terror, and yet so rich in mercy. I struggled with an inexplicable emotion. I sobbed convulsively while hot tears poured from my eyes. Then I ran out into the night: my spirit torn and purified.

Lenau, like Daniel Deronda, wonders at the possible origins of the strains, to be answered that they had been "handed down from grandfather to grandchild" and further ruminates that "such a song, redolent of a people's suffering, can hardly have been composed by one brain"; that it resulted "from the composite inspirations of hundreds."[113]

Lenau's passionate reaction to this "nightly" Jewish song (as he termed it!) was not the sole one during the nineteenth century. Rumors commented that Beethoven adopted it in his op. 131 string quartet *adagio quasi un poco andante* (sixth) movement; musically it does reverberate in it.[114] Later, we glimpsed it in Meyerbeer's confessional moment.[115] The German composer Max Bruch famously developed it in a highly sentimental way in his op. 47 cello piece; he learned it from his friend, the great Berlin synagogue cantor, Abraham Jacob Lichtenstein, and adapted it for the composition.[116] In that famous rhapsody, he also inserted a quote from Nathan-Byron's *Hebrew Melodies*. Curiously, it is a phrase from "Weep for Those" (underscored in chapter 3 through music example ex. app. 3; see appendix), itself a quote from an old Jewish melody— "Tsena Urena." The craze, at the time, for the authentic and the antique in various folklores benefited this classical Missinai tune—the "Kol Nidre," itself a living testimony of those times in which Jewish and Christian music were apparently divided.

Separating melody from text—Louis Lewandowski, the Cantor Lichtenstein's colleague (whom we met as Hermann Cohen's father-in-law) and collaborator in the Berlin synagogue, adapted his *Kol Nidre* to a new and highly elevated text for both Jews and Christians, Psalm 130, "Aus der Tiefe" (*De Profundis*).[117] Many more Jewish synagogal composers adorned the melody with their melismatic imagery in their manuscripts and collections; Jewish music, in this case, seemed to atone for the problematic text it matches, and maybe also for other Jewish "transgressions," both vocal and ritual.[118]

Reik went in the opposite direction. Hailing the melody, he saw it as a symptom of its vexed text, and delved into its possible meaning. He grouped prevalent Jewish rebuttals of the Kol Nidre accusation under four categories, which he deemed unsatisfactory. They include: (1) a general defense of swearing and oath-taking in Jewish laws, stressing their sanctity and inviolability (that's right, he says, but it only aggravates the dissonance); (2) an exegetic argument, interpreting the Kol Nidre formula as concerning only obligations one imposes upon oneself and not in relation to another person (a belated apology, he contends, evading the historical roots of the custom); (3) a historical argument, viewing the formula as an internal Jewish expression of reacceptance of transgressors— "lip Christians"—into the holy congregation, as in the time of the Inquisition (but vows taken under duress, Reik argues, were never considered in Judaism or any other impartial legal system as valid anyway); (4) a psychological claim, relegating oath-taking to general primitive swearing/cursing customs, which people tend to undertake upon themselves in an act of prejudicial defense, precisely during the intense days of repentance, such as the Day of Atonement. This, Reik asserts, goes in a more promising direction.

Reik deepens the argument psychoanalytically, in terms already familiar to the reader. For him the text is a symptom of an archaic custom, that of the *B'rith* or covenant,[119] undertaken between two parties (two persons, peoples, God and person, and so forth) entailing asseveration, curse, and a symbolic action, which includes slaying of sacrificial animals. The B'rith ritual represents an "intermediate form which has developed historically from the primitive forms of the totem meal." We are back into the primordial parricide and the guilt it evokes, in relation to which the B'rith is a vow not to repeat it, and a promise—by the "murdered" god—to protect his devotees.[120] Now, the self-imprecation—part of the B'rith complex—is directed toward the potential perpetrators of the crime (if they commit it, so and so will happen to them), betraying the compulsion to repeat the crime. Here Reik connects the ancient ritual with neurotic symptoms, with obsessional thoughts of annulling one's own decrees. Such thoughts often cause a displacement of affect, releasing defensive thoughts of how to prevent the transgression into the prime mental object of the patient. In the life of obsessional neurotics, "who value their oaths and promises so scrupulously and over-conscientiously, there comes a moment when they attempt to get rid of their whole obsession, and they declare their oaths and promises invalid in advance." Again, a return of the repressed; such a distorted return, Reik maintains, is a common phenomenon of many a devout person, of monks who would "think of blasphemies in the midst of their prayers" and ascetics "tempted to commit the worst kind of sins in their deepest contrition." Kol Nidre, though in appearance an extension of the defense against temptation, is in reality, Reik concludes, an invocation to God, a confession that we, "a congregation of perjurers," feel within us the wish "not to keep oath and vows." Recited elliptically, clarifies Reik, it guards against a full recognition of the obsessive thoughts and their nature.

Reik returns to the "deeply affecting melody," now stressing that its power derives from "the secret feelings which have become unconscious," and adds:

> The music brings adequately to expression the revolutionary wish of the congregation and their subsequent anxiety; the soft broken rhythms reflect their deep remorse and contrition. Thus the song is really full of terror and mercy, as Lenau has observed.[121]

The elements in common with Reik's shofar exegesis need not be explicated, but there is one component—important for the author—that Kol Nidre possesses much more straightforwardly than the shofar: as a syndrome, it is found also in Christianity, especially in the "Catholic forms of repentance of the Middle Ages." In the present history, this comment is intriguing; Reik brings to bear as evidence various Catholic prayers (such as *Confiteor, Kyrie Eleison*) but adds to this also Lewandowski's *Kol Nidre / De Profundis*, which unveils, he contends, more explicitly than the original text, the same devotional vein![122]

Taken hither and thither, we are back in those grim moments of the old Catholic customs of Good Friday (themselves reminiscent of prevalent Jewish rites), discussed in chapter 1.

Apparently, Schoenberg-Sonderling's approach to the ritual and its historicized imagery seems the exact opposite. This is manifest in Schoenberg's treatment of the melody and its connotative import: his perception of it betrays his ambivalence to the tradition; unlike Reik and many other contemporary Jews, his synagogal experience—if he had any—did not leave a memorable, meaningful imprint on him. Certainly, the Kol Nidre melody was not among his favorites. It suffers, he writes, "from monotony and sentimentality," brought about

> by the circumstance that it is composed in a minor-like church mode. At the time the Kol Nidrey [*sic*] originated there was seemingly no discrimination between the emotional effect of major and minor. No doubt, Bach would have composed it in major, because to him, as to us, minor expressed mournful and touching emotions. Certainly in the 16th century this melody expressed dignity, seriousness, solemnity and awe. Today we feel, if not the contrary, so at least the discrepancy between the solemnity of the words [!] and the sentimentality in which they are presented.[123]

Incongruence again, but so different from that purported by Reik. It concerns, firstly, Schoenberg's awareness of (Western) music's historicized semantic fields and secondly, his appreciation of the text as dignified and solemn, rather than as penitent and contrite. While he was basically right in the first point—the expressive language of Western music underwent a tremendous change since the sixteenth century—he partially erred in relation to the particular import of the melody, viewed within its own musical surrounding. Nor did he consider the progression within the melody from minor to major tonal districts. Above all, he missed the wholesomeness and connectivity of the ritual as performed in Ashkenazi synagogues, especially its role as grand overture to the holy day, and that which it had emotionally accumulated over time, beyond its underlying written text.[124]

But maybe even more surprising is the way Schoenberg treats the text. He acknowledges the anti-Semitic assaults, defending the Jewish case by the "general argument" Reik refutes. ("[This view] stands in contradiction to the high morality of all Jewish laws").[125] Gone are all the repressed layers Reik ascribed to it; the ancient formula appears clear and bright to the composer, who wishes to musically enhance these qualities. For that he had to "fix" the melody, which, besides its faulty semantics, he also found structurally deficient. "We are

Ex. 6.4. Arnold Schoenberg, paradigmatic layout of cantors' versions of
"Kol Nidre," _Kritischer Bericht, Chorwerke,_ 16.

accustomed," writes the composer, "that melodies are 'built up' onto a certain climax. Nothing of this kind can be observed in this melody. It ends without any musical reason. . . . This is very insatisfactory [*sic*]."[126]

This "aesthetically incorrect" judgment determines Schoenberg's attitude toward the musical matrix of his composition, which is deeply connected with its avowed theological core. Meticulously comparing extant versions of the melody, thus isolating structural notes, he wished to distill a musical substance out of them (ex. 6.4 contains a specimen of this matrix, containing an essential motif, also discussed in chapter 4).[127]

This procedure, which may recall the ordering of a twelve-tone row for composing a work in that technique, is however differently motivated: deriving "essence" from "impure" surplus,[128] it acquires an emblematic standing, highlighted by Sonderling's prose. The work opens with the following lines, recited by the "Rabbi" (narrator):

> The Kabalah tells a legend: At the beginning God said:
>   "Let there be light." Out of space a flame burst out.
>   God crushed that light to atoms.
>   Myriads of sparks are hidden in our world, but not all of us behold them.
>   The self-glorious, who walks arrogantly upright, will never perceive one;
>   but the meek and modest, eyes downcast, he sees it: "A light is sown for
>   the pious."

The distilled melody stands to its empirical versions like the sparks of light to the material world in which they were dispersed. The composer's task, like that of the pious person, is to collect them. Composing becomes thus part of a great Tikkun, or fixing the world, a leading theurgical idea of the Kabbala, and later Hasidism (which practically encouraged the selection of spiritually worthy musical material from previous "non-kosher" moorings).[129] Light turns into music not only allegorically, but also synaesthetically. Schoenberg resplendently rehearses his synaesthetic lessons, from his "modernist" years, to create the smashing prelude of the work, including a moment of musical creation of light. That moment refers to the enlightened musical light-making in Handel's, Haydn's, and Mendelssohn's works, discussed above. In Schoenberg, however, this moment consists of noise rather than of triadic harmony, comprising the entire twelve-tone gamut and carried through strident orchestration (m. 32). By virtue of all this, the universalistic expression of the Enlightenment composers, turns, in Schoenberg's work, into a cosmopolitan gesture emerging from within the particular, emblematic group of an eternal Jewish congregation.

Major motifs of the "Kol Nidre" melody will appear on the musical surface; the text itself will be carried in an English adaptation of the Aramaic original. Intelligibility matters here. Previous antinomies will be reconciled. The old text is fully integrated with the new one, which further aggrandizes it. This is how its first part starts, incorporating Moses' theology within a communal system of Aron's (the italicized words are those radically different from the original):

> All vows, oaths, promises and plights of any kind, wherewith we pledged ourselves *counter to our inherited faith in God, Who is One, Everlasting, Unseen, Unfathomable,* we declare these null and void.

And this further continues:

> *We repent that these obligations have estranged us from the sacred task we are chosen for.*

To this the chorus replies: "We repent."

Now all becomes clear. The interpretation takes the text away from all the apologetic arguments Reik had rejected. It is forward-looking, indeed, but within a binding theological framework, which clearly separates good from bad vows, sacred task (of the chosen) from mundane activities. It connects with the aesthetic theology Schoenberg seems to have been in search of since his early "synaesthetic" period, and with the important verse he did not include in his opera: "I will be what I will be." Don't predetermine your spiritual progress. Leave your soul open to the infinite divine. Neither Hermann Cohen nor Rosenzweig would oppose this reading of the ancient formula.[130]

The incorporation of Moses' negative theology within Aron's communal system has further compositorial realization, attenuating antinomies that underlie their previous antagonistic operatic encounter in the Schoenbergian universe within a comprehensive whole: whereas in *Moses und Aron* the twelve-tone technique seems to negate conventional tonal patterns, now tonal patterns guide the basic motivic figurations. Old forms—a choral texture, a refrain, responsorial elements that in the operatic work are more haphazard or concealed, are here boldly playing their part, assisting congregation both internal (the embedded chorus) and external (the synagogal one). The tension between an oratorio and an opera, between presentation of an idealized, temporally meandering dramatis personae (as in oratorio) and concrete, fictive, and clearly historicized ones (as in opera) is solved by the concrete and ever-present participants of the renewed ritual. The speech versus melody antinomy is disentangled between the reciting Rabbi (himself fully rhythmically contained in the music) and the singing people. They are fully attuned to each other, and do not cut into different sonic ideals.

These multiple reconciliations can be exemplified by different sections of the work. The overarching structural element will serve it most comprehensively: the text, according to the liturgical tradition, is thrice repeated. In prevalent Ashkenazi synagogal practice, the hazzan usually starts sotto voce, increasing volume in each repetition, an effect often achieved also through elevation by a tone or a half tone. Schoenberg keeps this custom within his tonal structure, perceptually working it into the musical motifs, by means of twelve-tone procedures. This divides the work into a clear three-partite edifice, in which the first part is the Rabbi plus orchestral accompaniment simulating a virtual choir; the second and the third are carried by the chorus, alternating with the Rabbi. This gives clear advantage to the choir, the congregation, and supports its ritualistic character.[131]

Are indeed all conflictual matters resolved? Does substituting ethnic assembly for cosmopolitan siblinghood—which nonetheless is committed to universal mission[132]—make this possible, or maybe it is the egalitarian spirit of the New World, which now presides over it all? And if so good and reconciling, why did it not become the kind of oeuvre its creator designated it to be—a work for actual worship? Only once it was so performed—on the original Yom Kippur of 1938; later ritual performances of the work, if there were any, are not registered in extant documents.[133] Lazare Saminsky, whom Schoenberg addressed in 1941 with the idea of the work being adopted by the Reform synagogal union, responded negatively. Equipped with various practical reasons, his stronger one seemed to be that the text differs too much from the standard version of the Reform Jews.[134]

This is all true, but the crux of the matter is that Schoenberg, an outsider to his own tradition, did not really grasp the nature of the ceremony as performed in the synagogue, fragmentary indeed, "illogical" in Western terms, entertaining an expressive language that only partially overlaps with the common Western one. Profoundly traditional, the actual ceremony must also reflect changing times and places, and, guided by the Ba'al Tefila or hazzan, reverberates the plights and mood of the present prayers. A fully composed and highly synchronized work does not fit into such a ritual practice. That of Schoenberg even less, being too ceremonious, too complete, even for Reform Jews. In that sense, Schoenberg remained an outsider from all worlds, again, not unlike Spinoza. But by so doing he was able to erect a sonic monument, which sealed a glorious and turbulent period of composers of Jewish origin in Europe, and opened a new horizon for those, like him, who wished to integrate into new worlds.

About a month after the *Kol Nidre* premiere had taken place, the Kristallnacht events erupted. Both Schoenberg and Sonderling, who left family and friends in Europe, were highly shaken. There were barely synagogues left in Germany after that well-orchestrated night of hooliganism. The *Lärm*, though smothered, became more violent than ever. Schoenberg, like Sonderling, anxious for the remaining family members who were still there, endeavored to acquire for them American affidavits, and was about to sketch his *Kristallnacht* fugue. And within that darkness, Jewish synagogal "noise"—as ultimate noise—was heard for the last time.[135]

7

THE END: ESSENTIALIZING JEWISH NOISE IN NAZI MOVIES

[I am Saul and] you are my David, should I become sick and melancholic, you must banish my bad dreams by your playing! I assure you that, unlike Saul, I will never throw the spear at you.

—*Goethe to F. Mendelssohn*

"The End." She sits in the darkened cinema; these are her first exposures to the fantasies of the cinematic medium. Even before she knows what conventions are, when her knowledge of English is rudimentary, she learns what it means: the end of the plot, the end of two or more hours of fantasy, with heroes whose lives and emotions she has been ardently involved in. Now these characters go their own ways, carry on with actions she will no longer be privy to, though she is free to imagine. Many internal signs lead to this inevitable ending point—itself further enhanced by musical signals—the theater's lights coming back up, the commotion of people rising from their seats. The Hebrew characters are not late to appear on the screen and confirm all this: "*Ha-sof,*" they announce. Sometimes it appears in French, *Fin.* Upon opening the doors from the cinema to the street, she is always hit by daylight, by the fact that the world continues as it has done before, indifferent to that which has so excitingly transpired in the fantastic in-between.

Most of the film endings she watches at the time are happy ones: *Mary Poppins, The Sound of Music, Oliver.* Sometimes they are not so happy. Does it already occur to her, at that stage, that *Ha-sof* is also the word chosen to denote that which became inexorably final? *Ha-pitron ha-sofi.* The Final Solution. She

340

cannot recall when she has first learned about that *Sof*; it seemed as if she has ever known it. It was engraved in the names her parents gave her, after her father's two young cousins, the girls Ruth and Miriam (Kober), born in Amsterdam, who ended their lives in Auschwitz. This took place twelve years before she was born; as a child, it seemed a long time ago.

As a child and youth she never imagined she would ever return to Germany, to her parents' birthplace. But then it happened; because of music, musicology, and projects she became involved in. Again and again she found herself there, most of all in that intense, variegated, and internally turbulent city—Berlin. The year now is 2005; she is engaged, in Berlin, in that Jewish noise project. Together with a close friend, she sits in the National Film Archive where they are watching together the most sequestered films in Federal Germany, *Jud Süß* and *Der ewige Jude*.[1] Watching and being watched by a plump German lady, the situation seems both *unheimlich* and *out*landish.[2] For everyone knows that these illicit objects can be easily ordered over the Internet. *Der ewige Jude* is then allowed to be taken out. *Jud Süß* is not. They try to understand the logic; after all, the first is a "documentary," and more blatantly anti-Semitic. Maybe, they reflect, that was its weakness, the reason why, unlike *Süß*, it did not become a blockbuster when it was issued, on 28 November, 1940.[3]

Jud Süß was a great success. When it was first released to the German public, a month before, in September 1940, that first audience's impulsive reaction, upon watching the scene of the Jews' entrance to Stuttgart with all their belongings was: "Drive the Jews out of Kurfürstendamm!"[4] And off Kurfürstendamm they sit now, watching the film. It was a great success, they learn, because it was a good, even a *very good* movie. So good that many years later, old Germans, all Nazi condemners, would tell Linda Schulte-Sasse that, of course, the movie was "terrible Nazi propaganda" *but* "today's actors aren't nearly as good as Werner Krauss"[5] and "today's movies are violent(!) and trashy."[6] It was so good that it was deliberately used to enlist public and military support for the actual deportation of Jews out of Germany, eastwards, out of the ghettos, to death camps: "Facts" (this movie was deemed, by the Nazis, "historical") turned to fiction—they also categorized it as "feature"—turned to facts. Very hard facts.[7]

This is also the end, with very hard facts, of the vocal fiction, or fictions, this book has addressed. Like other monuments and edifices built by the Nazis, the movie aimed to remain for a long time and justify the colossal act of annihilation. No wonder aforementioned modes and themes, elaborated in vocal fictions of noise and harmony, found there their ultimate consolidation. In recent years, the movie was thoroughly researched by various scholars; its sonic components were identified, but never analyzed in depth.[8] Among the film's quintessential elements, the sonic components frame it in a sophisticated, "state of the art" way, insinuating that which seemed never to have been hushed in German culture, even in its most enlightened days—the noise allegation.

In Nazi Germany the noise allegation became outspoken again. The Wagnerian "musical Judaism" was powerfully revoked, giving rise to a regulative policy against Jewish musicians, composers, dead and alive, as well as against their supporters. Furthermore, this was accompanied by a systematic rewriting of German music history by eminent musicologists, aimed at eradicating the Jewish presence and the Jewish contribution to the making of the great German tradition. This had immediate implications on the cultural life of the period: absurdities were inevitable, and attempts such as commissioning a substitute for the Mendelssohnian *Midsummer-Night's Dream* proved to be a failure. Smoother, as we have seen, was the adaptation of a German Fascist text to the biblical oratorios of Handel. By and large, inconsistencies in Nazi policy regarding its avowed musical canon, with changing regulations as to the approved and the condemned (including Wagner's own oeuvre, *Parsifal*), continued well into the war years.

Considered in broader terms, Jews became increasingly identified as public noise-makers, while Aryans were characterized as quiet, orderly, and disciplined, as Yaron Jean has shown. A report of the Bavarian police dated April 1936, tells of a group of vociferous, card-playing Jews that infuriated their German neighbors who were trying to listen to the Führer's speech from a nearby radio.[9] The juxtaposition of these two elements—Jewish noise and Hitler's voice—in the Nazi imaginaries was crucial. The incredible technical apparatus built to make Hitler's "raging baritone" omnipresent all over the Reich is well documented. The powerful impact of this voice, as Hanfstängel reported, was, from the very beginning of its bearer's career, among his most consciously employed "equipment":[10] "In the past," wrote Hitler, "you have heard the voice of a man and he touched deeply in your heart. It evoked you, and you followed it . . . even before you have ever seen the face to which it belongs. You have heard this voice alone, and despite that you followed it."[11] They had indeed, and continued, misled by this Pied Piper, himself believing his vocality to be an embodiment of quintessential German culture—an incarnation of Wagner.[12] Playing his pipe, like the figure in the legend transcribed by the Brothers Grimm, he first drove the town's "rats" to the nearby river, and then led the town's children to their own catastrophic doom. Only that he, in the present story, made up the rat plague, and was vengeful towards his own people's offspring from the very start.[13]

PLOT AND NOISE: BASIC COORDINATES AND STRATEGIES

It is within these multiple frameworks that the following analysis of the sonic configurations in *Jud Süß* should be considered. The fictional ("historical") plot is situated in Joseph Süß Oppenheimer's early eighteenth-century Württemberg (a sample of its more faithful, anti-Semitic modern rendition in Lion Feuchtwanger's 1925 novel was included in the transfigured ethnographies discussed in chapter 3).[14] The movie's director, Veit Harlan, exploited extant fictional and historical sources for his own needs.[15] He presents his script as follows:

> The film begins in 1733 with Karl Alexander's accession to power as Duke of Württemberg. Lacking enough money to buy a celebratory gift for his wife, the Duke sends his envoy von Remchingen to Joseph Süss Oppenheimer in Frankfurt's Jewish Ghetto. Süss ingratiates himself with the Duke by extending him credit on a necklace in exchange for permission to enter the capital city of Stuttgart, which heretofore has been prohibited to Jews. Süss becomes the Duke's financial advisor, and continues to finance the latter's representational excesses (an opera, a ballet, and a retinue) denied by the Estates. To compensate Süss, the Duke grants him control of the roads of Württemberg. Süss enrages the people by taxing every bridge, gate, and street heavily. He persuades the Duke to lift the ban on Jews entering Stuttgart, as well as to seek absolute power by staging a *coup d'état* with the help of foreign soldiers hired with Jewish money. When Estate-Counselor Sturm rejects Süss's offer to marry his daughter Dorothea, Süss has Sturm arrested as a traitor. Dorothea is hastily married to her lover Karl Faber, who is also arrested for planning a revolt. She visits Süss in his chamber, begging him to free her husband and father. Süss rapes her, after which she drowns herself. The Duke dies suddenly, whereupon the power of Württemberg falls into the hands of the Estates, who arrest Süss and hang him for having carnal relations with a gentile woman.[16]

Oppenheimer was hanged in 1738, five years before Moses Mendelssohn entered Berlin's gates (the movie remains faithful to these dates). The historical embeddedness of the story, just before Jews entered into (Christian) German society—becoming less and less identifiable as Others—is the movie's most crucial hinge. The film attempts to reify this point in time, in which an ideal, pure German culture was not yet defiled by the Jewish element. Not coincidentally does it overlap with the main temporal axes of the present book, only that here the gaze has been directed precisely to the temporal mingling—real, imaginary, phantasmagoric—of Jewish and Christian existence, as embodied in Jewish and Christian sonorities.

The strategies the film deploys to conjure up this fictitious historical reverse, which the cinematographic ones further enhance, correspond, however, to some of those explored throughout the book. Firstly, it makes use of the documentary genre to validate its fictive ethnography, along the matrix's coordinates highlighted in chapter 3 (extending between insider/outsider, real/fictive, benevolent/malevolent, traditional/transfigured positions). This resolves in a combination of rubrics not specified before, coalescing outsider-malevolent-"fictional"-traditional positions. Secondly, it plays with motives (and motifs) of (Jewish) revenge and (Christian) compassion, inherent, as we have seen, in the noise allegation. Thirdly, it highlights Jewish *Mauscheln* talk, from which modern Jews (including Harlan's Süß, in most of the movie), attempted so much to exempt themselves. It also enlists dramatic models of the Age of Enlightenment, such as that of the "bourgeois tragedy," founded by Lessing and Schiller, which the movie, as Schulte-Sasse persuasively showed, depoliticizes and re-politicizes according to ideological needs.[17] Lessing came in, involuntarily, through his works in other genres, as did Mozart, Wagner, and Puccini.[18]

More particularly, we found the movie rehearsing themes such as the move from the *Judenrein* era (in Stuttgart) onto the famous Judengasse in Frankfurt (which hosted more than a few of the previous vocal fictions and "ethnographies"), from which the duke's ambassador transfers Süß into areas forbidden to him, to satisfy his master's financial desires. It brings together, in the same "homey" space, the Jew and the harlot (like the Jew in the 1820 English caricature who went to "Sin-agog"—see figure 3.5). It draws on repulsive animalistic epithets for Jews (locusts in *Jud Süß* and rats in *Der ewige Jude*), recalling Kafka's self-allegorizing mice.[19] As in Halévy's *La Juive*, it also makes use of the Jew's treasure chest, encasing Christian jewelry (a crown bearing a cross, and similar objects), aimed to entice innocent Christians (and overpower them). In all these and their like, the movie activates fictional, dramatic, and vocal strategies for bolstering exclusiveness. It urges the expulsion of real and metaphoric noisy Jewish elements, portrayed as endangering German harmony on both its sexual/familial and political/communal levels.

It is the conjugation of such encoded fictional imaginaries that makes the film into the enthrallment it became for so many Germans at the time. In the spirit of Slavoj Žižek's political-film theory, one may claim for a case where the phantasmic was willfully penetrating reality as a programmatic desideratum, enhancing policy well under way, itself established on the obfuscated boundaries of the real and the illusionary.[20] The fortuity of this conjugation (or partial lack of it) replicates the golden-calf syndrome, as expounded in the previous chapter, in putting together diversities that can act with or against one another, enhancing authors' intentions or clashing with them. Several writers have noticed that some of the movies' strategies do indeed create an inherent ambivalence that points to the cracks between ideology, reality, and the fantastic, phantasmal elements enlisted for bridging them.

This ambivalence concerns the elusive, twofold Jewish inside-outsider constitution, which the movie aimed to annihilate on account of its hypocritical nature (this is the explicit theme of *Der ewige Jude*). The Jew can thus enter disguised into the holy of holies of civil German society, cunningly obliterating it from within, because of his being "me and not me" and one "who both embodies for others and pursues for himself forbidden desire," as Schulte-Sasse claims, being as such, in James Donald's phrasing, a symptom of "the instability of culture, the impossibility of its closure or perfection."[21] This is exacerbated in the film through the paradox its casting procedures expose, a paradox we will explore later.

DEFINING MUSICAL FRAMES

It is here that music, a nomadic and slippery phenomenon, as maintained throughout this book, is paradoxically summoned to fixate the unfixable. It operates through a clear associative structure, which is established by the film's opening frames. In each of the main junctures of the movie, a marked musical moment, mostly diegetic, signals the exacerbation of Süß' scheme, resolving only in the final scene of his execution and its aftermath.

Preceding the movie's opening images, a serious, determined minor brass fanfare heralds that regardless of what is going to be heard or seen, you, the German spectator, are safely contained by the proper sounds. Hear the following foreign vocal sounds as but a quote, and remember who the final winner is, but be alert — the fanfaric music forewarns — there is danger here. These quoted sounds should threaten and repel you, arouse you to action, induce your legitimation of certain exploits. Comprising a genuine Jewish synagogal voice, the sounds are framed by the Jewish *ḥanukiah* with eight burning candles against a background of the Jewish star and lions. Listen to the yell the voice emits, the nauseating lament it intones. Don't fret, however, for you will not be able to grasp its content, beyond the general apprehension of a certain whining; this music does not resemble any of the sonic schemes you are familiar with.[22]

But if you happen to be an insider, you may discern that this voice is reciting:

הוּא יוֹשִׁיעֵנוּ וְיִגְאָלֵנוּ שֵׁנִית וְיַשְׁמִיעֵנוּ בְּרַחֲמָיו לְעֵינֵי [כָּל חַי]

(. . . [he is our savior], and will save us and redeem us again, and will let us hear, in his compassion, before the eyes [of all living]), from Shabbat and the Holidays' (Musaf) Kᵉdushah.[23] How did the film producers, you wonder, come to choose precisely these loaded phrases, carrying the promise of the prophetic revelation of the God of the Jews' compassionate redeeming *sound* in front of the entire world? (The bracketed words are not uttered here.)

This Ba'al Tᵉfila, or cantor, does not really sing or recite; rather his delivery borders on the verge of weeping, howling, ululating, in the manner of the Sᵉliḥa (litany) mode, or *steiger*, associated with those heartrending sections of the Days of Awe liturgy. (He opens with the small range of a fourth, through the minor third [1 to 3 and 4], gradually extending to 5, with many wavering, trill-like motions, pitching higher though never alighting on a clear note, but to wail back down to the *finalis*, on iterating, sobbing notes.)[24] The frame dissolves to the credits, and on the Bᵉraḥamav (in his mercy) melisma the serious fanfare reenters, resulting in actual cacophony, which also brings into the previous "Jewish" frame a *Der Stürmer*[25] stereotyped figure (fig. 7.1—compare the "Sinagog Jew," fig. 3.5) as an alleged agency of this vocation. His wailing (on *lᵉ-einey*, before the eyes)—we see his lips moving—is finally abducted by the fanfaric orchestra, leading to a major-chord cadence, free of any Jewish disruption.[26]

From within this sonic confusion, soft, clean, relaxing sounds come forth, executed by string instruments and further taken up by woodwinds, silenc-

Fig. 7.1. "Oriental" Jew davening, Veit Harlan (*Jud Süß*).
Courtesy of International Historic Films, Inc.

Fig. 7.2. Dorothea and Christian performing "All' mein'
Gedanken," Veit Harlan (*Jud Süß*). Courtesy of
International Historic Films, Inc.

ing other voices. Connoting innocence, hope, light, these tones are familiar to German insiders (including German Jews, were they allowed to watch the film). A minor hue is smuggled in, conveying, à la Wagner, future trouble; but the major mode then takes over and, introduced by bells' toll, transports us to Württemberg's council where the Duke swears in, while the music hushes (this is a serious business, like Sarastro's convention of priests for sober consultation). Diegetic sounds—court fanfares and public commotion—irrupt into the scene, as it dissolves into the ensuing street ceremonies. Noise, indeed, but now the "right" kind, punctuated with a Parsifalian tolling of bells, heralding the enthronement of Duke Karl Alexander—a memorable day for the Swabians.

From the collective we move into the homely, the familial, through the "innocent" theme, likewise diegetically loaded. What could be more heartening and romantic than a musical scene featuring a very young, Aryan-looking, dirndl-dressed sweet woman, singing to the harpsichord accompaniment of a similarly classic Germanic-looking, gentle, yet determined young man (fig. 7.2)?[27] Those who have identified the melody in its previous instrumental rendition are now fulfilling their unwitting expectation: yes, it is *our* old familiar German song: "All' mein' Gedanken" with its well-known text ("All my thoughts that I have are for you, you, the chosen, sole consolation, stay with me . . . you, you, you . . . from you I will never depart"), calling for our identification with the attractive protagonists, Dorothea Sturm (Kristina Söderbaum) and Christian Faber

(Malte Jaeger). We hum the melody, smile upon Dorothea's somewhat hesitant singing, well supported by her beloved coach, allowing for a stroke of affection in the third phrase of this square song to close it on a cadence leading to a real kiss.

Some of us may know that this is an "original" song, first included in the 1450 *Lochamer Liederbuch* (see music example ex. 7.1); others are familiar with Johannes Brahms' adaptation of it, in his famous folk song collection. The fact that the melody is so simple—almost like a nursery rhyme—enhances, in this instance, the feeling of its authenticity, its association with the roots of German music, a "Hans Sacksian" item surviving all that has transpired since and remaining untainted. The simplicity projected onto (and from) the girl, which accentuates her childish manners, her need of instruction by the male figures—father and future husband—becomes an allegory of the unguided nation in need of a *Führer*, resembling Wagner's Elsa, according to the composer's own view.[28]

The bundle of binaries evoked by the contrasting Jewish and German "melodies" creates a scheme to be fulfilled dramatically. It heightens the dichotomy already found in Thomas Rowlandson's 1803 caricature (see fig. 2.4) between the vigorous, structured, genuine English folk tune and the weak, illogical, and capricious Jewish vocalization, metonymically projected onto the visual appearance of their respective singers. Here, the clean sonorities of the harpsichord, with its evident baroque and domestic, *heimisch* lure further enhance the trope of connectedness and clarity vis-à-vis those of detachment and murkiness.

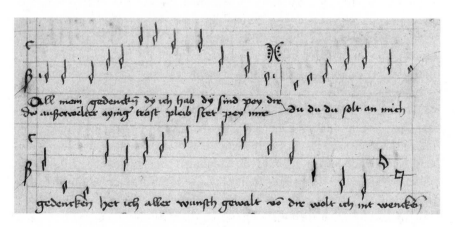

Ex. 7.1. "All' mein' Gedanken," *Lochamer Liederbuch*, 1450.
Courtesy of bpk/SBB, Musikabteilung mit Mendelssohn-Archiv,
Staatsbibliothek zu Berlin—Preußischer Kulturbesitz.

THE SCHEMES AND IRONIES OF THE SONIC NARRATIVE

The music also halts when we reach the Frankfurt Judengasse with von Remchingen, the Duke's ambassador. The negotiation with the Jew and his journey to the forbidden Stuttgart have nothing to do with music either, though the reasons are not those of the previous oath-taking scene. It will recommence in a crucial moment, dramatic and cinematic: when the Jew—now officiating as the Duke's treasurer—turns his money into elegant, twirling ballerinas.

This moment of dissolve recalls Tchaikovsky's *Nutcracker* animation from Walt Disney's *Fantasia*, released in the same year. The music, in line with the fictional time, is, however, French rococo. Subtly, it insinuates Wagner's idea of Judaism in music: don't be misled by such sweet music. It is empty and commercial, like all the music "modern" Jews—Mendelssohn, Meyerbeer, Offenbach—had produced. Similarly, don't be misled by the European look and the French etiquette that the Court Jew acquired. Connoisseurs will recognize the difference. They did: unlike the eighteenth-century protagonists in Lessing's *Die Juden* (fictionally contemporaneous) who could not fathom their traveler's real (Jewish) identity, this traveler's pedigree is revealed, on the spot, by deft Faber. He even ventriloquizes, almost *verbatim*, the words Lessing put in *his* astonished protagonists' mouths: "Das ist ein Jude." And when evidence (brought by naïve Dorothea) seems to contradict his verdict—he repeats it with a different (and typically German) vocal emphasis: "Das *ist* ein Jude."[29] But since the actor—the racial laws did not allow otherwise—was an Aryan (however a swarthy one), a rupture broke out within ideology, differently projected on fantastic fiction and legal reality.

More gallant music will be heard in the "Don Giovanni" scene, later transpiring in the palace, in which "Leporello" (the Jew) protects his "Don" (the Duke) in the latter's sexcapades. Concomitantly, he himself will be engaged in grabbing poor Zerlina/Dorothea to quench his own lust—both sexual and vindictive—but her Masetto (Faber) will rescue her, this time, to Süß' dismal and increasingly rancorous dismay.

A nondiegetic, Wagnerian *Götterdämmerung*-like music will signal Süß' cruel demolition of the blacksmith Hans Bogner's house, foreshadowing the revengeful Jew's own impending ruin. This omen is reinforced by Bogner's ensuing execution, also musically accentuated: music in its punitive task, now appearing through a massive drum roll. This turns into another cause for exacerbating stratagems: by the Duke's decree, the following scene will focus on the Jew's fellow-people entering Stuttgart. Opportunity for an ethnographic moment, again cacophonic: against the background of a foreboding leitmotif (which will extend into the next scene of the council meeting, connecting the two), a long procession of humble "Jews," seen from behind, proceeds toward the now familiar city gates. The diegetic music is piling up on this background motif, realistically performed by an unseen singer who later becomes visible: our bearded cantor with protruding lips and large nose, from the opening frames.

As for the music, however—could the average German viewer perceive that it has no connection whatsoever to the previous music, or does it all sound like "noise," as a disruption or interference, in the "theory of information" sense of the word? If you happen to be at home also in this Jewish subculture, you will be surprised, for this nonliturgical music is a Zionist "landscape and homeland" song: the Song of the Camel (a genre of its own, in the Yishuv of the twenties and thirties).[30] You wonder how this somewhat childish "Gamal G'mali" found its way here, and what its use was meant to communicate.

The search for an orientalist idiom in the film should not surprise us, however; its roots in the history of Western music's "otherness" is well documented. In *The Eternal Jew*, it conspicuously adorns the "Palestinian" Jewish part, functioning as another mode of degradation. And yet it seems to belong among those items that subvert the authors' intentions, leading their narrative along unintended paths.

Composed by Yedidya Admon (1927), the song comprises a simple, almost childish refrain: "Camel, my Camel, you are my friend in the coarse sand" (ex. 7.2). This refrain is wedded to two verse "strophes," borrowed from Balaam's prophecy on the people of Israel (Numbers 24). Only the first is performed here, voicing the words: "How goodly are thy tents, O Jacob, thy dwellings, O Israel!" Someone played it sarcastically—or was it an unconscious choice? The irony, in any event, is twofold and bitter: for this Gentile prophet, Balaam, was a "hater of Israel," and, as the Midrash reflects, "wanted to curse [Israel], and found himself blessing [them]."

The irony becomes even more exacerbated when the musical element is considered. The song is a classic specimen of the orientalist trend in the "invented tradition" of Hebrew folk songs, an organic and vital part of the Zionist enterprise, aimed at drawing Jews out of Europe, towards the imagined desertlike Palestina-Eretz-Yisrael.[31] Accordingly, this emerging corpus reverts no more to the liturgical Jewish modes that dominated much of the Jewish music discussed in this volume. Its modality is of a different type—in the present case it ranges between the natural minor and the Dorian modes (the region of "church" or pseudo-Greek modes, as Harold Powers termed them), readapted for this made-up musical lore. The glissando in the fourth measure enhances the oriental flavor of the special Arabic term *zifzif* (coarse sand) and imitates the call of

Ex. 7.2. Yedidya Admon, "Gamal G'mali," from
Jacob Schönberg (ed.) *Shirej Eretz
Israel*, 87–88.

the rider to his animal, while the syncopated rhythm of the first four measures takes the melody into the realm of a slow hora ("in the tempo of the camel"). The last four measures give vent to the voice of the rider in the wasteland, now in the Dorian mode, to squarely close it—as befits a folk song—in the original tonality and melodic line.

A group of full-fledged, mostly European-born composers, all ideologically oriented, were involved, since the beginning of the twentieth century, in the making of a Hebrew song corpus, distinguished from both Western European tradition and the Jewish exilic one. They searched for a sonority that would reflect both their landscape imaginaries and the Zionist enterprise, drawing on oriental sources—both Arabic and Jewish—in accordance with the dictates of the Sephardic pronounced Hebrew.[32] The song was included among many others in the highly popular *Shirej Eretz Israel* by Jacob Schönberg, published in Berlin in the 1930s, which achieved a biblical status for many Zionist groups in Germany and other German-speaking communities and countries.[33]

The irony is deepened when Schönberg's description of his project is considered (written in 1935). Clearly deriving from the Herderian *Volksgeist* ideas, it points to the parallel and interrelated motions of the Zionist and the Nazi movements that brought the twain to some inevitable encounters in the prewar years.[34] Jacob Schönberg's text also echoes elements from Hermann Cohen's appraisal of the Jewish recitative, while planting it on an "independent [musical] soil," subtly differentiating the exilic from the "rooted" musical element:

> [T]he musical form of the Hebrew song does not have a limiting unity. The conventional notation is not able to properly express the melody of the Jewish song in general, and that of the oriental one in particular. Apart from dance melody, whose musical rhythm is defined, the Jewish song does not depend on a predetermined measure. . . . The acquaintance with the special musical character of the Hebrew folk song and the deep penetration into its musical feeling are prerequisites for a deep knowledge of the various expressions of its spirit. As the Hebrew nation is dispersed among the gentiles, so finds its psychological substance a faithful echo in her many songs. The new Hebrew Eretz-Yisraeli song has an independent character, and it is created out of an enormous will to build new life. It is related to the work of redeeming the homeland's soil. We see here the roots and seeds for a natural development of the Hebrew folk song.[35]

True, while most of these complicated meanings would have been lost on the average Nazi German viewer of the film, it was left there for posterity. At the time, the song could function as a metonymical mark of the search for country and nationhood, for those who planned to leave this inferno and did not manage to, as would soon become clear. Their voice, in any event, reaches us even today, creating an insiders' oratorical moment, as do other musical items, in this and the subsequent quotations addressed below.

The next stage in the "Jew's progress," again "Jewish-musically" signaled, follows Süß' advice to his Duke to disperse his rebellious council, recruiting, instead, mercenaries, so as to become an absolute sovereign. The financial support for this hired armed force should be drawn from his fellow Jews, he schemes, and the Rabbi must give his blessing to it. Süß enters the synagogue in the midst of a festival. The Jews are gathered there, vigorously engaged in "heterophonic chant-mumbling." The ark is open; a Torah scroll is taken out and the cantor, with a nobler look than our former singer, solemnly recites a tune derived from the High Holidays' motifs (ex. 7.3): "Sh^{e}ma Yisrael . . . Hear, O Israel: the Lord our God, the Lord is one."

We have heard the famous verse from secretary Levy's lips in one of the troubled moments in an earlier scene, but here it functions differently. The festival is Simchat Torah: The Joy of the Torah. It is the very last day in the series of Tishrei Festivals, commencing with Rosh Hashanah. Not burdened anymore with notions of repentance and judgment, the holiday marks the annual opening of the Torah reading cycle, celebrated, among other things, by dancing with all the scrolls stored in the ark (not in this staged ritual, however, which uses only one), through seven major encirclements (*Hakafot*) of the *Bima*, each including many rounds. The hazzan initiates the ritual with the opening "Shᵉma Yisrael," the congregation iterates—but Süß has already grabbed the Rabbi for a private consultation, urging him to consent to his plan. The people's celebratory singing voices continue to emerge from below (repeating the same verse, over and over again, not according to custom, which includes the reciting of a series of verses), and when Rabbi Loew concedes, Süß joins the dancing people together with the Rabbi (fig. 7.3). Now the men (according to Jewish law, women are not allowed to take part) dance to a typical Hasidic *niggun*, singing the major *piyyut* of the day: "Sisu Ve-simḥu Be-simḥat Torah" (delight and be merry in joy of the Torah). Musically, these two units are not connected; the first is old, maybe even part of the Missinai Niggunim, and is

Ex. 7.3. Shᵉma Yisrael, transcription from "extra Jew's"
fake davening in Harlan's *Jud Süß*.

Fig. 7.3. Süß participates in Simḥat Torah's dances, Veit Harlan
(*Jud Süß*). The "Rabbi" stands in front of him. Courtesy of
International Historic Films, Inc.

liturgical, while the melody of the second—the text itself is paraliturgical and its tune not obligatory—was then, at the most, two hundred years in use. While the dance fades, the "oriental" Jew from the previous musical scenes reappears, rounding off the scene with an ongoing "ululation" (or jubilation, depending on the listener's viewpoint); this again is not an organic conclusion of the ritual, but rather a staged cadence.

CRIME AND PUNISHMENT

We reverse back to Dorothea's harpsichord. Now she is singing and playing alone, no man to support her (her father was arrested by the Jew, her hastily wedded husband is recruited for the revolutionary enterprise), and upon the third phrase she closes the notebook and breaks down. She will never resume the music.

The introductory juxtaposition is, thus, reinforced: Jews, however vociferous, are stronger; Christians, though harmonious, weaker. Jewish music is triumphant; German music is in defeat, relying on the feminine, weak element and thus collapsing. We are back in the "feminine zone" visited several times in the present study; this one proves most stereotyped. Upon hearing her "Mario" (Faber) screaming, under the pressure of (Süß' messengers') torture, this "Tosca" (Dorothea) will not be as resourceful as her great Italian (and formidably musical) counterpart. She will fall into that brutal man's lap, and from there, in a far less heroic suicidal action than that of the diva—hurl herself to her death in the river.

At least her dead body will inspire manly spirits. The funeral march (could they hear it?—the music is seemingly nondiegetic but seems nonetheless to direct their steps, thus functioning as a "heavenly heard" music) will resemble that of heroic Siegfried, in the most elaborate symphonic number of the entire film. Unlike that of Siegfried, this march is composed of permutations of one and the same "All' mein' Gedanken" motif, driving the action to its dissonant (however harmonic cliché) conclusion, whose dramatic meaning is "throwing out the Jew." As in *Don Giovanni*, this will not take place through a direct causal chain, for, while the mourners are marching toward the palace, its people are engaged in a hedonistic, Jewicized ball, wrapped with Mozartian music. Like Don Giovanni, the Jewish rogue also demands a deus ex machina to forestall his extermination—in this case, the Duke's (historically warranted) sudden death (here related to his fury at his rebellious subjects). The last punitive action against the Jew will indeed restore order. Like the scoundrel in many of the Grimms' stories, the Jew reverts to his initial state, even begins to *mauscheln*, losing the gloss of courtly finesse he had acquired in between.

And the music—German music—after this purge, could it be restored? Familial harmony has not been recovered—the film insists upon its fractures—only a bereaved father, Sturm, now assuming leadership, faces his (nondiegetic) audience, in a counter gesture to that of wise Nathan's judge, reaching those future witnesses and viewers, in a music-less oratorical moment:[36]

> Every Jew must leave Württemberg in three days. Jews are banned from all Württemberg from February 4th, 1738. May our descendents hold firmly to this too, so they can save themselves much sorrow and save their goods and life and the blood of their children and their children's children—

And a solemn fanfare, still drawing on "All' mein Gedanken," seals it all, to the very End.

German music, that amazing, glorified legacy reduced to a tiny, primitive *Weise* (it even provides the tune to the organ accompaniment in the church wedding ritual)—how and why? Curiously, the Jewish music that is presented here is far more variegated. Apart from the fanfaric coronation and execution music, the little "All' mein' Gedanken" comprises all the rest of the diegetic music, and a large part of the nondiegetic, as if all German music, perhaps from the movie's historical time onwards, had become a *Mischung*, racially mixed music, defiling the pure Aryan element. Historically, as this book attests, there is something to this tacit claim, though Mozart and his generation can be so "blamed" only through a weird, retrospective act. This is, perhaps, the golden calf's revenge: Goebbels and collaborators wished to highlight an *Urjudentum*, or primitive Judaism;[37] they ended up with a primitive Germanism. The great musical tradition whose major line of development coincides more or less with the span of time during which Jews penetrated German society, became suspect. (The use in *Der ewige Jude* of Bach's famous Toccata in D to juxtapose true art to the degenerate is likewise caught in a paradox, for it unwittingly "competed" with the opening number in Walt Disney's *Fantasia* of that year, which Americanized, if not globalized, the piece).[38] This accounts for much of the confusion prevailing in Nazi times up until the end of the Third Reich regarding "right" and "wrong" musical repertories.

EXTRA JEWS

We remain then with extra Jewish music, and with musical extra Jews. Who were these extras and where did it all take place? The answer to these questions, following Tegel's meticulous archival research, is clear, and does make sense: they are not Jews from the Lublin ghetto as was formerly held (though preparations in that direction were well under way at a certain point); they are Jews from Prague—"extra" Jews who were hired for the movie (this was not publicized; Goebbels disclaimed the participation of any actor with "Jewish blood" in the film).[39] Very few of these Jews survived the war. They collaborated,[40] and the reasons could have been many and rather obvious at this time for Jews in conquered Prague. Unlike their (real Jewish) counterparts in *Der ewige Jude*, they were not forced to cooperate, though, as Tegel notes, they obviously performed under duress.[41] Some, however—we know at least of those from the Zionist Beit He-ḥalutz—willfully chose to stay away.

Still most testimonies concur that Harlan treated his extras properly. He was even moved by their synagogal music![42] And yet he knew well—too well—what his masters wanted from him. The fact that his extras turned out to be "modern" Prague Jews, rather than the *Ostjuden* of East Poland, has some poignant implications in the present history.

The place in which the synagogal scene unfolds is a replica of the famous *Altneuschul* of the renowned Maharal, Rabbi Judah Loew (!) ben Bezalel (1525–1608). This is meant to be easily identifiable, and documents concur.[43] Apparently it is not *"unsere Synagoge,"* the one in which Kafka's animal dwelled. Yet those recruited for the enterprise are from that Jewish milieu. They complained, we learn, about the fact that they had to dance to Hasidic tunes; that was not their style of worship: they were "modern Jews."[44] And yet they knew how to perform the way insiders do. Was the choice to repeat the "Shᵉma Yisrael" several times (unlike the "correct" ritual) their idea, to emphasize to subsequent connoisseurs that this is not a "real" one? Or maybe Kafka's animal, before it too had to find a new abode, was evoking the repetition of this ultimate verse (Jews used to voice it before their sacrificial act), sharing with them the still unspeakable knowledge of their impending future? And who devised the opening "mumbling" shot? This, it seems, could come from Nazi agents, as was the demand for rocking the body's upper part, for they searched precisely for these elements in the "real" ethnographic footage they took in Lodz for *Der ewige Jude*.

The *Gamal G'mali* performance betrays another element: the singer (Harlan, in his trial, could not recall his name),[45] whether the bearded figure or someone else who did his dubbing, must have learned the melody from an "insider," say, a Zionist messenger from Palestine, or a recording.[46] For he sings according to the composer's (unwritten) intention, in the Eretz-Israeli performance practice noted above. Moments of choice thus lurk from in-between the scenario, staging, and editing, conferring an unwitting subjectivity onto those who were supposed to be totally deprived of it. This becomes even more accentuated when compared to their Lodz coreligionists, in *Der ewige Jude*, who, to a certain extent, were their camera's victims, for better or for worse—usually for worse. For they had to live up to all the noise stereotypes we mentioned throughout the book, which the camera revealed as the ultimate abjection: the swaying of the body, the allegedly unmusical whining of the cantor, the buzz and mumbling of the congregation (stronger than the Prague counterpart's), the "strange" ritual props—*Tᵉphilin* and *Tallit*, and so forth.

Yet these too may be assessed from a posterior, insider perspective. What really takes place in the synagogal section of this "documentary," ritually and musically, is a collage of footage from basically three services, between which the movie alternates, obviously without acknowledgment.[47] It seems to have taken place in the period during the Days of Awe, as attested not only by the liturgy and music, but also by the embroidered inscription on the ark's curtain: "Our Father and King, open the gates of heaven to our prayers."[48] Other parts draw from daily prayers of this season: the men are adorned with *Tᵉphilin*, carrying parts of *Sᵉliḥot* (in their typical tunes); then there is a part, again, from Friday night (Shabbat) service—we hear the last verses (except for the following bracketed parts of Psalm 29) in the traditional, solemn minor mode recitative, delivered by a highly competent and musical cantor: ["The Lord sat enthroned at the flood]; yea, the Lord sitteth as King for ever. The Lord will give strength unto His people; [the Lord will bless his people with peace"]. Their import, in the present context, is again unwittingly poignant. There is also a section of the removal of the Torah from the ark, on a Saturday or Holiday morning. All this is performed by people who are quite oblivious to the camera; a rare and rather authentic record of the services of these doomed Jews. We can only bemoan the fact that it is all too short and cursory and that the voice-over eclipses our actual hearing.

The contiguity of the synagogal scene of *Der ewige Jude* with that of the cruel Jewish slaughtering ritual cannot, in the context of the present book, be eschewed. It seems to brace the line of argument drawn in the previous chapter: noise and totemic rites are interconnected, if not interchangeable. Here, the noises of the dying bull and that of the synagogue become one. In the association this movie wishes to engrave in its viewers, the bull is indeed the (Egyptian) German god (Germans are presented as the animal-loving nation); Jewish noise is interpreted by the narrator as a non-service, an antireligious form (in the spirit of Edelmann, but without any relativism or humor, however sarcastic).

But by rendering the Jews as the epitome of civilization's usurpers, the Nazi authorities exposed their own precarious position. Kafka's slaughter scene from the *altes Blatt* comes to mind, and, confronting this sequence, one wonders who the barbarian is, and who the cultured group. If slaughtering customs and "noisy" prayer are precisely the embodiment, as Reik argued, of a law-based culture struggling with its own archaic-arcane sense of guilt and culpability, their distorted representation in *Der ewige Jude* could betray the Nazis' ultimate program to establish a brutal nature-culture society. Based on an imagined, quasi-incestuous solidarity, it meant to forgo all human contracts, as Jean-Gérard Bursztein argues.[49] The Nazi authorities' ambivalent position vis-à-vis the slaughter scene betrays their own hesitations, whether this would transmit onto their audience, without exposing too blatantly their own shameful prospects. Their audience, indeed, recoiled from the scene more than from its referents (the Jews), and voted with their feet; the movie, as indicated above, was a fiasco. In any event, even if among that audience there were those who read the inscription on the movie screen, it might have been, at that point, too late to affect, even slightly, the course of ensuing events.

* * *

It should be counted among the oddities of history, and the mysteries of human consciousness, that a Nazi phantasmagoric notion of the purification of German music from its Jewish element would resonate in a monumental oeuvre of the kind the anti-Nazi political exile Thomas Mann was completing while Third Reich Germany precipitated itself to its final doom. Neighboring in remote California, not far away from Adorno and Schoenberg (among other renowned refugees and émigrés), Mann eventually bequeathed to a postwar world his *Doktor Faustus*[50]—a monumental oratorical work in prose (narrated by a "Catholic evangelist," Dr. Phil. Severus Zeitblom), an epitome of a baroque tragedy, a *Trauerspiel* of the kind the author's tragic contemporary, Walter Benjamin, so powerfully theorized.

At the beginning, Mann laid the foundations for a possible world and a probable narrative—"the like of it happens," as another contemporary, the Austrian Robert Musil, defined it in *his* historical novel, *Der Mann ohne Eigenschaften*. This world is situated in recognizable landscapes and cityscapes; its historico-cultural circumstances were familiar to readers coming from its parallel "real" world, who would also be acquainted with its prevalent codes of behavior and common modes of speech (those of early twentieth-century Germany). Life threads of historical composers, philosophers, and writers interweave to form the hero's predicament and the life course of those surrounding him; the works he composed and others that are mentioned, both musical and literary, are either modeled on existing ones or actually allude to them. Yet these plot components are interlaced with odd, quasi-magical scripts, symbolic names, and archetypal, mythical elements. Working together, they transform the fictive world into a baroque-allegorical sphere, which, according to Benjamin, is basically revolving on doom and decline, culminating in the passion story of an individual—saint or criminal—verging on apocalypse.

The individual is Adrian Leverkühn, composer. He makes a pact with a Satan, or a Mephistopheles, to attain the kind of artistic achievements that lie outside his scope, such that would clearly detach him from old bourgeois forms— and cliché sentiments—he both detests and craves. Just before this fatal event, he hits upon a musical invention: a twelve-tone method, one that was forged by its historical creator, Arnold Schoenberg, for apparently similar reasons (about a "dozen years later"). Eventually, the work becomes ruptured in its own *mise en abîme*—the oratorio *Lamentation of Doctor Faustus*, the imagined composer's final work, which signifies and hastens his ultimate collapse, to later coincide with that of Nazi Germany. Though completed, the oeuvre was never performed.

This is not the place to recount the tragic events befalling this final alter ego of the Jewish composer, nor to assess his imaginary aural worlds in relation with that of his model. Neither is it the place to examine the eventual complaints of the "original" ego—Schoenberg—who felt doubly betrayed: both by his disciple's (Berg) disciple Theodor Adorno—who transmitted that script of twelve-tone music (never a secret one) to the writer—and by the latter, who omitted any reference to the historical composer. But it is a place for briefly noting that the huge historical Germanic space this Faustian opus lays out—again finding the Reformation as the point of departure for all crucial unfolding of this culture and "race"—is basically *judenrein*.

Jews are orbiting in this space: there is a one-time popping up of a learned, "sharply religious" Talmudist Dr. Carlebach—the Orthodox Rabbi of "Kaiseraschern";[51] a more profound acquaintance with a disgusting Dr. Chaim Breisacher—an anticulture philosopher of culture; and a gallant, ridiculous music entrepreneur ("looking more fashionable than you and me") by the name of Saul Fitelberg (a shtetl Jew assimilated into a French, "progressive" world). And there is a "real" Otto Klemperer who fictionally conducted in Frankfurt, 1925, Leverkühn's *Apocalypsis cum figuris* (the kind of work Klemperer performed at the time in Berlin). There is a brief mention of Mahler and Mendelssohn as sources of inspiration for the fictional composer, and a rather degrading allusion to Meyerbeer. Moreover, there is even a typical acknowledgment of a Jewish audience's sensitive openness to Adrian's music (reminiscent of Wagner's adoration by Jews) and their general "musicality." These can be all summed up as stereotyping Jewish presence, concomitantly, insinuating their noisy—now in the sense of parasitical—essence.[52]

Surely Mann did not directly mean it—himself the husband of Katia Pringsheim, daughter of a prominent, secular Jewish family of intellectuals.

Yet that which *is* essential—Schoenberg's creative journey, which he embarked upon, *qua* Austrian Jew, twice inside-outsider of German culture (now labeled/libeled *entartete* [degenerate] *Musik*)—was appropriated, confiscated by Mann's authorial voice as purely German, as thoroughly originating from old Teutonic worlds and underworlds. As if the enterprise of this fictional creator could have been undertaken, say, by a descendent of Bach or Handel, *ohne Juden* around; as though his achievements, the new compositional strategies, his oratorical bent, his pitting of word and tone against each other could have been products emerging from within the historical furnaces of Thuringia or Bavaria, their theological legacies, familial heritages, and literary lore. All this without the Jews ever having lived there, fertilizing this culture with their learning, prayers, and ideas, their commerce, science, and art: their forms of life and death. And without their voices—concerted and deserted, expressive of joy and sorrow, articulating dream, devotion, and devastation.

EPILOGUE: REFLECTIONS ON THE INTERSECTING BOUNDARIES OF VOICE AND COMMUNITY

No time to rejoice for those who walk among noise and deny the voice

—*T. S. Eliot*, Ash Wednesday V

A lingering and tortuous history of sonic entanglements between Jews and Christians arrives to its abrupt ending. It revolved around visions, vocalities, and verbal expressions that reverberated and reflected one another in ways the author of this book could only dimly have anticipated. Of this history, beginning some time in the High Middle Ages, the last two hundred years—marked between the fictive 1738 and the factual 1938 to 1940—were the most crucial. These are the years that Harlan's *Jud Süß*, epitomized in Sturm's oratorical harangue, wished to rewrite, replay, without Jewish interference, vocal and otherwise.

But Sturm was wrong; or maybe only partially. He was wrong because the infiltration of the "defiled" elements started long before. He himself marked that time: in front of the Duke and the council, he quoted Luther's 1542–43 behest "to set fire to their synagogues,"[1] conferring theological weight to his otherwise *bürgerlich* civil repute. (From his distant shore, also Thomas Mann marked this epochal moment as the gestation of quintessential German music.) The omnipresent "All' mein' Gedanken" in the movie soundtrack from the 1450 *Lochamer Liederbuch* pushes this time mark even earlier. The two dates are connected: for the creation of his new liturgical canon, Luther, as has been already indicated, based a considerable part of his chorale melodies on German lieder contrafacta. It was also noted that Jews, at that time, began to borrow auditory capital from Christian neighbors more systematically, and gradually and sporadically adopted its related apparatus, including musical notation, compositional strategies, and polyphonic structures. The theological sanctioning of such appropriation, which transpired about that time, mainly in kabbalistic circles, eventually supported, in the eastern part of Europe, the Hasidic musical revolution. Building its musical corpus largely through non-Jewish contrafacta, this became, in due time, another source of "authentic" Jewish music.

A remote descendant of such sanctioning theology reverberates in Sonder-ling-Schoenberg's *Kol Nidre*. Schoenberg also marked the sixteenth century as a watershed in the making of Ashkenazi Jewish music (following common opinions), though his explanations as to this turn remain problematic. Scholars of Ashkenazi Jewish music have sensed a similar periodization, although it is still lacking in substance. The main implication of this demarcation for the present history is that only since that time do we begin to form a clearer (and better documented) notion of (Ashkenazi) Jewish music, which becomes increasingly lucid in the course of the eighteenth century and thereafter. Everything that unfolded before the sixteenth century appears open to sometimes wild conjectures.

Treading on this uncertain ground (as I did too, in the book's opening chapter) presupposes acknowledgment of the largely dissociated picture of that time, as attested by the traces—partly bequeathed and partly rediscovered—left by this period for much later generations. Among the noise accusation traces, narrative and fictional elements loom large. And yet, despite the horrifying endings of these narratives, no Jew, as far as we know (unlike those charged with ritual murder), was executed on the grounds of his unmusical, "murderous" behavior. Still, rather than foment hospitality, these stories arguably exacerbated the hostility of Christians towards Jews. Moreover, vocal/musical disparateness between the communities prevailed and, since that time and henceforth, became increasingly acknowledged, determined by divergent psycho-theological preferences and determining dissociated senti-*mentalities*. The question as to the kind of reciprocity that transpired, nevertheless, between the musics of the adversarial communities, prior to or following the mutual sonic prohibitions, remains open to further study.

If, indeed, the *Christian* Reformation unlatched the spiritual mobility of music, rendering sonic dams more permeable, and, concomitantly, more communal and cross-communal, the eventual reformation of the *Jewish* autochthonous "noisy" legacy should be regarded as its belated wave. A proponent of the latter movement, Gustav Karpeles (1848–1909), even celebrated the connection of the two musical movements, by stating, in his address at the celebration of "Herr Lewandowski's fiftieth anniversary as director of music," how Luther proved the conciliatory power of music to stand "high above the barriers raised by religious differences."[2] Yet the indigenous sonic element that it aimed to amend persisted, in both reality and fiction, and not only in "aboriginal" contexts, such as east European shtetls. Concomitantly, the incriminating noisy element found new expression, preoccupying those who thought it was long overcome by the "harmonization" of the two cultures.

All this brings us to the last major query of this study: how to historicize the *longue durée* of these vocal fictions of noise and harmony. If this "story" mainly resides in imagined constructions and reconstructions—whether benign or malicious—what kind of historical weight should one ascribe to it? Should we consider it, indeed, as a continuous unfolding, or else, as a broken, loosely connected string of events or creations? More particularly, to what extent may the psychoanalytic terms, endeared by Reik, and interspersed, however haphazardly, throughout the book, lend themselves to such historicization? These series of questions touch upon one of the major queries that run through the book: what kind of encounter, of modern insiders and outsiders, did the resurfacing of the noise accusation entail, after all? And, last but not least, what kind of repercussions has it left, beyond its own *durée*, that is, on postmodern sonic cultures?

While I cannot do full justice to all these questions, I believe that the first four underlie trails mapped throughout the book. For a general historical assessment, it is tempting to make use of grand syndromes, such as the one recently introduced by the French philosopher Jacques Rancière.[3] Rancière proposed a scheme of threefold "artistic regimes" governing the political "distribution of the sensible" in Western tradition. Though he only cursorily referred to the aural dimension, and despite running the risk of overgeneralization, his three epochal divisions (briefly mentioned in chapter 2) may serve, in our case, to access three perspectives. These divisions include, first, the *ethical* regime of images (or, alternatively, the theocratic regime), according to which the aesthetic is subsumed under the examination of images (of the divine) and the right to produce such images. Platonic in its essence, our medieval sonic contests, on both sides of the fence, neatly fall within this division. The second division, termed by Rancière the poetic or the regime of *representations* in the arts, follows, isolating artistic imitations from forms of discourse abiding by "law" or "truth." This (Aristotelian) regime is engaged in the "distribution of resemblances according to principles of verisimilitude, appropriateness, or correspondences." From the *Merchant* through *Madre Ebrea*, including also the later *Juden* and *Nathan der Weise*, the call to abide by rules of genre and psychological realism relativized and ironicized fictional characters, whether friends or foes. This effected the loosening of the libelous grip in that period, coinciding with other ideological shifts.

The third division, a Schillerian *aesthetic* regime, apparently frees art from rules (epitomized, presumably, by Walther von Stolzing's "master-singing" against a literal [and ululating] Beckmesser), relegating it to the unintentional and the unconscious. Art, in this regime, becomes identified with life itself, both of the individual and the political community, performing their own subjectivities. "Expressive relationships" are probed in a suspended past (a medieval Seder, a Bach Passion, or the "Songs of Zion in a Foreign Land") and unfathomed future. In the language used in the present book, these orientations are tantamount to a strong predisposition for oratorical genres and moments, which may serve, however, contradictory political goals.

Schematic as this periodization appears in this brief presentation, it seems to make sense of ruptures, juxtapositions, and associations introduced throughout the book, and to indicate the embeddedness of this history in major trends and transformations of European cultural history. Inasmuch as a cultural history is, first and foremost, a history of imagined and performed constructs, the metamorphoses of the music libel against the Jews play a significant role in it, highlighting some of its major predicaments. Determining first, who possesses proper sounds, moving then to the ways sounds shape difference, this cultural history finally contributes its part to our understanding of why the sonic becomes crucial in the making of political entities as well as in their deconstruction.

This brings us to a consideration of imaginaries conceived in psychoanalytic terms, mainly those connected with trauma, the return of the repressed, or the flashing back of the dissociated (two opposing alternatives), and to explore the ways in which they fare as modes of connectivity, outside clinical premises, that is, in grand historical narratives. To what extent, one should ask, did the noise accusations and their repercussions partake in a traumatic perception of Ashkenazi Jewry of their own history (according to the assessment of certain historians), that is, the incessant haunting of its distressful pasts within the (unredeemed) experienced presents? In other words, could the works and events related in the book's first chapter have been historically conceivable outside their vexed, however fragmented, re-collection by modern authors? If such a process is far from being exceptional in modern historiography (especially with regard to subalterns' history), what kind of working through or out (of) this past characterizes our case, and how does this affect our understanding of this unfolding in terms of historical realism?

The theory of trauma is highly contested, and the pitfalls of applying it to a history of a collective, rather than individuals, have been long noted. The following lines cannot do even meager justice to the richness of these discussions and their related caveats, and yet some of the ideas raised in this connection may suggest a possible insight into our "case." If for Reik the roots of the shofar's tremorous appeal lie in the repression of a catastrophic trauma, later theoreticians and practitioners, including Freud himself, would hesitate to ascribe to traumatic occurrences any encoded (symbolized) content, which can be, as such, repressed. Analyzing the genealogy of the concept through the twentieth century, Ruth Leys discerns a theoretical line linking traumatic dissociation to preverbal emotional identifications with an immediate other, in a preliminary dyad (of parent/caregiver and baby).[4] Preceding the distinction between subject and object, this developmental stage is characterized also in terms of *sympathetic* bonding and *mimetic* connectivity. Trauma is aligned to a moment in which primordial identification is breached, shattering the protective shield provided by the primal dyad. The effacement of boundaries will subsequently resurface at analogous moments of breach, when the self becomes a victim of aggression enacted within an original or substitute mimetic binding, involving, as such, a sense of identification with a perpetrator. Experienced thereafter mainly through involuntary repetition of fragmented experience, a healing process may take place, when a subject begins to rehabilitate itself through a *diegetic* process: a narrative reorganization of the dissociated elements, which, however incoherent, may facilitate the resumption of the lost context and lead to a better bounded agency.

Subject to all the necessary qualifications of shifting from the interactions between individuals to those between communities (which are still made up of individual cases) this kind of breach and eventual healing may help to enunciate the interrelations between trauma, vocalities, and sympathy in our account. The imitative self-immolation of the adversarial communities, each in relation to itself and its reflected other, is a case in point, that of historical fragmentation is another. One may further ascribe the narrative impulse beyond the unfolding of this history to the attempt to work through dispersed sonic elements, and discern the strong bent, on the side of accusers, to connect the noise defamation to the question of the limits and limitations of compassion. But at this point one may ask, with Ruth Ginsburg, "whose trauma is it, anyway"?[5] Is it the aggressor's trauma, whether insider or outsider (as implied by Reik's "Shofar" and Freud's *Moses and Monotheism*) or that of the victim? And if shared by both, as the notion of sympathetic bonding (or binding) indicates, how is it related to subsequent elaborations of the concept of sympathy, pivotal in the unfolding of the music libel history?

Replacing, momentarily, sympathy with symbiosis may help us reassess themes and arguments raised in relation to the medieval "counternarratives" and their musico-theological counterpoints within this larger historical and conceptual framework, and further fathom their *longue durée*. Whereas the millennia-long development of symbiotic relations of Jews and Christians has become a truism, and has already been connected to a psychoanalytic discourse, the vocal element sharpens this claim and gives it a twist. The preverbal quality of vocal expression emerges throughout the book in various contexts and connections, from the Prioress' infantile harangue to Rousseau's primordial speech and from Mirah's primal intonations to Schoenberg's Sprechgesang/Sprechstimme. In recent experimental research, it has become amply clear that rudimentary vocal dialogues between parent and baby are crucial for the normal affective bonding of the developing human being.[6] Prior to any symbolic communication, attentive vocal reciprocation may "go deeper into us than other things" as Mirah Lapidoth sensitized us, providing the basic sensory infrastructure on which the sympathetic self grows (as Paul de Man helped us to conceive, at a certain point along the way). When world and words subsequently engage the developing subject in various encoded ways, affective vocalities, for better or for worse, are still vital in effecting a reconnection to primal layers of attachment. Skipping symbolizations, they cannot be repressed as such, in unconscious recesses of the mind, and, a fortiori, they cannot "return" at a later stage as their inadvertent symptoms. But they may intertwine with the traumatic, which likewise floats unsymbolized. The immediacy of cries, weeping, and lament upon an inconceivable infliction befalling human beings may point to a shared etiology, or even, to a mechanism enabling a release of the affective charges through vocal expression.

Abiding by reciprocality, the vocal is thus both inside and outside us, evoking self-expressions as well as comforting or excruciating external intonations. The ever-present, unfathomable synagogal animal in Kafka's tale may stand for it, as for the irretrievable memory of what begot it. Its observer can only generally grasp it, in trauma-laden words akin to those expressed by the above-quoted Karpeles: the "endless, oppressive, anxious wail, sounding adown, through two thousand years, like a long-drawn sigh, reverberating in far-reaching echoes: 'How long, O Lord, how long!'"[7]

This accentuates the course reiterated throughout the book, that of sacrifice (the source of trauma) to weeping (lament), to partially conventionalized liturgical system, preserving its vitality through nonstrict norms of performance (producing heterophonic mumbling). It adds up to the notion that this kind of reaction carries with it its own modes of commemoration, allowing for affective release which is never fully detached from the originating events. These vocal expressions create, in turn, internal paths of sympathy and contagion, superseding those that have been (traumatically) severed by the atrocious acts, themselves perceived only unstably and retroactively.

Such a retroactive perception, that regards the reshaping of the synagogal soundscape as part of the (internal) therapeutic process of the community as a whole (rather than in terms of adopting external ideals), is exemplified in an 1835 address by Abraham Geiger, the renowned *Wissenschaft des Judentums* scholar. Geiger summons many of the noise accusation's ingredients, explaining that with the burden of "cries of fear" that "resound round about us . . . where the ear had grown deaf to harmony, where men desire only to sigh and to beat their breasts so that the God of mercy may withhold His chastising hand," there is no possibility to renew ancient beauty, solemnity, and dignity, no emancipatory path.[8] An operative conclusion follows, proposing, maybe all too easily, the dismembering of the centuries-long vicious circle of abasement.

The complexity of the vocal phenomenon, what it stood for and how it functioned, reverberates in a reverse mode on the side of the aggressors. Harmoniousness serves thus a highly defensive social structure for the latter, blocking reactive sonorities from infiltrating their space, rendering them bland and uniform. Rationalized in politico-theological terms (perfidious Jews are crying loud to their forsaking God), changing aesthetic and historical conditions such as aesthetic relativism, ethnographic realism, and satirical hyperbolism, while enervating its sting, still maintained the underlying affective force of this sonic economy.

The proposed conceptual framework may also account for the powerful emotional impact that the rise of the ethics of compassion and the aesthetics of the beautiful and the sublime had, in the course of the Enlightenment, on inheritors of these vocal cultures. A shared sympathetic universe appealed to Jews who were formerly banished from it into their humiliating community of sympathy, especially since it was wedded to a universalizing aesthetics, which still cherished (subjective) lachrymose moments. Even then, Jews and Gentiles attuned differently to these new possibilities. Questions of pity and compassion, as we have seen, divided friends of the Lessing-Mendelssohn's caliber, with the latter among the first to apprehend compassion's perils, even within its new ecumenical frame. It was as though he could prefigure the Schopenhauer-Wagner condescending approach, and the sinister recoupling of compassion with abhorrence. Mendelssohn seems to opt for the "sympathetic" direction developed by Smith, a direction that his grandson Felix practically adopted, and that George Eliot would further elaborate and refine. The British egalitarian spirit could thus bear poignant synergetic moments of vocal reciprocity, such as those yielded by Nathan and Byron's collaboration. These moments left their imprint on a society that still resounded with its notorious music libels' past, even throughout the nineteenth century.

That the rise of Jewish musicians to the forefront of the European stage would coincide with that of nationalist and protoracist ideologies, reawakening dormant phobias, seems almost predetermined by the above entanglements. This coincidence ever exposed the tenuousness of the sympathetic texture of interfaith relations, and unwittingly bolstered intrafaith bonds, even if formulated in harmonistic-ecumenical terms, as in the case of Lewandowski, celebrated by both Karpeles and Hermann Cohen. The striving to normalize the abnormal, rendering the Jewish case a universal paradigm, is typical of many of the post-Wagnerian reactions to the allegation, and mostly of our modernist Viennese authors. Some, like Reik, reversed the order: they opted for abnormalizing the normal, turning Christian harmony into an existential noise. Freud himself, in his conceptualization of trauma, undecidedly oscillated between these two options, as expounded by Ginsburg.[9] These options, rendered in the present book as harmonizing noise, on the one hand, or cacophonizing harmony, on the other, pertain to various interpretations of the origin of sound proper, and of proper sounds, connecting as such the psychoanalytical with the theological and the aesthetic, and all with the particular sonic. With some ruminations on these connections I conclude the major part of the epilogue.

"Proper sounds" are what triggered the paradox entailed in the process of "assimilating" Jewish music (and other minorities' music)—concerning the extent to which it could retain an identity recognized by its "possessors" despite reformatory measures that recurred in various contexts in the nineteenth century and beyond. Jews who favored that cross-breed realized that there were (Jewish) noisy elements they wished to dispose of, and—to borrow Vogel's ominous formulation—(Christian) "black tar" vocalities they preferred to avoid, and in between a thin edge of a "decorated" aural hybrid. It was Heine, among both contemporary insiders and outsiders, who could perceive, ahead of his time, the inherent tension between the syncretic (and thus "noisy") nature of all indigenous musical traditions and their capacity to configure, nevertheless, specific ethnic attachments, designating shared origins.

As was pointed out, Rousseau and Herder (following a host of contemporary philosophers and men of letters) opened a path, theoretical and practical, in this direction, for their concept of origins bypasses, to a large extent, issues of national genealogy, patriotism, and priority. Moreover, it was the Jean Jacques from Calvinist Geneva who ridiculed Gregorian chant as vociferous and lumbering, which, moreover, he considered as the source of the unwholesome music of Western polyphony. (Dr. Chaim Breisacher, the fictional Jewish autodidact from *Dr. Faustus,* was of the same mind.) Claims to harmony became, from that point, suspicious, until they reached in our time even the defamatory assessment (in line with Kafka's premonitions) that homogenous, "harmonious" systems are basically cruel, "building as they are on the horror of disorder and noise," as Michel Serres put it.[10]

In the nineteenth century, as part of the general "sentimental" proclivity, origins were sought on both the individual and the collective levels, sometimes complementing, sometimes contradicting each other. The *alte Weise,* or old tune, epitomized in *Tristan and Isolde's* act III—an evocation of primordial memories through a dimming consciousness, enabling deep integrative psychic processes—was the reverse side of the search for old tunes on the idealized national level, which were thought to activate similar processes on its related collective unconscious. Curiously, insiders' jargon in the Jewish cantorial realm branded their long inherited and sanctified *Nussaḥ*: *Weise.*

On both individual and collective levels, origins were connected to cherished aesthetic categories from the authentic to the sublime, through the pastoral and the archaic, to the primitive and the primeval. It is the latter pair that seemed to pave the way for the eventual modernist integration of noise into aesthetics, converging industrial, anthropological, and psychoanalytical elements. The abject, the bestial, and the criminal thus found their path into music through various modes of sonic transgression, transmigration, and transplantation. Some authors, mainly of Jewish affiliation, were driven thereby to delve deeply into the productive implications that "meaningful noises" carry for art, polity, and spirit, apparently transcending the former politico-theological distribution of the aural. All in all, sound proper seemed to detach from "proper" sounds, scarifying a conventional sublime for less ready-made satisfactions.

Yet the question of origins never left the stage. The plethora of "origin assumptions," opened through the audial perspectives of this book, may be thus summarized: in the beginning there was a harmonious being and pattern, and as such it was imparted onto the universe, the planets, world music. In an alternative beginning—epitomized in *Moses und Aron*—there were unsynchronized sounds (heterophony); in them music and speech were undivided. God thus communicated His word. In yet another beginning there were deeply ingrained melodies, "All' mein' Gedanken," and other *alte Weisen,* including Missinai Niggunim; they constituted our psychic makeup for generations to come. In the very beginning, however, there were sonic animalistic molecules, not quite distinguishable as such, and certainly not semantically discernable. In another primordial beginning such molecules were of divine descent, myriads of one unified voice that broke down into infinite sound units, and human beings were exhorted to salvage them in their great effort of *Tikkun Olam* (as Schoenberg would in his *Kol Nidre*). Or rather: in the ultimate beginning, there was an archaic bull-god, and it was slaughtered by a younger and more progressive god, whose sounds were full of moaning and repentance. In a more mundane (or is it again mythological?) beginning there was a quiet civilization (one symbolized by a bountiful E-flat *Rheingold* chord) and only modern technology and the boisterous rhythm of life defiled it with noise. Finally, the order, to quote again Michel Serres, has capsized: "In the beginning was noise." God never attempted to create a world devoid of difference.

All these versions of sonic geneses were suggested, or intimated, in the preceding pages. They intrigue, challenge, and enable different lines of creativity; they react to voices, works, events, and ideas in their vicinity. They suggest alternative ontologies, epistemologies, utopias, dystopias, sublime beings, and dismal existences. They bespeak the primacy of the audial over the visual, and point, therefore, to another origin, maybe the vexed origin of the entire history enfolded in these pages: who were those who first heard God's voice, direct and unmediated, on the Holy Mount of Revelation? The Midrash, as we have seen in chapter 2, was unequi*vocal* about the righteous addressees of the Voice (sounded as noise to others). Yet, once they became the world's excommunicated Cains, was their audial revelation transferred onto the faithful believers of the (new) God? Old and New Christians could hold, with T. S. Eliot, that there is "[n]o time to rejoice for those who walk among noise and deny the voice."[11] Pinpointing their identity was not necessary; that was part and parcel of the persistence of the signifier "Jew" throughout many generations and surroundings.

Further reflection on the above genealogies may reveal that they elaborate, negate, or bypass that moment of (assumed) collective sonic revelation. Even the Passions lend themselves to such a reading, to a claim of establishing a point of beginning, one that involves a communal witnessing of the murder of God, the bemoaning it triggers, and its pervasive reenactment and reconnection with the ecclesia and its believers. This may explain, from yet another angle, the ubiquity of oratorical moments throughout the vocal fictions that have populated this book, whether exclusive and competitive or inclusive and reconciling.

What became of Jewish sound in Europe in the aftermath of the events and fictions brought forward in this volume, once the Nazis' stratagem to purge their Europe from its clamor so nightmarishly succeeded? There are poignant attempts, by writers and musicians, Jews and others, to grapple with this sonic vacuum, aiming beyond "the Shriek of Silence"[12] that filled the European air years after the mass murder of Jews, to summon the living voices of Jewish pasts that were forever lost. Momentous as they are, the capacious boundaries of the present book cannot contain them. Moving beyond the Jewish scene, it should be once again emphasized that the seemingly unruly sonic-performative practices that have characterized it are far from being a unique Jewish spécialité. "Clapping, screaming and shouting that may seem jarring to the untrained ear" characterize other groups, maybe similarly engaged in cohesive solidarities and spontaneous communicative norms, sounding as noise to outsiders. The last quotation is, in fact, Barack Obama's autobiographical account of his cherished affiliation with the Trinity Church in Chicago. This, however, brings us back to Jewish predilections: it points to a long-term affinity between African-American and Jewish-American sonic cultures that brought about glorified moments of musical collaborations and coalescences throughout the twentieth century.

This elective affinity could explain, perhaps, why even an American Jew such as Leon Wieseltier could associate the sound of church bells with "a vexing triumphalist sound—the pealing of history," from which his honor as a Jew, he writes, required him to recoil. "When the tintinnabulations of the Church of St. Francis Xavier on Avenue O reached my ears," he relates, "they brought the message that I was a member of a minority."[13] Later, he reflects, listening once to a Christian choir, in an alma mater Oxford college, he would perceive the beauty of it with pain, to later dissociate religion—even Christianity—from beauty. His punch line lies, however, elsewhere: it moves into Harvard Yard, where Muslim vocalities of calling to prayer (*Adhan*), would sound to some as "an infringement upon the liberty of others." Advocating the *Adhan* case, the literary editor of the *New Republic* finds it necessary to sensitize his readers, even toward the end of the first decade of the present millennium, to the fact that an open civil space will always sound cacophonous.

If this is true in liberal America, in the Middle Eastern part of the globe it is all the more so. This brings me—the girl who wished to hear the stars' sweet music and lived through poignant moments in the Polish ("noisy") Ashkenazi synagogue of her parents; who thirstily sipped, at different hours, "passion" Christian music and otherwise; she who grew under the shadow of two young girls, brutally killed because of their Jewishness, some years before she was born, and with a mother who ever heard the songs of Hitler *Jugend*, sung in her childhood by classmates; the present musicologist from Mt. Scopus in Jerusalem, overlooking the city from its eastern end—to utter a few final words, from the present time and place, however momentary and ever-changing as it is.

In the autumnal period in Jerusalem—the graceful days of soft light and open hearts—Rosh Hashanah's shofar blows, ululating from every corner, often mingling with *Adhan* calls, described by an Israeli writer as "a strong wailing that breaks out from the entire city, like a crying voice that turns to heaven and forcefully springs from the big city that is spread on the mountains."[14] Longing for the heavenly spheres, the customary peal of church bells, stemming from the city's spires and towers, tuned their sounds to this polyphony of faiths and liturgies.[15] Apparently the city seems capable of bearing them, despite complaints to the contrary, local and otherwise. Whether mutual lamentation can be heard—this is another question.

These days, the variegated musical life of the deeply divided city rarely brings together—whether in concerts or other performances—an audience from its eastern and western parts. But it has inspired musicians, in the last decades, as in other parts of Israel/Palestine, to engage in a musical dialogue of difference. This sonic openness—an assortment of music from different origins, yet distinguished by an "oriental" character—whether Muslim, Jewish, or Christian, originated in diasporas whose musical affiliations with their surroundings were less colored by accusations and humiliation than the Ashkenazi one. Here and now such dialogues involve people of motley backgrounds. Moving on the waves of "world music" trends, they seem to transcend them, in quest of the lost and the unborn; to combine diverse musicalities and their related harmonies, sentiments, noises. They mark an arena, a habitat of reciprocal listening and aural mingling. At the same time, international research is conducted for the recording of an unconscious Old City's soundscape, eluding surveillance.[16]

Questions of identity ever arise, and are not easily resolved. In all cases, issues of sonic hegemony, including that of Western classical music, should be openly discussed, as they are in certain quarters.[17] Political issues cannot be settled there: the medium's lack of apparent semantics is both an advantage and a drawback in such sonic encounters. They skip linguistic barriers and forestall controversies, but often leave the sounds hovering, unconnected to realities. In the meantime, demonstrators' drums are heard accompanying bold political slogans. Harmonious existence is deemed utopian, if not oppressive, yet one still hopes, at least, for a better orchestrated cacophonous, or even, in one's wildest dreams, heterophonic coexistence.

Appendix of Music Examples

Ex. app. 1. J. S. Bach, *St. Matthew Passion* I, 29: chorale:
"O Mensch bewein' dein' Sünde groß," mm. 1–14.

Ex. app. 2. George Frideric Handel, *Israel in Egypt* I, 8:
chorus: "He sent a thick darkness," mm. 1–28.

"Oh weep for those."

Braham & Nathan.

Largo con Espressione

Oh weep for those that wept by Babel's stream, Whose shrines are desolate, whose land a dream, Weep for the harp of Judah's broken shell_ Mourn where their God hath dwelt the Godless dwell! And where shall Israel lave her bleeding feet And where shall Zi_ _on's songs again seem

Ex. app. 3. Isaac Nathan and Lord Byron, *Hebrew Melodies,*
"Oh! Weep for Those" (complete).

We sate down and wept.

Nathan.

Lamentevole
Expressivo

We sate down and wept

We sate down and

by the wa-ters of Ba---bel, and thought of the day When our

wept by the wa-ters of Ba---bel, and thought of the day When our

foe, from the hue of his slaughters, Made Salem's high pla . . . . . ces his prey; And

foe, from the hue of his slaughters, Made Salem's high pla . . . . . . ces his prey;

ye, oh her de-solate de-solate daugh-ters! Were scat———ter'd all

And ye, oh her de-solate daugh-ters! Were scat———

weep———ing a-way. While sadly we gaz'd on the ri-ver———

———ter'd all weeping a-way. While sad-ly we gaz'd on the

roll'd on in free-dom be-low, They demanded the song; but, oh never oh never That

ri-ver which roll'd on in freedom below, They demanded the song; but, oh never oh never That

triumph the stranger shall know! They demanded the so———

triumph the stranger shall know! They demanded the so———

Ex. app. 4. Isaac Nathan and Lord Byron, *Hebrew Melodies*,
"We Sate Down and Wept" (complete).

Brogni

Si la ri-gueur et la ven-gean - ce

leur font ha - ir - - - - - - ta sain - te loi,

que le par-don, que la clé-men - ce, mon

Ex. app. 5. Jacques Fromental Halévy, *La Juive* I, 2: cavatina:
"Si la rigueur" (Brogni), mm. 1–24.

Ex. app. 6. Gregorio Allegri, *Miserere*, opening, mm. 1–15.
Adapted and arranged by Ivor Atkins (London: Novello & Company, 1951).
This musical rendition follows the British mode of performance—in language
and texture—thus coming closer to the musical image that Eliot and her
readers would have experienced.

Ex. app. 7. Kabbalat Shabbat, "Lechu nᵉranena" (Psalm 95, Idelsohn, *Thesaurus* 7: no. 28), close to Ogutsch, *Der Frankfurter Kantor*, no. 41.

Ex. app. 8. Arnold Schoenberg, one of two earlier versions of the
"Wasteland Ritornello" melody.
From Arnold Schoenberg, *Moses und Aron: Oper in drei Akten, kritischer Bericht*, ed.
Christian Martin Schmidt (Mainz: Schott's Soehne, 1977–98), 112.
The letters and numbers above the notes stand for the permutation of the
row from which the melody is taken.

*) Eventuell von ϕ gesprochen; in diesem Fall spielt die Harfe die Gesangsnoten.

Ex. app. 9. Arnold Schoenberg, *Moses und Aron* II, 5, mm. 1043–44:
the "Wasteland" (flute) theme is now taken by the oboe.

NOTES

INTRODUCTION

1. The Jews' expulsion from England in 1290 (after a long series of notorious and ob-scure ritual-murder accusations against them), as well as their gradual resettlement from the mid-seventeenth century to full citizenship two hundred years later (with Baron Lionel de Rothschild taking his seat as the first Jewish member of Parliament in 1858), neatly coincides with the major chronological outlines of the history related here.

2. One famous and almost isolated known case of a non-Jew's interest in and respect for Jewish musical heritage is that of the German humanist and Hebraist Johann Reuchlin, whose rendition of the biblical tropes was published by the priest Johann Böschenstein in 1518. See Hanoch Avenary, *The Ashkenazi Tradition of Biblical Chant between 1500 and 1900: Documentation and Musical Analysis* (Tel Aviv: Tel Aviv University, Faculty of Fine Arts, School of Jewish Studies, 1978).

3. On the eventual influence of this Sephardic music in northern Europe see Israel Adler, *Musical Life and Traditions of the Portuguese Jewish Community of Amsterdam in the 18th Century* (Jerusalem: The Hebrew University Magnes Press, 1974), and Edwin Seroussi, *Spanish-Portuguese Synagogue Music in Nineteenth-Century Reform Sources from Hamburg: Ancient Tradition in the Dawn of Modernity* (Jerusalem: The Hebrew University Magnes Press, 1996).

4. On this vast subject see, for example, Don Harrán, "Tradition and Innovation in Jew-ish Music of the Later Renaissance," *Journal of Musicology* 7 (Winter 1989): 107–30, and in *Salamone Rossi: Jewish Musician in Late Renaissance Mantua* (Oxford: Oxford University Press, 1999).

5. The term *soundscape* was introduced to Jewish music research by Edwin Seroussi, in a keynote address at the opening of the conference on Jewish music at the City University of London, April 1997, later published in revised form as "La dimensione del suono nelle sinagoghe del Marocco," *EM — Rivista degli Archivi di Etnomusico-logia dell'Accademia Nazionale di Santa Cecilia*, 2/2 (2006), 109–125. It opens with

the statement that in replacing *music* with *soundscape* the author seeks to refer "to all sonic phenomena of the synagogue," suggesting "a comprehensive approach that tackles the complexity of the liturgical event as a whole, including all nonverbal sonic occurrences included in it," as that which comprise a 'Jewish liturgical music.'"

6. For a detailed and extensive survey of particular aesthetic categories, see Karlheinz Barck, Martin Fontius, et al., *Ästhetische Grundbegriffe*, vol. 1–7 (Stuttgart: J. B. Metzler, 2000–2005).

7. On this development see Carl Dahlhaus' classical study, *The Idea of Absolute Music*, trans. Roger Lustig (Chicago: University of Chicago Press, 1989).

8. This is extensively discussed in Ruth Katz's and Ruth HaCohen's *Tuning the Mind: Connecting Aesthetics to Cognitive Science* (New Brunswick, NJ: Transaction, 2003).

9. In comparison and contrast to the concept of the "hermeneutic Jew," used by Jeremy Cohen in *Living Letters of the Law: Ideas of the Jews in Medieval Christianity* (Berkeley: University of California Press, 1999), of Hannah Arendt's "The Jew as Pariah: A Hidden Tradition," in Hannah Arendt, *The Jew as Pariah, Jewish Identity and Politics in the Modern Age* (New York: Grove, 1978), 69–75, or of the Jew as an epistemological category, used by David Nirenberg in *The Figure of the Jew: from Ancient Egypt to the Present* (provisional title) (New York: Norton, forthcoming), mine is not only ideological (like Cohen's), it is also as generative, inexplicit, and transformative as Nirenberg's "epistemological" Jew, and sometimes as personal and reactive as Arendt's Jew as pariah.

10. Associating art with benevolence was a major aesthetic presupposition, especially in eighteenth-century England; see Katz and HaCohen, *Tuning the Mind*, chapter 5.

11. In the following I concentrate more on the musical than on the literary arena, since (1) there are several basic common denominators shared by the two arts in this period, such as the idealization of *Volksgeist*, psychological realism, the predilection for the fantastic, and the emphasis on "lamps" (originality) rather than "mirrors" (imitation), to allude to M. H. Abrams' famous dichotomy; (2) the poetry and literature of the time—especially those works discussed in this volume—are marked by the famous aspiration of the arts "to the condition of music"; and (3) in the works of literature discussed, the reflection of music as medium and some of its select genres and styles are a major concern.

12. In terms of their relations to their favorite authors, there was of course a difference between middle-class Jews and middle-class non-Jews. But there is enough evidence to suggest that many Jews viewed Jewish authors (such as Heine) as Germans, and were not disturbed by their Jewish affiliation. When their perception was more mixed it refers to the inseparability, for many Jews, of being Jewish and being German. On the entrance of Jews into the musical arena during the nineteenth century, mainly as performers, see also Ezra Mendelssohn, "On the Jewish Presence in Nineteenth-Century European Musical Life," *Modern Jews and Their Musical Agendas: Studies in Contemporary Jewry* 9, ed. Ezra Mendelssohn, (New York: Oxford University Press, 1993), 3–16.

13. See chapter 4.

14. My conception of "fictive worlds" relies on a variety of thinkers, from Leibniz and Baumgarten to Walterstorff, Walton, and Riffaterre, but it is less closed and monadic

than most of their conceptions. Also, and related to this, distinctions between possible and fictive worlds (crucial to Walton) collapse when worlds are viewed as connected through networks of recursive and intertextual links, as I believe they are. On recursion in this regard see Douglas Hofstadter, *Gödel, Escher, Bach: An Eternal Golden Braid* (London: Penguin, 1979).

15. Ernst Cassirer in *The Philosophy of Symbolic Form,* 3 vols., trans. R. Manheim (New Haven: Yale University Press, 1955) and Nelson Goodman, especially in *Ways of Worldmaking* (Indianapolis: Hacket, 1978), though entertaining different philosophical premises, emphasize these tendencies of "worlds."

16. In Ruth HaCohen, "The Music of Sympathy in the Arts of the Baroque; or the Use of Difference to Overcome Indifference," *Poetics Today* 22/3 (2001): 607–50.

17. John L. Austin's famous speech acts theory in *How to Do Things with Words* (Oxford: Oxford University Press, [1963] 1986) and its elaboration by John Searle, in, for example, *Expression and Meaning: Studies in the Theory of Speech Acts* (Cambridge: Cambridge University Press, 1979) inspires the first sense of "performative speech acts." The second, related to identity, follows Judith Butler's interpretation of the theory in her "Performative Acts and Gender Constitution: An Essay in Phenomenology and Feminist Theory," in *Performing Feminisms: Feminist Critical Theory and Theatre,* ed. Sue-Ellen Case (Baltimore: Johns Hopkins University Press, 1990), 270–81.

18. Taking Fredric Jameson's classic *The Political Unconscious: Narrative as a Socially Symbolic Act* (London: Methuen, 1981) as a point of departure, this study offers a less structural and hierarchized reading of what I would define as "the political or the politico-theological surface or threshold of consciousness." This is especially pertinent to music's nonlexical expressive specificities, which can isomorphically pinpoint the undulation of its emotional referent without categorizing it. Bypassing the symbolic while retaining cognitive substance, it negotiates layers of consciousness differently.

19. It was only in sixteenth-century Italy that Jews began to grapple theoretically with harmoniousness in its Western definition, a concept that they were ready to apply to contemporary polyphony insofar as it was considered to be modeled after the music of Solomon's Temple. The Hebrew treatise *Higgayôn Be-ḵinnôr* ("The Melody of the Lyre") by Judah ben Joseph Moscato (1530–90) may be regarded as the most systematic attempt to merge Jewish and classical ideas of world harmony. The treatise was printed in 1588–89 in Venice, republished in Israel Adler's *Hebrew Writings Concerning Music in Manuscripts and Printed Books from Geonic Times up to 1800* (Munich: G. Henle, 1975) (text in Hebrew), 221–39.

CHAPTER 1. RECIPROCATED RITUALS AND NOISY ENCOUNTERS

1. David M. Schiller, *Bloch, Schoenberg, and Bernstein: Assimilating Jewish Music* (Oxford: Oxford University Press, 2003), 25 (italics added).

2. Imaginaries stand here, following Yaron Ezrahi's conceptualization in *Necessary Fictions: Democracy after Modernity* (forthcoming), for collective, rather nonexplicated cultural-mental configurations, which regulate behavior.

3. See Simon Schwartzfuchs, "The Place of the Crusades in Jewish History," in *Culture and Society in Medieval Jewry: Studies Dedicated to the Memory of Haim Hillel Ben-Sasson*, ed. Menachem Ben-Sasson et al. (Jerusalem: Zalman Shazar Center for Jewish Studies, 1989), 251–69, as quoted in Jeremy Cohen, "A 1096 Complex? Constructing the First Crusade," in *Jews and Christians in Twelfth-Century Europe*, ed. Michael A. Signer and John Van Engen (Notre Dame: University of Notre Dame Press, 2001), 14. For the chronicles see Shlomo Eidelberg, trans. and ed., *The Jews and the Crusaders: The Hebrew Chronicles of the First and Second Crusades* (Madison: University of Wisconsin Press, 1977).

4. The term, introduced by the historian Zvi Yavetz, was later used by Peter Schäfer in *Judeophobia: Attitudes towards the Jews in the Ancient World* (Cambridge, MA: Harvard University Press, 1998) and many others.

5. See the above-quoted edited volume *Jews and Christians in Twelfth-Century Europe*, for a variety of approaches to and contexts of direct and indirect contacts.

6. For a succinct summary of modes of contact and mutual avoidance see John Van Engen, "Introduction: Jews and Christians Together in the Twelfth Century," in *Jews and Christians in Twelfth-Century Europe*, 1–8. Of interest in the present context is the direct contact that transpired within the "feminine zone" of Christian wet nurses and Jewish mothers, which involved also unavoidable musical contact, as it stems from certain prohibitions quoted below. On these contacts see Elisheva Baumgarten, *Mothers and Children: Jewish Family Life in Medieval Europe* (Princeton: Princeton University Press, 2004), chapter 4.

7. See Robert Suckale's pathbreaking article, "Über den Anteil christlicher Maler an der Ausmalung hebräischer Handschfriften der Gothik in Bayern," in *Geschichte und Kultur der Juden in Bayern*, ed. Manfred Treml and Josef Kirmeier (Munich: K. G. Saur, 1988), 123–34; Sarit Shalev Eyni, "Jerusalem and the Temple in Hebrew illuminated manuscripts: Jewish thought and Christian influence," in ed. M. Perani, *L'interculturalità dell'ebraismo* (Ravenna: Longo, 2004), 173–91; and "Cosmological Signs in Calculating the Time of Redemption: The Christian Crucifixion and the Jewish New Moon of Nissan," *Viator: Medieval and Renaissance Studies* 35 (2004): 265–87.

8. See Ezra Fleischer, *Hebrew Liturgical Poetry in the Middle Ages* (Jerusalem: Keter, 1975). The marginal borrowings relate to certain strophic patterns or rhyme schemes typical of medieval German poetry; in this they paralleled musical borrowing from the Minnesinger. I thank Yehoshua Granat for advising me on this matter. Recently he has exemplified such a local influence in the famous Hanukkah hymn "Maoz Tsur" in his lecture "Maoz Tsur: Between Contents and Form," given at the Hebrew University, Jerusalem, 7 December 2010.

9. For earlier possible exchanges see note 13 below.

10. Johan Huizinga, *The Waning of the Middle Ages* (New York: Courier Dover Publications, [1924] 1998), 2.

11. Ibid.

12. As it seems to emerge from the more conspicuous cases of musical borrowing in this context, as extensively argued by Abraham Z. Idelsohn, in *Thesaurus of Hebrew*

Oriental Melodies (The Traditional Songs of South German Jews) (Leipzig: Friedrich Hofmeister, 1933), 7:xxxv–xxxviii.

13. Idelsohn argues that the competition between the communities started earlier, and still in the ninth century the Jews were the source of imitation; see Abraham Z. Idelsohn, *Jewish Music in Its Historical Development* (New York: Schocken, [1929] 1967), 130 and *Thesaurus* 7:ix–x. There is a piece of evidence to this effect in Gregory I's instruction to the Bishops of Formi and Fundi "to stop the Jews from having their celebrations" if indeed "the voice from that place is being heard at the church's entrance." Yet he concomitantly admonished them to "manage [the Jews'] affairs without any obstructions." See Amnon Linder, ed., *The Jews in the Legal Sources of the Early Middle Ages* (Detroit: Wayne State University Press, 1997), 422–23. I thank Amitai Spitzer for this reference. Other earlier sources, quoted below, point to an aversion to synagogal sonorities. For the late medieval source quoted above see Israel Jacob Yuval, *"Two Nations in Your Womb"—Perception of Jews and Christians in Late Antiquity and the Middle Ages*, trans. Barbara Harshav and Jonathan Chipman (Berkeley: University of California Press, 2006), 204. For an etymological analysis and modern implications and resonation of this phrase, see chapter 3 and 6 below.

14. In Mary Douglas, *Purity and Danger: An Analysis of Concepts of Pollution and Taboo* (London: Routledge and Kegan Paul, 1966).

15. To clarify, *ghetto* is the etymological source of *fare un ghetto* and not the other way around. *Ghetto* derives from *gettare* (to pour or cast), related to the presence of foundries in the area of the ghetto in Venice. See Benjamin C. I. Ravid, "From Geographical Realia to Historiographical Symbol: The Odyssey of the Word *Ghetto*," in David B. Ruderman, ed., *Essential Papers on Jewish Culture in Renaissance and Baroque Italy* (New York: New York University Press, 1992), 376. An insiders' folk etymology connected *ghetto* with the Hebrew *ghet*, divorce, as experienced by Jews in relation to their Christian neighbors. See Kenneth Stow, *Theatre of Acculturation: The Roman Ghetto in the Sixteenth Century* (Seattle: University of Washington Press, 2001), 96–97. I thank Ghil'ad Zuckermann and Manuela Consonni for their help in this matter.

16. See Stow, *Jewish Dogs: An Image and Its Interpreters* (Stanford: Stanford University Press, 2006), 31.

17. Chrysostom's *Adverseus Judaeus* contains a few acrimonious attacks on the synagogue as worse than theater and brothel, a den of robbers, a place of demons, desolated by God, and hence deprived of past musicality. Chrysostom's language and theological insinuations must have urged later generations to view it as aurally contaminated. See *The Fathers of the Church: St. John Chrysostom, Discourses against Judaizing Christians*, trans. Paul W. Harkins (Washington: Catholic University of America Press, 1979), Discourse I, sec. II (7); sec. III (1); sec. IV (2); sec. VI (2); and Dis. IV, sec. VII (3–5). I thank Yifat Monnickendam for helping me to locate these references.

18. See Stow, *Jewish Dogs*, 31, also 94–95, and references.

19. As in the case of Goethe-Mendelssohn's *Erste Walpurgisnacht* briefly discussed in chapter 4. I am grateful to Talia Trainin for calling my attention to these important etymological connections.

20. See http://www.ajudaica.com/guide_shofar.php (accessed 5 June 2008).

21. For more complaints about Jewish chanting see William Chester Jordan, *The French Monarchy and the Jews: From Philip Augustus to the Last Capetians* (Philadelphia: University of Pennsylvania Press, 1989), 17. For sonic interactions of late medieval Spanish communities with their non-Jewish environments, and noise accusations on their behalf, see Edwin Seroussi's rich discussion in "Music in Medieval Ibero-Jewish Society," *Hispania Judaica Bulletin* 5 (2007): 5–67.

22. The case of the twelfth-century Obadiah the Proselyte (Johannes of Oppido) from Italy/Normandy, whose notational scripts to two Hebrew *piyyutim* and five psalmodic verses were found in the Cairo Geniza, is exceptional and solitary. Interestingly, they were written probably in North Africa and not in Europe. See Israel Adler, "Synagogue chants of the 12th century; the music notations of Obadiah the proselyte," *Ariel* 15 (1966): 27–41; and Hanoch Avenary, "Paradigms of Arabic Musical Modes in the Genizah Fragment Cambridge T.S. N.S. 90, 4," in *Yuval* 4, eds. Israel Adler and Bathja Bayer (Jerusalem: The Hebrew University Magnes Press, 1982): 11–28. For another exceptional case see plate 1.

23. Possibly, as Doron Mendels and Arye Edrei have recently argued, these newcomers were of different religious bents—they were "Talmudic" Jews, abiding by the complex system of Jewish rabbinic law. Arye Edrei and Doron Mendels, "A Split Jewish Diaspora: Its Dramatic Consequences," (I & II) *Journal for the Study of the Pseudoepigrapha* 16/2 (2007): 91–137; 17/3 (2008): 163–87; idem, *Zweierlei Diaspora: Zur Spaltung der antiken jüdischen Welt* (Göttingen: Vandenhoeck & Ruprecht, 2010).

24. For the fascinating history of *Minhag Ashkenaz* see Israel M. Ta-Shma, *Early Franco-German Ritual and Custom* (Jerusalem: The Hebrew University Magnes Press, 1992) [Hebrew].

25. See Boaz Tarsi, "Voices in the Sanctuary: Musical Practices of the American Synagogue," *Conservative Judaism* 55/1, 2002: 71–72.

26. The epigraph to the present chapter is an example to this effect.

27. As reflected by major Jewish authorities, see below.

28. Defined by Boaz Tarsi and myself, in relation to this corpus, as "the knowing how to perform sonic sequences and combinations of various kinds and forms and carry them through," in "Ashkenazi Liturgical Music: Analysis of Modes of Operation in Historical and Cognitive Perspectives," paper delivered at the Fifteenth World Congress of Jewish Studies, Jerusalem, August 2–6, 2009.

29. We will elaborate on this point in a publication related to the paper mentioned in the preceding note.

30. The famous "Kol Nidre" tune, traditionally considered as a part of this group of melodies, is dated to the fifteenth century.

31. *Sefer Ḥasidim* ("The Book of the Pious") (Bologna edition), ed. Reuven Margaliot (Jerusalem: Mosad Harav Kook, 1957 [Hebrew]), 241, sec. 302. Written by Rabbi Yehudah He-ḥasid, the book is considered among the most important Jewish creations of the late Middle Ages. There are many unanswered queries concerning this musical oral tradition that cannot be addressed here. The terminology of Missinai was com-

mon, for example, among the modern Hasidim, as reported by Yaakov Mazor in "The Power of the Niggun in Hassidic Thought and Its Roles in Religious and Social Life," in *Yuval: Studies of the Jewish Music Research Centre* VII, (*Studies in Honour of Israel Adler*), ed. Eliyahu Schleifer and Edwin Seroussi (Jerusalem: The Hebrew University Magnes Press, 2002), 43 (Hebrew part). On the possible origins and characteristics of Missinai tunes see A. Z. Idelsohn, "Der Missinai-Gesang der deutschen Synagoge," in *Zeitschrift für Musikwissenschaft* 8 (1926), 449; Idelsohn, *Hebrew Oriental Melodies* 7, xxix–xxxvi for the selection of the more archaic elements from melodies, the biblical trope layers within which they lie, and also for possible affinities to the Minnesinger's melodies (suggesting a "phonosemantic" matching to Missinai). See also Idelsohn, *Jewish Music*, 136; on the dominance of the lamentative element in synagogal music see ibid., 74–78. See also Eric Werner's speculations in *A Voice Still Heard . . . The Sacred Songs of the Ashkenazic Jews* (University Park: Pennsylvania State University Press, 1976), chap. 3. Many of the claims these pioneer scholars maintain need to be revisited, and yet they contain valuable insights that cannot be easily dismissed.

32. The historical transformation this music map underwent from the twelfth to the twentieth century, though pertinent to the story here told, is too complicated to be surveyed here.

33. The adaptation of the notational signs so as to scripturally translate the set of pitches (later also the rhythms) of a given piece, guaranteed its (musical) identity in all performances, faithful to the script. The symbolic requirements such a system fulfills were famously discussed by Nelson Goodman in *Languages of Art* (Indianapolis: Bobbs-Merrill, 1968) and further historicized by Ruth Katz in *A Language of Its Own: Sense and Meaning in the Making of Western Art Music* (Chicago: University of Chicago Press, 2009), 21–41.

34. Oscillations between moments of uniformity versus variety prevailed nonetheless, especially in the Office realm. See Andrew Hughes, "Late Medieval Plainchant for the Divine Office," *The New Oxford History of Music: Music as Concept and Practice in the Late Middle Ages*, ed. Reinhard Strohm and Bonnie J. Blackburn (Oxford: Oxford University Press, 2001) III.1: 33–43.

35. By Augustinian temporal unfolding I mean his conception of a "becoming harmony," which Spitzer juxtaposes to St. Ambros' "simultaneous harmony." Leo Spitzer, *Classical and Christian Ideas of World Harmony: Prolegomena to an Interpretation of the Word "Stimmung"* (Baltimore: Johns Hopkins University Press, 1963), 22–33. For the ways in which the technico-musical dimension of St. Augustine's theological aesthetic conception is realized, see his *De Musica*, in Ruth Katz and Carl Dahlhaus' *Contemplating Music: Source Readings in the Aesthetics of Music*, vol. 2, *Import* (New York: Pendragon Press, 1989), 10–31. See also Paul Ricoeur, *Time and Narrative*, trans. K. Blamey and D. Pellauer (Chicago: University of Chicago Press, 1988), 3:12–22.

36. The melodies of the Ordinary of the Mass originated as congregational songs, which later were taken by the *scholia* (church choir) as reflected in more elaborated melodies from that period, which, nevertheless, usually retain their communal character. See Willy Apel, *Gregorian Chant* (Bloomington: Indiana University Press, 1958), 27.

37. Some instances of the Communion—neumatic (with few and short melismas)—are very short, yet as a whole it cannot be characterized as a distinct genre. See Apel, *Gregorian Chant*, 311–12.

38. See Miri Rubin, *Gentile Tales* (Philadelphia: University of Pennsylvania Press, 2004), 22.

39. Sarah Beckwith, "Ritual, Church and Theatre: Medieval Dramas of the Sacramental Body," in David Aers, ed. *Culture and History, 1350–1600: Essays on English Communities, Identities, and Writing* (New York: Harvester Wheatsheaf, 1992), 65–89.

40. See Spitzer, *Classical and Christian Ideas*, and Simeon K. Henninger, *Touches of Sweet Harmony* (San Marino, California: Huntington Library, 1974).

41. Spitzer's starting point for his research into classical and Christian ideas of world harmony is the etymology of the German word *Stimmung* (atmosphere; air; mood); a derivative of *Stimme* (voice), it bred an array of lexemes—Germanic translations of Latin words for concepts such as concord, concert, consent, and conciliation. What is unique to the German word, writes Spitzer, and missing in other European languages, is that it stands for the expression of "the unity of feelings experienced by man face to face with his environment (a landscape, nature, one's fellow man) and would comprehend and weld together the objective (factual) and the subjective (psychological) into one harmonious unity" (Spitzer, *Classical and Christian Ideas*), 5. The existence of such a semantic space in the German language is vital to the book's main argument.

42. See Bruce W. Holsinger, *Music, Body, and Desire in Medieval Culture: Hildegard of Bingen to Chaucer* (Stanford: Stanford University Press, 2001), 269.

43. This dichotomy was maintained by John of Afflighem and elaborated even further by Adam Scot. See Charles Burnett, "Perceiving Sound in the Middle Ages," in *Hearing History: A Reader*, ed. Mark M. Smith (Athens: University of Georgia Press, 2004), 70, 82 (italics added).

44. Leo Spitzer, "Patterns of Thought and of Etymology, I. Nausea>OF(>Eng.) Noise," *Word* I/3 (1945), 260–276. One should not overlook the year of publication of Spitzer's article, which also contains some revealing emotional autobiographical testimonies (270, n. 11), regarding introvert versus extrovert Jewish mourning decorum.

45. Esther Cohen, *The Modulated Scream: Pain in Late Medieval Culture* (Chicago: University of Chicago Press, 2010), 191. I thank the author for letting me read her manuscript before publication.

46. As in the JPS 1917 translation: "Why are the nations in an uproar? And why do the peoples mutter in vain?"

47. Miri Rubin, *Gentile Tales*, 36. See also Kenneth Stow, *Jewish Dogs*, 173. The motif, now in the contest of Catholics and Protestants, recurs in a fantastic story by Heinrich von Kleist, "Die Heligie Cäcilie, oder die Gewalt der Musik" ("Holy Cecilia, or the Power of Music"). See his *Sämtliche Werke und Briefe* (Munich: Deutscher Taschenbuch, 2001), 216–28.

48. Regarding such accusations see Idelsohn, *Thesaurus* 7:10.

49. In this sense, the first Jewish ritual murder libels are considered a turning point in Christian attitudes towards Jews. As Gavin I. Langmuir argued in "Thomas of Monmouth: Detector of Ritual Murder," *Speculum* 59 (1984), 820–46, the creation of this

specific fantasy marks the transition from "anti-Judaism" to "anti-Semitism." Controversies among scholars notwithstanding, it is agreed that a change in *imagining* Jews came about at this moment.

50. See Yuval, *Two Nations*, 135–204. After Yuval first published his thesis in "Vengeance and Damnation, Blood and Defamation: From Jewish Martyrdom to Blood Libel Accusation," *Zion* 58 (1993), 33–90 (in Hebrew), the first wave of polemics that ensued was published in the subsequent issues of *Zion*. See also Moshe Lazar, "The Lamb and the Scapegoat: The Dehumanization of the Jews in Medieval Propaganda Imagery," in *Anti-Semitism in Times of Crisis*, ed. Sander Gillman and Steven Katz (New York: New York University Press, 1991), 38–80.

51. This is the main structural correlative in the host desecration accusation, as indicated by Rubin. See especially chapter 2 of her *Gentile Tales*.

52. See David Nirenberg, "The Rhineland Massacres of Jews in the First Crusade: Memories Medieval and Modern," in *Medieval Concepts of the Past: Ritual, Memory and Historiography*, ed. Gerd Althoff, Johannes Fried, and Patrick Geary (Cambridge: Cambridge University Press, 2002), 279–309.

53. On the ways whereby modes of memory and commemoration established in the Middle Ages (especially in the wake of the Jewish martyrdom associated with the Crusades) determined modern forms of memory and identity, see the classical (and controversial) study of Yosef Yerushalmi, *Zakhor: Jewish History and Jewish Memory* (Washington: University of Washington Press, [1982] 1996).

54. The term *Seder* in Hebrew means "order," and, as such, relates to the ordered program of the night, organized according to preestablished headings, consisting of ritual actions and illocutions.

55. Originally, the Eucharist (as it was celebrated through the Mass) took place in the evening; only later was it shifted to the morning hours.

56. See Don Handelman, *Models and Mirrors: Towards an Anthropology of Public Events* (New York: Berghahn, [1990] 1998), 15.

57. Whether this was indeed the case has been of course a cause for debate, but it was at least the assumption of three Gospels and many of the church fathers, and this is sufficient evidence for our purpose.

58. Gershom Scholem, *On the Kabbalah and Its Symbolism*, trans. Ralph Manheim (New York: Schocken, 1965), 121.

59. The two are preceded by Palm Sunday, on which, in the Roman Church, the Passion story according to Matthew (26–27) is fully recited. The scriptural lessons of the Christian Church and its relations to the parallel Jewish holidays are discussed in Eric Werner's ambitious and controversial *The Sacred Bridge: The Interdependence of Liturgy and Music in Synagogue and Church during the First Millennium* (London: Dennis Dobson, 1959), 50–101. More recent comparative studies of the two liturgies include Paul Bradshaw, *The Making of Jewish and Christian Worship* (Notre Dame: University of Notre Dame Press, 1991); and *Life Cycles in Jewish and Christian Worship* (Notre Dame: University of Notre Dame Press, 1996); I thank Israel Yuval for these references. For how consequential the simultaneity of these holidays could become, see Miri Rubin, *Gentile Tales*, 45.

60. Yuval, in his *Two Nations*, 71–107, has boldly shown the mutual reflectivity in the process of the crystallization of the two festivals and their respective rituals, bringing evidence to the effect that the Seder, as set in the Haggadah, was by and large conceived as a rebuttal of the increasingly spreading Christian rituals commemorating Jesus' crucifixion. In this interpretation, which regards the Haggadah as a Jewish "counter-Gospel," Yuval follows Robert Eisler and especially David Daube, whose research was never officially published.

61. The gradual replacement of sacrificial rituals performed in the Temple by illocutionary acts such as prayers, recitations, teaching, and learning was already part of a general, encompassing trend in Judaism preceding the destruction of the Second Temple in 70 CE. Soon after this event, these vicarious acts—especially the substitution of the sacrifices by the three major daily prayers and the "supplementary" (*Mussaf*) of Shabbat and Holidays—became the rule in all (rabbinically oriented) Jewish communities.

62. Rabban Gamliel (the Second) started his presidency of the Jewish Sanhedrin in Yavne ten years after the destruction of the Temple. Beyond this important quote, he was responsible for establishing the main framework of the Seder evening, once the sacrifice ritual in the Temple could no longer be performed.

63. For the complex history of the text see Daniel Goldschmidt, *The Passover Haggadah: Its Sources and History* (Jerusalem: Bialik, 1969); Shmuel Safrai and Zeev Safrai, *The Sages Haggadah, Passover's Haggadah* (Jerusalem: Karta, 1998) [both in Hebrew].

64. I kept the male grammatical form in this discussion, in accordance with most of the Haggadah's illocutionary addresses, though women's and girls' participation in the Seder is almost as compulsory as that of the men and boys.

65. Yerushalmi, *Zakhor*, 44. First person singular is relatively rare in the Haggadah.

66. This list of speech acts can be divided, following John Searle, into illocutions whose "words match the world" and others that urge the "world to match the words"; this kind of oscillation between past and future, between given realities and those promised and expected, is the linguistic embodiment of the major theological thrust of this night. Most of them are what Searle calls performative speech acts, i.e., illocutionary verbs that precede the illocutionary act itself such as promise, state, order. See John R. Searle, *Expression and Meaning: Studies in the Theory of Speech Acts* (Cambridge: Cambridge University Press, 1979), 3–7.

67. There are several concluding parts in the Haggadah, which make "the middle" more important than the finale. On the emphasis on "middles" in salvation stories in contrast to salvation stories leading to definite closure, see chapter 5.

68. "Adonai Malach" can be schematically characterized by a basically major/Mixolydian mode (manifest by an arpeggio progression), with a bent towards the second (minor) degree, and a minor upper third, but it is more than that, as *steiger* does not fully correspond with *mode*, itself a fuzzy concept. It rather coincides with what Boaz Tarsi and I term as "mode of conduct," see n. 28 above.

69. On the tunes of the Haggadah, see Eric Werner's rich discussion in *A Voice*, 147–67.

70. The scroll itself does not effectively conclude its own "story" but instead leaves the lovers to roam their ways. The allegorical rendition of the text has similar parallels in Christianity. The relation of the two traditions has been richly investigated.

71. The tone is typically anti-Christological.

72. See T. P. Gilmartin, transcribed by Joseph P. Thomas in *The Catholic Encyclopedia*, vol. 6 (New York: Robert Appleton, 1909); online edition, 2003 by K. Knight, http:// www.newadvent.org/cathen/06643a.htm for the official view of the Catholic church at the beginning of the twentieth century, attesting to the entrenched notion of the Jewish origin of this highly consecrated ritual.

73. On the precarious existence of converts in late medieval Europe see Rubin, *Gentile Tales*, 88. See also J. M. Elukin, "From Jew to Christian? Conversion and immutability in medieval Europe," in *Varieties of Religious Conversion in the Middle Ages*, ed. J. Muldoon (Gainesville: University Press of Florida, 1997), 171–89.

74. The vulnerability of the church in relation to identity and boundaries, expressed in the Holy Week events and ceremonies, is emphasized by Nirenberg in his research on Good Friday riots against the Jews in fourteenth-century Spain: "Christian competitive anxieties were never greater than during Holy Week and the period surrounding it." David Nirenberg, *Communities of Violence: Persecution of Minorities in the Middle Ages* (Princeton: Princeton University Press, 1996), 220. See also Rubin, *Gentile Tales*, 29.

75. These series appear, for the first time, in a Roman ordo only in the fourteenth century, but the retention of that part called the *Trisagion* in Greek goes to show that it had found a place in the Catholic Good Friday service much earlier.

76. An interesting case is the missal *I-Lc 606* (early eleventh century), which contains instructions for stylized action and rubrics that read "almost like stage directions." This information was obtained from Ruth Steiner and Keith Falconer, "Reproaches [Improperia]," *Grove Music Online*, ed. L. Macy; accessed 10 September 2005 (http:// www.grovemusic.com). It also dates the earliest musical version of the *Improperia* to the tenth century. This article avoids mentioning the Jewish element.

77. See *The Sacred Bridge* 1: 224, 453; Werner further elaborated on the theme in the second volume of the book (New York: Ktav Publishing House, 1984) in a chapter entitled "Two Hymns for Passover and Good Friday," based on two earlier articles. Containing painstaking comparisons of the Dayyenu text with the *Improperia*, including what seems like some brilliant suggestions of the source of the *Improperia*, his analysis was severely criticized, e.g., by Peter Jeffery in "Werner's *The Sacred Bridge* Volume 2: A Review Essay," *Jewish Quarterly Review* 77/4 (1987): 289–91.

78. P. Morrisroe, transcribed by Christine J. Murray, *The Catholic Encyclopedia*, vol. 7, 1910 by Robert Appleton Company; online edition 2003 by K. Knight (http://www .newadvent.org/cathen/07703a.htm).

79. See chapter 5 below and Ruth HaCohen, "Intricate Temporalities: The Transfiguration of Proper and 'Improper' Sounds from Christian to Jewish Environments," in *Given World and Time: Temporalities in Context*, ed. Tyrus Miller (Budapest: CEU University Press, 2008), 81–103. It should be emphasized that the Catholic Church's

approach in this connection has changed since WWII, as decided officially in the 1962–65 Vatican Council II. For the particular change concerning the *Improperia* see "Good Friday Reproaches (Improperia)," *Bishops' Committee on the Liturgy Newsletter* (March 1980) and related debates in a few websites.

80. "Pour out Your wrath upon the nations that do not know Thee and on the kingdoms that do not call on Thy Name. For they have devoured Yaakov and laid waste his dwelling place. Pour out Thy indignation upon them, and let Thy fierce anger overtake them. Pursue them with wrath, and destroy them from beneath the heavens of the Lord." *The Yeshiva University Haggada*, eds. Steven F. Cohen and Kenneth Brander (Jerusalem: Koren, 1985).

81. Daniel Goldschmidt, *The Passover Haggadah*, 179. For an encompassing historical survey of the Jewish imprecations on this and other holidays and the Gentiles' reactions see Yuval, "Vengeance and Damnation," 50–63, *Two Nations*, chapter 3.

82. The iconography related to these verses in the Haggadah—the Messiah's ass carrying Jews to Jerusalem—inspired later Christian iconography: that of the Jew's she-swine (Judensau) which was pictorially associated with the image of the famous "child-martyr" Simeon of Trent (1475), murdered, as it were, by the Jews. See Isaiah Schachar, *The Judensau: A Medieval Anti-Jewish Motif and Its History* (London: University of London, The Warburg Institute, 1974).

83. See John Stevens, *Words and Music in the Middle Ages: Song, Narrative, Dance and Drama, 1050–1350* (Cambridge: Cambridge University Press, 1986), 333–34.

84. Already in the *Liber Usualis* version of 1937 the anti-Jewish line does not appear.

85. "Lord, in the ghetto swarm the hordes of Jews. / They come from Poland and are all refugees. // I know they held your Trial, [Lord]; / But believe me, they aren't completely bad. // They sit in shops, under copper lamps, / Sell old clothes, books, arms, and [stamps]. // Rembrandt loved to paint them in their cast-off clothes. / Me, tonight I pawned a microscope. // Alas, Lord, after Easter you won't be here anymore! / Have pity on the Jews in their hovels, Lord." Blaise Cendrars, *Complete Poems*, trans. Ron Padgett (Berkeley: University of California Press, 1992), 6–7.

86. "*Dic nobis, Maria, quid vidisti in via?*" / "The humble morning light, shivering." // "*Dic nobis, Maria, quid vidisti in via?*" / "A wild whiteness, like hands quivering." // "*Dic nobis, Maria, quid vidisti in via?*" / "The augury of spring, in my breast, throbbing." Cendrars, *Complete Poems*, 235 (French), 10 (English).

87. The lines I have in mind are: "I would have liked to enter a church Lord; / But there are no bells in this city, Lord. // I think of the silent bells—where are the ancient bells? / Where are the anthems and sweet canticles? // Where are the long offices and the beautiful canticles? / Where are the litanies and the music?" (ibid., 9–10).

88. This is musically achieved, among other ways, by his use of an ostinato motif of pentatonic-diatonic scales soaring in a high register (centered on E), played against a middle-range chromatic short configuration, using perfect or semiperfect harmonic intervals as tonal points of reference in the orchestral accompaniment; a chromatic progression of sixth chords; a repetition of these sonorities in various combinations and rhythmic configurations, always within a crystal-clear texture, avoiding close dis-

sonant clashes. All this creates a rich and somewhat distant background to the simple recitative lines of the voice.

89. For the religious drama in various contexts and regions see Peter Meredith and John Tailby, *The Staging of Religious Drama in Europe and the Later Middle Ages* (Kalamazoo: Western Michigan University, 1990).

90. Stevens, *Words and Music*, 321; the high voice of the Jews comes up again, directly or obliquely, in modern works such as Franz Kafka's "Josefine, die Sängerin oder Das Volk der Mäuse" (Josephine the Singer, or the Mouse Folk, 1924) and with the concept of *mauscheln*. Actually, Jews, at least in Spain, could take real part in the medieval renditions of the Passion, as musicians or dancers. This astonishing fact is known through the intervention of the church council (in Valladolid, 1322), who forbade this practice. This phenomenon, related to funereal practices, is also known from Jewish sources. See Nirenberg, *Communities of Violence*, 215.

91. See Marshall Blakemore Evans, *The Passion Play of Lucerne: an Historical and Critical Introduction* (New York: Modern Language Association of America, 1943) and Werner, *A Voice*, 104–9.

92. For the thirty-three to thirty-four extant versions of the "plot"—itself a subgenre of the so-called Miracles of Our Lady—see the encompassing study by Carleton Brown, *Study of the Miracle of Our Lady, Told by Chaucer's Prioress*, in the Second Series of Chaucer Society Publications: (no. 45) 1910.

93. This applies mainly to the two Marian antiphons mentioned above, rather than to the *Gaude*. These antiphons (out of surviving four) are the earliest known Marian antiphons and were probably composed by Hermannus Contractus (1015–54); see Willi Apel, *Gregorian Chant*, 404. As Richard Hoppin maintains, it is their "modernity" (in terms of the musical features mentioned above) that earned them their prominent liturgical position and place in the affections of composers throughout the Middle Ages and Renaissance. See Richard H. Hoppin, *Medieval Music* (New York: Norton, 1978), 104. Their unique musical character, especially that of the "Salve Regina," is further discussed by Fred Büttner, in "Zur Geschichte der Marienantiphon 'Salve regina,'" *Archiv für Musikwissenschaft* 46 (1989), 257–70, who sums up a century of musicological research on this topic in the attempt to analyze the reasons for the predominance of the Dorian melody (uncharacteristic of Ashkenazi synagogal music) over others in relation to this antiphon.

94. Brown, *Study of the Miracle of Our Lady*, 38. I thank Esther Cohen for helping me with this translation. This, of course, runs counter to the Jews' attraction to these church melodies, according to other stories. Some of the versions solve this paradox by maintaining that the grounds for the murderous act was the Jews' resentment towards the text rather than the music, and they keep an assumption that the Jews could understand the Latin language (through translation, language proximity, and the like).

95. See especially the introduction and chapter 3.

96. Kenneth Stow, "Medieval Jews on Christianity," *Rivista di Storia del Cristianesimo* 4/1 (2007): 73–100.

97. See *Megillat Ahimaaz*, ed. Benjamin Klar (Jerusalem: Tarshish, 1974).

98. In the Ashkenazi pronunciation.

99. See Yerushalmi, *Zakhor*, 48–52.

100. Yoseph HaCohen, *Emek Habaca*, ed. and trans. into German by M. Wiener (Leipzig, 1858), 8 (Hebrew) and 31 (German). The grammatical pun on *no'am* (sweetness, agreeableness) and *ne'ima* (melody, tune) derives from the Bible and the language of the oldest part of the service: the K^{e}dushah. Etymologically, according to Michal Ephratt, it is a case of a homonym, coming from two different proto-Semitic roots. See Michal Ephratt, *Needed Words: The Lexical Innovations of Yonatan Ratosh* (Ramat Gan: Bar Ilan University Press, 2010, in Hebrew), 480. In the Bible, *no'am* is associated with God's grace, thus defeating the opposing "noisy" attributes, reconnecting Jewish melody with harmonious grace. The word *yyiḥud* (in: "Veydanu biyyiḥud ki alenu leshabe'aḥ haya") is likewise rich in connotations. The juxtaposition between the Blois story and Chaucer's is noticed by several scholars, including Yuval, *Two Nations*, 209, who brings in Habermann's source, *Sefer G^{e}zerot Ashkenaz V^{e}tsorfat* (Jerusalem: Tarshish, 1945), 142–3. The two versions are very similar (Habermann's book is even more poignant in phrasing: Velo shamanu k^{e}no'am han^e'ima hahee). The year and place of the republication of *Emek Habaca* should be regarded as part of the *Wissenschaft des Judentums* enterprise; more particularly, of a conscious attempt to publish "Jüdische Chroniken und Reisewerke" (Jewish chronicals and travelogues). Its author, the sixteenth-century Yoseph HaCohen, is considered by Yerushalmi as a "restrained messianic" (*Zakhor*, 64). Habermann's book is a typical post-Shoah, Jerusalem publication.

101. This is further assessed in Hanoch Avenary's painstaking comparison of the "Aleinu" tune's versions as sung by various eighteenth- and nineteenth-century cantors, from which one can further extrapolate its essential melodic structure. See Hanoch Avenary, "The Cantorial Fantasia of the Eighteenth and Nineteenth Centuries," *Yuval* 1 (1968): 65–85. A thorough analysis of the tune, in the context of other old Ashkenazi melodies and *Nussaḥ*, might throw light on the infrastructure of Ashkenazi Jewish music and of the Missinai tunes in particular.

102. See Idelsohn, *Jewish Music*, 148 for the example. The numbers above the notes are Idelsohn's, indicating motivic structure. In his *Thesaurus* 6 (190, no. 6) there is another version of Beer, influenced by the prevalent (classical) musical style. In vol. 7, devoted to the traditional songs of south-German Jews (p. 76, no. 201), an anonymous version, closer to the one above but more elaborate, is presented.

103. Hélène Wagenaar-Nolthenium, "Der *Planctus Iudei* und der Gesang jüdischer Märtyrer in Blois anno 1171," in Pierre Gallais and Yves-Jean Riou, eds., *Mélanges offerts à René Crozet* (Poitiers: Société d'Études Médiévale, 1966), 2:881–85. The resemblance is however musically arguable (too scant and local), and leaves the enduring question of origin open; see ex. 1.8 and discussion below. For the dramatic context of the *Spiel*, see Lee Patterson, "'The Living Witnesses of Our Redemption': Martyrdom and Imitation in Chaucer's *Prioress' Tale*," *Journal of Medieval and Early Modern Studies* 31/3 (2001), 533.

104. See Carleton Brown "The Prioress' Tale" in *Sources and Analogues of Chaucer's Canterbury Tales*, ed. W. F. Bryan and Germaine Dempster (London: Routledge & Kegan Paul, [1941] 1958), 447–85; Walter Morris Hart, "Some Old French Miracles of Our

Lady and Chaucer's *Prioress Tale*," in *The Charles Mills Gayley Anniversary Papers* (Berkeley: University of California Press, 1922), 31–53.

105. For part of this history see Lawrence Besserman's trenchant article, "Ideology, Antisemitism, and Chaucer's *Prioress' Tale*," *The Chaucer Review* 36/1 (2001): 48–72.

106. Lee Patterson, "The Living Witnesses," 516 (original italics). On the centrality of Chaucer's ironic, if not satirical stance see also Michael Calabrese's "Performing the Prioress: 'Conscience' and Responsibility in Studies of Chaucer's Prioress' Tale," *Texas Studies in Literature and Language* 44/1 (2002): 73–74, 82.

107. Ibid., 521.

108. The choice of the early age of seven is deliberate in Chaucer's version of the story, which some critics consider as related to "a desire on the part of Chaucer to show a soul possessed by religious cravings at an age before he would be influenced by *book lernynge*" (Spitzer, *Classical and Christian Ideas*, 52); others as reflecting ethnographic fact (Brown, *Study of the Miracle of Our Lady*, 126–36). Patterson considered the liminality of this age ("The Living Witness," 514) as did Louise O. Fradenburg before him in "Criticism, anti-Semitism, and the Prioress' Tale," *Exemplaria* 1 (1989): 101. In *Music, Body, and Desire in Medieval Culture*, Bruce Holsinger further delves into the violent aspects of musical education in the late Middle Ages in general, and its repercussions in the tale in particular (as in lines 272–75). For the musical education of such choirboys in late medieval Europe see also Yossi Maurey's "Music and Ceremony in Saint Martin of Tours, 1205–1500: The Interplay of Pilgrimage, Kingdom and Liturgy" (PhD diss., University of Chicago, 2004), chap. 2; Hughes, "Late Medieval Plainchant," 33.

109. Geoffrey Chaucer, *Canterbury Tales*, ed. A. C. Cawley (London: Dent & Sons, 1958), 377. Brown (*Sources and Analogues*, 452–55) unravels the influence of ritual murder stories (especially that of William of Norwich) on the tragic ending in the specific group of British stories to which the "Prioress' Tale" belongs.

110. As Holsinger, *Music, Body and Desire*, 285–6 insightfully notices.

111. Transcribed from *Liber Usualis*, 1266, see especially the second long melisma on "Virgo." There is another story related to this hymn, which likewise reveals a sensitive element regarding the Jewish proximity to Christian vocal treasures. See Brown, *Study of the Miracle of Our Lady*, 72.

112. Fradenburg, "Criticism," 82. Even those who criticized Fradenburg's pathbreaking article could not resist the power of this claim. Fradenburg interestingly capsizes some of Yuval's arguments, though not necessarily contradicting him, even prior to their publication. She maintains that the story shows that "the violence done to children of 'Cristen blood' by 'Cristen folk' is being attributed to the Jewish scapegoat" (105).

113. Idelsohn, *Thesaurus* 7:xxxi.

114. Brown, *Study of the Miracle of Our Lady*, 13.

115. The element of geographical proximity recurs in most of the versions.

116. See Ivan G. Marcus, "The Dynamics of Jewish Renaissance and Renewal in the Twelfth Century," in *Jews and Christians in Twelfth-Century Europe*, 33.

117. Gilles Deleuze and Felix Guattari, *A Thousand Plateaus: Capitalism and Schizophrenia*, trans. Brian Massumi (London: Athlone Press, 1988), chap. 11. On the Christian

fear of being influenced by the Jews in these matters see Idelsohn, *Jewish Music*, 130–32. The analysis of the phenomenon of transgressing communal boundaries through musical means could be benefited by cultural sociological theories of symbolic space such as Georg Simmel's "Bridge and Door," in *Simmel on Culture*, ed. David Frisby and Mike Featherstone (London: Sage, 1997), 170–74 and by case studies such as Galit Hasan-Rokem's *Tales of the Neighborhood: Jewish Narrative Dialogues in Late Antiquity* (Berkeley: University of California Press, 2003).

118. See Burnett, "Perceiving Sound in the Middle Ages," 72.

119. Noticed by Calabrese, "Performing the Prioress," 67.

120. Satan appears also in a late version of the story (turn of the sixteenth century), the Toledo story, but there the child is conquered by him. See Brown, *Study of the Miracle of Our Lady* 45, 109. The countertransference of melodies from one abject territory to another (Jewish territories—Jewish privy—Christian cemetery) is noteworthy.

121. Issuing with St. Augustine's famous "musical" confession and achieving one of its best-known climaxes in Thomas Mann's *Doktor Faustus*, briefly discussed in chapter 7.

122. As in the Hanukkah hymn "Maoz Tsur," which, according to Hanoch Avenary in "The Ma'oz Zur Tune: New Facts for Its History," *Encounters of East and West in Music* (Tel Aviv: Tel Aviv University, 1979), 175–185, was constructed, sometime in the fifteenth century, "as a mosaic of motives popular in Central Europe" (182). His convincing article aims to mend the rather entrenched notion, from Eduard Birnbaum onward, that the tune is a sixteenth-century conflation of two German religious songs into the famous "Maoz Tsur" tune of Hanukkah: the "Nun freut Euch Ihr Lieben Christen" and "Nun werd ich hören singen" (Idelsohn, *Jewish Music*), 171–4. It should be marked that even these rather late borrowings happened within a paraliturgical sphere. I thank Israel Yuval for the reference to Avenary's article.

123. Fradenburg, "Criticism," 94.

124. In more particular technical terms, *diabolus in musica* refers to the interval of triton, which was theoretically (but never practically) forbidden in church music, but which would inevitably became more dominant in Jewish music, once a *steiger* such as "Ahavah Raba" was adopted in synagogal music.

125. This antiphon is prevalent in Brown's group C, and Chaucer was probably not familiar with other possibilities. See Brown, *Study of the Miracle of Our Lady*, 112. The controversial text in the "Gaude" appears in the verse: "Erubescat iudeus infelix." Ibid., 63, 71.

126. *Sefer Ḥasidim*, pp. 302, 459, 211 respectively. Sec. 768 (p. 459) also adds an insider comment about noise in the synagogue: "one said to his friend who was raising his voice, 'say that in a lower voice, like our voices, and equalize your voice to ours,' and he said 'I raise my voice to concentrate (*lekhaven*) in my prayer since I know how to concentrate when I raise my voice.'" The author praises him for that. This practice has contributed its part to the special "noisy" soundscape of the Ashkenazi synagogue and is in effect in certain communities even today.

127. The spiritual power of the textless melody will be fully recognized and dwelled upon in Judaism much later (especially in relation to modern Hasidism), legitimizing all

sources, provided their reterritorialization is properly made. For the process in an earlier Sephardic culture see Edwin Seroussi, "Music in Medieval," 46–47.

128. An Old Norse version includes the following: "The clerk sings the verse loudly. Since its pitch goes highest where the words are most offensive to the Jews, they hear it in the synagogues." Brown, ibid., *Study of the Miracle of Our Lady* 26.

129. I refer here to the entrenched custom of the reading of the Esther Scroll on Purim, to make great noise whenever the name of Haman is mentioned. This goes back to early medieval times, and to other forms of violence practiced by Jews, whether subdued or blatant; see Eliot Horowitz, "The Rite to Be Reckless: On the Perpetration and Interpretation of Purim Violence," *Poetics Today* 15 (1994): 9–54.

130. See above. W. Robertson Smith's *The Religion of the Semites* (1899) was Freud's main source for his *Totem and Taboo*; see Theodor Reik, in *Ritual, Psycho-Analytic Studies*, trans. Douglas Bryan (New York: International Universities Press, 1958), 301. Phono-semantic matchings are diagnosed and discussed in Ghil'ad Zuckermann, *Language Contact and Lexical Enrichment in Israeli Hebrew* (Houndmills: Palgrave Macmillan, 2003).

131. Jacques Attali, *Noise: The Political Economy of Music*, trans. Brian Massumi (Minneapolis: University of Minnesota Press, 1985), 25–26.

132. The martyrdom of the First Crusade was considered horrendous by Jews more than eight hundred years after the event. That is how it was characterized by my maternal grandmother Berta Bracha Ehrentreu-Fraenkel (1895–1965) before WWII in Munich, her birthplace. Her family from her mother's side (the Feuchtwangers from Fürth, expelled from Feuchtwangen in 1555) dwelled in Ashkenaz for generations. While this kind of recollection was interpreted by some as a sign of continuous memory, others could claim the opposite. Thus Nirenberg argues (in "The Rhineland Massacres of Jews", 295–99), relying among others on Ismar Elbogen's *Jewish Liturgy: A Comprehensive History*, trans. Raimond P. Scheindlin (Philadelphia, PA: The Jewish Publication Society, [1913] 1933), that the partially forgotten traumatic events returned as a repressed memory in the wake of the *Wissenschaft des Judentums* and later with the rise to power of National Socialism, which coincides with the dates of my grandmother's recollections.

133. For antecedents of these motifs in Jewish literature of late antiquity and the early Middle Ages, see Galit Hasan-Rokem, *Web of Life: Folklore and Midrash in Rabbinic Literature*, trans. Batya Stein (Stanford: Stanford University Press, 2000).

134. Nathan's compassionate deed, in turn, is indirectly criticized by the Christian patriarch in what could originally be interpreted as a Jewish martyro-logic: "Denn besser, / Es wäre hier im Elend umgekommen, / Als daß zu seinem ewigen Verderben / Es so gerettet ward." *Nathan der Weise*, VI.ii.2546–49.

135. George Eliot, *Daniel Deronda*, ed. Terence Cave (London: Penguin, [1876] 2003), 222. This motif returns several times in the novel.

136. http://www.museodelprado.es/en/the-collection/online-gallery/on-line-gallery/obra/the-fountain-of-grace-and-the-triumph-of-the-church-over-the-synagogue/?no_cache=1 (accessed 12 March 2010).

137. See Josua Bruyn, in "A Puzzling Picture at Oberlin: The Fountain of Life," *Allen Memorial Art Museum Bulletin* 16/1 (1958): 12–13 (http://www.oberlin.edu/amam/Spanish_FountainofLife.htm#C), accessed 12 March 2010. Bruyn contended that the three texted objects held by Jews contain specific psalm verses, of which I have discerned none. But since he was describing the Oberlin counterpart of this painting (which I have not observed closely), it could be the case (though unlikely) that the two diverge at this point. Gibberish Hebrew script is a recurrent phenomenon in medieval paintings, and a sign of Jews' abasement, though the period under discussion shows signs of change. See Shalom Sabar, "Between Calvinists and Jews: Hebrew Script in Rembrandt's Art," *Beyond the Yellow Badge: Anti-Judaism and Antisemitism in Medieval and Early Modern Visual Culture*, ed. Mitchell B. Merback (Leiden: Brill, 2008), 271–72.

138. David Nirenberg brilliantly analyzes the paradoxes inherent in the painting's pictorial realism attributed to the Christian perception of Jewish letters and literalness in "The Jewishness of Christian Art," in *Judaism and Christian Art: Aesthetic Anxieties from the Catacombs to Colonialism*, ed. Herbert L. Kessler and David Nirenberg (Philadelphia: University of Pennsylvania Press, 2011, 387–428).

139. Martin Luther, "Von den Juden und ihren Lügen" ("About the Jews and Their Lies"), in Luther, *Sämtliche Schriften*, vol. 20, "Reformationsschriften," ed. Dr. Johann Georg Walch, trans. Dagmar C. G. Lorenz (St. Louis, Missouri: Lutherischer Concordia Verlag, 1890), 1990.

140. The basic work on Lutheran music is still Friedrich Blume's *Protestant Church Music* (New York: Norton, 1974). See also Rebecca Wagner Oettinger, *Music as Propaganda in the German Reformation* (Aldershot: Ashgate, 2001).

141. See Moshe Idel's publications on this subject: "The Magical and Theurgic Interpretation of Music in Jewish Sources from the Renaissance to Hassidism," *Yuval* 4 (1982): 33–62; "Music and Prophetic Kabbalah," *Yuval* 4 (1982): 150–69; "Kabbalah and Music," *Judaism and Art*, ed. David Cassuto (Ramat Gan: Bar Ilan University Press, 1988–89), 289–75 (Hebrew); "Conceptualization of Music in Jewish Mysticism" in *Enchanting Powers*, ed. Lawrence E. Sullivan (Cambridge, MA: Harvard University Press, 1997), 159–88.

142. Rich interpretations of this kind are Spitzer's in *Classical and Christian Ideas*; John Hollander's in *The Untuning of the Sky: Ideas of Music in English Poetry, 1500–1700* (New York: Norton, 1961), 137, 150–53; and Simeon Kahn Henninger's, who based the title of an abovementioned book on the potent line "Touches of sweet harmony." Of the three, Spitzer's reveals an awareness of the implicit Jewish element.

143. For the ways whereby the universal and inclusive turn into the particular and exclusive, see Mark Shell, *Children of the Earth: Literature, Politics and Nationhood* (Oxford: Oxford University Press, 1993). An opposite course is marked by Thomas Carlyle in his *Sartor Resartus*, where "the immeasurable circumambient realm of Nothingness and Night" is the realm of the courageous, uncategorized wanderer who explores "hidden treasurers" long before it becomes a shared continent for all.

144. For the "Jewish crime" as was held in Shakespeare's time, see James Shapiro's instructive discussion in *Shakespeare and the Jews* (New York: Columbia, 1997), 89–111

and also David Nirenberg's *The Figure of the Jew: From Ancient Egypt to the Present* [provisional title] (New York: Norton, forthcoming) for a rich discussion of the work within the context of traditional Christian anti-Jewish epistemology.

145. According to the *Oxford English Dictionary*, this denotation was introduced in the late sixteenth century—Shakespeare's time.

146. See *The Merchant of Venice*, ed. M. M. Mahood (Cambridge: Cambridge University Press, 1987), 50; on Miller's reply to his critics on this provocative production see Helen Krich Chinoy, "The Director as Mythagog: Jonathan Miller Talks about Directing Shakespeare," *Shakespeare Quarterly* 27 (1976): 7–14.

147. He delves into the Orphic myth of music up to the lines: "Their savage eyes turned to a modest gaze / By the sweet power of music" and then skips to "mark the music." In the first part he skips from "such harmony is in immortal souls" to the end.

148. Galit Hasan-Rokem suggested to me that the irony in this case applies also to Jessica as Lorenzo's wife—a woman caught between two masters, two faiths, and two contradictory sets of sentiments.

149. In Denis Carey's 1953 production, Antonio's persistent melancholy was emphasized, as it has been in many recent productions. See Mahood, *The Merchant*, 42.

150. Heinrich Heine, "Shakespeares Mädchen und Frauen," *Werke und Briefe in zehn Bänden*, ed. Hans Kaufmann (Berlin and Weimar: Aufbau, 1972), 4:543 (http://www.zeno.org/Literatur/M/Heine,+Heinrich/Essays+III%3A+Aufs%C3%A4tze+und+Streitschriften).

151. See Harrán, "'Barucaba' as an Emblem for Jewishness in Early Italian Art Music," *Jewish Quarterly Review* 98/3 (2008): 328–54. This article analyzes the three extant works featuring synagogal "Barucaba" linguistically and partially also musically, and speculates on the phenomenon's origins and aftermath.

152. Orazio Vecchi, *L'Amfiparnaso: A New Edition of the Music with Historical and Analytical Essays*, ed. Cecil Adkins (Chapel Hill: University of North Carolina Press, 1977), 74. I made use of this edition for my analysis. I thank Yifat Simpson for introducing me to this work. The first to relate to this work in connection with musical representations of Jews was perhaps Alfred Einstein in Daniel Jütte, "Judendarstellungen in der Musik. Ein vergessener Text Alfred Einsteins," in *PaRDeS, Informationsblatt der Vereinigung für Jüdische Studien* 10 (2005): 11–14. Ideologically, his article is close in spirit to the studies of another Jewish émigré, Leo Spitzer.

153. In contrast to these nonsensical invocations, the crucial words in this "transaction"— *Moscogn* (pawn), *podem* (the act of its cashing), *Sabba* (Sabbat), *sinagoga*—remained almost undistorted. For a detailed account and possible renditions of the nonsensical words, see Harrán, "Barucaba," 342.

154. See Archibald T. Davidson and Willi Apel, *Historical Anthology of Music* (Cambridge, MA: Harvard University Press, 1950), 1:108, 227.

155. There is a possibility that the Hebrew chorus was intended as a satire on contemporary Catholic polyphony, as Gino Roncaglia once suggested (in *Orazio Vecchi, Contributi nel 4°centenario* [Modena, 1950] as quoted in *L'Amfiparnaso*, 101). But this only stresses the assessment that Jews became a model for the musically ridiculous.

156. As discussed by Don Harrán, "The Levi Dynasty: Three Generations of Jewish Musicians in Sixteenth-Century Mantua," in *"Uomo sagace": Judah Moscato and Jewish Culture in the Renaissance*, ed. Gianfranco Miletto, Adam Shear, and Giuseppe Veltri (Leiden and Boston: Brill, forthcoming).

157. Adriano Banchieri, *Barca di Venezia per Padova*, urtext edition, ed. Filomena A. de Luca (Bologna: Ut Orpheus, 1998). A relativist perspective is tenable even in the "Prioress' Tale" (see Calabrese, "Performing the Prioress," 72).

158. See Ruth HaCohen, "The Music of Sympathy," *Poetics Today* 22/3 (2001): 634–37.

159. Analysis is based on the facsimile score, Christ Church MS 83, 27–32; translation follows the one in the booklet for the CD *Lamenti Barocchi* 3 (Naxos, 8553320), 30–33.

160. In *L'incoronazione di Poppea*, I, iii.

161. Another contemporary example, which seems to convey a similar though more subtle lesson, is Alessandro Scarlatti's oratorio, *Hagar and Ismael* (1684), in which Sarah functions as the uncompassionate Hebrew mother (Sara) and the title roles prefigure the Virgin Mary and Christ.

CHAPTER 2. RETHINKING AND ENACTING SYMPATHETIC WORLDS

1. Jacques Rancière, in *The Politics of Aesthetics: The Distribution of the Sensible*, trans. Gabriel Rockhill (New York: Continuum, 2004).

2. This predicament trapped even Nazi propaganda, as we shall see in chapter 7.

3. Rich discussions of the period along its ideological and social changes can be found in Michael A. Meyer's *The Origins of the Modern Jew: Jewish Identity and European Culture in Germany, 1749–1824* (Detroit: Wayne State University Press, 1967), Jonathan M. Hess, *Germans, Jews and the Claims of Modernity* (New Haven: Yale University Press, 2002); *Deutsch-Jüdische Geschichte in der Neuzeit*, ed. Michael A. Meyer (Munich: Leo Beck Institute, 1996), vols. 1–2 (appeared simultaneously in German and Hebrew), to mention but a few examples.

4. The "Lavater affair" took place during 1769, when Johann Kaspar Lavater, a Swiss theologian, challenged Mendelssohn by calling him either to publicly refute Christianity or to join it. This forced Mendelssohn to explain his stubborn adherence to Judaism. Series of letters ensued, in which more people were involved and which eventually gave rise to Mendelssohn's famous treatise *Jerusalem* (*Schriften*, III). In this treatise, Mendelssohn developed his vision of the ideal society, where religion and tolerance are interconnected. See Meyer, *The Origins*, chapter II. See also Alexander Altmann, *Moses Mendelssohn: A Biographical Study* (Philadelphia: Jewish Publication Society, 1973), chapter 3 and Hess, *Germans, Jews*, 97–105.

5. On Plato's harsh judgment of compassion see Ruth HaCohen, "The Music of Sympathy in the Arts of the Baroque; or the Use of Difference to Overcome Indifference," *Poetics Today* 22/3 (2001): 609; see also Clifford Orwin, "Rousseau and the Discovery of Political Compassion," in *The Legacy of Rousseau*, ed. Clifford Orwin and Nathan Tarcov (Chicago: University of Chicago Press, 1997), 297.

6. For an elaborate survey of the Christian view see Joachim Koffler, *Mit-Leid, Geschichte und Problematik eines ethischen Grundwortes* (Würzburg: Echter, 2001).

7. In fact, those dealing with compassion went beyond rationalism (as associated with the Leibniz-Wolff school) or empiricism (as associated with Lock and Hume, though Hume's contribution to the concept of sympathy is of prime importance to its later elaborations). Shaftsbury, more of a neo-Platonist than an empiricist, was an important inspiration. See also James Engell, *The Creative Imagination: Enlightenment to Romanticism* (Cambridge, MA: Harvard University Press, 1981), 143–60.

8. Clifford Orwin goes even beyond this to claim that theological compassion is in fact charity, that "to love one's fellow as Christ loves him is to strive to the salvation of the soul. Compassion, by contrast, is purely human and is altogether this-worldly . . . a natural sentiment which attests to the goodness or innocence of our nature" ("Rousseau," 296). Culturally, historically, and theologically speaking, I see this distinction as an overstatement, especially with regard to the kind of compassion practiced within certain Lutheran traditions, as will become clearer in the following.

9. Descartes analyzed the composite nature of this passion in the framework of his theory of emotions in his *Passions de l'âme* of 1649. See René Descartes, *The Passions of the Soul*, in *The Philosophical Writings of Descartes*, trans. J. Cottingham, R. Stoothoff, and D. Murdoch (Cambridge: Cambridge University Press, 1985), vol. 1, sec. 185–88, 395.

10. It seems that Adam Smith refers to this statement, or to a similar one by Mendelssohn, when he mentions that "a late ingenious and subtle philosopher thought it necessary to prove, by arguments, that we had a real sympathy with Joy, and that congratulation was a principle of the human heart." Smith, *The Theory of Moral Sentiments* (New York: Prometheus, 2000), 60.

11. Moses Mendelssohn, in *Ästhetische Schriften in Auswahl*, ed. Otto F. Best (Darmstadt: Wissenschaftliche Buchgesellschaft, [1761] 1974).

12. Apart from Mendelssohn's original contributions to *Mitleid*, he also translated Rousseau's *First and Second Discourses*, which discuss compassion.

13. Gotthold Ephraim Lessing, Moses Mendelssohn, Friedrich Nicolai, *Briefwechsel über das Trauerspiel* [1756/57], ed. Jochen Schulte-Sasse (Munich: Winkler, 1972), 55. The mutual development of the conception regarding the boundaries of compassion in the German orbit, especially in relation to Mendelssohn and Lessing, is discussed by Reinhart Meyer-Kalkus in "Apotheose und Kritik des Mitleids: Lessing und Mendelssohn," *Berlin Debatte Initial* 17 (2006), 36–49.

14. Rousseau's ideas of sympathy appear in his various writings of which those furnishing the discussion below are *The First and Second Discourses*, ed. Roger D. Masters (New York: St. Martin's, 1964); *Essay on the Origin of Languages*, in *On the Origin of Language*, trans. John H. Moran and Alexander Gode (Chicago: University of Chicago Press, 1966); and *Politics and the Arts, Letter to M. d'Alembert on the Theatre*, trans. Allan Bloom (Ithaca: Cornell University Press, 1960). Smith's *Theory of Moral Sentiment* was first published in 1754.

15. Jacques Derrida, *Of Grammatology*, corrected edition, trans. Gayatri Chakravorty Spivak (Baltimore: Johns Hopkins University Press, 1998), 185. See also Orwin, "Rousseau," 297.

16. Orwin elaborates some of Derrida's claims, though he never mentions him. He, in any case, emphasizes that imagination develops only with reason, and it is only then that it salvages bestial compassion from its "obscurity" (300–301). It is important also to add here Orwin's emphasis on what he considers as the peak of Rousseau's presentation of pity, that is, his evocation of the great cosmopolitan soul, "who rises furthest above the conventions that hamper the rest of us like blinders" (301).

17. Paul de Man, "The Rhetoric of Blindness: Jacques Derrida's Reading of Rousseau," in *Blindness and Insight: Essays in the Rhetoric of Contemporary Criticism*, (Minneapolis: University of Minnesota Press, [1971] 1983), 123–25. De Man elaborated his ideas as part of his famous controversy with Derrida's interpretation to Rousseau's ideas in the *Grammatology*. Rousseau's insights regarding music's unique cognitive and semiotic character could be influenced by Daniel Webb's profound treatise on the correspondences between music and poetry (1769). See Ruth Katz and Ruth HaCohen, *Tuning the Mind: Connecting Aesthetics to Cognitive Science* (New Brunswick, NJ: Transaction, 2003), 210–21 and Katz and HaCohen, eds., *The Arts in Mind: Pioneering Texts of a Coterie of British Men of Letters* (New Brunswick, NJ: Transaction, 2003), 256–327.

18. Rousseau, *Essay on the Origin*, 57.

19. Ibid., 8.

20. de Man, "The Rhetoric," 128.

21. Ibid., 132.

22. See Rousseau, *Essay on the Origin*, chapter 19.

23. See Smith, *Theory*, especially section I, chapter IV; section III, chapter 1.

24. Ibid., 66.

25. Ibid., 5, 14; Rousseau's attack on the theater appears in his *Politics and the Arts*, 24–25.

26. See K. C. Cole, *Sympathetic Vibrations: Reflections on Physics as a Way of Life* (New York: Bantam, 1985), 263–76, and HaCohen, "The Music of Sympathy," 626–27.

27. Smith, *Theory*, 67–68, 69.

28. See Smith, *Theory*, 14 and my discussion of Wagner's ideas in chapter 5.

29. On this connection and other related issues see James Chandler's instructive discussion in "Moving Accidents: The Emergence of Sentimental Probability," in *The Age of Cultural Revolutions*, eds. Colin Jones and Dror Wahrman (Berkeley: University of California Press, 2001), 137–70.

30. See Smith, *Theory*, "Of Duty"; I am grateful to James Chandler for calling my attention to this important caveat. For an insightful discussion of the transition from "naïve" to "sentimental" compassion/sympathy and its challenges in the modern and postmodern world see Geoffrey Hartman, "The Sympathy Paradox," in *The Fateful Question of Culture* (New York: Columbia University Press, 1997), chapter 5.

31. This is discussed in his *Hamburgische Dramaturgie* (Stuttgart: Alfred Kröner, 1958), pp. 290–311, 318–26.

32. As they surfaced in the *Kohelet Mussar* affair—a moral journal he initiated and edited (only two issues were published). See Meir Gilon, *Mendelssohn's 'Kohelet Mussar'*

and Its Historical Context (Jerusalem: The Israel Academy of Sciences and Humanities, 1979, in Hebrew).

33. See Mendelssohn, *Sendschreiben*, 80, as quoted in Meyer-Kalkus, "Apotheose und Kritik," 40.

34. The premiere of this production took place in Berlin in 1999. I also attended a performance of the same in Berlin, 2005, which both musically and dramatically was less convincing.

35. They consciously make noise throughout, e.g., when their noisy flight from Jesus after the incarceration (in the opening ritornello of the great chorus "O Mensch, bewein' dein' Sünde groß") stresses the mimetic element of the ritornello's basic motif, concretizing the discordant elements from which it derives. This dissolves the "harmoniousness" attributed to Bach's music through its traditional affiliation with Renaissance (*stile antico*) polyphonic writing.

36. The following passage from the production's program notes (of 2005) attests to the designers' intentions: "In September 27, 1941 the sixteen-year-old Zvi Michalowski was about to be murdered with over 3000 other Lithuanian Jews. He had fallen into the pit a fraction of a second before [the discharge of] the volley of shots which killed those standing with him. At night he crept out of the mass grave and fled to the next village. A farmer who opened the door saw the naked boy, covered with blood, and said/yelled: 'Jew, go back to the grave where you belong!'—Desperate, [the youngster] finally implored an old widow: 'I am your Lord, Jesus Christ,' he said. 'I came down from the cross. Look at me—the blood, the pain, the suffering of the innocent. Let me in.' The widow, recalls Zvi, fell at his feet and hid him for three days. Then the [resurrected] young man set off for the forest. There he survived the war as a partisan." Borrowed from Martin Gilbert, *The Holocaust* (New York: Holt, Reinhart & Winston, 1986), 27); it is an extract from Yaffa Eliach's controversial *Hasidic Tales of the Holocaust* (London: Oxford University Press, 1982).

37. The directors' attempt to bind the role of these "abstract voices," embedded in Bach's score, to biblical personae seems to derive from Mendelssohn's theological aesthetic conception (following Schleiermacher's) concerning these voices.

38. The Italian *cori spezzati* principle (literally: divided choruses) infiltrated Lutheran Germany via Heinrich Schütz and other composers, mainly from Venice. The extent to which Bach puts this principle to use in the *St. Matthew Passion* is beyond all antecedents and contrasts with its decline among Bach's contemporaries. For a concise description of the historical vocal forces that Bach mobilized for the production of the work, see Daniel R. Melamed, *Hearing Bach's Passions* (New York: Oxford University Press, 2005). As Christopher Wolff stresses, the special effect of the double forces of the work (two choirs, two organs, two orchestras) in Bach's time "by no means went unnoticed." See Wolff, *Johann Sebastian Bach: The Learned Musician* (Oxford: Oxford University Press, 2000), 298. For a semiotic analysis of these forces in terms of the genres, gestures, fictional planes, and recursive nets they inhabit, see Ruth HaCohen, "Fictional Planes and Their Interplay: The Alchemy of Forms and Emotions in *St. Matthew Passion*," in *Music and Signs: Semiotic and Cognitive Studies in Music*, ed. Ioannis Zannos (Bratislava: ASCO Art and Science, 1999), 416–34.

39. In the Israeli performance, the choir was the Estonian National Choir, but this did not interfere with the general impression that the entire production was German.

40. The original verses from the Song of Songs (3, 11) are: "Go out, O daughters of Zion, and look upon King Solomon, with the crown with which his mother crowned him, on the day of his wedding, on the day of the gladness of his heart." The first number of the second part similarly paraphrases a Song of Songs verse.

41. Albert Schweitzer's hermeneutic approach, previously disparaged, can now be partially supported by recent rhetorical and semiotic research.

42. The text of the chorale is worth quoting here: "O Lamm Gottes, unschuldig, / am Stamm des Kreuzes geschlachtet, / Allzeit erfunden geduldig, / Wiewohl du warest verachtet. // All' Sünd' hast Du getragen, / Sonst müssten wir verzagen, / Erbarm' dich unser, O Jesu." (O lamb of God, unspotted, / Upon the Cross Thou art slaughtered, / Serene and ever patient, / Tho' scorned and cruelly tortured. // All sin for our sake bearing, / Else would we die despairing, / Have pity on us, O Jesus.) The aloofness of this choral melody is expressed, among other ways, by its distinct G-major tonality soaring above the E minor below. The key words through which the "earthly" events are either affirmed or negated—*Unschuld* (innocence), *Geduld* (patience), *erbarm' dich* (have mercy), and so on—will be later taken up by various individual voices. In the overture itself, the soprano chorale "geduldig" coincides with the chorus "sehet die Geduld" ("see the patience," mm. 44–46); the chorale's "unschuldig" is met with the responsive "auf unser Schuld" only in the second part, after which it is repeated several times (from m. 61).

43. I found three reviews of the 1999 premiere, two of which were very favorable regarding both the production and the music (Subill Mahlke, "Jesus Christ Opernstar," *Tagesspiegel* 4 April 1999 and Wolfgang Schreiber, "Die Kerle um Jesus," *Süddeutsche Zeitung*, 78, 4 April 1999, 17), and another that expressed a very disapproving view on both aspects (Klaus Georg Koch, "Jesus lieb mich," *Berliner Zeitung*, 6 April 1999, 11). The only extant Israeli review was highly acclamatory in terms of the conception (and was more critical respecting the musical aspects). See Hagai Hitron, "Excitement with Reserve," *Haaretz Daily Newspaper*, 20 February, 2002. The staging of oratorios was a common practice at the beginning of the twentieth century. See Winton Dean, *Handel's Dramatic Oratorios and Masques* (London: Oxford University Press, 1959), 8.

44. Günther Uecker and Götz Friedrich's article (formerly at http://www.deutsche operberlin.de/home/index.html).

45. Christopher Hogwood, in "Den Zeitgenossen nahegebracht," in the program notes of the production (*Johann Sebastian Bach, Matthäus-Passion* Deutsche Oper, 1999, 21). Christopher Hogwood was the conductor of the 1999 production. Mendelssohn's urtext or full score is now preserved in the Bodleian Library, Oxford (Ms. M. D. Mendelssohn c. 68).

46. In the above program notes.

47. Eduard Devrient, *Meine Erinnerungen an Felix Mendelsssohn-Bartholdy und seine Briefe an mich* (Leipzig, 1872), 62. Jeffrey S. Sposato, in "The Price of Assimilation: The Oratorios of Felix Mendelssohn and the Nineteenth-Century Anti-Semitic Tradi-

tion" (PhD diss., Brandeis University, 2000), 73, rightly criticizes Natalia MacFarren's translation, in Eduard Devrient, *My Recollections of Felix Mendelssohn Bartholdy and His Letters to Me*, trans. Natalia MacFarren (New York: Vienna House, 1972), 57, of the poignant *Komödiant* as "actor" and *ein Judenjunge* as "Jew," which takes the edge off their sarcastic flavor.

48. Larry Todd in *Mendelssohn: A Life in Music* (Oxford: Oxford University Press, 2003), 122–23 follows A. B. Marx's testimony on this account. It is Peter Ward Jones who surmised that the occasion was Felix's birthday, whereas Devrient tells us it was an 1823 Christmas present. It is improbable that this Jewish grandmother gave her grandson a Christmas gift, though there is a possibility that it was a Hanukkah present (if Hanukkah presents were customary in these Jewish circles at that early time). See Rudolf Elvers and Peter Ward Jones, "Das Musikalienverzeichnis von Fanny und Felix Mendelssohn Bartholdy," *Mendelssohn Studien* 8 (1993): 85–104.

49. Cherished in partial performances in many private gatherings at the Mendelssohns, as told by Devrient and others.

50. Pölschau himself had purchased the work from the estate of C. F. G. Schwenke, C. P. E. Bach's successor in Hamburg. It had belonged to the family since 1799; see Todd, *Mendelssohn*, 123–24. See also Martin Geck, *Die Wiederentdeckung der Matthäuspassion im 19. Jahrhundert. Die zeitgenössischen Dokumente und ihre ideengeschichtliche Deutung* (Regensburg: Gustav Bosse, 1967), 18–19. The view of music as a divine art was also part of the Mendelssohns' legacy, as attested by Moses Mendelssohn's deep attraction to and love of music, expressed, in one of several instances, in an (anonymous) treatise on the construction of the well-tempered pianoforte. See Altmann, *Moses Mendelssohn*, 60, 66–67; for the treatise's English text, introduced and annotated, see David Halperin, "To Please Both the Ear and the Eye: Moses Mendelssohn, Equal Temperament and the Delian Problem," in *Yuval: Studies of the Jewish Music Research Centre VII (Studies in Honour of Israel Adler)*, ed. Eliyahu Schleifer and Edwin Seroussi (Jerusalem: The Hebrew University Magnes Press, 2002), 442–67.

51. Sarah Levy, Babette's sister, was a favorite student of Wilhelm Friedemann Bach; Lea Mendelssohn (Felix's mother) herself was an avid student of this tradition, as attested by Adolph Bernhard Marx, a Jew himself and the leading musical theorist of his time, who held a long and significant relationship with Mendelssohn (Geck, *Die Wiederentdeckung*, 18). For an important assessment of Sarah Levy's role in Berlin musical life and the Bach cult see Peter Wollny, "Sara Levy and the Making of Musical Taste in Berlin," *Musical Quarterly* 77/4 (1993), 651–88. See also Wollny's recent study, *Ein förmlicher Sebastian und Philipp Emanuel Bach-Kultus: Sara Levy und ihr musikalisches Wirken* (Wiesbaden: Breitkopf & Härtel, 2010). Other very well-known Bach devotees of the intermediate generation were members of the Baron van Swieten circle in Vienna of the 1780s, which included Mozart and Haydn. In Berlin, it was the Singakademie under Zelter that commenced a "Bach fever" at the turn of the century. Of those who wrote about the anecdote of the gift, Geck was the most sensitive to this remarkable historical moment: "A worldly, artistically exposed Jewess, who grew up in the Berlin Bach tradition, was among the first to anticipate the dynamic

of the probably most powerful and well-known work of musical Lutheranism." Geck himself, however, could have been influenced by Marx, who sensed the historical importance of this gift: "Only the wish of Mendelssohn's grandmother to grant her grandson a present of an unknown musical work brought it into Mendelssohn's possession and effected the production of the genuine score" (*Die Wiederentdeckung,* 19, 21).

52. This is known through Friedrich Nicolai's report (mentioned above, himself a distinguished intellectual and theoretician of music, who also befriended Moses Mendelssohn), which states: "Herr Daniel Itzig . . . besitzt eine auserlesene Sammlung von Gemälden; unter denselben . . . Moses schlägt den Felsen von Beschey; ein großer Prospekt von vielen Personen von Canaletto; . . . Ganymed von Rubens; Herkules und Omphale aus Rubens Schule; . . . Eli und Elkana, der seinen Sohn Samuel bringt, von Gerbrand van den Ekhout [*sic*]; ein Familienstück von Peter Hals" (Mr. Daniel Itzig owns an exquisite collection of paintings, among them *Moses Strikes the Rocks* by Beschey, a big panorama with many people by Canaletto, *Ganymede* by Rubens, *Hercules and Omphale* from the school of Rubens, *Eli and Elkana, who brings his son Samuel,* by Gerbrand van den Eeckhout; a family piece by Peter Hals). From *Beschreibung der Königlichen Residenzstädte Berlin und Potsdam* (Berlin, 1786) 2, 839, as quoted in Mordechai Breuer and Michael Graetz, *Deutsch-Jüdische Geschichte in der Neuzeit* I 1600–1780 (Munich: C. H. Beck, 1996), 255.

53. Interestingly, Leo Spitzer's study of noise etymology starts with the Vulgate's translation of Numbers 21:5: "for there is no bread, and there is no water; and our soul [*anima*] loatheth [*nauseat*] this light bread." This event follows the one in Qades, depicted in Beschey's painting, itself caused by a previous complaint (a loud lament!). See Leo Spitzer, "Patterns of Thought and of Etymology, I. Nausea>OF(>Eng.) Noise," *Word* I/3 (1945), 262.

54. See Tzvetan Todorov, "The Origin of Genres," in *Modern Genre Theory,* ed. David Duff (London: Longman, 2000), 193–209; for a similar thesis see also Fredric Jameson's instructive discussion in *The Political Unconscious: Narrative as a Socially Symbolic Act* (London: Methuen, 1981).

55. It is not surprising that a tradition that had established itself on St. Augustine's theological teachings would celebrate such a complex temporal construction. See Paul Ricoeur's "The Time of the Soul and the Time of the Worlds: The Dispute between Augustine and Aristotle," in his *Time and Narrative,* trans. Kathleen Blamey and David Pellauer (Chicago: University of Chicago Press, [1985] 1988), 3:21–22.

56. The term *Oratorium,* however, was only rarely applied in Lutheran Germany, as Christoph Wolff claims in "Under the Spell of Opera? Bach's Oratorio Trilogy," *Bach Perspectives* 8 (2011): 5. I thank the author for letting me read the article before publication.

57. For a more extensive elaboration of this theoretical framework in relation to the *St. Matthew Passion,* see Ruth HaCohen, "Fictional Planes and Their Interplay," and HaCohen, "The Dramaturgy of Religious Emotions in Bach's Cantatas: Aristotelian Processes in Neoplatonic Frames," in *Understanding Bach* 4 (2009): 33–54 (http://

www.bachnetwork.co.uk/ub4/hacohen.pdf). Close to my approach is the richly elaborate article of Naomi Cumming, "The Subjectivities of Erbarme Dich," *Music Analysis* 16/1 (1997): 5–44.

58. Devrient, as quoted in Todd, *Mendelssohn*, 194. The virtual agents' role in Passion music did not originate with Bach. One of the first to so use it was the composer Johann Sebastiani, from Königsberg (1663–1672). See Kurt von Fischer, *Die Passion, Musik Zwischen Kunst und Kirche* (Kassel: Bärenreiter/Metzler, 1997).

59. See HaCohen, "Dramaturgy," for a discussion of the concept of Dasein in a similar context.

60. The term "show forth" is used by James Joyce's Stephen Dedalus in his definition of "epiphany," which appears to share some features with "oratorical moments."

61. Walter Benjamin, *Ursprung des deutschen Trauerspiels*, in *Gesammelte Schriften*, ed. Rolf Tiedemann and Hermann Schweppenhäuser (Frankfurt am Main: Suhrkamp, 1978), 1:230, trans. John Osborne as *The Origin of German Tragic Drama* (New York: Verso, 1988), 49. The whole concept of *Entstehung* and *Ursprung* is pertinent here, as its dialectics comprises the historical and the metaphysical in a unique way.

62. This is the tradition Eric Chafe refers to in his attempt to unearth the "tonal allegory" of Bach's great oratorical legacy in his *Tonal Allegory in the Vocal Music of J. S. Bach* (Berkeley: University of California Press, 1991). However important this perspective, it tends to eschew the vital and subversive role a work of art can play vis-à-vis its tradition. On the epistemological problem of such an allegorical reading of texts and its political implications, see Fredric Jameson's *Political Unconscious*.

63. Cumming, "The Subjectivities."

64. For this history see Geck, *Die Wiederentdeckung* and Celia Applegate, *Bach in Berlin: Nation and Culture in Mendelssohn's Revival of the "St. Matthew Passion"* (Cornell: Cornell University Press, 2005).

65. See Michael Marissen, "Religious Aims in Mendelssohn's 1829 Berlin-Singakademie Performances of Bach's *St. Matthew Passion*," *Musical Quarterly* 77 (1993): 718–26; Sposato, *The Price of Assimilation: Felix Mendelssohn and the Nineteenth-Century Anti-Semitic Tradition* (Oxford: Oxford University Press, 2006), 41–42.

66. Sposato, ibid., 111, relies on Friedrich Schleiermacher, *Der christliche Glaube 1821–22: Studienausgabe*, ed. Hermann Peiter (Berlin: Walter de Gruyter, 1984) 2:207–209.

67. The numbers refer to the *Neue Bach-Ausgabe*; this holds also for the *St. John Passion*. The abbreviation NBA will be omitted from subsequent references.

68. Ulrich Leisinger, in "Form and Functions of the Choral Movements in J. S. Bach's *St. Matthew Passion*," *Bach Studies* 2, ed. Daniel R. Melamed (Cambridge: Cambridge University Press, 1995), 70–84, interprets the dissection of this number into two separate expressive entities as related to the Baroque doctrine of affection, which "does not allow for the representation of two antithetical human passions at the same time" (79). I think that this movement proves the opposite, i.e., that the two are represented as unfolding simultaneously, as do many other antithetical human passions in the Baroque (as they are represented, for example, in Poussin's great scene paintings). What differentiates this movement from, say, a Mozart ensemble is that the personae

to whom contrasting passions are attributed do not share the same arena of action, i.e., they do not interact with each other or try to influence one another with regards to a shared state of affairs.

69. It is with Spitta that the tradition of viewing this aria in terms of action (walking) seems to issue. The ground for this symbolic interpretation is a rhetorical tradition that originated in the Baroque.

70. Movements with similar accompaniment (the so-called *bassetchen* arias) in the *Passion* have a similar expressive quality, as Chafe showed in *Tonal Allegory*, 350–51.

71. John Butt, *Bach's Dialogue with Modernity: Perspectives on the Passions* (Cambridge: Cambridge University Press, 2010), 162. I am grateful to the author for letting me read this valuable manuscript before publication.

72. Laurence D. Dreyfus, "The Metaphorical Soloist: Concerted Organ Parts in Bach's Cantatas," *Early Music* 13 (1985): 237–47.

73. Bach succeeded in extending and condensing the ritornello to befit his semiotic program. One of his devices was to set the pedal point in the tonic (and not in the dominant) and thus to turn this section of the theme into a final or semifinal gesture. The latter enabled him to overlap this part with a new beginning of the ritornello cycle, which commences with a pedal point in the tonic.

74. Following Heinz Kohut's definition of empathy as "vicarious introspection" and connecting it to the idea of Christ's sacrifice as an act of "vicarious atonement."

75. For Marx the work was "a living church service of the congregation . . . already in the rehearsals with reduced forces the artistic and religious sense of the participants was highly stimulated." For more contemporary reactions, see Marissen, "Religious Aims," 720 and Applegate, *Bach in Berlin*.

76. Meyerbeer tried never to miss an annual performance of the work. See *The Diaries of Giacomo Meyerbeer* (1791–1839), 3 vols., trans. and ed. Robert Ignatius Letellier (Madison, NJ: Fairleigh Dickinson University Press, 2000–2002), 1:45.

77. Ludwig Rellstab, *Vossische Zeitung*, 13 March 1829; quoted in Todd, *Mendelssohn*, 198 (n. 164).

78. His adherence to his Jewish origins found expression in early days in the famous "Mendelssohn-Bartholdy" name affair. On the seriousness of Mendelssohn's admiration for Moses Mendelssohn's work, see Leon Botstein, "Neoclassicism, Romanticism, and Emancipation: The Origins of Felix Mendelssohn's Aesthetic Outlook," in *The Mendelssohn Companion*, ed. Douglass Seaton (Westport: Greenwood Press, 2001), 4–5.

79. Jeffrey S. Sposato, "Creative Writing: The [Self-] Identification of Mendelssohn as Jew," *Musical Quarterly* 82/1 (1998): 204.

80. He becomes more tentative in the "second round" of this debate, published as Jeffrey S. Sposato, "Mendelssohn, Paulus and the Jews: A Response to Leon Botstein and Michael P. Steinberg," *Musical Quarterly* 83/2 (1999): 280–91.

81. Leon Botstein, "Mendelssohn and the Jews," *Musical Quarterly* 82 (1998): 211.

82. In the following issue of the journal: Michael P. Steinberg, "Mendelssohn's Music and German-Jewish Culture: An Intervention," *Musical Quarterly* 83/1 (1999): 31–44; the same argument, elaborated, is included in *The Cambridge Companion to Men-*

delssohn as "Mendelssohn and Judaism," 26–41, later published as part of his *Listening to Reason: Culture, Subjectivity, and Nineteenth-Century Music* (Princeton: Princeton University Press, 2006). Steinberg admirably "intervened" in the above debate, bringing more evidence (e.g., the composer's investment in the *Antigone* themes) as well as strong theoretical claims to the "nonexclusive" and "unstable" question of Mendelssohn's identity, contextualizing it within the general modern "German-Jewish" culture. The serious attitude of the Mendelssohns toward (Christian) New Year (reminiscent of Rosh Hashanah) manifests such instability. See Steinberg, "Mendelssohn and Judaism," 40.

83. It can be further argued that the multilayering of the work forms the basis for the changing nature of communities and individuals that have opened their hearts and minds to its complex message in the course of its history of reception. For a philosophico-semiotic argument in support of this claim see Eero Tarasti, *Existential Semiotics* (Bloomington: Indiana University Press, 2000), especially 17–36. It is no coincidence that Tarasti chose to illustrate his views drawing on the *St. Matthew Passion* as a prime example. If, following Hans Blumenberg, "each hearing of the St. Matthew Passion seems to mark the refounding of an institution," the question is, of course, to what extent all these institutions cohere. Hans Blumenberg, *Matthäuspassion* (Frankfurt am Main: Suhrkamp, 1988), 48, as quoted in Butt, *Bach's Dialogue*, 103.

84. The academy began to rehearse part of the work already in the 1800s. See Todd, *Mendelssohn*, 42.

85. See Martin Staehelin, "*Elijah*, Johann Sebastian Bach, and the New Covenant: On the Aria "Es ist genug" in Felix Mendelssohn-Bartholdi's Oratorio *Elijah*," in *Mendelssohn and His World*, ed. Larry Todd, trans. Susan Gillespie (Princeton: Princeton University Press, 1991), 121–36.

86. Whether the defeat to Rungenhagen in the election was directly anti-Semitic or whether anti-Semitism was only indirectly insinuated on his behalf remains a debate among scholars. See W. A. Little, "Mendelssohn and the Berlin Singakademie: The Composer at the Crossroad," in *Mendelssohn and His World*, 65–86; Todd, *Mendelssohn*, 264–65.

87. A rich complementary assessment of the adventures of the work and its reception in modern times vis-à-vis its musico-dramatic contents is given by Butt, in *Bach's Dialogue*.

88. This is only implied in *St. John*. Michael Marissen, in *Lutheranism, Anti-Judaism, and Bach's "St. John Passion"* (New York: Oxford University Press, 1998), 26, 35, insists on the hermeneutical turn of the work in this direction.

89. This has been observed first by Friedrich Smend in "Die Johannes-Passion von Bach," *Bach Jahrbuch* 37 (1926), 105–28. See also Dagmar Hoffmann-Axthelm, "Bach und die *Perfida Iudaica*: Zur Symmetrie der Juden-Turbae in der Johannes-Passion," *Basler Jahrbuch für historische Musikpraxis* 13 (1989): 31–54.

90. Moments prefiguring the interactive parts of the *St. Matthew Passion* appear in the no. 24 bass aria with chorus "Eilt" (Hurry) with the "wohin" (whither) utterances by the choir (much less integrated than in the parallel "Golgatha" alto aria in the *St. Matthew Passion*, having a "childish" effect, as Friedrich Wilhelm Marpurg claimed

in 1750; see Marissen, *Lutheranism*, 32), and the bass aria with chorale (no. 32), "Mein treuer Heiland / Jesu, der du warest tot" (My precious Saviour / Jesus, you who were dead), but they take place within the same *Dasein* level—that of the believers, or eternal Christian community. (The translations are borrowed from the annotated translation of Marissen in *Lutheranism*.)

91. The liturgical centrality and importance of the Kᵉdushah section renders this verse a vocal "crown" of sorts, musically as well as liturgically.

92. Chafe, *Tonal Allegory*.

93. Chafe, ibid., and Marissen, *Lutheranism* 13.

94. See Jeremy Cohen, *Living Letter of the Law: Ideas of the Jews in Medieval Christianity* (Berkeley: University of California Press, 1999), chapter 1.

95. The creators of the Deutsche Oper *St. Matthew Passion* production were sensitive to this predicament, using the story of the Shoah survivor Zvi Michalowsky, quoted above (n. 36), as a motto to their program notes.

96. See Marissen's discussion in *Lutheranism*, especially pp. 28–36. Though some of his arguments are well taken, he seems to me not to be attentive enough to the harsh dissonant setting of the central turba sections with their up and down chromatic bass when the Jews shout (no. 16b [23]): "Wäre dieser nicht ein Übeltäter, wir hätten dir ihn nicht überantwortet" (Were this one not an evildoer, we would not have given him over to you) and (16d [25]): "Wir dürfen niemand töten" (We are not allowed to put anyone to death).

97. The *Improperia* section or a parallel prayer against the perfidious Jews central to the Catholic liturgy of Good Friday (as we have seen in chapter 1) was not practiced in the Lutheran services in eighteenth-century Leipzig and its surroundings. See Marissen, *Lutheranism*, 33. Raymond Erickson, following the contributions of Arno Herzig and Jacob Goldberg, has elaborated on the Leipzig theologians' 1714 *Gutachten* denouncing the traditional ritual murder accusation as lacking any historical or (Jewish) religious basis ("In the Defense of the Jews: Leipzig Theologians in the Early Enlightenment," forthcoming, *Musical Quarterly*). I thank the author for permission to refer to this paper before publication.

98. Marissen, *Lutheranism*, 16.

99. Franz Rosenzweig, *Der Stern der Erlösung*, part 3 (Frankfurt: Suhrkamp, [1976] 1988); *The Star of Redemption*, trans. William W. Hallo, book 3 (Boston: Beacon, [1971] 1972).

100. See chapter 3 below.

101. Substitutions included Jehuda Halevy's "O Gott, nach dir allein steht mein Verlangen" (O God, towards you alone goes my desire) for the aria "Betrachte, meine Seele, mit ängstlichem Vergnügen" (Ponder, my soul, with anxious pleasure) no. 19 (31) and "Weltende" by Else Lasker-Schüler for "Es ist vollbracht." For further details, see Almut Sh. Bruckstein and Ruth HaCohen, "An Experiment in Reception and Conception: Re-texting Bach's *St John Passion* for Good Friday 2005," in *Understanding Bach* 1 (2006): 87–88 (http://www.bachnetwork.co.uk/ub1/hacohen2.pdf). On the difficulties of performing the work in the church as part of current liturgy see Marissen, *Lutheranism*, 6; and regarding how to perform anti-Semitic music responsibly

nowadays, see Richard Taruskin, "Text and Act," in Taruskin, *Text and Act: Essays on Music and Performance* (New York: Oxford University Press, 1995), 353–58.

102. Gotthold Ephraim Lessing, *Die Juden. Ein Lustspiel in einem Aufzug verfertigt im Jahr 1749* (Stuttgart: Philipp Reclam, [1981] 2002), 44. In the following translations from Lessing's works I drew on Noel Clark's English translation, Gotthold Ephraim Lessing, *Two Jewish Plays: The Jews, Nathan the Wise* (London: Oberon, 2002), though I chose to deviate from it in various places.

103. The sextet takes place in the third act of Mozart's opera, when Marcellina and Bartolo recognize Figaro as their lost son and he recognizes them as his parents. The small drama that takes place there concerns the entrance of Susanna, his betrothed, who had been absent at that moment of recognition and misinterprets it. This is not the only affinity between the two comic plays, the most important of which is the fact that it is the noble person, rather than the buffa characters, who must learn the lesson; here the prejudiced baron, there the lascivious count.

104. The more farcical tone opted for this rejoinder in George Tabori's (in the "Berliner Ensemble," 2005) interpretation seems to me less intuitive. In any event, as Wilfried Barner comments, the young lady is innocent of the anti-Jewish sentiments harbored by the other participants. See his "Lessings *Die Juden* im Zusammenhang seines Frühwerks" (*Lessing Yearbook Supplement: Humanität und Dialog* (Detroit: Wayne State University Press, 1982), 203.

105. See Barner, ibid., for the centrality of the battle against the prejudices endorsing discrimination of groups, including women and actors, in Lessing's early work and thought.

106. It was published, however, only in 1754, the year in which Lessing met Mendelssohn—the cause for the mistaken conflation of the traveler with the Jewish philosopher by many scholars.

107. Lessing's decision to set the drama in a contemporary German context is discussed in Wilhelm Grosse's epilogue to the edition I used (Lessing, Die Juden, 70–88).

108. See the dialogue between Michel Stich and Martin Krumm, in scene i.

109. See Johannes Wallmann, "The Reception of Luther's Writings on the Jews from the Reformation to the End of the 19th Century," *Lutheran Quarterly* (new series) 1/1 (1987): 72–97.

110. Scene ii (p. 9). Compare this to the Baron's diatribe against the Jews, which is no less dramatically ironic, likewise "ethnographically" reflective, though with fewer directly religious overtones and more "modern" ones (e.g., the physiognomic claim), scene iii, line 21.

111. This in itself can be interpreted as having homoerotic overtones, as interpreted by George Tabori in the 2004–5 production mentioned above.

112. In Genesis 21:22–23, Abimelech, king of Gerar, and Phicol, his army commander, said to Abraham, "God is with thou in all that thou doest. Now therefore swear unto me here by God that thou wilt not deal falsely with me, nor with my son, nor with my son's son, but according to the kindness that I have done unto thee, thou shalt do unto me, and to the land wherein thou hast sojourned." This appeal leads to the treaty between them.

113. See chapter 5.
114. See *Writing Culture: The Poetics and Politics of Ethnography*, ed. James Clifford and George E. Marcus (Berkeley: University of California Press, 1986), 98–121, for the manner in which allegory could burst forth from realism or even ethnological narrative. Galit Hasan-Rokem uses this dialectic to address "The Emergence of Theological Concepts from Everyday Life: Jews and Christians in Roman Galilee or: Rabbinical Ethnography and Allegorical Tales" (unpublished manuscript), in an essay that brought these theoretical discussions to my awareness. The ethnological basis of this text is evident, as in Krumm's diatribe against the Jews, quoted above. See also Barner's "Lessings *Die Juden*," 194–95, for the "empirical" character of the psychological reality of Lessing's early works.
115. Scene 22, p. 44. (English edition: 52.)
116. Scene 22, p. 45. (English edition: 53.) These lines bring us back to the musical affinity with *The Marriage of Figaro*, alluded to above, and to the genre which both relate to and transcend through Enlightenment morality. As with *Figaro*, here too the nobleman shakes off some of his prejudices through a costumed trial taught by *mezzo carattere*.
117. This and the following German quotations are borrowed from G. E. Lessing's *Nathan der Weise* (Stuttgart: Phillip Reclam, [1964] 2000). For the English version see again Noel Clark's translation in *Two Jewish Plays: The Jews, Nathan the Wise*. As in the instance of *The Jews*, I allowed myself to alter his translation slightly when deemed necessary.
118. These connections have frequently been mentioned in the scholarly literature since the eighteenth century. Again, vocal resonance in the recognition moment in the last scene of *Nathan the Wise* calls to mind the resonating voices of *Figaro*'s sextet, here also containing the exclamation of family relation with the fitting pronoun: *ihr Bruder, mein Bruder, ihr Bruder*, and so on, the musicality of which is reinforced through the blank-verse unfolding.
119. This double appearance of the voice first as imagined, then as real, again echoes verses from the Song of Songs 2:8, 5:2, which is verbally and narratively connected.
120. IV.vii.3052–53, and compare the above discussion of the relevant legacy of Rousseau. Lessing's emphasis here on "the gentle voice of reason" (*die sanfte Stimme der Vernunft*), however, may reflect a later phase of Lessing's conception of compassion affected by Mendelssohn's ideas.
121. See Hannah Arendt's foreword in "On Humanity in Dark Times: Thoughts about Lessing," in Gotthold Ephraim Lessing's *Nathan the Wise, Minna von Barnhelm, and Other Plays and Writings*, ed. Peter Demetz (New York: Continuum, 1994), vii–xx. Alan Mittleman, in "Toleration, Liberty and Truth: A Parable" *Harvard Theological Review* 95/4 (2002): 353–72, cogently criticizes her main claim. See also Michael P. Steinberg's instructive discussion of this text in *Judaism Musical and Unmusical* (Chicago: University of Chicago Press, 2007), 30–31.
122. The 1998–99 *Schauspielhaus* Hanover production of the play, as described by Sarah Bryant-Bertail ("Theatre as Heterotopia: Lessing's *Nathan the Wise*," *Assaph* 16 (2000): 91–108), made a fascinating experiment in a possible imaginary sonoric dimension of

the play. "The music," she writes, "functions as a triple signifier of traditional Jewish and Arabic folk culture, and contemporary Euro-American mass culture. Although the musicians are always visible, their music evokes unseen spaces as it wordlessly tells the stories of Nathan and many Others. It is impossible to know whether to read the sound as coming from the past, future, or present. Thus a disquieting question is evoked: are these stories behind us, yet to come, or all around us now?" (96). Such insights are consonant with the arguments I raise here. Of interest are also the reflections of Erik Gedeon, the composer of this production, in Bryant-Bertail, "Theatre as Heterotopia," 98.

123. This is emphasized in Michael Radford's 2004 *Merchant of Venice*, title role played by Al Pacino.

124. See *The Tempest*, I.ii.

125. The biblical expression "dust and ashes" is uttered by both Abraham and Job in their own theodicy, addressed to God.

126. This Hannah or Miriam Bat Tanhum sacrificed her seven sons to avoid worshipping Greek idols. Before her youngest child is taken away to be executed, she kisses and tells him, "Go to Abraham your father and tell him for me, 'You built one altar; I built seven. In the end, you did not sacrifice your son; I sacrificed seven'" (*Lamentation (Ekha) Rabba*, sec. 1).

127. The parable, in brief: a family had a tradition of the father bequeathing a precious opal heirloom ring to his most beloved son, who thereby became his true inheritor and future head of the family. The ring also had the mysterious power that whoever wore the ring faithfully was beloved by God and man. In one generation, this tradition was broken by a father who loved his three sons equally. Before he came to die, he secretly asked a craftsman to create two more rings identical to the family heirloom, which he separately distributed, unable anymore to distinguish between them himself. Once he passed away, the sons realized that each possessed a ring. For the way in which they overcame this predicament, and how Lessing/Nathan compared this to the strife among the monotheistic religions, see below.

128. In his 1864 lecture, published as *Lessing's Nathan der Weise. Ein Vortrag* (Bonn: Emil Strauss, 1886, reprinted several times until the end of the nineteenth century), David Friedrich Strauss (whose book on Jesus' life George Eliot translated into English) traces the political-religious circumstances that brought Lessing to draw on Boccaccio's *Decameron* parable and to transcend it. For a more recent close comparison, see Heinz Politzer, "Lessings Parabel von den drei Ringen," *German Quarterly* 31/3 (1958): 161–77.

129. Unlike the golden and silver caskets, the leaden one—whose paleness moves Bassanio "more than eloquence"—is neither hypocritical nor deceptive (III.ii). While such wisdom—humans' final, and most concealed one—seems compatible with Freud's association of the leaden casket with silence and death (in his "Theme of the Three Caskets"), Portia's musical soliloquy refers to these themes more ambiguously, or even defensively.

130. In his letter to Mersenne; see René Descartes, *Philosophical Letters*, trans. and ed. Anthony Kenny (Minneapolis: University of Minnesota Press, [1970] 1981).

131. Though her argument relates particularly to notated music, Ruth Katz's claim, in tune with Portia's, about how music expresses that which it metaphorically possesses (following Nelson Goodman's *Languages of Art*), is relevant to music bearing more flexible criteria of identity. See *Divining the Powers of Music: Aesthetic Theory and the Origins of Opera* (New York: Pendragon, 1986). See also the discussion in chapter 1, on Deleuze's and Guattari's concept of deterritorialized/reterritorialized music.

132. This emptiness is what distinguishes Lessing's adaptation of the parable (in comparison with both Bocaccio and the sixteenth-century Hebrew version of Shlomo Ibn Verga in *Shevet Yehuda*). See Mittleman, "Toleration, Liberty and Truth."

133. Indeed they do; from this perspective it is interesting to consider the reception of the play in various cultures and milieus. Only briefly touched upon in my discussion, it is the subject of various studies; Chaim Shoham's "*Nathan der Weise* unter Seinesgleichen: Zur Rezeption Lessings in der hebräischen Literatur des 19. Jahrhunderts in Osteuropa" [*Lessing Yearbook* 12 (1980–1), 1–30] is of interest in the present context.

134. Strong support for the interpretation suggested here comes from Robert S. Leventhal's fascinating analysis of Lessing's hermeneutical approach, ever confronting historical tradition and textual authority in its insistence on a dialogical, historicist interpretation of truth, as it emerges from his theoretical writings as well as from his reading of the play, and especially the "performative" aspects of the ring parable. See Robert S. Leventhal "The Parable as Performance: Interpretation, Cultural Transmission and Political Strategy in Lessing's *Nathan der Weise*," *German Quarterly* 61/4 (1988): 502–27.

135. See B Zevahim 116:1 and Mekhilta.

136. See Mittleman, "Toleration, Liberty and Truth."

137. This is the way the scene was staged by Claus Peymann in the Berliner Ensemble production, 2004–5. This comes close to Jessica in Miller's *Merchant of Venice* production, discussed in chapter 1.

138. For the popularity of these works throughout the nineteenth century, see Howard Elbert Smither, *A History of the Oratorio*, vol. 4, *The Oratorio in the Nineteenth and Twentieth Centuries* (Chapel Hill: University of North Carolina Press, 2000), 4. In his career as conductor, musical entrepreneur, and editor (he edited *Israel in Egypt*), Mendelssohn was involved with Handel's oratorios throughout, especially *Israel in Egypt*, *Samson*, *Messiah*, *Solomon*, *Judas Maccabeus*, and *Joshua*.

139. The cultural infrastructure that fostered the creation of these works is elaborated in Alexander H. Shapiro, "'Drama of an Infinitely Superior Nature': Handel's Early English Oratorios and the Religious Sublime," *Music & Letters* 74/2 (1993): 215–45 and in Ruth Smith, *Handel's Oratorios and Eighteenth-Century Thought* (Cambridge: Cambridge University Press, 1995). The popularity and high esteem of an oratorio central to our story—*Israel in Egypt*—was perhaps at its peak in the Victorian England of George Eliot. Among the admiring critics of the time, Howard D. Weinbrot, in *Britannia's Issue: The Rise of Literature from Dryden to Ossian* (Cambridge: Cambridge University Press, 1993), 432, regards G. A. Macfarran's review and analysis as the best of its kind. See *Great Handel Festival, at the Crystal Palace, June 13th, 17th, and 19th,*

1857. *Israel in Egypt: An Oratorio . . . By George Frederic Handel. With an Analysis of the Oratorio, Written Expressly for the Sacred Harmonic Society By G. A. Macfarran* (London 1857).

140. See Shapiro, "Drama," 231 and Linda Colley, *Britons: Forging the Nation, 1707–1837* (New Haven: Yale University Press, 1992), chap. 1. On the Hebraic fever of the time see Weinbrot, *Britannia's Issue*, 405–445.

141. Robert Tate, *An Essay for Promoting of Psalmody*, 34, 37–38, quoted in Shapiro, "Drama," 231.

142. Milton's "At a Solemn Music" is perhaps the best example of its kind and could indeed serve as a model. For religious musicalized poetry of seventeenth-century England see John Hollander, *The Untuning of the Sky: Ideas of Music in English Poetry, 1500–1700* (Princeton: Princeton University Press, 1961).

143. In a 1733 ode by Aaron Hill, quoted in Shapiro, "Drama," 238.

144. See Smith, *Handel's Oratorios*, 234.

145. Ibid., 234–36. This relates to revisions of the biblical stories in both primary (Bible and Apocrypha) and secondary sources (as adapted by Milton, Racine, and so on).

146. Weinbrot, *Britannia's Issue*, 416. This also involved an attempt to create a Hebraic genealogy of the British people, ibid., 418. It was James Harrington in his 1656 *Commonwealth of Oceana* that fixed the model for the British nation on the biblical "Jewish Nation" for the English republican tradition to come.

147. The philosemitic attitude contained at least two important contemporary ingredients. The first ingredient was socioeconomic: in the wake of the rise of capitalism, the role of the Jews as commercial mediators on an international scale loomed large, in addition to their actual crediting capabilities, which proved crucial at critical moments. (A case in point is Samson Gideon's leading role in calming the severe financial crisis of 1745, reminiscent of and perhaps a model for Lessing's Nathan.) The second ingredient was mostly cultural and was related to the Jews' position as intelligent outsiders in a society seeking to reconcile its diverse parts. For the decline of the process of naturalization in the so-called Jew bill case of 1753 see Thomas W. Perry, *Public Opinion, Propaganda, and Politics in Eighteenth-Century England: A Study of the Jew Bill of 1753* (Cambridge, MA: Harvard University Press, 1962). See also Todd M. Endelman, *The Jews of Georgian England 1714–1830: Tradition and Change in a Liberal Society* (Philadelphia: Jewish Publication Society of America, 1979). Alexander Ringer added details in this connection as background to Handel's positive rendition of the Jewish cause, especially in *Judea Maccabeus*. See his "Handel and the Jews," *Music & Letters* 42/1 (1961): 26–27. Ringer's argument, as part of a major trend to favorably connect Handel to the Jews, was quite persuasively rebutted by David Hunter, in "George Frideric Handel and the Jews: Fact, Fiction and the Tolerances of Scholarship," in *For the Love of Music: Festschrift in Honor of Theodore Front on His 90th Birthday*, ed. Darwin F. Scott (Lucca: Lim Antiqua, 2002), 5–28. I thank Uri Erman for calling my attention to this article. Michael Marissen, in "Rejoicing against Judaism in Handel's *Messiah*," *Journal of Musicology* 24/2 (2007): 167–93, claimed anti-Semitic insinuations in the *Messiah*, provoking a wave of harsh reactions.

148. The openness of the oratorio to a variety of ideological interpretations is emphasized by Smith in _Handel's Oratorios_, 296, and was subsequently considered within a different political context by Pamela Potter in "The Politicization of Handel and His Oratorios in the Weimar Republic, the Third Reich, and the Early Years of the German Democratic Republic," _Musical Quarterly_ 85/2 (2001): 311–41. "Occasional" is used here in the sense of its primary meaning at the time, "constituting or serving as the occasion or cause of something" (_OED_); many commissioned musical works (and most of Handel's oratorios) belong to this category. One of Handel's oratorios is even called the _Occasional Oratorio_ (1746), in which the memorable line "Oh liberty, thou choicest treasure, seat of virtue, source of pleasure" seems to express the composer's commitment to liberal, rational values.

149. Quoted in _Anglia Judaica: Or the History and Antiquities of the Jews in England_ (1738), 135–36, as cited by Weinbrot, _Britannia's Issue_, 422. This could have been a source for Eliot's approach to Jewish martyrdom, discussed in chapter 1.

150. First and foremost in _Judas Maccabeus_. In any event, we are speaking of audience after Handel's time, following Hunter's arguments in "George Frideric Handel and the Jews."

151. The emphasis on Hebrew sources and original Hebrew writings, the preference for the Bible over the Talmud, the reverting to biblical time and the temporal ellipsis of the period of exile (or in the case of Zionism, negating exile and diasporic existence) were common ideological interests of both interrelated, though not identical movements.

152. The order of names here follows the Hebrew Bible order of books and their traditional grouping.

153. As such, they coincided with utopian conceptions that have emerged since the early nineteenth century, as expressed by the St. Simonians and other groups.

154. Many contemporary British men of letters held in highest esteem as the prime models for sublime poetry the biblical Song of Songs and the Song of the Sea, the book of Job and, above all, the story of Joseph much above certain Greek mythologies. They considered them bolder and more synthetic than the latter in their powerful wedding of natural and supernatural, everyday existence and the most extraordinary ideas and images, compelling readers to become participants, even actors on stage. They also regarded English blank verse—highly esteemed at the time—as close to Hebrew metrical verse. See Weinbrot, _Britannia's Issue_, 423–31.

155. Handel was searching for a sublime expression, as the following quote demonstrates: "I have . . . endeavoured to shew, that the English Language, which is so expressive of the sublimest Sentiments, is the best adapted of any to the full and solemn kind of Musick." (Handel's letter to _The Daily Advertiser_, 17 January 1745, quoted in Dean, _Handel's Dramatic Oratorios_, 64.)

156. (Original italics.) See Immanuel Kant, _The Critique of Judgement_, trans. James Creed Meredith (Oxford: Clarendon Press, [1952] 1986, sec. 52), 190–91; for the original see _Kritik der Urteilskraft_ (Frankfurt: Suhrkamp, 1977), 264.

157. The genre, as deployed by Bach, Handel, Mendelssohn, and others includes, as a matter of fact, the "didactic poem" and rhymed, quasi-tragic element, thus embody-

ing even further Kant's category of the sublime. The element of amusement, which relates to the fact that Handel's oratorios were performed in playhouses rather than churches, evoked much criticism at the time, but also some enthusiastic reactions. See Weinbrot, *Britannia's Issue*, 435.

158. See Hugo Leichtentritt, "Handel's Harmonic Art," in *Musical Quarterly* 21 (1935): 208–23, an essay that still offers valuable insights.

159. Stanley Fish, *How Milton Works* (Cambridge, MA: The Belknap Press of Harvard University Press, 2001), 391–414.

160. Handel's educational background in pietistic Halle prompted him in this direction, at least according to Ringer, "Handel and the Jews," 17–20; evidence is not too strong, but neither does other evidence clearly point in the opposite direction.

161. In contrast, the chorus of *Samson Agonistes* only after a long soliloquy and upon Samson's entreaty, articulates the rather miserly: "To visit or bewail thee, or if better, / Counsel or Consolation we may bring, / Salve to thy Sores, apt words have power to swage / The tumors of a troubl'd mind, / And are as Balm to fester'd wounds. See John Milton, *Complete Poems and Major Prose*, ed. Meritt Y. Hughes (Indianapolis: Odyssey Press, 1957), 554, ll. 182–86.

162. This musical icon of loneliness appears already in his first aria (lament): "Torments, alas! are not confin'd to heart, or head, or breast!" becoming the opening gesture of the following "Total eclipse!" It is no wonder that writers found the Handelian *Samson* more human than the Miltonian one: "[Handel] presents his characters as he sees them, tempers their failings with charity, and leaves us to exercise our own judgment," writes Percy M. Young in *The Oratorios of Handel* (London: P. Dobson, 1949), 123. Dean (*Handel's Dramatic Oratorios*, 42) similarly maintains that "[Handel's] profound sympathy for human suffering shines through his entire work."

163. Dean, *Handel's Dramatic Oratorios*, 40. The distinction between the two roles led Hanns Niedecken Gebhard in 1923 to use an offstage "observation choir" as well as an onstage "action" choir in his staging of *Saul*. See Potter, "The Politicization of Handel," 315.

164. This choir could be the inspiration of Haydn's parallel choir: "Und der Geist Gottes schwebte . . . es werde Licht" from *Die Schöpfung* (*The Creation*) of 1798, whose widespread popularity, particularly among Jews, throughout the nineteenth century and beyond, is also a case in point in this history. Schoenberg's interpretation of the verse in his *Kol Nidre* (1938) seems to owe something to both. See below, chapter 6.

165. From John Lightfoot's *Works* 1, 1014, published posthumously in 1682, as quoted by Weinbrot, *Britannia's Issue*, 413 (original italics).

166. The text is a paraphrase of Milton's "At a Solemn Music."

167. Handel's music distinguishes between sympathetic and unsympathetic dialogues, but not between "positive" and "negative" characters. Cf., for example, the duet of Samson and Delilah "Traitor to Love" and that between Delilah and her Virgin companion "My/Her faith and truth." The "excommunication" of Harapha from this order interestingly parallels that of the banishment of Grandcourt in Eliot's' *Daniel Deronda*, in particular from a certain point in the plot and onward.

168. That music works through pleasure was a major premise of central British aestheticians of the eighteenth century. Though outwardly apolitical, this aesthetics paradoxically coincides with the thoroughly political aesthetics of Bertolt Brecht that mocked the role of music in the old theatre as "culinary," but still regarded its entertaining elements in the revolutionary "epic theatre" as contributing to the *Verfremdung* effect through a sharp distinction between content and form. See Bertolt Brecht, "The Modern Theatre is an Epic Theatre," in *The Essence of Opera*, ed. Ulrich Weisstein (New York: Norton, 1964), 334–44. The following discussion can serve as an explanation of this paradox.

169. See Dean, *Handel's Dramatic Oratorios*, 331.

170. *The Magic Flute, Lohengrin,* and *The Great Dictator* are discussed from this point of view in Ruth HaCohen's "'Never Ask Me What My Name Is': Distinct Meaning and Obscured Message in the Music of Wagner," in *The Restless Reich*, ed. Oded Heilbronner (Jerusalem: The Hebrew University Magnes Press, 1998), 475–96 (Hebrew).

171. See the discussion on the *Unheimliche* in chapter 6.

172. Martin O. Stern, "How do you like America?" 69 (Leo Baeck Institute, 1999) partially quoted in Lily Hirsch, *A Jewish Orchestra in Nazi Germany: Musical Politics and the Berlin Jewish Culture League* (Ann Arbor: University of Michigan Press, 2010), 107. For the full citation see Hirsch's "Imagining 'Jewish Music' in Nazi Germany: The Berlin Jüdischer Kulturbund and Musical Politics" (PhD diss., Duke University, 2006), 187.

173. Handel was among the few German composers whose music was certified by the Nazis as part of the League's repertoire. For its reception and place in the repertoire of the Jewish League, see Lily Hirsch, *A Jewish Orchestra*.

174. The *Reichsstelle für Musikbearbeitung*, an office of the Propaganda Ministry founded in 1941, was responsible for this, and commissioned Johannes Klöcking to revise the first two. The ideological reading and reinterpretation of the oratorios in this direction had already began in 1934. One of the first adaptations was made by Fritz Stein for the Olympic Games of 1936 in Berlin, who retitled the *Occasional Oratorio* as *Festoratorium*. See Potter, "The Politicization of Handel," 318–24.

175. The community-building aspect of Handel's oratorios has been noted by many, including Rudolf Steglich in "Händel und die Gegenwart," *Zeitschrift für Musik* 92 (1925), 336, who deployed Ferdinand Tönnies' famous distinction between *Gesellschaft* (society) and *Gemeinschaft* (community), claiming the advocated work as conducive to the reinforcement of the latter. The claim for enhancing democracy through these works was made by the eminent musicologist, Hermann Abert. See Potter, "The Politicization of Handel," 314.

176. The melody of the famous "Hail! The conquering hero comes" was set to various liturgical texts associated with Hanukkah and Passover. The first introduction of Handel's music in a synagogue was as early as 1766, in the rededication of the Great Synagogue in Duke's Place, with his "Coronation Anthem" reported in the *London Chronicle* of the time. See Ringer, "Handel and the Jews," 29.

177. Lamb's article was first published in the *London Magazine* of August 1821. The version of the work that was performed that evening was, accordingly, the earlier one, which includes this aria.

178. See Charles Lamb, "Imperfect Sympathies," *Essays of Elia*, in *Works*, ed. Alfred Ainger (Boston: Merrymount Press, 1888), 2:72–73.

179. This ancient aporia, as it continues to affect present-day politics, is poignantly explored by Jacques Derrida and Anne Dufourmantelle, *Of Hospitality: Anne Dufourmantelle Invites Jacques Derrida to Respond*, trans. Rachel Bowlby (Stanford: Stanford University Press, 2000).

180. Braham ceased to cherish his Jewish origin once embarking upon an operatic career. See his portrait as Orlando in Todd M. Endelman's *Radical Assimilation in English Jewish History 1656–1945* (Bloomington: Indiana University Press, 1990), 64.

181. For a discussion of the cultural context of the caricature, the opera, and the emotional turmoil it provoked in the Jewish community, see Alfred Rubens, *A Jewish Iconography*, rev. ed. (London: Nonpareil, 1981), 18. Shai Burstein aptly contextualizes this caricature and Braham's career in "Jewish Singing and Boxing in Georgian England," *Yuval: Studies of the Jewish Music Research Centre*, VII (*Studies in Honour of Israel Adler*), ed. Eliyahu Schleifer and Edwin Seroussi (Jerusalem: The Hebrew University Magnes Press, 2002), 425–39. Also, Uri Erman is completing a master's thesis temporarily titled "In Music on a Wondering World He Burst": Jewish Opera Singers in Late Georgian England (Hebrew University). Upon wrapping up the present book, I noticed that Judith W. Page likewise connected Lamb and Rowlandson within her own *Imperfect Sympathies: Jews and Judaism in British Romantic Literature and Culture* (New York: Palgrave Macmillan, 2004), 40–46, bringing to the discussion fresh perspectives and insights. The term *mauscheln* (referring both to Moses and to *Maus*, mouse) was one of the forms used to ridicule Yiddish and the way it affected Jews' pronunciation of European languages.

CHAPTER 3. NOISE IN THE HOUSE OF PRAYER

1. Theodor Reik, "Das Shofar," in *Das Ritual, Psychoanalytische Studien*, 1928, trans. Douglas Bryan as "The Shofar," in *Ritual: Psycho-Analytic Studies* (New York: International Universities Press, 1958), 235. I have corrected the above translation, as it falls into a typical and telling pit: translating *Judenschul* for "Jewish school." *Schule*—in German, a derogatory word for synagogue—normally denotes "school," but certainly not in this context. The translator either wished to avoid anti-Semitic connotations or was unaware of this peculiar mid-European context. In any event, this mistranslation demonstrates how the story narrated here is basically a European one that by and large was not recognized by Americans. This does not mean that it did not cross the Atlantic; Henry Ford was continuing this strain in "Jewish Jazz Becomes Our National Music," chapter 11 of *The International Jew*, the first in the four-volume series, published by Ford, and admired by Hitler. I thank Nita Schechet for this reference.

2. See Reik's beautiful description of a childhood experience in "Kol Nidrei," *Ritual: Psycho-Analytic Studies*, 167–68, discussed in chapter 6 below.

3. David Vogel, *Married Life, a Novel* (Jerusalem: Keter, 1986) trans. Dalya Bilu (London: Halban, 1998). On Vogel see http://www.ithl.org.il/author_info.asp?id=279 and Gershon Shaked, "David Vogel: A Hebrew Novelist in Vienna," in *Austrians and Jews*

in the Twentieth Century: From Franz Joseph to Waldheim, ed. Robert S. Wistrich (New York: St. Martin's, 1992), 97–112.

4. Leo Spitzer, "Patterns of Thought and of Etymology, I. Nausea>OF(>Eng.) Noise," *Word* I/3 (1945), 273.

5. The *Wahrig Kompaktwörterbuch der deutschen Sprache* (Munich: Wissen Media, 2002) from which this definition derives, contains a politically correct vestige of this anti-Semitic expression. The example it gives for the second meaning of the word is *Der Lärm auf dem Schulhof*—noise in the schoolyard—which, strangely enough, resembles the wrong—similarly euphemistic?—translation of Reik's text into English, quoted in n. 1 above. While working on this project I was told by a few people, among whom were the author Y. Michal Bodemann and the Israeli political scientist Prof. Benny Neuberger, who went to elementary school in West Germany in the 1950s, that *Lärm wie in einer Judenschule* was often used by teachers who were annoyed by the children's noise and commotion. Benny Neuberger, whose parents immigrated to Germany after WWII, remarked that his very presence in class sensitized the teachers to the political incorrectness of this phrase. The phrase sounds familiar also to the younger German generation.

6. The word *Lärm* recurs nine times in Luther's translation of the Hebrew Bible and only once in the New Testament. In the translation of the Hebrew Bible *Lärm* is the word standing for a variety of Hebrew words (*hamon, sha'on, t^{e}ru'ah, t^{e}shu'ot*) always connoting masses, or a mob, usually defeated.

7. I heard this joke from Bilha Sammet, born in Poland c. 1920. This joke appears also in Druyanov's *Book of Jokes*, vol. 1 (Tel Aviv: Dvir, 1963 [in Hebrew]), 324, in a self-deprecating way. I thank Shai Burstyn for this reference. A related joke is told by Reik himself: "An old man during the service on the Day of Atonement rebukes one of those praying, who is beating his breast very violently and very loudly, confessing his sinfulness and remorse, in these words: 'Young man, force will do nothing with Him up there'" (*Ritual*, 225).

8. The central shofar ritual takes place on Rosh Hashanah, the Jewish New Year, a two-day festival in which, according to law and custom, about a hundred blasts are performed on each day (provided it does not fall on Shabbat). As a spiritual preparation for the High Holidays, the shofar—a simple, nonperforated ram's horn—is blasted briefly every day throughout the entire preceding month of Elul. Lastly, a long blast (or a series of short blasts) is performed as a sign of the end of Yom Kippur.

9. Vogel, *Married Life*, 283; in the Hebrew original, 198. Robert Musil's *Der Mann ohne Eigenschaften* (*The Man without Qualities*), chapter 1, contains a corresponding depiction of poignant impressions of the noise of modern Vienna. Unsurprisingly, it is more ironic and less desperate than that of his Jewish contemporary. *Married Life* is replete with vocalities and sonic signs of various kinds, creating a rich texture that significantly marks the narrative trajectories.

10. A metamorphosis so poignantly elaborated by T. S. Eliot's epoch-making *The Waste Land* (1922), a poem probing the borderland of music and noise (including Wagner's *Tristan*), as in the repeated line: "What is that noise?" This twilight zone seems to mark the unintelligibility of existence, the dissolution of meaning as modern angst. Of

special relevance here are the lines connecting lament with urban (or maybe eschato-logical) noise. "What is that sound high in the air / Murmur of maternal lamentation . . . What is the city over the mountains / Cracks and reforms and bursts in the violet air / Falling towers / Jerusalem Athens Alexandria / Vienna London / Unreal."

11. Yaron Jean's PhD diss., "'Hearing Maps': Noise, Technology and Auditory Perception in Germany 1914–1945" (The Hebrew University of Jerusalem, 2005, in Hebrew), tells a fascinating and often horrific story of German society and culture of and between the wars from the point of view of its changing soundscape, as it was affected by technology. The story of Germany, unique as it is, throws light on the noisy world of modernism in general. This is further supported by Alain Corbin's *Village Bells: Sound and Meaning in the 19th-Century French Countryside* (New York: Columbia University Press, 1998), which tells the story of the struggle to maintain the premodern soundscape in nineteenth-century France.

12. Mahler's ambiguous relation to "Jewish music" is revealed in the following anecdote narrated by Natalie Bauer-Lechner: "Around the age of three, Mahler was taken to the synagogue by his parents. Suddenly he interrupted the singing of the community with shouts and screams: 'Be quiet, be quiet, that's horrible!' And when, from his mother's arms, he succeeded in stopping everything, when the whole congregation was in consternation and had all stopped singing, he demanded—singing a verse for them—that they should all sing 'Eits a binkel Kasi [Hrasi?], one of his favourite songs from earliest childhood." In Norman Lebrecht, *Mahler Remembered* (New York: Norton, 1987), 11–12. The story may be interpreted in various ways, but its persistence contains a germ of Mahler's possible aversion to the sound of a Jewish house of prayer, exacerbated, no doubt, by the standard anti-Semitic accusations. Norman Lebrecht comments that the song is untraced, and as the story was told by Mahler to an Austrian Gentile, unfamiliar with either Czech or Hebrew, it could be perhaps the Hebrew "Etz ḥayyim hi" ("A tree of life is she, the Torah," a psalm sung when the Torah scrolls are returned to the Ark, before Musaf, on Shabbat, and Festivals), that, as Lebrecht rightly observes, could create "a strong impression on the young." Lebrecht provides an alternative suggestion—that it could be a Moravian song "At'se pinkl házi" ("The bundle should swing back and forth") popular in Prague in the 1860s (ibid.). These divergent surmises point to the complex background of Mahler's musical childhood, a complexity well reflected in his work.

13. The dialectical and dialogical relations between profession and confession are ana-lyzed by Jacques Derrida in "The University without Condition" in *Without Alibi*, ed. and trans. Peggy Kamuf (Stanford: Stanford University Press, 2002), 202–37. The trope of confession is central to Reik's later work, see, for example, *The Compulsion to Confess* (1925) and the autobiographical study, *Fragments of a Great Confession* (1949).

14. Reik, *Ritual*, 259.

15. Leo Spitzer left Vienna as a young man to study in Germany. Later on, like many of his contemporaries, he immigrated to the United States. See Helmut Hatzfeld "Necrol-ogy: Leo Spitzer (1887–1960)," (*Hispanic Review* 29/1, 1961), 54–57. Something about the background of his work during wartime, including his work on harmony (see next note) can be indirectly inferred from Kader Konuk, "Jewish-German Philologists in

Turkish Exile: Leo Spitzer and Erich Auerbach," in *Exile and Otherness: New Approaches to the Experience of the Nazi Refugees*, ed. Alexander Stephan (Oxford: Peter Lang, 2005), 31–47.

16. Spitzer quotes the *New Yorker's* description of the Shiite Day of Ushra, whose ritual consists of a group of "a hundred men and women, ragged and stripped to the waist, marching about, chanting songs and beating their breasts" ("Patterns of Thought," 269). A counterimage can be seen, and heard, in the "noisy" "Dies Irae" procession in Ingmar Bergman's *Seventh Seal* (fictionally taking place in the fourteenth century), a vociferous self-image of the Christian community.

17. Sander Gilman, *Jewish Self-Hatred: Anti-Semitism and the Hidden Language of the Jews* (Baltimore: Johns Hopkins University Press, 1988).

18. See Spitzer, "Patterns of Thought" 272–73.

19. Vogel, *Married Life*, 211.

20. *The New Shorter OED*, Oxford, 1993.

21. As embodied in two famous works: young Schoenberg's *Verklärte Nacht* (*Transfigured Night*) of 1899 and young Richard Strauss' *Tod und Verklärung* (*Death and Transfiguration*), composed a decade earlier. Transfiguration in relation to fin-de-siècle Viennese art is further discussed in chapter 6.

22. Music as punishment became a hot topic recently. See for example Lily E. Hirsch, "Weaponizing Classical Music: Crime Prevention and Symbolic Power in the Age of Repetition," *Journal of Popular Music Studies* 19/4 (2007): 342–58.

23. "Dissenting" Christian and Jewish groups—Lutheran, Hasidic, and nineteenth-century Liberal communities—all used contrafacta of various sorts as part of constructing their new religious identity. See also chapter 1.

24. "Aus Johann Christian Edelmanns von ihm selbst aufgesetzten Lebenslauf," (November 1749), published in the volume *Pietismus und Rationalismus*, ed. Marianne Beyer-Fröhlich (Leipzig: Philipp Reclam, 1933), 108–37. The italics in the following extracts are mine. Regarding the Frankfurt custom, see Mordechai Breuer, "Besonderheiten des alten Frankfurter Synagogengesangs" *Jüdische Kultur in Frankfurt am Main von den Anfängen bis zur Gegenwart*, ed. K. E. Grözinger (Wiesbaden: Harrassowitz, 1997), 91–100, and Salman Geiger, *Divre qehillot* (Frankfurt am Main, 1862). See also Benjamin Shlomo Hamburger, *Shorshei Minhag Ashkenaz* (Bnei Brak: Machon Moreshet Ashkenaz, 1995 [Hebrew]), for the centrality of Frankfurt tradition in Ashkenazi custom (*Minhag*).

25. See n. 1 to this chapter.

26. Called *almemor* or *almemar* in insiders' descriptions (from Arabic *al-minbar*).

27. See chapter 1.

28. Cf. chapter 5, in Eliot's description of Deronda's synagogal experience. On Rosh Hashanah there is also one such "Aleinu" kneeling (on each of the two days of the holiday).

29. The question of a shared heritage will be entertained by a later writer, reporting from the very same synagogue (George Eliot via Daniel Deronda). For a benevolent description of an indigenous tribe's "noisy" worship in sixteenth-century Brazil by Jean

de Léry see Michel de Certeau, *The Certeau Reader*, ed. Graham Ward (Oxford: Wiley-Blackwell, 2000), 143–48.

30. That is the spirit of his entire report, which extends to the pietists, the "inspirational-ists," and others. See "Aus Johann Christian Edelmanns," 108–12; 116–37.

31. Charles Burney, *Dr. Burney's Musical Tours in Europe*, ed. Percy A. Scholes (New York: Oxford University Press, 1959), 2:229–30. As with Edelmann, I have italicized words denoting or connoting noise and weird behavior. For rich contextualization of this report (though itself only briefly discussed) in relation to Burney's musical journeys (fascinatingly compared with those of the colonial musical adventures of Captain Cook), see Vanessa Agnew, *Enlightenment Orpheus: The Power of Music in Other Worlds* (New York: Oxford University Press, 2008).

32. In a very different, semipastoral context, the "murmuring of innumerable bees" can add a part to a polyphony of sweet, harmonious voices, as in Alfred Tennyson's famous "Come Down, O Maid."

33. On the popularity of Jewish singers in England about that time see Shai Burstyn, "Jewish Singing and Boxing in Georgian England," in *Yuval* VII, *Studies in Honour of Israel Adler* (Jerusalem: The Hebrew University Magnes Press, 2002), 425–41.

34. See Israel Adler, *La Pratique musicale savante: dans quelques communautés juives en Europe aux 17e et 18e siècles* (Paris: Mouton, 1966), chap. 1.

35. Vocal music for several voices written in independent parts, usually performed with-out instrumental accompaniment. On the Portuguese practice see also Edwin Se-roussi, "The Ancient Modernity of the Liturgical Music of the Portuguese Synagogue in Amsterdam," *Jewish Studies and the European Academic World. Plenary Lectures Read at the VIIth Congress of the European Association for Jewish Studies (EAJS) Am-sterdam, July 2002*, ed. Albert van der Heide and Irene E. Zwiep (Paris, Louvain, and Dudley, MA: Peeters, 2005), 15–21.

36. Several studies shed light on the practices of the Portuguese synagogue in Amster-dam. See in particular Israel Adler, *Musical life and traditions of the Portuguese Jewish community of Amsterdam in the XVIIIth century* (Jerusalem: The Hebrew University Magnes Press, 1974).

37. As Idelsohn claims, the Ashkenazi synagogue in Amsterdam introduced this tech-nique as early as 1700. See Abraham Z. Idelsohn, *Jewish Music in Its Historical De-velopment* (New York: Schocken, [1929] 1967), 207. The word *meshorerim* designates the role of the Levites as singers in the Jewish Temple and is thus used also in the language of the ancient *piyyut*; see chapter 5. In the internal Jewish debate, such as Hanoch ben Abraham from Posen, *Sefer Reshit Bikurim* (Frankfurt 1708), 29, a homi-letic book, they are also called *Klei homos* (instruments of robbery), an abbreviation of Hazzan, Meshorer, Singer (more ubiquitously—Hazzan, Bass, Singer), attesting to their ambiguous standing in some of the communities. See Daniel S. Katz, "A Pro-legomenon to the Study of the Performance Practice of Synagogue Music Involving M'shor'rim," *Journal of Synagogue Music* 24/2 (1995): 35–79. The decline of this prac-tice is surveyed in Geoffrey Goldberg, "The Training of *Hazzanim* in Nineteenth-Century Germany," in *Yuval: Studies of the Jewish Music Research Centre* VII (*Studies*

in Honour of Israel Adler) vol. 7, ed. Eliyahu Schleifer and Edwin Seroussi (Jerusalem: The Hebrew University Magnes Press, 2002), 299–306.

38. See Idelsohn, *Thesaurus of Hebrew Oriental Melodies*, vol. 6, *The Synagogue Song of the German Jews in the 18th Century* (Leipzig: Friedrich Hofmeister, 1932), 222. Idelsohn discussed these phenomena also in "Song and Singers of the Synagogue in the 18th Century," in *Hebrew Union College Jubilee Volume* (Cincinnati: 1925), 419–22. For the practice of Hazzan, Meshorer (bass), Singer see also Hanoch Avenary, in Raphael Patai, *Studies in Biblical and Jewish Folklore*, ed. Francis Lee Utley and Dov Noy (New York: Haskell, [1960] 1973), 187–98.

39. On Weintraub, see Hanoch Avenary, "A Way of a Hazzan to the West: The Autobiography of Hirsch Weintraub," *Tatslil* 4 (1969), 124–27 (Hebrew), and Andreas Nachamas and Susanne Stähr, "Die vergessene Revolution, der lange Weg des Louis Lewandowski," *Menorah* 3 (1992), 248.

40. Burney, ibid., 229.

41. Running divisions: the technique, prevalent in English music, of breaking up a melody, or a "ground," usually by a melodious instrument (flute, viol, but also voice) into quick figures and passages.

42. This, again, brings us to the crucial difference, following Mittleman and others, between liberal and tolerant societies.

43. Cf. the presence of the menorah in Heine's *Rabbi of Bacharach*, quoted below, and later in *Jud Süß* (chapter 7), where it clearly functions as a Jewish stereotype.

44. While it is true that cantors at the time began to write their compositions and recitation in Western musical notation, they used them mostly for training, and for preserving and disseminating their music. Edwin Seroussi (to whom I am grateful also for showing me the lithograph of the 1790 synagogue) suggested to me that this could be the reading of the Megillah (Esther) on Purim. This can explain the size and spread of the scroll, the general gaiety and laughs, and the turbans, and maybe the two cantors: one is a reader of the Megillah and the other the actual hazzan. The noisy soundscape of Purim, as known since the Middle Ages (see chapter 1) could have been, indeed, an apt trigger for a visual rendition of this sort.

45. For details of this lithograph, see Alfred Rubens, *A Jewish Iconography*, rev. ed. (London: Nonpareil, 1981), 134, and idem, *A History of Jewish Costume* (London: Peter Owen, 1973), 142.

46. Quoted in Judith W. Page, *Imperfect Sympathies: Jews and Judaism in British Romantic Literature and Culture* (New York: Palgrave Macmillan, 2004), 19.

47. Some of the details (such as wearing the tallit) in Edelmann's report do not fit the customs of the day; but as we have seen, his description must have been partially nourished by rumors and prejudices.

48. Heymann Steinthal, *Über Juden und Judentum*, ed. Gustav Karpeles (Berlin: M. Popplauer, 1906), 300. I am grateful to the late Dieter Adelmann for calling my attention to this important report.

49. *Borchu:* Bless (as a command, second person plural); *Boroch:* blessed is (He).

50. See chapter 5.

51. In the case of Steinthal, it finds expression in his eventual choice to engage in *Wissenschaft des Judentums* and his concept, which he shared with Maurice Lazarus, of *Völkerpsychologie*—psychology of peoples, according to which "nationality could be acquired only by an act of will and by a conscious identification with the deeds and the creative, expressive forms of the nation—its mother tongue, which was the indispensable organ in the creation of reality and the receptacle of its deepest loyalties, and its aesthetic creations in which the soul of a people was given visible shape." See Uriel Tal, *Christians and Jews in Germany: Religion, Politics, and Ideology in the Second Reich, 1870–1914* (Ithaca: Cornell University Press, 1975), 98–99, and notice the similarity to Wagner's presuppositions, as discussed in chapter 5. This concept was advocated as part of the internal Jewish debate in the wake of the "culture war" waged between 1871 and 1875. The paradoxes inherent in the positions of progressive Jews concerning the rational basis of the desired liberal regime, one that would acknowledge religious minorities' right of worship, is expressed in the case of Steinthal's "double loyalty" to particularistic Jewish sentiments and general national (German) values.

52. "Wie schnitt das *ach bi* des dritten Verses, das volle a mit dem Brustlaute ch und daruf das scharfe i durch das Herz! Ja, es gibt keinen Schmerz wie mein Schmerz." Steinthal refers here to Lamentations 3:3, "Ach bi yashuv yahafokh yado kol ha-yom"—(Only against me he turns his hand again and again the whole day long). Interestingly, he phonosemantically transposed the Hebrew *ach* (meaning here "only") as the German sigh, *ach* (as in "Ach, nun ist mein Jesus hin," in Bach's *St. Matthew Passion*, no. 30). For this linguistic phenomenon see Ghil'ad Zuckermann, *Language Contact and Lexical Enrichment in Israeli Hebrew* (London: Palgrave Macmillan, 2003).

53. Among Feuchtwanger's sources were two Orthodox Jewish novels: Salomon Kohn, *Ein Deutscher Minister: Roman aus dem achtzehnten Jarhhundert* (Cincinnati: Bolock, 1885), and Markus Lehmann, *Süß Oppenheimer: eine jüdische Erzählung* (Mainz: Hofbuchdruckerei, 1871), not to mention dozens of non-Jewish renditions of the story, starting with Wilhelm Hauff's *Jud Süß* of 1828. (A rich and rather alienated, nonfictional description of a synagogal service by a modern inside-outsider, the composer Ernest Bloch, of his visit to a Hasidic synagogue, is brought by Klára Móricz, in *Jewish Identities: Nationalism, Racism, and Utopianism in Twentieth-Century Music* (Berkeley: University of California Press, 2008), 162–63.

54. Lion Feuchtwanger, *Jud Süß* (Berlin: Aufbau Taschenbuch, 1999), 232–33; trans. as *Jew Süss*, by Willa and Edwin Muir (London: Henry Pordes, 1927), 203–4. Feuchtwanger himself came from a non-Orthodox background in Munich, but was exposed to some Jewish education. In the large Feuchtwanger clan in Munich many were at the time devotedly observant (like my great-grandmother, Ida Ehrentreu (née Feuchtwanger, his father's cousin).

55. Feuchtwanger is acquainted with the two kinds of ritual garments, the tallit and the *Kittel*, the latter worn on Yom Kippur and by bridegrooms, as a reminder of shrouds.

56. Again, the phonosemantic affinity to the Hebrew idiom: *Besell* (lit. the house of God, see Genesis 28:19)—in Ashkenazi pronunciation—(*Bet-El* in the Sephardic) cannot be overlooked.

57. A verse discussed by Reik, see above.
58. Walter Benjamin, "On the Concept of History" in *Illuminations,* trans. Henry Zone (London: Fontana, 1968). Benjamin's entire thesis fits in well here. Instructively, the motto of this thesis "re-sounds" a line from the Brecht/Weill *Three Penny Opera,* "Consider the darkness and the great cold / In this vale which resounds with mystery"; the sound of the defeated as part of the aesthetics of the night thus stands as the inspiration for this major idea.
59. *Wozzeck,* based on George Büchner's *Woyzeck* (1836–37), sympathetically and critically tells the story of Wozzeck, a systematically exploited and traumatized soldier. Like Berg, Feuchtwanger had problems finding a publisher for his work (in the case of Berg the issue also concerned the performance itself), and similarly knocked at reluctant doors for several years until he found an open one; these two monumental works were then overwhelmingly acclaimed in and beyond Germany. On the reception of *Jud Süß* see Giesela Lüttig, "Zu diesem Band," *Jud Süß,* 473–74.
60. On the contemporary replacement of *Jewish* by *Israelite* see chapter 4.
61. Hanoch Avenary, ed., *Kantor Salomon Sulzer und Seine Zeit, Eine Dokumentation* (Sigmaringen: Jan Thorbeck, 1985), 23.
62. The Jewish community in Hohenems is known to have preserved the old Ashkenazi musical tradition. Sulzer was initiated into his profession by the local cantor and, after a few years at the yeshiva in Endigen, he studied both the old *nussah* and some innovations introduced over recent generations with cantors in south Germany. He also studied theory and harmony of Western music in Karlsruhe. At the age of sixteen, he was appointed cantor of his hometown. While in Vienna, he furthered his studies of music with Ignaz von Seyfried, a friend and disciple of Beethoven. See Eric Werner, *A Voice Still Heard . . . The Sacred Songs of the Ashkenazi Jews* (University Park: Pennsylvania State University Press, 1976), 209–19, and Aron Marko Rothmüller, *The Music of the Jews* (Cranbury, NJ: A. S. Barnes, 1975), 124–39.
63. Later in his life, Sulzer advocated its introduction; see Avenary, ed., *Kantor Salomon Sulzer,* 166–67.
64. For this and more biographical details see A. L. Ringer, "Salomon Sulzer, Joseph Mainzer and the Romantic a cappella Movement," *Studia Musicologica* 11, Fasc. 1/4, Bence Szabolsci, Septuagenario (1969), 355–70. Avenary, ed., *Kantor Salomon Sulzer,* 55–60; Werner, *A Voice,* 206–9. Werner argues that it is due to Mannheimer's charismatic personality that the Viennese and related communities achieved a unified, manageable *ritus* that helped preserve them in the face of internal and external crises. The opening of the Jewish-sanctioned soundscape to non-Jewish ears is discussed by Philip Bohlman, "Composing the Cantorate: Westernizing Europe's Other Within," in *Western Music and Its Others: Difference, Representation, and Appropriation in Music,* ed. Georgina Born and David Hesmondhalgh (Berkeley: University of California Press, 2000), 187–212, arguing for the opening of the cantorial music into a "public space." His claim that it was "the first time the sanctuary was truly a public space" is warranted by the fact that synagogal music did enjoy more public interest (including for example a generous review of *Schir Zion* 2 by the renowned music critic Eduard Hanslick); but

it was usually considered merely a curiosity and had never become public as had other music institutions (opera, church music, and so on).

65. Avenary, ed., *Kantor Salomon Sulzer*, 23–25.

66. See Goldberg, "The Training of *Hazzanim.*"This was by far not always the case. State authorities often pitted themselves against reform, seeing it in some way as a perditious movement (Richard Wagner is a good example of this as well). See Michael A. Meyer, *Response to Modernity: a History of the Reform Movement in Judaism* (New York: Oxford University Press, 1988).

67. The preacher Mannheimer was not allowed by the authorities to introduce any change in the established Jewish *Ritus*; see Avenary, ed., *Kantor Salomon Sulzer*, 63.

68. See Avenary, ed., *Kantor Salomon Sulzer*, 9. Uttered on the occasion of the fortieth anniversary of Sulzer's appointment to office, these words were published in the important newspaper *Neue Freie Presse* (no. 563) after the favorable review by Hanslick on Sulzer's *Schir Zion 2*, previously published in the same paper (issue no. 551).

69. Salomon Sulzer, *Schir Zion: Ein Cyklus religiöser Gesänge zum gottesdienstlichen Gebrauche der Israeliten* (Vienna: self-published, 1840). The second part followed in 1865. *Schir Zion*—the Song of Zion, the title of Salomon Sulzer's main collection of liturgical compositions, derives from the famous Psalm 137 (3–4), "By the water of Babylon": "For there our captors required of us songs, and our tormentors, mirth, saying, 'Sing us one of the songs of Zion!' How shall we sing the Lord's song in a foreign land?" (see the epigraph to this chapter). This verse became a source of tropes and paraphrases for the authors addressed in the rest of this chapter.

70. See *Schir Zion*, 180. The text is a quote from Exodus 34:6–7 citing Moses' announcement upon witnessing God's (private) revelation to him: "The Lord, the Lord, God merciful and gracious, long-suffering, and abundant in goodness and truth; keeping mercy unto the thousandth generation, forgiving iniquity and transgression and sin." Known as the Thirteen Attributes, the rest of the verse contains the less merciful aspects of God. The opening words themselves ("*Adonai, Adonai*"), hitherto considered to be "noisy" Hebrew words—are here redeemed through harmonization; see chapter 1 and Vecchi's example there.

71. Sulzer's friendship with Schubert yielded, among other things, the choral setting by Schubert of Psalm 92, ("tôw l'hôdôs ladônoj"), for the Friday night (Kabbalat Shabbat) service, commissioned by Sulzer. See Elaine Brody, "Schubert and Sulzer revisited: a recapitulation of the events leading to Schubert's setting in Hebrew of Psalm XCII, D. 953," in *Schubert Studies: Problems of Style and Chronology*, ed. Eva Badura-Skoda and Peter Branscombe (Cambridge: Cambridge University Press, 1982), 47–60.

72. Cf. the opening gesture of Pamina's aria "Ach, ich fühl's" from Mozart's *Magic Flute* (1791), which is followed by a poignant octave leap, developing into a highly expressive melodic line. This opening gesture is discussed in the context of the Baroque figures *saltus* and *passus duriusculus* in Katz and HaCohen, *Tuning the Mind: Connecting Aesthetic Theory to Cognitive Science* (New Brunswick, NJ: Transaction, 2003), 113–22.

73. This too is recognized in insider Jewish practice.

74. Shocked by the "hep hep" pogroms of 1819, Börne coined this expression that became quite widespread. It appears in his *Sämtliche Schriften*, 1, 510, quoted in Amos Elon, *The Pity of It All: A History of Jews in Germany, 1745–1933* (New York: Henry Holt, 2002), 134. See also Gilman, *Jewish Self-Hatred*, 148–167.

75. Semiotically, if functions as synecdoche, designating this tonal structure (rather ubiquitous in Sulzer's oeuvres) as standing for the renewed Jewish life in central Europe.

76. In the south German (Jewish) pronunciation reflected in the transliteration: "Ono tôwo l'fonecho t'fillosenu w'al tisallem mi-t'chinosenu sche-en onu asse fonim u-sche [*sic*] ôref lômar l'fonecho ªdônoj elôhenu we-lôhe ªvôsenu zadikim ªnachnu we-lô chotonu ªvol ªnachnu chotonu." (Hide not Thyself from our supplication for we are neither so arrogant nor so hardened as to say before Thee, O Lord our God and God of our fathers, "we are righteous and have not sinned"; verily, we have sinned.) *High Holiday Prayer Book*, ed. and trans. Morris Silverman (Hartford, CT: United Synagogue of America, 1972), 239.

77. Semantically marked as a reinforced "optimistic" progression.

78. A moment captured, for example, in Heine's first *Hebrew Melodies* poem "Princess Shabbat" (see n. 108 below).

79. This idea and several examples of such motifs are presented in what Tarsi initially termed "universal motifs." See Boaz Tarsi, "Tonality and Motivic Interrelationships in the Performance Practice of *Nusach*," *Journal of Synagogue Music* 21/1:21–24; these motifs are not mode-dependent; they can be found throughout the repertoire in various liturgical contexts.

80. The last words of Eicha (Lamentations) mentioned above, variously set to music by Jewish composers of this school. The polyphonic setting of such pieces is interpreted by Bohlman as "a metonymy for the many voices now constituting the Jewish community" (Bohlman, "Composing Cantorate," 198). While the Jewish community by and large became more diverse, the mostly homophonic settings of the "new music" bespeak an aspiration to homogenization of soundscape, replacing, as we have seen, the old heterophonic practices which implied an undisciplined service, expressing a preference for the prevalent Christian music's sonority.

81. For his criticism of Reform Judaism and its imitation of Christianity as comprising "tortoise soup without tortoise," see Heine's letter to Immanuel Wohlwill, 1 April 1823, in *Confessio Judaica*, 13. For his critical views on Felix Mendelssohn, see "Heinrich Heine on Mendelssohn," selected and introduced by Leon Botstein, in *Mendelssohn and His World*, ed. R. Larry Todd (Princeton: Princeton University Press, 1991), 352–63. Especially poignant are the lines in his letter to Ferdinand Lassalle (February 1846): "I cannot forgive this man whose independence is assured by financial circumstances, for serving the Pietists with his great, enormous talent" (ibid., 356).

82. For a comprehensive survey of the movement see Ismar Schorsch, *From Text to Context: The Turn to History in Modern Judaism* (Hanover, NH: published for Brandeis University Press by University Press of New England, 1994). A hitherto unknown document related to the group's major agenda has been recently published in Elon's *The Pity*, 113. For Heine's appreciation of the group, see "Ludwig Marcus: Denkworte"

in *Heinrich Heine: Gesammelte Werke* 7, 250. Similar ideas to those detailed below, this time regarding smell rather than sound, are purported by Sander L. Gilman in *Inscribing the Other* (Lincoln: University of Nebraska Press, 1991), chap. 5: "Heine, Nietzsche and the Idea of the Jew: The Other and the Self."

83. Hannah Arendt, *The Jew as Pariah*, 68.

84. Idelsohn's reaction to Sulzer betrays a general antagonism to the enterprise of the renewal of Jewish cantorial music. He claimed that the Jewish element in Sulzer's works is no more authentic than orientalism is in Rimsky-Korsakov's or Saint-Saëns' music, yet it is foreign enough for non-Jews to count as Jewish. Werner's rebuttal of these charges is well taken. See Idelsohn, *Jewish Music*, 254, and Werner, *A Voice*, 217–18.

85. Elliott Schreiber, "Tainted Sources: The Subversion of the Grimms' Ideology of the Folktale in Heinrich Heine's *Der Rabbi von Bacherach*," *German Quarterly* 78/1 (2005): 23–44.

86. Translation is quoted from *The Complete Poems of Heinrich Heine*, trans. Hal Draper (Oxford: Oxford University Press, 1982), 580–83.

87. See, for example, the opening recitative of Musica in Monteverdi's *Orfeo* (1607), or the description of Walhalla's *Wunschmädchen*.

88. Operatically, the old man plays the role of a servant or an old man disenchanting a naïve woman about the true nature of her beloved, such as Leporello towards Elvira in the famous catalogue aria; like Elvira, also our nun is consequently dumb-founded.

89. It seems that what started as a general cultural practice in Germany since the seventeenth century, became "Jewish" when theatrical life grew more established. Fictional Mirah Lapidoth's father may have been related to such wandering groups, at least initially (see chapter 5 below). Later, Kafka was attracted to touring Yiddish theatrical groups and rendered the notion a trope. See Galili Shahar "Der Erzähler auf der Galerie, Franz Kafka und die dramaturgische Figur," *Weimarer Beiträge* 4 (2003): 516–33.

90. The term *niggun* (in Hebrew and the Yiddish form) denotes, literally, "tune" (as in Missinai Niggunim). It connotes authenticity, if not sacredness, as in connection with Hasidic tunes.

91. This is another way to connect Heine to Arendt's claim regarding Heine as the only emancipated Jew, at once "both a German and a Jew" (Arendt, *The Jew as Pariah*, 72–75). See also Jost Hermand, "One Identity Is Not Enough: Heine's Legacy to Germans, Jews and Liberals," in *Heinrich Heine and the Occident: Multiple Identities, Multiple Receptions*, ed. Peter Uwe Hohendahl and Sander L. Gilman (Lincoln: University of Nebraska Press, 1991).

92. Rowlandson seems to closely follow a description such as Walter Scott's Isaac, in *Ivanhoe* (quoted in Page, *Imperfect Sympathies*, 11). It attests to the kind of attraction the synagogue could exert at the time, but also to the bewilderment such encounters bred on both sides (see Rubens, *A Jewish Iconography*, 97, cat. no. 926).

93. Liszt's entire text, entitled—following Wagner—"Judentum in der Musik," can be found in Avenary, ed., *Kantor Salomon Sulzer*, 154–58. This translation, with slight changes, is from Werner, *A Voice*, 215.

94. Contemporary British criticism of Byron's *Hebrew Melodies* (discussed below) drifts in this direction, accusing the poet of polluting and profaning the sacred song and of "mental prostitution." See *A Selection of Hebrew Melodies, Ancient and Modern*, by Isaac Nathan and Lord Byron, ed. Frederick Burwick and Paul Douglass (Tuscaloosa: University of Alabama Press, 1988), 16.

95. "Among the uncanny things that oppressed me as a boy, and even as a youth, were especially the conditions in the Jewish quarter, actually called Jews' Lane since it consisted of little more than a single street, which in early times had apparently been crammed like a kennel between the town wall and the moat. Its narrowness, filth, the swarms of people, *the disagreeable sound of the accent*—all of it together made the most unpleasant impression, even if one only looked in at the gate while passing by. It was a long time before I ventured to go in alone, and, once I had escaped the importunities of all those people persistently demanding or offering something to haggle over, I was not eager to return. Also some old tales hovered darkly before my young mind about the Jews' cruelty to Christian children, tales we had seen horribly illustrated in Gottfried's *Chronicle*. And although in more recent times one had a better opinion of them, an extraordinary witness was borne against them nevertheless in the big mocking picture that was still rather clearly to be seen, to their disgrace, on a wall of the arch under the bridge tower; for it had not been painted by some mischievous private person, but by official order [meaning, the *Judensau*].

    Nevertheless, they were God's chosen people and, however this may have come about, walking reminders of the most ancient times. Moreover, they were also human beings, industrious and affable, and even their obstinacy in clinging to their old customs commanded respect. The Christian boy who encountered them in Fisherman's Field on a Sabbath paid some friendly attention to them. Therefore I was extremely curious to see their school [should be: *synagogue* R. H.], had attended a circumcision and a wedding, and gotten myself an idea of the Feast of Tabernacles [Sukkot]. I was well received everywhere, well entertained, and invited to return, for influential persons either took me there or recommended me." Johann Wolfgang Goethe, *From My Life: Poetry and Truth*, trans. Robert R. Heitner (New York: Suhrkamp, 1987), 119–20 (italics added).

    Despite stereotypical anti-Semitic notions ironically mediated, Goethe's report is likewise affected by the new ethnographic impulse. Unfortunately, it does not contain any specific details about his experience at the synagogue, at the circumcision ceremony, or in the Sukkah. It is interesting to compare his account with that of Ludwig Börne—an outside-insider—upon his visit to the lane on Passover morning, at about that time. See "Jugendarbeiten Ludwig Börne's über jüdische Dinge" (aus dessen Nachlass herausgegeben von G. Schnapper-Arndt) in *Zeitschrift für die Geschichte der Juden in Deutschland* 2 (1888): 375–80.

96. See Heinrich Heine, *Der Rabbi von Bacherach. Ein Fragment*, Zweites Kapitel (http://www.heinrich-heine.net/rabbi2.htm), and *The Rabbi of Bacharach*, trans. Charles Godfrey Leland, The Project Gutenberg e-book of The German Classics of The Nineteenth and Twentieth Centuries, vol. 6 (http://www.gutenberg.org/files/12473/12473.txt). I introduced slight changes and some additions to this translation.

97. This mixture of imaginings is aptly analyzed in Schreiber's "Tainted Sources."
98. Ibid., 37. Nightingales, together with other voices of nature, are also central in some of the medieval elaborations of world harmony ideas. See Spitzer, *Classical and Christian Ideas*, 199–204. From a forward-looking perspective, Heine anticipates here a Joycean epiphany, though from a bit more ironic distance: "Its soul, its whatness, leaps to us from the vestment of its appearance. The soul of the commonest object, the structure of which is so adjusted, seems to us radiant. The object achieves its epiphany." James Joyce, *Stephen Hero* (Norfolk CN: New Directions, 1963), 213.
99. Heine was alerted to this by the blood libel in Damascus in 1840, an event thoroughly studied by Jonathan Frankel in *The Damascus Affair: "Ritual Murder," Politics, and the Jews in 1840* (Cambridge: Cambridge University Press, 1997). See Schreiber, "Tainted Sources," 30 and Ritchie Robertson, *Heine* (London: Halban, 1988), 85–86. This will be taken up in the following chapter.
100. Bluma Goldstein, "Heine's 'Hebrew Melodies': A Politics and Poetics of Diaspora," in *Heinrich Heine's Contested Identities*, ed. Jost Hermand and Robert C. Holub (New York: Peter Lang, 1999), 49–68.
101. Here Goldstein follows Daniel Boyarin and Jonathan Boyarin in their article, "Diaspora: Generation and the Ground for Jewish Identity," *Critical Inquiry* 19/4 (1993): 693–724, which celebrates the diasporic existence of North American Jews, condemning Zionism. She also makes use of James Clifford's by now classic study "Diaspora" in *Routes: Travel and Translation in the Late Twentieth Century* (Cambridge, MA: Harvard University Press, 1997), 244–78. What is problematic here is the outright enlisting of Heine for this ideology, the unwarranted parallelism between medieval Spain, nineteenth-century Germany and late twentieth-century United States, and the reduction of a complicated poetical statement to a dichotomous juxtaposition of "out-of-homeland" cultures and contexts. I find more persuasive Gilman's discussion of these poems in terms of Heine's complex, ambivalent grappling with his own status as a Jewish poet in the German language. See Gilman, *Jewish Self-Hatred*, 179–88.
102. See the likewise self-reflective and ars poetical "My Poetry," in Ch. N. Bialik, *Poems*, ed. Avner Holtzman (Tel Aviv: Dvir, 2004), 189, especially the image of the cricket's song. For an English translation, see *Chaim Nachman Bialik: Selected Poems*, bilingual edition, trans. Ruth Nevo (Tel Aviv: Dvir, 1981), 14.
103. See Heinrich Heine, "Ludwig Börne," in *Heinrich Heine Sämtliche Werke* (Leipzig: Insel Verlag, 1913), 8, 366. A pictorial equivalent of this trope and mood is *By the Waters of Babylon* (1832) by the convert (and Nazarene painter) Eduard Bendemann, which, however, as Richard I. Cohen maintains in *Jewish Icons: Art and Society in Modern Europe* (Berkeley: University of California Press, 1998), 160, is "marked by an overdose of sentimentalism" reflecting predominant Christian attitudes.
104. *Untergang* is also the last, highly contested word of Wagner's *Judentum in der Musik*, which carries Heine's idea one step further. It is Wagner who undertook to musicalize Heine's *Ahasver* (*The Flying Dutchman*) — the Wandering Jew — and who sought to let him sink, either through total assimilation or through other ways of annihilation, as some critics claim. See chapter 5, n. 92.

105. At the time he wrote the poem, Heine was already suffering from a chronic terminal illness.

106. I refer to "Auf Flügeln des Gesanges." Written by Heine in 1822, the poem contains the following memorable, orientalist/escapist lines: "Auf Flügeln des Gesanges / Herzliebchen, trag ich dich fort, / Fort nach den Fluren des Ganges, / Dort weiß ich den schönsten Ort"—enhanced by Mendelssohn's soaring 6/8, major-minor setting. For a different interpretation of the song, see Susan Youens, "Mendelssohn's Songs" in *The Cambridge Companion to Mendelssohn*, ed. Peter Mercer-Taylor (Cambridge: Cambridge University Press, 2004), 192–95.

107. See Goldstein, "Heine's 'Hebrew Melodies,'" 65, n. 8.

108. This exchange of text and melody is the essence of Nathan's and Byron's cycles; in Heine it unfolds, for example, in his famous parody of Beethoven-Schiller's *Ode to Joy* in his first *Melodie*, "Prinzessin Sabbat" ("Princess Shabbat"), praising the Jewish *schalet* (Shabbat's special dish, the famous *cholent* or *tshoolnt*) and, in the same poem, the "Lecho daudi" *piyyut* of the Kabbalat Shabbat service.

109. For the entire collection, see Isaac Nathan's *A selection of Hebrew melodies, ancient and modern [music]: newly arranged . . . with appropriate symphonies and accompaniments* (London: J. Fentum, 1860). The title includes the following caption: "the poetry written expressly for the work by Lord Byron." For a modern facsimile, see Burwick and Douglass, eds., *A Selection of Hebrew Melodies*. In the introduction, "The Creation of 'Hebrew' Melodies" (1–39), the editors give valuable data about the main strivings behind this project, such as Nathan's ambition to be recognized as a professional musician and his unavailing struggle against surrounding anti-Semitic prejudices.

110. Ibid., 7. Nathan's announcement appeared in the May 1813 issue of *The Gentleman's Magazine*.

111. Ibid., 8.

112. See a caricature and an allusion to John Braham's singing in chapter 2.

113. Collaboration of poet and composer of this kind was rare at the time. Curiously, it foreshadows procedures prevalent in modern Hebrew folk song. See Ruth HaCohen, "'To Hear the Singing and Prayer': From Words to Music and from Music to Words in the Israeli Song Culture," in *Jerusalem Studies in Literature* 20 (2006): 13–37 (Hebrew).

114. Several scholars have attempted to identify the tunes of the collection. See the summary in Burwick and Douglass, eds., *A Selection of Hebrew Melodies*, 13. On the sources of "Maoz Tsur," see chapter 1, n. 122. This case accentuates the migratory nature of melodies in general and of the Jewish-Christian ones, since about the fifteenth century, in particular.

115. Ibid., 3.

116. Benedetto Marcello's collaboration or mediation between Jewish "informants" and the poet Giustiniani is an antecedent of sorts. Nineteenth-century familiarity with Marcello's Psalm is well documented. See Edwin Seroussi, "In Search of Jewish Musical Antiquity in the 18th-century Venetian Ghetto: Reconsidering the Hebrew Melodies in Benedetto Marcello's Estro Poetico-Armonico," *Jewish Quarterly Review* 93/1–2 (2002): 149–200; Don Harrán, "The Hebrew Exemplum as a Force of Renewal in

18th-century Musical Thought: The Case of Benedetto Marcello and His Collection of Psalms," in *Music in the Mirror: Reflections on the History of Music Theory and Literature for the 21st Century*, eds. Andreas Geiger and Thomas J. Mathiesen (London, 2002), 143–94. Ravel's *Three Hebrew Melodies* and Shostakovich's *Jewish Songs* draw on indigenous Hebrew/Jewish melodies but are not undertaking such an exchange.

117. For a curious anecdote on this matter see http://www.smerus.pwp.blueyonder.co.uk/byron.htm.

118. "The days are done" contains an allusion to Judea and is close in spirit to Handel's *Samson*.

119. See *Jewish Encyclopedia* u.vv. "Nathan, Isaac," "Priestly Blessing." See also Eliyahu Schleifer, "The Priestly Blessing in the Ashkenazi Synagogue: Ritual and Chant," in *Yuval* VII, 268.

120. This famous melody is transcribed, among other places, in Abraham Baer (1834–1894), *Baal Tefillah, Der praktische Vorbeter*, 2nd ed. (Frankfurt: J. Kauffmann, 1883), 175 (3. Weise).

121. See Boaz Tarsi, "Toward a Clearer Definition of the Magen Avot Mode," *Musica Judaica* 16 (2001–2002): 61–63.

122. Burwick and Douglass rightly note that tonal changes in the cycle are made more pronounced through "shifting," in accordance with prevalent melodic patterns of the synagogue (36).

123. The "Leoni Yigdal" is so called after its transcriber, Meyer Lyon, the chief singer of the Great Synagogue in London. Nathan quoted it in his *Essay on the History and Theory of Music and on the Qualities, Capabilities and Management of the Human Voice* (London: B. Whittaker, 1823), 45–46, a book worth investigation in the present context. The text contains the following appraisal: "At the time the celebrated Leoni sang at the synagogue, he gave such general delight by his execution of this melody, that it was adapted to English words for the service of the Protestant church, and has since been published in a collection of Psalms, and named after Leoni." Idelsohn, in a posthumously published article, added that Leoni gave it in 1772 to the Wesleyan clergyman Thomas Oliver, and the latter composed an English text for it ("God of Abraham, Praise") that "is printed to this day in the Episcopalian songbook." See "The Magen-Ovos-Mode," *Hebrew Union College Annual* 14 (1939): 563–64.

CHAPTER 4. "JEWS (AND JEWESSES) LIKE YOU AND ME"

1. *Les juifs, en Allemagne, en France, sont des gens comme vous et moi; leur religion, leurs mœurs sont tellement fondues dans le mouvement social auquel ils s'agrègent que tout ce qui fait le juif a disparu, sauf son habileté commerciale, son avidité; mais son avidité met des gants jaunes, son habileté se francise: il est poëte comme Heine, musicien comme Mayer-Beer et Halévy, collectionneur comme les Fould, généreux comme Les Rostschild [sic]; tandis que, dès Cracovie, les vrais talmudistes se manifestent.* Honoré de Balzac, *Lettre sur Kiew, fragment inédit*, 1847 (Paris: Lapina, 1927), 39.

2. "Balzac himself always speaks of his characters as of natural phenomena, and when he wants to describe his artistic intentions, he never speaks of his psychology, but always

of his sociology, of his natural history of society and of the function of the individual in the life of the social body. He became, anyhow, the master of the social novel, if not as the 'doctor of the social sciences,' as he described himself, yet as the founder of the new conception of man, according to which 'the individual exists only in relation to society.'" Arnold Hauser, *Social History of Art* (London: Routledge & Kegan Paul, 1962) 2:25. An antimonarchist, Balzac was an avowed liberal and religious tolerant, as were many others in his circle. See Alan Barrie Spitzer, *The French Generation of 1820* (Princeton: Princeton University Press, 1987), 5–6.

3. In France Jews were granted full civil rights by the National Assembly in 1791.

4. Hannah Arendt, *The Jew as Pariah: Jewish Identity and Politics in the Modern Age* (New York: Grove, 1978), 63. For the characteristics of this generation see also her *Rahel Varnhagen, The Life of a Jewess*, ed. Liliane Weissberg, trans. Richard and Clara Winston (Baltimore: Johns Hopkins University Press, 1997), especially 87–88. For the process of assimilation, see the classical studies of Jacob Katz, *Out of the Ghetto: The Social Background of Emancipation* (Cambridge, MA: Harvard University Press, 1973) and *Tradition and Crisis: Jewish Society at the End of the Middle Ages* trans. B. D. Cooperman (New York: Schocken, [1961] 1974).

5. For Heine, the noncategorizability of a writer in terms of his political stances was a crucial ideological matter. See Thomas Pfau, *Romantic Moods: Paranoia, Trauma and Melancholy, 1790–1840* (Baltimore: Johns Hopkins University Press, 2005), 385.

6. This is related in Balzac's description of his Kiev trip on Rosh Hashanah, recounted in the letter quoted above.

7. The term *Ostjuden* became widespread only in the early twentieth century, and the stereotype was not in common use before the mid-nineteenth century, when the process of de-ghettoization of German Jews was well under way; yet the process started earlier. For the dialectics of this stereotyped internal Jewish dichotomy, see Steven Aschheim, *Brothers and Strangers: The East European Jew in German and German Jewish Consciousness 1800–1923* (Madison: University of Wisconsin Press 1982); idem., "The Eastern European Jew and German Jewish Identity," *Studies in Contemporary Jewry* I, ed. Jonathan Frankel (Bloomington: Indiana University Press, 1984), 3–25; Sander L. Gilman, *Jewish Self-Hatred: Anti-Semitism and the Hidden Language of the Jews* (Baltimore: Johns Hopkins University Press, 1988), 270–86. See also Paul Mendes-Flohr, "Fin-de-Siècle Orientalism, the *Ostjuden*, and the Aesthetics of Jewish Self-Affirmation," *Studies in Contemporary Jewry* I, 96–139. The great German Jewish historian, Heinrich Graetz, is a prime example of the condescending, if not derogatory, treatment of eastern European Jews. See Aschheim "The Eastern European Jew," 23, n. 20. In France, this dichotomy engendered the distinction between *juif* and *israélite*; Halévy, for one, viewed the figure of "his" Éléazar—who is led by hatred and vengeance, as *juif* rather than *israélite*. See Diana R. Hallman, *The Politics of Halévy's La Juive: Opera, Liberalism, and Anti-Semitism in Nineteenth-Century France* (Cambridge: Cambridge University Press, 2002), 193.

8. See Thomas Schmidt-Beste, "Felix Mendelssohn Bartholdy and Heinrich Heine," *Heine-Jahrbuch* 39 (2000), 111–34. Heine mocks Mendelssohn on several occasions, e.g., chapter 16 of *Deutschland: Ein Wintermärchen*. For its English translation see

Leon Botstein, "Heinrich Heine on Mendelssohn," selected and introduced by Leon Botstein, in *Mendelssohn and His World*, ed. R. Larry Todd (Princeton: Princeton University Press, 1991), 353. The tumultuous relations between Meyerbeer and Heine, which included Heine's evaluation of Halévy, were partially recorded by Heine himself, and were further investigated by several scholars. His poignant phrases against other composers appeared mainly in his "Musical Feuilletons." See "Heinrich Heine's Musical Feuilletons," *Musical Quarterly* 8 (1922): 115–59; 273–95; 435–68.

9. The comparison between the two was not unprecedented in their own time. Even Fanny (Felix's sister) would wonder at the coincidental premiering of *St. Paul* and *The Huguenots* and a critic named Lyser would defend the two from their diametrically opposed adversaries (see George Feder, "Sacred Music" in *The Mendelssohn Companion*, ed. Douglass Seaton (Westport: Greenwood Press, 2001), 259.

10. For a rich survey of Meyerbeer's relation to Halévy, see Robert Ignatius Letellier, "Meyerbeer and Halévy: Relations between Two Masters of the French Grand Opera, A Talk for the Bicentennial Celebration of the Birth of Jacques-Fromental-Elie Halévy, New York 11 April 1999," (http://www.meyerbeer.com/mey-halevy.htm). The inscription Meyerbeer engraved on the monument he donated for Halévy in 1862 is most telling in this connection: "Shalom ba-olam dear Jacques-Fromental-Elie. May you rest in beatitude, and may we soon be able to celebrate your life through knowing and loving the hidden treasures of your slumbering scores." Its first two Hebrew words (peace in the world) connect the two through their Jewish affiliation; the rest attests to Meyerbeer's awareness that his younger colleague never received the recognition he deserved.

11. For a rare article in this direction see Frieder Reininghaus, "Zwei Emanzipationswege aus Berlin. Anmerkungen zum Verhältnis Meyerbeers und Mendelssohns," in *Giacomo Meyerbeer, Musik als Welterfahrung, Heinz Becker zum 70. Geburtstag*, ed. Jürgen Schläder (Munich: Ricordi, 1995), 223–36.

12. The concept of moods as an historical entity is central in Thomas Pfau's study mentioned in n. 5 above. He himself follows Heidegger's concept of *Stimmung*, which the latter regards as a social construct one is born into and is always surrounded by. This is of special interest in connection to the theory of emotions in music, and will be used in this sense in the following chapter. For a succinct exposition of Heidegger's concept of mood, see Charles Guignon, "Moods in Heidegger's Being and Time," in *What is an Emotion? Classic and Contemporary Readings*, ed. Robert C. Solomon (Oxford: Oxford University Press, 2003), 181–90.

13. For the sociohistorical characteristics of the French scene, relevant to all except Mendelssohn, see Spitzer, *The French Generation of 1820*. Wolf Lepenies, in *Melancholy and Society*, trans. Jeremy Gaines and Doris Jones (Cambridge, MA: Harvard University Press, 1992), 151–54, views the parallel German Vormärz generation as dominated by a melancholic mood, which served them as a "means of self-confirmation out of the inhibition of action" (related to a forestalled social development, strict surveillance of universities, and censorship of writing). Such generational melancholy, Pfau tells us, had a heteronomous rather than autonomous affect that determined the mental make-up of its subjects. The "unconscious other" of this affect, he argues, was

ressentiment—a Nietzschean category that he reads back to Heine. See, Pfau *Romantic Moods*, 393, 405. Anti-Semitism easily flourished in such sociocultural soil.

14. The interest of Meyerbeer in the politics of his time is documented in his diaries. For the ideas and activities of the Halévy brothers, see below.

15. According to Karl August Varnhagen von Ense's report, the ten-year-old Felix was a victim of a "hep hep" rioters' attack or jest in 1819 Berlin. Recent research casts doubt on this account, but certainly the atmosphere in Berlin at the time was not auspicious for this *Neuchrist* family. See Todd, *Mendelssohn*, 50–51.

16. The social makeup of his mother's salon in connection with other Berliner salons is surveyed, with rich bibliography, by Klaus Wolfgang Niemöller, in "Meyerbeer und die Berliner Salons," *Giacomo Meyerbeer, Musik als Welterfahrung* (see n. 11 above), 173–81. For a vivid description and a cultural analysis of it within the context of the Jewish women's musical salon see, respectively, Emily D. Bilsky and Emily Braun, *Jewish Women and Their Salons: The Power of Conversation* (New York and New Haven: The Jewish Museum and Yale University Press, 2005), 38–49, and Leon Botstein, "Music, Femininity, and Jewish Identity: The Tradition and Legacy of the Salon," in ibid., 159–70. Meyerbeer's rich social affiliations and acquaintances are documented in his diaries. See *The Diaries of Giacomo Meyerbeer: 1791–1839*, 3 vols., trans. and ed. Robert Ignatius Letellier (Madison, NJ: Fairleigh Dickinson University Press, 2000–2002).

17. See Joan L. Thomson, "Giacomo Meyerbeer: The Jew and his Relationship with Richard Wagner" in *Musica Judaica* 1 (1975/6): 57–58; Hanoch Avenary, ed. *Kantor Salomon Sulzer und Seine Zeit, Eine Dokumentation* (Sigmaringen: Jan Thorbeck, 1985), 24. For the design of Jacob Beer's home synagogue see Bilsky and Braun, *Jewish Women*, 42.

18. See Letellier, *The Diaries of Giacomo Meyerbeer* 1:53–54.

19. Ibid., 52. Michael (1800–1833), the youngest of four sons and a gifted playwright, gave vent to their feeling of nonbelonging in his tragedy *Der Paria* (1828)—a play about an unfortunate hero of a despised Indian caste, commended by no less than Goethe himself.

20. Meyerbeer's letter to his wife, according to Thomson's "Meyerbeer and Wagner," 61.

21. Theodor Uhlig, "Der Prophet von Meyerbeer," *Neue Zeischrift für Musik* (appearing in installments from February to April 1850: 11; 17; 33; 34). The text is partially reprinted in Jens Malte Fischer, *Richard Wagners "Das Judentum in der Musik": Eine kritische Dokumentation als Beitrag zur Geschichte des Antisemitismus* (Frankfurt: Insel, 2000), 208–9. For his influence on Wagner see chapter 6 and below.

22. The phrase "unity within variety" was coined by Francis Hutcheson, but he did not invent it. See Francis Hutcheson, *An Inquiry Concerning Beauty, Order, Harmony, Design*, [1725] ed. Peter Kivy (The Hague: Martinus Nijhoff, 1973); Ruth Katz and Ruth HaCohen, *Tuning the Mind, Connecting Aesthetics to Cognitive Science* (New Brunswick, NJ: Transaction, 2003), 183–242.

23. This aesthetic category predominates in some favorite works of Mendelssohn such as the scherzo from *A Midsummer Night's Dream*, the scherzo from Piano Trio op. 49 in D minor, and several lieder.

24. Mendelssohn's commitment to the idea of the classical genres is discussed by Carl Dahlhaus in "Mendelssohn und die musikalische Gattungstradition," in *Das Problem Mendelssohn*, ed. C. Dahlhaus (Regensburg: G. Bosse, 1974), 55–60; see also Leon Botstein, "Neoclassicism, Romanticism, and Emancipation: The Origins of Felix Mendelssohn's Aesthetic Outlook," in *The Mendelssohn Companion*, ed. Douglass Seaton (Westport; Greenwood Press, 2001), 1–24; and the critical essay of Albrecht Riethmüller, "'Das Problem Mendelssohn,'" *Archiv für Musikwissenschaft* 59/3 (2002): 210–21.

25. See Thomas Pfau, "From Mediation to Medium: Aesthetic and Anthropological Dimensions of the Image (Bild) and the Crisis of Bildung in German Modernism," *Modernist Culture* 1/2 (2005): 141–80.

26. See Luc Boltanski, *Distant Suffering: Morality, Media and Politics*, trans. Graham Burchell (Cambridge: Cambridge University Press, 1999), 121.

27. Ibid., 123.

28. Ibid., 122.

29. Friedrich von Schiller, *Über die ästhetische Erziehung des Menschen* (1794). For an English translation on the Internet, see http://www.fordham.edu/halsall/mod/schiller-education.html.

30. See Johann Jakob Engel, *Schriften, Reden und ästhetische Versuche* (Frankfurt, 1857), 4:136–52. For the English translation see *Contemplating Music: Source Readings in the Aesthetics of Music*, vol. 3 *Essence*, ed. Ruth Katz and Carl Dahlhaus (New York: Pendragon, 1992), 128–140. Engel's ideas were known also in England, through the translation of "Ideen zu einer Mimik" by Henry Siddons, published in London in 1822 as *Practical illustrations of rhetorical gesture and action: adapted to the English drama, from a work on the subject by M. Engel.* Meyerbeer's deep interest in the treatise is expressed in his diaries; see Letellier, *Diaries of Giacomo Meyerbeer*, 3:327 (entry: July 1815).

31. For Webb's treatise, see Ruth Katz and Ruth HaCohen, eds., *The Arts in Mind, Pioneering Texts of a Coterie of British Men of Letters* (New Brunswick, NJ: Transaction, 2003): 251–324. His text was translated into German in 1771.

32. Engel explicates how working through the various musical parameters such as key, melody, movement, and harmony enables the endless variations so necessary for the minute depiction of sentiments. These ideas go in the direction of modern theories of the semiotics of music.

33. Engel follows Webb in a few other matters, and like him, he also may have consulted Descartes' theory of emotions, or received the latter ideas through Webb.

34. As was famously expounded by Susanne Langer in her various writings on music aesthetics.

35. The idea that the Vormärz Jews in Berlin were "wary of words" is a point made also by Susan Youens in "Mendelssohn's Songs," *The Cambridge Companion to Mendelssohn*, ed. Peter Mercer-Taylor (Cambridge: Cambridge University Press, 2004), 189.

36. Letter from Berlin, dated 15 October 1842, in *Briefe*, ed. R. Elvers (Frankfurt, 1984), 2:337–38 as translated by Youens, in "Mendelssohn's Songs," 190.

37. Cone's analysis (whose point of departure is Schubert's *Erlkönig*) aimed at a semiotic deconstruction of the lied as artistic medium, yet was justifiably criticized for its reification of the authorial voice. See E. T. Cone, *The Composer's Voice* (Berkeley: University of California Press, 1974), 1–40.

38. Engel, "Über die Musikalische Malerei," in *Contemplating Music*, 135. The idea, though not in connection with music, was explicated by Descartes in *Passions of the Soul*, in *The Philosophical Writings of Descartes*, trans. Robert Stoothoff (Cambridge: Cambridge University Press, 1985), 1 (sec. 39): 343.

39. See Michael P. Steinberg, *Listening to Reason* (Princeton: Princeton University Press, 2006), 1–17. The idea of the multivalent point of view of an observer is usually ascribed to the revolutionary techniques of seventeenth-century Dutch painters, especially Saenredam, as argued by Svetlana Alpers in *The Art of Describing: Dutch Art in the Seventeenth Century* (Chicago: University of Chicago Press, 1984), 64–69. An even more pertinent example, drawn from the cultural milieu discussed here and involving the painter's own subjectivity (and not only an "arbitrary" external point of view) is, according to Michael Fried, a group of Courbet's paintings, mainly self-portraits. See Michael Fried, *Courbet's Realism* (Chicago: University of Chicago Press, 1990).

40. Heine wrote it in 1830 as part of the cycle *Neuer Frühling*.

41. Eric Werner, *Mendelssohn, a New Image of the Composer and His Age*, trans. Dika Newlin (London: Free Press of Glencoe, 1963), 273. It is not clear from Werner's account whether Hegel directly instructed Mendelssohn regarding this caveat or whether the composer inferred it from the lessons he attended, or from Hegel's writings, with which he was acquainted. See ibid., 79. For Hegel's ideas in this regard see Katz and Dahlhaus, *Contemplating Music*, 1: 333–58.

42. For this general approach in Mendelssohn see, for example, Youens, "Mendelssohn's Songs," 191.

43. He was part of a politically and culturally conservative movement (a group that included people with different political commitments, such as his relative Friedrich Schlegel, Achim von Arnim, and Clemens Brentano) that sought to transcend politics altogether in their poetical worldview.

44. Interestingly, the song, in the beautiful translation of the nationalistically ambivalent poet Lea Goldberg, became since the days of the Yishuv a favorite of choirs expressing a romantic, Zionist, "anti-exile" spirit.

45. As Laurence Kramer has shown in "The Lied as Cultural Practice," in *Classical Music and Postmodern Knowledge* (Berkeley: University of California Press, 1995), 143–73, Mendelssohn's Goethe lieder comprise a group of their own, all featuring a feminine subjectivity addressed to their distant beloved. Goethe, a tutor and benefactor of the young composer, becomes, according to Kramer's interpretation, the latent addressee of these letters-songs sent by an effeminate disciple who seeks, through the artistic signs he wove in the poem, cultural-artistic approval. Mendelssohn's search for such approval and reception by the prince of German culture attests to an existential distress exceeding the general ennui characteristic of this generation of artists and *gebildet* persons in Germany.

46. I refer in particular to Schoenberg's *Book of the Hanging Gardens* op. 15 (1908–9), set to a selection of Stefan George's poems bearing this name. See the discussion of these songs, addressed from a related point of view in Carl Schorske, *Fin-de-Siècle Vienna: Politics and Culture* (Cambridge: Cambridge University Press, 1981), 344–64, and below, chapter 6.

47. Wagner maintains this "accusation" in particular towards Mendelssohn. Karl Kraus is one of the most quoted authorities on a similar notion about Heine. Nietzsche, saw, on the other hand, Heine's "sweet and passionate music" in highly positive terms. See Friedrich Wilhelm Nietzsche, *Ecce Homo: How to Become What You Are*, trans. Duncan Large (Oxford: Oxford University Press, 2007), 25. Heine saw poetic craftsmanship as crucial for the political mission of art; see Pfau, *Romantic Moods*, 383.

48. Pfau, *Romantic Moods*, 411.

49. Heine, *Schriften*, in Frederick H. Martens (trans.), "Heinrich Heine's Musical Feuilletons," *Musical Quarterly* 8 (1922), 463.

50. This complex process is the subject of a few of Sander Gilman's studies; see his *Jewish Self-Hatred*, and even closer to the topics here discussed is "The Jewish Voice: Chicken Soup or the Penalties of Sounding Too Jewish," in *The Jew's Body* (London: Routledge, 1991), 20–37.

51. In his work *The Entire Jewish Faith* (1531), the convert Antonius Margaritha, by then a follower of Luther, includes this anti-Jewish accusation; see Gilman, *Jewish Self-Hatred*, 63–64.

52. Pfau, *Romantic Moods*, 428–71.

53. A similar opinion is expressed by Letellier: "One should note that both Mahler and Schoenberg, the precursors of these composers [Ulman, Zemlinsky, Korngold, and so on] and both Jews who rejected their religion but still suffered from anti-Semitism all their lives, wrote music expressive of their sense of personal and artistic isolation and its attendant neurosis. The harmonic, melodic, and structural boldness of the musical language of *Le Prophète* and *L'Étoile du Nord* ought perhaps to be understood in the same light" (Letellier, *Diaries of Giacomo Meyerbeer*, 1:77, n. 231). An interesting case of a prodigy of the first generation of Jewish composers who turned out to be a musical recluse is the composer Charles-Valentin Alkan, Wagner's exact contemporary (1813–88), who was highly conscious of his Jewish legacy.

54. See Doron Mendels, "How was antiquity treated in societies with Hellenistic heritage? And why did the Rabbis avoid writing history?" in *Antiquity in Antiquity: Jewish and Christian Pasts in the Greco-Roman World*, eds. Gregg Gardner and Kevin Osterloh (Tuebingen: Mohr Siebeck, 2008).

55. Ludwig Rellstab's novel *1812* features a dirty, villainous Jew, who stands in striking contrast to the indigenous virtuous German heroes.

56. This did not prevent, perhaps it even compelled them, to search for stability and legitimation in terms of their own careers through institutional positions and belonging, though they did not necessarily find there the kind of security they craved.

57. On Saint Simon's ideas see Paul Ricoeur, *Lectures on Ideology and Utopia*, ed. George H. Taylor (New York: Columbia University Press, 1986), 285–300, and Ralph P. Locke, *Music, Musicians and the Saint-Simonians* (Chicago: University of Chicago

Press, 1986). Leon Halévy (the composer's brother), a poet and author of prominence, was pivotal in formulating some of these ideas, hailing the role of art in the new revolutionary society (ibid. 37–42; and Hallman, *The Politics*, 73–107).

58. Meyerbeer was exposed to the influence of Saint Simon's followers, and even Mendelssohn's encounter with some of their ideas influenced his worldview, though he totally rejected others. See Locke, *Music, Musicians and the Saint-Simonians*, 94–97; 107–113.

59. In the French Opéra, that was a real political problem, which engaged both hegemonic and dissident minds, as Jane Fulcher's thick tapestry of the circumstances and reactions related to *The Prophet*'s premier and subsequent performances reveals. See *The Nation's Image: French Grand Opera as Politics and Politicized Art* (Cambridge: Cambridge University Press, 1987), 122–163.

60. The writings of Wilhelm Heinse (1746–1803) are known for this association. See the discussion of the etymology of *Lärm* in chapter 3.

61. Carl Dahlhaus, *Nineteenth-Century Music*, trans. J. Bradford Robinson (Berkeley: University of California Press, [1980] 1989), 124–34. Interestingly, Dahlhaus' treatment of the subject is imbued with a Benjaminian "saving the phenomenon" ethics. He quotes Benjamin (from the *Arcades Project*) and draws on his ideas as a general backdrop to his discussion, and also applies his concept of "shock" in analyzing the phenomenon itself. Prior to Wagner, both Schumann and Mendelssohn criticized Meyerbeer's operas on various aesthetic grounds, e.g., Schumann's disparagement of *Les Huguenots*: "It is too much for a good protestant when he hears his most hallowed song bawled forth from the stage, too much for him when the bloodiest drama in the history of his church is reduced to a rustic farce simply to earn money and notoriety. The thing is outrageous from beginning to end, from the overture with its silly religiosity to the end, when we are all supposed to be burned alive. What is left after *Les Huguenots* but actually to execute criminals on the stage and to make a public exhibition of whores?" For the original German, see Robert Schumann, *Gesammelte Schriften über Musik und Musiker* (Wiesbaden, [1854] 1985), 1–2:221–22. The translation follows Tom Kaufman in "Why did Meyerbeer and Halévy fall from grace and what can be done about it?" (http://www.meyerbeer.com./kaufman.htm). For Wagner's attacks in *Oper und Drama* see his *Sämtliche Schriften und Dichtungen*, 5th ed. (Leipzig: Breitkopf und Härtel, 1911) 3:229, 296.

62. Dahlhaus, *Nineteenth-Century Music*, 125. Dahlhaus likewise emphasizes the place of the picturesque in the genre.

63. Ibid., 127. Dahlhaus insists that events related to the July Monarchy were already regarded by contemporaries as a turning point in the history of the genre, hence it is the works from that stage—mainly Auber's, Rossini's, and Meyerbeer's—that became its paradigmatic specimens. But it is Meyerbeer who became, together with the main librettist and dramaturge Eugene Scribe (and director Luis Veron, and architect Henri Duponchel), the main rulers in this dominion. The triumphs in the thirties of both Meyerbeer's *Robert le Diable* and Halévy's *La Juive* were among the main factors that transformed the Opéra at the time into a successful, lucrative institution. See Fulcher, *The Nation's Image*, and Barbier, *Opera in Paris 1800–1850*, trans. Robert Lu-

oma (Portland: Amadeus Press, [1987] 1995), 38–62. This book contains the following aesthetically categorizing sentences: "A real crisis lay behind the successful facades of Meyerbeer and Halévy. The works of these two consigned the other great works of the repertoire to oblivion, and with the tacit agreement of the authorities, smothered the creativity of talented younger composers, who were forced to live unrecognized and ignored" (83). Do we have here a subdued anti-Semitism of the sort Heine put in poor Spontini's mouth (quoted as epigraph above)? The statement is not backed by reference of any kind.

64. It is the attempt to balance the "references to the historical and contemporary," as Jane Fulcher puts it (*The Nation's Image*: 93), that renders this operatic moment into an "oratorical" one.

65. See Tarsi, "Toward a Clearer Definition of the Magen Avot," *Musica Judaica* 16 (2001–2002): 61–63. Cf. Idelsohn, *Thesaurus* 7:15–16, no. 46–48. See also chapter 3 in the present book, in the discussion of Nathan's melody to "We sate down and wept." As it turns out, I am not the first to hear this section as an oral allusion to the traditional Magen Avot (or "Vayekhulu") tune. The renowned cantor Pinchas Minkowsky seems to refer to that section as modeled after "Vayekhulu" in his article on "Ḥazzanut" in Judah David Eisenstein (ed.), *Otzar Israel: A Hebrew Encyclopedia* (New York: Pardes, [1906–1913] 1951), 4:264. I thank Boaz Tarsi for this reference.

66. *Der jüdische Cantor* 1879, no. 26. This statement was made in reference to the question of whether to include an organ in the service, discussed in chapter 3. The question was not halakhic: Meyerbeer "allowed" the use of flutes and horns, "similar to those used in Solomon's Temple." The entire letter is of interest here, since it opens with a curious phrase professing that the organ is a Christian instrument. Meyerbeer proceeds, "I consider it my merit that, in accordance with Mendelssohn-Bartholdy, I arranged in Berlin an a cappella choir only." Idelsohn, who quotes this letter, rightly refers it to the services organized in the Beer's home during 1815–17, which means that Mendelssohn was at the time a boy of eight, at the most. But if this is true, then we have here outstanding evidence of the exposure of Mendelssohn to synagogal practice at an age that must have instigated a significant memory. See Idelsohn, *Jewish Music*, 512, and for the political circumstances see Tina Frühauf, *The Organ and Its Music in German-Jewish Culture* (New York: Oxford University Press, 2009), 29.

67. Explicated by Lessing in his famous *Laocoön* (1776); for an interesting application of these principles in relation to Mendelssohn's *St. Paul* see Michael P. Steinberg, "Mendelssohn and Judaism," *The Cambridge Companion to Mendelssohn* (Cambridge: Cambridge University Press, 2004), 39.

68. See *The Rabbi of Bacharach*, second chapter.

69. For a discussion of the three assimilatory phases indicated by this thrice repeated injunction (related to the group of visual images to which they refer) see Florian Krobb, "'Mach die Augen zu, Schöne Sara': Zur Gestaltung der Jüdischen Assimilationsproblematik in Heines *Der Rabbi von Bacherach*," *German Life and Letters* 47/2 (1994): 167–81.

70. The Jewish massacre referred to here took place in 1349 in Frankfurt. The number of people killed is not known. It is interesting, in connection with the present chapter, that the movement of the flagellants was forbidden by Pope Clement VI, and then

rehabilitated by the Council of Constance in 1417 (the background events of *La Juive*).

71. This famous council of 1414–18 (the fifteenth ecumenical council of the Roman Catholic Church) aimed to bring to an end the Great Schism of the papacy. It is usually agreed that though the council's endeavors to carry out church reforms were of little effect, its acts against the Hussites and Lollards were consequential. John Huss was allowed to defend his cause before the council members, yet, despite a guarantee of safe-conduct, he was condemned as a heretic and burned at the stake. This background infiltrates the opera's plot, but, as in *Les Huguenots* and *Le Prophète*, emphasizes that "at stake" in all these works was the general theme of religious tolerance.

72. This production was generated in cooperation with the New Israeli Opera, Tel Aviv, and was premiered there in 2000. A live DVD rendition was produced in 2003 (with Neil Shicoff as Éléazar, Krassimira Stoyanova as Rachel; produced by Günther Krämer). Renewed interest in the opera is exemplified in the title of Raphael Mostel's 2003 review in the *Forward* (21 November 2003): "After 70 Years, 'The Jewess' Captivates Once Again" (http://www.highbeam.com/doc/1P1–89108932.html) and reveals a change in sensibilities also evident in other recent productions of works discussed in the present book.

73. This part is skipped in the opera. My reference below to the score and libretto is based on the edition of *La Juive: Opéra en cinq actes d'Eugene Scribe, musique de F. Halévy*, ed. Karl Leich-Galland (Saarbruecken: Musik-Edition Lucie Galland, 1985).

74. The simultaneous, synaesthetic nature of the Ambrosian hymn and its community-enhancing role is analyzed in Leo Spitzer, *Classical and Christian Ideas of World Harmony, Prolegomena to an Interpretation of the Word "Stimmung"* (Baltimore: Johns Hopkins University Press, 1963), 23–28.

75. The transition from the real to the symbolic is tonal—from E-flat major it slides to C major and back, through a tritonal progression, allowing for the reappearance of the final part of the hymn as a closing part (as though it continued to be sung while the protagonists exchange their utterances), and metrical—the common meter allows for a breaking into triplets and semiquavers in the dramatic exchange, resuming the quavers and minims for the conclusive hymnal singing. Other tonalities will ensue, but they are all tightly connected to the E-flat center (with F minor leading to F major for the finale, and C minor for the treatment of the "Jew's noise").

76. All of these were popular in France at the time. They are thoroughly discussed in Hallman, *The Politics*, chapter 5. Scott's influence was powerful also on Heine, especially in *The Rabbi*, as Florian Krobb maintains, while making a clear distinction between the epic closure of Scott's text and Heine's open, or even, to borrow Nita Schechet's terms, highly "fissured" work. See Nita Schechet, *Narrative Fissures: Reading and Rhetoric* (Madison, NJ: Fairleigh Dickinson University Press, 2005).

77. See Samuel Naumbourg, *Semiroth Israel, Chants religieux des Israélites: contenant la liturgie complète de la synagogue dès temps les plus reculés jusqu'à nos jours (dédiés au Consistoire Israélite de la Circonscription de Paris)* (Paris: Chez L'auteur, 1847), no. 152 ("Vajhi binsoa hooron," a cappella; no. 300 [Psalm 122], a paraliturgical three-

part chorus — both pieces following the *meshorerim* practice — the latter orchestrated with organ and harp). Halévy's *rapport* in the preface is instructive, giving an artistic cachet to the volume much in the spirit of Sulzer and company. ("M. Naumbourg m'a paru réunir toutes les qualités désirables, et j'espère qu'il exercera une heureuse influence sur l'exécution des chants religieux dans nos Temples, trop souvent aban-donnés à une déplorable routine. M. Naumbourg a recueilli un grand nombre de chants traditionnels qu'il importe de conserver dans la liturgie, et qui sont parvenus jusqu'à nous sans rien perdre du double caractère qu'ils tirent de leur antique origine et de leur pieuse destination.")

78. By the modulation to A-flat, the Hosanna chorus originally followed that of the *Te Deum*. I agree with Hallman's claim (*The Politics*, 164) that in the final version of the opera the impact of the juxtaposition of Christians and Jews becomes more effective.

79. Their separateness is highlighted through tonal means: their serenade (in the frame-work of C major) drags them into sharp keys, which then are reconstituted (D major, though with a deviation to Phrygian A) when his voice appears (to her) in public.

80. This becomes again an ambiguous trait, for this artistic capability turns out to be non-Jewish when real identity is revealed. On the question of the Jew as a category of nonvisual sensitivities, consult, among others, Richard I. Cohen, *Jewish Icons: Art and Society in Modern Europe* (Berkeley: University of California Press, 1998), Kalman P. Bland, *The Artless Jew: Medieval and Modern Affirmations and Denials of the Visual* (Princeton: Princeton University Press, 2001) and Margaret Olin, *The Nation without Art: Examining Modern Discourses on Jewish Art* (Lincoln: University of Nebraska Press, 2001).

81. The idiom of Rachel's music can be considered "Jewish" — starting with a regular D major phrase (to the words: "Ô surprise nouvelle!"), it changes, in the fourth mea-sure, to Phrygian on A (to the words: "cette horde cruelle, ces soldats menaçants à son ordre obéissent et devant lui fléchissent, désarmés et tremblant"), emphasizing the augmented second, in a treading, almost recitative unfolding, modulating back to D. It ends with a gradual, diatonic fall from G to D also typical to such melodic unfolding.

82. Spinoza's theologico-political ideas are discussed in connection with Schoenberg's *Moses und Aron* in chapter 6.

83. Through the enharmonic move of Brogni, to the precinct of B, meeting the choir on the diminished part of its dominant seventh ("Ah! Pour notre ville"), and moving back enharmonically to the ceremonial C minor–E-flat for the entrance of Brogni.

84. As if she were an immortal Homeric deity, the epithet *schöne* is always attached to her name.

85. The description is worthy of George Eliot's portrait of Mirah or her like in the sym-pathetic, historicized depiction of features and expression; Eliot, as is evident from *Daniel Deronda*, was deeply impressed by Heine's "Jewish" works.

86. Even an innocent melody by Haydn, featuring in the famous slow movement of his string quartet, op. 76 no. 3, could turn into a Nazi "Deutschland über alles" hymn

(whereas in Rossini's *Il Viaggio a Reims* (1825) it functions, in a pan-European banquet, as a benign German anthem). See also the discussion of *Lohengrin*'s overture in chapter 2.

87. Wagner, as reported by Cosima, praised the Seder scene which, as he said, "contains the best expression of the Jewish character." See Cosima Wagner, *Tagebücher 2, 1878–1883* (Munich: P. Piper, 1977), June 1882.

88. Contrary to Hallman's suggestion (*The Politics*, 181), the harp was not traditionally "linked to Jewish musical practice," and yet it could play such a role in popular culture, as the anti-Semitic caricature of fig. 4.2 indicates. Practically, the harp was newly endorsed by Naumbourg, relying on its frequent mention in Psalms (as Hallman notes). Its accompaniment in Éléazar's cavatina aims to connote Jewish music with mellowness and harmony. Interestingly, the harp also plays a significant role in Meyerbeer's Prophet's imagination.

89. For his psalms' rendition to the synagogue see Naumbourg, *Chants religieux des Israélites*.

90. Especially the antique, highly poetical *piyyut*'s line that opens the cantor's part after the silent prayer: "Oḥila la-'El" (I hope for the Lord). Cf. also Heine's confusion of the two holidays, in his description of Passover's liturgy discussed in chapter 3.

91. See chapter 1.

92. The *mysterium tremendum* moment in the analysis of the phenomenology of "the sacred" is explicated by Rudolf Otto in his famous *Das Heilige* (Munich: C. H. Beck'sche, [1917] 1958), chap. 4.

93. The affinity of these two *mysterium tremendum* moments and their possible genealogies is discussed by Eric Werner in *The Sacred Bridge: The Interdependence of Liturgy and Music in Synagogue and Church during the First Millennium* (London: Denis Dobson, 1959), 1:252–55. He himself based his investigation on Armand (Ahron) Kaminka's study from 1906. Recently two studies have independently taken up this comparative query from different perspectives. One is Israel Yuval's "The Seventh Seal and Man's Hand's Seal: From John of Patmos to the Story of Rabbi Amnon" (I thank the author for allowing me to read it before publication; it was published in part in Israel Yuval, "Gedichte und Geschichte als Weltgericht. Unetane tokef, Dies irae und Amnon von Mainz," *Kalonymos Beiträge zur deutsch-jüdischen Geschichte aus dem Salomon Ludwig Steinheim-Institut* 8/4 (2005): 1–6. The other is my "Updating Horror: Changing Sound Imagery in the Jewish and Christian 'Day of Judgment,'" delivered at the symposium "Mysterium Tremendum: Horror and the Aesthetics of Religious Experience," Wissenschaftskolleg zu Berlin, Berlin, December 2002.

94. In Hebrew this line is terser, reminiscent of the Latin.

95. This Greek word, meaning "excommunication" in this context, was brought into Christian use through a translation of the Hebrew word *ḥerem*, which had a similar meaning to that of the original Greek: things offered to God (in the temple) and forbidden in other contexts (as in Leviticus 27:28), but which also, as in Greek, denotes an abomination that should be banned (Deuteronomy 7:26)—used thus by St. Paul and the early church fathers. See *International Standard Bible Encyclopedia*, ed.

Geoffrey W. Bromiley (Grand Rapids, MI: William B. Eerdmans, 1979) 1:29. This interrelated etymology attests again to the thick interlacement between these two religions.

96. Staged by Sidney Lumet and added as a bonus feature in the DVD of *La Juive* mentioned in n. 72.

97. See Hallman, *The Politics*, 152–54. The change of a "happy ending" of this kind to the one of martyrdom and immolation calls to mind the change Wagner introduced into the finale of *Götterdämmerung*. This could have been affected (among other things), perhaps unconsciously, by the change effected in *La Juive* (if he knew about that change).

98. Cf. (prosodically and thematically) Eichendorff's earnest Romanticism in *Mondnacht* (set to music by Schumann, Lied no. 5 of op. 39 *Liederkreis*) "und meine Seele spannte weit ihre Flügel aus."

99. Oppenheim, a smart businessman, knows what type of illustration would appeal to potential readers, as Barbara Gilbert writes. See Barbara C. Gilbert, "Moritz Oppenheim's Illustrations to *Stories from Jewish Family Life* by Salomon Hermann Mosenthal," in *Moritz Daniel Oppenheim, Die Entdeckung des Jüdischen Selbstbewußtseins in der Kunst / Jewish Identity in 19th-century Art*, eds. George Heuberger and Anton Merk, bilingual edition (Frankfurt am Main: Wienand, 1999), 257.

100. Frederic V. Grunfeld, *Prophets Without Honour: A Background to Freud, Kafka, Einstein and Their World* (London: Hutchinson, 1979). For a critical reading of this work, see Robert Alter, *Commentary*, 1980.

101. The motto of Grunfeld's book is the famous quote from Matthew 13:57: "A prophet is not without honor except in his hometown and in his own household," a proverb largely adopted in Jewish circles.

102. To name two writers who shared this view—the famous American sociologist who long preceded Grunfeld—Thorstein Veblen, in "The Intellectual Pre-eminence of Jews in Modern Europe," in *The Portable Veblen*, ed. Max Lerner (New York: Viking, [1919] 1958) (I thank Elihu Katz for this reference), and the recent book by Yuri Slezkine, *The Jewish Century* (Princeton: Princeton University Press, 2004) which offers a comprehensive overview of the twentieth century in similar terms.

103. Mendelssohn began his long affair with the work on *Elijah* as early as 1837, soon after the premiere of *St. Paul*, and was long preoccupied with the making of its libretto. He continued to rework the score beyond its premiere. For a good summary of this story see Friedhelm Krummacher, "Art—History—Religion: On Mendelssohn's Oratorios *St. Paul* and *Elijah*," in *The Mendelssohn Companion*, ed. Douglass Seaton, 323–30, and Andreas Eichhorn, *Felix Mendelssohn Bartholdy: Elias* (Kassel: Bärenreiter, 2005), 18–33. The making of the libretto with its various working versions is analyzed in Jeffrey S. Sposato, *The Price of Assimilation: Felix Mendelssohn and the Nineteenth-Century Anti-Semitic Tradition* (Oxford: Oxford University Press, 2006), 115–28. One finds strikingly similar circumstances surrounding Meyerbeer's making of *The Prophet*, in both the convoluted creation of the libretto and a long odyssey on the way to composition and production. See Reiner Zimmermann, *Giacomo Meyerbeer,*

Eine Biographie nach Dokumenten, trans. Eva Zimmermann (Berlin: Henschel, 1991), 253–78; Robert Ignatius Letellier's discussion in *The Operas of Giacomo Meyerbeer*, (Madison, NJ: Fairleigh Dickinson University Press, 2006), 181–210, of the dramatic inspirations of Scribe and Meyerbeer, pinpoints the libretto's unique psychological and moral depth. For the political and social implications of the opera see Fulcher, *The Nation Image*, chapter 3. See also Alan Armstrong, "Meyerbeer's 'Le Prophète': A history of its composition and early performances" (PhD diss., Ohio State University, 1990), and Matthias Brzoska, "Remarks about Meyerbeer's *Le Prophète*" (http://www .meyerbeer.com/Brzoska_040914_Prophete.htm) (accessed 16 August 2006). It is of interest to note that Scribe's original title for the opera was *The Anabaptists*, and that it was Meyerbeer who changed it later to the ambiguous title, *The Prophet*.

104. A severe but differentiating critic was the renowned Otto Jahn, who claimed that the renouncing of the epic, narrative element in the oratorio — which he deems essential in the genre — to rely on direct speech alone "required [a] constantly heightened degree of characterization which often comes into conflict with its object or disintegrates into details and wearies us." Otto Jahn, "Über Felix Mendelssohn Bartholdy's Oratorium Elias," *Gesammelte Aufsätze über Musik* (Leipzig 1848) 45, as quoted in E. Werner, *Mendelssohn*, 459; tellingly, Werner accepts many of his claims. For more contemporary German reviews see Krummacher, "Art — History — Religion," 328–29.

105. Among other things, the effect of electrical light, by Léon Foucault, was introduced on a European stage at the premiere of the opera.

106. Mendelssohn told his English librettist, William Bartholomew, the following: "I wanted to have the colour of a Chorale, and I felt that I could not do without it, and yet I did not like to have a Chorale." Quoted in F. G. Edwards, *The History of Mendelssohn's Oratorio "Elijah"* (London, 1896; repr. New York: AMS Press, 1976), 106. See also Larry R. Todd, "On Mendelssohn's Sacred Music, Real and Imaginary," in *The Cambridge Companion to Mendelssohn*, 174–76.

107. The turn into a more "objective" plateau is achieved among other things by a progression that goes against the "cabaletta" grain, that is, instead of accelerating motion as in the cabaletta form it is often slowed down, if not halted, by a sustained chordal unfolding, even more protracted than in a traditional chorale. Also the use of an organ in these parts accentuates the religiosity of these elements. Krummacher ("Art — History — Religion," 340) also insists on the individual subjective character of these "sublime" parts.

108. Mendelssohn could have learned about the theological affinity between the two through Friedrich Wilhelm Krummacher, a most effective preacher of the time, whose sermon "The Flight into the Desert" he might have read. See Staehelin: "*Elijah*, Johann Sebastian Bach, and the New Covenant," 128. For other aspects of a possible Christological reading of the text, see Sposato, *Price of Assimilation*, 128–146.

109. The announcing numbers are 6 (the Angel); 10 (Elijah, preceded by the series of opening chords); 19 (Obadjah); the soprano aria no. 21; 23 (Elijah); no. 27 (tenor); no. 30 (Angel); 33 (Elijah); and no. 40 (soprano). Reference here and below are to Felix Mendelssohn Bartholdy, *Elias – Elijah* op. 70, *Oratorium nach Worten des*

Alten Testaments, Study Score, ed. Larry Todd (Stuttgart: Stuttgarter Mendelssohn-Ausgaben, 1995).

110. Mendelssohn only once negotiated the idea of composing music (Psalms 24, 48, 100) for a Jewish service, the consecration of the new building of the Hamburg Neues Tempel in 1844; as Todd recently argued, it seems that it yielded nothing for the synagogue (no. 100, claims Todd, was probably meant for the Berlin Cathedral). See Todd, "On Mendelssohn's Sacred Music," 171.

111. E. Werner (*Mendelssohn*, 471) argued that the melody of "Behold God the Lord passed by!" (no. 34)—of the main revelation to Elijah—is modeled on a Jewish melody sung since the fifteenth century for the Thirteen Divine Attributes of the Days of Awe, referred to above. He unfortunately does not mention his source.

112. *St. Paul* is also relevant to the present history, however. See my "Between Noise and Harmony: The Oratorical Moment in the Musical Entanglements of Jews and Christians," *Critical Inquiry* 32/2 (2006): 274–75.

113. Felix Mendelssohn, *Briefe 1833–1847*, 460 as quoted in Feder, "Sacred Music," *The Mendelssohn Companion*, 260.

114. Though he felt "like J. S. Bach" when he wrote the work, as he famously reported.

115. The parallel verse in Bach is *Herr, unser Herrscher, dessen Ruhm in allen Landen herrlich ist!* (O Lord, our Lord, how majestic is your name in all the earth!) For a discussion of this movement see chapter 2.

116. Interestingly, the word *curse* in the King James' translation (used by Mendelssohn in the English version of this text) stands for the Hebrew word *ḥerem* in its negative meaning, discussed above (see n. 95). The German *Bann* is closer to the Hebrew.

117. There is again a compelling Jewish juxtaposition of which Mendelssohn was probably incognizant: the following number, "Holy, holy, holy" (the Trisagion) appears in the Days of Awe liturgy (*musaf*) right after the *piyyut* "Unᵉtane tokef" mentioned above, which likewise quotes the "still small voice." A comparison to Christ's revelation to Paul in *St. Paul* is pertinent but beyond the scope of this chapter.

118. That Felix Mendelssohn could have entertained such an epistemological worldview, following his grandfather in this matter, is more than a probable hypothesis. See Botstein, "Neoclassicism, Romanticism."

119. The famous book by the Danish philosopher was published (pseudonymously under Johannes di Silentio[!]) in 1843 and engages with the antipodal, if not contradictory demands of ethics and faith, with the paradigm of Abraham's sacrifice of Isaac.

120. In the words of George Herbert's "Prayer" (1633).

121. Franz Rosenzweig, *Der Stern der Erlösung*, part 2 (Frankfurt: Suhrkamp, [1976] 1988), 205.

122. The letter is quoted in chapter 6, below.

123. On Mendelssohn's popularity in the Jewish Culture League see Lily A. Hirsch, *A Jewish Orchestra in Nazi Germany: Musical Politics and the Berlin Jewish Culture League* (Michigan: University of Michigan Press, 2010). Ringer's report is mentioned in Leon Botstein's "Mendelssohn and the Jews," *Musical Quarterly* 82 (1998), 213. I thank Yonatan Dayan for providng me with the text of Ringer's report.

124. The historical figure Jean of Leyden (1509–1536), an innkeeper and tailor, became famous as an orator. In Münster, he became the head of the Anabaptists, set up a "kingdom of Zion," with polygamy and community of goods. In 1535 the city was taken by the Bishop of Münster, and Jean and his accomplices were executed.

125. The four Protestant brothers in Heinrich von Kleist's "The Holy Cecilia or the Power of Music," who were vocally cursed for their iconoclastic attack on the convent in Aachen and condemned forever to intone the "Gloria in Excelsis Deo" at midnight in a "terrible and hideous voice," might have influenced this scene (later the Anabaptists' music becomes more variegated). Meyerbeer, the literate composer, could have been familiar with the story that was published in *Berliner Abendblätter* n. 40–42, Nov. 1810.

126. For how contemporary socialists and their opponents viewed these rebels see Fulcher, *The Nation*, 154.

127. See Letellier, *Operas of Giacomo Meyerbeer*, 189–90.

128. The libretto's English translation is based, with minor alterations, on the text featured in the booklet to the *Le Prophète* CD (performed by the Royal Philharmonic Orchestra, conducted by Henry Lewis CBS M3K 79400, name of translator not mentioned). Reference to the music is based on *Le Prophète . . . Partition Piano et Chant* (Paris: G. Brandus, Dufour et Cie, c. 1855).

129. Ibid., 123 and 127.

130. Uhlig, "Der Prophet von Meyerbeer." This claim appears in the last installment, issue no. 35, 30 April 1850, 179–80.

131. See Giacomo Meyerbeer, *Briefwechsel und Tagebücher*, 7 vols., ed. and annot. by Heinz Becker and Gudrun Becker (Berlin: W. de Gruyter, 1960–2004), vol. 2 (1970), 207.

132. "I saw this work of Meyerbeer's break upon the world like the dawn heralding this day of disgraceful desolation," he first intimated. Later, he complained how "sickened he was by this performance," that he left in the middle of an act despite the embarrassment it caused him. Richard Wagner, *My Life* (London: Constable, [1911] 1963), 528. His letter to Uhlig is quoted in Letellier, *Operas of Meyerbeer*, 296. In contradistinction to Wagner, Liszt was highly stimulated by the opera to arrange what is considered his most substantial musical response to any such work.

133. The categories of the naïve versus the sentimental were introduced into the cultural discourse by Schiller in his famous treatise "On Naïve and Sentimental Poetry" (1800). The trio has indeed Mozartian qualities (cf. *Così fan tutte*).

134. Gounod, for one, wrote in his memoirs that the audience's response in the premiere oscillated between shock and enthusiasm, and that one had the impression that the hall prepared itself for a revolution; he also noted that Berlioz burst into tears (perhaps despite himself). The Escudier brothers, on the other hand, complained about a lack of melody, about *noise*, "and that the audience searched with magnifier for beauties . . . the sublime . . . [to] find only peculiarities, blockishness; the poetic breath, the melodic inspiration lack entirely." See Zimmerman, *Meyerbeer*, 270, 277 for other instructive reviews. For a highly favorable *Times* review (of the London premiere in 1849) see http://www.meyerbeer.com/Prophrev.htm.

CHAPTER 5. THE JUDENGASSE SYNAGOGUE
VERSUS THE TEMPLE OF THE GRAIL

1. The description of the encounter of the Leweses and the Wagners is based on the following sources: *The George Eliot Letters*, ed. Gordon S. Haight, 9 vols. (New Haven: Yale University Press, 1954–78); David C. Large and William Weber, *Wagnerism in European Culture and Politics* (Ithaca: Cornell University Press, 1984), 248; Ronald Taylor's *Richard Wagner: His Life, Art and Thought* (London: Paul Elik, 1979), 226. Cosima's remark is taken from her diaries, Cosima Wagner, *Tagebücher* 2, 1878–1883 (Munich: P. Piper, 1977), 1081 (30.12.1882). On 18.2.1881 we find the following sentence: "After the meal G. Eliot's portrait evoked disgust because of its ugliness."

2. George Eliot, "Liszt, Wagner and Weimar," *Essays of George Eliot*, ed. Thomas Pinney (New York: Columbia University Press, 1963), 102–3. It is worth noting that prudent Eliot qualifies her own criticism. Aware of Wagner's greatness as an artist who opened new ways within the operatic tradition, she candidly wondered whether she herself had been stricken by a blindness that prevented her from recognizing the full power of the new "sun."

3. Nietzsche would subscribe, especially in connection with *Parsifal*. See "The Case of Wagner," in *The Birth of Tragedy and the Case of Wagner*, trans. Walter Kaufman (New York: Vintage, 1967).

4. See Jacob Katz, *The Darker Side of Genius: Richard Wagner's Anti-Semitism* (Hanover, NH: Published for Brandeis University Press by University Press of New England, 1986). According to Rose (Paul Lawrence Rose, *Wagner: Race and Revolution* [London: Faber and Faber, 1992]), Wagner's anti-Semitism was exacerbated in these years, and was colored in typical racial hues. However, his textual analyses are problematic, and I would like to adhere to Katz's "weaker" version of Wagner's anti-Semitism, which seems to me fairer and sounder. Dieter Borchmeyer, in "The Question of Anti-Semitism," in *Wagner Handbook*, ed. U. Müller and P. Wapnewseki, trans. ed. by J. Deathridge (Cambridge, MA: Harvard University Press, 1992), 166–85, holds a similar opinion.

5. In her article "The Modern Hep! Hep! Hep!" in *Impressions of Theophrastus Such*, ed. Nancy Henry (Iowa City: University of Iowa Press, [1879] 1994), 143–65, Eliot endeavors to rebut well-known anti-Semitic arguments, but never mentions whose views she discusses. Her sensitivity to the subject and her familiarity with cultural life in Germany in general and with Wagner in particular renders the latter as potentially one of her invisible contenders.

6. The studies of Rose in *Wagner: Race and Revolution*; of Jean-Jacques Nattiez in *Wagner Androgyne: A Study in Interpretation*, trans. Stewart Spencer (Princeton: Princeton University Press, 1993); David J. Levin, "Reading Beckmesser Reading: Antisemitism and Aesthetic Practice in The Mastersingers of Nuremberg," *New German Critique* 69 (1996): 127–46; and Barry Millington's "Nuremberg Trial: Is There Anti-Semitism in *Die Meistersinger?*," *Cambridge Opera Journal* 3/3 (1991): 247–60, are examples of this approach. The last two are of special interest in connection with the present study, as they touch directly on the representation of "Jewish noise" by a major Wagnerian character: Beckmesser.

7. Beryl Gray, *George Eliot and Music* (New York: St. Martin's, 1989), 100. The musical interest in this rich novel exceeds the limits of the present study. Ruth Solie recently researched the evidence in the novel "about the understanding of music history in circulation among the Victorian bourgeoisie," especially as it relates to dialectic and complementary notions of evolution and heritage (canonization). This engagement yields instructive insights, some of which are in line with my arguments in the present chapter. Of special interest is her assessment of Wagner's reception in England at the time. Solie brings ironic evidence of an association of Wagner and Eliot by a contemporary attending the first festival at Bayreuth in 1876, noting "the minute development of tone and character painting which makes Wagner the George Eliot of music." Ruth Solie, "*Daniel Deronda* as Music Historiography," in *Music in Other Words: Victorian Conversations* (Berkeley: University of California Press, 2004), 163.

8. The processes of the liberalization of music-making (in relation to commercial, social, and aesthetic factors) had already begun in Italy and England in the seventeenth century, but became prominent in Germany only toward the end of the following century.

9. Katz considers treatises such as those of Bruno Bauer, Eduard Meyer, Heinrich Laube, and Karl Marx among the most influential (see *The Darker Side*, chapter 2). It is not entirely clear whether the latter's influence on Wagner in this matter was direct or indirect. See also Borchmeyer, "The Question of Anti-Semitism," 180.

10. See "Der Prophet von Meyerbeer," in *Neue Zeitschrift für Musik* 33 (April 23 1950), 170.

11. Rose has a similar argument but, because he addresses the question of anti-Semitism in isolation, he misses the implications of this argument from a general cultural point of view. Slavoj Žižek emphasizes that "Wagner's rejection of the society of exchange, which provides the basis of his anti-Semitism, amounts to an attempt to regain the prelapsarian balance," linking it with the most comprehensive structure of meaning of the Wagnerian work. See Slavoj Žižek, "'There is no Sexual Relationship': Wagner as a Lacanian," *New German Critique* 69 (1996), 13.

12. See Wagner, "Das Judentum in der Musik," in Jens Malte Fischer, *Richard Wagners "Das Judentum in der Musik," Eine kritische Dokumentation als Beitrag zur Geschichte des Antisemitismus* (Frankfurt: Insel, 2000) 144–96. It should be noted that Wagner uses essence (*Wesen*) more than substance (*Inhalt*). I use the term "substance" in this connection to refer to the Platonic assumption underlying Wagner's conception of real human "essence," which has a definite ontological status for him. The essentializing trend in relation to Jews increasingly permeated scholarly circles in Germany towards the end of the century, as with those dealing with the sources of "Jew baiting" (*Judenhetzen*) in antiquity. See Peter Schäfer, *Judeophobia, Attitudes toward the Jews in the Ancient World* (Cambridge, MA: Harvard University Press, 1998), 1–6. It also affected Jewish circles; see Uriel Tal, *Christians and Jews in Germany: Religion, Politics, and Ideology in the Second Reich, 1870–1914* (Ithaca: Cornell University Press, 1975).

13. At this point Wagner veers deliberately from the aesthetics of the Enlightenment. Denying the imagination an autonomous role, he also rejects the Kantian harmony

between reason and imagination, realized in its purest form in "independent beauty." Such enlightened, disinterested contemplation is replaced, by him, with spiritual effervescence, which transcends the individual consciousness permeating the community's mythological and historical mental spaces.

14. "Sehr natürlich gerät im Gesange, als dem lebhaftesten und unwiderleglich wahrsten Ausdrucke des persönlichen Empfindungswesens," Wagner, "Das Judentum in der Musik," in J. M. Fischer, *Richard Wagners "Das Judentum in der Musik,"* 152.

15. J. Katz, *The Darker Side*, 38.

16. It seems to me that Heine was Wagner's main source in this regard, especially his treatise entitled "Ludwig Börne," in *Sämtliche Werke* 6 (Munich: Georg Müller, 1925).

17. See Michel Foucault in *The Order of Things* (New York: Vantage, 1972), 17–25 and Ruth HaCohen, "The Music of Sympathy in the Arts of the Baroque; or The Use of Difference to Overcome Indifference," *Poetics Today* 22/3 (2001): 607–50.

18. Quoted from a letter to Hans von Bülow, 26 October 1854, in *Selected Letters of Richard Wagner*, trans. and ed. Stewart Spencer and Barry Millington (London: Dent & Sons, 1987), 322.

19. See Carl E. Schorske, "The Quest for the Grail: Wagner and Morris" in *The Critical Spirit: Essays in Honor of Herbert Marcuse*, ed. R. H. Wolff and B. Moore (Boston: Beacon, 1967), 220–28. Seventy years later, this ideational fabric received an explicitly racial anchorage, as expressed in Jung's writings. According to Jung, the collective unconscious is woven out of basic visions or archetypes. More than Wagner, Jung denied the creative autonomy of the individual and viewed the origin of artistic creation in entrenched systems, the legacy of forefathers and race. It was because of this that Jews, according to Jung, could not be part of the eternal Aryan myth, since they had not inherited the spiritual elements of this world. Moreover, they endeavored, and were still attempting, to estrange the Aryan people from their rich cultural worlds through their mythless, religious Jewish rationalism. See Richard Noll, *The Arian Christ: The Secret Life of Carl Jung* (New York: Random House, 1997); *Parsifal's* influence on his worldview is discussed in pp. 143–46.

20. Schopenhauer discusses this issue in two treatises—*On the Basis of Morality* (Oxford: Berghahn, 1995); and "Religion," in *Essays from Parerga and Paralipomena*, trans. T. Bailey Saunders (London: G. Allen and Unwin, 1951), 85–95. Schopenhauer's claims against the Jews are discussed by Nathan Rotenstreich in *Jews and German Philosophy* (New York: Schocken, 1984), 174–96.

21. See Richard Wagner, *Tagebuchblätter und Briefe an Mathilde Wesendonck*, 1853–71, introd. and annot. by R. Sternfeld (Berlin: Deutsche Buch-Gemeinschaft), 84; the translation is from *Selected Letters of Richard Wagner*, 422.

22. Ibid., 86–88 (German) and 423–24 (English). *Parsifal* had not yet been composed, but Wagner is dated to have started to conceive the work on Good Friday, 1857 (a year before the letter). The name is still spelled by Wagner in the medieval form: Parzival.

23. In "Das Judentum in der Musik" (see J. M. Fischer, *Richard Wagners "Das Judentum in der Musik,"* 151). Wagner writes that nothing will evoke a heated emotional response in the Jew. He later adds that baptism makes this even worse, completely isolating the Jew and rendering him "the most heartless of all human beings to such a degree that

even the former sympathy we had for the tragic fate of his tribe was bound to be lost" ("... und ihm zum herzlosesten aller Menschen in einem Grade zu machen, daß wir selbst die frühre Symapthie für das tragische Geschick seines Stammes verlieren mußten," 154).

24. For Coleridge's opposite position see Thomas M. Greene, "Coleridge and the Energy of Asking," *English Literary History* 62/4 (1995), 907–31.

25. See Marc Shell, *Children of the Earth: Literature, Politics, and Nationhood* (New York: Oxford University Press, 1993).

26. In this he follows a genuine German tradition, including Lessing, Schiller, and other great dramatists. For Lessing's and Rousseau's respective ideas on theatrical compassion, see chapter 2.

27. In Ruth HaCohen and Naphtali Wagner, "The Gestural Power of the Wagnerian Leitmotifs: Self-Promoting Jingles or Self-Contained Expressions?" *Orbis Musicae* 13 (2003): 185–95, we attempted to demonstrate how Wagner's shared motivic gestures yield a nuanced language of intersubjectivity. This, however, is mainly elaborated between those who seek sameness (as in the case of Tristan and Isolde), if not incestuous relations (Sieglinde and Siegmund).

28. David Marshall's two books—*The Figure of Theater: Shaftesbury, Defoe, Adam Smith, and George Eliot* (New York: Columbia University Press, 1986) and *The Surprising Effects of Sympathy: Marivaux, Diderot, Rousseau, and Mary Shelley* (Chicago: University of Chicago Press, 1988)—grapple with this tradition in theater, literature, and ideas.

29. See Geoffrey Hartman, "The Sympathy Paradox," in *The Fateful Question of Culture* (New York: Columbia University Press: 1997), 141–64.

30. Only few contemporaries understood her unique approach: "Art has a moral purpose; the purpose is to widen human sympathy; this can be achieved only by giving a true picture of life," summarizes Thomas A. Noble regarding Eliot's enterprise. For these and other contemporary statements in relation to Eliot's concept of sympathy, see Suzanne Graver, *George Eliot and Community: A Study in Social Theory and Fictional Form* (Berkeley: University of California Press, 1984), 264.

31. Michael Tanner compares Wagner to Eliot from this point of view; he maintains that "[Wagner's] view of people [is] as saved or damned, sheep or goats. He seems ... in this respect like Shakespeare and Dickens, and unlike George Eliot who is always nudging us not to be vengeful about, say, Hetty Prynne [*sic*] or Rosamond Vincy, because they have been spoilt by other people whose bad tendencies in turn are explicable by the way they were brought up, etc.; the sole exception in her oeuvre— and a very powerful one—is Grandcourt, one of the most convincing figures of evil that realistic literature has to show and one for whom no explanation is offered and no extenuation." Michael Tanner, "The Total Work of Art," in *The Wagner Companion*, ed. Peter Burbridge and Richard Sutton (London: Faber and Faber, 1978), 156–57.

32. Chap. 32, 364 (italics added); all quotations from *Daniel Deronda* are from Terence Cave's annotated edition, with reference to chapter and page number. See George Eliot, *Daniel Deronda*, ed. Terence Cave (London: Penguin, 1995).

33. The OED gives the following definitions of *sentiment* since the seventeenth century, and before it acquired some negative connotations: "(1) The sum of feelings of a person or group on a particular subject; an opinion, a point of view, an attitude. (2) A *mental* feeling, an emotion; (3) A thought or view coloured by or based on emotion; the feeling or meaning intended by a passage, the sense of a statement; and (4) emotional or tender feelings collectively, esp. as an influence; the tendency to be swayed by feeling rather than reason." The various dimensions of sentiment as captured in these definitions are all relevant to Eliot's use of the term, especially in its function as steering sympathy towards a more defined goal, shedding light on the mental and communal dimensions of its activation, its immediacy, and historicity. The theory of emotion and memory this concept entails seems to go back to Spinoza's ethico-political views. Of the latter, and its reflection in Eliot's way in *Daniel Deronda*, see Moira Gatens' illuminating essay, "The Politics of 'Presence' and 'Difference': Working Through Spinoza and Eliot," in *Visibile Women: Essays on Feminist Legal Theory and Political Philosophy*, eds. Susan James and Stephanie Palmer (Oxford: Hart, 2002), 160–74.

34. This is reinforced by the protagonists' allusions to various literary works, such as Shakespeare's *Winter's Tale*, which they perform as a tableau vivant, Tasso's *Rinaldo*, *The Thousand and One Nights*, and so forth. See Barry V. Qualls, "Speaking through Parable: Daniel Deronda" in *George Eliot: Modern Critical Views*, ed. Harold Bloom (New York: Chelsea House Publications, 1986), 205–6.

35. The tradition associating static landscapes with narcissistic being originates in Ovid, as Hermann Fränkel maintains in *Ovid. A Poet between Two Worlds* (Berkeley: University of California Press, 1945), 213.

36. These issues are discussed in Bernard J. Paris' "George Eliot's Religion of Humanity," in *George Eliot: A Collection of Critical Essays*, ed. George R. Creeger (Englewood Cliffs, NJ: Prentice Hall, 1970), 11–36.

37. This contemporary criticism is quoted in Graver, *George Eliot and Community*, 270–71.

38. See Graver, ibid.; the aesthetic background for these conceptions in British thought is discussed by James Engell, in *The Creative Imagination*, 143–60 and by Judith W. Page in *Imperfect Sympathies: Jews and Judaism in British Romantic Literature and Culture* (New York: Palgrave Macmillan, 2004), as particularly pertaining to the "Jewish question."

39. In her unpublished lecture "The Experimental Philosophy of George Eliot: Spinozistic and Feuerbachian Influences" (Wissenschaftskolleg zu Berlin, Berlin, 29 April 2008), Moira Gaten insightfully connects these philosophical legacies with Eliot's literary enterprise. I thank the author for letting me read the lecture before publication.

40. See Cave, introduction, in George Eliot, *Daniel Deronda*, xxiv–xxxii. Cave devoted an entire study to the tradition of Aristotelian recognition (*anagnorisis*), relevant to Eliot no less than to Wagner; see Terence Cave, *Recognition: A Study in Poetics* (Oxford: Oxford University Press, 1990). Qualls ("Speaking through Parable," 206) further traces this frame of reference to Tasso's *Gerusalemme liberata* and Handel's variation of this work in *Rinaldo*.

41. A formative experience of J. J. Rousseau, according to Jean Starobinski, which generated his moral, social, and aesthetic view, setting compassion at its center. See Jean Starobinski, *Jean-Jacques Rousseau: Transparency and Obstruction*, trans. A. Goldhammer (Chicago: University of Chicago Press, 1988).

42. Like Schopenhauer, Eliot interprets the biblical story of Hagar and Ishmael as an emblem of uncompassionate conduct, though she reverses the order: as far as she is concerned, the Jews are the cultural Ishmaelites, and hence their disposition to compassion, both as a group and as individuals. See chapter 36, 434.

43. At the beginning of the twentieth century, the traditional concept of sympathy is replaced by that of empathy. For an instructive discussion of the use of empathy in modern historical research, mainly in connection with traumatic subjects and events, see Dominic LaCapra, *Writing History, Writing Trauma* (Baltimore: Johns Hopkins University Press, 2001). Daniel Goleman in *Emotional Intelligence* (New York: Bantam, 1995), 116–19, summarizes modern psychological research into the cerebral dimension of empathic behavior, on which the above statement is based. The crucial role Heinz Kohut allots to empathy in his self psychology is also vital within this theoretical fabric as that which facilitates a therapist's understanding of a patient's inwardness, providing also a powerful curing tool. Interestingly, he also saw the horrors perpetrated against the Jewish people during WWII as a result of the Nazis' "empathy," or vicarious introspection, which enabled the torturers to know their victims thoroughly.

44. See my discussion of these issues in "The Music of Sympathy." See also Neil Hertz's inspiring discussion in "Poor Hetty," in *Compassion: The Culture and Politics of an Emotion*, ed. Lauren Berlant (New York: Routledge, 2004), 87–103, for the notion of narcissism in Eliot's earlier novels "and its relation to pity and pitilessness" (91).

45. She appears in this attire in Alessandro Farra, *Settenario* (1571), quoted in Louise Vinge, *The Narcissus Theme in Western European Literature up to the Early 19th Century* (Lund, Sweden: Gleerups, 1967).

46. As expressed in the following quote: "[H]e objected very strongly to the notion, which others had not allowed him to escape, that his appearance was of a kind to draw attention; and hints of this, intended to be complimentary, found an angry resonance in him, coming from mingled experiences, to which a clue had already been given. His own face in the glass had during many years been associated for him with thoughts of some one whom he must be like—one about whose character and lot he continually wondered, and never dared to ask" (chapter 17, 186).

47. The chapter's epigraph quotes Tennyson's paraphrase of these lines of Dante.

48. The role of "real" song, heard as such in all worlds (fictive, realistic, transcendental) is of a distinctive ontological status, as briefly elaborated in previous chapters.

49. "Mögen wir diese musikalische Gottesfeier in ihrer ursprünglichen Reinheit auch noch so edel und erhaben uns vorzustellen gesonnen sein, so müssen wir desto bestimmter ersehen, daß diese Reinheit nur in allerwiderwärtigster Trübung auf uns gekommen ist: hier hat sich seit Jahrtausenden Nichts aus innerer Lebensfülle weiterentwickelt, sondern Alles ist, wie im Judentum überhaupt, in Gehalt und Form starr haften geblieben. Eine Form, welche nie durch Erneuerung des Gehaltes belebt

wird, zerfällt aber; ein Ausdruck, dessen Inhalt längst nicht mehr lebendiges Gefühl ist, wird sinnlos und verzerrt sich. Wer hat nicht Gelegenheit gehabt, von der Fratze des gottesdienstlichen Gesanges in einer eigentlichen Volks-Synagoge sich zu über-zeugen? Wer ist nicht von der widerwärtigsten Empfindung, gemischt von Grauen-haftigkeit and Lächerlichkeit, ergriffen worden beim Anhören jenes Sinn und Geist verwirrenden *Gegurgels, Gejodels und Geplappers,* das keine absichtliche Karikatur widerlicher zu entstellen vermag, als es sich hier mit vollem, naivem Ernste darbie-tet?" Richard Wagner, "Das Judentum in der Musik," in J. M. Fischer, *Richard Wag-ners "Das Judentum in der Musik,"* 158–59 (italics added).

50. It is clear, here as elsewhere, that Eliot's narrator's voice is not patronizing nor is it transcendental, but, as Qualls writes, "[i]t is not the eye of a Dickens narrator looking on the Dedlock [*sic*] world of Chesney World, nor that of a Carlyle sitting in judg-ment on the French revolution. It is more Virgil's shade, leading us towards the vision which will allow us to say, 'There is a lower and higher!'" (Qualls, "Speaking through Parable," 220.)

51. Similarly to Eliot (and in line with Heine and others), Wagner also maintains that the Reform prayer is a "vain effort coming from above . . . unable to root itself below," and that it lacks the ability to renew "the old purity" of the Jewish prayers. See Wagner, "Das Judentum in der Musik," in J. M. Fischer, *Richard Wagners "Das Judentum in der Musik,"* 159. As mentioned in chapter 4, Wagner's praise of Halévy's Seder scene as "the best expression of Jewish character" (which, as we saw, is very much in the spirit of this Reform music) shows how Wagner in the present case was just reiterating what others had said.

52. Eliot emphasizes this with the awareness that, in the wake of the Counter-Reforma-tion, the aesthetic politics that subsists in the Christian works to which she alludes—Palestrina's and Allegri's—aimed to render the text audible and intelligible, as back-ground to the music. In *George Eliot's Daniel Deronda Notebooks,* ed. Jane Irwin (Cambridge: Cambridge University Press, 1996), 440–42, one finds some remarks to this effect.

53. That this was Eliot's intention can be inferred from the fact that she also endeavors to give more than a flavor of the delivered music in other places and works. Thus, for example, the musical reader can imagine Leopardi's fictive musical work that Mirah sings in her "audition" for Klesmer (in chapter 39). See also Gray, *George Eliot and Music,* 111 and Ruth Solie, "*Daniel Deronda* as Music Historiography."

54. The improvisatory technique in which it was sung, entitled *super librum,* was known as a special proficiency unique to the pope's chapel, to which the performance of Al-legri's *Miserere* was confined.

55. In this she capsizes the principle she advocated in her later combative article against anti-Semitism ("The Modern Hep! Hep! Hep!"), likewise aiming to rebut prejudice. Here is the text: "To discern likeness amidst diversity, it is well known, does not re-quire so fine a mental edge as the discerning of diversity amidst general sameness. The primary rough classification depends on the prominent resemblances of things: the progress is towards fine and finer discrimination according to minute differences. Yet even at this stage of European culture one's attention is continually drawn to the

prevalence of that grosser mental sloth which makes people dull to the most ordinary prompting of comparison—the bringing together because of their likeness. . . . To take only the subject of the Jews: it would be difficult to find a form of bad reasoning about them which has not been heard in conversation or been admitted to the dignity of print: but the neglect of resemblances is a common property of dullness which unites all the various points of view—the prejudiced, the puerile, the spiteful, and the abysmally ignorant" (ibid., 143).

56. The musical-ritual distinctiveness of the Orthodox Frankfurt community is surveyed in Mordechai Breuer, "Besonderheiten des alten Frankfurter Synagogengesangs," *Jüdische Kultur in Frankfurt am Main von den Anfängen bis zur Gegenwart*, ed. K. E. Grözinger (Wiesbaden: Harrassowitz, 1997), 91–100. In addition to his personal knowledge (he grew up in this community), Breuer makes use of books written by insiders, especially two: that of Salman Geiger, *Divre Qehillot*, and Fabian Ogutsch, *Der Frankfurter Kantor, Sammlung der traditionellen Frankfurter synagogalen Gesänge*, ed. J. B. Levy (Frankfurt am Main: J. Kauffmann, 1930), from which some of the following examples are taken (pp. 16–22); this collection reflects turn-of-the-century practice. In 1873, Eliot and Lewes visited synagogues in Germany, the singing in which they enjoyed, as Lewes noted in his diary. See Cave's note on p. 828 in his *Daniel Deronda* edition.

57. This psalm entered the Catholic service rather late (its first polyphonic renditions date to the early sixteenth century).

58. For a thorough study of the circumstances surrounding the work's genesis and its basic musical configurations, see Julius J. Amann, *Allegris Miserere und die Aufführungspraxis in der Sixtina, nach Reiseberichten und Musikhandschriften* (Regensburg: Birkeneck, 1935); see also Frederick Hammond, *Music and Spectacle in Baroque Rome* (New Haven: Yale University Press, 1994).

59. Eliot is, however, cautious not to include the bare Gregorian chant, which sounded to her, in historian John Pyke Hulla's formulation, as a "strange, dull, uncouth sort of stuff," in contradistinction to the sublime polyphony through which the "discords" of the self may be "quenched by meeting harmonies," as expressed in one of her poems. This evidence is brought by Gray, *George Eliot and Music*, 116 and in Irwin, ed., *George Eliot's Daniel Deronda Notebooks*, 441.

60. Idelsohn's characterization of the *steiger* goes in this direction (*Thesaurus* vol. 7, xx–xxi), which some of his examples do not fully realize. This stems, among other things, from the fact that cantors' manuscripts from which he borrows his examples (including those of examples 5.2c and app. 7) are not full renditions of the performative scope of the *steiger*/mode.

61. The *Arvit steiger* is thus labeled due to the lack of a more coherent theory of Ashkenazi Jewish modes. It is basically a natural diatonic minor, extending between two dominants and characterized by stepwise progression with occasional leaps (dominant–tonic; dominant–dominant) and slight majorization towards the cadences. For Ogutsch's example see ex. app. 7 and *Der Frankfurter Kantor*, 19.

62. A practice continuing that of "Aleinu (Olenu) Leshabeaḥ," discussed in chapter 1.

63. See chapter 2.

64. On the superiority of voice and dialogue to vision in religious discourse, see Walter Ong, *The Presence of the Word: Some Prolegomena for Cultural and Religious History* (New Haven: Yale University Press, 1967). That Rabelais' book preoccupied Eliot at the time we can learn from her notebooks, 319. The relevant chapters in François Rabelais' *Gargantua and Pantagruel* are 55–56: "How on the high seas Pantagruel heard some unfrozen words," and "How among the frozen words Pantagruel found some lusty jests."

65. See preface. Kaufmann was not Eliot's sole source, of course; she was an avid reader of his predecessors in this movement, including Zunz, Geiger, and Graetz and was also in close contact with Oscar Deutsch (1827–1873). It is more than a curious coincidence that Kaufmann was the first to publish a comprehensive study on the eleventh-century *Ahimaaz Scroll* (referred to in chapter 1).

66. One might argue that these parts were understood only by a Jewish audience, as manifest in the reception of the book by the Zionist Jewish community. But Eliot's original aim was to address her book first and foremost to a general, that is, mainly Christian British audience.

67. On Beethoven's work, see the following note. Gordigiani was a popular Italian composer in the first half of the century; Schubert's pieces were sung by Daniel himself in his recitals, as related in chapter 37, thus reinforcing the reverberating effect between the two.

68. The aria Mirah sings is from the scene and aria "Ah perfido," op. 65. The choice of music set to the eternal narrative of a forsaken woman is not coincidental: "For pity's sake, do not bid me farewell; / bereft of you, what shall I do? / You well know, my beloved, / that I shall die of grief. / Cruel one! Do you wish me to die? / Have you no pity for me? / Why do you so harshly repay / the one who adores you? / Say, all of you, whether in such distress / I do not deserve pity?" (The text is by the renowned Pietro Metastasio; the translation, by Lionel Salter, is taken from the booklet accompanying John Eliot Gardiner's Archiv Produktion recording of the work, CD no. 435 391–2.) The figure of the forsaken, lamenting woman is a prime archetype in opera, embodying another aspect of the mythological structure, revealed in this novel, of women who act through music. Echo is a related type. Mirah's sirenic, benevolent power complements this structure. See Ruth HaCohen, "Between Eurydice and the Sirens: A Study of the Feminine Sphere of Action in Wagner's *Ring*," *Motar* 1997 (5): 131–40 (Hebrew). The dominating affect of this aria (in major) is not of revenge or lament, but that of tenderness, longing, and pleading, signaling reciprocal compassion.

69. Parsifal's "orient-ation" is to India, rather than Jerusalem, as Wagner had already formulated it in 1848. See Roger Hollinrake, *Nietzsche, Wagner and the Philosophy of Pessimism* (London: Allen and Unwin, 1982), 129.

70. In this, Parsifal, like Siegfried and Elsa before him, is the optimal subject to be "educated," or to put it from a critical perspective (e.g., that of Nietzsche), to be manipulated by his leader. In contradistinction to the other two, Parsifal himself eventually becomes a leader and savior of others.

71. *Parsifal*'s comprehensive meaning is ever interpreted anew. While modernist scholars such as Carl Dahlhaus, in *Richard Wagner's Music Dramas*, trans. Mary Whittall

(Cambridge: Cambridge University Press, 1979), Arnold Whittall, in "The Music," in Lucy Beckett, *Richard Wagner: Parsifal* (Cambridge: Cambridge University Press, 1981), 61–86, and Michael Tanner, in *Wagner* (London: Flamingo, 1997), have sought to purge the work of its Christian elements and assert its motivic and structural cohesion as an embodiment of pure aesthetic principles, postmodern interpreters wish to view such cohesion as the root of social and personal wounds, which are exposed on the work's surface. Whereas Žižek ("'There is no Sexual Relationship'") emphasizes the predicament of the incestuous knights' society that repudiates any contact with Otherness and Others, Tomlinson (following Adorno) argues that the overall, transformative cohesion of the work is a reflection of the extreme exchange-consciousness of postcapitalist society (Gary Tomlinson, *Metaphysical Song: An Essay on Opera* [Princeton: Princeton University Press, 1999], 127–42).

72. Since the Enlightenment, the arpeggio, a chord unfolding melodically, has constituted the tightest relation between melody and harmony—the utmost expression of a pure, musical nature.

73. The fact that Eliot likewise chose to foreground *communion* bespeaks a similar urge to trace the relation of the individual to a possible and meaningful community of belonging and sacrifice, dialoguing with an entrenched Christian lore; see also chapter 1.

74. This translation is taken from the ESV and is typical of the Christological understanding of this famous verse; Jewish translations sometimes choose to retain the Hebrew name of the savior as a sacred coinage: "For a child is born unto us, a son is given unto us; and the government is upon his shoulder; and his name is called Pele-joez-el-gibbor-Abi-ad-sar-shalom" (JPS, 1917).

75. The main motif of Schumann's "Stirb, Lieb' und Freud'" (op. 35, no. 2) connoting celestial spirituality, is akin to the faith motif, though differently worked out; instructively, its poem (by Justinius Körner) shares with Chaucer's "Prioress' Tale" the total devotion of a virgin (here a woman), forgoing earthly love, to the Virgin Mary, who likewise miraculously bequeathes grace on her in public. This sonoric icon could have affected Wagner, a thematic borrower, who would have carried along their import. The motif thus winds up a circle of Christian celestial harmoniousness, entertained by those who are contained within its shell (his other well-known inspiration for the Grail motif) could have been Mendelssohn's reformation-symphony "Dresden Amen" theme, but semiotically it goes beyond that, as Carolyn Abbate indicates in *In Search of Opera* (Princeton: Princeton University Press, 2001), 127–28.

76. Nietzsche, who otherwise condemned the work (in *The Case of Wagner*) for, among other things, its compassionate surplus, was fascinated by its overture; does this relate to its nonconclusiveness, whose opposite in the Wagnerian *Gesamtkunstwerk* he came to loathe?

77. An accurate title for the leitmotif would be a combination of all these: the prophecy of the coming of the "compassionate fool."

78. In that sense, the work is a "Catholicized" version of the *St. Matthew Passion*, to which it owes some crucial structural debts, such as the high-voiced gallery chorus referred to below.

79. Tehila Mishor ("'Real Music' in Opera: The Case of *The Tales of Hoffmann*," unpublished master's thesis, Hebrew University of Jerusalem, 2008, in Hebrew) has insightfully suggested to view such moments of "real" music in the Lacanian term of *le point de caption*—the "quilting point" (Seminar iii), where the perpetual sliding of signifiers and signified reaches a momentary firm "stapling"—similar to the one made in a quilt to connect its two sides. While in verbal texts such moments are created through particular semantic encounters of words and meaning, in opera, she claims, it is achieved in each performance of "real music," so prevalent in this medium. Such moments, she continues, following Lacan, enable the further streaming of the unsynchronized semantic entities—the musical and the dramatic—that builds the main body of the work's semiotics.

80. See Abbate, *In Search of Opera*, 136, and for the whole section that brilliantly analyzes the music of the scene. If this indeed stands, as Abbate argues, for the spectral presence of the absent father (Titurel), then, combined with Mladen Dolar's claim that this refusing-to-die father's voice resembles a shofar's sound (in "The Object Voice," in *Gaze and Voice as Love Objects*, ed. Renata Salecl and Slavoj Žižek [Durham: Duke University Press, 1996], 25–26), we are getting close to Theodor Reik's psychoanalytic reading of the ancient Jewish ritual of this "primitive horn" (discussed in chapters 3 and 6 of the present study). Though the sin and repentance symptomized by these vocalities are very differently framed and solved by Reik, this unwitting thematic proximity bespeaks again how thoroughly entangled "Jewish noise" became in European modern culture.

81. As quoted in Abbate, ibid., 138.

82. A similar case is perhaps the parallelism of signifcant portions of the first and fourth acts in Puccini's *La Bohème*.

83. Similar to Tonio Kröger in Thomas Mann's sonata-form novella of that title.

84. *Notebooks 1865–1869*, 2, as quoted in Darrel Mansell, "George Eliot's Conception of Form," in *George Eliot: A Collection of Critical Essays*, ed. G. R. Creeger (Englewood Cliffs, NJ: Prentice-Hall, 1970), 67. The importance of "middles" in musical works is a leading idea in Michael Beckerman's scholarly work: see "The Strange Landscape of Middles," in *The Oxford Handbook of the New Cultural History of Music*, ed. Jane Fulcher (New York: Oxford University Press, forthcoming).

85. This divergent world-and-work structuring of the two artists—one that calls for total immersion, assuming what Freud would later term the temptation of the oceanic, and the other that fends off such oneness—is interestingly reflected in Freud's own elective lineage with John Stuart Mill, as Michael P. Steinberg poignantly argues; see his "The Family Romances of Sigmund Freud," *Judaism Musical and Unmusical* (Chicago: University of Chicago Press, 2007), chapter 2. For Eliot's Spinozist legacy see Gatens, "The Politics of 'Presence' and 'Difference.'"

86. As claimed by Adam Smith in his essay on the imitative arts. See Ruth Katz and Ruth HaCohen, *The Arts in Mind: Pioneering Texts of a Coterie of British Men of Letters* (New Brunswick, NJ: Transaction, 2003), 369–421.

87. The element of free choice is central in *Daniel Deronda*, as reflected in the stances the author gives Ezra-Mordecai regarding the concerns of Judaism (chapter 42).

88. On the musical aspect of Feuerbach's philosophy and its appeal to Wagner, see Ruth Solie, *Music in Other Words*, 162.

89. This is the main line of argument in Moira Gaten's research project, represented in the above-quoted "The Experimental Philosophy of George Eliot."

90. Within the British political context, this stance is what brought Eliot to side with the conservative position at this period of her life. She seems to rightly understand the danger of the cosmopolitan view that became prevalent among liberal circles in England, and its paradoxically inherent racist potential. She insisted that while Britain has no right to enforce its political domination on other cultures, it should concurrently oppose the liberal view that condemns national emotions as barbaric. On this issue see Bernard Semmel, *George Eliot and the Politics of National Inheritance* (Oxford: Oxford University Press, 1994). This appraisal only slightly mitigates Edward Said's well-known criticism of the author's "Zionist" approach (as expressed by Mordecai in the novel), relating to what Said deemed as a typical view by "Gentile and Jewish versions of [proto] Zionism: their view of the Holy Land as essentially empty of inhabitants, not because there were no inhabitants . . . but because their status as sovereign and human inhabitants was systematically denied." See "Zionism from the Standpoint of Its Victims" (1979), in *The Edward Said Reader*, eds. Moustafa Bayoumi and Andrew Rubin (New York: Vintage Books, 2000) (http://homes.chass.utoronto.ca/~ikalmar/illustex/said%20zionism.htm).

91. Both Daniel's mother, Princess Halm-Eberstein (formerly, before her conversion and marriage, called by the Sephardic Jewish name "Alcharisi") and Gwendolyn are left behind in this world of redeeming males. The mother's voice is strong enough in criticizing the men dominating the Jewish world with which Daniel chooses so emphatically to identify, and in confrontation with him the woman's voice is not delegitimized, despite the characterization of possible deficiencies in her personality. Eliot is anticipating here major trends in twentieth-century feminist Jewish thought, as Solie rightly observes (*Music in Other Words*, 173). Daniel's mother is an embodiment of the Wagnerian conception of Jewish assimilation, including her contempt for synagogal rituals.

92. In the debate regarding the meaning of the famous last words of Wagner's invective (Aber denkt, daß nur Eines eure Erlösung von dem auf Euch lastenden Fluche sein kann: Die Erlösung Ahasvers, der *Untergang!*), I side with Katz and Borchmeyer, whose historical and textual caution prevented them from ascribing the idea of genocide to Wagner. It should be likewise noted that Wagner sometimes expressed himself in contradictory terms, considering Judaism a cultural superior to Germanness, and that Judaism alone can equal Germanness in its role in global history. See Borchmeyer, "The Question," 180.

93. The centrality of orphanage/orphanhood as a psychoanalytic concept, in Anna Freud's postwar enterprises, is insightfully analyzed by Suzanne Stewart-Steinberg in *Imaginary Socialities: Four Essays on Anna Freud, Psychoanalysis and Politics* (Ithaca: Cornell University Press, forthcoming). Competing with the Oedipalian legacy of her father, argues Stewart-Steinberg, the daughter questions the universality of trajectories of libidinal cathexis as he conceived them, revealing the contingency of kinship relations

and variety of modes of growth, expression, and socialization they entail. I find these ideas of high relevance to questions of sympathy, compassion, leadership, community, and their relations to our main heroes' partial orphanhood, their interrelations, and the special social-political roles they undertake. I thank Suzanne Stewart-Steinberg for allowing me to read her manuscript before publication. A more contemporary orphaned group is that which populated the fictional American *Pequod*, also trapped in the predicament of compassion and sympathy, as beautifully construed in Ilana Pardes' *Melville's Bibles* (Berkeley: University of California Press, 2008), chapter 5.

CHAPTER 6. THE AESTHETIC THEOLOGY OF MULTIVOCALITY

1. Examples for "mythological subjectivism" can be found in works as different as Henrik Ibsen's *When We Dead Awaken* (1899)—which Thomas Mann (in *Essays by Thomas Mann* [New York: Vintage, 1947], 200) called, together with *Parsifal*, "celestial old-men's works" or, much later, the second book of Robert Musil's *Der Mann ohne Eigenschaften* (an author otherwise suspicious of Wagner), again glorifying incestuous relations. The couple in *Verklärte Nacht* is another example, all involving sacralization of sorts.

2. See Laurence Dreyfus' "Hermann Levi's Shame and *Parsifal's* Guilt: A Critique of Essentialism in Biography and Criticism," in *Cambridge Opera Journal* 6/2 (1994): 125–45 for a poignantly critical revisiting of this fascinating case. Interesting for the present chapter is the evidence regarding Wagner's apellation of Levi as his "alter ego"! (ibid., 131–32).

3. See, for example, Benedictus Levita's (pseudonym of Weissler, a Jewish attorney from Halle) 1900 article "Die Erlösung des Judentums" (The Salvation of Judaism [and/or Jewry]) for the following lines: "Certainly, anyone who still tolerates the chattering and sing-song in his synagogue instead of grasping the treasures of German church music . . . must certainly appear as an alien to the German." Quoted in Moshe Lazar, "Arnold Schoenberg and His Doubles: A Psychodramatic Journey to His Roots," *Journal of the Arnold Schoenberg Institute*, 18/1–2 (1994), 13. See also Ludwig Wittgenstein, *Culture and Value*, ed. G. H. von Wright (Chicago: University of Chicago Press, 1980), especially his dispersed comments on Mendelssohn.

4. See Thomas Pfau, "From Mediation to Medium: Aesthetic and Anthropological Dimensions of the Image (Bild) and the Crisis of Bildung in German Modernism," *Modernist Culture* 1/2 (2005), 141–80. The sociocultural backgrounds of some of these composers were discussed by Leon Botstein in a series of articles, such as his "Music and the Critique of Culture: Arnold Schoenberg, Heinrich Schenker, and the Emergence of Modernism in Fin-de-Siècle Vienna," in *Constructive Dissonance: Arnold Schoenberg and the Transformation of Twentieth-Century Culture*, ed. Juliane Brand and Christopher Hailey (Berkeley: University of California Press, 1997), 3–22.

5. For the impingement of Catholic culture on Austrian Jews, see Michael P. Steinberg, "The Catholic Culture of the Austrian Jews," in: *The Meaning of the Salzburg Festival: Austria as Theater and Ideology 1890–1939* (Ithaca: Cornell University Press, 1990), 179–81.

6. For the case of anti-Semitism against Mahler see, for example, Jens Malte Fischer, "Gustav Mahler und das 'Judentum in der Musik' in *Merkur, Deutsche Zeitschrift für europäisches Denken* 581 (1997), 665–80, and Susan M. Filler, "Mahler as a Jew in the Literature," in *Dika Caecilia: Essays for Dika Newlin*, ed. Theodore Albrecht (Kansas City: Park College Department of Music, 1988), 66–85. For the case of Schoenberg, see Leon Botstein, "Arnold Schoenberg: Language, Modernism and Jewish Identity," in *Austrians and Jews in the Twentieth Century: From Franz Joseph to Waldheim*, ed. Robert S. Wistrich (New York: St. Martin's, 1992), 162–83 and cited literature.

7. For the Kandinsky-Schoenberg correspondence between 15 April and 4 May 1923 (the last one, critically poignant, was Schoenberg's) see *Arnold Schoenberg, Wassily Kandinsky: Letters, Pictures, and Documents*, ed. Jelena Hahl-Koch, trans. John C. Crawford (London: Faber and Faber, 1984), 75–82.

8. See Albrecht Dümling, "The Target of Racial Purity, The 'Degenerate Music' Exhibition in Düsseldorf, 1938," in *Art, Culture, and Media under the Third Reich*, ed. Richard A. Etlin (Chicago: University of Chicago Press, 2002), 43–72, and Richard Begam, "Modernism as Degeneracy: Schoenberg's "Moses und Aron," *Modernist Cultures* 3/1 (2007): 33–56.

9. This close company comprises some of the following family relations: Schoenberg married Mathilde Zemlinsky; Mahler met Alma at Zemlinsky's place.

10. These are further analyzed in Ruth HaCohen, "Reflections and Inflections of the Transfiguring Self. On the Music of the Unheimliche in the Works of Schoenberg and Mahler," in *Österreich-Konzeptionen und jüdisches Selbstverständnis, Identitäts-Transfigurationen im 19. und 20. Jahrhundert*, ed. Hanni Mitelmann and Armin A. Wallas (*Conditio Judaica* 35), (Tübingen: Max Niemeyer, 2001), 115–40.

11. Sigmund Freud, "The 'Uncanny'," in *Art and Literature*, The Penguin Freud Library, ed. Albert Dickson (London: Penguin, [1919] 1985), 14:356.

12. Eddy Zemach, "Unconscious Mind or Conscious Minds?," *Midwest Studies in Philosophy* 10 (1986): 121–49. In recent years a growing literature on these alternative psychologists has emerged. For the famous case history of Morton Prince see Ruth Leys, *Trauma: A Genealogy* (Chicago: University of Chicago Press, 2000), chapter 2. Some of the controversies are described in *The Freud Encyclopedia: Theory, Therapy, and Culture*, 2nd ed., ed. Edward Erwin (London: Taylor & Francis, 2002), s.v. "Repression." See also Ann Taves' rich discussion in "Religious Experience and the Divisible Self: William James (and Frederic Myers) as Theorist(s) of Religion," *Journal of the American Academy of Religion* 71/ 2 (2003): 303–26.

13. Quoted by Bryan R. Simms, in "Whose Idea Was *Erwartung?*" in *Constructive Dissonance*, 105–6 (original italics).

14. Ibid.

15. In Jacques Derrida's *Memoirs of the Blind: The Self-Portrait and Other Ruins*, trans. Pascale-Anne Brault and Michael Naas (Chicago: University of Chicago Press, 1993).

16. See chapter 1.

17. See Jonathan Dunsby, *Schoenberg: Pierrot Lunaire* (Cambridge: Cambridge University Press, 1992); Reinhold Brinkman, "The Fool as Paradigm: Schoenberg's *Pierrot*

Lunaire and the Modern Artist," in *Schoenberg and Kandinsky: An Historical Encounter*, ed. Konrad Boehmer (Amsterdam: Harwood Academic Publishers, 1997), 139–67; and HaCohen, "Reflections and Inflections of the Transfiguring Self."

18. From a letter to Richard Dehmel, 13 December 1912, quoted in Joachim Birke, "Richard Dehmel und Arnold Schönberg, Ein Briefwechsel," *Die Musikforschung* 11/3 (1958): 279–85. For translation, see *A Schoenberg Reader: Documents of a Life*, ed. Joseph Auner (New Haven: Yale University Press, 2003), 119.

19. For details concerning the chronology of the composition, see Jean Marie Christensen, "Arnold Schoenberg's Oratorio *Die Jakobsleiter*," 2 vols. (PhD diss., University of California at Los Angeles, 1979).

20. The eager expectation of Schoenberg's students, especially Webern, of the text and the music of the work, and its enthusiastic reception by them, speaks volumes about its special spiritual artistic value for that circle. See ibid., 8–43.

21. Translation by Gabriele Cervone, from the booklet to Arnold Schoenberg, *Die Jakobsleiter, Symphony No. 1, Begleitmusik zu einer Lichtspielszene* audio CD, performed by the BBC Singers and Symphony Orchestra, conducted by Pierre Boulez, Sony Classical, SMK 48 462, p. 20. This passage is often interpreted as foreshadowing the multidimensional, nondirectional, twelve-tone techniques. For the full libretto of the oratorio, including the noncomposed part, see Christensen, "Arnold Schoenberg's Oratorio."

22. As documented in Franz Rosenzweig's critical-ironic essay, *Understanding the Sick and the Healthy: A View of World, Man, and God*, trans. Nahum Glatzer (Cambridge, MA: Harvard University Press, 1999).

23. See Jennifer Shaw, "Androgyny and the Eternal Feminine in Schoenberg's Oratorio *Die Jakobsleiter*," in *Political and Religious Ideas in the Works of Arnold Schoenberg*, ed. Charlotte M. Cross and Russell A. Berman (New York: Garland Publishing, 2000), 61–83. Important in this regard are Schoenberg's inspirational models, the most significant of which are Balzac's *Sériphîta*, and the writings of the eighteenth-century mystic, Emanuel Swedenborg (familiar to him through August Strindberg's works). Schoenberg was cognizant of the debates, in the wake of Weininger's influential misogynistic text, also through his reading of essays in *Die Fackel* by Karl Kraus (with whom Schoenberg was on close terms; the Jewish "liminality" of these writers was noted by many).

24. This conclusion, observed the authorized editor of the work's score, Winfried Zillig (1905–1963)—although completion of the entire text eluded the author—"is one of the most impressive endings in the whole of Occidental music." Quoted in Arnold Schoenberg, *Die Jakobsleiter, Oratorium*, scored for performance by Winfried Zillig, revised by Rudolf Stephan (fragment; Vienna: Universal Edition, 1977), unspecified page.

25. Hermann Cohen, "Deutschtum und Judentum," in *Jüdische Schriften* in 2 vols., ed. Bruno von Strauss (Berlin: C. A. Schwetschke, 1924) 2:251.

26. On this double affiliation see Michael P. Steinberg, "Grounds Zero," in *Judaism Musical and Unmusical* (Chicago: University of Chicago Press, 2007), 177–92.

27. In the winter of 1913–14, A. Z. Idelsohn came to visit the old Cohen, who could have been at the time already engaged with writing the essay. Idelsohn, as he reports,

sang to him several "authentic" tunes from the Days of Awe prayers, which deeply moved him; as a consequence he fell from his seat and passed out. When he revived he muttered: "Ich weiß selbst nicht, was das ist. Die hebräische Melodie ist es, die mein Herz erschüttert. Sie haben, mein Freund, eine unheilbare Wunde im Herzen berührt . . . Aber dank . . . Ich danke Ihnen sehr! Mein Geist ist neu belebt." (I don't know myself what it is. The Hebrew melody it is, that has shaken my heart. They have, my friend, the capacity to touch the heart's unrecovered wound. . . . But thanks . . . I thank you very much! My spirit is revived.) The episode (quoted in Hartwig Wiedebach, "Hebräisches 'Fühlen,' Hermann Cohens Deutung des *Schma' Jisra'el/*"Höre Israel," *Kalonymos, Beiträge zur deutsch-jüdischen Geschichte aus dem Salomon Ludwig Steinheim-Institut* 6/2, [2003], 1–4) accentuates, nonetheless, the built-in tension, in the philosopher's own perception, between the indigenous Jewish and that which had become musically more acculturated.

28. See Howard Elbert Smither, *A History of the Oratorio*, vol. 4, *The Oratorio in the Nineteenth and Twentieth Centuries* (Chapel Hill: University of North Carolina Press, 2000), 13.

29. In Ethan Haimo, *Schoenberg's Serial Odyssey: The Evolution of His Twelve-Tone Method 1914–1928* (Oxford: Clarendon Press, 1990).

30. Quoted from Josef Rufer, "Hommage à Schoenberg," in Egbert M. Ennulat, ed., *Arnold Schoenberg Correspondence: A Collection of Translated and Annotated Letters Exchanged with Guido Adler, Pablo Casals, Emanuel Feuermann and Olin Downes* (Metuchen, NJ: Scarecrow Press, 1991), 2.

31. For the way the twelve-tone method evolved from this work see Haimo, *Schoenberg's Serial Odyssey*, 60–64.

32. He found it prepared for him by Oscar Wilde's eponymous play, from which he borrowed his libretto, verbatim—in this scene with but few omissions. Though bearing a clearly anti-Semitic tone, Wilde's text does not directly refer to noise, as it was not meant to be performed polyphonically. For the interpretation of this scene of Jewish noise in Strauss' *Salome*, within the framework of other fin-de-siècle "perversions," especially homosexuality and its effect on voice, see Sander Gilman, "Strauss and the Pervert," *Reading Opera*, ed. Arthur Groos and Roger Parker (Princeton: Princeton University Press: 1988), 306–27. Musically, the noisy elements are conspicuous, despite a generally tumultuous score, and well within the legacy of staging "noisy Jews."

33. See Vogel, *Married Life*, Hebrew original, 71–72, 306; English translation, 102–3, 448.

34. See Ernst Pawel, *The Nightmare of Reason: A Life of Franz Kafka* (New York: Farrar, Straus & Giroux, 1984), 53–61. A no less poignant criticism against the "wishy-washy" Jewish rituals of assimilated Jews was made by Gershom Scholem in his youth—see his *Von Berlin nach Jerusalem, Jugenderinnerungen*, trans. M. Brocke and A. Schatz (Frankfurt: Suhrkamp, 1997).

35. Ambros' *History of Music* was first published in 1862.

36. Theodor Reik, "Das Schofar," in *Das Ritual, Psychoanalytische Studien*, 1928, trans. Douglas Bryan as "The Shofar," in *Ritual: Psycho-Analytic Studies* (New York: International Universities Press, 1958), 221–22.

37. Ibid., 236–7, and cf. Steinthal's Tish'a' be'Av report, chapter 3 for an awareness of moments of rare silence in the synagogue.

38. Reik, *Ritual*, 237.

39. Ibid., 239; see also 268 and 272; the latter is of special interest in its "repetition with difference" of former themes.

40. The semiotic mapping of Ashkenazi Jewish music has rarely been discussed in the scholarly literature, but its elaborate semantic markedness can be interpreted through the intersections of coordinates of text, occasion, performing norms on musical variables.

41. Reik, *Ritual*, 266.

42. Visually it also imitates his phallus, but this is more marginal to Reik's argument.

43. Reik, *Ritual*, 267 (original italics).

44. Ibid., 259

45. This orphan Orpheus (as some etymologies hold), a professional lamenter of darkness (as others propound), was, according to another version, as Oderberg writes, "the son of Oiagros and grandson of Charops to whom the god Dionysos had given instruction in rites and ceremonies connected with the Mysteries. Oiagros succeeded his father, and later Orpheus inherited those responsibilities." I. M. Oderberg, "Creative Power in Orphic Myths," *Sunrise Magazine*, February/March 1989 (http://www.theosophy-nw .org/theosnw/world/med/my-imo3.htm) (accessed 15 July 2008). Though Reik does not mention these sources, they likewise reverberate with themes pertinent to vocal fictions of noise and harmony in general, and Reik's theory in particular.

46. For the story see Franz Kafka, *The Complete Stories*, ed. Nahum N. Glatzer (New York: Schocken, 1971); the translation of this story is by Willa and Edwin Muir. For the quote from Elias Canetti see his *Kafka's Other Trial: The Letters to Felice*, trans. Christopher Middleton (London: Calder and Boyars, 1974), 88.

47. Canetti, *Kafka's Other Trial*, 87.

48. See chapter 1.

49. Gilles Deleuze and Félix Guattari, *Kafka: Toward a Minor Literature*, trans. Dana Polan (Minneapolis: University of Minnesota Press, 1986).

50. Ibid., 13. The rhizome is a basic concept in Deleuze's and Guattari's thought, standing for nonhierarchical, nondichotomous modes of representing and interpreting data, allowing for horizontal and transspecies connections and flows in various orbits of life and knowledge.

51. Ibid.

52. Ibid., 21.

53. In Carl Dahlhaus, *Realism in Nineteenth-Century Music*, trans. Mary Whittall (Cambridge: Cambridge University Press, 1985), 115.

54. As translated by Joseph Kresh, *Diaries of Franz Kafka* (New York: Schocken, 1948), entry of 15 December 1910, 33. For the German see The Kafka Project, by Mauro Nervi (http://www.kafka.org/index.php?h2). The sonic otherness this expression betrays, whether related to the real or dressed-up "Negro," may be considered as part of the defamation of Jews as "white Negroes" documented at least since the rise of modern anti-Semitism; but unlike "self-hating Jews" working in the scheme Gilman

describes in *Jewish Self-Hatred, Anti-Semitism and the Hidden Language of the Jews* (Baltimore: Johns Hopkins University Press, 1988), 6–12, Kafka saw himself as "black," an association in line with his other sonic (self) projections. On Kafka and *mauscheln*, ibid., 283–84.

55. See "In unserer Synagoge . . . " in *Franz Kafka Erzählungen und andere ausgewählte Prosa*, ed. Roger Hermes (Frankfurt: Fischer, 1996), 408. Translation, with changes, from *Parables and Paradoxes* (in German and English), trans. Ernst Kaiser and Eithne Wilkins (New York: Schocken, 1958), 57.

56. Ibid.

57. See Thomas Mann, *Doktor Faustus: Das Leben des deutschen Tonsetzers Adrian Leverkühn, erzählt von einem Freunde* (Frankfurt: Fischer, [1947] 1999), 85.

58. Franz Kafka, *The Complete Stories*, 284. (This story was translated by W. and E. Muir.)

59. This story brings out the liminality of musical power as a feminine zone (see chapter 4) while alluding to certain Jewish traits. On the former see Ruth V. Gross, "Of Mice and Women: Reflections on a Discourse in Kafka's 'Josefine, die Sängerin oder das Volk der Mäuse,'" *The Germanic Review* 60/2 (1985): 59–68.

60. Franz Rosenzweig, *The Star of Redemption*, trans. William W. Hallo (Boston: Beacon, [1971] 1972), 360.

61. Deleuze and Guattari, *Kafka*, 21–22.

62. This itself may stand as the cause for the deep feelings emanating from Kafka's own music, own "dialectic lyrics," as the poet-novelist Paul Goodman—a highly sensitive reader of Kafka's—put it; see his *Kafka's Prayer* (New York: Vanguard, 1947), 240–42.

63. *Moses und Aron*, I.i.

64. See Carl Dahlhaus, "Schoenberg's Aesthetic Theology," in *Schoenberg and the New Music*, trans. Derrick Puffet and Alfred Clayton (Cambridge: Cambridge University Press, 1987), 81–93.

65. These ideas are further explored in my "Sounds of Revelation: Aesthetic-Political Theology in Schoenberg's *Moses und Aron*," in *Modernist Cultures* 1/2 (Winter 2005): 110–40.

66. The score of the work referred to here is *Moses und Aron, Oper in drei Akten*, Studienpartitur (Mainz: B. Schott's Söhne, 1958). I have used the English translation (embedded in the score) by Milton Babbitt.

67. See Schoenberg's essays on his creative growth in Leonard Stein (ed.) *Style and Idea: Selected Writings of Arnold Schoenberg* (Berkeley: University of California Press, 1975), part I. This "mechanical" invention is only to some extent parallel to the Kafkaesque machines, deconstructed by Deleuze and Guattari; the attraction of Schoenberg and Kafka to machines, by and large, is not exceptional in that age of mechanical production.

68. See Ruth HaCohen, "Psychoanalysis and the Music of Charisma in the *Moseses* of Freud and Schoenberg," in *New Perspectives on Freud's "Moses and Monotheism,"* ed. Ruth Ginsburg and Ilana Pardes (*Conditio Judaica* 60), (Tübingen: Max Niemeyer, 2006), 177–95.

69. This statement, of course, does not take into consideration a history of reception that further transforms the import of the art object.

70. For the history of the golem legend, see Moshe Idel, *Golem, Jewish Magical and Mystical Traditions on the Artificial Anthropoid* (Albany: State University of New York Press, 1990).

71. W. J. T. Mitchell, *What Do Pictures Want: The Lives and Loves of Images* (Chicago: University of Chicago Press, 2005).

72. The classical works in this trend are R. Strauss's *Salome*, Debussy's *Pelléas et Mélisande*, and Berg's *Wozzeck*.

73. Once this chapter was written, I found in Paul Goodman's text on Kafka, mentioned above, the following statement, which refers to the affinities of the kind I aimed to uncover between Schoenberg and his "alter egos." Commenting on Kafka's conception of the *dis*harmony of the world, Goodman argues: "Every writer discovers his antinomies; mostly then he proceeds from them to grasp the matter in a different way, avoiding the antinomies or reconciling them. . . . But Kafka comes to freeze the antinomies to become the corpse of the world, in which we support our life and breath, such as it is" (*Kafka's Prayer*, 233–35).

74. See Bluma Goldstein, *Reinscribing Moses: Heine, Kafka, Freud, and Schoenberg in a European Wilderness* (Cambridge, MA: Harvard University Press, 1992), 137–68. Goldstein meticulously discusses the various interpretations of the musicless act. See also the insightful essay by Jan Assmann, "Die Mosaische Unterscheidung in Schönbergs *Moses und Aron*," program notes (Berlin: Staatsoper Unter den Linden, 2004), 15–24.

75. "Ewig in Gottes Wort ist sein Geist! Der Wortlaut ist nur Erscheinungsform; dem Augenblick angepasst, den Erfordernissen der Wüstenwanderung." Quoted from Arnold Schoenberg, *Der Biblische Weg: Schauspiel in drei Akten* (http://www.usc.edu/libraries/archives/schoenberg/bibliweg.htm). The English translation is Bluma Goldstein's, *Reinscribing*, 145.

76. An accusation concerning literalness/materialism versus allegorism/spiritualism, which Christians and Jews leveled against each other, is brought out in the context of this drama between the Orthodox David Asseino and the Liberal Jew—the leader Max Aruns.

77. Quoted in Peter Gradenwitz, "The Religious Works of Arnold Schoenberg," *The Music Review*, 21/1 (1960), 19. Schoenberg here unknowingly echoes Lord Warburton, the author of the *Divine Legation of Moses*, who, already in 1738, situated biblical narrative and prophecy in a cultural phase that communicated through palpable images and embodied actions, in contrast to subsequent, more abstract modes of thought and communication.

78. This is featured above all in the three magical signs Aron performs, in the water he brings forth from the rock (as deduced from Moses' complaint), and in the pillars of smoke and of fire, likewise associated with biblical Moshe.

79. At the time of the composition of the opera, Schoenberg probably owned two translations of the Bible—Luther's and Simon Bernfeld's. When I find it instructive I refer the reader to both translations. Another curious book in his library is Yoseph HaCohen's *Emek Habaca*, mentioned in chapter 1 in connection with the Blois "Olenu" memoir.

80. I refer here to his letter to Eidlitz, of 15 March 1933, *Ausgewählte Briefe* ed. Erwin Stein (Mainz: B. Schott's Söhne, 1958), 188, which gives vent to his struggling with

two incomprehensibly contradictory versions of what he believed to be the same story—Moses' smiting/ speaking to the rock (respectively in Exodus 17:1–7, Numbers
20:1–13). Quoted in Goldstein, *Reinscribing*, 206, n. 62.

81. Menachem Lorberbaum, "Spinoza's Theological-Political Problem," *Journal of Hebraic Political Studies* 1 (2006), 222.

82. In this it is different from musical works of the tonal era, which are tonally more continuous in relation to each other and thus sometimes exchangeable.

83. See Theodor W. Adorno, "Sacred Fragment: Schoenberg's *Moses und Aron*," in *Quasi
una Fantasia, Essays on Modern Music*, trans. Rodney Livingstone (New York: Verso,
1992), 225–48.

84. Pamela White's pioneering study of the work contains analysis of leitmotivic elements
in the opera that sometimes overlooks the perceptual constraint of leitmotifs (i.e., they
should be distinctly profiled) crucial for their communicative efficiency. See Pamela
C. White, *Schoenberg and the God-Idea: The Opera "Moses und Aron"* (Ann Arbor:
University of Michigan Research Press, 1985), 160–225.

85. Michael Cherlin, "Dramaturgy and Mirror Imagery in Schönberg's *Moses und Aron*:
Two Paradigmatic Interval Palindromes," *Perspectives of New Music* 29/2 1991, 56.
Cherlin allegorizes this erroneous ascription of new grammatical operations to an
older musical one as the misunderstanding of Moses' words by Aron and the people.
This will be differently interpreted below.

86. In order to illustrate this question, I suggest the following comparison: when Shakespeare's protagonists shift from blank verse to rhyming verse before they exit—what
does it disclose about their consciousness? Of course, not a technical knowledge, but
rather the awareness that they are concluding an interaction, an occurrence, moving
elsewhere. The spectator, sensitive to this cadential element, more readily reflects on
it as a closed unit. The phenomenology of protagonist and spectator is thus different
and yet closely interrelated.

87. Philippe Lacoue-Labarthe, *Musica Ficta (Figures of Wagner)*, trans. Felicia McCarren
(Stanford: Stanford University Press, 1994), 117–45.

88. David Lewin was probably the first to pursue this line of argument, which was rarely
touched upon by later scholars, when remarking that "the problem posed by the
drama is not whether Moses or Aron is 'right,' but rather how God can be brought to
the Volk." See his "*Moses und Aron*: Some General Remarks, and Analytic Notes," in
Perspectives on Schoenberg and Stravinsky eds. Benjamin Boretz and Edward T. Cone
(New York: Norton, 1972), 62.

89. See Leon Botstein's "Arnold Schoenberg: Language," 177–80, for a poignant discussion of the work's affiliation with *Parsifal*.

90. In the Passion tradition (e.g., *St. Matthew Passion*) *turba* stands for the chorus sections
representing the voices of the many in the biblical story—priests, people, disciples—
treated by musically realistic means (rhythmical fugato sections).

91. Hemiola—the rhythmic relation of three notes in the time of two.

92. Are they walking towards each other as the Bible, and later the people in scene III
imply? No instructions in the score itself are given as to how they should behave during this opening part.

93. Act I, m. 208: "Reinige dein Denken, lös' es von Wertlosem, weihe es Waherm" (Purify your thinking. Free it from worthless things. Let it be righteous), he says in a rather Wagnerian way; and then, no longer sung: "Kein andrer Gewinn dankt deine Opfer"—(no other reward is returned for your sacrifice). Latham has shown that this moment takes place when the energetic flow of the dialogue of the two reaches its most intensive point, and coordinates with Aron's "spoken" moment, thus signifying a moment of emotional annoyance. It also manifests Moses' capability to sing, to express "worldly" emotions and hence his refusal to routinely do that "normally." See Edward Latham, "The Prophet and the Pitchman: Dramatic Structure and Its Musical Elucidation in *Moses und Aron*, Act I, scene 2" in *Political and Religious Ideas in the Works of Arnold Schoenberg*, 131–58.

94. "Auch du würdest dies Volk lieben, hättest du gesehen, wie es lebt, wenn es sehen, fühlen hoffen darf."

95. "Umschreibend, ohne auszusprechen: Verbote, furchterregend, doch befolgbar, sichern das Bestehen, die Notwendigkeit verklärend: Gebote, hart, doch hoffnungserweckend, verankern den Gedanken. Unbewußt wird getan, wie du willst."

96. Note that Aron correlates emotions with restrictions and commandments the way Spinoza does. Baruch Spinoza, *Political Treatise*, in *A Political-Theological Treatise and a Political Treatise*, trans. R. H. M. Elwes (New York: Dover, 1951), chap. 5, 74. Musically speaking, the metamorphosis the ritornello undergoes seems to bear a tonal equivalent of the subjunctive mood of Aron's rhetoric.

97. Eli Zaretzky in "The Place of Psychoanalysis in the History of the Jews," paper read at the Jewish Studies program, University of Texas, Austin, TX, 25 February 2004; Jüdisches Museum, Berlin, Germany, February 2005. I thank Eli Zaretzky for allowing me to quote from this paper. The idea of Jewishness as openness was prevalent at the time, and was expressed by many, e.g., Franz Werfel as quoted by Alma Mahler in her diary, 31 July 1918, in Alma Mahler-Werfel, *Mein Leben* (Frankfurt am Main: Fischer, 1998), 106.

98. Goldstein, *Reinscribing*, 154.

99. See Shlomo Pines, "Spinoza's *Tractatus Theologico-Politicus*, Maimonides and Kant," in *Studies in the History of Jewish Philosophy, The Transmission of Texts and Ideas*, (Jerusalem: Bialik Institute, 1977, in Hebrew), 306–49. Pines relies especially on chapter 14 in Spinoza's treatise. His argument is supported by Lorberbaum, "Spinoza's Theological-Political Problem," 212, in which he claims that Spinoza advocates a "polity congenital to individuals seeking their own good and not a polity charged with realizing human perfection."

100. Spinoza, *Political Treatise*, 287.

101. This is further elaborated and musically illustrated in HaCohen, "Psychoanalysis and the Music of Charisma."

102. Gebhardt, *Spinoza, Opera* (Heidelberg 1925), chapter 1, p. 21, as quoted in Pines, "Spinoza's *Tractatus*," 314.

103. No copy of Spinoza's treatises is to be found, however, in Schoenberg's library, but his ideas could have reached him through other channels, such as his acquaintance and correspondence with Jacob Klatzkin, well known for his Hebrew translation of

Spinoza's *Ethics*. Any comparison between Spinoza and Schoenberg should of course take into consideration that unlike Spinoza, Schoenberg was not a democrat, and, like many of the Weimer generation Jewish intellectuals, adhered to a certain form of enlightened autocracy, that in his case orients itself in those years into the Zionist revisionist ideology of Jabotinksy. Still, Schoenberg was pluralist and, despite his tendency to take extreme ideological positions, was not dogmatic in his philosophical inclinations.

104. In the opening of chapter 1 this group of historians is briefly surveyed.

105. Leo Strauss, "Preface to Spinoza's Critique of Religion" in *Liberalism Ancient and Modern* (Ithaca: Cornell University Press, 1968), 242–59.

106. Carl Dahlhaus, *Schoenberg and the New Music*, 167.

107. For a comprehensive discussion of his attempts in this direction see Alexander Ringer, *Arnold Schoenberg: The Composer as a Jew* (Oxford: Clarendon Press, 1990), 116–49. Klára Móricz, in *Jewish Identities: Nationalism, Racism, and Utopianism in Twentieth-Century Music* (Berkeley: University of California Press, 2008) added to the picture much to indict the composer for a seriously protofascist orientation in the thirties, most of which, however, remained unpublished. Her contribution is subject to the reservation that it is not contextualized within a prevailing discourse in related intellectual circles, and suffers from "backshadowing" from a vantage point of our knowledge of the aftermath of the turbulent thirties and in relation to Schoenberg's earlier work.

108. Rabbenu Tam's (twelfth-century) version of the prayer contains also an annulment of vows for the year to come. It was adopted by the communities of Ashkenazi, oriental Sephardic, and Yemenite Jewry. This is considered by Reik as part of the apologetic rebuttal of the anti-Jewish allegations.

109. (For a concise account of this history see for example http://www.jewishencyclopedia.com/view.jsp?artid=340&letter=K); *Encyclopaedia Judaica*, 2nd ed. s.v. "Kol Nidrei."

110. Reik, *Ritual*, trans. Douglas Bryan, 167–219; 168.

111. For an even richer synaesthetic and vocally resplendent description of Yom Kippur eve in a Galician town, see Shmuel Y. Agnon, *Yamim Nora'im (Days of Awe)*, (Jerusalem: Shocken, 1968, in Hebrew), preface, unnumbered.

112. Reik, *Ritual*, 170.

113. According to Karl Beck's *Diaries* as quoted in Reik, *Ritual*, 170.

114. First violin, last quarter note of m. 6; for extant documents and hypotheses regarding these events and connections, see Avenary, *Kantor Salomon Sulzer und seine Zeit, Eine Dokumentation* (Sigmaringen: Jan Thorbeck, 1985), 48–51. Beethoven was approached in 1826 by the Viennese new Jewish community's representatives to compose a cantata for the consecration of the new synagogue.

115. See chapter 4.

116. See Sabine Lichtenstein, "Abraham Jacob Lichtenstein: eine jüdische Quelle fuer Carl Loewe und Max Bruch," *Die Musikforschung* 49/4 (1996): 349–67.

117. Recited daily in the ten days ("asseret yᵉmey tᵉshuva") extending from Rosh Hashanah to Yom Kippur.

118. This calls for a full analysis of the melody from the point of view of its expressive values through the joint perspectives of Jewish musical tradition and the classical Western one which I hope to carry out in a subsequent study.

119. The Hebrew word (*B^erit*) stands in the Bible for different kinds of covenants and agreements, including circumcision, the receiving of the Torah at the Sinai revelation, as well as for more mundane contracts.

120. For the explanation of the paradox entailed by this relation see Reik, *Ritual*, 191.

121. Reik, *Ritual*, 203–4.

122. Ibid., 211.

123. Arnold Schönberg, *Kritischer Bericht, Skizzen, Fragmente; Abteilung V: Chorwerke*, Reihe B, Band 19, ed. Christian Martin Schmidt (Mainz: B. Schott's Söhne, 1977), ix.

124. For an insiders' evaluation of the importance of the traditional melody see Agnon, *Yamim Nora'im*, 290.

125. Schönberg, *Kritischer Bericht*, xiii (translated from German).

126. ibid.

127. He spoke about seven; there actually are but four or five.

128. Schoenberg's terms, in *Kritischer Bericht*, xi.

129. See Yaakov Mazor, "The Power of the Niggun in Hassidic Thought and Its Roles in Religious and Social Life," in *Yuval: Studies of the Jewish Music Research Centre*, 26–53 (Hebrew).

130. I refer the reader to Cohen's impressive chapter on the Day of Atonement in Hermann Cohen, *Religion der Vernunft* (chap. xii). On Rosenzweig's special experience on 1913 Yom Kippur, and the centrality of the day in his thought, see Nahum Norbert Glatzer, *Franz Rosenzweig: His Life and Thought* (Indianapolis: Hacket, [1961] 1998), xvii–xx. See also Paul Mendes-Flohr, "Rosenzweig" in *A Companion to Continental Philosophy*, ed. Simon Critchley and William Ralph Schroeder (Oxford: Blackwell, 1998), 319–39.

131. For details of this construction, see Steven J. Cahn's enlightening analysis in "'Kol Nidre' in America," *Journal of the Arnold Schoenberg Center* 4 (2002): 203–18.

132. In addition to the text itself, which clearly discloses such spirit, Schoenberg explicitly wrote the following to Lazare Saminsky (on 6 February 1941) about the piece: "Ich glaube, meine Textfassung bringt die [Versöhnungstags]-Idee mit der Moral aller Andersgläubigen in Einklang, der wir Juden genauso unterliegen wie alle andern Menschen." Quoted from *Arnold Schönberg 1874–1951. Lebensgeschichte in Begegnungen*, ed. Nuria Nono-Schoenberg (Klagenfurt: Ritter, 1998), 351.

133. Eric Werner's review of the European premiere of the work is worth mentioning in this connection. See "France," *Musical Quarterly* 44/2 (1958): 242–44.

134. *Arnold Schönberg 1874–1951*, 351. Schoenberg's disappointment is expressed in a letter to Paul Dessau; see Schönberg, *Kritischer Bericht*, xii.

135. See Severine Neff, "Schoenberg's *Kristallnacht* Fugue: Contrapuntal Exercise or Unknown Piece?" *Musical Quarterly* 86/1 (2002): 117–48.

CHAPTER 7. THE END

1. The friend is Galit Hasan-Rokem, to whom the author is grateful. I wish also to acknowledge my gratitude to Roger Hurwitz who first pointed out to me the relevance of these films to the "Jewish noise" project.

2. No less bizarre, in this connection, is the framing of *Jud Süß* by its 1984 American commercial distributor, who chose to describe the film as "the most controversial motion picture of all times." The International Historic Films company reproduced it on DVD 2008, with an appropriate framing, including an informative and thoughtful essay by David Culbert.

3. For an explanation of this flop regarding both text (the film) and context (cinema go-ers' habits and expectations, and so on) see Stig Hornshøj-Møller and David Culbert, "*Der ewige Jude* (1940): Joseph Goebbels' Unequaled Monument to Anti-Semitism" in the *Historical Journal of Film, Radio and Television* 12/1 (1992): 49–52.

4. The movie was premiered in Venice (!) on 5 September 1940, and first shown in Ger-many on 24 September, attended by Goebbels and other leading Nazi officials; the following day the press praised the movie as "the decisive breakthrough in creating cinematic art out of our National Socialist ideology"; from David Welch, *Propaganda and the German Cinema* (Oxford: Clarendon Press, 1983), 290–91.

5. That famous German actor, whose features and stature could easily pass for a cari-caturized Jewish appearance, played the role of several stereotyped Jews in the film: secretary Levy, Rabbi Loew, Butcher Isaak, and the old man at the window, essential-izing their "kind." Krauss also played Shylock in a Max Reinhardt guest production at the 1937 Salzburg Festival, claiming (in his postwar trial) that Goebbels had used this against him. See Susan Tegel, "'The Demonic Effect': Veit Harlan's Use of Jew-ish Extras in *Jud Süss* (1940)," *Holocaust and Genocide Studies* 14/2 (2000), 236. In this sense, the movie goes in the opposite direction from Chaplin's *Great Dictator* of the same year, whose double casting as "Hynkel" and the Jewish Barber aims to blur categorizations.

6. Linda Schulte-Sasse, *Entertaining the Third Reich: Illusions of Wholeness in Nazi Cinema* (Durham, N.C.: Duke University Press, 1996), 50. Schulte-Sasse stresses that this "schizoid 'yes, but' attitude might offer a more complicated lesson about the way such texts 'work' or, in some cases, don't" (ibid.). This idea guides her throughout her profound analysis of the film.

7. The director of the movie, Veit Harlan, who became, due to that success, the chief director of the Third Reich's movies, was also the only one in the production to be later tried (1949) for crimes against humanity, but was acquitted. For details of his and related collaborators' and witnesses' arguments in the trial see Tegel's "'The De-monic Effect.'" Over twenty million people watched the movie at the time. See Gerd Albrecht, *Film im Dritten Reich: Eine Dokumentation* (Karlsruhe: Doku, 1979), 251. Heinrich Himmler made it compulsory viewing for the SS and the police. Recently, a richly investigated and highly acclaimed documentary on Harlan and his "oeuvre," *Harlan—In the Shadow of Jew Süss* (2008) was produced by Felix Moeller.

8. The faithful identification, including the tracing of performers and performance con-text was made by Susan Tegel, in her abovementioned article.

9. See Yaron Jean, "'Hearing Maps': Noise, Technology and Auditory Perception in Ger-many 1914–1945" (PhD diss., Hebrew University of Jerusalem, 2005, in Hebrew), 234. An interesting, amazingly similar, however contradictory description (the *German* card players and others in the restaurants were blatantly oblivious to Goering's speech

on the radio) is found in Victor Klemperer's *Ich will Zeugnis ablegen bis zum letzten. Tagebücher 1933–1945* (Berlin: Aufbau, 1995), entry of 11 September 1938.

10. Werner Maser, *Hitler: Legend, Myth, and Reality*, trans. Peter and Betty Ross (New York: Harper and Row, 1973).

11. Quoted in Jean-Gérard Bursztein, *Hitler, la Tyrannie et la Psychanalyse: Essai sur la Destruction de la Civilisation* (Paris: Nouvelles Études Freudiennes, 1998).

12. Again the famous balloon scene from Chaplin's *Great Dictator* (fictionally) teaches us about the Führer's subjectivity in this respect, itself well documented. Thus Ernst Hanfstängel reports: "Wagner's music had simply become second nature to him. I would even maintain that there were marked parallels between the structure of the *Mastersingers* prelude and his speeches. In both cases the same interweaving of leit-motifs, wealth of embellishment, counterpoint and finally the powerful outburst like the sound of trombones at Wagner's act endings and Liszt's rhapsodic finales." Quoted in Jeremy Tambling, *Opera and the Culture of Fascism* (Oxford: Oxford University Press, 1996), 4–5.

13. About these vengeful actions see Bursztein in *Hitler, la Tyrannie et la Psychanalyse*.

14. Feuchtwanger's novel gave birth also to a British movie more benevolent to Jews, *Jew Suess*, of 1934.

15. It was dramatized by Ludwig Metzger, Eberhard Möller, and Harlan himself; music, except for the Jewish parts, was composed by Wolfgang Zeller. *Der ewige Jude* was directed by Fritz Hippler.

16. Quoted from Schulte-Sasse, *Entertaining the Third Reich*, 51–52.

17. Her discussion concentrates on Lessing's *Emilia Galotti* and Schiller's *Kabale und Liebe*; see Schulte-Sasse, *Entertaining the Third Reich*, 52–62.

18. The movie also plays on the biblical Joseph and Mordecai stories (from Genesis and the Scroll of Esther, respectively); the latter is even alluded to in the rabbi's debate with Süß.

19. See Régine Michal Friedman, "Juden-Ratten—Von der Rassistischen Metonymie zur tierischen Metapher in Fritz Hipplers Film 'Der ewige Jude,'" in *Frauen und Film* 47 (1989): 24–35.

20. Such ideas are elaborated by Slavoj Žižek, in, among other places, his *Welcome to the Desert of the Real: Five Essays on September 11 and Related Dates* (London: Verso, 2002). For the use of edited footage and newsreels to create false reality effects in *Der ewige Jude* see Joan Clinefelter, "A Cinematic Construction of Nazi Anti-Semitism: The Documentary *der Ewige Jude*," in *Cultural History Through a National Socialist Lens: Essays on the Cinema of the Third Reich*, ed. Robert C. Reimer (Rochester, NY: Camden House, 2000), 133–54.

21. The quotations from Schulte-Sasse and James Donald's "The Fantastic, the Sublime and the Popular, Or, What's at Stake in Vampire Films?" in *Fantasy and the Cinema*, ed. James Donald (London: British Film Institute, 1989), 233–51, are both borrowed from Schulte-Sasse's *Entertaining the Third Reich*, 82.

22. The Nazi reaction to Jewish music was unfolded in a review in the *Angriff*: "A strange mixture of word and sound . . . as alien to our ears as remotest Asia" (the original German word is *Asiatentum*); see Tegel, "The Demonic Effect," 223. Even a postwar

critical scholar such as Dorothea Hollstein, in *"Jud Suss" und die Deutschen: antisemitische Vorurteile im nationalsozialistischen Spielfilm* (Frankfurt: Ullstein Materialien, 1983), described the Jewish music in the film as "unpleasant and repellent" (98), a fact she de-essentializes, nevertheless, by ascribing it to the filmmakers' intentions.

23. Tegel believes this was taken from a recording, and I concur, especially because of the preceding organ. She is also right in designating it as Hungarian Jewish.

24. The mode title (like most others in Jewish Ashkenazi music) is an insiders' term. See Idelsohn, *Thesaurus* 7:27 and examples.

25. *Der Stürmer,* "The Stormer" (or "The Attacker"), a weekly Nazi tabloid published by Julius Streicher from 1923 to the end of WWII, notorious for its mocking caricatures of Jews with exaggerated facial features and misshapen bodies.

26. One of the "extra Jews," he was also cast in the other two major musical moments: the Jews' entrance to Stuttgart and the (Simḥat Torah) synagogal ritual; see below.

27. For the ideological import of keyboard instruments in bourgeois domestic imagery see Richard Leppert, *Music and Image: Domesticity, Ideology and Socio-cultural Formation in 18th-Century England* (Cambridge: Cambridge University Press, 1988).

28. See chapter 2 above and Carl E. Schorske, "The Quest for the Grail: Wagner and Morris" in *The Critical Spirit: Essays in Honor of Herbert Marcuse,* ed. Kurt H. Wolff and B. Moore (Boston: Beacon, 1967), 220–28.

29. Another moment that stands in striking opposition to Lessing's play is Süß' scheme to marry Dorothea and her father's refusal, which kindles a series of reactions, leading to Sturm's arrest, the riot, and so forth. As I was told by documentary filmmaker Felix Moeller, Harlan rehearsed the "das ist ein Jude" lines with Jaeger many times.

30. See Natan Shahar, *Song O Song Rise and Soar* (Ben Shemen: Modan, 2006, in Hebrew), 130–33.

31. See Shai Burstyn, "Inventing Musical Tradition: The Case of the Hebrew (Folk) Song," *Orbis Musicae* 13 (2003), 127–36.

32. This is unlike the liturgical pieces discussed throughout this volume, which follow, in the main, the Ashkenazi stresses and pronunciation. Admon's conscious search for the oriental flavor is exemplified in this song, though in a detail which the German edition of Schönberg chose to omit: the second B-flat should in fact be B natural. In that way, writes Burstyn, Admon, attempting to "capture something of the microtonic quality of oriental melos, . . . employed chromatic melodic permutations of certain otherwise diatonic scale degrees. . . . Admon was certain he had achieved the oriental effect intuitively rather than consciously." Endowed with a pleasant tenor voice, he would "engage in 'vocal exercises,' as he used to call them." Ibid., 130.

33. Also in Prague itself, as we learn from Shmuel Bloch's testimony, quoted by Zvi Semel in "Enigma of Survival: Verdi's Requiem in Terezin (1944)" (master's thesis, Hebrew University, 2007, in Hebrew), 123. See also the preface to this book.

34. One typical example, out of many, is my mother's reaction to the Zionist songs she was exposed to at the time. A fourteen-year-old girl when leaving Germany for Palestine, after two years in a Nazified Gymnasium in Munich, surrounded by Hitler Youth—once exposed to the culture of Hebrew song she felt, "and we too have such songs!" Whenever I heard this anecdote from her, her voice was filled with the joy of surprise and admiration. Regarding the common sources of the national idea in music

see Carl Dahlhaus, "Nationalism and Music," in *Between Romanticism and Modernism: Four Studies in the Music of the Later Nineteenth Century*, trans. Mary Whittall (Berkeley: University of California Press, 1989), 79–102. The encounters of Nazi and Zionist interests in prewar years in the musical realm are addressed in Lily Hirsch, *A Jewish Orchestra in Nazi Germany: Musical Politics and the Berlin Jewish Culture League* (Michigan: University of Michigan Press, 2010).

35. Jakob Schönberg (ed.) *Shirej Eretz Israel* (Berlin: Jüdischer Verlag, 1938), 5.

36. I take issue here with Steve Neale ("Propaganda," *Screen* 18 [1977], 31), who views this gesture of "beyondness" as threatening to rupture the film's boundaries, becoming blatant propaganda. Regarded against the background of the oratorical tradition, this seems to me as a moment of community bonding and elevation.

37. Tegel, "The Demonic Effect," 218.

38. Of course, German audiences of the time never saw the Disney piece. Again, oriental music accompanies the footage for the *entartete Kunst* section in the *ewige Jude*; the juxtaposition is obvious. The "composer" of this film was freelance musician Franz R. Friedl.

39. Tegel, "The Demonic Effect," 221. The extras were paid; see ibid., 230. Goebbels understood the power of these sources, and even before the war broke out he searched for ways to reach the Polish Jewish communities for what seemed to him invaluable propaganda material. But he had to wait, while Poland was still independent (not for long, as we know). Then he received his desired ethnographic object in even a preferable, condensed, shape. For Jews enclosed in the ghettos became more representative of their own (debased) qualities, in addition to the fact that they became so accessible. This was a major idea behind *Der ewige Jude*: the crew went through the newly wrought ghettos—Warsaw, Lublin, Lodz—and shot all the original footage of the film. See Hornshøj-Møller and Culbert, "*Der ewige Jude*," 41.

40. According to the postwar testimony of Alfred Braun (another professional producing the film), they even cooperated with "evident pleasure and eagerness" (ibid., 229).

41. Ibid., 228.

42. Ibid., 220; when still in Lublin, the original site of their "musical ethnography," Conny Carstensen, one of Harlan's assistants (his real name was Friedrich Wirth) reported (as part of his defense, in 1949, and that is how this testimony should be appraised) that the "chief rabbi" assembled a choir who sang "beautiful songs in the synagogue, from which he was "so overwhelmed that tears came." (Also, in Prague the singers were professional.) The conditions in the Lublin ghetto at that early time were already "generally frightful," according to the German team members; ibid., 228.

43. Ibid., 227.

44. Ibid., 230.

45. Ibid., 228.

46. Ibid., 223. The recording was done in Paris in 1930.

47. I am not discussing the Purim meal scene, for this is footage taken from the Yiddish film *Der Purimspieler* (1937), directed by Joseph Green, and thus relates to a different category.

48. This apparently contradicts the facts documented by Hornshøj-Møller and Culbert ("*Der ewige Jude*," p. 53, n. 6), that the synagogue and ritual slaughter scenes were

filmed on 11–13 October 1939, which that year fell on 28–30 of Tishri, that is, after the Tishri Holidays. My explanation for these later dates includes the following considerations: (1) The S^eliḥot mode could have been revoked on Thursday, 29 October, and Friday night could have taken place on 30 October evening; (2) these dates would be compatible also with their extracting twice the Torah from the ark, on Thursday and Friday, which was Rosh Ḥodesh (the festive first day of the month, Marḥeshvan in this case); (3) the special ark curtain could have remained from the holidays, because things were inevitably mixed up during the first holidays celebrated after the occupation of Poland and the setting up of the ghettos.

49. Bursztein, *Hitler, la Tyrannie et la Psychanalyse.* See also Louis Dumont, "The Totalitarian Disease: Individualism and Racism in Adolf Hitler's Representations," in his *Essays on Individualism: Modern Ideology in Anthropological Perspective* (Chicago: University of Chicago Press, 1986), 149–79.

50. *Doktor Faustus. Das Leben des deutschen Tonsetzers Adrian Leverkühn, erzählt von einem Freunde* (*Doctor Faustus: The Life of the German Composer Adrian Leverkühn as Told by a Friend*) (Frankfurt: Fischer, [1947] 1999).

51. My great-grandfather, Rabbi Hanoch Ehrentreu, the Orthodox Rabbi of Munich at the time Mann lived there, might have been his model for this figure. See Michael Brocke and Julius Carlebach sel. A. (eds.): *Biographisches Handbuch der Rabbiner Teil II. Die Rabbiner im Deutschen Reich 1871–1945*, vol. 2: *Aach-Juspa* (Munich: Saur, 2006), 171. I am grateful to Michael K. Silber for this reference.

52. Following the French etymology of the word, as explicated by Michel Serres, in *The Parasite*, trans. Lawrence R. Schehr (Minneapolis: University of Minnesota Press, [1980] 2007), which throws light also on Wagner's insinuations, discussed in chapter 5. I thank Suzanne Stewart-Steinberg for calling my attention to this insightful essay.

EPILOGUE

1. For reference see chapter 1.

2. Gustav Karpeles, "The Music of the Synagogue," in *Jewish Literature and Other Essays* (Philadelphia: Jewish Publication Society of America, 1895), 377, an e-book [#27901] (http://www.gutenberg.org/files/27901/27901-h/27901-h.htm#Page_369).

3. As adumbrated in Jacques Rancière, *The Politics of Aesthetics: The Distribution of the Sensible*, trans. Gabriel Rockhill (New York: Continuum, 2004); the following discussion refers to chapter 2.

4. Ruth Leys, *Trauma: A Genealogy* (Chicago: University of Chicago Press, 2000), 27–40.

5. Ruth Ginsburg, "Whose Trauma Is It Anyway? Some Reflections on Freud's Traumatic History," in *New Perspectives on Freud's "Moses and Monotheism*," ed. Ruth Ginsburg and Ilana Pardes (*Conditio Judaica* 60, Tübingen: Max Niemeyer, 2006), 77–91.

6. As discussed in Adva Frank-Schwebel, "The Sonic Dimension of the Psychoanalytic Encounter: An Interdisciplinary Analysis Integrating Psychoanalysis, Music Theory and Developmental Theory" (PhD diss., Hebrew University of Jerusalem, 2010).

7. Karpeles, "The Music of the Synagogue," 374.

8. "Present-Day Judaism and Its Intellectual Trends," *Abraham Geiger and Liberal Judaism: The Challenge of the 19th Century*, ed. Max Wiener, trans. Ernst J. Schlochauer (Philadelphia: Jewish Publication Society of America, 1962), 207. I am grateful to Richard I. Cohen for this reference.

9. Ginsburg, "Whose Trauma," 88. The question concerning individual versus collective trauma, in the present context, remains open. Dominick LaCapra has proposed a distinction between "trauma of absence" (individual) and the "trauma of loss" (historical), which engender, in turn, melancholy vs. mourning respectively. See *Writing History, Writing Trauma* (Baltimore: Johns Hopkins University Press, 2001), 43–85. The main concentration in the present study on individual, creative reaction to a collective stereotype, transcending mourning, seems to thwart this neat division, which LaCapra himself tends to suspect.

10. See Michel Serres, *The Parasite*, trans. Lawrence R. Schehr (Minneapolis: University of Minnesota Press, [1980] 2007), 14.

11. See epigraph to the present chapter.

12. See David Patterson's *The Shriek of Silence: A Phenomenology of the Holocaust Novel* (Lexington: University Press of Kentucky, 1992).

13. Leon Wieseltier, "Ring the Bells," *The New Republic*, 23 April 2008.

14. Ariel Hirschfeld, *Ha'aretz Magazine*, 16.03.2007. Avner Dorman, in *Jerusalem Mix*, 2007 (for oboe, clarinet, bassoon, horn, and piano, premiered at the International Chamber Music Festival of 2007) impressively composed *Adhans* into his score.

15. Interestingly, the bells of the German churches in Jerusalem were purported, by Kaiser Wilhelm II at the turn of the twentieth century, to attune to each other.

16. Conducted by Abigail Wood, and colleagues from SOAS (School of Oriental and African Studies), London, 2009–10.

17. As in Rachel Beckles-Willson's forthcoming book.

INDEX